Project Management Casebook

Project Management Casebook

EDITORS

David I. Cleland,
Karen M. Bursic,
Richard Puerzer, and
A. Yaroslav Vlasak

Library of Congress Cataloging-in-Publication Data

Project management casebook / edited by David I. Cleland ... [et al.].
     p.   cm.
    Includes bibliographical references.
    ISBN: 1–880410–45–1 (pbk.)
    1. Industrial project management––Case studies. I. Cleland,
David I.
HD69.P75P728   1997
658.4'04––dc21   97–3116
                                        CIP

Book Team

Editor-in-Chief: James S. Pennypacker
Book Designer: Michelle Owen
Copyeditor: Toni D. Knott
Copyeditor: Amy Goretsky
Copyeditor: Mark S.Parker
Cover design by: James S. Pennypacker and Dewey Messer
Production Coordinator: Mark S. Parker
Acquisitions Editor: Bobby R. Hensley

PMI books are available at special quantity discounts to use as premiums and
sales promotions, or for use in corporate training programs. For more
information, please write to the Business Manager, PMI Publishing Division,
40 Colonial Square, Sylva, NC 28779. Or contact your local bookstore.

The paper used in this book complies with the Permanent Paper Standard
issued by the National Information Standards Organization (Z39.48—1984).

10 9 8 7 6 5 4 3 2

Table of Contents

Acknowledgments

Our deep appreciation to the authors of the articles and papers who unknowingly provided the source material for this book. Also thanks to our students, clients, and colleagues, who through their questions and discussions prompted us to recognize the need for a casebook in project management that could be used as a key supplement for training future students.

Our profound thanks to Jim Pennypacker, Publisher/Editor-In-Chief, PMI Publications Division, who shared our vision for a casebook to augment the classroom experiences afforded to students of project management.

We thank Dr. Henry Wolfe, Chairman of the Industrial Engineering Department, and Dr. Gerald D. Holder, Dean of the School of Engineering, University of Pittsburgh, who provided the environment that made the development of this casebook possible.

Finally, a note of special thanks to Claire Zubritzky whose superb administrative work facilitated the development of this casebook.

Preface

Project Management is an idea whose time has come.

Project teams are becoming commonplace as key elements of organization design to deal with change in contemporary organizations. The use of project and other types of teams have modified the theory and practice of management as today's organizations plan and implement strategies to change products, services, and organizational processes. The key challenge facing contemporary managers is how to maintain ongoing efficiency and effectiveness in existing capabilities—and at the same time develop new initiatives to prepare the enterprise for survival and growth in uncertain times through the use of project management initiatives.

The extraordinary growth of project management has created the critical need for case-related instructional material to use in developing competencies in people by way of the knowledge, skills, and attitudes needed to perform effectively as members of project teams. Then too, those functional and general managers who use projects as building blocks in the design and execution of organizational strategies need instruction on how projects can be used to develop and execute strategic initiatives in preparing the organization for its uncertain future. It is to these purposes that this casebook is dedicated.

The casebook contains articles and symposia papers drawn from the literature of the Project Management Institute (PMI). Select pieces have been included from the *Project Management Journal, PM Network* magazine, and from the *Proceedings* of PMI's Annual Seminars & Symposia. A few articles, rich in project management information, have been included from other prestigious journals.

Since its founding in 1969, PMI has taken a commanding lead in the conceptualization and development of a body of knowledge about project management. For clarity, in 1987 it published the *Project Management Body of Knowledge,* which is known as the *PMBOK.* This was updated and expanded in 1996 and published as the *Guide to the Project Management Body of Knowledge,* or *PMBOK Guide.* In some literature, references are also made to the PMBOK, which would represent the sum of project management knowledge written and unwritten.

Each of the articles and papers selected include important information regarding the fundamentals of project management. Following each article or paper is a series of questions to guide the reader's analysis and maximize the learning process. Included in the questions are suggestions as to where the reader can look in the *PMBOK Guide* for insight into the particular project management techniques used, or challenges posed, by the project.

The cases can be used in senior undergraduate or graduate project management programs. The casebook is adaptable for use in short training courses. The cases illustrate how and why projects are used in a wide variety of organizational settings. Readers will be exposed to both successful and not-so-successful project management practices. By understanding what works and what does not work in project management, readers are given an opportunity to reach their own conclusions about the nature of project management philosophy in their personal and professional lives.

According to *Business Week* magazine, "Companies that learn the secrets of creating cross-functional teams are winning the battle for global market share and profits. Those that don't are losing out." With this statement *Business Week* has captured the prevailing attitude concerning the use of alternative teams as an essential element of organizational design to improve operational and strategy performance of the enterprise. Reengineering teams, benchmarking teams, concurrent engineering teams, and self-managed production teams are a few of the types of teams that are changing the way contemporary organizations are managed—often with striking improvements in the efficiency and effectiveness of the enterprise.

Project management has provided the strategic pathway for the emergence of these alternative teams. In this book the editors have provided several cases dealing with the use of alternative teams in the strategic management of the enterprise to enable the user to experience how such teams can improve organizational performance. The cases should also help the reader to recognize that cross-functional and cross-organizational teams are highly versatile strategic resources and key elements in the design and execution of strategic management initiatives.

The casebook editors hope this book will provide meaningful information to its readers. In doing so the knowledge, skills, and attitudes concerning project and team management will be enhanced.

The casebook is organized in six sections:

Planning—How to develop the objectives, goals, and strategies for projects.

Organizing—Considerations involved in the development of an organizational design for the management of projects.

Motivating—The design of strategies to bring out the best in people serving on and working with project teams.

Directing—How to develop effective leadership styles in the management of projects.

Controlling—Developing and executing the means for monitoring, evaluating, and controlling the use of resources to support project purposes.

General—A grouping of cases reflecting broader issues in project management.

Dr. David I. Cleland, University of Pittsburgh
Dr. Karen M. Bursic, University of Pittsburgh
Richard Puerzer, Hofstra University
A. Yaroslav Vlasak, University of Pittsburgh

Pittsburgh, Pennsylvania
September 30, 1997

PLANNING

1
PLANNING

1995 PMI International Project of the Year

The Benfield Column Repair Project

Ian Boggon, PMP, General Manager, INTENS SA

PM Network, February 1996, pp. 25–30

At 12:30 P.M. on Tuesday, March 8, 1994, a fire broke out in the carbonate regeneration column in the Benfield Unit of the Gas Circuit at Sasol Three, one of the factories of Sasol, a leading South African coal, chemical, and crude-oil company. The column, which was open for repairs and maintenance during the annual factory shutdown, is used to process hydrogen. It is one crucial component in a long chain of equipment that converts coal to oil and chemicals. Without it, a large section of the factory could not function, resulting in a considerable loss of income.

A damage investigation revealed that buckling in the shell of the column had caused it to bend in the middle to such an extent that the top of the steam chimney was 500 mm (20 inches) off-center, making the 70 m (231 feet) column resemble the Leaning Tower of Pisa.

Decision analysis revealed that, to get the plant safely back online in the shortest possible time, the damaged portion of the shell would have to be

GROUND RULES

- The project will be schedule driven, not cost driven.
- There is NO float on this project.
- Plan to reduce scheduled times, not be governed by them.
- The project will be a team effort with Sastech and Sasol Operations as partners, assisted by Sasdiens and CBI.
- Safety will not be compromised at any stage during the project.
- Quality will not be compromised at any stage during the project.
- Technical decisions will be authorized by Mr. J.D. Bosch and Dr. J.H. Snyders.
- Process decisions will be authorized by Mr. A.S. du Toit and Dr. J.H. Snyders.
- Resources will not be considered as a limitation.
- Commitments will be adhered to.
- Communication will be continuous at all levels.
- Sasol Mechanical Maintenance and Production will be notified of all work *before* it takes place in the unit.

cut out and replaced. The main component of the project, therefore, was to strip out the original shell, fabricate a new section, reinstall the column, and re-commission the unit.

And all this was to be accomplished in forty-seven days.

The project team. Sastech, a subsidiary of the Sasol Group of Companies, was requested to undertake the repair at 8:00 A.M. on Thursday, March 10. The Sastech project team consisted of a project manager, a senior project engineer, a cost engineer, and a planner. The total team, however, had twenty-seven members: four process engineers, six mechanical engineers, a pressure vessel specialist, a metallurgist, a welding engineer, a pipe stress engineer, a piping draftsman, a mechanical draftsman, a structural engineer, a structural draftsman, three quality assurance inspectors, a commercial contract officer, and a commercial procurement officer. Members were drawn from Sastech, Sasol Three, Sasdiens, Chicago Bridge and Iron Works (the original fabricators of the column), and from suppliers of the equipment and material.

CBI was contracted to remove, fabricate, and replace the vessel, with Sasdiens providing the rigging, piping, electrical, and associated work. Some of the CBI engineers involved when Sasol Three was built fourteen years ago now worked on the repair. The cutting up and removal of the damaged sections of the column was a combined effort between CBI and Sasdiens.

Within fifteen minutes of receiving the contract, CBI had contacted employees from six sites in the United States, Saudi Arabia, Turkey, and South Africa and were faxing drawings from their head office, placing provisional orders for material, completing the rigging study, and arranging delivery of the massive spreader beam to be used to lift off and replace the damaged and new sections. This speed of response set the standard for everyone involved.

The column was handed back to production on Sunday, April 3, at 12:30 P.M., certified as "ready for commissioning." The project completion certificate was signed on Friday, April 8, at 4:30 P.M.—fifteen days ahead of schedule.

Special management methods. Conventional project management techniques were not sufficient to ensure that the work was carried out in the shortest possible time. Two areas were identified as requiring special attention: *innovation and creativity*, and *enthusiasm and commitment*. Because

Project Statistics

```
Disabling injuries . . . . . . . . . . . . . . . . . . . . . . . . . . . 0
Welding rods burned . . . . . . . . . . . . . . . . . . . . . 3,500 kg
X-rays shot . . . . . . . . . . . . . . . . . . . . . . . . Over 1,000
Packing rings loaded . . . . . . . . . . . . . . . . . . 157 tonnes
Bottles of cola consumed . . . . . . . . . . . . . . . . . . 15,000
Companies supplying material/equipment . . . . . . . . . . . . . 12
Budget . . . . . . . . . . . . . . . . . . . R23.3 mil ($85.3 million)
Amount under budget . . . . . . . . . . . . R5.9 mil ($21.6 million)
Hamburgers eaten . . . . . . . . . . . . . . . . . . . . . . 12,000
Contractors employed . . . . . . . . . . . . . . . . . . . . . . 12
Activities in the schedule . . . . . . . . . . . . . . . . . . . 450
People involved . . . . . . . . . . . . . . . . . . . . . . . . 700
Project duration . . . . . . . . . . . . . . . . . . . . . 25 days
Days cut from the schedule . . . . . . . . . . . . . . . . . . . 15
```

the time frame was short, any time saved on individual tasks would have a direct effect on the overall project duration.

But because the majority of the workforce had been involved in the maintenance shutdown when the fire started, they were locked into a mindset that the schedule governs the duration of each task and a successful task is perceived as one that is completed "on time." On the first day of the repair project, two people were overheard saying that they had "plenty of time" to finish a particular task. It was explained to them that, for this project, they would be given credit for work finished *ahead* of schedule rather than *on* schedule.

This story was recounted at the next meeting, and supervisors were asked to pass the message on to their teams. The result was incredible. People came up with ideas for saving even five minutes—unheard of under normal circumstances. Such was the enthusiasm created in the workforce that this became the dominant culture. On the third day, when a new supervisor joining the team said that he would start first thing in the morning, there was an immediate uproar, with everyone in the meeting shouting that he should begin immediately!

It was agreed at the beginning of the project that to get the commitment of everyone involved, they had to know what was going on at all times. This was achieved in a number of ways.

A list of ground rules, developed in conjunction with the client's senior management team, was distributed to everyone on the project. Any decision, even if unconventional, could be accepted if it complied with these rules. For example, the welding foreman hired welders from a rival company rather than delay completion of a task because the ground rule stated that resources could not be considered as a limitation.

A board was put up outside the command center caravan and updated twice daily. When people performed well, their names were posted there. This was a real morale booster. The project team was located on-site and was present before the night shift finished in the morning and after it started at night. Visits were frequently made during the night, removing the feeling of isolation normally associated with this shift. The project team also made a commitment to visit every crew at least twice a day to give feedback and encouragement. Frequent visits were also made to off-site supervisors. Each member of the project team had a pager and the crews were encouraged to make contact at any time of the day or night, which helped to speed up the decision-making process.

From the first meeting, we encouraged innovation and creativity. Even silly ideas were examined in case they produced a worthwhile solution. This continuous push for innovative ideas produced numerous time-saving solutions.

Each person was encouraged to work for the benefit of the project as a whole and not for his or her own interest. The person responsible for a critical path activity would get help voluntarily from all other members in the team because he or she understood that to shorten the critical path would also shorten the total project. This concept was so successful that at one stage a fistfight nearly broke out because three different artisans wanted to work on one particular section of scaffold at the same time, such was their enthusiasm for the job.

A policy of "Accept It ... Or Change It ... But Never Complain About It" kept meetings positive. In addition to the shift change meetings, communication sessions were convened twice a day when the activities of the next two days were discussed in minute detail.

This positive spirit created a dedicated project team that had many successes leading up to the overall success. Over one million Rands ($3.6 million) worth of material and equipment was ordered and not one single item was late. Each piece of piping fitted correctly the first time—and there were many hundreds of meters installed. The managing director of one company opened up his factory over the Easter weekend to supply urgently required material. The production department, swept up in the spirit of the project, applied the same principles to re-commissioning activities and slashed the previous record for bringing the plant safely back online. The human factor was what made the project a success.

Scope Management

The objective of the project was clear from the beginning: Bring the plant back online in the shortest possible time. The first step was to determine the exact scope of the repair. We had to determine if it was an option to simply do nothing. A communication link was set up between CBI and the Sastech process engineers, which involved working very long hours because of the ten-hour time difference between South Africa and the United States. Their decision analysis revealed that the optimum solution was to remove the damaged shell sections.

While they were deliberating, other scope functions were already running in parallel. A meeting was convened to identify that work which could be performed irrespective of the type of repair selected. Items that fell into this category included removing the damaged packing material, insulation, and cladding, which would have to be changed even if the decision was to do nothing. Tasks that could not wait for a formal decision before starting without affecting their overall duration, and therefore the duration of the project, also had to be identified.

Scope statement. The brief scope statement issued initially simply stated that part of the Benfield Unit was offline due to fire damage and that it must be repaired as soon as possible. Development of the scope statement from this single sentence to the final format was carried out in conjunction with the development of the work breakdown structure. In fact, the work breakdown structure formed the basis of the scope, quality, schedule, and cost control documents.

To reduce bureaucracy, only two aspects required management approval: technical and process decisions used to determine whether to repair the column or leave it in its damaged condition. The baseline plan therefore lay in the hands of the project team. There were no fundamental changes to the baseline plan throughout the project life-cycle apart from the fact that durations were reduced and the project was completed ahead of schedule.

Project plan and control system. Once the optimum course of action was decided upon, planning started in earnest. The first step was to develop a work breakdown structure. This was completed at open meetings with representatives from each interested party present. A brainstorming process was used, with each topic identified on a Post-it note and attached to a huge white board. Delegates were encouraged to shout out tasks as they came to mind. The meeting was adjourned once the ideas dried up. A second meeting was convened to fine-tune and accept the WBS. The WBS determined what had to be done and when it had to take place, as well as the logic associated with each task.

Everyone was aware from the start that a higher premium would be placed on team performance than on individual performance. That this concept was clearly understood was demonstrated during feedback sessions. As soon as a task was reported as being in trouble or not being completed ahead of schedule, the rest of those present immediately offered to help. This removed the fear of reporting negative feedback and raised the morale of the whole team.

On completion of the project, a series of post-project analysis meetings were convened with the major players. Although we thought we had fast-tracked this project to the last second, there were a number of problems which, if recognized, would have saved time on the critical path. For instance, we failed to consider religious faith when we drew up the schedule. A number of the welders and boilermakers employed on the fabrication of the new shell sections were Muslims whose religious festival of Ramadan fell right in the middle of the most critical portion of their work. By the time we realized the problem, it was too late to employ welders with the same track record of zero defects from other ethnic groups. We updated the planning checklist to include this topic in case the same situation arises in the future.

QUALITY MANAGEMENT

Quality was one of the ground rules of the project. Everyone employed on the project had previously worked within the Sasol quality system and was familiar with Sasol's forms and procedures. One aspect that emphasized how far team building had come was the cooperation between QC personnel and the artisans. Not once did the foreman or supervisor have to call out the QC people to do their work; they were ready and waiting for the artisan to finish each task. The artisans didn't rush off to the tea hut the minute their work was complete; they stayed behind and helped the inspectors by preparing and cleaning the material to be inspected. This was reciprocated by the inspectors who dropped their "That's failed ... fix it!" attitude and worked together with the artisan to identify problems and rectify them.

From a managerial point of view, normal quality-related steps were followed for each aspect of the project. The complete quality dossier for the project was signed off and filed before the close-out certificate was signed.

TIME MANAGEMENT

From the beginning it was clear that the project would be schedule-driven. There would be no constraints as far as resources were concerned and no "float" would be published. Tasks identified during the development of the WBS were given to the teams responsible for carrying out the work and they were asked to attach durations to them. This gave the teams ownership of the schedule; and who better to develop accurate durations than the people with the relevant experience?

In the initial stages a two-day look-ahead window was used, which allowed immediate tasks to continue while future tasks were being developed. Meetings were held twice a day in the initial stages as detail was developed and input into the program. Because of its user-friendliness, Microsoft Project for Windows was used as the scheduling tool at the beginning of the project.

The schedule was also used to identify resources with the potential to affect critical task durations. Resource utilization was continuously examined to make sure that the labor and equipment to perform each task in the shortest possible time was available. If a task had work for ten welders but only eight welding machines were available, two additional welding machines would be located, plus a standby. The standby philosophy also applied to labor.

COST MANAGEMENT

Project cost management principles employed on this job paid a handsome dividend. The initial budget was R23,300,000 ($85,278,000) and the final job cost was R17,414,945 ($63,738,698): a massive savings of 25.26 percent of the total project cost.

A cost control base was developed based on the existing Sastech system and established estimating and forecasting methods. Regular feedback was given to each cost center. A one-page cost report was developed and presented to management on a regular basis.

Costs were also reduced by using techniques like value analysis. One example of cost reduction due to value analysis was the saving of hundreds of meters of scaffolding required to weld the connecting piping to the column. The regulations state that you can either put men or equipment into a man-rider basket hung from a crane; you cannot have both. This regulation was challenged and a man-rider was developed specifically to carry men *and* equipment. Drawings were taken to the responsible government minister in Pretoria, who accepted the proposal. A prototype was fabricated on-site. It passed the required tests with flying colors and was immediately put into service. From conception of the idea to the approved piece of equipment being used on-site took only four days.

RISK MANAGEMENT

Risk management ranged from ad hoc discussions to formal Potential Deviation Analysis (PDA) studies. Some of the results of these studies included arranging to receive weather reports from two different weather stations twice daily, extending every scaffold to make it possible to drape tarpaulins over the tower in the event of rain, the extensive use of standby equipment and materials, extensive servicing of equipment in the early stages of the project, canceling Easter holidays for key personnel (not a single person objected to this measure), and having crane maintenance personnel permanently on-site during lifting operations. Formal PDA sessions were convened for operations such as the removal and replacement of the shell sections. These sessions were attended by representatives from the fire brigade, insurance companies, production, maintenance, loss control, projects, design, Sasol management, and everyone involved in the operation.

In order to minimize risk associated with design, all design information was verified by actual site measurement before being finalized. The small increase in time paid dividends in the fact that all designs fitted the first time, reducing rework to zero.

TEAM DEVELOPMENT AND HUMAN RESOURCES MANAGEMENT

For a team to function at its peak, each member must devote all his or her energy to the task at hand. If they are worried about things like working conditions and transport arrangements, they will not be able to devote all their efforts to the project. Thus, a simple plan, centered around communication and considering the "soft" issues of each team member, maximized the motivation of the workforce.

The huge hierarchical gap between team members at some of the meetings had to be recognized. On some occasions, participants ranged from the factory manager to site laborers, and lower-level team members tended not to contribute in such senior company, which stifled valuable input. Therefore, meeting attendees were very carefully selected.

One member of the project team was appointed to give feedback to management and one member of the management team was appointed to receive it. This reduced the risk of confusing or misleading information being propagated up the management ladder. Secondary information was always cleared with the contact person before it was accepted, eliminating rumors and exaggerations.

The "soft" issues of hourly-paid team members involved ensuring that transport was provided, that contractors' accommodations were acceptable, that lunch packs were provided for the entire project team every day, and that overtime hours were strictly controlled. This policy of "looking after the people and letting the people look after the job" really worked. One example: A welder flown in from the United States was accommodated in a well-appointed apartment. Expecting him to be more than satisfied, we were amazed to discover that he was not happy with his situation. He was on night shift and the apartment block was also home to a large number of noisy small children. The welder got virtually no sleep. He was moved to the more Spartan but quieter Sasol single quarters and his productivity shot up the next day.

PROCUREMENT MANAGEMENT

Only two main contracts were entered into, one for the repair of the pressure envelope of the column and the second for all the other ancillary work such as removing and replacing piping, painting, scaffolding, rigging, and cranage. Therefore, Sastech would have to trust contractors to work on a verbal instruction to proceed, followed in due course by a conventional written contract. There simply was not enough time to work any other way. All the steps used in conventional procurement and contract management were followed, but on an informal basis and in a very short time frame.

CBI, the fabricator and installer of the original column, was asked to provide a target price within three days and to follow this up within a further ten days with a fixed price. Sasdiens was selected for the remainder of the work because it was on-site, knew the Sasol systems, and was part of the Sasol organization. Its contract was on a rates basis with a governing target price.

In addition, ten smaller contractors were involved. We were honest with all of them, explaining the situation and asking them to proceed without official paperwork in cases where it could not be generated timely. Though risky, this paid off. The level of trust in Sastech was such that we were invited to attend the internal meetings of some of the contractors.

On the procurement side, one buyer was selected to handle all purchase orders. By using one person rather than a department we had accurate feedback when and where we needed it. The risk associated was that if anything happened to the buyer, we would lose continuity. We reduced this risk by asking the buyer to keep a handwritten diary of events on his desk at all times.

The approach adopted with suppliers was to go in aggressively to ensure that we were not taken advantage of in our vulnerable situation. Once we came to an agreement, we dropped the adversarial attitude. By including suppliers in the team, we reaped tremendous benefits. A number of suppliers worked at night, during weekends, and even during holidays.

COMMUNICATIONS MANAGEMENT

Most of the communications management techniques employed on this project are described elsewhere in this article—which is as it should be, since communication is at the heart of successful management of risk, scope, cost, and so on. Communications management, the golden thread that ran through the project, was the one aspect that received the greatest attention; yet, it was also the one where most improvements were identified during the post-project evaluation.

A number of important people were left out of the communications list altogether at the beginning. One example was the quality inspector from the supply depot. When the first consignment of material was requested, we discovered that the inspector had gone home without clearing the goods we urgently required. We phoned him and apologized for not keeping him informed about the repair and he was on-site within ten minutes, eager to do his part. This incident prompted a critical look at the communication list, which revealed a surprisingly high number of "missing" people. A checklist was developed to ensure that the problem will not reoccur on future projects.

The communication channels covered contractors and vendors, subordinates, peers, and management, with frequency and type of communication structured to suit each recipient. At its request, feedback to management was mostly verbal and restricted to once per day so that we were not burdened with unnecessary paperwork. The only written reports given to management were the cost report and the schedule. One senior manager passed on progress information to interested parties outside the Sasol organization and to the head office. This ensured that there was only one "horse's mouth."

Meeting notes that required follow-up were typed into a computer program designed specifically for expediting action items. Each person with follow-up actions informed the meeting secretary on completion of the task so that the program could be updated. This meant that meetings could be restricted to exception items, which saved precious minutes each day. At meetings a PC screen was projected on the wall of the conference room for everyone to read. Minutes were printed at the end of each meeting. Since no one wanted his or her name to be on the follow-up list after the specified completion date, a great deal of effort was expended to ensure that action items were worked off quickly.

The only other information covered at every meeting was safety. Safety representatives were encouraged to give feedback and recommendations, and it was made clear to everyone that safety was not negotiable and that safety-related threats must be resolved on-site as soon as they were identified.

The project team spent a minimum of fourteen hours per day on-site. Talking to the workforce was an excellent way to pass on and receive information. As the level of familiarity increased, the quantity of information flow increased proportionally, confirming the maxim that the simplest solutions are the best.

CONCLUSION

The November 1993 issue of *Chemical Processing* contained an article entitled "'Fast Track' Approach Replaces Tower in Record Time." The column in question was 6 feet (1.83 m) in diameter and 140 feet (42.6 m) high. This compares to our column, which was 5.8 m (19 feet) in diameter and 70 m (231 feet) high. Their work was completed in ten weeks, a new record, according to the article. Our work was completed in only twenty-five days! This was the only other project of its kind that we could find to use as a benchmark; but it gives a good indication of what was achieved.

The project is over, but it lives on in the form of accumulated knowledge and lessons learned to be used on all future projects.

Study Questions

THE BENFIELD COLUMN REPAIR PROJECT

1. A work breakdown structure was used in the project management of the project described in this case. According to the *PMBOK Guide,* what is the concept of the work breakdown structure?

2. The work breakdown structure is described as a key for the scope management of the project. Describe the process used in this project to develop the WBS.

3. The author of this case presents communications management as "the golden thread which ran through the project." If the supplier relationships were less trustful, how would this have changed the management and success of the project?

4. This project challenged the way in which things are usually done, and based its success on what were considered special management methods. Mention a couple of the examples from the project which you think reflect these "special" practices.

5. How did the project build commitment from every member of the team? List several reasons for this commitment.

Food Waste Composting at Larry's Markets

Brant Rogers, Environmental Affairs Manager, Larry's Markets

PM Network, February 1995, pp. 32–33

The food waste composting project at Larry's Markets became one of the country's first when it began in the fall of 1991. The project is part of the company's comprehensive environmental program that includes recycling, waste reduction, energy conservation, water management, environmental landscaping, environmental product evaluation, community project support, and more.

Food waste composting was proposed in mid-1991 as a potential cost saving measure and method of reducing the company's impact on the natural environment. According to 1991 waste audits, 3000 tons of byproducts (e.g., garbage, cardboard, food waste, plastics, glass, etc.) were produced by the company's five stores during a typical year. Of this, over 700 tons per year were estimated to be compostable, and most of the compostable material was produced in the stores' produce and floral departments.

The project's mission was to capture all of the produce and floral department byproducts for composting by late 1993. Because food waste composting projects were virtually unknown, one of the project's first objectives was to find project team members to haul and compost Larry's byproducts.

Another fundamental objective of the project was to have the composting function well within the normal day-to-day activities of the company. To accomplish this, the project team included management staff of all stores.

As full-scale composting began in early 1992, the volume of material grew rapidly. In 1992 about 350 tons were composted. In 1993 almost 700 tons were composted. As the amount of material composted grew, the amount of material going to landfills decreased proportionately. In 1991, 2,000 tons of garbage were produced. In 1992 about 1,250 tons were produced, and in 1993 about 1,050 tons were produced. The proportion of the byproduct stream going to landfill declined significantly from 69 percent in 1991 to 47 percent in 1992 and to 36 percent in 1993.

In addition, Larry's began using the finished compost for landscaping. A new Larry's store in Tukwila, Washington, which opened in July 1993, used the compost in the topsoil of its large landscape. Also, Larry's B.I.O. Scapes landscaping staff uses the compost on the company's other landscapes, including an organic apple orchard and herb garden at its Kirkland, Washington, store.

As a result of the project, Larry's had reached a 64 percent recycling rate, exceeding the 50 percent goal for King County in 1995 and also Washington State's 60 percent goal for the year 2000. Also, the project has saved the company over $20,000 per year in garbage fees and has been a source of

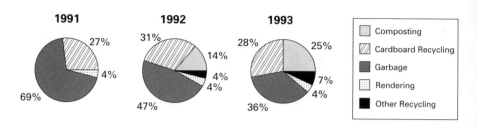

pride to employees and customers who are sensitive to environmental problems. Larry's received numerous letters, customer comments, and awards from local government and environmental groups for its efforts.

Study Questions

FOOD WASTE COMPOSTING AT LARRY'S MARKETS

1. The case description contains the following statement: "The project's mission was to capture all of the produce and floral department byproducts for composting by late 1993." The words mission, vision, objectives, and goals are very frequently used in management. What are their definitions and differences? Also, what were these for the Larry's Markets project?

2. Would this project be termed a success even if it meant no economic gain but the same environmental gain? If you were developing the proposal for this project given only the non-economic gain, how would you "sell" it to stakeholders?

3. This effort began as a project. In its current state, it is an ongoing effort by the company with no end in sight. Review the definition of a project and answer the following question: How can it be determined that an effort need no longer be managed as a project?

4. The outcome of this project was outstanding. What do you think are the primary reasons for this success?

Winning the Sydney to Hobart: A Case Study in Project Management

Lynn Crawford, University of Technology, Sydney

PMI *Proceedings*, 1993, pp. 53–59

INTRODUCTION

Campaigning for an ocean classic yacht race is a project. The campaign has a starting point which can be defined and the end of the race is the end of the project (1). It involves a process which requires management if the objectives are to be defined and achieved. Unlike many other projects where success may be open to debate and achievement of objectives may be unclear, this is a project in which project success or failure is as clear as the race results. As an interesting and atypical project type, it provides excellent opportunities to illustrate, examine, and question the application and operation of the project management framework.

The project was successful. The objectives were achieved; the races were won. This paper will briefly present, as a project, the campaign which culminated in the winning of both the 1992 Sydney to Hobart Yacht Race and the 1992 Kodak Asia Pacific Ocean Racing Championship. The phases of the project life-cycle—concept, development, execution, and finishing (2); the four basic project management functions—management of scope, quality, time, and cost; and the other essential project management functions—human resource management, communications management, contract/procurement management, and risk management—will be discussed in relation to the project.

As a case study, a project management framework is applied to the project, in retrospect. Many project managers tackle their tasks without conscious reference to the various project management frameworks developed by theorists. This project was carried out by a project initiator with many years experience and a reputation for success in leading projects in the corporate and financial field. Application of a rigorous and systematic process to a project outside his normal field of activity was both instinctive and a major reason for initiation of the project. However, the project process used does not necessarily fall neatly into accepted project management frameworks. Interpretation of the project in terms of project management theory is open to fruitful debate which provides project managers with useful insights to apply in planning and evaluating their own projects. An interesting question for debate is: What stage in this project can be regarded as execution or implementation in the project life-cycle? Is it the point at which

- the decision was made on the type of boat to be procured? or
- a commitment was made to acquire the boat? or
- the race entry was lodged? or
- the race started?

This case study adopts the acquisition of the boat for the race as the point marking the start of the execution phase, but other interpretations could be equally valid.

The project demonstrates the value of strategies which can be applied to a wide range of project types.

PROJECT LIFE-CYCLE

The project life-cycle (3) is used here to provide a summary of the major activities undertaken throughout the project. The phases and activities will be covered at varying levels of detail in the balance of the paper (see Figure 1).

PHASE 1: CONCEPT

Identification of Needs and Opportunities

Projects arise in response to an identified need. In February 1992, a former corporate high flyer and keen sailor, decided that he needed a new boat. His current yacht, "a 10.2 m speed machine, designed by Ben Lexcen, called *The Pink Boat*" (4) was then four years old and no longer competitive. Important bits, like the mast, were falling over too often when the boat was pushed too hard. There was no longer any point in persevering with it in serious racing.

With excellent timing, the project initiator had retired from the corporate rat race at the height of the boom. Accustomed to a high-pressure business environment in which he had enjoyed considerable success, the project initiator had begun to miss the challenges of corporate life. Spurred on by the need to replace his current yacht, he decided to address his need for a new challenge by using his planning, organizational, financial, and general business skills to achieve success in a totally unrelated field—yacht racing.

In taking on this challenge he held a strong belief that winning in yacht racing is at least 80 percent over before you even get to a race—40 percent in the choice and setting up of the boat and 40 percent in selection and training of the crew. On this basis, 80 percent of the challenge of winning can be directly controlled, leaving 20 percent, the actual race, subject to unpredictable factors, primarily weather.

Hence, there was:
- a need for a new boat, which would be exciting and pleasurable to sail
- a need for challenge.

At the same time, the project initiator had identified an opportunity. By February 1992, the International Offshore Rule (IOR) was "still regarded as the grand prix rule of international racing, but rapidly losing worldwide popularity" (5). Although major regattas were still being run under IOR handicapping rules, there was rapid development of cruiser/racer fleets using the International Measurement System (IMS) for handicapping.

From the 1930s until the late 1980s, serious offshore racing had been conducted under IOR rules. By the late 1980s the IOR rules, as a measurement formula for handicapping boats, were out of date, relatively inflexible, and had given rise to fundamentally bad boat design resulting from efforts to cheat the rules. The IMS is based on the use of software (Velocity Prediction Programme), which, when fed with enough data about boats in a competition, can predict the theoretical maximum speed of any boat on any point under

Concept	Development	Execution	Finishing
Identification of Need and Opportunity **Initial Risk Assessment** **Review Alternative Approaches** **Scope Management** • Definition of project objectives: —Time —Cost —Quality	**Boat** • Select boat design —Performance and market research • Decide acquisition strategy **Project Team** • Establish initial project team **Communications** • Monitor project environment **Prepare Project Plan** **Risk Assessment**	**Boat** • Procure boat • Fit out boat **Project Team** • Commit crew • Train crew **Testing** • Test boat and crew **Administration** • Ensure rule compliance • Lodge race entries **Risk Assessment** **Communications** • Monitor project environment • Manage public relations	**Start race 1** • Continually tune boat and crew • Review, establish, and implement strategy for each race **Finish race 5** (Each race a separate project or subproject)

FIGURE 1   **PROJECT LIFE-CYCLE FOR OCEAN RACE CAMPAIGN**

predicted or actual wind conditions. Boats designed for IMS racing were proving cheaper, faster, and more enjoyable to sail. As Bruce Farr, one of the top half dozen boat designers in the world, and a leader in design of boats specifically for IMS racing, said:

> In our early IMS designs we simply chose what we believed were good boat styles and designed as well as we could.... This approach yields boats that are very fast for their size, inexpensive relative to size (and especially to performance), an absolute pleasure to sail, and simply a lot of fun (6).

Although Australia was lagging behind the rest of the world in converting from IOR to IMS, it was fairly certain that IMS would eventually dominate.

The opportunity for someone looking for challenge, excitement, and a "modern, fast, seaworthy, and far less expensive ocean racer" (7) was to take the lead in IMS by campaigning a yacht purposely designed and built for IMS racing.

Having identified the needs and the opportunity, the next conscious step was definition of the project scope including objectives.

But in doing this, the project initiator recognized, as all project managers should, that opportunities have corresponding risks. Assessment and addressing of risk should begin at project definition.

His first instincts in response to the need and the opportunity was to replace his current boat with one in which he could enjoy sailing and winning. Being based in Australia, the obvious high profile race to aim to win was the Sydney to Hobart, conducted each year, starting on Boxing Day, the day after Christmas Day. Before deciding on project scope, however, the project initiator assessed the risks.

Initial Risk Assessment

Determination of project success on the results of one race, the Sydney to Hobart, over a distance of 630 miles (8), constituted a significant risk, due to the unpredictable and uncontrollable effects of weather conditions over considerable time (approximately three days) and distance. This could be offset by aiming to win the 1992 Kodak Asia Pacific Ocean Racing Championships which comprised five races, four of which were sailed out of Sydney Harbour in December, over distances between twelve to fifty miles, and less subject to unpredictable and uncontrollable conditions as they were sailed basically in the same weather. The Sydney to Hobart, although a race in its own right which could be entered and won independently on the Asia Pacific Championship, is the fifth and final race in the Asia Pacific Championship and carries double points. An objective of winning the 1992 Kodak Asia Pacific Ocean Racing Championship reduced the risk profile of the project.

Although it seemed likely, based on international precedent, that IMS division winners would be recognized in the Asia Pacific Championships and the Sydney to Hobart Yacht Race, it was not until mid-1992 that the race organizers finally decided to give dual status for IOR and IMS handicap winners. This constituted a risk at the outset of the project.

Even if the decision was made to recognize IMS division winners, there was no guarantee, early in 1992, that there would be no further change to IMS rules. They were then, and are still, subject to change which might impact on the competitiveness of boats designed specifically for IMS. It was possible that decisions could be made to adopt one design or special rules for a major regatta.

There was no established precedent for interpretation of rules. An established and entrenched IOR fleet could cause adverse pressures in rule application and interpretation. This would need constant monitoring and potentially require lobbying.

There was a strong risk that it might not be possible to be ready for competition in December 1992. The time constraints were extremely tight. In any case, there would be little time for tuning the boat and tuning and training the crew. It would be necessary to plan for aborting the project at any point if time constraints became unachievable.

There was a significant risk of potential embarrassment through failure to achieve project objectives.

Review Alternative Approaches

A possible alternative which was considered was the replacement of the current boat with a really good IOR boat to be campaigned in the 1992 Asia Pacific series, then sold and replaced by a purpose built IMS boat once the IMS rules had settled down and IMS racing was well established.

Although this alternative avoided risks involved in making a commitment to IMS before its future was settled, and the possibility of running out of time for the 1992 series, it was rejected because:
• The sale price of IOR boats was plummeting (e.g., one four-year-old IOR yacht had cost $600,000 to build and had recently been sold for $80,000), and "the competitive nature of IOR design quickly rendered them obsolete for international competition" (9).

• The project initiator/manager considered IMS boats more sensible in design and more pleasurable to sail than IOR boats. Sailing pleasure was a need of the initiator.

Scope Management—Project Definition

The project initiator clearly recognized both the risks and the opportunities. His career to date had been characterized by successes based on identifying, dealing with, and taking well calculated risks. His withdrawal from corporate life had been based on timely risk identification and effective risk management. With full recognition of the risks involved, he was attracted by:

• the opportunity to be *first* winner in a new IMS handicap division in the Asia Pacific Championships and Sydney to Hobart Yacht Race—a position in history
• the opportunity to enjoy sailing a state-of-the-art ocean racer
• the opportunity to be a leader and winner—an irresistible combination
• the opportunity to attract a first rate crew inherent in having a leading edge boat

The overall objective by which successful conclusion of the project would be judged was, therefore, defined as:

• to win the 1992 Asia Pacific Championships in the IMS division.

Project scope would include:

• acquisition of a boat purpose built for racing under IMS handicap rules
• establishment and training of a crew to race the boat
• competition in the 1992 Asia Pacific Championships, commencing in December 1992, under IMS handicap rules
• preparedness to abort the project at any stage if it became evident that the objectives could not be achieved.

Time management. Time was of the essence. The race series would begin on December 18, 1992. No extensions would be possible.

Quality management. Winning the race series in the IMS division would be dependent upon satisfying quality objectives. Choice and fit out of boat and selection of crew would be driven by the need for highest quality in order to achieve the overall project objective. Sailing pleasure was a quality objective.

Cost management. Due to the financial resources available to the project initiator, cost was subsidiary in importance to time and quality objectives in achievement of the overall project objective. In deciding on a purpose built IMS boat as against IOR, cost management had already been exercised to some extent as purpose built IMS boats cost significantly less than top of the range IOR boats.

PHASE 2: DEVELOPMENT

Project Team

The primary decision-maker was the project initiator/manager/potential owner and captain. He was assisted and advised at all stages by the crew of his current boat—*The Pink Boat*—and he had, over the years, established an expert advisory panel of experienced sailors, crew members, sail makers, boat designers, and builders.

The initial project team comprised the project initiator and a long-time colleague and crew member of his current boat, who was seven times world champion in different boats, and sought after as a crew member in ocean racing. The third and vital member was the owner of one of Sydney's top sail lofts.

The role of the initial project team was the selection of the boat and the rest of the crew.

An important and delicate issue of human resource management was the decision as to which members of the crew of the current boat would be involved in the project team and crew for this particular project.

Boat

The primary activity in the development stage of this project was the selection of the boat. This required considerable and extensive research.

A study of all IMS events around the world, and specifically the winners, indicated that Bruce Farr 44-foot designs were dominant. The 44-foot Farr-designed *Gaucho*, a yacht designed specifically to compete under IMS rules, had beaten all other IMS boats so soundly that it had led the establishment of a new breed of boat on the international sailing scene in what had become known as the "Gaucho Revolution." The project initiator/manager spent time with Bruce Farr and sailed on *Gaucho* in March 1993.

On the basis of race performance it would have been reasonable to follow the *Gaucho* lead and decide on a proven 44-foot Farr design. Farr had designed a 40-foot IMS boat, but at this stage it had not been built or raced. Examination of empirical data from previous races and advice from experts suggested that for the distance and weather conditions of the 630-mile Sydney to Hobart race a 40-foot boat was an optimum size in terms of performance, comfort, and ability to withstand varying weather conditions.

Factors considered were: The 44-foot *Gaucho* design was proven, with an unblemished record, but it required twelve to fourteen people to sail it (heavy crew requirement/commitment), and it was more expensive than the 40-foot design.

The project initiator/manager was really looking for a "sportscar style" boat—fast, with plenty of sail—and considered the proven 44-foot Farr design a little too big, a little too conservative, and a little too expensive. He was attracted to the as yet unbuilt and untried 40-foot design. While attracted by the 40-foot Farr design, the project initiator/manager recognized the inherent risk.

He continued his research, finding out all he could about potential builders, as it appeared most likely that he would have to arrange for a yacht to be built, regardless of the design chosen.

Gaucho had been built in Argentina, but this presented problems of transport and communication. An Australian or New Zealand builder was preferred for these reasons. Research suggested that a New Zealand builder might be most attractive in cost terms, as labor rates were sufficiently lower than in Australia, to offset the 25 percent tax which would apply. Two New Zealand builders were visited and assessed.

By May/June 1992 a decision had still not been made and the project initiator/manager was considering abandoning the project, or rather modifying the objective to aim for the equivalent 1993 race series. However, while market research and evaluation had been proceeding, Mick Cookson of Cooksons in New Zealand, had decided to build himself a 40-foot Farr design. This boat, *High Five*, was finished in June 1992 and won the Kenwood Cup in July. It proved to be very much as the project initiator/manager had expected—a sportscar style ocean racer, with large sail area, and a challenge to sail.

Spurred on by the success of *High Five*, Cookson started building another 40-foot Farr on a speculative basis. The project initiator/manager was able to negotiate an extremely favorable fixed price to take over the boat Cookson had under construction.

The final selection of the design and procurement method or acquisition strategy were, therefore, decided virtually simultaneously. The decision minimized risk as far as possible. The 40-foot Farr design had been proven by the performance of *High Five*. A time advantage was achieved as the new boat was already under construction.

PHASE 3: EXECUTION

Boat

Procure boat. The agreement for procurement of the boat was signed in August 1992 and the boat completed, for the amount initially agreed, at the end of October 1993.

Fit out boat. On completion of the boat, a skeleton crew, including the project initiator/manager and his top two crew members, flew to New Zealand to oversee initial fit out and trial the boat, spending three days sailing the boat with the crew from *High Five*. Full support and assistance were given by Cooksons and the experienced crew which had sailed *High Five* successfully in the Kenwood Cup. Once it was trialled, and they were happy with the set up, they marked settings, dismantled the boat, and had it shipped to Australia. Training with full crew began in early November 1992. The aim was to optimize the IMS rating through adjustment of set up, trimming, and weight.

Other aspects which had to be decided and arranged before the boat left the Cookson yard were the color scheme for the boat—and most importantly, the name. Much consultation resulted in adoption of the name *Assassin* which reflected the level of opposition and depth of feeling against this bold new breed on the ocean racing scene. Public relations had become a key issue.

Project Team

Commit and train crew. The selection and securing of the crew were as important as selection and securing of the boat. All key crew members were committed prior to the commitment to the boat. The right combination of boat, crew, commitment, and conditions were identified as essential to success of the project.

IMS rules provide the opportunity to choose the crew weight, and a decision was made to establish a crew of nine.

Crew, or team, members were carefully selected for particular positions based on previous experience and track record, motivation, and commitment and ability to work well together. Roles were clearly defined and agreed to by project team members.

The project initiator/manager fostered team relationships, watching the various personalities, keeping the peace, and relieving tensions when required.

Team motivation was assured by the nature of the campaign and the team members selected. All team members really liked sailing and took it seriously in career terms. The campaign was established as the leading edge in yachting. This would be one of the first purpose built IMS boats, and the first time that there would be an IMS handicap division winner in the Sydney to Hobart Yacht Race, one of the world's most prestigious ocean racing competitions. With a leading-edge boat and top crew there was a real chance of winning. The better the boat and the crew, the more fun there is in sailing. Team members had the opportunity of enjoying good sailing while improving their own skills and enhancing their yachting careers and reputation.

Administration and Control

The race entry had to be lodged correctly and prior to the official closing date of October 31, 1993.

Developments in IMS rules, and their interpretation and application, both internationally and in particular, locally, for the Sydney to Hobart race had to be monitored constantly. This was not difficult due to close and active participation in the yachting community and through the boat builders who had a vested interest in the ultimate performance of the boat. Compliance of the boat through construction and in set up and tuning, with IMS handicap rules, was ensured.

There were five certifications required to enable entry. These were carried out a couple of weeks before the first race in order to allow time for changes if necessary. Most of the certifications were purely objective, but accommodation regulations were open to interpretation and careful lobbying was required to ensure that attempts by entrenched interests did not cause difficulties in this area.

PHASE 4: FINISHING

Prior to the start of the Sydney to Hobart race on December 27, 1992, *Assassin* raced successfully in the four lead-up races of the 1992 Kodak Asia Pacific Ocean Racing Championship. At the end of the fourth race *Assassin* was leading the IMS point score in the Asia Pacific Championship. The team members were feeling like winners. The boat had been well tuned. Morale and excitement were high.

The Sydney to Hobart was worth double points. A good start to the race was important for morale, and *Assassin* made "a classic windward end start" (10), winning the start from other boats at that end of the line by two boat lengths and surviving "a spirited luffing incident" (11) with another boat. Going out to sea it was well positioned in sixth place and was well ahead of boats it had to beat on handicap. "Helmsman on *Assassin*, Bob Fraser, on his 14th Sydney-Hobart, had the best summation of. ... the 630-nautical-mile dash south: It was a windy, wet, cold, 'never do another one' sort of Hobart race (12)." The project initiator/manager's comment was that "it was a pretty tough Hobart. We had two reefs in the main and a storm jib up for probably two thirds of the race. It just went on and on and on (13)." The Farr IMS designs perform best upwind, but only 3–4 percent of the race was to windward. The project initiator/manager claimed that time spent in selecting the crew and developing teamwork was well rewarded by the team's ability to achieve a winning performance "despite the fact that conditions did not suit the boat's full strength" (14). The boat remained dry and intact throughout the race.

The strategy chosen and adhered to for the race was to sail as close as possible to the rhumb line and always sail the favored tack or gibe rather than chase weather systems (15).

THE RESULTS

The project was an undisputed success. *Assassin* won in the 48th Sydney to Hobart Yacht Race and with it the 1992 Kodak Asia Pacific Championship in the IMS division.

CONCLUSION

Project Success—Objectives Achieved

The project initiator/manager and the project team were proven right in their decision to campaign for an IMS win. In the Sydney to Hobart "the number of IMS entries (61) over IOR (34) reflected the acceptance of the new rule (16)." As it turned out, the IMS division proved far stronger than the traditional IOR division. This may well not have been the case, and this possibility had been identified as a definite area of risk in the initial assessment for the project.

The decision to procure and race a boat purpose built to IMS rules was clearly justified as:
• Leadership in the field made it possible to secure the best possible crew.
• The combination of boat and crew made it possible to achieve a historic win in the first ever IMS division of the Sydney to Hobart.

The decision to procure a Farr-designed boat was justified not only by the win of *Assassin* but by Farr designs winning all three divisions in the race.

The decision to procure a 40-foot Farr IMS design was justified by the win of the 40-foot *Assassin* over its close rival, the Farr 50-foot IMS design, *Morning Mist III*, which had secured a crew of equal calibre to *Assassin* as the first of the Farr IMS 50s to be launched.

Project Strategies for Project Success

This case study of a clearly successful project demonstrates a number of strategies which can be applied to a wide range of project types.

Characteristics vital to the success of this project were:
• extensive market research prior to major decisions (selection of boat)
• extensive risk assessment at all stages including modification of the key project objective in order to reduce risk (key objective changed from winning the Sydney to Hobart to winning the five-race Asia Pacific series)
• identifying an opportunity (taking the risk in competing on new race rules—IMS)
• securing the best possible project team (crew)
• committing key team members early and involving them in major project decisions (e.g., selection of boat)
• constant monitoring of the project environment (rule changes and interpretations)

- treating each of the five races in the Asia Pacific series as a project with project performance feedback from each race being fed back into strategy and tuning of the boat and crew for the next race (or subproject)
- motivation of the project team through project objectives and project quality (the crew was committed and motivated by the excitement of winning and by knowing that it was a top-flight crew, sailing a superbly fitted leading edge boat).

Another interesting aspect of the case study is that the project initiator was prepared to abort the project at any stage rather than sacrifice quality. For instance, he was not prepared to make a decision on the boat for the campaign without extensive research as to the most suitable design. This may have meant that insufficient time remained for the achievement of the project for 1992 in which case he would have revised his objectives.

According to the project life-cycle interpretation adopted, nearly 50 percent of the project duration was spent in the concept and development phases. This combined with the undoubted success of the project supports, and the importance of effort devoted to initial stages of projects to their ultimate success.

REFERENCES

1. Wideman, R. M. 1987. "The Framework: Part 1 The Rationale." *Project Management Body of Knowledge.* Upper Darby, PA: Project Management Institute, p. 1–1.

2. Ibid.

3. Ibid.

4. Wolfe, K., and P. Campbell. "Vanguard of Change." *Club Marine* 8, no. 1, p. 10.

5. Campbell, P. 1993. "A New Era of Ocean Yacht Racing." *Offshore Yachting.* The Cruising Yacht Club of Australia. Feb.–Mar., p. 11.

6. Farr, B. 1993. "The IMS in 1993—Coming of Age." *Seahorse.* The Official Magazine of the Royal Ocean Racing Club. June, Issue 160, p. 47.

7. Campbell, P. 1993. "A New Era of Ocean Yacht Racing." *Offshore Yachting.* The Cruising Yacht Club of Australia. Feb.–Mar., p. 10.

8. Gore, P. (Ed.). 1988. *The Eighties' Greatest Yacht Races.* Sydney: Robertsbridge Limited.

9. Campbell, P. 1993. "A New Era of Ocean Yacht Racing." *Offshore Yachting.* The Cruising Yacht Club of Australia. Feb.–Mar., p. 11.

10. *The Sun-Herald.* Dec. 27, 1992, p. 67.

11. Wolfe, K., and P. Campbell. "Vanguard of Change." *Club Marine* 8, no. 1, p. 9.

12. Ross, B. 1993. "Wet and Windy." *Australian Sailing.* Feb., p. 28.

13. Ibid., p. 34.

14. Ibid., p. 35.

15. Mundle, R. 1993. "Rags to Riches." *Modern Boating.* Mar., p. 26.

16. Ibid., p. 27.

Study Questions

WINNING THE SYDNEY TO HOBART: A CASE STUDY IN PROJECT MANAGEMENT

1. The project initiator believes that winning a yacht race depends 80 percent on the preparation stage and only 20 percent on the effort in the actual race. Einstein was quoted as saying that a creation is 10 percent inspiration and 90 percent perspiration. Which of these statements do you agree with? Why, given a project management context?

2. This project essentially describes a job-shop point of view. How might the creation of a fleet of championship boats change the described project life-cycle?

3. Cost management was described as subsidiary to time and quality objectives for this project. If this situation had been different, i.e., a restrictive boat budget, how might the project results have changed?

4. Had this same project analysis been performed on another boat in the Sydney to Hobart, how might it have pointed out any deficiencies in the project process?

5. The case mentions the importance of meeting the requirements of five different certifications along with careful lobbying in order to enable entry of the yacht into the races. All projects face these kinds of challenges. Review the literature to develop your own model for dealing with these issues.

Kodak's New Focus

Mark Maremont

Business Week, January 30, 1995, pp. 62–68

Not long after taking the helm of Eastman Kodak Co. in late 1993, George M. C. Fisher bought a new house.

Not just any house. He and his wife, Ann, chose a spacious estate on East Avenue, a boulevard that strikes out from the center of Rochester, N. Y., and meanders into the suburbs. On the very same road, a few miles closer to town, sits another house once owned by a Kodak chairman named George: the fifty-room mansion built in 1905 by George Eastman, the company's visionary founder. Coincidence? Fisher thinks it could be more like destiny.

Acutely aware that the responsibility for restoring Eastman's legacy rests on his shoulders, Fisher has mentioned their common address on more than one occasion. He often jokingly refers to Eastman as "the other George." And he likes to point out the parallels between his strategy and the game plan of Kodak's founder, who combined technological genius with something in short supply at the company recently—marketing vision.

Not many executives would compare themselves to one of the icons of American industry. But George Fisher, 54, doesn't lack self-confidence. In giving up his CEO post at fast-growing Motorola Inc. to come to Kodak, he traded a virtually sure thing for one of America's toughest management challenges. Kodak has spent billions on research and development, diversification, and repeated restructurings. Fisher's immediate predecessor, Kay R. Whitmore, implemented no fewer than three reorganizations—yet Kodak earned less in 1993 than it had in 1982. Although blessed with a powerhouse brand name, it seemed trapped in the slow-growth photography industry, hobbled by huge debts, a dysfunctional management culture, and a dispirited workforce.

It's too early to say whether Fisher can yet lay claim to the other George's crown. But after barely a year at the helm, Kodak's new chief has clearly shaken up the sluggish giant as never before. He has sold off its health-care businesses and refocused the company around its core imaging business. Asset sales have also allowed him to slash the photography giant's debt load from a burdensome $7.5 billion in 1993 to an estimated $1.5 billion last year.

Far less tangible but no less crucial to Kodak's future has been Fisher's progress in reinvigorating a bloated, hierarchical management. He has started to tackle Kodak's matrix management system, which deflected responsibility for poor performance. And although morale is still shaky, Fisher has given staffers hope that the company has a future beyond repeated restructurings. "I'd call George's first year a spectacular success," says University of Michigan management professor C. K. Prahalad, who has consulted for both

Fisher's Bold Beginning

Focused Strategy   Company had been floundering, unsure which businesses to pursue. Fisher decided imaging was key to the future and sold Kodak's health and household-products arms.

Created Digital Imaging Unit   With product development and sales scattered among divisions, digital effort was ill-focused. Fisher gathered most of the talent into one division and hired an experienced computer marketing executive to head it.

Repaired Balance Sheet   By selling off businesses, notably the Sterling drug operation, he has slashed the company's total debt from $7.5 billion to $1.5 billion. Photography cash machine is now available to fund growth, not debt payments.

Improved Morale   After years of restructuring and uncertain direction, employees were disheartened. By stressing bright future and improving communication, Fisher has perked up spirits.

Began Overhauling Culture   By stressing accountability, quality, and cycle time, Fisher is beginning to transform Kodak's slow-moving culture. Made pay more dependent on performance.

... And The Challenges Ahead

Re-Ignite Growth   Fisher believes Kodak can double its growth rate in photography, a tough challenge in slow-growing global market. Key target: Asia, especially China, where Kodak lags behind Fuji.

Hire New Talent   Company needs outside blood. So far, Fisher has hired a new CEO and head of digital imaging. Badly needs marketing depth.

Improve Customer Focus   Kodak still is driven by engineering mentality that devises products first before finding buyers. Company must become more market savvy.

Sign Joint Ventures   Kodak can't do it alone in digital arena. Company has to expand its technology base. Fisher's platinum rolodex should work here. Promise of big announcements in 1995.

Cut Costs Further   Plenty of fat still around. Big targets include receivables, inventories, corporate overhead. No way Kodak can compete in digital arena with its high cost structure.

Kodak and Motorola. "He has cleaned up the company and created a new spirit, a new willingness to compete. He has laid the foundation."

Now, Fisher has to deliver. His strategy, as outlined in several lengthy interviews with *Business Week*, is fairly straightforward. First, he'll continue to work on Kodak's culture and costs. "There are textbook types of things that are wrong with this company," he says. "Decisions are too slow. People don't take risks." So Fisher is applying lessons learned at Motorola. By focusing on basics such as quality, customer needs, and shorter product-development time, he hopes to squeeze out costs and produce a more dynamic culture. He says results should start to show this year, but he believes it'll take three to five years to see dramatic progress.

The go-slow approach stands in sharp contrast to the rapid-fire job cuts and reorganizations practiced by many other CEOs who parachute into troubled companies. But Fisher thinks cost-cutting edicts from on high don't work well. He prefers to set tough goals, then let his managers decide how to achieve them. Moreover, Fisher fears drastic action could kill Kodak's golden goose: its consumer photography operation, which produces 75 percent of its operating profit on just 42 percent of its revenue. "There's no need to take a business with the share and profitability we have and screw it up by replacing experienced managers and injecting outsiders," he says.

That leads to his second goal: re-ignite growth. Fisher is convinced that Kodak's traditional film and paper business can grow at 7–9 percent annually for the next decade, about double the growth rate in recent years. How? In part, through expansion in the fast-moving economies of Asia, where Kodak has been badly lagging archrival Fuji Photo Film Co. And he sees dramatic growth in barely tapped developing markets such as Russia, India, and Brazil. "Half the people in the world have yet to take their first picture," says Fisher. "The opportunity is huge, and it's nothing fancy. We just have to sell yellow boxes of film."

Step-By-Step

Fisher is also counting on strong growth from Kodak's thus-far disjointed entry into the digital imaging market. Kodak's boss has gathered the company's far-flung digital projects into a single division and hired Carl Gustin, a former Apple Computer Inc. and Digital Equipment Corp. marketing executive, to head the unit. By embracing digital technology, he hopes to enhance photography and encourage more picture-taking. "The future is not some harebrained scheme of the digital Information Highway or something," he says. "It's a step-by-step progression of enhancing photography using digital technology."

The new emphasis on digital technology is already producing results. Early in 1995, Kodak will relaunch its poorly marketed Photo CD product to make it more useful to millions of desktop personal computer users. Another promising product is the new CopyPrint station, which uses digital technology to make enlargements from ordinary prints. None is exactly revolutionary. But again, the model is Motorola, which succeeded by pushing low-cost electronics items that turned into hits. "I'd bet we have at least one home run of the sort Motorola hit in cellular telephones," says Fisher.

It's a tantalizing turnaround plan. But so far, critics complain, progress is slow. Few on Wall Street expect good news on Jan. 31 when Kodak announces its 1994 results. The company has already hinted at more restructuring changes. Analyst B. Alex Henderson of Prudential Securities Inc. estimates that Kodak's earnings from continuing operations fell 4 percent last year, to $953 million, as its revenues rose by 7 percent, to $13.7 billion. At around 48, Kodak stock is little changed since Fisher's arrival in December 1993.

Tougher Than Moto

Even some Fisher boosters caution that he has taken on a monumental task. The core photography business is brutal, marked by growing capacity and falling prices. Just to keep profits flat, Kodak needs to cut manufacturing costs substantially every year. "This is a tougher challenge than Motorola," says Richard S. Braddock, former chairman of Medco Containment Services Inc. and a Kodak outside director. "Kodak has very high shares and high

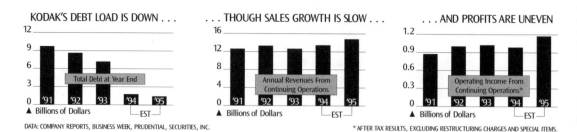

KODAK'S DEBT LOAD IS DOWN . . .

12
9
6
3
0   '91 '92 '93 '94 '95
▲ Billions of Dollars   └─EST─┘

Total Debt at Year End

DATA: COMPANY REPORTS, BUSINESS WEEK, PRUDENTIAL, SECURITIES, INC.

. . . THOUGH SALES GROWTH IS SLOW . . .

16
12
8
4
0   '91 '92 '93 '94 '95
▲ Billions of Dollars   └─EST─┘

Annual Revenues From
Continuing Operations

. . . AND PROFITS ARE UNEVEN

1.2
0.9
0.6
0.3
0   '91 '92 '93 '94 '95
▲ Billions of Dollars   └─EST─┘

Operating Income From
Continuing Operations*

* AFTER TAX RESULTS, EXCLUDING RESTRUCTURING CHARGES AND SPECIAL ITEMS.

margins. That's a difficult combination. While trying to be aggressive, you're also trying to defend what you have."

In the digital imaging arena, Kodak has a very different problem: It's just one of many hopefuls in a nascent industry. By its own count, Kodak faces no fewer than 599 global competitors working on optical storage technology that could challenge its Photo CD. And other rivals are chasing after the emerging digital market. Casio, for example, just introduced a $700, feature-laden digital camera. In other niches, ranging from scanners to printers, Kodak faces such giants as Canon, Fujitsu, Sony, and Hewlett-Packard. "Kodak has some good technology," says Jacques P. Kauffmann, an imaging consultant in Wilmette, Ill. "But they haven't yet shown any outstanding products. So far, they're just one player among many."

And fixing a deeply ingrained culture in a company with 88,000 employees could prove harder than Fisher realizes. Lower-level staffers complain that the changes haven't tiered down to them, decision-making is still painstakingly slow, and they remain concerned about Kodak's direction. Many skeptics would agree with the assessment of a longtime institutional investor in Kodak: "Fisher is a great manager in a tough environment," he says. "In a situation like that, very often the environment wins."

Still, even the naysayers aren't about to count Fisher out. Few CEOs boast his credentials as a technologist and manager. After getting his Ph.D. in applied mathematics from Brown University, he started as a scientist at Bell Labs. In 1976, he moved into management at Motorola, where he quickly made his mark as head of the pager division by breaking into the Japanese market. In 1988, Fisher took on the CEO's title.

As Motorola's CEO, Fisher excelled at motivating people, pushing decision-making down, and picking among the company's many promising technologies. Profits more than doubled during his tenure. But when the Kodak search committee came calling, Fisher was ready to listen. "I was already a success," he recalls. "But I was too young to begin to think about the end of my career. This was a chance to take a great company, like Kodak, that was having some transient problems, and build it back up into one of the world's greatest companies." A $2 million salary, $5 million signing bonus, and some juicy stock options helped seal the deal.

Once he arrived, it didn't take Fisher long to focus on Kodak's most visible problem: its balance sheet, weighed down by nearly $7.5 billion in debt. Much of that was the result of past acquisitions, notably Sterling Drug Inc. in 1988. A lot of the cash being generated by photography was going to service debt instead of funding new products and businesses. "We were going to milk the imaging business to death," says Fisher. By February 1994, he decided on a dramatic measure: sell the sprawling health and household-products divisions.

Kodak's New-Product Offensive

Advanced Photographic System "Smart" film and camera to be introduced in 1996. Stores data, such as shutter speed, on film as each picture is taken, permitting much finer processing and printing

Improved Single-Use Camera To be introduced in the United States this spring. Sleek plastic design and better flash mark big improvement over old disposable cameras.

Photo CD Relaunch planned for March 1995. Kodak will seek to revive product by marketing it to desktop-computer users.

Thermal Printers Kodak's $10,000 thermal printer is a market leader, producing near-photographic-quality prints. Company aims to get $1,000 version to market in 1996.

Copyprint Station Allows consumers to make high-quality copies and enlargements from ordinary prints, not negatives. In hundreds of photo stores already. Combines a digital scanner, PC, and thermal printer.

Quicktake Camera Introduced in mid-1994. Has Apple's name on it, but Kodak makes it. First low-cost (about $700) digital camera for desktop applications.

Royal Gold Film Replacement for flagging high-end Ektar film is doing well.

Custodial Mentality

The resulting auctions brought in $7.9 billion. By yearend, Kodak's debt was down to $1.5 billion, cutting annual interest payments by 80 percent, to $120 million, while freeing up much of the company's cash flow to back Fisher's new strategy. Just as important, the massive sale transformed Kodak from a conglomerate to a narrowly focused imaging company, making it easier to manage.

Kodak executives say the quick decision to sell the nonimaging operations was vintage Fisher. He rarely handles a piece of paper twice and usually gives executives a decision on the spot. That's a dramatic change at a company where "paralysis by analysis" had become an art. "People can study a problem around here forever," says Leo J. Thomas, the executive vice-president who heads the imaging group. "George has a willingness to use the 80/20 rule," which holds that it's O.K. to be right just 80 percent of the time if you act quickly.

The push for quick decision-making is part of a broad campaign by Fisher to overhaul Kodak's lethargic culture. When Fisher arrived, he found an insular company that venerated authority and frowned on confrontation. "It was so hierarchically oriented that everybody looked to the guy above him for what needed to be done," he says. That led to diffusion of responsibility: "How can you hold a person accountable if you've had three overrides on his decision?" he asks. Having been beaten down so long, he says, Kodak developed a custodial mentality geared to protecting current businesses rather than seeking new frontiers. "Why is Kodak in such a state of doldrums and Motorola so vibrant?" he asks. "One drives for growth, and the other doesn't.

You have a different mental attitude when you drive for growth. You don't just try to figure out how to manage your way through existing markets."

To help break down the rigid hierarchy and get his message across to all layers of the company, Fisher has turned himself into ambassador of informality. Low-key, genial, he almost never raises his voice or shows anger. Past Kodak CEOs tended to be aloof and autocratic. But managers liken Fisher's style to that of a coach—or parent. "It's like talking to your father," says Carl F. Kohrt, general manager of the $1.6 billion health sciences unit. "You don't want to disappoint him."

Fisher is also far more accessible and visible than previous Kodak CEOs. He frequently pops in on researchers for updates on projects and chats casually with staffers in the cafeteria where he breakfasts almost every workday—invariably on a bowl of Special K cereal and a mug of coffee. Employees are invited to send him E-mail messages, and they do—as many as thirty a day. His secretary prints them out, and he usually responds the next day with handwritten notes on the printouts—a personal touch staffers seem to appreciate.

More important, Fisher is trying to teach his managers that Kodak's ultimate fate rests on them. During management presentations, Fisher often flashes a slide with a single word on it: accountability. Kodak managers have frequently missed targets by a mile and suffered no consequences—but no longer, Fisher vows. In the annual planning process for this year, he worked hard with executives on coming up with realistic numbers and has been adamant that he will hold laggards responsible. And in late January, he plans to announce a new management-compensation structure that will tie pay more closely with performance. Kodak won't discuss details.

Kodak executives concede that many employees are reeling from the shift in direction. Staffers are also angered by a Fisher-ordered cutback in benefits last summer. And an announcement in December that 800 more jobs would be cut at the Kodak Park manufacturing complex in Rochester has further soured the air. "People's feelings about the company are still on a roller coaster," says Kohrt.

But Kodak execs say there's progress. In the labs, Kodak never used to measure the time it took to complete projects or even how fast they were progressing. With Fisher's emphasis on cycle time, managers have set up formal gauges.

The labs are key because the new, improved Kodak will need things to sell. Fisher has been spending a disproportionate amount of time on a subject dear to his technologist's heart: digital imaging. The term has been around since the late 1970s, when Kodak executives first realized that chemical-based photography faced a new rival. Images could be captured with digital cameras, stored on computer disks, altered with software, and zapped around by phone wires.

Kodak began frantically spending huge sums on digital imaging R&D—as much as $5 billion over the past decade. But by the time Fisher arrived, little had emerged from the labs. Some executives were gung ho, others fearful of introducing digital gear that would cannibalize high-margin film and paper sales. To compound the problem, product development and sales efforts were scattered over more than a dozen divisions.

At one point, Kodak was working, on twenty-three separate digital-scanner projects. Fisher ended the debate. Kodak would push full-speed into digital imaging: "And if that eats up some of the film business, so be it." He also folded most digital efforts into a new Digital & Applied Imaging Division. To run it, he turned to Gustin, one of several outsiders Fisher hired to help him revitalize Kodak's management. An ebullient former advertising executive who talks at a rapid clip, Gustin says he was amazed at the technology languishing in Kodak's closet. Outsiders agree that Kodak has top technology in several key digital imaging areas. Among them are color-management software to ensure true reproduction and charged-couple devices (CCDS) that act as the eyes for digital cameras and scanners. One big problem, Gustin quickly surmised, was lack of marketing ability. To help overcome that drawback, Gustin is on the verge of hiring a half-dozen experienced computer marketing executives. Fisher has also hired former Apple Chairman John Sculley as a part-time marketing consultant in the digital-imaging area.

Thanks to the reorganization, Gustin claims he and his team will soon silence critics who believe stodgy Kodak is incapable of achieving the six-month development cycles typical in the computer industry. Back in November, Gustin says, he started a project to develop a $1,000 desktop version of a four-month-old, $10,000 color thermal printer that spits out high-quality color images on special paper using a heat-transfer process. That version weighs about 60 pounds and has 500 parts. In less than a month, he says, Kodak engineers built a 14-pound, sixty-five-part prototype with better performance specs.

Gustin promises a raft of new digital products early next year. In addition to the less expensive thermal printer, he's aiming to introduce a $300 digital scanner and a digital camera in the $300 range. Apple's QuickTake digital camera made by Kodak is among the cheapest now on the market, at $700. Gustin's division had revenues of about $500 million in 1994, roughly 4 percent of Kodak's total sales. Gustin has told Fisher that it will grow by 67 percent in 1995 and will take another leap the following year. Meanwhile, Gustin is looking to resurrect Kodak's faltering Photo CD project. Launched in mid-1992, it was badly misdirected at the consumer market as a high-tech way to see photos on TV. But few photo buffs wanted to spend about $1 to transfer each snapshot to a compact disk. In March Kodak will relaunch Photo CD, this time aimed at the PC user. By adding software to each Photo CD platter, Kodak plans to make it easier to retrieve photos and use them in electronic documents. A personnel manager, for example, could load a Photo CD with pictures of employees into a CD-Rom drive and create an organizational chart complete with photos.

Although digital imaging embraces everything from Sega video games to on-demand cable-TV movies, Kodak is sticking mostly to its historical niche of color still images. That's a plenty big enough market, says Gustin, who says Kodak wants to make it cheap and easy for people to use high-quality images in everything from real estate listing sheets to school essays. But Kodak doesn't have the clout or the technology to do it alone. That's why Fisher and Gus have been trying to get other industry players to adopt Kodak's technologies as standards in the computer and multimedia worlds. Fisher's platinum Rolodex of information-industry contacts has been crucial in the hunt. He has used his contacts at the University of Illinois' National Center for Supercomputing Applications in a drive to get Photo CD accepted as a standard for sending images over the Internet. He has also met with other corporate heavyweights, among them Microsoft's Bill Gates and Scott McNealy of Sun Microsystems, to discuss licensing and partnership deals.

Microsoft will include Kodak's color management standards in its Windows '95 operating system. Kodak also says it's working with leading telecom companies on ways to make it easier to send images over phone lines. And on Jan. 17, Kodak said it would license a technology from Live Picture Inc. that will speed image processing on Photo CDs. Other deals should be announced in the first quarter.

Again, while the strategy sounds fascinating, skeptics abound. Bob Goldstein, president of ZZYZX Visual Systems, a Los Angeles imaging lab, is one of the leading Photo CD users in the country. But he has been frustrated because key enhancements, such as the ability to encrypt images, have been repeatedly promised by Kodak but never delivered. "I'm going to reserve judgment until I see the products actually hitting the street," he says.

Transformation

Others point out that Kodak has never been good at manufacturing electronic gear in high volumes and low cost. Nearly all of its equipment is aimed at the less competitive, pricey end of the market, from copiers to scanners. And when Kodak tried to sell consumer products in the past—8mm camcorders, videotape, even batteries—it quickly dropped out when the competition got too stiff. "They're going into a totally different business, with totally different distribution channels and much slimmer margins," says one former Kodak executive. "They have an incredibly long road ahead."

Fisher concedes Kodak is still feeling its way in the digital world. His aim is to get an array of new products and services to the markets, figure which ones work, and make a course correction. Meanwhile, Fisher is counting on a revolutionary new film and camera system to expand the consumer photography market. Developed in partnership with five Japanese companies, including Fuji, Canon, and Nikon, the Advanced Photographic System (APS) is scheduled for launch in early 1996. Its drop-in film cartridges will eliminate the problem of misloading. More important, APS cameras will digitally record information such as shutter speed and aperture on a magnetic strip running across the film spool. That data will help a new generation of photo-processing gear churn out better prints.

Based on the growth spurt that accompanied prior new film standards, such as the Instamatic, 110, and Disc formats, Kodak sees a nice uptick in film and camera sales. But with heavy investment needed to start APS production, it's less certain that profits will surge as quickly. APS could displace higher-margin, traditional 35mm sales. Another danger: Kodak developed the Disc and 110 film standards itself. This time, it will be in a foot race with the Japanese. Still, as he demonstrated at Motorola, Fisher isn't afraid of Japanese competition. Indeed, he has made expansion into Asia and developing markets, often dominated by Fuji, another top priority.

His view is that Kodak, which has close to half of the global photography market, has missed big growth opportunities outside the United States. "For some reason, and I don't fully understand why, we went to sleep," says Fisher. Kodak won't discuss details of the new market push, but Fisher has already made three trips to China. And he appointed one of Kodak's most senior executives, Executive Vice-President William Prezzano, to head a new thrust into China, Taiwan, and Hong Kong.

It's all part of the broad transformation Fisher believes is finally taking hold at Kodak. In a recent speech to a group of employees, he concluded with this quote from Niccolò Machiavelli's *The Prince:* "There is nothing more difficult to take in hand, more perilous to conduct, or more uncertain in its success, than to take the lead in the introduction of a new order of things." Or, he added, more invigorating. But then, if Fisher didn't want a challenge, he would still be chairman of Motorola.

Study Questions

KODAK'S NEW FOCUS

1. Since George Fisher was named as the new CEO of Kodak in 1993, many changes have taken place. Is there any resemblance between a new administration taking over a company and the undertaking of a new project?

2. Many symptoms of poor management can be identified from the case including large debt, slow decision-making, multiple reorganizations, avoidance of risk taking, disjointed efforts, etc. However, what was the real problem Kodak was facing before 1993?

3. New Kodak CEO George Fisher is described as taking a slow approach to reorganizing Kodak. He claims that he is doing this in order to preserve Kodak's successful business segments. By doing this, the scope of the reorganization effort is controlled and focused. Draw comparisons between this method of change and the *PMBOK Guide* section 5, Project Scope Management.

4. How are the use of Kodak's new measures concerning project progression and completion going to affect these projects and their management? What are some of the intangible or cultural effects? What guidelines can be used to ensure that this is done effectively?

5. Kodak has obviously had many successful products, but is described as bad at developing products aimed at the less costly consumer market. How might its project management be focused to address these markets?

6. Fisher's managerial style is described as rather informal, resembling that of a coach or parent. How do you feel about this type of leader?

Managing Kuwait Oil Fields Reconstruction Projects

Mehdi Adib, Bechtel Corporation

PMI Canada *Proceedings*, 1994, pp. 184–90

INTRODUCTION

The Iraqi invasion of Kuwait took place in August of 1990 with the liberation in February 1991 following the Gulf War. Almost all of the country's oil production facilities suffered extensive damage.

The Kuwait Oil Company's (KOC) oil field reconstruction project that was planned, executed, and managed by Bechtel International was actually conceived in November 1990 in London, England. Planning and organizing the reconstruction of the oil facilities continued throughout the war in London, Houston, San Francisco, Dubai, and Riyadh. This was during the occupation but prior to the liberation. No one knew at that time what the true magnitude of the work would be; however, some tasks could be identified and front-end planning and procurement for these tasks started immediately. The scope of the restoration work was obviously increased tremendously by the damage incurred from the oil field fires that started at the end of the war.

Bechtel project management personnel arrived in Kuwait on March 4, 1991, three days after the allied troops had completed their initial sweep of Kuwait City. The main objective of this team was to organize and manage the fire-fighting effort, This phase of the project was named Al-Awada (Arabic for return).

The vivid scenes shown by the newspaper, magazine, and television reports came alive for Bechtel project personnel. The days were dark with smoke from the fires blocking the sun, oil droplets filled the air, clean water and sanitary systems were not working, power plants were down, transportation was minimal as tires were a precious commodity, and food was very scarce. Initial accommodation was in refurbished ship quarters and in some vandalized apartment complexes without water and electricity, no more than a foam mattress on the floor, and a long hike up a darkened staircase. In addition to these problems, booby traps, land and water mines, unexploded shells and rockets, and other ordnance had littered the country. The temperatures in summer consistently were above 50° C in shade (seldom below 37° C at night), exposing the people in the field to temperatures of 55–58° C in many locations, and hotter nearer to the fires. Just providing drinking water was a major undertaking. John Oakland, senior vice president of Bechtel Corporation, who served as the manager of projects in Kuwait, remarked, "This campaign, which was well covered by the international news media, was one of the most complex engineering and construction efforts in history (1)." However, the following assignment, which was the reconstruction of the

Kuwait oil fields, was an even bigger and more challenging task. The project management of the oil production facilities reconstruction, which was named Al-Tameer (Arabic for rebuild), is the subject of this report.

Status of the Facilities

The state of the two million bpd oil export industry in Kuwait after the completion of the fire-fighting effort was as follows:
* Six-hundred-forty-seven wells had burned in total, 751 wells were damaged.
* Twenty-six oil gathering, separation, and production centers were damaged or totally destroyed.
* One marine export facility and its related single point mooring was totally destroyed, and the second marine export facility was partially damaged and out of commission.
* The equivalent of ten million barrels of crude oil storage tankage had been destroyed.
* The Shuaiba refinery was totally destroyed.
* A crude unit in the Mina Al Ahmadi Refinery was completely destroyed. The rest of the refinery was partially damaged and the refinery was out of commission.
* The Mina Abdullah Refinery was partially damaged and the units were not operable.
* All communication towers and networks were destroyed.
* Most of the working population had either fled or were in hiding.

AL-TAMEER PROJECT

After the successful completion of the fire-fighting effort, KOC invited Bechtel to present its plan for the reconstruction of the oil fields production and exporting facilities damaged during the war, starting work by November 1990. KOC's goal was to be able to produce 2 million bpd of oil by September 1992.

PLANNING AND ORGANIZATION

The planning and organizing effort for the Al-Tameer project started with the Bechtel team that was already on-site as part of the Al-Awada project fire-fighting effort.

An organization totally different from the Al-Awada project was required to scope, estimate, plan, execute, and turn over operational facilities to KOC. This organization had to be self sufficient and be able to fully support and service a massive work force of more than 16,000 people.

The main organization was divided into five main functions. One was to support KOC's future five-year budget planning with identification, scoping, and planning future projects. This was named KOC Major Projects Group. The other four groups consisted of:
* manager Al-Tameer projects, responsible for all planning and project management, as well as engineering and procurement
* manager coordination, responsible for scheduling, cost control, estimating, project reporting, public and community relations, and other relevant functions

- manager services, responsible for providing all the required support services for the project team including explosive and ordnance demolition group
- manager operation, responsible for field execution of all the defined work.

A damage assessment and scoping team consisting of engineers, planners, and estimators walked every foot of the oil fields production and exporting facilities preparing a scope of work, cost estimate, a plan and schedule of work for each facility.

The planning was based on a back to front scheduling defining the dates and production goals first, working backward to see when the drilling effort and facilities reconstruction work had to start to meet this goal. This approach also determined the required manpower and helped with direct hire and subcontracting plans.

The overall plan defined the sequence of the work and prioritized the resources to make sure facilities with least damage were first priority for completion.

The master schedule was developed based on nine subproject organization work breakdown structures (WBS):

- oil recovery
- tankage south
- North Kuwait
- pipelines/flowlines
- power, buildings, cathodic protection
- marine facilities
- desalters
- South gathering centers
- West gathering centers.

Each subproject having its task force, budget, schedule, and its priority on resources identified was headed by a project manager. The Al-Tameer project organization chart is shown in Figure 1.

The teams were integrated with available KOC personnel who performed some of the project functions. Each subproject team was supported by local functional managers to provide them with staff and resources to execute the work. The key driver behind the plan was meeting the schedule and the production capacity.

EXECUTION

The project execution consisted of three main functions: detail engineering, procurement, and construction management.

Detail Engineering

Engineering and construction teams worked very closely during the planning phase to determine the best and most expedient way of rebuilding some of the facilities. This close collaboration continued until construction was complete.

More than 200 designers and engineers worked in the makeshift project offices at various sites, with strong central support from a base that was set up in an old war-damaged girl's school. This was later transferred to a newly constructed KOC engineering building. Additionally, a team of more than

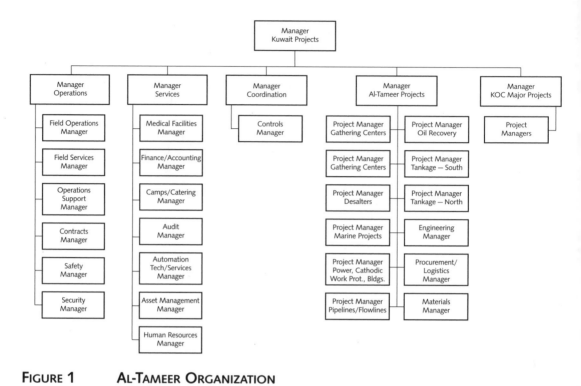

FIGURE 1   AL-TAMEER ORGANIZATION

200 engineers from various Bechtel regional offices worldwide provided continuous support and specialized expertise.

The main deliverables of the engineering teams were construction drawings, construction packages, and material requisitions and technical bid tabs. This effort was not limited to oil production and exporting facilities; it included some of the necessary infrastructure required for the day-to-day operation of KOC. Offices, warehouses, guest houses, employees housing, roads, power, water, etc., were all part of the scope of the work.

Because most of the original drawings and specifications were destroyed during the war, field sketches and measurements had to be used. A total engineering effort of 450,000 hours resulted in 4,500 major drawings.

One totally new and fully modularized gathering facility (GC-17) was designed and built in Houston, Texas, and shipped to the sites. Other facilities were designed for rebuild based on their original concept, but modernized wherever possible. Some of the units were very old and were upgraded with the more modern versions of the equipment available. A more extensive use of distributed control systems and automation was one of the key areas that was upgraded.

Procurement

The project procurement group was established in full force during the fire-fighting phase of the project to provide resources for that very important effort. In the Al-Tameer phase the team was further expanded to support the massive procurement and contracting effort that was required to meet the target schedule. In addition, inventory control and warehousing material were also part of the procurement team's area of responsibility.

The procurement team was also responsible for incorporating all the material into KOC's automated material and inventory control system. The procurement effort driving the execution phase was centralized, and it was divided into three main areas:
- material management
- contracts management
- warehouse management.

Material management included purchasing, inspection, expediting, and traffic and logistics. Contracting included formation and administration. Warehouse management included central warehouses and satellite warehouses.

The procurement team had three main goals within the project's overall objective:
- ensure the right material and resources were available in time to meet the schedule
- maximize the use of available local resources to assist in rebuilding the local economy
- ensure sure final warehouse inventory met KOC's material coding and identification system.

The size and the particular nature of the project required that the procurement team be divided between material management—reporting to the manager of projects—and contracts management—reporting to the manager of construction. This arrangement facilitated the communication and management of site contractors' work with Bechtel's direct hire construction work.

Material Management

Project managers were responsible for development and processing of the material requisitions for their areas of responsibility. Orders over $100,000 required further approval by KOC's manager of the Al-Tameer project.

Almost everything required for the execution of the project had to be imported from outside the country. At the early phases of the project the port facilities, custom facilities, and other services required for the proper importation of goods and services were not functioning. Bechtel established a staging area in Jebel Ali port of Dubai (UAE) to receive, inspect, and accept material. Utilizing much smaller vessels and boats, Bechtel then transported goods from Dubai to various Kuwait ports depending on availability and cargo size. This plan also included most of the air freighted material.

Because timely delivery of the material was critical to meeting the project schedule, a very detailed material requisitioning plan had to be developed identifying every required detail. This plan was then incorporated into Bechtel's worldwide Procurement Tracking System (PTS) that enabled all Bechtel offices to monitor and follow through each order until it reached the site.

At later stages of the project when Kuwait ports and custom facilities became functional the above arrangements were changed and everything was imported directly into Kuwait. During this period more than 26,000 purchase orders were issued, and more than 520,000 tons of material were imported utilizing 742 aircraft and sea-going vessels.

Warehousing Management

One of the key activities of the warehousing management team was to incorporate the variety of material that was left behind after the war and the fire-fighting phase with newly ordered and engineering-specified material. Also, by continuously adjusting and monitoring quantities and specifications they could respond very quickly to emergency and out-of-schedule circumstances.

The engineering and warehouse both utilized a common software (PCMC) to identify, locate, and quantify most of the bulk material making sure that when the material was required it would be made available immediately.

Contract Management

Although due to scheduled requirement reconstruction of some of the flow line, all of the gathering centers and booster stations were performed by Bechtel direct hires, nevertheless more than 300 major construction contracts and 650 equipment rental agreements were issued by the contract management team during the Al-Tameer project phase.

The contract formulation team worked as a central group serving all subprojects. The contract administration group managed the administration work more by function than by area. Project managers were ultimately the responsible parties for the contractor work in their areas, receiving the necessary support and services from these two centralized teams.

Construction Management

Al-Tameer was probably one of the most challenging construction projects ever managed by Bechtel. The work required provision of labor, equipment, and support facilities in fifty-five locations and in four different parts of the country—North fields, South (marine facilities and refineries), West fields, and Burgan fields.

The work involved construction of drill pads; roads for heavy rig transportation; well heads; flow lines; gathering centers; gas booster stations; oil storage tanks; water supply, distribution and storage; and marine export terminal and loading facilities. In addition, KOC's own infrastructure—offices, housing, clubs and restaurants, warehouses and buildings, telecommunication, etc.—had to be reconstructed.

Construction efforts were divided between direct hire construction and subcontracted work. The total scope of work was divided into nine construction areas, each managed by a field superintendent. Each superintendent was responsible for both direct hire execution as well as field administration of the subcontractor's scope of work within his area. Construction superintendents were supported by the central construction group that was the functional group supporting a project matrix team. Prioritization of resources and construction equipment was one of the major functions of the central construction team.

Field construction teams were comprised of multinational forces (from thirty-six countries) with totally different cultures, languages, and performance capabilities. Catering and other cultural requirements had to be addressed to ensure each group could perform its function satisfactorily.

Each task had to be "tailor made" to suit the team available. It was important that planning of the manpower and resources take into consideration availability of the right foreman and support group to be able to communicate and perform work with each team.

SUMMARY

Approximately 1,000,000 hours in the regional offices and 4,000,000 hours in Kuwait were spent for project management/engineering/construction management during the first two phases of this project. Field labor hours were 50,000,000.

These project manhours were spent within the following project schedule milestones:
- start of planning   November 1990
- start implementation in Kuwait   March 1991
- project completion   June 1993.

The sources of the project personnel were various. A total of 16,000 workers from thirty-six countries on five continents were involved in this massive effort. The countries that participated in the supply of manpower to this reconstruction included Kuwait, the United States, Great Britain, Canada, France, Australia, Belgium, Holland, Germany, Ireland, New Zealand, Mexico, Saudi Arabia, Egypt, Iran, Lebanon, Bahrain, Yugoslavia, Colombia, Indonesia, Nigeria, Bangladesh, Brazil, Afghanistan, the Philippines, India, Djibouti, Sri Lanka, Somalia, Syria, Tanzania, Thailand, Tunisia, Pakistan, Trinidad, and Sierra Leone.

ACCOMPLISHMENTS

- The work was conducted in fifty-five locations that included fields in the north of Kuwait on the border with Iraq, west and south of Kuwait on the borders with Saudi Arabia and Iraq, and in the refineries and loading facilities along the coast and offshore.
- Five hundred square miles of land were swept and cleared of unexploded ordnance. More than 23,000 pieces of explosive devices were destroyed by explosive ordnance disposal teams. Although all work areas were swept, the risk from undetectable ordnance was ever present and some fatalities did occur.
- More than 26,000 purchase orders and 300 major construction contracts and 650 equipment rental agreements were awarded during Phases I and II of the project. (A more normal project performed over the same time frame may have 4,000 to 6,000 purchase orders.)
- A complete communication system dedicated to the oil industry was installed that included twenty-three satellite telephone systems, 4,500 telephones, and 2,000 portable radios.
- A twenty-four-hour health care and safety program was established that included two helicopter medivac teams, a forty-bed hospital, a dental clinic, and a team of approximately 100 professional medical personnel on duty at seven medical stations.
- More than 5,800 pieces of field operating equipment ranging from the larger bulldozers, cranes, trucks, front-end loaders, and heavy industrial

equipment to ambulances, pickup trucks, cars, buses, and other support vehicles were shipped to the job sites. These pieces of equipment were purchased from twelve different countries.

• A total of 742 aircraft and sea-going vessels were deployed to ship more than 520,000 tons of equipment and material to Kuwait in support of this project.

• Six full-service dining halls with catering support staff provided about 3,500,000 meals for the workers during the fire-fighting campaign and 10,000,000 meals during the reconstruction phase. Menus were established to cater to the different ethnic backgrounds.

• Provisions and housing for 12,000 manual and 2,000 non-manual Bechtel employees were provided. All of the members of project management and their support teams, over 200 design and engineering personnel and about 200 procurement, administration, and subcontracts management teams, were resident in Kuwait.

• Construction of a number of permanent offices, workshops, warehouses, maintenance shops, and housing complexes for KOC was completed at the same time.

• Fire-fighting efforts originally involved the four major international teams of Boots & Coots, Red Adair, Safety Boss, and Wild Well Control. They were later joined by an additional twenty-three teams from Kuwait, Iran, China, Hungary, Great Britain, France, Canada, Romania, and Russia.

• Four hundred kilometers of water and oil pipelines were installed during fire-fighting efforts. Water lines and pumping stations could deliver 25,000,000 gallons a day to fire sites. Each of 360 lagoons was excavated, lined, and filled with 1,000,000 gallons of water for use in fire-fighting.

• Drilling pads and access roads were constructed for 700 new and workover wells.

• Three-thousand kilometers of new flowlines were constructed.

• One-thousand kilometers of new and refurbished pipelines were installed.

• Fifteen crude gathering centers, including a totally new and modularized early production facility, were assessed, designed, and constructed.

• Three gas booster stations were constructed

• Restoration and reconstruction of the marine loading terminals, offshore terminals, and SPM were completed.

• Construction of more than 10,000,000 barrels of new crude oil storage tankage was managed.

• Restoration of overhead and underground electrical power transmission and distribution system and cathodic protection system within the oil fields was completed.

• Construction/repair and operation of water systems (fresh, brackish, and salt water) were completed.

• Construction and operation of oil recovery systems and facilities that collected and treated more than 25,000,000 barrels of weathered crude were completed.

KEY MILESTONES

Some of the more notable milestones in the program were:
- The last fire was extinguished and the well was capped on November 6, 1991, eight months after the arrival of the first Bechtel team on-site.
- The first postwar oil was pumped from two of the original gathering centers on May 26, 1991.
- By December 1991, more than 400,000 barrels of oil per day were being produced from the rehabilitated facilities.
- By April 1993, more than 11,000,000 barrels of weathered crude had been reclaimed from oil pits and lakes, and processed through the field treatment centers and the refinery.
- By the end of June 1993, eighteen of the original centers were back in operation, with all the production goals achieved as scheduled.

REFERENCES

1. Oakland, J.A. 1994. "Al-Tameer: The Reconstruction of Kuwait." *PM Network.* May, pp. 14–21.

Study Questions

MANAGING KUWAIT OIL FIELDS RECONSTRUCTION PROJECTS

1. This project was a major undertaking. The challenges it faced ranged from providing the basics for being able to live in the desert (water and shelter) to finding creative methods for getting imports into the country through non-traditional routes. From the author's point of view, the project went rather smoothly. To which factors do you attribute the success of this project?

2. This case describes an enormous undertaking made up of many different projects. Which of these projects can be considered the most important? Why?

3. One of the regular outputs of the development of the project plan is the work breakdown structure. Define the work breakdown structure and its benefits.

4. How were the multinational relationships handled in this project?

5. This project was handled by the Bechtel Corporation, a private company, and not the Kuwaiti government. List some of the advantages to this project being handled privately and not publicly.

6. Figure 1 shows the organization chart of the Al-Tameer project. What kind of organization does this represent?

Managing Resources and Communicating Results of Sydney's $7 Billion Clean Waterways Program

Larry Johnson, Consultant to the Sydney Water Board's Clean Waterways Program
Richard Wankmuller, Consultant to the Sydney Water Board's Clean Waterways Program

PMI *Proceedings*, 1992, pp. 127–33

INTRODUCTION AND BACKGROUND

Sydney, Australia, is renowned for its beautiful ocean beaches and scenic harbor. However, a population growth of over five percent between 1986 and 1991, combined with outdated wastewater facilities, has threatened the beauty of the region with serious pollution problems. In response to the problems, the Government of New South Wales and the Sydney Water Board made a commitment to clean up the beaches and waterways within twenty years by launching the $7 billion (1991 $AUS) Clean Waterways Program (CWP).

The CWP covers a wide range of projects including:
- upgrading of sewage treatment plants
- establishing beneficial use of sludge
- reduction of sewer inflow and infiltration
- reduction of sewage overflows
- reduction of odors and emissions
- restoration of urban bushland
- control of urban and rural runoff.

This paper demonstrates the innovative project management techniques that are being used to manage the resources of this environmental program.

Managing People and Projects

Over 1,000 people are working on the CWP at many locations all over the Sydney Region. The program is managed from the Pollution Abatement Branch of the Water Board. The planning portions of the program are organized into functional teams which address specific areas of work such as sludge management, odor reduction, plant operations optimization, and sewage treatment planning, just to name a few. With such a broad scope of work spread over this region, it is imperative that the people and projects of the CWP be carefully organized and managed to ensure successful delivery.

Management plans. All CWP teams are required to prepare management plans (MPs) which are used to define the scope of work and to outline the general rules and guidelines for performing their work. The MP's also inform CWP management of exactly what each team will be working on, thus avoiding possible duplication and avoiding any false expectations. The MPs contain these key elements:

- mission statement
- objectives
- targets
- work breakdown structure
- budgets
- baseline schedules.

A discussion of each of these elements follows.

Mission statements create a positive teamwork atmosphere. The mission statement is comprised of one or two sentences which describe the main goal of the team's work. The mission statement is typically signed by all members of the team to create a positive teamwork atmosphere and to signify ownership and dedication to the work described within the MP.

Objectives summarize project goals. Work objectives are a list of goals of the team and are tied back directly to the objectives of the CWP. For example, one objective of the Plant Operations Optimization Team is to develop standard operating procedures at the sewage treatment plants. This objective can be tied directly back to one of the CWP objectives which is to increase the reliability of operation of sewage treatment plants.

Targets state when and to what level. Targets narrow down the scope of the objectives and indicate specifically when and to what level the objectives will be met. This sets the resource requirements needed to meet the objectives. For the standard operating procedure objective example stated above, one of the targets was to deliver the final standard operating procedure for influent screens at North Head Sewage Treatment Plant by April 1, 1992.

Work breakdown structure organizes the work. The work breakdown structure (WBS) organizes the work of a project into a formal outlining of how the work will be accomplished. The objectives and targets are often used as part of the structure. The WBS is very important when laying out the structure of the baseline schedule. Figure 1 shows the WBS of the Plant Operations Optimization work at North Head STP.

Budgets establish resource availability. Budgets establish the resource availability for each project and can be measured both in manhours and dollars. Budgets are extremely important because they define the maximum limit of people and funds available to perform work contained in each project.

Baseline schedules are a project manager's road map to achieving a successful project. Baseline schedules are one of the most important parts of the MP and often take the most time to prepare. The objectives, targets, and WBS are all used in developing the baseline schedule. They are used to identify detail schedule activities, work products (deliverables), and key events (milestones). Detailed activity durations are kept short enough to make it easy to identify physical percent complete when updating. Shorter durations also ensure objective and accurate updating of project schedules. Planning-type project deliverables such as concept design reports, technical memoranda, facility plans, and environmental impact reports are also added to the schedule. Important milestones such as groundbreaking and ribbon cutting events are also identified and included so that they can be incorporated into media plans.

Responsibility and resource loaded schedules are critical. Responsibility assignments and estimated resources necessary to complete each detail

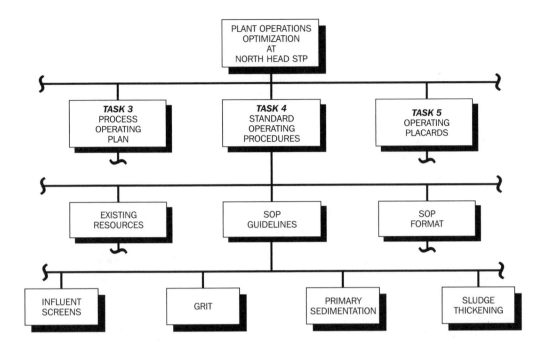

FIGURE 1 **PLANT OPERATIONS OPTIMIZATION WORK BREAKDOWN STRUCTURE**

activity are determined by project managers. Resources, which are measured in work-hours, dollars, or both, are loaded into the project schedule. They cover project staff costs as well as outside costs including special consultants and construction.

Realistic, achievable schedules represent a key to success. CWP project control specialists spend many hours working one-on-one with each team developing realistic and achievable baseline schedules. Several revisions are often necessary before the baseline schedules are accepted by project staff and management. When completed, project staff, project managers, and clients all "buy into" or take ownership in the baseline schedule. Realistic, achievable schedules that the entire project team is committed to will have the greatest probability for success.

Controlling Projects

Earned value methods evaluate performance of CWP projects. Performance of CWP projects is measured by how well they are progressing against the baseline schedule and budget. Earned value techniques are used to measure performance. As work progresses, the baseline value for completed activities is earned. Earned value obtained for each detailed activity is calculated by multiplying the physical percent complete by the budgeted cost of that activity. The earned value for the entire project is calculated by adding the earned value for all detailed activities on the project.

This information is gathered through monthly meetings when project control specialists interview each project manager to determine the status of each activity on the schedule. Actual start and end dates are documented for completed activities, and start dates, physical percent complete, and forecasted end dates are determined for partially completed activities. Actual

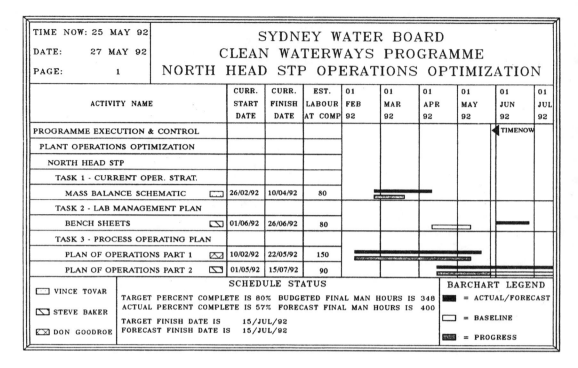

ACTIVITY NAME	CURR. START DATE	CURR. FINISH DATE	EST. LABOUR AT COMP	01 FEB 92	01 MAR 92	01 APR 92	01 MAY 92	01 JUN 92	01 JUL 92
PROGRAMME EXECUTION & CONTROL								TIMENOW	
PLANT OPERATIONS OPTIMIZATION									
NORTH HEAD STP									
TASK 1 - CURRENT OPER. STRAT.									
MASS BALANCE SCHEMATIC	26/02/92	10/04/92	80						
TASK 2 - LAB MANAGEMENT PLAN									
BENCH SHEETS	01/06/92	26/06/92	80						
TASK 3 - PROCESS OPERATING PLAN									
PLAN OF OPERATIONS PART 1	10/02/92	22/05/92	150						
PLAN OF OPERATIONS PART 2	01/05/92	15/07/92	90						

TIME NOW: 25 MAY 92
DATE: 27 MAY 92
PAGE: 1

SYDNEY WATER BOARD
CLEAN WATERWAYS PROGRAMME
NORTH HEAD STP OPERATIONS OPTIMIZATION

SCHEDULE STATUS

TARGET PERCENT COMPLETE IS 80%   BUDGETED FINAL MAN HOURS IS 348
ACTUAL PERCENT COMPLETE IS 57%   FORECAST FINAL MAN HOURS IS 400

TARGET FINISH DATE IS   15/JUL/92
FORECAST FINISH DATE IS   15/JUL/92

VINCE TOVAR
STEVE BAKER
DON GOODROE

BARCHART LEGEND

= ACTUAL/FORECAST
= BASELINE
= PROGRESS

FIGURE 2   DETAILED SCHEDULE REPORT

costs are obtained from the CWP cost accounting system, and all update information is entered into the project management software program for processing.

The CWP detailed schedule report is the project manager's most important guide. The first monthly report to be prepared is the first draft of the detailed schedule report like the one shown in Figure 2. It gives the project manager the first look at the schedule and budget status of the project. The first draft of the detailed schedule report calculates the forecasted final cost of each activity already started based on performance to date by using the following formula:

FFC = AC/PC, where:

FFC = Forecasted Final Cost

AC = Actual Cost To Date

PC = Physical Percent Complete (e.g., 50 percent = .50)

For CWP reporting, if the forecast final cost for a particular activity is less than 90 percent of the budgeted final cost, it is printed on the report in green. If the forecast final cost is more than 110 percent of the budgeted final cost it is printed in red.

This first draft of the report highlights areas of work that are over or under spending and ahead or behind schedule, and also gives the project manager an opportunity to re-forecast any future costs before the final report is published. There may be several revisions made to the detailed schedule report before the final report is ready for distribution.

The CWP deliverable schedule report keeps the client informed. Work products or deliverables produced by the project team are tracked using the

TIME NOW: 25 MAY 92 / DATE: 27 MAY 92 / PAGE: 1	SYDNEY WATER BOARD CLEAN WATERWAYS PROGRAMME NORTH HEAD STP OPERATIONS OPTIMIZATION							

ACTIVITY NAME	BASE. FINISH DATE	ACT. /F'CAST FINISH	01 FEB 92	01 MAR 92	01 APR 92	01 MAY 92	01 JUN 92	01 JUL 92
PROGRAMME EXECUTION & CONTROL							◀TIMENOW	
PLANT OPERATIONS OPTIMIZATION								
NORTH HEAD STP								
TASK 1 - CURRENT OPER. STRAT.								
DELIVER MASS BALANCE SCHEMATIC	10/04/92	10/04/92			△			
TASK 2 - LAB MANAGEMENT PLAN								
DELIVER BENCH SHEETS	26/06/92	26/06/92					△	
TASK 3 - PROCESS OPERATING PLAN								
DELIVER PLAN OF OPERATIONS PART 1	22/05/92	22/05/92				△		
DELIVER PLAN OF OPERATIONS PART 2	15/07/92	15/07/92						△

☐ VINCE TOVAR   ◨ STEVE BAKER   ⊠ DON GOODROE

FIGURE 3   DELIVERABLE SCHEDULE REPORT

deliverable schedule report such as the one shown in Figure 3. This report is electronically generated from the detailed project schedule and documents when work products such as reports and technical memorandum are completed and delivered. These reports are particularly useful to CWP clients who must coordinate their resources so that work products can be reviewed in a timely manner. This report also gives the project team a sense of accomplishment as they see work products being delivered to the client throughout the project

The CWP one-page summary schedule report tells it all. The one-page summary schedule report, like the one shown in Figure 4, includes information CWP managers want to know for each project. The upper half of the report contains a summary or roll-up schedule for the project. The physical percent complete for each area of work is electronically calculated from the status of detailed schedule activities and is printed to the right of the start and end dates. Progress is shown by filling in the baseline bar to the date that the physical percent complete would have been reached in the baseline schedule. The lower right portion of the report contains the earned value analysis showing the baseline cost curve (dashed line), actual/forecasted cost curve (solid line), and earned value achieved for each reporting period (vertical cross-hatched columns). The lower title block includes total project statistics including earned value percentages to date and budgeted and forecasted final costs. Text highlighting accomplishments, upcoming milestones, key issues, as well as schedule and budget status notes, are added to the report making it a very compact and comprehensive one-page presentation. These one-page reports are used in project control report books distributed to CWP management and are used in staff meetings when discussing progress for each project.

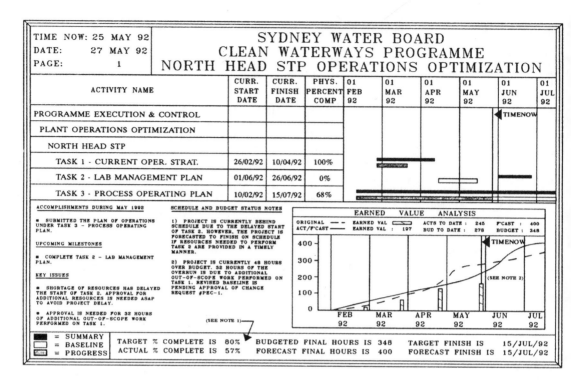

FIGURE 4   ONE PAGE SUMMARY SCHEDULE REPORT

Schedule and budget problems are hard to avoid. CWP schedule and budget problems can be identified from all three schedule reports described above. As with all schedule and budget problems it is important to identify them at an early stage while they are small and manageable. The project controls team and project managers keep a sharp eye on the earned value curve of projects looking for schedule and budget slips. Most schedule and budget problems encountered on the CWP arise from performing out-of-scope work and underestimated baseline schedule durations and budgets. CWP staff meetings are used as a forum for project managers to present schedule and budget problems and to propose schedule and budget recovery plans and/or change requests for their projects. The project controls team works with project managers to develop their change requests and recovery plans.

PROJECT PRIORITIZATION WITH LIMITED FUNDING

One limiting resource on the CWP is available funding. In order to decide how best to administer the program under this limiting factor a project prioritization method was developed for identifying those projects that should receive funding over those that could be delayed, downsized, or deleted. For the overall CWP this prioritization procedure is still being refined. However, for the early phases of the program the prioritization procedure for projects funded by a separate source has been well established. It includes a number of different factors, all of which were accounted for in reviewing the overall priority of any given project. These factors included:

- significance of environmental enhancement
- qualifications to perform work
- community needs
- impact on public health
- cost benefit (compared to alternative solutions)
- ability to measure project effectiveness (by use of performance indicators)
- ability to accomplish environmental improvement by June 1994
- political commitment
- population benefiting
- comparability with strategic plans and/or broader policy directions
- community recognition.

While each of these factors are important, some are more important than others. Accordingly, the prioritization incorporates a weighted distribution for each of the factors. This distribution allows each item to have a maximum score of between five and fifteen depending on its relative importance to the goals of the program. The net effect is those factors that are more important to the goals of the program contribute more points towards the total score for any particular project. The result is that those projects with the highest score are the highest candidates for the limited funds.

This procedure is used in trying to decide which projects should be funded when the available funding is limited. It not only allows the program manager to make decisions on which projects should proceed but it provides a list of standby projects to be drawn from as reallocation becomes possible. This type of analysis is very important in order to ensure the limited funds are being applied in the most effective manner possible.

It is important to note that the project prioritization procedure has to be tailored to the goals and the intended outcome of the environmental program.

COMMUNICATING RESULTS

Clear internal and external communications are the lifeline of program implementation. Internal communications are vitally important to keep not only the staff that are working on the program informed of the progress and key issues, but to keep the remaining staff in the organization aware of the progress and the need for the program that is under way. External communications are equally important because public input is critical to delivering outcomes that benefit the population as a whole. Public input is also important because it generates support for the program. A review of some of the methods of both internal and external communications follows.

Internal Communications

Monthly progress report binders make it easy to keep managers up to date. CWP project managers use monthly progress report binders to communicate the progress to both the CWP management and to the clients of the Sydney Water Board. These progress reports contain text highlighting major accomplishments, upcoming milestones, and key issues for each of the projects within the program. They also contain the progress schedules described earlier in this paper.

The progress reports also include a list of major deliverables for each project. This list identifies what work products will be delivered through the life of the project and includes a copy of each of the major deliverables that have been completed. For any deliverable that exceeds twenty-five pages only the executive summary and the table of contents for the work product is included in this report. However, the table of contents includes a reference to where the full deliverable work product could be found in the program library.

The binders are updated monthly by inserting the new sections into the existing binders within each of the senior managers' offices. This ensures that the senior managers will be brought up to date on project performance quickly even if they do not take the time to review the information on a monthly basis.

The monthly manager's report keeps senior management informed. In addition to the progress reports, a monthly manager's report is forwarded to the managing director of the water board and the members of the appointed board. This report documents the major accomplishments of the program for the month. It focuses on key strategic issues. The issues are targeted at key items that either the managing director or the appointed board need to know about or could help the program manager resolve.

External Communications

Media plans gain public support and promote public participation. Early on in development of the CWP a media plan was developed for communicating early successes of the program. This media plan focused on those major accomplishments that could be reached within the first year of the program and was a very important tool in gaining public support

By generating public support for the program it was hoped that the media plan would motivate people to participate in the community consultation process and provide their input. This input was needed to help determine which options for the long-term upgrade of Sydney's wastewater system would be supported by the local community.

The media plan was also used to communicate the scope of the CWP to the public. Accordingly, it targeted the major components of the program and attempted to show some early improvements in each of the major areas.

For instance, the CWP goals are to provide an incremental environmental improvement on a yearly basis. Since the environment is made up of three major factors, air, land, and water, each of these areas was targeted in the media plan. For improvements to the air, the odor reduction program accomplishments were stressed. For improvements to the land, some of the major accomplishments within the sludge beneficial re-use program were highlighted. For improvements to the water, major accomplishments towards improving effluent quality from sewage treatment plants was stressed.

The media plan included a detailed schedule that portrayed the type of announcements and media events that would be available from the first year of the program. This schedule allowed immediate identification of when the Community Consultation Team could expect to be able to have some of these "good news" stories available for the local media. It also allowed some rationalization of the timing of each media event so that the program could manage messages sent and received by the public.

While literally hundreds of projects were going on during the first year, the media plan summarized all of this work into eight targeted projects. For each of these projects a detailed media plan was written that addressed the key issues and the media opportunity.

It should be noted that these plans did not preclude other good news stories from occurring. They simply ensured that a focused effort was made to release selected key messages to the community.

Quarterly and annual reports provide accountability. Another method for communicating program results and indicating the scope of the CWP are the quarterly and annual reports. The annual report is a legislative requirement, and it reviews the entire program and the accomplishments and progress made to date. It comments on each of the major objectives of the program and reviews the progress of each project currently under way. The quarterly report has a similar format to the annual report but only comments on those projects where major accomplishments have been made during the last quarter.

Accordingly, the annual report also serves as the public accountability tool for the status of the program and how the money is being spent on a yearly basis. On the other hand, the quarterly reports are strictly informational, but are used as a policy vehicle within the organization.

Both reports include graphical representation of performance indicators. The indicators are chosen to represent the progress being made under each objective of the program. For example, one performance indicator for reduction in beach pollution is the percentage of time that pollution is visibly present on beaches. Figure 5 graphically shows how the ocean outfalls at Malabar and Bondi STPs have improved the beach pollution indicators at several local beaches between the summers of 1989–90 and the summers of 1990–91.

The reports also include a market survey. The public is asked to fill out these surveys after reading the report so that the program can ensure that public requirements are continually being addressed.

Good news stories educate the public and gain its support. Another effective external communication is the publishing of good news stories. The CWP uses a number of different mediums to transmit these good news stories. These mediums range from TV and newspapers to local community bulletins put out by the water board. The stories are generally targeted at specific audiences such as a local electoral district or a neighborhood where the issue may be of particular concern.

One medium which is economical to produce and provides some very good benefits is the neighborhood news publication. The water board is using this community bulletin extensively throughout the local neighborhood surrounding the major treatment plants. This medium has proved to be a very effective way of reaching the local community and generating feedback. The neighborhood news publications are directly mailed to all people in the surrounding areas of the major treatment plants. This direct mail campaign ensures that the people most affected by the local facility can be kept up to date and informed not only of progress, but when opportunities for community consultation occur.

Since launching the CWP, numerous opportunities have been taken to help create media interest in water board issues. These included familiarizing the local and regional newspaper journalists with the program. The opportunities also included informal meetings within the offices of the water board as well as off-site meetings to look at projects that were part of the CWP. This effort continues in order to help ensure that journalists are continually aware of

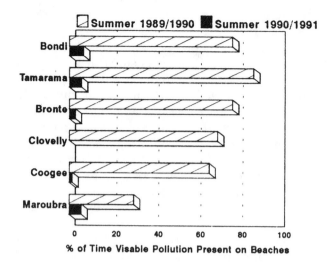

% of Time Visable Pollution Present on Beaches

FIGURE 5   **HOW BEACH POLLUTION INDICATORS HAVE IMPROVED SINCE COMMISSIONING OF OCEAN OUTFALLS**

what the program is trying to accomplish as well as what it has accomplished. It is hoped that this realization will help the journalists be prepared to report accurately and completely on any of the good news stories that may be generated by the program.

SUMMARY

This paper includes a discussion of the need for accurate and complete management plans that include an earned value analysis for detailed project control. It was pointed out that this earned value analysis is vitally important in obtaining an objective analysis of the status of a project at a given point in time. This is critical to successful project delivery especially in an environment where resources can change continuously. It is also important so that it is not necessary to rely on the subjective analysis of individual project managers as to whether schedules and budgets are being maintained.

The prioritization technique gives an indication of the types of methods that can be used to prioritize projects that are competing for the same source of funding. This technique became very important in the early stages of the Clean Waterways Program in order to rationalize which projects would be funded. The paper also stresses that the prioritization technique must be tailored to the individual program and the requirements, needs, and stated objectives of that program.

The paper also includes a discussion of the need for accurate and timely internal and external communications. It was pointed out that internal communications were equally important to external communications so that the organization is aware of the progress being made within the program. This awareness is very important in order to ensure that the program maintains its identity and the commitment of key staff throughout the organization.

It should be noted that within the confines of this paper the authors could not hope to present all of the project control and communication techniques being used within the CWP. They simply tried to present some of the more critical issues. There are many other key techniques being used by project managers throughout the CWP and, accordingly, if one would like more information, contact the authors directly, or contact the Sydney Water Board's communication officer in Sydney, Australia.

Study Questions

MANAGING RESOURCES AND COMMUNICATING RESULTS OF SYDNEY'S $7 BILLION CLEAN WATERWAYS PROGRAM

1. The case presents three of the reports used to control the project's development. Section 10.3 of the *PMBOK Guide,* Performance Reporting, lists the elements that a performance report should include. Evaluate the detailed schedule report depicted in Figure 2 using the *PMBOK Guide* standards.

2. The case mentions the difficulties of scheduling and budgeting due to out-of-scope activities and poor estimates of baseline schedule duration and budgets. How should the project manager control the undertaking of activities which are out of the project's scope?

3. Define and highlight the differences between a project's mission, objectives, and goals and provide examples from the case.

4. Define what is meant by a "media plan" and list elements that should be contained within it. Discuss the importance of good external communications.

5. Is the one-page summary schedule report shown in Figure 4 an effective means of communication?

Making Affordable Housing Attainable through Modern Project Management

Paul L. Berg, Enterprise Builders, Inc.

PM Network, August 1994, pp. 12–18

To the everyday observer, Deer Meadow, a Bloomfield, Connecticut, family-oriented apartment community, appears to be an "upscale" condominium complex. In reality, it is an affordable housing project, one that shows how modern project management (MPM) can assist in realizing the social objectives of local government.

Governor Lowell Weicker's desire to provide quality, affordable housing in the state of Connecticut helped make this project a reality. Funding was provided through the state's Department of Housing under Connecticut's Private Rental Investment Mortgage and Equity Program (PRIME) and from Connecticut Housing Finance Authority (CHFA).

Developer Marc S. Levine's goal was to create an attractive living environment and to offer units at both market rates and at lower rentals, affordable to families whose incomes did not exceed 60 percent of the area's median. Mr. Levine's dream is more remarkable when you realize this was around 1990, a time when new construction was at an all-time low in Connecticut and when attaining funding for new projects was next to impossible! Nevertheless, he successfully accomplished land acquisition, financing, and planning and zoning approvals.

It was at this point that Enterprise Builders came on board as construction manager/general contractor. We had to quickly pick up the ball and provide value engineering, conceptual estimating, budgets, breakdowns of trades, and a guarantee of price for the project in an intense period of just a few weeks. In addition to budget information, we had to submit our Affirmative Action Program to CHFA for review. Our contract included a Minority Hiring Agreement and Affirmative Action Goal, requiring that we sign minority subcontractors for at least 20 percent of the total construction contract. All this information had to be submitted and CHFA's strict requirements met before approval was given for us to proceed with the construction phase of the project.

The scope of our phase of the project involved construction of a low-density housing development consisting of five buildings on a 13.5-acre rural site. It would contain forty-eight two- and three-bedroom, garden-style apartments ranging in size from 1,000 to 1,300 square feet. The plans called for children's play areas, ample parking, and attractive landscaping.

The project team consisted of the owner/developer, the design architect from Texas, a local architect as project administrator, an on-site representative from CHFA, engineers, and Enterprise Builders as construction manager/general contractor. With so many people, agencies, and distances involved, there was a larger margin for errors, confusion, and for getting off schedule. The team established clear lines of communication and defined roles:

• to construct the project within the budget of $3.75 million
• to stay on or ahead of schedule
• to perform as a team in the best interests of the project
• to anticipate the needs of the project and identify potential problems before they occurred
• to end with a satisfied client.

The project team agreed that the schedule must be rigorously adhered to in order for each of the five buildings to be ready for tenants to move in by the predetermined dates. We all felt the pressure of completing the project on time so that the developer could take advantage of tax credit incentives available to him. Added to this, CHFA made it clear that there would be no change orders on this project!

With clear understanding by all parties of the task ahead, ground was broken in February 1992, approximately one month later than originally planned.

Mike McNaboe of Enterprise Builders headed up the project team for the construction phase. An experienced project manager, Mike knew that planning and predicting time durations were crucial. He conceptualized how the buildings would be sequenced to maximize trade coordination. He then generated a CPM schedule which could be updated on an as-needed basis to reflect any changes. The scheduling data from the first building was dissected to search for additional ways to save time through optimizing the construction sequence and resource allocation.

Everyone involved in the project lived by the CPM schedule. We tied it into all of the subcontractors' contract agreements. Mike McNaboe distributed updates regularly to team members, subcontractors, and foremen. Goals were agreed on. Progress was checked and compared to the original CPM schedule at all meetings. Each day, feedback was solicited from the tradepersons on ways to improve the construction schedule for their particular crafts. We utilized checklists accumulated from lessons learned in past experiences to make sure that routine items were not overlooked. We have found if we keep a list of successful steps to follow, then success becomes routine. It also frees the mind to solve potential new problems or to find improvements to the established routine.

Given the economic climate at the time of construction, there was an element of risk involved in selecting subcontractors who were financially stable and who would be around to complete the project. Using the construction management approach on this project made it possible for us to draw from a prequalified list of quality subcontractors and minority firms and still realize the advantages of competitive bidding. Additionally, we required all major subcontractors to provide payment and performance bonds as protection against failure to perform or failure to pay their labor or material suppliers. Where bonds were not requested, our financial department would follow-up on second- and third-tier subs to ensure they were being paid.

At the start of construction, we encountered problems due to the condition of the site, which was surrounded by wetlands. Much of the material was unsuitable for structural bearing. Special engineering was required and the layout of the project had to be modified to make the site stable and structurally sound. We rushed stone in and placed it under the footings of some of

The attractive design of this family-oriented apartment community makes it appear to be an "upscale" condominium complex. It was completed in less than eight months, a month ahead of schedule, and $300,000 under budget.

the buildings. Cost savings through value engineering helped to create a contingency to pay for this unforeseen condition.

Constructing the project adjacent to protected wetlands had raised concerns from local environmentalists. An environmental site assessment had been made by the developer, who promised to take special precautions not to disturb the wetlands area and its wildlife. Our contract actually required us to construct birdhouses and place them in trees in protected areas to encourage the nesting of certain types of birds.

Another challenge of scope management was creating an attractive exterior appearance for affordable housing. Mike McNaboe researched a variety of materials and alternatives, examined them for cost, delivery, constructability, and quality and sent them to the architect, The Steinberg Collaborative of Dallas, Texas. The design incorporates building materials which provide a pleasing environment for renters: vinyl siding, larger trim, and Palladium

The words of a tenant who just moved in said it all —"I live in a palace!"

windows. The result was an attractive exterior in a color scheme characteristic of New England. Reduced cost also had to be balanced against maintainability and workability. A number of options were rejected because the long-term costs were not worth the savings.

Quality starts at the foundation of a building. Mike McNaboe and on-site superintendent John Woodward achieved a high caliber of workmanship on this project by continual follow-up and consistently demanding a quality finished product. They carefully tracked the relationships of the physical components to ensure everything would fit perfectly. They knew from past experience the importance of visualizing how the space would be used to anticipate the owner's needs. They also had to take into account elements that were outside our scope of work (special utilities, telephone, cable TV) and to make sure nothing would be dysfunctional to the end user. Their object was always to anticipate and identify potential problems before they occurred.

John Woodward, project superintendent, was responsible for coordinating sub-subcontractors' work crews and ensuring that materials and equipment were delivered on time and in the right sequence. Good subcontractors can anticipate what the following trade will need. When subcontractors move their crews from an area, they can leave it in such a way that it is easier for the next subcontractor to perform the next activity. Delays from work having to be undone, stored materials and equipment having to be moved, etc., can be avoided, greatly assisting in accelerating the schedule. Clear communication from John facilitated people working together and the project kept moving. Work had to be performed just once and correctly!

Each project superintendent has his own individual style of keeping a project on track. There are, however, some common traits that occur with successful superintendents like John Woodward:

Among the services a government or community can provide, affordable housing is every bit as necessary as good schools, fire and police protection, public transportation, and other basic services. Deer Meadow is an important development because of the need it serves and because of the example it sets.

• A seasoned, working knowledge of construction details accumulated over the years from a variety of construction projects.

• An attitude of approaching each project as an unique opportunity to become better educated in the intricacies of the subtrades; the best superintendents ask, listen, and discuss rather than tell and yell.

• The ability to *plan* overall objectives to achieve specific milestones along the way and organize them into short-term goals for each trade.

• The ability to *effectively communicate* and discuss the plan in weekly coordination meetings. To set assertive goals and work out objections and objectives so that the goals can be met.

• The habit of walking around daily to follow up personally on the accomplishment of tasks, goals, and schedules; effective follow-up puts a supervisor in control.

• The ability to regularly review achievements and identify new problems at weekly meetings, which is a result of planning, organizing, communicating and controlling—in that order; if a superintendent finds himself yelling a lot, you can bet he skipped one of these four steps.

Job site safety was a prime concern of the project team. The members established and implemented basic safety guidelines:

• Weekly safety meetings would be held to identify potential problems.

• It was agreed never to sacrifice safety for production.

• The project manager was to walk the site weekly and follow up on his findings with the superintendent and subcontractors.

• The superintendent was to hold regular safety meetings with all foremen.

• The project manager and superintendent were to set good examples of safety for the workers.

Deer Meadow was successfully completed in October 1992, over one month ahead of schedule and almost $300,000 under budget.

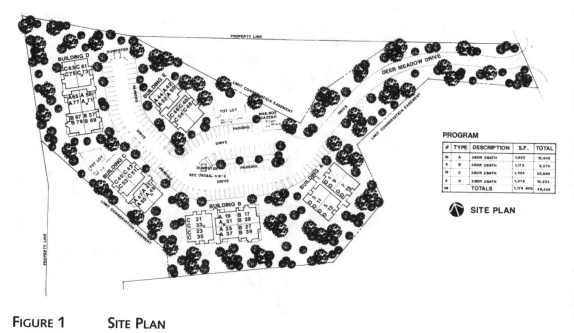

PROGRAM

#	TYPE	DESCRIPTION	S.F.	TOTAL
16	A	2BDR 2BATH	1,003	16,048
8	B	2BDR 2BATH	1,172	9,376
16	C	3BDR 2BATH	1,305	20,880
8	D	3BDR 2BATH	1,278	10,224
48		TOTALS	1,179 AVG	56,528

SITE PLAN

FIGURE 1   SITE PLAN

Many times I've been asked why Deer Meadow was so successful. We strive for teamwork on all our projects, but this was something special! Maybe we had an exceptional group of mature, responsible people who could set aside their own egos and put the project first. It was a pleasure to work with the owner, architects, engineers, and agencies, who at all times maintained an attitude of fairness, cooperation, and partnership.

From conception through completion, it takes many people, agencies, and professions to complete a project such as Deer Meadow. The state of Connecticut, developer Marc S. Levine, Enterprise Builders, the architects, the engineers, the various agencies, all had a role and the opportunity to be the leader for a portion of the project.

As evidence of the successful precedent set by the Deer Meadow project, we recently completed Country Place, another affordable housing project in Connecticut for the same developer and with the same project team. This project was valued at $8.75 million and set on a 50-acre site. We were able to draw on our experience at Deer Meadow to attain a smooth and successful completion on this larger project. Clear and complete communication and follow-up every step of the way is what makes a job run smoothly. A lot of effort goes into making a job look easy to the outside observer.

Another achievement was that Enterprise Builders and the team on the Deer Meadow project were honored as "Project Team of the Year" from the Southern New England PMI Chapter, 1992/93.

Possibly the greatest satisfaction experienced by the team was the positive sociological impact we felt in helping make affordable housing available to families who would not otherwise have the opportunity to live in such pleasant surroundings. The words of a tenant who had just moved into a new apartment said it all — "I live in a palace!"

Possibly the greatest satisfaction for the project team was helping make affordable housing available to families who would not otherwise have the opportunity to live in such pleasant surroundings.

MARC S. LEVINE, DEVELOPER

What is really required for a project such as Deer Meadow to be successful is a team effort, not only in terms of design and construction, but also from the financial establishments and municipalities that enable the permit and development process to go smoothly.

We were able to put together an excellent financing package, the key elements of which were the favorable second mortgage from the Department of Housing and the equity proceeds that came from the sale of low income housing tax credits.

It's exciting to see the result, which is a beautiful project, integrated economically and racially—economically in that it combines market rate units with tax credit assisted units. The apartment complex is full and operating on a virtually trouble-free basis.

What we are able to do with a complex like this is to scatter affordable housing into the suburbs instead of concentrating them in the cities with all the ensuing problems.

Projects such as Deer Meadow allow families of modest means to raise their children in safe and attractive surroundings.

COMMISSIONER HENRY S. SCHERER, JR., CONNECTICUT DEPARTMENT OF HOUSING

We all know that decent housing is central to a decent quality of life. Among all the services a government or community can provide, a stock of affordable housing is every bit as necessary as good schools, fire and police protection, public transportation, and other basic services.

Deer Meadow is an important development because of the need it serves and because of the example it sets. It is an outstanding example of the private/public partnership working to benefit the community. The quality of this housing proves that by working together we can meet the affordable housing needs of rural and suburban communities.

For Deer Meadow, the Connecticut Housing Finance Authority provided the first mortgage, the Department of Housing provided the second mortgage, and the development received nearly one million dollars in federal low-income housing tax credits. But as we all know, housing does not get developed without the commitment of the local government, the developer, and so many dedicated parties.

The Department of Housing does not have powers of initiation. Regardless of what needs assessments indicate, we must rely on proposals from nonprofits and developers like Marc Levine.

In the current economy, some have questioned the need for affordable housing. In some areas there are high vacancy rates for rental units. But as the Brookings Institute has said, "There is no housing shortage. There is, however, a shortage of affordable housing." And the vacancy rates do not reflect an abundance of affordable units, but rather the fact that many in our society simply cannot afford private market rents without some form of subsidy.

Some of the impediments to affordable housing production are the misconceptions that surround our product. I am confident that if we could gather the opponents together and bring them to Deer Meadow, their opposition would be defused by the weight of the evidence before their eyes. This project transformed a vacant parcel of land into much-needed housing.

Government has a responsibility to make sure that our citizens are stakeholders in our society. For low-income families, it means providing a chance to become stakeholders. Making sure that our citizens have that essential stake in their society by creating affordable housing is both a challenge and an opportunity. As I see these beautiful apartments, I believe that we have accepted the challenge and that we are seizing the opportunity.

I submit that to continue to do so is as imperative to our future as to our society. As John Kennedy said in his inaugural address, "If a free society cannot help the many who are poor, it cannot save the few who are rich."

Connecticut's affordable housing is a good product, and as everyone can see, it is housing that belongs in any backyard.

MICHAEL McNABOE, PROJECT MANAGER, ENTERPRISE BUILDERS, INC.

Our experience on the Deer Meadow project allowed us to apply what we learned to a much larger project for the same developer and with the same team.
* We continually refined the CPM schedule and input feedback from everyone involved.
* We made an aggressive commitment to a completion date and worked to ensure we kept this commitment.
* We continually looked for ways to optimize the sequencing of construction and logistics of the various trades.
* We had learned the benefits of establishing a good relationship with the local utility companies early so that they would respond on schedule.

- We checked the source of materials from second- and third-tier subcontractors to ensure that deliveries were on time and that materials came from the same manufacturing facility.
- We also made sure that subcontractors were making payments to second- and third-tier subcontractors to make sure that money paid was flowing to its intended source, thus avoiding liens at the end of the job.

The most simple, yet most complex, element to explain about the success of this project was working with a team that allowed us to do our job as project managers. They simply let the construction management process work. They made decisions in a timely manner, responded to questions, and kept approvals moving. They reacted immediately and cooperatively and worked towards a common goal that was always in the best interest of the project.

ENTERPRISE BUILDERS, INC.

Enterprise Builders, Inc. is a merit shop general contractor and construction management firm located in Simsbury, Connecticut. Incorporated in 1984, Enterprise Builders is primarily involved in commercial, industrial, and institutional projects with construction values ranging from $1–20 million. The firm has access to $50 million in overall bonding capacity and is experienced and qualified to respond to competitively bid projects as well as negotiated and design/build contracts for private and public sector clients throughout New England.

Enterprise Builders' philosophy is that only through the team approach of owner, architect, and builder can a project be successfully completed. The firm is committed to leadership in the field and to establishing a reputation of excellence, integrity, service, and value in the marketplace.

In addition to a steady workload for prestigious clients, Enterprise Builders has received such project awards as "Excellence in Construction" from Associated Builders & Contractors, "Project Team of the Year" from the Southern New England PMI Chapter, and several safety awards. In 1989, the firm made the "Inc. 500" list of fastest growing companies in America, and in 1991 was one of four companies in Connecticut to receive the "Blue Chip Initiative" award for resourcefulness in business.

Study Questions

MAKING AFFORDABLE HOUSING ATTAINABLE THROUGH MODERN PROJECT MANAGEMENT

1. The author identifies some of the most important skills or abilities of a superintendent that help to keep a project on track. Which are those? Can you add some?

2. The case stresses the importance of planning as crucial to the success of the project. During the planning phase of a project it is necessary to develop a strategy that addresses all the issues that can influence the project. What are the topics that the planning strategy should cover?

3. The project team put special effort into the fulfillment of the schedule so the tenants would be able to move on the predetermined dates. Therefore time durations were crucial for the completion of this goal. What are the techniques more frequently used to estimate activity duration?

4. What two or three scope management factors were most critical to the success of this project? Why?

Goal Definition and Performance Indicators in Soft Projects: Building a Competitive Intelligence System

François Lacasse, Université du Québec à Hull

PMI Canada *Proceedings*, 1986, pp. 247–52

INTRODUCTION

This paper describes a "soft" project: the setting up of a competitive intelligence system (CIS) in an agency of government. This case serves to illustrate:
• how project management methods can be successfully applied to situations where the objectives are, at the outset, relatively unclear
• how success requirements were determined and subsequently used to keep the project on track and how, even in nebulous areas such as "managerial technology," such indicators can be selected and applied
• how performance indicators need to be tackled early on for purposes of control and, more importantly, for sharpening the planning and implementation processes.

After describing the context of the project, we review the project itself. The conclusion draws some lessons on the specifics of managing soft projects.

THE CONTEXT AND THE PROJECT

The government agency where the project took place is concerned with tourism; its mandate is similar to other governmental tourism bodies throughout the world, that is, marketing and promotion, assistance to private sector industries related to tourism (grants, technical support, standards, etc.). The organization is structured into three divisions: marketing, product development and research, and policy (including most data collection and analysis). The rivalry between divisions is relatively high, and coordination requires substantial resources.

The competitive intelligence system project idea flowed from a complete review and strategic reorientation launched in 1984. This reorientation called for a clearer role definition and a more commercially aggressive stance for the organization (i.e., concentrate all efforts first on expanding Canadian exports, limit its domestic role to helping a small set of Canadian destinations compete directly with foreign destinations).

In this context, the need was felt by management for a competitive intelligence system to generate high quality information for itself and the various line managers.

As with all such systems, this CIS was to inform management about the actions and the intentions of Canada's chief competitors for tourist dollars in markets identified as among the most promising (e.g., Pacific Rim countries). This intelligence was to focus on other countries' marketing strategies and on trends in new tourist products. When arrayed against information on the evolving state of Canadian attractions, such intelligence was intended to provide 1) a continual monitoring of how Canadian destinations were likely to fare in the competition for tourist dollars, and 2) early identification of threats and opportunities in this sector.

Initial Goals, Assumptions, and Structures

In its original formulation, the goal of the project was: "to have in place, fully operational, within two years a complete CIS which would be at least as good as the best ones existing in the private sector."

The first project plan, described below, made the following assumptions, albeit implicitly:

• A clear set of rules or a dominant model for setting up and successfully running a CIS existed in large corporations.

• This "proven technology" could be imported without extensive modification.

• The key feature of a CIS was the collection, storage, and retrieval of information (i.e., the core of the project consists of designing and setting up this "machinery").

• A CIS was basically an outgrowth of the research/data collection function (i.e., line managers and top management were its relatively passive consumers rather than active participants/producers).

The project management structure was under the responsibility of the head of research and planning. Two teams were set up, one internal to the organization, the other made up of consultants. As indicated in Figure 1, the internal team was to proceed immediately with reorganizing the data gathering and analysis functions (from the library to EDP). As well as laying the groundwork for the system, the internal team was also given the task of preaching the new gospel to the rest of the organization.

The external team was responsible for the overall design of the system, for ensuring that it met the quality and completeness standard of "best business practices" in the field, for defining the final implementation strategy, and for providing technical assistance during the last implementation phases, at which time it would merge with the internal team. The very existence of an external team was seen as an expression of top management's commitment to the project: this team was totally insulated from "crises" and emergencies.

The coordination structure was both simple and rigid: at least every other week, the two teams would meet to assess progress and report to the overall project coordinator.

The key feature of this project structure was that implementation and planning were, in practice, to proceed simultaneously. For insurance, the internal team would busy itself with reorganizing the library, part of the EDP and research function, and with pre-marketing potential CIS clients, while the external team was working on refining knowledge of the exact structure of private CIS to be borrowed, establishing performance criteria (project and system), and designing the system's implementation primarily for participants (functions) other than those reached by the internal team. The success of the project itself was predicated on 1) rigorous determination of the CIS features to be copied, 2) precision in formulating instructions to personnel, 3) good choice of computers, and 4) fast and efficient training/recruitment.

On the Brink of Disaster

Within a matter of weeks it became obvious that the project was heading for serious trouble if its structure and purposes were not modified. The assumed clarity of goals, as summarized above in four assumptions, evaporated as soon as they were confronted with reality. Serious organizational resistance was encountered in all implementation aspects: unrealistic budgetary requests; demands for highly detailed instructions (not forthcoming) on what to collect, how, and why; drift into turf battles ("Research power grab has to be resisted."); apparent lack of interest from potential CIS clients, both internal and external; etc.

The situation was no better within the external team. The "easy" job of establishing the fine points of what constituted a good private CIS proved quite difficult. Getting on with the "real" job of designing its integration into the organization was consequently stalled. Contrary to initial expectations, no single dominant private sector model of a CIS existed. Indeed a bewildering array of techniques, managerial practices, and structures existed, all loosely termed "CIS."

The project had clearly been underplanned. The goal, which in fact was a rather delicate change in a strategic management process, had been treated as if it were the purchase and installation of a well-known machine. The hasty partial implementation attempts had forgotten that "building blocks" cannot be put together before consensus is reached on plans for the whole structure. Even more importantly, the realization had come too late that a CIS constituted not only an addition to the organization, but also a change in its modus operandi. Competitive intelligence systems (CIS) were differently organized in various companies essentially because, wherever they had been successful, they had become embedded into existing strategic decision processes and so had been molded by a particular company's culture and environment.

Consequently, the management of the project had to be guided as much by determinants for successfully effecting organizational changes as by technical indicators. In practice, to be successful as a project, the setting up of a CIS had to:
• meet needs felt at lower levels (specially those of middle line management)
• be designed for and perceived as allowing improvement in job performance—with the appropriate rewards
• be inspired by "best business practices" (to give it legitimacy), and fit into the organization's culture and mandate (congruence)
• be part "owned" by the people who would have to run and use it; that is, they must have a say in its design and implementation.

THE PROJECT: SECOND WIND AND PRELIMINARY RESULTS

The above considerations for a successful project led to a drastic reorganization in terms of goals, progress (success) indicators, and distribution of tasks.

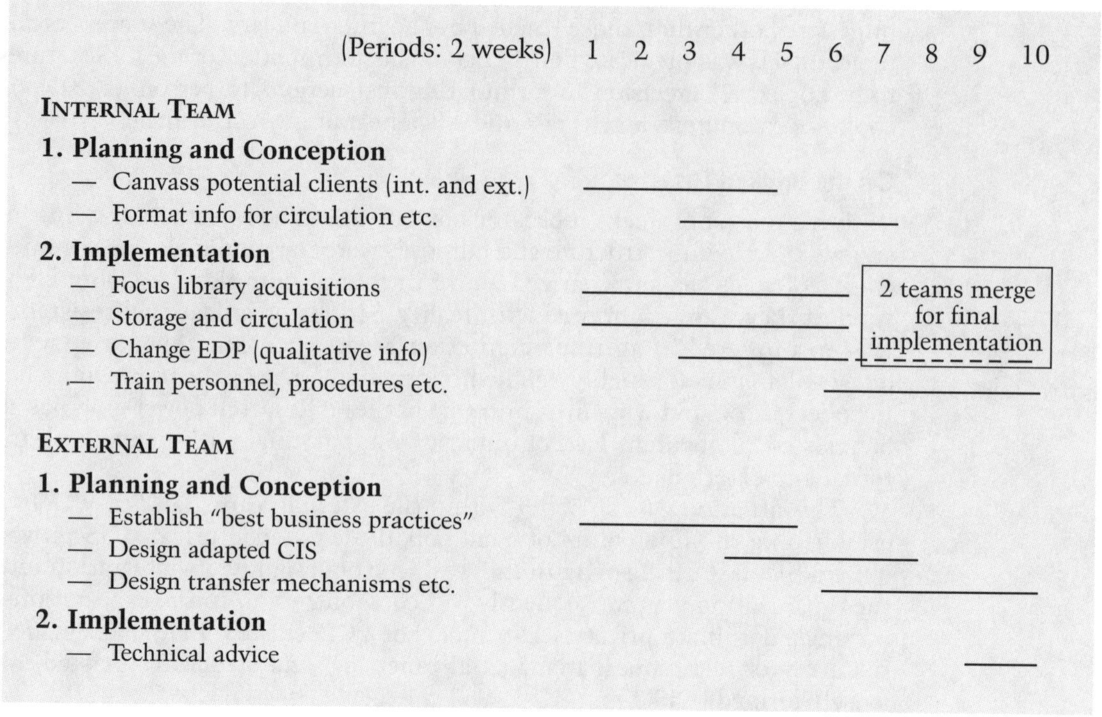

(Periods: 2 weeks)   1   2   3   4   5   6   7   8   9   10

INTERNAL TEAM

1. Planning and Conception
— Canvass potential clients (int. and ext.)
— Format info for circulation etc.

2. Implementation
— Focus library acquisitions
— Storage and circulation
— Change EDP (qualitative info)
— Train personnel, procedures etc.

> 2 teams merge for final implementation

EXTERNAL TEAM

1. Planning and Conception
— Establish "best business practices"
— Design adapted CIS
— Design transfer mechanisms etc.

2. Implementation
— Technical advice

FIGURE 1   INITIAL PROJECT STRUCTURE AND TASKS (SUMMARY)

Deadlines and budget were only slightly modified, since the problems had been detected early.

Briefly, the revamped project focused on:
- distinguishing those best business practices which were essential to implement within the organization (external team)
- defining options for the rest of the system, specifically, practices which might be useful but were not essential; the basis for selecting these options was to be their "fit" within the organization (external team).

As the work progressed on those two aspects, the internal team was to float the various options, obtain informal reactions to the fit between them and the interested parties within the organization, and transmit feedback to the other project team. The partial implementation measures envisaged at the outset were dropped.

First and foremost, in terms of goal definition, a classification of "best business practices" emerged, clearly separating the necessary characteristics of a CIS from those which were really options (see Figure 2). The criterion used for this classification was simple: Only practices which were observed in all or virtually all companies running successful CIS, despite variations in company size, business environment, and industry, were considered to be compulsory features of a CIS. The criteria were equally straightforward for deciding whether a CIS was successful: survival for more than five years and top management satisfaction with it.

Figure 2 confirms the wisdom of postponing the partial "technical" implementation. Indeed, it is on those very "technical" characteristics that clear "best business practices" did not exist; "best" was simply what was

	1	2	3	4	5	6
Practices:	Specialized staff collects	Collection: for line staff	Comput-erized system	Qualitative information	Sources	Use of outside commercial services
1. Uniform across organizations ("necessary")		X		X		
2. Varies according to circumstances ("discretionary")	X		X		X	X

	7	8	9	10	11	12
Practices:	Divisional location	Single leader (account-ability)	Line managers dominate analysis	Standard format for dissemi-nation	Integration (collection and analysis)	Much resources in focusing info collection (mini-projects)
1. Uniform across organizations ("necessary")		X	X			X
2. Varies according to circumstances ("discretionary")	X			X	X	

FIGURE 2   NECESSARY VERSUS DISCRETIONARY PRACTICES IN SUCCESSFUL PRIVATE CIS

most convenient to a particular organization. For instance, the choice between specialized information gathering personnel and information collection by line personnel or between computerized and manual systems proved to be discretionary, instead of necessary, features of a good CIS.

No less important results were that in virtually all observed instances:
• The key element in a successful CIS was that rather ill-defined step called analysis; i.e., the crucial link in the system was the quality of the analysis of the information not, as was believed at the outset, the collection stage. This confirmed the key role of line involvement as a requirement for success.
• To keep costs under tight control in information gathering and to minimize the risks of flooding the organization with papers and meetings, the dominant requirement was that the quest for information be *very carefully* targeted. This meant that small-scale competitive assessments had to be conducted to define the identity of competitors and the threats and opportunities they represented; that is to say the system involves a series of mini-projects. This requirement for what otherwise would be an ongoing activity provided the most practical avenue for building feedback mechanisms right into the CIS. For instance, the users (line and top management) would be involved in requesting such assessments and line personnel in providing them.

IMPLEMENTATION

The original intent, at least implicitly, had been to proceed in standard mechanical fashion according to the following sequence: define techniques, explain them to selected personnel (training), review budgets and make adjustments, assign tasks and responsibilities, and introduce control a few months later. Given the now more precise goals and awareness of key organizational/behavioral constraints, the sequence and the approach had to be altered. The following sequence emerged:

• Formulate and present options to the management team (costs, structures) both for the ultimate design of a CIS adapted to the organization and for the implementation strategy.

• Test the feasibility of the options selected on personnel involved and adjust accordingly (involves extensive information dissemination).

• Provide support services and follow-up mechanisms for the people initially involved in the CIS.

In practice, the implementation was quite different from what had been envisaged: The approach selected relied on imitation and competition inside the organization via a series of mini-projects carried out by small teams of *volunteers* drawn from all three divisions within the organization. Essentially to ensure relevant collection and analysis of information, in a setting where employees had no direct commercial contact with tourists, it was decided to keep specialized CIS staff to a minimum. The bulk of the work would be done by line personnel, involving the three divisions. This choice meant that feedback and integration would be maximized.

The implementation consisted essentially of providing guidelines, money and technical support, and an evaluation framework for these mini-projects. For instance, the following was communicated to the staff.

• CIS was a high priority and its concrete input was needed.

• Teams of volunteers were needed of no more than three to four people which had to include personnel from each division.

• Each team would submit a short project proposal to the CIS team (e.g., to analyze the competition facing Canadian western ski resorts and to design and implement a cost efficient system for subsequent monitoring of this segment); they would assume the responsibility—initially at least—for running this monitoring system.

• Within one week management would select a few proposals/teams and negotiate budgets, rewards (trips, good evaluations, etc.), deadlines (no longer than three months), time allocation with respect to "normal" line duties, and the amount of support required from the original external and internal teams.

• At least two other rounds of such mini-projects would be called for, each time with more precise criteria for selecting and judging the success of the mini-projects. For instance, after the results of the first round were in, a primitive standardized format for circulating the intelligence (i.e., preliminary diagnosis of threats and opportunities on the basis of information gathered) to line managers and for allowing them to provide feedback both in terms of additional information needed and of their judgment of the reliability of the intelligence provided was developed.

• By the end of the first year the entire CIS was to be in place (i.e., it should spread like wildfire, it was hoped).

This implementation strategy provided:
- solid control of costs, since each mini-project was controlled separately
- a sense of "ownership" throughout the organization of the CIS by various individuals whose diligence and commitment could not be commanded but who would respond favorably to incentives, competition, and technical support
- a gradual transition from what some had seen as a power grab by one division under the guise of a "newfangled system" to a standard operating procedure for deciding what information to use (and how) in the normal course of managerial decision-making.

The project was a success insofar as the CIS became a reality, gained acceptance, and met the basic criteria of adapting proven private-sector techniques and exhibiting good control of costs and deadlines—by the standards of organizational changes. The ultimate success of the new CIS belongs to the elusive realm of "improved management strategy and tactics." It will not be possible to ascertain its impact for a number of years.

CONCLUSION: THE LESSONS

1. First and foremost, this experiment showed how useful a systematic project management framework can be even in relatively unstructured situations. For instance, the original intent of management could have been carried out by decree: change in unit and job descriptions, purchases of new data gathering and processing equipment, etc. Those moves would have been costly and would have required very extensive (and protracted) changes and soul searching within the newly established structures and responsibilities. The attendant risks of low morale and of line managers dismissing the whole idea as harebrained were very high. Furthermore, the approach allowed for early detection and use of relevant performance indicators.

2. When applying project management methods to organizational and strategic changes, the approach must devote more resources and time to what is usually termed "the planning phase." Defining in operational terms the goal of the project becomes a rather detailed first implementation step. This flexibility leads to a sequential approach to both goal definition and implementation. In most soft projects, it has to be accepted that the initial formulation of the objective cannot be much more than a general direction, that the indicators of success have to be systematically devised early on by the project team.

3. The common problems associated with project termination are exacerbated in "soft" cases. For instance, in the project reviewed above, should the end be taken as when the CIS was in place (How big does it then have to be?) or was it when it was running smoothly (How smooth?) or when it had demonstrated that the CIS could deliver what it was hoped for (i.e., better marketing and development strategies and tactics)? The difficulty in using any of these criteria led to an arbitrary definition of the end: After one year of implementation and three series of (volunteer-led) mini-projects, it was deemed to be no longer a project, but rather a normal activity.

4. "Soft" organizational change projects constitute a fascinating field for refining project management methods. Namely, research is needed to design better, more systematic paths toward goals which are progressively defined as the project unfolds.

REFERENCES

1. Anderson, J., and R. Narasimhan. 1979. "Assessing Project Implementation Risk: A Methodical Approach." *Management Science.* June.

2. Clark, C.H. 1980. *Idea Management: How to Motivate Creativity and Innovation.* AMACOM.

3. Cleland, D.I., and W.R.King. 1975. "Competitive Business Intelligence Systems." *Business Horizons.* Dec., pp. 19–29.

4. Conrath, D.W., and G. du Roure. 1977. "Organisational Implications of Comprehensive Communication Information Systems: Some Conjectures." Discussion Paper. Centre d'etude et de Recherche sur les Organisations et la Gestion. Institut d'administration des Entreprises, Aix-en-Provence.

5. Fuld, L.M. 1985. *Competitor Intelligence: How to Get It. How to Use It.* New York.

6. Gordon, I. 1982. "Your Survival Kit: Competitive Intelligence." *Business Quarterly* 47, no. 2, Aug., pp. 65–67.

7. Jaffe, E.D. 1975. "Multinational Marketing Intelligence: An Information Requirements Model." *Administrative Science Quarterly.* September, pp. 53–60.

8. Kaiser, M.M. 1984. *Understanding the Competition: a Practical Guide to Competitive Analysis.* Michael M. Kaiser Associates, p. 98.

9. Kerzner, H. 1980. "Evaluation Techniques in Project Management." *Journal of Systems Management.* Feb.

10. Lederman, L.L. 1984. "Foresight Activities in the U.S.A.: Time for a Re-Assessement?" *Long Range Planning* 17, no. 3, pp. 41–50.

11. MacMillan, I. C. 1982. "Seizing Competitive Initiative." *Journal of Business Strategy* 2, no. 4, Spring, pp. 43–57.

12. McNamee, P. 1984. "Competitive Analysis Using Matrix Displays." *Long Range Planning,* vol. 17, no. 3, pp. 98–114.

13. Meredith, J.R. 1981. "The Implementation of Computer Based Systems." *Journal of Operations Management.* Oct.

14. Moravec, M. 1979. "How Organizational Development Can Help and Hinder Project Managers." *Project Management Quarterly.* Sept.

15. Nutt, P.C. 1982. "Hybrid Planning Methods." *Academy of Management Review.* July.

16. Pearce, F.T. 1976. "Business Intelligence Systems: The Need, Development and Integration." *Industrial Marketing Management* 5, no. 2 and 3, June, pp. 115–138.

17. Piercy, N. 1979. "Behavioral Constraints on Marketing Information Systems." *European Journal of Marketing* 13, no. 8, pp. 261–70.

18. ———. 1980. "Marketing Information Systems: Theory vs. Practice." *Quarterly Review of Marketing* 6, no.1, pp. 16–24.

19. Rubinstein, A.H.; Chabrebarty, A.K.; O'Keafe, R.D.; Souder, W.E.; and M.C.Young. 1976. "Factors Influencing Innovation Success at the Project Level." *Resource Management* 19, May, pp. 15–20.

20. Schonberger, R.J. 1980. "MIS Design: A Contingency Approach." *Management Information Systems Quarterly* 4 no. 1, pp. 13–20.

21. Stuckenbruck, L.C., ed. 1981. *The Implementation of Project Management: The Professionals Handbook.* Project Management Institute, Addison-Wesley.

22. Tushman, M.L., and D.A. Nadler. 1978. "Information Processing as an Integrating Concept in Organizational Design." *Academy of Management Review* 3 no. 3, pp. 613–24.

23. Wren, D.A., and D. Voich, Jr. 1984. *Management: Process, Structure and Behavior.* New York: Wiley.

Study Questions

GOAL DEFINITION AND PERFORMANCE INDICATORS ON SOFT PROJECTS: BUILDING A COMPETITIVE INTELLIGENCE SYSTEM

1. Describe some of the scope management problems created by using one goal statement as the sole guiding factor on the project in this case. Define scope management for any project.

2. Briefly describe how the original project management team(s) were organized. Identify some of the problems resulting from operating under this structure.

3. What were some of the specific problems originally encountered by the project teams?

4. What were the keys to project success as cited in the case? What other factors influence the success or failure of a project?

5. Describe the eventual implementation strategy used on this project. What are some potential problems of this approach?

ORGANIZING

2
ORGANIZING

Communication Risk Management in Municipal Government Projects: City of New Orleans Computer-Aided Dispatch System Project

Michael Newell, Orleans Parish Communication District

PMI *Proceedings*, 1995, pp. 224–33

INTRODUCTION

Communications among municipal government agencies has its own set of special problems. This project proved to be an excellent platform to showcase these problems and it involved the development of a computer system that would be used by the city of New Orleans police, fire, and emergency medical departments.

These agencies are traditionally very private about their activities and normally do not share information or standardize on common procedures. In the development of this project it was critical that the three agencies compromise on system requirements and standardize on the use of the system.

In addition to the problems involved in communicating between different parts of the city government, excellent communications between the city's project team and the vendor were essential.

Background

A dispatch system is used to assign vehicles that are in the field to where they are needed in a timely way. This is usually done through the use of a very high frequency radio system. A computer-aided dispatch (CAD) system is used to aid the dispatcher in carrying out this function and to supply an audit trail to show the history of the incident.

The New Orleans Police Department installed its first computer-aided dispatch system in 1978. At the time this was a state-of-the-art dispatch system. By 1987 the system was no longer state-of-the-art and the anticipated capacity of the system had been far exceeded. The age and overuse of the system led to frequent system crashes and slow response times. The city was unable to pay the monthly maintenance charges on the system which had increased as the system got older.

A new project was organized and a set of requirements was written. The person assigned to manage this project, an employee of the Police MIS Department, was given this project as an addition to his normal duties. The user requirements were written without much involvement of the users and without very much detail.

The normal bidding process was used and bids were received from several potential vendors. The lowest bidder was significantly lower than any of the bidders. This bidder was selected on the basis of having the lowest bid and a contract was signed. Relatively little was done to evaluate the vendor's ability to get the job done.

Shortly after contract signing, the vendor shipped all of the required hardware to the communications center. This allowed the vendor, a software development house, to bill the city for the hardware and use the profit margin of selling the hardware to finance the software development. The cost to the city for this hardware was $425,000, approximately half of the value of the contract. This is a common practice in computer systems development and should be avoided if possible.

Since the bid process requires the selection of vendors based on price alone and assumes that all vendors are providing essentially the same product or service, an unqualified bidder could easily become the selected vendor. This is exactly what took place.

The selected vendor for this project deliberately low bid the project in order to allow him to make an entry into the business. By having a large site like the city of New Orleans use his product successfully, the vendor would acquire a powerful selling tool for additional future sites and at the same time gain experience in the development of a CAD product.

This turned out to be a bad decision all around. The vendor was never able to develop the software to a point when the requirements could even be closely met and the response time of what was developed was much too slow to be used effectively. Ultimately, after significant delays and missed milestones, it became clear that the vendor would not be able to produce the promised software without additional funding from the city.

Additional funding was considered throwing good money after bad and it was decided to litigate for the recovery of the cost of the computer hardware and continue the project with another vendor. This caused an additional three-year delay of the project but allowed for a recovery of $300,000 and retained position of the computer hardware.

The computer hardware had, during all this time, become obsolete and was not of much value. Although, the hardware, two Tandem Corporation Non-Stop II computers, and all of the associated peripherals, had never been operated. New and faster units were available from Tandem. Tandem, like many other computer hardware vendors, had significantly raised the price of maintenance on these now obsolete computers. This is one way of forcing the customer to upgrade to the new equipment. This significantly reduced the value of these computers. In addition, the computers were somewhat special purpose and primarily used in the banking industry.

Many alternatives were tried to find some way of utilizing these computers. An attempt was made to sell them to a company outside the United States via a used computer broker. Ads were run in trade journals, and an attempt was made to donate them to another branch of city government. In all these attempts, the best offer that was received was one to take them off our hands at no charge and not charge us for the removal.

WHAT IS COMPUTER-AIDED DISPATCH?

The enhanced 911 telephone system, in use in the city of New Orleans since 1984, allows the city's population easy access to the public safety service providers of police, fire, and emergency medical. By having one number, nationwide, that is simple to remember and used to access any of the emergency services, the public is assured the fastest possible access to the service providers. The public is not required to look up or remember a separate number for police, fire, or emergency medical, and the same number can be used when a person travels from one community to another.

The Enhanced 911 system displays the street address where the call is being made from. This is known as the automatic location information (ALI). This information is critically important in the event that the caller does not give the location of the emergency or hangs up the telephone suddenly. New Orleans Police policy is to send a unit to this location immediately to investigate. Many lives have been saved through this feature.

In the city of New Orleans, all 911 calls are answered by a police department call taker. This person determines first if the call is truly an emergency and then whether police, fire, emergency medical, or a combination of all three are required. If fire or emergency medical services are required, the police call taker has the ability to transfer/conference the call to fire and/or emergency medical and can also stay on the line as well. When this is done the ALI information accompanies the transfer of the call.

Fire and emergency medical calls are received very quickly from police by their respective emergency operators and the appropriate response can be made. In this way each agency is responsible for dispatching its own appropriate units to the emergency.

Once a call is received by any agency and the location and type of emergency is determined, the radio dispatcher can dispatch the appropriate response. Police generally only dispatch a one- or two-man vehicle; emergency medical generally only dispatch an ambulance or, in extreme emergencies, an emergency medical supervisor. The Fire Department has a much more complicated response depending on the type of fire, location, and risk to life and property. The Fire Department also has a much larger choice of the type of equipment to be selected for dispatch.

The computer-aided dispatch system links all of the dispatch and call-taking functions of the public safety agencies together. By using the computer to retrieve the appropriate information for the call taker and dispatcher, much time can be saved and there is a higher assurance that the appropriate equipment response will be made.

Call Taker Functions

When a 911 call is received it is issued to the operator who has been available the longest. In this way 911 calls are evenly distributed to the call takers. The telephone number, address, and whether it is a business or residence of the phone that is used is automatically loaded onto the CAD work station.

The call taker now asks the person calling what type of emergency there is and enters this information. Once this is done the CAD computer searches its database and verifies that the address is one that is valid. If the exact address and street name are not valid, the computer displays possible matches to the address. For example, if the address entered was 301 Broad Street, the computer would return with 301 S. Broad Street and 301 N. Broad Street. The call taker would then select the correct street address.

The address and the type of emergency are all that is required to enter the call. The call taker generally remains on the phone with the caller while the computer relays the information to the radio dispatch person. The call taker continues to take down information from the caller and each time adds it to the call electronically and passes the information to the dispatcher. This is done automatically even though the call taker and dispatcher may be located no where near one another.

Dispatcher Functions

Meanwhile the computer uses the location and type of emergency information already recorded to recommend the appropriate level of response. The response is sometimes dependent on the incident type such as an armed robbery in progress or a house fire, and sometimes dependent on the location of the incident such as a house fire at a nursing home or a house fire in a residence. The CAD system takes these things into consideration and makes the appropriate recommendation to the dispatcher. The dispatcher considers the computer recommendation and either accepts it or makes her own recommendation.

In addition, the computer also displays any pertinent information known about the location, in the form of premise information. This information may indicate that there has been a previous fire at this location, that it is a possible narcotics location, or that the residents might be armed. The dispatcher can relay this information to the units responding. The system also searches a predefined radius around the incident to determine whether there are any other incidents being worked by this or another agency. In many emergencies, such as a fire, there will be several calls to the communication center for the same emergency. This duplicate call-checking feature allows the dispatcher to be aware of another agency's involvement in the area as well as the possibility that this is an incident that is already being worked by the agency.

There is a computer-generated map that displays the incident location in the center of the screen and the user-defined area around that incident. The map displays have been physically verified and are the most accurate representation of the city available. The map displays not only the incident being worked but any other activity by any other agency in the displayed area.

A global positioning system-based automatic vehicle location system shows the position of all public safety vehicles within one minute of their actual positions. The accuracy of the position is within 50 feet. This system allows the dispatcher to know exactly where all vehicles are at any given time and allows for the proper selection of vehicles to respond to an emergency. This system can display the relative travel time of several units from their actual positions to the site of the incident.

Mobile data terminals round out the equipment complement. These computer terminals allow the person in the field to directly contact the central computer. In addition to being used to update the status of field units, the Police Department units can make inquiries such as suspect or license plate checks without interfering with the dispatcher's normal duties. The Fire Department also has the capability to operate a mobile printer on board the fire engine to send text and graphic information directly to the engine company while enroute.

All transactions in the CAD system take place in less than two seconds and an audit trail, including the time of day and the operator ID and name, are recorded for every transaction that is made on the system. The audit trail is extremely detailed and audit records are made even to the fact that a warning notice was displayed to the operator and that it was viewed.

Supervisor Functions

When a serious emergency occurs, such as a multiple alarm fire or a serious crime, the CAD system automatically generates a list of persons within the city who should be notified. These persons might include the superintendent of police, superintendent of fire, the mayor, the electric company, etc.

These notification lists are pre-planned and loaded into the CAD system. When the appropriate incident occurs, the lists are automatically sent to the work station of the persons responsible for making the notified persons aware of the emergency. More than one person can be doing this simultaneously and the CAD system keeps track of who has and has not been notified so that no time is lost by two people calling the same person.

Multiple deployment plans can be entered into the system. This means that the deployment of emergency vehicles can be changed depending on the time of day or the day of the week. At different times of the day or night the likelihood of an emergency becomes greater in some areas and less in others. It is important to allow for the deployment of emergency units to minimize the response time for a particular emergency.

CAD PROJECT RESTARTED

Once the litigation over the failed project was complete a new project could be initiated. This time, instead of assigning the project to one of the people already on staff at one of the public safety agencies or the city's MIS department, it was determined to hire a professional project manager. Through PSM Consulting, I was hired in as a consultant to be the project manager. One of the deciding issues in the interview process was my conviction that project management methodology could be applied to any type of project and that the project manager need not have experience in the area directly as long as this is done. This was important since there are very few people available who have experience in this area.

Forming the Project Team

As project manager, the first thing to do was to set up a project team. This was felt to be of critical importance since reviewing the files from the previously failed project led to the conclusion that many of the users were inadequately informed of the project's progress and were not allowed to participate in the development of the system requirements. The first objective was to ensure that all of the users would have a means of communicating their wishes to the project manager.

The formation of the project team was done by selecting team members from every agency in the city that would have a stake in the results of the project. This meant that a large number of individuals would be very inexperienced in project management and management practices in general. Persons were selected from the MIS, police, fire, and emergency management departments. While my previous project management experience prepared me for dealing with difficult user groups, I had never been in a position where some of the attendees at meetings wore guns, as was the case whenever the police were involved.

When forming a project team there are usually some territorial issues involved. My previous experience had taught me how to deal with departmental disagreements but never to the extent that I experienced here. The police, fire, and emergency departments were not only physically separated by several miles but had operated as separate agencies for their entire existence.

The agency spending the money for this project, the Orleans Parish Communication District, had the unique privilege of not holding allegiance to any of the city's agencies and, in fact, is chartered as a parish (county) agency by the state. As such, we could not be coerced into doing anything through the use of city politics.

Conflict Resolution Issues

Since all of the agencies were part of the city of New Orleans government, conflict resolution was difficult to achieve through traditional means. The superintendents of the police and fire departments report directly to the mayor. The director of the Emergency Medical Department reports to the director of the Health Department who, in turn, reports to the mayor. The single point of conflict resolution was therefore the mayor and access to the mayor was very limited. In fact, any conflict that had to be resolved at this level had to first be brought to the chief administrative officer (CAO) who would then take the matter up with the mayor.

The situation that frequently developed was that a meeting could be held with all of the persons that had the knowledge to make a decision and these people were quite willing to reach compromises and agreements. But, if the decision required the expenditure of funds, decisions had to be carried to the superintendent level. If the decision required exceeding the departmental budget, the decision had to be brought to the CAO or the mayor. Decision requests to the CAO tended to be delayed great periods of time because of other more pressing problems. Experience showed that any decision that could not be resolved within the project team did not get resolved at all.

An example of this type of problem was the employment of a person to manage the graphic information systems (GIS) and maps. The Fire Department agreed to hire this person and use him to service the GIS requirement for the police, fire, and emergency medical. When it was determined that this would require an additional person above the Fire Department's budget, the Fire Department kicked it to the CAO and no action was taken. After one year, this position remains unfilled.

Informal Communications Issues

In the communications area there were several issues causing derogatory opinions about each other's department. These varying opinions frequently caused jealousy and bad feelings.

Environment. Police dispatchers handle approximately 600,000 calls for service each year. This means that on many days a police dispatcher must handle an average of one call per minute. A typical emergency medical dispatcher handles an average of one call every five minutes and a Fire Department dispatcher handles an average of one call per hour.

Fire dispatchers' salaries were considerably higher than either police or emergency medical dispatchers. The Police Department personnel felt this was unfair since all of their calls were emergencies and that life and property were always at stake. The emergency medical personnel felt that this was unfair since each of them had to be a certified emergency medical technician.

The working environment at the Police Department was not nearly as pleasant as at the other two agencies. Police Department personnel have a small unequipped break room while the fire and emergency medical personnel each have a full kitchen and break room.

Communicating with the individuals of the project team was difficult because of the level of inexperience in project management as well as the distances involved. Personnel on the project team were located in six different geographic locations about the city. Telephone communications proved impossible since none of the team members ever seemed to be in their office. Broadcasting fax through a fax/modem proved to be the most effective means of communication.

Geography. Each of the persons on the project team was generally located in a different part of the city. City Hall was located in the central part of the city; police headquarters was located north of City Hall about three miles; Fire Department headquarters was located about three miles east of City Hall; fire communications center and the emergency medical communications center were located about six miles north of city hall. Persons located at City Hall were generally located on different floors.

Fortunately about the time this project got under way, Fax/Modem boards for PCs became very reasonably priced. This became the primary communication device for formal and informal communications. Each person on the project team, it was found out, had close access to a Fax machine. After some initial getting used to, most of the communication between team members outside meetings was through the use of Fax.

This could not have been done using a normal fax machine or by personally delivering each memo. The city mail system proved to be unreliable and not fast enough to be practical. The time factor for visiting each of the project team sites could take most of a morning or afternoon. By utilizing the PC/Fax/Modem combination, memos could be written one time and automatically distributed to the project team members after hours. This proved to be a tremendous savings in time and effort and all of the team members had hard copy information in front of them.

Formal Communications Issues

Meetings. Once the team had been formed, a set of requirements for the system had to be drafted. These requirements were begun from scratch to ensure that all of the project team members fully understood and agreed to the requirements definition. It was also important for the project manager to fully understand the workings of the departments and how the system would be utilized. Both of these things were accomplished at the same time since each requirement had to be explained thoroughly to the project manager before he could formally enter it into the requirements list.

Many hours in team meetings resulted in a 300-page requirements definition document that was understood and agreed to by the entire project team. It was possible to create a sense of teamwork among the project team through the use of these meetings. Members of the project team felt that they were truly responsible for the ultimate system, and as such learned to work together even on issues that had been serious disagreements in the past.

Documents. It was determined that the system could best be procured by using a request for proposal (RFP) instead of the normal bid process. This process has its pros and cons.

The bid process. In a bid process, the specifications for the system you are purchasing are quite specific. The potential vendor simply gives you the price for the items you have required. You may easily find yourself in the position of requiring the bidder to quote something that is more expensive and less useful than an alternative. In the area of computer systems, this is frequently the case. In the process of purchasing the CAD system, the original quotes and specifications would have called for the use of 386 PCs as the operator work stations. By the time the equipment was actually delivered, the 486/66 was the state-of-the-art PC to be used. In a neighboring city this actually took place. A bid was written for CAD equipment and the thirty-seven workstations were quoted as 386/25 PCs. By the time the vendor was selected, contract negotiated and equipment delivered, 486 PCs were available, much faster, and more capable, and less expensive. However, because this was a bid process, the bidding would have to have been reopened to all potential vendors if the specifications would have been changed. This would have resulted in another contract negotiated and another delay in the process and then it might be that the Pentium computers would have been available.

All bidders in this process are guaranteed that fairness in selection will be followed since it is a pure quantitative measurement between vendors' prices. There is assumed to be no difference between any vendor's offering.

The RFP process. In the RFP process the specifications are more functional than specific. In other words the buyer writes down what he expects the system to do but not how he expects it to be done. By writing functional requirements, the potential vendor has some options as to how the system will actually work. It is critically important that the functional requirements be very specific.

The principal problem here is one of communication. The functional specifications must be extremely clear to the potential vendor and written down in an extremely explicit manner. This communication is actually more difficult than a bid since in a bid specification, all bidders are given exactly the same information and equipment and software selection is quite specific.

In the RFP process, the potential vendors have much more freedom to design something that exceeds the requirements in a favorable way. This, of course, means that there will be another document, from each proposer, explaining what his system will actually do and how it will do it.

In the process of selecting a vendor for our CAD system, we began with twenty-four possible vendors; four actually prepared proposals. Each proposal was 2–4 feet thick. The size of the proposals made the evaluation process complex and difficult but resulted in the selection of the best possible system for the money involved.

Evaluation. The evaluation process was completed in three steps: three days of oral review for each vendor, submission of a best and final proposal, and final evaluation using a value matrix.

Three-day oral review. Each potential vendor was required to participate in a three-day, maximum, presentation to the project team. The potential vendors were invited to bring any demonstration equipment or presentation tools and personnel that they thought would enhance their possibility of winning the contract award.

Each potential vendor temporarily installed a fully operational CAD system and presented the functionality of their system. During this time the project team was able to ask specific questions about each system and gain confidence in the potential vendor's ability to actually do the work.

The only difficulty in this part of the process was coordinating the large number of personnel involved and scheduling times when everyone was available. All of the potential vendors, of course, wanted to be the last one to present so that they could leave a lasting impression and respond to questions that their predecessors had failed to answer satisfactorily.

Best and final proposal. After the oral reviews were completed, a list of changes to the original specifications in the RFP were written. This allowed us to eliminate the items which all potential vendors indicated were either too expensive or not practical.

By using the revisions feature in Microsoft Word, clear distinctions could be made between the original RFP and the revised RFP. This allowed us to communicate the changes fairly to each potential vendor.

A listing of each numbered paragraph in the RFP was extracted. Each potential vendor was required to respond to each paragraph by checking a box to indicate that she fully complied with the paragraph, that she would modify the system so that it did comply, or that she would not modify the system so that it would comply.

VENDOR COMMUNICATIONS ISSUES

Using the RFP

In spite of all the effort that was made to ensure that the potential vendors and the chosen vendor completely understood the requirements of the system, the above described process was followed and then elaborated on. Each potential vendor, and later the chosen vendor, did not really accept the requirements.

In retrospect, I feel that the participants all felt that their already developed systems would satisfy our needs without much modification. They bet on the fact that they would be able to convince us, when the systems were delivered, that they would work "as is." Our user group, however, was quite firm on these points.

It is critical for buyers using the RFP process to understand that an enormous effort must be spent carefully explaining to any potential vendor what requirements must be met and making sure that they understand these to be requirements and not wish lists.

Submitting Proposals

When proposals are submitted most potential vendors seem to think that they will be evaluated by weight. Each of the proposals that we received for the project came in several three ring binders that when stacked totaled more than three feet.

Proposals Did Not Follow the Format of the RFP

In the RFP, in order to allow easier review by the project team, we required all submitters to use the same numbering scheme to address requirements and features of their system. So, if we had a paragraph 3.2.4 that referred to a specific requirement, the proposer could use the same paragraph number. If the proposer needed additional paragraphs, he could be added using additional levels.

In spite of having detailed instructions, the proposers ignored this. Their response to this problem was that no one had ever asked them to follow any special format. Their respective sales departments had, over the years, formed formats that they thought were adequate and sellable and would not deviate.

Since all of the proposers had this fault, it became a choice of rejecting all of the proposals and forcing them to be resubmitted or accepting them. We chose to accept this problem since the cost to us and the proposers in terms of time and money seemed to outweigh the inconvenience that the project team would have in reviewing the proposals.

In retrospect, the RFP should have been more detailed and specific about the format of submitted proposals since this would save an enormous amount of time on the part of the project team in the review of the proposals.

Best and Final Proposals

After the project team reviewed the proposals, the proposers were invited to a three day, if needed, oral review of their proposals.

Forcing a Checklist

To reduce and eliminate the possible misunderstanding of the requirements on the part of the proposer a checklist was made. This list was a paragraph by paragraph work sheet for each proposer. The proposer was required to go down the checklist and indicate that she fully complied to the requirement in every way, or that she would not comply with the requirement at all, or that she would comply with the requirement only if additional money, above the already stated amount, was paid.

All potential vendors filled out the checklists and indicated compliance to each requirement. We were suspicious that all of the proposers submitted compliance so easily.

Final interviews were granted to all proposers to review the requirements one final time and again all proposers agreed to their statements of compliance.

The Statement of Work

Once the vendor had been selected, the vendor submitted a statement of work (SOW) for the project. When this was done, the vendor submitted a standard statement of work normally used by him in this type of project. The SOW was to be the controlling document for the work to be done on the project and took precedence over all other documents except the contract itself.

This statement of work was very unacceptable to us. The format of the SOW was completely different from any previous document and a boiler plate description of all the features was given. None of the requirements was addressed directly.

The problem was solved by forcing the vendor to cut and paste the entire request for proposal into the SOW and add the appropriate text from his SOW. In this way all of the requirements were included in the SOW, as well as the vendor's comments.

PROJECT MANAGEMENT

Microsoft Project

The RFP required that any selected vendor use Microsoft Project of the latest version throughout the project and submit the current schedule, on floppy, at any project review meetings.

This proved to be a great timesaver for the project manager since it enabled us to keep our own project schedule on MS Project and integrate ours with the vendor schedule. In this way the users could see a nicely organized schedule that kept all related tasks together.

At first vendors resisted this idea but once they purchased the software and got used to using it they became devoted users. The chosen vendor used this software for other projects in her corporation and standardized on its use within the company.

Change Orders

This project was funded with a very small contingency factor. This was done by emphasizing that there would be no additional funds available for changes.

In the case of many government contracts, there is a strong tendency on the part of the vendor to try to submit the lowest initial cost for the project and then make large profit margins on the expected changes made during the development of the project.

We hoped to avoid this problem by explaining in some detail to each potential vendor that we intended to have no changes or overruns in the project and that we intended to budget all of the money for the project up front.

We were nearly successful in this. Since we told the vendors that the budgeted money for the project was all there would be, we asked them to submit their best and final proposals with a number of optional modifications which may or may not be purchased. We then budgeted for the basic system, adding as many of the options as possible until the available money was committed to the budget for the project. Of course, even though we forced the vendor into a turnkey position, there was still additional money spent that was unexpected. We were able to keep the unplanned expenditures to less than one percent of the project budget.

Early Delivery of Hardware

All vendors of this type of product operate on a tight budget. The projects take one to four years of sales and negotiating before contract signing. During this time the potential vendors spend large amounts of money in sales and promotion of their products to the potential buyer. None of this money and effort is recouped until contract signing. For this reason, the vendor has a strong incentive to deliver any hardware as early as possible and collect the money due. He can then pay his suppliers and use the profit to offset his negative cash flow. One way to avoid part of this problem was to require an acceptance test before any hardware delivery.

Acceptance testing. The method used to prevent this problem was to require that an acceptance test be performed using the actual software to perform the test.

The acceptance test method used for this system was to create a simulated load on the system of four times the expected peak load and then measure the system response times using the most often used commands. In most cases, since this is truly a real time, online system, this was a response time of less than two seconds.

The mainframe computers were set up at the vendor's location and personal computers were used to create a load. These PCs were set up to simulate the typing that a public safety operator would actually perform. By varying a timer, the load could be adjusted. This was accomplished using five PCs. A sixth PC was used to test and measure the specific commands. Each command was submitted to the system on top of the load simulation and its time measured. The cycle for all commands was repeated thirty-five times to gather statistically meaningful results. The allowed performance specification was to have the average response time plus three standard deviations below 2.0 seconds.

This requirement was met at the vendor's facility and allowed for the equipment to be shipped to our site and installed.

Penalty Clauses

We used a penalty clause to create incentive for the vendor to finish the project on time. This was a simple device of requiring the vendor to submit a project completion date at the time of best and final proposals. Each day beyond the project completion date would have $1,000 deducted for each day of delay.

The proposers all added 90 to 180 days to their expected completion dates to avoid payment of the penalty clause. We felt that this was an acceptable way to allow the vendor to build a buffer in the schedule. If the vendors were not allowed to build an identified delay at the end of the project, they would have added delay into all of the scheduled activities of the project, guaranteeing that the project would be finished later than the best completion date.

An additional incentive was created by requiring that the vendor include in his proposal a prepaid maintenance and warranty of one year after system acceptance. By doing this, the maintenance charges for the system hardware and software, totaling $15,000 per month, or about $500 per day, would not go into effect until one year after system acceptance. So, any delay from the earliest possible system acceptance would result in a cost to the vendor of $500 per day. Thus, the vendor had a strong incentive to complete the project as soon as possible.

It is important that this incentive began to save or cost the vendor for every day the project was completed early or late. The cost was real as well, since much of the maintenance was the monthly maintenance on the mainframe computers and associated hardware and this money had to be paid each month from our vendor to his vendors.

Acceptance testing. Acceptance testing of the system comprised two parts, the final acceptance performance test and the final acceptance reliability test.

Performance test. The performance test was simply a repeat of the performance test performed at the vendor's site some months earlier. We did not expect any problems in this test. If the system had performed adequately before at the vendor's location, there should have been no problems when it had been installed on our site.

This test was conducted and improvements of 25 percent were evident in the test. This was attributed to the fact that when the mainframe computers were bought they were the first delivered of an entire new line and that significant improvements had been made in the computers operating system.

Reliability test. A reliability test requiring the vendor to operate the system using actual operators in a live, real-use condition continuously, twenty-four-hours per day, with no loss of the system availability to the operator, was required. The vendor was required to complete these continuous forty-five days of operation within seventy-five days. At this point final acceptance of the system would take place.

POST PROJECT EVALUATION

On Time

The project was completed on time. It is felt that the use of the double penalty clause described above allowed the vendor to have sufficient motivation to get the required resources to complete the project on time. Issues of disagreement were able to be settled between the two project managers and then the solutions to problems brought to management.

Under Budget

This project was completed nearly exactly on budget. This was primarily due to the careful explanation to the vendor that the project was a turnkey project and that the vendor was responsible for the performance of the system for the stated price regardless of the final cost to the vendor. If the vendor agreed to meet the functional performance required and the equipment or software he proposed did not work, it was his responsibility to find the proper hardware and make it work.

SUMMARY

The success or failure of a project of this type depends on the ability of the project team to communicate effectively with the vendor's project team. This communication begins with the requirements definition and ends at final acceptance. In this project, the requirements definition, or the setting of all goals and objectives in extreme detail, was accomplished. Because of the vendor's desire to sell a product and minimize the cost of producing it, the vendor has a great incentive to interpret any requirements in a way that will minimize her effort and cost.

The RFP process has the potential to see that the buyer gets the most for his dollar, but with it comes the responsibility of making an extremely detailed list of requirements that cannot be misunderstood even if intentionally misunderstood.

Oral reviews give the potential vendors time to present their products in their best light and give them the opportunity to answer questions in detail after the proposals have been read.

It is important to have vendor proposals submitted in a format and structure that is consistent with the requirements definition and the other proposers.

Penalty clauses are an effective means of creating incentive in the vendor. An even more effective method is to have reward clauses for completing the project early or with added features.

Specific performance test criteria are extremely important and should not be subject to any interpretation. The performance test must be relevant to the actual system use when actually in service.

Study Questions

COMMUNICATING RISK MANAGEMENT IN MUNICIPAL GOVERNMENT PROJECTS: CITY OF NEW ORLEANS COMPUTER-AIDED DISPATCH SYSTEM PROJECT

1. The *PMBOK Guide*, section 2.4, Key General Management Skills, describes the most important personal tools of a project manager. Which of these skills do you think were the most valuable in the project management of this project?

2. The *PMBOK Guide*, section 10, Project Communications Management, analyzes a project's communications process in four main phases. List communication challenges the project faced and classify these challenges in the different phases.

3. What was the project manager's main challenge in completing the project?

4. Explain the difficulties of managing a project involving stakeholders with different objectives in the project, i.e., the relationship between the vendor and customer.

5. Would the standardization of the procurement methods described in the case serve the city well in the future? Would you recommend that project managers be required for similar tasks in the future? Where do you draw the line on the necessity of using project management?

Cape Town's Olympic Bid:
A Race Against the Clock

Project Pro, March 1996, pp. 7–10

The official contenders for the 2004 Olympic Games are now known. The formidable line-up comprises: Athens (Greece), Buenos Aires (Argentina), Cape Town (South Africa), Istanbul (Turkey), Lille (France), Rio de Janeiro (Brazil), Rome (Italy), San Juan (Puerto Rico), Seville (Spain), Stockholm (Sweden), and St Petersburg (Russia). The Cape Town Olympic bid team is racing against the clock to complete the voluminous bid documents, which must be submitted by August 15, 1996. What are the chances that Cape Town's bid will be named the winner in little more than a year in September 1997?

AN EMOTIONAL FAVORITE

Africa is the only continent that has never hosted the Olympic Games so there is a lot of emotional support for Cape Town's bid, which is even stronger now that Cairo has decided not to bid for 2004.

There are presently 106 International Olympic Committee (IOC) members who vote on which city is to be awarded the games. Of these, nineteen are from African countries so one would expect Cape Town to be 18 percent of the way there. However, the lobbying process is so intense and persuasive that members may not even vote for a city in their own country, let alone a city at the tip of Africa.

Hosting the Olympic Games is, however, big business and the decision to award the Olympics to a city is based on hard-nosed aspects such as finance, technology, infrastructure, environment, management skills, etc. Only if all these factors are equal, could the emotional appeal of Cape Town tip the scales in its favor. There was tremendous emotional support for Athens, which hosted the first Olympics in 1896, to host the 1996 Centennial Games, but they lost out to a very professional bid from Atlanta, which emphasized their project management approach to staging this massive project.

Managing the Bid

Chris Ball, CEO of the CT 2004 Bid Committee, was instrumental in raising a R10 million sponsorship from Mercedes-Benz SA. Part of that package was the agreement of Manfred Gundlach, a manager from Daimler-Benz Aerospace, to establish a management information center and to track the progress of Cape Town's bid.

"My task is to catch all the activities we have to perform," says Gundlach, "whether driven by the Bid Manual, or driven by national RDP programs and the regional development needs of the Western Cape. We need to get all this information on board, structure it in a logical manner and transfer it all into schedules which *will* ultimately be presented in the form of a bar chart that will identify who has to do what over what period of time; milestones; and interfaces with other organisations."

The bid team is using standard well-known software wherever possible as there is very limited time for training. Microsoft Project 4.0 was chosen because it is such a popular and universally accepted package. The name of the game is time, resources, and meeting deadlines—so although the position of project manager does not officially exist in the Bid Committee, Gundlach has become the focus of the activities that comprise the traditional project manager role.

So Much to Do ... So Little Time

The momentum of the original bid under the leadership of Raymond Ackerman came to a grinding halt at the beginning of 1995 when the new team challenged legitimacy.

"Cape Town has to do more in a shorter period of time than other Olympic cities," says Gundlach. "When we started, we had two years in which to plan, but now we only have one year, of which four to five months can be taken off because the information for the bid documents needs to be professionally compiled and printed in two languages (French and English)—a time consuming process. Our draft document has to be completed by April 1996."

This wouldn't be as tough if Cape Town was situated in a First World country, but we are at a distinct disadvantage to Rome, for instance, which has much of the necessary infrastructure to stage the games already in place. Rome is a *very* strong contender for 2004 as they have the wealthiest of the National Olympic Committees and one of the most influential. They hosted the games in 1960 and basically only need to upgrade their existing facilities, while Cape Town is still agonizing over whether to site the Olympic Stadium in Culemborg at the foot of table mountain, or 20 km west in Wingfield. Initial studies by the bid team suggest that Wingfield would be most feasible for the Olympic Stadium, rowing course, and athletes' village. Culemborg may get the media center and officials/media village.

Like Barcelona, Cape Town has an enormous amount of infrastructure to prepare for the games. Government and local authorities still seem hesitant to wholeheartedly throw their weight behind the Cape Town bid, unlike Barcelona, where a massive $21 billion was committed to the games project as a catalyst to large-scale urban redevelopment.

Prior to 1992, Barcelona was considered a backwater. Now it has been rated by Healey and Baker, British real estate multinational firm, as the sixth best city in Europe to locate a business. A survey of 500 top executives showed appreciation for Barcelona's availability and quality of office space, quality of life, good internal and external communications, and inner city transport. Barcelona's economy is booming, with the major thrust coming from the housing construction sector, which showed a 53 percent growth in the number of houses constructed in 1995, compared to 1994. Just what Cape Town and South Africa need!

	LOW SCENARIO		HIGH SCENARIO	
	Western Cape	RSA	Western Cape	RSA
	R Billion		R Billion	
Up to 2004	4.50	13.80	6.90	21.80
Up to 2010	5.90	17.00	8.90	29.80

The average between the low and the high scenarios up to 2004 is R17.8 billion.

FIGURE 1   IMPACT OF HOSTING THE OLYMPIC GAMES ON THE GDP

CRITICAL SUCCESS FACTORS

A high-quality bid is the key success factor. The standard of modern-day bids is so high that Cape Town has no chance of winning if its bid documents are substandard in any respect.

The baseline standard for hosting the Olympic Games has progressively been raised over the decades. Atlanta and Sydney have now set such a high standard that only First World countries are capable of hosting the games.

Cape Town has consulted the IOC on more appropriate standards for an African bid, which was well received, but there are still organizations within the Olympic family who want First-World standards throughout. A compromise will have to be found so that high-tech facilities can either be sold off or be suitable for local use after the games.

Fifty-five people are presently working full time in the Cape Town Olympic Bid Office and many people are, of course, working on a voluntary basis, boosting the workforce to between seventy and ninety people from time to time. The organization uses a task-team approach where a full-time bid member will act as a team leader with professionals from local firms donating their time to support the Bid Office. Taking all these people into account, the total work force is approximately 500. If Cape Town is awarded the games, this figure could peak at 1,000 full-time staff in 2004.

COUNTING THE COSTS ... AND BENEFITS!

The Bid Committee needs R75 million to fund their effort up to September 1997, and R60 million has already been committed by the private sector.

The biggest and most difficult question to quantify is what the total economic impact will be on the gross domestic product if Cape Town gets the games. A preliminary study by KPMG (SA) and NN Gobodo & Co. adopted a high/low scenario approach to estimating the impact (see Figure 1). Up to 2004, the impact on South Africa should be between R13.8 billion and R21.8 billion (base date 1995). The benefits, however, still continue to flow in after the games and should be between R17.0 billion and R29.8 billion up to 2010, with about 110,000 jobs being created.

Preliminary Operating Budget	RM 1995
Total Revenue	**4210.00**
Television and International Marketing	2747.00
(US $ Based)	
Local Marketing	983.00
Ticket Sales	480.00
Total Expenditure	**(2908.00)**
Games Operations	(2493.00)
Events Management	(415.00)
Gross Surplus	**1302.00**
Sports Facilities	(504.00)
Housing Subsidy*	(150.00)
Contingency	(554.00)
Net Surplus	**94.00**

*Housing will be built by the private sector and is estimated to cost R1040 million. A contribution from the operating budget of R150 million will be made to underpin the selling price of the houses.

FIGURE 2   PRELIMINARY OPERATING BUDGET

Television revenue is a major money spinner for any Olympic Games. Rupert Murdoch is reported to have offered $2 billion for the European TV rights alone, but the IOC declined it in order to enable as many viewers as possible to see the games on TV. The American and European TV rights have been sold for $1.26 billion and Cape Town's would be $600 million. Cape Town is budgeting for a R2.75 billion revenue from TV rights and international marketing, giving a gross surplus of R1.30 billion (see Figure 2). Deducting the cost of sports facilities (R.50 billion), a housing subsidy (R.15 billion) to reduce the selling price of R1.04 billion worth of housing to be built by the private sector and a contingency (R.55 billion) leaves a net surplus of R.94 billion.

There has been speculation that the cabinet and the National Executive Committee of the ANC are split over the bid. This has been denied by Minister of Sport, Steve Tswete.

According to Mike Fuller, regional director of Ernst & Young, who is responsible for the bid's accounting and financial control, there should certainly be no financial reason for the government not to support hosting the games in Cape Town. "We are asking government for R978 million, which will generate between R5 billion to R9 billion in tax revenue for them over the next decade. The Games will cause the economy to grow, create jobs, have a positive tax impact and economic merit."

A Spirit of Giving

"Where possible, we have tried to negotiate our operation on a cash-free basis," says Fuller. "For example, our office space in the Metlife Building and Dock House has been donated by the owners; we have free petrol accounts from Caltex; Vodacom has given us cellphones; and SAA will provide air tickets."

There has been an excellent response from the big six professional accounting firms: Ernst & Young, Coopers & Lybrand, Price Waterhouse, KPMG, Deloittes, and Arthur Andersen who have seconded staff for the duration of the bid or will execute work at cost (not charging for man-hours).

There are over fifty project teams busy planning Olympic facilities on a voluntary basis, which amounts to a R30 million donation of professional fees.

Eskom, as the electricity supplier, will be a key infrastructure player through the course of the bid.

"Eskom will provide support to the Cape Town 2004 bid by helping to plan for infrastructure requirements and other related services," says Eskom's Chief Executive Allen Morgan.

"The bid is a golden opportunity to place South Africa firmly in the global arena. Eskom applauds the South African endeavor to win the bid. We will assist with support in kind: we will help to plan the infrastructure which will be needed and we will place our marketing expertise, staff and information sources at the disposal of the Committee. This assistance in kind is valued at R2.5 million. Whatever happens, our efforts will not be fruitless. All the work we contribute will be useful in strengthening and extending the electricity supply facilities in the Western Cape, something which will be needed in the future."

Eskom will make use of the forward planning needed for the submission of the bid book to help realize its vision of providing the world's lowest-cost electricity for growth and prosperity.

The Last Hurdle

Once the bid documents are submitted in August this year, Cape Town will be girding itself for the next hurdle in March 1997, when the IOC will cut the list of candidate cities down to only four.

Cape Town is favored to clear this hurdle, but which city breasts the tape in September 1997 remains to be seen.

Study Questions

CAPE TOWN'S OLYMPIC BID: A RACE AGAINST THE CLOCK

1. Although the Olympics is an entertainment and sporting event, it is very much tied with financial performance. As a project manager, what are the main steps in assuring proper project cost management, and assuring economic success?

2. Obviously, hosting the Olympic Games could be economically beneficial to Cape Town. Given this, how much of a risk is the investment in preparing the bid? How would the efforts completed to create the bid document be best used to aid the city if Cape Town is not awarded as the host city of the 2004 Olympic Games?

3. Benchmarking can be used in this project, i.e., matching Atlanta's preparation effort. How can this be beneficial in the management of the project?

4. This case was written in 1996. If possible, update the results of the bidding process for the 2004 Olympic Games, focusing on South Africa's bid. From your research, what were the strengths and/or weaknesses responsible for the success/failure of its bid?

5. In the case, Mr. Gundlach describes his task as "to catch all of the activities we have to perform." Do you see this description as having any resemblance to a project management endeavor?

6. A work breakdown structure (WBS) is the backbone of the project management of any project. According to the *PMBOK Guide*, what is the concept of the WBS? Do you see any resemblance between the work done in developing the Olympic bid and the WBS?

Sydney 2000 Olympic Games:
A Project Management Perspective

David Eager, University of Technology, Sydney

PMI *Proceedings*, 1997, pp. 227–31

SUMMARY

The Sydney 2000 Olympic Games is a large-scale and very complex project involving a diverse range of activities and large numbers of people. Given the nature and vast scale of this project, sound and exemplary project management techniques and principles are essential for its success. The strict time constraints set for the project increase the difficulties of managing cost and quality. The project will be regarded as successful if it is finished to time, on budget, and to the required quality. Good quality means meeting the needs specified by the organizer, to the standard and specification laid down, with a predictable degree of reliability and uniformity, at a price consistent with the organizer's budget and to the satisfaction of the end users. This review discusses issues that need to be addressed to make this project a success.

INTRODUCTION

The Sydney 2000 Olympic Games will be held between Friday, September 15, and Sunday, October 1, 2000, in Sydney's spring.

Sydney, competing against bids from four other cities, was awarded the right to host the games of the 26th modern Olympiad after a vote by the members of the International Olympic Committee in Monte Carlo in September 1993.

The bid was prepared by Sydney Olympics Bid Limited which drew on funds from the private and public sectors and worked in close cooperation with the Australian Olympic Committee. It enjoyed broad public support with 90 percent of the people across Australia supporting the bid. More than 100,000 volunteers offered their services. The bid was centered on the theme *Share the Spirit* and called on the people of Sydney to join in the excitement of the bid, and invited the world to come and share the spirit of Sydney at the Olympic Games in the year 2000. The bid also included a comprehensive set of environmental guidelines recognizing the principle of ecologically sustainable development. The guidelines promote energy conservation; water conservation; waste avoidance and minimization; protection of air, water, and soil from pollution; and protection of significant natural and cultural environments.

SOME SIGNIFICANT FEATURES

The New South Wales Government underwrites the games and is responsible for the provision of new permanent venues and facilities needed for the games. It also provides support services particularly in the areas of transport, security, and health care. The construction of new sporting facilities and refurbishment of existing facilities for the games is being undertaken by the State Government's Olympic Coordination Authority, namely: Sydney Organizing Committee for the Olympic Games (SOCOG).

Staging of the 2000 Games is the responsibility of SOCOG which was established in November 1993 by legislation in the New South Wales Parliament.

The Sydney Para-Olympic Organizing Committee will stage the Para-Olympic Games following the Olympic Games and will draw extensively on SOCOG expertise in its games organization.

Sydney's Olympic plan is based on a commitment to provide the right conditions for athletes to perform at their optimum levels. For the first time in Olympic history, all athletes will live together in one village, and many will be within walking distance of the venues for their events.

Except for some football preliminaries, all Olympic events are planned to be held in metropolitan Sydney in venues within thirty minutes travel from the Olympic Village. No training facility will be more than forty-five minutes away from the village. The focus is mainly on two Olympic zones, namely: the Sydney Olympic Park, situated at Homebush Bay about 14 km west of the Sydney city center; and the Sydney Harbor zone, located near the Sydney city center and accessible by road, rail, and ferry from Sydney Olympic Park.

A series of test events in the years preceding the Olympic Games is planned with the aim of trialling the Olympic venues, training the technical officials and volunteers who will help conduct the events at the Olympic Games, and selectively trialling arrangements for accreditation, transport, security, broadcasting, media, and other services.

INFRASTRUCTURE—PREPARATION WORK FOR THE GAMES

A significant number of Sydney's Olympic venues already exist. Most of the remaining facilities required for the games will be constructed as part of the redevelopment program being undertaken at Homebush Bay.

Key elements of the Homebush Bay area include the construction of new sporting facilities, establishment of a new showground and major exhibition center, development of residential and retail areas, and the establishment of a commercial center for high technology industries. A main press center and the Olympic village with accommodation for 10,000 athletes and team officials also comes under the umbrella of the Olympic Park.

Recently completed major transport projects such as Sydney Harbor Tunnel, M4 and M5 Motorways, and Glebe Island bridge, together with the major projects currently in progress, such as City West Development, Ultimo-Pyrmont light rail system, Airport City Link, and the railway loop line to link the Olympic Park with the Sydney rail network's main western rail line, will ensure that an effective transport system will be available for the Olympic Games.

Telecommunications infrastructure, such as Integrated Services Digital Network (ISDN), Intelligent Networks (IN), and Cellular Mobile Telephone Service (CMTS), together with Broadband ISDN (B-ISDN), currently being established are considered sufficient to successfully service the international and domestic demand of the games.

During Sydney's bid, a campaign to register volunteers was conducted by the St. George Bank which attracted more than 100,000 people. Sydney will require 35,000 people from all walks of life to form a volunteer workforce essential for the smooth running of the games.

Revenue for the games is expected primarily from television rights fees, sponsorships, coin marketing royalties, licensing fees, and ticket sales.

It is estimated that during the period 1994–2004 the Olympics could add A$7.3 billion to Australia's gross domestic product, create 150,000 full- and part-time jobs, and bring an extra 1.3 million visitors to Australia. In order to safeguard sponsorship fees and sponsors and licensees benefits from ambush marketing, the New South Wales Government has legislated the Sydney 2000 Games (Indicia and Images) Protection Bill 1996.

DEFINITION OF THE PROJECT

The objective of the Sydney Olympic Games Program is to stage the year 2000 Olympic Games at specified locations in Sydney. Although the New South Wales Government is underwriting the project activities, there is no clearly defined client for the program. There are many stakeholders and customers, including the citizens of New South Wales, the New South Wales Government, the Australian people, the International Olympic Organization, the international community as a whole, the athletes, and Australian and international business communities. The scope of the project comprises organizing all the games and ceremonies, putting in place technology and resources required to stage the games, public relations, and fundraising. Criteria for the success of the project include trouble-free performance of the games, the level of public enthusiasm and enjoyment generated by the activities and resultant sustained economic activity generated within New South Wales and Australia, and continued interest in Olympic Games for the future.

SOCOG was appointed to manage the project by legislation. In addition to SOCOG there are other organizations that directly contribute to the success of the games. International Olympic Committee, Australian Olympic Committee, Sydney City Council, and Olympic Coordination Authority (New South Wales Government) have been made party to the host city contract. Olympic Coordination Authority is responsible for all the infrastructure projects, almost all of which are not being built specifically for the Olympic Games. These projects are either already under way or are being reprogrammed to accommodate the games. Completion of these projects on time is vital to the success of the Olympic Games. The general rule-of-thumb used by the Government has been to relocate infrastructure projects initially external to the games under the games umbrella.

The infrastructure construction is the responsibility of the government and is overseen by the Olympic Coordination Authority. To make matters more complicated, the scope of work of SOCOG is restricted to organization of the events. The games budget in nominal terms is A$1.847 billion (US$1.4 billion).

There is an explicit need to control the cost of all its activities very carefully. Any major cost overruns will alienate the public and will have adverse effects on the success of the games.

The project can be broken in to the following major areas of work (as a work breakdown structure):

- events
- venues and facilities including accommodation
- transport
- media facilities and coordination
- telecommunications
- security arrangements
- medical care
- human resources including volunteers
- cultural Olympiad
- pre-games training
- information-technology projects
- opening and closing ceremonies
- public relations
- financing
- test games and trial events
- sponsorship management and control of ambush marketing.

Each of these items could be treated as a project in its own right. Further, an enormous coordination effort will be required to ensure these, and therefore, the entire games project, are delivered on time.

CRITICAL PROJECT DIMENSIONS

Time is the most critical dimension of the Sydney 2000 Olympic Games project. As the project must be completed and ready for staging the Olympic Games on the stipulated dates, any shortcomings in the time dimension will have to be offset by sacrificing the other two dimensions, namely: cost and quality. However, performance on all three dimensions is vital for the success of the project.

Time Dimension

Sydney is fortunate in having sufficient infrastructure capacity either existing or under construction to cater for an event of this magnitude. It is anticipated that the infrastructure projects under construction will be completed well in advance of the commencement of the Olympic Games. Any delays in the completion dates could be accommodated without much difficulty. The criticality of the time dimension applies mainly to other activities and timing of individual activities such as events, opening and closing ceremonies, and so on. To ensure that the time dimension is achieved, the Sydney Organizing Committee for the Olympic Games has adopted strategies such as: holding frequent coordination meetings with the organizations and parties responsible for delivering the required items, setting target dates well in advance of the main event, designing test events, and trialling events as milestones for the critical items.

For the construction projects, estimation of the time dimension should be relatively straightforward. Expertise is available within the construction industry to produce reasonable estimates. Critical path methods, precedence block diagrams, and program evaluation and review are employed to control the uncertainties in the time dimension. Proper plans must be prepared for these construction activities. All persons who may be affected by these programs should have an opportunity to comment on the plan. Instruments should be put in place to monitor the progress against the program continually. The program should include enough leeway or float to allow minor problems to be accommodated without causing major changes to the timing of the overall program. Elements which are expected to have most impact on the program must be identified and defined as early as possible, and an adequate series of milestones must be established to allow monitoring of the progress of the program.

At this early stage of the program or the project life-cycle the time required to complete tasks for particular events introduce uncertainties. These uncertainties are related to the nature of the tasks involved. Some non-construction projects—such as developing software to monitor the games' progress, establishing the games database and systems to disseminate the information to general public—have larger uncertainties inherent in the system. Some new technologies may have to be developed to adapt to the advances in the way the information is distributed to the public and media. For example, the Atlanta 1996 Olympic Games had a dedicated Internet facility to give the public access to games information. Since Internet technologies are changing very rapidly, the way information is given out to the public may also change in line with advances in technology. It is difficult to predict what these advances may involve until much closer to the actual event. However, a comprehensive information technology strategic plan is essential to safeguard against these rapid changes. It has been said that one Internet year is equivalent to seven earth years, hence the three years that lie ahead for Sydney 2000 Olympic is equivalent to twenty-one years of Internet development, quite a daunting time scale to anticipate. But anticipating and facing this is nevertheless necessary.

Certain other programs such as cultural events and the opening and closing ceremony performances are based on inspirations. The time dimension of inspirations is quite difficult to anticipate. Allowing sufficient time for inspirations to prosper, while necessary, will severely restrict the possible lead times on these programs. Time, cost, and quality dimensions on these kinds of activities are tightly interrelated. Sufficient safeguards need to be incorporated so that persons involved do not get carried away, and ego conflicts are avoided. Several alternative proposals may have to be developed beyond the conceptual stage to select the best. Such an exercise could add to the overall cost of these activities, and compromises may need to be negotiated.

Activities that have several unknowns, by their very nature, need to be planned toward the later stage of the project life-cycle. The time dimension becomes extremely critical for these activities.

COST DIMENSION

The cost estimates of the construction projects are not reflected in the games budget as the infrastructure projects are undertaken outside the games project.

Sydney's games budget is based on conservative assumptions and estimates of games receipts and payments. Receipts are mainly from television rights and international and local participation (8). The financial planning process included:

• consultations with both national and international experts in the fields relevant to both receipts and payments
• consultations with the Barcelona Organizing Committee, the International Olympic Committee, and the Australian Olympic Committee
• review and analysis of results and budgets from previous games and bid candidature
• independent analysis of construction costs by quantity surveyors, Rider Hunt
• independent review of the estimates by auditors, Price Waterhouse.

SOCOG has stated that the NSW Audit Office has conducted a detailed review of the games budget, concluding that "the bid estimates have been developed following the due process, the assumptions were considered sound, the procedures adopted for developing the estimates were rigorous, and the processes used to develop the estimates were appropriate for the purpose (8)."

SOCOG has also advised that the factors influencing the process included (8):

• bipartisan support for the games, both at federal and state government levels
• the support of trade unions, minimizing the risk of construction disputes
• Australia's low level of inflation
• process undertaken by Sydney to implement procedures for accommodation price control, particularly in relation to hotel tariffs.

The NSW Audit Office cost estimates appear to have been produced using appropriate methodologies. However, even though the cost estimates were prepared using appropriate methodologies it is necessary to develop strict cost control mechanisms in order to keep the overall project costs to the minimum. It is worth noting that the major portion of the games budget is for the events and ceremonies, and the nature of these programs is such that there are considerable uncertainties inherent in these items. Further, the time and cost dimensions of these events are tightly interrelated. Consequently, any slippage in timing of the programming, training, and testing of these activities could lead to large cost escalations.

Due to the predicted rapid change in technology it is highly likely that there will be variations in requirements or design. As a general rule, it is undesirable to allow too many such changes, since they are a major source of cost escalation in any project and especially in projects such as this. Some variations may be to a cost advantage, but this is the exception rather than the norm.

Economic and social factors will also play a major part in cost escalation in the games budget. Currently, the games project enjoys overwhelming public support, thus minimizing the risk of labor strikes and other legal conflicts. However, if not managed properly, the tide could turn leading to spiralling cost escalations. For example, SOCOG is negotiating with the hotel industry to ensure stable room rates for the period in time surrounding the games.

Cost escalations would lead to disillusionment among the public and would diminish the public appeal of the games thus affecting public support and a vital source of volunteer games staff. Any cost overrun will have to be met by the taxpayer, as the New South Wales Government has underwritten the Host City Contract. This could also become a major political issue. Maintaining the costs within budget is vital to the games' success.

QUALITY DIMENSION

This is the most difficult dimension of the project to define. The quality is threefold:
- good quality versus high quality
- fit for purpose
- conforming to the customer requirement.

As part of the host city contract the International Olympic Committee has specified certain quality requirements for the Sydney 2000 Olympic Games. The New South Wales Government has specified certain environmental guidelines that all Olympic ventures should follow. Within the public mind there is also a concept of the level of quality and excellence the Olympic Games should achieve. The SOCOG itself will set its own quality standards mainly in performing its duties. Sponsors will demand a certain quality standard. Some of these standards are currently only at the conceptual stage. As the project progresses through its life-cycle these standards need to emerge. Each program component will have its own definition of quality and standards.

One of the major areas a quality which should not be underestimated nor forgotten is the aspect of security. Responsibility for management of Olympic Games security lies with the Olympic Security Planning and Implementation Group (OSPIG). It would appear that there is a significant weakness in the security planning process in that it lacks coordinated project control. Rather than being developed as a strategic program, activities are being undertaken as disparate tactical operations. This has occurred because *Olympic Security* is being used to expand existing programs rather than being managed as a separate program. The focus has been on integrating existing activities to provide security for the games, rather than on developing an effective games security plan and then integrating existing programs when practical.

Wherever there is public involvement in large projects, it is generally not sufficient to have good quality or fit for purpose quality. The public demands very high quality standards. The quality of the game events is likely to be judged by the absence of delays and clockwork precision with which the public expects events to proceed. In the case of transport, quality is judged by lack of traffic jams and holdups. The quality of security will be judged by perceived public safety and lack of incidents such as terrorism.

In construction projects quality can be clearly defined, for example, as fit for purpose or conforming to strict environmental guidelines. In projects such as the games there are difficulties in defining quality, particularly in the early stages of the development cycle. For example, quality of performances and ceremonies might be measured by how spectacular they are, how precisely orchestrated, and how much they appeal to majority audiences. Qualitative criteria such as these are not easy to quantify or to monitor in early stages of the development cycle.

Adoption of total quality management techniques in these programs could improve the quality of the delivered Olympic Games. The essential ingredients of a total quality management system are: quality of the product as the ultimate goal; quality management process; quality assurance systems; and attitude.

Where clear specifications and well-defined standards are difficult to formulate, engaging experienced personnel and experts may be particularly desirable. The product (e.g., events or performances) should be thoroughly tested prior to the games, allowing ample time to make necessary modifications at least cost.

A good management process is vital to the delivery of a high quality product. It is necessary to establish milestones and set procedures for the management process to achieve quality.

As mentioned above, cost and quality are closely related. Quality comes at a price. This applies particularly to a project like the Olympic Games when completion on time is critical, and the cost of failure is extremely high for any of the items included in the project.

Only through closely controlled quality management processes and early identification of the possibility of failure can the success of the program be ensured. Several safeguards have been put in place both by the International Olympic Committee and the New South Wales Government to ensure the delivery of the games is to an acceptable quality.

CONCLUSIONS

The Sydney 2000 Olympic Games is a venture that requires considerable use of project management techniques and skills to make it a success. The large scale and very nature of the event requires good time management and the control of all three project dimensions: time, cost, and quality.

All three dimensions of the project are interrelated, and careful monitoring is needed at every stage of the project life-cycle. The estimates of the initial bid were prepared carefully and thoroughly with adequate checks and safeguards. During the bid stage and subsequent stages there was no leeway for varying the time dimension. This restriction, however, applies only to the delivery of the overall project. If the program is broken down into manageable items of work, the time dimension becomes something that can be manipulated. Careful programming and identifying proper milestones can improve the time management of the project.

The quality of the games project is vital for its success, and the project requires careful orchestration. Quality control can be achieved using proven project management delivery techniques. Some activities of the games have a very high correlation of time and quality. Such events should be identified early in the planning process and test methods developed. Quality is hard to impose on events such as performances which involve subjective qualitative judgments. However, excellence can still be achieved with proper planning and commitment of the personnel involved.

The cost aspect of the project is closely interrelated to the time and quality aspects. In the Olympic Games project if a compromise has to be made, the cost aspect will be the first dimension that will be sacrificed.

Good communications are vital to the success of the project and to effective control of all three dimensions. Trial games and test programs will serve to control all three dimensions and should be treated seriously. The planned trials in the coming years will be an excellent opportunity to monitor, control, or correct any deficiencies in the project.

REFERENCES

1. Badiru, A.B., and P.S. Pulat. 1994. *Comprehensive Project Management: Integrating Optimisation Models, Management Principles and Computers.* Upper Saddle River, NJ: Prentice Hall.

2. Birner, W., Geddes, M., and C. Hastings. 1994. *Project Leadership.* Aldershot, UK: Gower Publishing.

3. Burke, R. 1994. *Project Management: Planning and Control.* New York: John Wiley & Sons.

4. Davison, I. 1994. *Project Procedures Handbook.* Hypertext Publishing.

5. Eager, D.M. 1996. *Project Management 49002 Notes.* Graduate School of Engineering, UTS Printing Services.

6. Nicholas, J.M. 1990. *Managing Business and Engineering Projects—Concepts and Implementation.* Upper Saddle River, NJ: Prentice Hall.

7. Meredith, J.R., and S. J. Mantel. 1995. *Project Management: A Managerial Approach.* New York: John Wiley & Sons.

8. Sydney Organizing Committee of the Olympic Games (SOCOG). 1996. Fact Sheets. September.

9. Turner, R.J. 1993. *The Handbook of Project-Based Management.* New York: McGraw-Hill.

Study Questions

SYDNEY 2000 OLYMPIC GAMES: A PROJECT MANAGEMENT PERSPECTIVE

1. Why is time management critical to the Sydney 2000 Olympics Games project?

2. By what yardsticks will the Sydney 2000 Olympics Games project be measured, and how will it be considered a success? Give examples to illustrate your answer.

3. Why is project scope management so important to the Sydney 2000 Olympic Games project? Illustrate your answer with some examples from projects that you have studied or worked on and draw parallels.

4. A project is said to be successful if the work is finished on time, to cost, and to quality. We understand clearly how to measure time and cost-days and dollars-but few people have a clear idea of what they mean by quality in the context of projects. Discuss the concept of quality with specific reference to the Sydney 2000 Olympic Games project.

Strategic Project Control Initiatives

Jose Herrero, Senior Project Director, Fluor Daniel
Dev Hundal, Principal Project Control Specialist, Fluor Daniel
Paul Russel, Senior Project Controls Engineer, Fluor Daniel

PMI Canada *Proceedings*, 1996, pp. 5–10

ABSTRACT

This paper describes the implementation of a project controls philosophy to minimize the total installed cost of a world-scale petrochemical project in Alberta. Three strategic initiatives which resulted in major cost and schedule savings are discussed:
- A very early focus on planning and identifying major risks and opportunities.
- Planning/scheduling work packages based on 3-D design partitions were used to manage the design through hydrotesting cycle for piping, reducing the project critical path.
- Implementation of project management tools was directed towards accelerating the transition from construction to systems completion.

Project Background

The Prentiss II project is an Ethylene Oxide/Glycol facility that uses Union Carbide proprietary technology. Fluor Daniel provided engineering, procurement, and construction (EPC) services for this facility, located in Alberta, Canada.

The prime requirement of the project (1) was to construct the specified plant for minimum cost, i.e., a truly "cost driven" project. The project management team, therefore, adopted as its main strategy for success the minimization of "total installed cost." The emphasis from the beginning was on *total* cost impact of all major decisions.

After commencement of the project, Union Carbide decided to use a new technology, resulting in a three-month delay to the issue of detailed process design packages. As a result, the project team realized that significant changes to normal work processes would be required to recuperate the delay and still minimize the total installed cost.

All major project execution decisions were scrutinized against this criteria.

STRATEGY TO MINIMIZE TOTAL INSTALLED COST

A simplified work process for implementation of the above strategy is shown in Figure 1.

Alignment/team building sessions were held very early in the project, involving key personnel from the client and the contractor, with the whole team buying into the primary objective of minimizing total cost. These meetings continued throughout the project duration, eventually involving

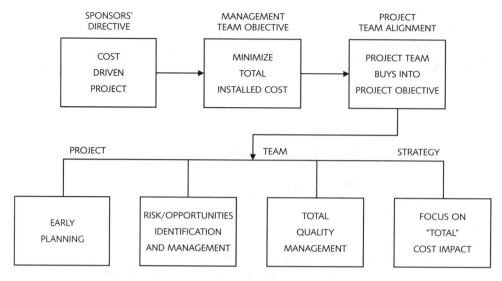

FIGURE 1   STRATEGY TO MINIMIZE TOTAL INSTALLED COST

construction management, key suppliers, subcontractors, and the construction crafts (trade unions).

A team strategy to achieve the prime requirement was formulated with emphasis on the four areas of early planning, risk and opportunity evaluation, total quality management, and focus on the reduction of total installed cost.

Early Planning

Critical equipment (long delivery) was identified and action plans for engineering and procurement were formulated to improve deliveries:

• Eight major equipment items were identified.

• Some of the heavy pieces of equipment needed to be delivered during a "transportation window" (December 1992 through February 1993) dictated by load restrictions on Canadian roads in spring.

• Other equipment had extended deliveries and needed to be ordered at a very early stage of engineering. Special efforts were made by the project team (client and contractor) to specify this equipment early, so that purchase orders could be placed in a timely manner.

• Detailed transportation plans were prepared for all critical items.

The project execution plan was developed and documented. This listed the overall execution strategies and detailed plans for project management, engineering, materials management, construction management, and project controls.

The project objective, the key driving forces, project execution risks, and strategic objectives were defined, and the project scope was documented.

Candidates for modularization and pre-assembly were identified based on previous experience and input from construction management, using brainstorming sessions and continuous evaluation of overall cost effectiveness.

The main pipe racks, the substation building, and the main analyzer building are some of the items which were modularized, with an overall cost savings of $2.5 million.

Risk and Opportunity Evaluation

Team meetings were held in the engineering office and at the construction site to assess risks and opportunities "to go," using brainstorming techniques.

Major areas of risks and opportunities for cost savings were identified; for example:

• Due to the delay in finalization of process design, there was considerable risk that underground facilities and foundations would not be completed before "freeze up." This would have resulted in very significant cost increases. A work process to release scope defining documents in advance of the detailed process packages was developed to avoid this risk.

• As mentioned previously, there was a major risk that heavy equipment, if delayed, could not be transported to site until the following winter. Extra efforts were used in expediting and supporting the fabrication to achieve the desired delivery.

• A risk that hydrotesting was being pushed into the winter period due to the delay in process packages was identified. A number of actions was implemented to minimize the amount of hydrotesting that would have to be done under winter conditions.

• Our assessment of cost savings/avoidance achieved by managing these risks and opportunities was $3.5 million.

Total Quality Management

This subject is addressed in more detail in a previous paper (2). The main components of the quality plan relating to cost were:

• Many existing work processes were documented, analyzed, and improved for project execution, avoiding duplication and saving cost.

• Project strategic objectives (key result areas) were identified and action plans formulated to achieve success in the following areas:

  • "out of the ground" before freeze up in 1992
  • procurement of critical items (cost, delivery, quality)
  • execution of critical subcontracts (cost, schedule, quality)
  • timely receipt and approval of vendor data
  • timely completion of turnover packages.

• A value awareness plan was implemented with prompt recognition and reward for successful (Betterway) ideas. Documented cost savings/cost avoidance due to this value awareness plan reached $18 million on the project.

• An earned incentive plan for the contractor enabled cash incentives to be earned for superior performance in the areas of safety, cost, and quality. The project team's focus on cost savings and avoidances (lump sum mentality) was heightened by the fact that 25 percent of the total incentives received by the contractor were shared by the staff.

Focus on "Total Installed Cost"

Following brainstorming sessions and subsequent analysis, a written "Strategy to Minimize Total Installed Cost" was adopted, addressing key elements of engineering, procurement, and construction with specific directions to achieve the objectives. This document was widely distributed and updated regularly. Some of the elements were:

- enhancement of field productivity (each 1 percent improvement = $0.5 million savings) by ensuring availability of drawings, materials, tools, and construction equipment *before* starting work in any package
- management of overtime
- just-in-time staffing and timely destaffing
- minimization of winter work.

Key schedule targets—for example, delivery of pipe rack modules, completion of piping isometrics, and delivery of fabricated piping spools, installation of piping spools, and delivery of the modularized substation—were monitored on a weekly basis.

Alternative courses of action were evaluated on an ongoing basis, and plans were modified where necessary to achieve minimum total cost. For example, craft manpower in January and February 1994 was reduced significantly from the original plan to minimize the impact of poor productivity due to severe winter weather.

Detailed "completion and demobilization plans" were made for final stages of construction to ensure timely and cost-effective turnover of systems as well as timely demobilization of temporary facilities to maximize cost savings.

The bottom line: The net result of all the proactive strategies adopted by the project team resulted in a 10 percent cost underrun, timely completion, and high job satisfaction by all participants.

Planning and Scheduling Work Packages

The main obstacle to shortening the overall duration of a project comes from the transitions that must be made between design (which begins with process or utility systems) to construction (which is done by physical area), and back to completion, which is again by process or utility systems.

The method used to smooth the transition from design to construction on the Prentiss II project was the designation of construction planning areas called work packages (WPs). Careful thought was given to the setting of planning areas that were meaningful to both design and construction. On this project, construction WPs were set as physical areas to coincide with the boundaries of each 3-D design partition (see Figure 2). Some of the reasons that 3-D design partitions proved to be optimal WPs were:

- The size of partitions was limited to permit efficient design of piping isometrics (typically sixty to 100 isometrics).
- In construction, this meant that each partition would be manned by one piping crew or less, making it an ideal size for manpower planning.
- The monitoring paperwork was minimized by incorporating the WP number in all documentation and databases associated with an isometric or spool.
- The detailed bill of material electronically downloaded from the 3-D design system to the material control system also contained the WP number against each record.
- The pipe fabrication shop database was electronically downloaded (by special arrangement with the pipe fabricator) via modem, and the fabrication status (by WP) was obtained on a weekly basis. This was a real help in construction planning, as the latest fabrication status was available almost online.

Once the work package boundaries had been defined, specific target dates were set for the start of piping erection for each WP. These dates were set to provide firm targets for design and procurement using the following assumptions:

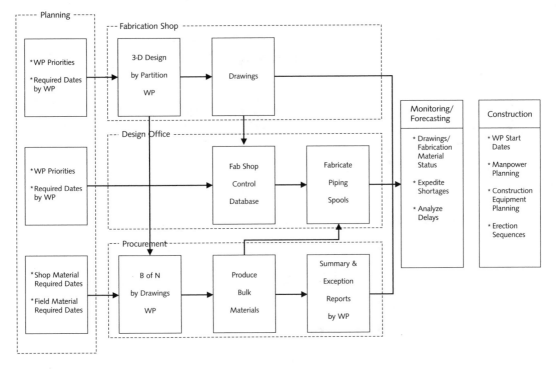

FIGURE 2   **PLANNING AND SCHEDULING WORK PACKAGES (WP'S)**

- To begin piping erection in a work package:
  - *All* columns must be set and plumbed, all heat exchangers set, and all pumps set and aligned.
  - *All* piping spools should have been delivered to site, together with all field destination bulk materials.
  - The pipe rack module adjacent to the WP must be placed and aligned, and any steel structures complete.
- Piping design targets for issue of *all* isometrics for a WP were set twelve weeks earlier than the construction start dates to allow for fabrication. Procurement targets were set to have *all* shop destination bulk materials delivered to the fabrication shop *at the same time,* prior to start of fabrication.

The results of this planning strategy were firm target dates for the issue of ISOs for forty-six construction work packages, the delivery of bulk materials to both shop and field, and the commencement of above-ground piping erection, which spanned an eighteen-week period.

During the monitoring phase of the plan, a weekly report was produced detailing the isometric issue status, and shop and field bulk material delivery status, and fabrication status for each WP planned and forecast dates were reported for ISO issue, material delivery, and construction start.

At site, a detailed plan was developed for each spool to be erected within each WP and progress monitored at a detailed and summary level weekly. In practice, piping erection began in a WP when 70 to 90 percent of the spools were on-site and the fabrication status indicated that the remainder were nearing completion.

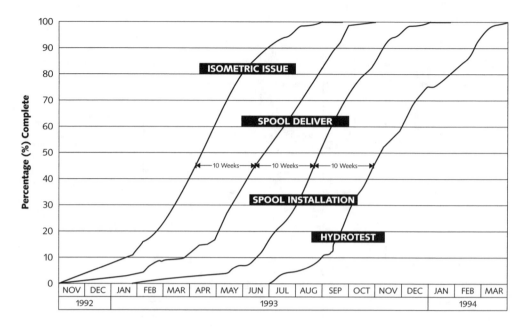

FIGURE 3   PROJECT PIPING PERFORMANCE

Benefits:
• Early in the engineering stage, the design team had clear targets for piping isometric production that were meaningful to all disciplines.
• The use of small WPs did not impose a burden of paperwork because the alignment with 3-D design partitions allowed the WP number to be associated with each element electronically.
• The effect of delays to any component of the construction plan, i.e., isometric production, design changes, bulk material deliveries, or mechanical equipment deliveries could be quickly and meaningfully assessed; corrective action could be decisively implemented.
• The most significant benefit was in day-to-day construction planning. In the early stages of construction, each area general foreman had a reliable method of directing crews to specific areas, knowing that the work could continue uninterrupted.

    In cases where construction began before material was 100 percent on-site, means were available to identify pipe spools or bulk material items that were missing, and the "drop dead" date they would be required to avoid affecting productivity in the area. Spool and bulk material exceptions were identified to expediting with target dates for delivery to allow work to proceed in the WP without interruption.
• The ability to accurately plan mobilization dates and manpower requirements by WP meant that although the workforce on the Prentiss II project was increased to peak levels very rapidly, it was achieved in a well managed manner that avoided many of the productivity losses associated with rapid workforce build-up.

    The total piping crew built up from seventy-five to 450 in a thirteen-week period, an average increase of twenty-nine workers per week over the period. In the same period, actual productivity averaged 5 percent higher than budgeted.

The bottom line (see Figure 3) showed the duration from isometric issue to hydrotest on the Prentiss II project consistently averaged thirty-one weeks over the life of the project. The best comparison for this is a 3-D project of comparable size that did not implement the 3-D work package planning system and achieved an average of forty-three weeks from ISO issue to hydrotest.

We feel strongly that the difference resulted in a twelve-week reduction in the overall project duration and is repeatable on other projects. This equated to a savings of approximately $1.5 million in indirect field costs on this project, and opportunities still exist for further improvement in each step of the process.

PLANNING STRATEGY FOR COMPLETION PHASE

The strategy used on the Prentiss II project to facilitate the transition from construction to completion phase included manpower and progress forecasting and monitoring for each turnover package (TOP). This forecast, which was based on the completion schedule, accurately reflected the specific resources required for completion of each utility and process system, set weekly targets for performance, and provided timely and accurate feedback on whether completion goals were being accomplished. This was made possible by the preparation of turnover piping and instrument flow diagrams very early in the project and identification of packages in detail.

Again, the ability to correlate data from a number of different databases was crucial to the successful implementation of this strategy. The backbone of the system was the field progress reporting system (FPRS). Briefly, the FPRS was a database that contained the budgeted workhours for all material installation or labor operations shown on "approved for construction" drawings on the project, and a milestone breakdown of the work hours. The FPRS was updated for progress of individual items every week, and formed the basis for reporting of physical progress at both detailed and summary levels.

The exercise of defining the TOPs began in the design office by entering the TOP number as a field in all applicable design databases, in much the same way that the WP was a field in these databases (see Figure 4). This included the isometric log, instrument index, and several electrical databases for wire and cable drawings. These databases were then sorted by TOP to provide the detailed listing of drawings and information required for the physical turnover package to be assembled for transmittal to the client at mechanical completion of each package. Simultaneously, this TOP data was added to the FPRS databases. Progress (percent complete) and earned and "to go" work hours could now be summarized by TOP for all construction activities specifically related to completion of the TOP.

The workhours "to go" for each craft were then spread over the remaining duration in the commissioning schedule to support the individual mechanical completion dates and manpower requirements (and percent complete forecast) for each TOP summarized by craft and area. Status against this forecast involved no additional work for the field control team other than running a different set of summary reports; i.e., progress summarized by TOP.

This technique provided construction supervision with not only a very clear road map of the manpower resources required to achieve the project completion schedule, but also weekly feedback on which TOPs were on target, and

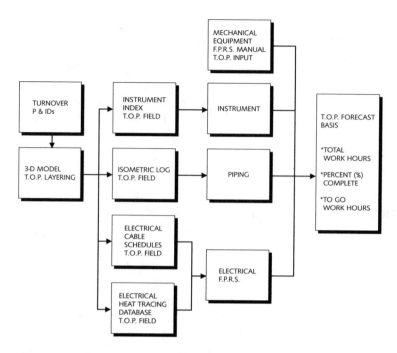

FIGURE 4   **PLANNING STRATEGY FOR COMPLETION PHASE**

where progress on a specific TOP was falling behind, and exactly which craft or area required additional resources.

The bottom line: A measure of the effectiveness of this strategy in easing and focusing the transition from the construction to completion phase of the project is again illustrated in Figure 3. Let us assume that the duration from spool installation, which is a construction phase activity primarily planned and executed by physical area, and hydrotesting, which is a completion phase activity planned and executed by utility and process system, represents effectiveness of shifting from one phase to the other. On the Prentiss II Project, this duration was consistently eleven weeks; the figure for a comparable project was eighteen weeks. This equates to a saving of approximately $1.1 million in indirect field costs.

CONCLUSIONS

The above strategies of minimizing total installed cost, work packaging, and completion planning benefited the Prentiss II project as follows:
- completion of the project ahead of schedule with an *overall cost savings of over 10 percent* of the total installed cost
- recuperation of the project schedule after an initial three-month delay, with no adverse cost impact
- outstanding quality and safety results.

We strongly believe the results on the Prentiss II project are repeatable and achievable on any project if similar strategies are applied. Further incremental improvements are possible through work process analysis, in particular in developing and sharing information and planning data between the design office, material fabricators and suppliers, and the construction site.

REFERENCES

1. Herreo, J.C., and H.G. Weil. 1994. "Strategies for Improving Team Behaviour and Attitudes. Results in Major Petrochemical EPC Project." INTERNET, 12th World Congress on Project Management. Oslo, Norway.

2. Herreo, J.C., and H.G. Weil. 1993. "How to Apply TQM to a Major Petrochemical Construction Project." PMI Regional Symposium *Proceedings.* Calgary, Alberta, Canada, pp. 223–43.

Study Questions

STRATEGIC PROJECT CONTROL INITIATIVES

1. The prime requirement of this project was clearly established. It was to minimize the total installed cost. The management of the project, in order to achieve this requirement and fulfill this project's objective, followed the strategy presented in Figure 1. Discuss the analogy between this strategy and the project management processes: initiating, planning, executing, controlling, and closing listed in the *PMBOK Guide*, section 3.2, Process Groups.

2. The case described a significant amount of planning as having gone into the project. How did this planning help to reduce costs?

3. The risk and opportunity evaluation completed for this project identified several potential scheduling problems. How does this evaluation and its effect on scheduling affect cost management?

4. The author stresses the importance of facilitating the transition between construction and completion (executing to closing the project). How did the project managers deal with this challenge?

5. Though the construction of this facility was "cost-driven," cost management was not the only project management area used in the administration of the project. Mention at least two other project management areas involved in the making of this project.

6. This case describes how the natural environment affects all aspects of how the project work is done. Compare and contrast how these natural environmental risks are analogous to risks in other types of environments (public relations, political, etc.).

Libya: Redefining Challenge

Gordon Mahovsky, Project General Manager, RASCO Project

PMI Canada *Proceedings*, 1996, pp. 88–91

ABSTRACT

This paper describes the impact of international politics on project planning and execution. The direct effects experienced on other peripheral issues such as communications, travel and logistics, human resource maintenance, and cultural differences are also discussed.

The outbreak of civil war in the former Yugoslavia, coupled with the imposition of United Nations sanctions against Libya, have had a dramatic effect on the ability of both the owner and contractors to maintain project momentum. These events have significantly altered the original project execution plan and schedule, and to date the political situation can best be described as anything but helpful. It has challenged the very heart of our project management control system.

INTRODUCTION

In 1990, Monenco AGRA Inc. was awarded a contract for a $1 billion ethylene unit downstream expansion in Libya for the Ras Lanuf Oil and Gas Processing Company—the RASCO project. Although Monenco had been working on numerous industrial projects in North Africa and the Middle East, the RASCO Project was the first major hydrocarbon project to be undertaken by the company in this part of the world.

Ever since the onset of activity, the concepts of challenge and project management have certainly taken on new meaning. The traditional issues of scope definition, change order management, and project controls have proven to be quite routine and fade in order of difficulty to international politics and the normally peripheral issues such as communications, travel and logistics, human resource maintenance, and the management of cultural differences. The objective of this paper is to share some of these unique experiences.

THE PROJECT

The project is located at an existing refinery complex at Ras Lanuf, Libya, on the Gulf of Sirte. Figure 1 shows the location relative to the major centers of Tripoli and Benghazi.

At present, the unit produces both refined crude oil and ethylene products. The desire to increase the value-added potential of the complex has prompted the owner to add ethylene downstream units consisting of both petrochemical and polymer units which include:

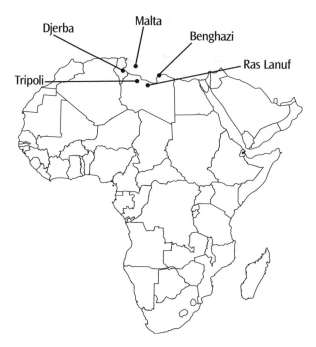

FIGURE 1   PROJECT LOCATION

- petrochemical units (LSTK-1) (to be awarded)
- polypropylene unit (LSTK-2) (to be awarded)
- polyethylene unit (LSTK-3) (Korea/England)
- tank farm and flares (Package A) (Korea)
- polymer handling and film plant (Package B) (Korea)
- desalination unit (Package C) (Italy)
- nitrogen unit (Package D) (Germany)
- hydrogen unit (Package E) (to be awarded).

SCOPE OF WORK

The essence of Monenco's activities being performed under this contract can be summarized as follows:
- owner's representative and overall project management
- engineering
  - detailed design of utilities and interconnecting facilities between new units and existing units
- tendering
  - including subcontract negotiations
- procurement
  - procurement of materials for the interconnect facilities
  - inspection and expediting of subcontractor supplied equipment and materials
- coordination of all EPC activities on the project
  - review and approval of subcontractor design
- on-site construction management.

When considering the size and complexity of the new units to be added and the all encompassing scope of work, the project team faced an enormous challenge, even under normal circumstances. Circumstances, however, turned out to be anything but normal and serve as proof to the fact that project management must be adaptive and innovative in order to meet the challenge of the unexpected.

INTERNATIONAL POLITICS

International politics, more than any other single factor has affected almost every aspect of the RASCO project. Its effect on the traditional key control parameters of cost and schedule are immense. Its effects, direct and indirect, on the seldom mentioned issues of communications, travel and logistics, human resources, and cultural differences have added complexity to an already intricate situation.

When Monenco was awarded the RASCO project, tendering activities had advanced to the point when LSTK-1, the petrochemical complex, was nearing the award stage. When the bid evaluations and follow-up clarifications were completed, the contract was awarded, and made effective, to Energoinvest, an engineering company from the former Yugoslavia. As final preparations for contract kickoff approached, so did civil war. Efforts were made, time and again, to honor contractual obligations by both the owner and contractor, but eventually all efforts succumbed to the ravages of civil war, and resulted in the termination of the contract.

This was a serious setback to the project. The petrochemical complex, comprised of units to produce MTBE, Benzene, Butene-1, and Butadiene were the front end of a major expansion and should have been the first to be implemented. Bringing a contract from the initial bid stage through technical and commercial evaluations and arrangements of the letters of credit and bank guarantees had taken an average of twenty-seven months as a result of a very regimented bidding process. Similar concerns also arose in the early stages of the polyethylene unit LSTK-3 when political friction seemed to be on the increase between North and South Korea. However, the situation stabilized and that contract remained intact.

The United Nations sanction in 1992 dealt another major blow to project execution. There was a lengthy period during which the impact of the sanctions could not be defined. Any supplier with United States affiliations was susceptible to the effects of the sanctions. Existing lump sum, firm price contracts had been awarded based on selected suppliers, and there was now a danger of certain vendors not being able to continue supplying materials and equipment to the project. For some suppliers, production schedules were impeded, causing no end to contractual disputes regarding time to deliver.

For packages that were midway through the bidding process, delays were encountered as a result of the uncertainty of the impact of the sanctions. Suddenly, some "approved bidders" were no longer eligible as suppliers for goods and services to the project.

Alternate vendors had to be found in some cases while bidders struggled to maintain quoted prices and deliveries. The tendering process had turned into a project manager's worst nightmare. Arrangement of financial instruments,

Calgary, Alberta

Woking, England

Gustavsburg, Germany

Ras Lanuf, Libya

Seoul, Korea

FIGURE 2   MAIN PROJECT OFFICE LOCATIONS

such as letters of credit and bank guarantees required by the contracts, became inordinately complicated, resulting in further delays.

The cessation of air transportation into Libya added another twist that had not been envisaged at the start. Workers on fixed rotation schedules saw their time at home decreased by increased travel time. Employees became concerned about being able to travel home quickly on family matters. The logistics of shipping materials and equipment to site had to quickly change to meet the new political scenario.

From the very early stages of the project it became obvious that the original job schedule of twenty-eight months would never be realized, and the challenge of maintaining positive momentum was going to be immense.

COMMUNICATIONS

Communications, both personal and interoffice, are the heart of every successful project. Whether good or bad, they are always a factor. On the RASCO project, communications have been a critical issue, since project activities to date have been executed from offices scattered around the globe—Canada, England, Germany, Libya, Italy, and Korea. Figure 2 shows the location of these offices.

Global interoffice communications outside of Libya have been quite normal—phone, fax, telex, and computers. Communication links to site have not proven to be as reliable. Delays from two to three hours up to several days have been encountered. Receiving or sending correspondence by fax, although the preferred method, has been subject to the same problems as phone lines. Telex, surprisingly, has proven to be the most reliable and is still used today for the majority of incoming correspondence from the owner. Courier service is reliable, but slow. Calgary to Ras Lanuf, for example, is typically ten days.

The turnaround of documents and drawings to meet the contractual approval schedules between owner and contractors has been a major cause for concern. Typical approval cycles are twenty-one days, but this remains to be an enormous task. One solution attempted was the electronic transfer of drawings via the Internet. This has been tried and has worked very well between the contractor's and Monenco's offices, however, E-mail transfer to site is not possible. The traditional method of document submission by courier was therefore maintained.

Due to the volume of correspondence that accompanies a project of this size and complexity, an electronic mail distribution system was introduced in house. Up to 150 pages of correspondence are faxed daily to the Calgary office from around the world. With this system, the need for hard copies was greatly reduced and distribution to project staff made far more efficient. The system improved the staff's ability to retrieve records needed during the day-to-day administration of the project. Significant savings were realized in reproduction costs.

TRAVEL AND LOGISTICS

Of all the things that are affected by international politics and which have a direct bearing on the project staff, a major one is is travel—getting to and from the job site. When Monenco initially took over the RASCO project, travel to site was quite simple. Following a direct flight to Malta, the necessary visas were obtained, after which the journey would be continued the next day by air to Tripoli. After that, another one-hour flight on the following day was all that was needed to arrive at Ras Lanuf. An alternate route through Benghazi was also utilized, which was an easy three-hour drive to the site.

The introduction of the United Nations' sanctions in 1992 brought an immediate halt to this routine. Travel now is usually through Tunisia where the applications for entry visas are submitted. This can be one to three days, depending on many factors. Once visas are obtained, it is a short flight to Djerba and another overnight stay. From there, Tripoli is typically a five-hour drive assuming an easy Tunisia/Libya border crossing. From Tripoli, it is another eight-hour journey by car to Ras Lanuf.

In the early stages of the project, ferry service was also available between Malta and Tripoli. Although the service supposedly operated on a regular schedule, delays of up to three days in departure from Malta were sometimes experienced, adding more difficulty to the fourteen-hour crossing. However, this alternate travel mode was available if flights were missed or canceled in Malta.

The ferry service was in operation until mid-1995 when an international incident in Malta caused the service to be canceled. It resumed in January 1996 for a short time only, to be shut down again in March 1996. For construction staff on rotation, the journey remains an arduous task.

Visas for allowing entry into Libya can be obtained in either Malta or Tunisia. Monenco staff presently obtain their visas in Tunisia, although Malta had been used until late 1994. Both ninety-day business visas and permanent resident visas have been used, although the latter is probably the best arrangement for site construction staff.

Traveling to and from the job site does require more planning than usual due to the complexities of routing and the various modes of transportation. However, international travel is interesting and seeing new places and people has been exciting for the staff. A little known fact is that Libya has some of the best preserved Roman ruins in existence, another bonus to the traveler!

HUMAN RESOURCE MAINTENANCE

Maintaining momentum on a project is not just a matter of tight schedule control and man-hour monitoring. On a project which is subjected to many delays and interferences from factors beyond the control of the project team, morale becomes a very important consideration. Job satisfaction and staff motivation quickly become a priority with project management and are usually issues which are very difficult to handle.

In theory, people exert work effort to achieve task performance and as a result expect to receive work-related satisfaction. However, hard work has not necessarily meant achieving goals in a timely manner. Monenco has been fortunate in that most of the home office, and to a great extent the construction team, are permanent staff. As new opportunities within the company arise, most staff view the experience on the RASCO project as a stepping stone to these new opportunities and view the project assignment in this light.

Revisiting design concepts several times over has been unavoidable in certain situations, and the discipline learned from this has provided the stamina to endure the many road blocks prohibiting efficient execution of the scope of work.

The elongated project schedule has presented other problems relative to staff rotation and replacement on the project. Job history has become very important to all team members and having to recall earlier decisions made on design philosophy, contract negotiations, or on contract change requests is a frequent occurrence. As contract schedules extended, it became increasingly important to maintain the same project staff in the same capacities. Staff burnout, therefore, became an issue which had to be addressed by project management, especially in the home office. Field staff seem to be less prone to this phenomenon since construction activity produced changes on the job site, imparting the feeling of accomplishment.

Field staff have faced increased difficulty in making the most of their turnaround leave due to air travel restrictions into Libya, as previously outlined. Increasing travel time by one or two days only adds to an already stressful situation.

Monenco has been fortunate in that more than half of the home office team has been on the project from the beginning. Staff turnover in the field has been even less than the home office. LSTK-3 is nearing mechanical completion, Packages A, C, and D are well advanced, and both Packages B and Interconnect construction are progressing well. The fruits of their labor are in sight and this certainly appears to make a difference.

CULTURAL DIFFERENCES

The RASCO project has been an education in human relations and diplomacy. The job has brought together people from over a dozen countries and an even greater number of ethnic backgrounds.

With English as the official contractual language, communication, both written and oral, has provided challenges of its own. The word "yes" more than likely means "maybe"; "soon" has come to mean "sometime in the future"; and "on schedule" has had its own day in the sun. Contractual negotiations have become bogged down at times, certainly attributable to misunderstanding to some degree. Technically, P & ID reviews have been exceptionally difficult, highlighting the fact that both written and verbal communication can be equally challenging.

One eye opener on-site has been the various hiring practices undertaken by the different construction contractors, especially concerning allowable staff turnaround time for R&R. For Canadian and European companies, typically seventy-two days in and twenty-one days out has been the norm. This contrasts with other contractors' staff turnaround schedules of six months. Craft labor turnaround can run as long as one year and has been extended to overall job duration in some instances.

Work schedules have been established at ten hours per day, six days per week, with Friday being the designated day off. Overtime is allowed by special approval only. In spite of all the differences that exist, the work ethic on-site has been commendable. Cooperation among the various contractors is always prevalent and spills over into off-the-job activities. One can always count on help, if needed, for in-country travel, vehicle maintenance, assistance with visa applications, or whatever the need may be.

CLOSING REMARKS

The RASCO project has provided a most demanding and challenging environment in which the project team has had to demonstrate its ability to achieve project objectives, at times in the most difficult situations. International politics and its underlying effects on all aspects of the job is an ongoing issue to be faced daily. The difficulties associated with interoffice communications, travel, and logistics have been circumvented to a large degree. Rethinking of the manpower staffing plan, with a focus on maintaining job motivation and satisfaction, remains an important ongoing task. The opportunity of working with many different cultures around the world has certainly been a maturing experience for the staff which will, without a doubt, produce only positive results in future careers.

It is interesting to note that in meeting all of the challenges discussed in this paper, solutions have not been found in textbooks, project management software, latest research, or any other space-age adaptation. This project has demonstrated that, more than anything, people have made the difference and that the most powerful tool in project management today still remains to be the human mind.

Study Questions

LIBYA: REDEFINING CHALLENGE

1. Due to political changes, the management of this project was faced with completely different challenges than initially perceived. If, as a project manager, you are going to be involved with an endeavor with this characteristic, what management model would best suit your needs?

2. Human resources are discussed in this case, both from the staff/office and field staff/construction point of view. What are the difficulties and differences in managing these two different groups?

3. Can uncertainty such as the international political uncertainty described in this project be scheduled? When should project management identify and evaluate such risks?

4. The author mentions the procurement, transportation, communication, travel, and human resource problems faced in the course of the project. Among all of these problems listed, why did the job satisfaction and staff motivation become the priority of the project?

5. This case does not mention any problems in dealing with the Libyan government despite all of the international unrest surrounding Libya. How might the project management have successfully "sold" this project to the government?

6. The author ends the case with the phrase: "This project has demonstrated that, more than anything, people have made the difference and that the most powerful tool in project management today still remains to be the human mind." Do you agree with this statement?

Land Reserve Modernization Project:
The Future of Army Infrastructure

LCol. Foreman, Project Manager, Department of National Defense, Canada

PMI Canada *Proceedings*, 1996, pp. 101–7

ABSTRACT

This paper reviews how the Department of National Defense responded to recent federal government restraints in providing training facilities for its field personnel. The paper overviews the challenges and learnings the project team faced in the design and construction of a new $100 million Militia Training Support Centre (MTSC) at Meaford, Ontario.

INTRODUCTION

The present federal government fiscal restraint and personnel reductions have significantly affected the Department of National Defense (DND). The political sensitivities of DND's large percentage of the federal government's discretionary spending have dictated that the department maintain infrastructure and resources in areas that have no direct bearing on the operational activities within the Canadian Armed Forces, in particular, the army. Severe budgetary cutbacks now make it impossible for the army to maintain the status quo and to continue to use most of its infrastructure which is well beyond its economical life expectancy. In addition, the army commitment to the total force concept, meaning the interchangeability of the regular and reserve forces, has meant a reallocation of resources and a new requirement for infrastructure to support the reserve force. Putting these new facilities on the ground is an excellent example of implementing a complex construction project in today's ever-changing environment, as well as conforming to existing government regulations and policies.

BACKGROUND

Army reserve units have never had the appropriate resources allocated to enable them to properly train and prepare for their tasks. As a result, units spend most of their time and effort administering themselves into a training situation. In order to maximize field training time and to reinforce the government's White Paper on defense and the army's total force concept, the axiom of training on well-maintained centralized fleets of equipment was initiated. The concept of the militia training support centers (MTSC) in each of the four army areas across the country was approved and the land reserve modernization project was created and chartered to oversee the development, definition, implementation, manning, and equipping of the MTSCs across the country. MTSC Meaford was the first of these centers and the lead project in the program.

PROJECT REQUIREMENT

This unique army project was a completely new requirement for which no precedent existed. The MTSC Meaford project consisted of providing the infrastructure, manning, and equipping a facility that could support a training load of twenty-five-hundred militiamen per weekend (peak period). The requirement was to construct support facilities that would enable a combat team to arrive with personal gear and be in the field within one hour, completely kitted with vehicles and equipment, ready to perform operational taskings. Another requirement was that the facility had to be located within three-hours travel of the majority of militia units. This limited the site options to the long neglected, virtually greenfield site at the Camp Meaford Tank Range on Georgian Bay in central Ontario. The project was approved for construction in April 1992 at a cost of $105 million. Project implementation required that the political sensitivities of the depressed southern Ontario construction industry be accommodated as well as the strict adherence to government contracting regulations and policies. A further requirement was that the existing and evolving camp training capability and throughput had to be maintained throughout the delivery process.

PROJECT SCOPE

As the project was a greenfield site, the project team essentially built a complete town from the ground up including site services and layout, water and sewage treatment, fire hall, barrack blocks, lecture training facilities, mess halls, maintenance garages, supply complexes, POL distribution systems, vehicle wash facilities, and ammunition storage bunkers. Also included was a 1,000-man stand-alone summer camp facility to handle peak loads during the summer. Aside from the 2,500 trainee throughput, the site had to support a permanent staff of 250 and a training fleet of 300 combat vehicles.

PROJECT TEAM ORGANIZATION

The project charter set the team up as a self-accounting, independent, self-contained organization that was dedicated to cradle-to-grave implementation of the project. The project team organization chart is shown as Figure 1. Originally set up to implement four similar MTSC projects, the early success of the PMO resulted in assumption of more responsibilities and at the high point had a budget of plus $1 billion over the life of the program.

DESIGN IMPLEMENTATION

Contract Strategy

Design of the thirty-three different facilities was split between consultants, PWGSC, and in-house designs. The majority of projects were full design and site adaptations of previous designs, while some design/build contracts were awarded. Government policy in the depressed southern Ontario market stated that although the design was managed by PWGSC and done through a prime consultant, all local firms were to be given equal access to the work. This resulted in twenty-six different subconsultants producing designs as part of the team. This cross-pollination generated a competitive edge and pride of product that benefitted all firms which did not go bankrupt.

Design Review

The imposed system meant three levels of review of the originator's work. To gain efficiency of this cumbersome situation, the project manager had to become directly involved in controlling the situation and had to usurp some of the traditional design management roles. Only through team building and intimate cooperation were the tight deadlines achieved. The project manager also enforced the 80 percent solution which enabled a more timely evolution of the designs.

CONSTRUCTION CONTRACT STRATEGY

Again the project team was to ensure that local contractors were able to be competitive for all contracts. Despite the intention, the contracts ended up going to firms from the London area because of the union boundaries. The project ended up with eight major contractors and, ironically, with significantly fewer subcontractors in some disciplines. All contracts were awarded and supervised by DND's contracting agency, Defense Construction Canada (DCC), which created a special contract management team on-site. The key issue for the project team was to get best value for money from DCC's service and the prime consultant's CSA obligations. The multitude of shop drawings and change orders was dealt with under the team approach of the contractor or consultant never having to down tools for an answer. The daily site meetings and monthly team construction meetings kept ahead of the issues as team members were empowered to make decisions on the spot. What became obvious was that the builders were focused primarily on installation and that the actual operation and maintenance of building systems needed more contractor, as well as designer and supplier, interface to achieve the desired life-cycle end result. Due to the competitive nature of the Ontario construction industry at the time, three contractors sacrificed too much profit margin and were forced to default on their contracts. In all cases, the bonding companies assumed the responsibilities for completing the work. The common experience with bonding companies was positive as their "time is money approach" in some cases, because of quick team action, actually expedited the projects. It should be noted that all bonding company action commenced after major project cashflow had occurred. Had that not occurred, it could have been a different situation.

SCHEDULING AND COST CONTROL

The project work breakdown structure was developed by the project team and the first levels are shown in Figure 2. A cost control and scheduling consultant was retained and the schedule and accounting systems made compatible with DND's financial information system. Monthly team meetings at the

PMO office in Ottawa enabled timely decisions to be made and kept a current control of expenditures. Managing these decisions by variance proved to be the most effective way to deal with the situation. The overall project schedule is shown in Figure 3. A sample project status report is in Figure 4.

SITE REALITY

Construction Quality Management

On-site construction contract management and quality control were divided responsibilities. On-site construction contract inspection and administration by DCC site engineers and inspectors worked well. The number of inspectors, as determined by the DCC, was adequate for the majority of time. The quality of inspectors was, at times, sub-optimal. The quality of inspection and the resultant work accepted were occasionally below standard. Ultimately, the owner suffered beneficial occupancy delays or additional costs were incurred for contentious post-occupancy remedial work.

The site consultant supervisory assistance (CSA), less the DCC contract inspection and administration, was undertaken by the design consultant/sub-consultants. In particular, site inspectors required consultants for interpretation of the design documents, resolution of site condition problems, and designs related to scope of work changes. The consultants felt that they bore limited liability for the constructability of the design documentation, and that they required little involvement in daily site construction activity. As a result, efforts to mitigate or correct design misinterpretations, errors, or omissions became adversarial between consultants and the DCC site inspectors. Timely and effective communication and cooperation between DCC inspectors and consultants deteriorated, causing construction delays on-site. Inevitably, the project manager became personally involved in negotiating and constructively resolving issues, restoring effective team communication and providing leadership. A more formal approach to the "partnering concept" may have improved the commitment of all parties toward mutual conflict resolution during construction.

Scheduling/Time Management

The scheduled completion dates for the majority of contracts were not achieved due to contractor mismanagement. Delays in occupancy (not attributable to the owner) of three to twelve months occurred. Contractors in this group minimized resource allocations to contract sites, up to and including declarations of bankruptcy. Bonding companies completed ten of the thirty-three major construction contracts on-site. Government contract regulations precluded time or schedule-based contract bonuses or penalties. Only incremental cash costs borne by owner which were attributable to occupancy delays were contract claimable. The project manager was unable to provide significant incentives or penalties, beyond moral suasion, to alter the contractor's scheduling. Unfortunately, the end user ultimately suffered from the delay in beneficial occupancy.

PROJECT MANAGEMENT CHALLENGES

Life-cycle Costs

Facility designs were based upon the premise of minimum military requirement. That is, designs based upon a businesslike or commercial approach of satisfying the basic military operational requirement with a civilian standard commercial or industrial facility solution. The design solution needed to satisfy an optimization of capital construction costs and operating/maintenance costs to achieve a minimum life-cycle cost. Designers and end users often lost sight of achieving the aim of Minimum Military Requirement at minimum life-cycle cost, to the consternation of the project manager. Constant vigilance and value engineering by the project manager were required.

Cross Functional Issues

The MTSC continued to operate as a training facility during the construction period, at an increasing level of activity as new facilities became occupied. Although the facility users had originally understood and accepted that construction activity had priority over training, as the project progressed with more new facilities in use, the end users required constant reminders of the priority of site activity. The conflicting site functions were caused by the convergence on-site of two different chains of command with entirely different functions, objectives, and priorities. Anticipation of the conflict and early planning by preparation of a written agreement of site priorities assisted in ameliorating site management for the project manager.

Design Site Adaptation

In delivering the infrastructure to MTSC Meaford, the project management team remained mindful of an overall objective of reusing the facility designs in other parts of the country for future MTSCs. Site adaptation considerations of the facility design for future sites without compromising satisfying the requirements for the Meaford site remained a project management challenge.

Scope and Magnitude Uniqueness

The greenfield site and the uniqueness of the military requirement challenged the designers and the project managers. The combat vehicle dimensions and weight distribution and the military requirement for barrack rooms without doors confronted designers with unique challenges. Greenfield site development of the scope and magnitude of MTSC Meaford had not been undertaken by the army since the 1950s. The project management functions for the multiplicity of activities and contracts for the site remained a continual learning challenge.

State of the Ontario Construction Industry

Construction contracts were awarded through fixed-sum, bid-build DCC public tender. The Canadian economic cycle in general, and Ontario in particular, at the time provided a very competitive bidding environment. Tender prices below estimate account for the majority of the 23 percent under budget project expenditure. Winning contractors were primarily from southwest Ontario. Three contractors went bankrupt, which affected ten of thirty-three

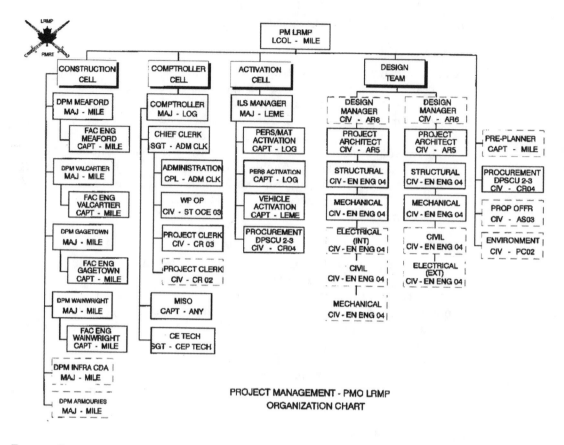

**PROJECT MANAGEMENT - PMO LRMP
ORGANIZATION CHART**

FIGURE 1

major construction contracts. The impact on the MTSC meant occupancy delays, while bonding companies assumed and completed contracts, a large number of warranty issues, and the potential for a higher-than-average incidence of latent defects. These may surface beyond the warranty period and may affect facility serviceability and operating costs.

MANNING AND EQUIPMENT

In addition to delivering the infrastructure, the project team was also mandated with establishing the manning levels and providing all of the stores and equipment to make the facility work. Within DND obtaining new manpower and equipment and orchestrating offsets and allocations is a thankless and never-ending paper chase at the best of times. The four-man activation cell went as far as setting up its own warehousing operation on a national level to capture stores and equipment being declared surplus from the closure of other DND facilities, in particular Canadian Forces Europe. This activity proved so successful that it was used to stockpile stores for the remaining three MTSCs. In the end, the project saved $4 million out of a $7.5 million budget.

LRMP PROJECT Expenses as at end Jul 95 Category	Budget	Expend Auth	Contractual	Paid to Date	Incurred to date	Forecast to complete	Forecast Final Cost	Period Change	Budget Variance
DSGN/CSA/CONST MGT	12900.6	12779.5	12731.1	12385.3	12377.1	419.3	12796.4	132.1	104.2
CONSTRUCTION	79591.1	58509.1	56597.8	54759.9	54474.8	4287	58761.8	317.7	20829.2
EQUIPMENT	8508.8	4232.3	4247.4	3924.9	3924.9	579.4	4504.3	28.3	4004.6
INTERIM ACCOMODATION	372.0	369.1	369.1	369.1	369.1		369.1		2.9
PMO MGT/ADM - DESIGN	739.7	714.3	714.3	714.3	714.3		714.3		25.4
PMO MGT/ADM - IMPLEMENT	2158.3	1902.5	1902.6	1498.3	1632.5	565.6	2198.1	32.7	-39.8
PM's CONTIGENCY	1516.0	125	125	29.4	29.4	1486.6	1516		
PROJECT TOTALS	105786.5	78631.8	76687.3	73681.2	73522.1	7337.9	80860.0	510.8	24926.5
	100.0%	74.3%	72.5%	69.7%	69.5%	6.9%	76.4%	0.5%	23.6%

FIGURE 2

Appendix 3

PROPERTY AND ROW	SITE DEVELOPMENT	MUNICIPAL/ UTILITIES SYSTEMS	NEW BUILDINGS /FACILITIES	EQUIPMENT	TEMPORARY CONSTRUCTION	CONSTRUCTION MANAGEMENT	DESIGN	MEAFORD PERSONNEL	PMO PROJECT MANAGEMENT
Acquisitions	Demolitions	Water Treatment Plant	CE/Transport	Training Equipment	Temporary Site Development	Tender Call and Award	Preliminary Design	Staffing	Coordinate Related Projects
ROW	Site Clearing and Leveling	Sewage Treatment Plant	CANEX	Commercial Vehicles	Temporary Site Services	Construction Contract Administration	Detailed Design	Training	Coordinate Ex- Project Tasks
Maintenance	Roadways	Hydro Substation	Medical Unit	MIU/DA	Temporary Accommodation	Consultant Supervisory ASSISS(CSA)	Acceptance	Service Contracts	Project Management Support
	Parking	Natural Gas Substation	M153 Quarters	Communications and ADP		Site Management and Cooordination			PMO General Administration
	Parade Square		M155 Quarters	Warehousing and Furnishings		Project Insurance			External Reporting
	Sports Fireld		M156 Quarters	Tools and test Equipment		Inspection			Manage Project Contingency
	Utilities Distribution System			Initial Provisioning and Spares		Quality Assurance			
	Fencing			SetUp					
	Landscaping								
	Hydro Powerline								

FIGURE 3

CONCLUSIONS

The MTSC Meaford opening ceremonies were held July 24, 1995, one year ahead of schedule and $21 million (23 percent) under budget. The strength of the success was in having dedicated project manager resources from the outset. The constant flow of communication from the PMO, prime consultant,

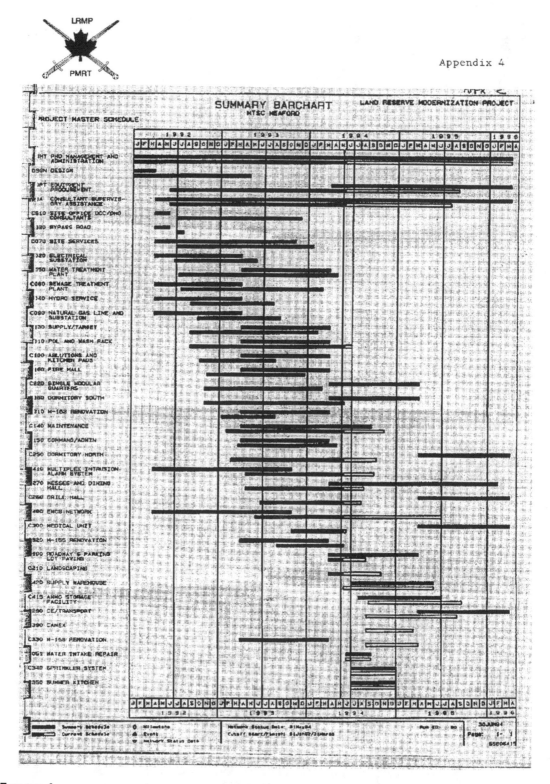

FIGURE 4

PWGSC, contractors, and Defense Construction Canada enabled the team to overcome the significant hurdles placed in its path. In spite of the unstable state of many of the design consultants and contractors, no disputes went to arbitration, more than 1,000 design changes were effected, and several major changes in the requirement were accommodated. Cost control and scheduling proved to be the link that brought it all together. However, the single most important factor was the desire and willingness to get things done on the part of the user, the PMO, the consultants, the contractors, PWGSC, and DCC.

Future Program

Three more MTSCs will be built in Valcartier PQ, Gagetown/Aldershot, and Wainwright AB using the site-adapted designs based on the Meaford experience. The Wainwright facilities will give an additional 1,500 man capacity to the existing infrastructure at a budgeted cost of $70 million. In addition, the project team has been given the additional responsibility of rebuilding Camp Wainwright, which was built as a temporary facility in the early 1940s. In all, construction costs will total some $200 million and will be budgeted over the next five years. But all that is another presentation. Needless to say, the project team, anxious to apply lessons learned, is looking forward to working in the West. As well, many of the staff come from this fine but often ignored area of the country.

Study Questions

LAND RESERVE MODERNIZATION PROJECT: THE FUTURE OF THE ARMY INFRASTRUCTURE

1. This project is described as unique, with a magnitude and scope not undertaken by the Canadian Army since the 1950s. How was this challenge taken?

2. Figure 1 of the case presents the project team organization. The author describes it as "a self-accounting, independent, self-contained organization that was dedicated to cradle-to-grave implementation of the project." Following the descriptions from section 2.3.3, Organization Structure, in the *PMBOK Guide*, what kind of organization was used for this project?

3. This project had three contractors go bankrupt during the course of the project. These three contractors were responsible for almost one-third of the construction work on the project. However, all of the work involved with the project was completed on schedule and under budget. Given what was presented in the case and your own thoughts, how was this achieved?

4. It is clear from the case that the project took advantage of the economic situation of the area in order to "get the best value for the money from DCCs." However, this triggered the undesired side effects of the bankruptcy of several companies, substandard quality requiring remedial work, and delays in the schedule. Was this the result of a component of project management not being carried out effectively?

5. The project management officer was able to manage well enough to receive more responsibilities and gain control over a budget of $1 billion despite the fact that the Meaford camp was not a complete success. To what do you attribute this apparent disparity in additional responsibility and success?

R&D in the Insurance Industry: PM Makes the Difference

Julie M. Wilson, Implementation Manager, Pacific Mutual Life Insurance Company

PMI *Proceedings*, 1992, pp. 223–31

INTRODUCTION

At Pacific Mutual Life Insurance Company (Pacific Mutual), researching, developing, and implementing insurance products ranged widely—nine months to five years—before a product entered the market. But that was before. The marketing environment for insurance products began rapid changing in the late 1970s based on:
- population declines in the United States and Canada
- aging baby boomers
- changing family structure
- more affluent and better educated consumers.

Specializing in corporate owned life insurance (COLI) for businesses, as well as individually owned insurance, Pacific Mutual often was tardy taking advantage of marketing opportunities due to its cumbersome and lengthy research and development efforts. Looking ahead to the need to develop additional diversified products for its product portfolio to meet sophisticated consumer needs, Pacific Mutual reengineered its research and development efforts.

Prior to 1987, the company experienced slow market introduction for its products whether designed for a specific client or designed for a broad client base. Development efforts swung back and forth between researching and designing a custom product for a specific individual or business to working on a non-custom product being designed for the general marketplace. Often the same staff working on a custom product was the same staff working on a regular product and morale suffered when priorities and work kept changing.

Questions were asked about the research and development efforts. Why don't products get to market on time and why aren't they complete? What needs to happen to help get products out the door faster yet achieve improved quality? How do we work on getting new products out the door and still maintain current servicing levels? How do we achieve a dramatic expansion of product portfolio while maximizing shrinking profit margins? What are the impacts on profitability?

This paper addresses the questions posed above. It also addresses the extensive reengineering effort which resulted in increased efficiency and effectiveness throughout the organization in its research and development efforts as well as the day-to-day functional service business environment. It will feature case studies of several types of products and how the use of cross-functional teams coupled with innovative project management methods continues to work in this service environment.

INDUSTRY BACKGROUND

Insurance has been around for about 2,000 years first starting with property insurance in the Mediterranean area when ships and their cargos were insured. Shipping was at best a hazardous venture, especially when long distances were involved and the likelihood of loss acted as a deterrent to trade. The fact that cargoes and ships could be insured encouraged people to risk their money in overseas trade. The resulting investments helped the shipping industry to flourish. The first life insurance company was called the "Corporation for Relief of Poor and Distressed Presbyterian Ministers and of the Poor and Distressed Widows and Children of Presbyterian Ministers" which was established in 1759. Now there are over 1,200 insurance companies in the United States and Canada marketing property and liability insurance as well as mutual funds and other investment products. This trend toward broadened financial services is having a continuous impact on every facet of the industry (1).

Today's marketing environment seldom permits a company's current product mix to remain effective for long. To stay competitive, a company must be able to adjust product mix so that it can continue to provide the kinds of products required to meet the changing needs of both current and potential clients and thus achieve the overall goals and objectives of the company. A company can change its product mix in three basic ways: develop new products, modify existing products, and delete weak or unwanted products (2).

In the early 1980s, when inflation was in the double digits and interest rates were there also, investors flocked to take advantage of earning high interest on their money. Junk bonds abounded. Staunch, conservative insurance companies were guaranteeing 4–5 percent interest. Insurance policyholders drew out their money either by completely surrendering their policies or by taking out low-cost loans preferring investment elsewhere. Insurance companies felt compelled to take on riskier investments to maintain their client bases and to offer more diversified products to attract new clients. Society was also changing in the United States and Canada. Populations were declining. The largest portion of the population, baby boomers, were aging. The traditional family structure was splintering.

As the 1980s rolled on, insurance owners' needs became more sophisticated as the need to preserve savings became increasingly important in accelerating inflationary times. They began earning more and they also were living longer. They waited to marry and didn't always remain married as long as their parents did. They had less children or no children as the two-income family became more prominent. In case of death, they still wanted the death insurance benefits (funeral expenses and paying off the home mortgage), but now it needed to cover both wage earners' lives. And consumers also began seeing for the first time the benefits of an insurance contract for investment and for use while they still lived (e.g., college tuition, home purchase, retirement savings). Pacific Mutual began gearing up to meet the new and rapidly changing consumer needs.

WHY PRODUCTS DIDN'T GET TO MARKET QUICKLY

Slow Research and Development

Research and development in the company was conducted in a sporadic, un-structured way as it had been done in the past when the need to get a new product out on the market lacked a sense of urgency. Products were not market sensitive and were expected to have a long life; therefore, there was no rush to get them to market, as the consumer need was known and stable.

The designing engineer of an insurance product, an actuary, tended to fine-tune for a long time. When interest rates and inflation became volatile, affecting financial investment futures, pricing products also became more difficult and volatile. Product specifications changed as Wall Street changed, and products simply weren't getting developed in a timely, structured manner.

No Development Methodology

There was no development methodology employed to research and develop products in the company. The actuary, as lead, worked with each department independently, controlling the outcome of the overall effort, trusting each department to produce what was needed. Often this technical lead had all the expertise to price and design the product but lacked the overall view of the impact of implementing the product in the company. With over twelve departments working on product pieces interpreting product needs different-ly, it was evident that the final product outcome was usually quite different from what the actuary had in mind.

Ineffective Timing and Resource Utilization

There were other signs that the way in which products were being re-searched and developed was not effective or efficient, creating increasing dis-satisfaction at all levels of the organization.

Experienced and highly skilled staff members did not work together as a team; rather, they were expected to complete their pieces of the product using their interpretations of what needed to be done. The phrase "on time" meant different things to each group of workers. Marketing often communicated to the agent producers that the product would be out on a certain date without confirming that it could, in fact, be done by all the affected home office departments. This lack of shared vision was not uncommon in the insurance industry.

During the development effort, the various departments rarely consulted with each other, except through the actuary. There were no group meetings or overall communications on the product. Ownership of the new product was nonexistent. Staff was held accountable for the functional administrative work, and work on new products was to be done "as time permitted." In short, appraisal of work performance emphasized day-to-day functional work—not new product work.

The level of satisfaction and cooperation between the functional departments at Pacific Mutual continued to decline.

Incomplete, Ever-Changing Product Specifications

Setting aside the volatility of pricing the product, the specifications were in-complete, non-specific, and not readily available to those who needed to know. They were usually developed with minimum interaction and dialogue with the affected departments. Initial specifications did not take into account the administrative data processing system, a major flaw in designing the product. And they kept changing—not only in the early stages of product development but even after market introduction of the product. This caused a backlog of modifications for the system and increasing burdens of manual work on the administrative staff.

Projects, Priorities, and Project Management

Projects and priorities revolving around the establishment and maintenance of automated data processing systems were recognized and firmly established in the data processing area of the company. Indeed, within the insurance industry, project management has existed for a long time when the earliest computers were eagerly embraced to handle the tremendous volumes of mathematical calculations and information handling prevalent in the insurance industry.

The systems department at Pacific Mutual had a system to define, prioritize, and maintain projects as negotiated by it with end-user departments for systems it developed and maintained. The system was the nucleus of the project. Less emphasis was placed on the business need resulting in the system being installed in the first place. The terms "project" and "project management" were exclusively associated with this department—and not always in a positive sense. As in other insurance companies, the data processing area was perceived as mysterious and foreign to its client departments. No one knew what the department really did because it was so highly specialized—everyone in it seemed to talk a different language. Its development methodology was perceived as too rigorous, too structured, and too inflexible.

Projects going on which were non-systems driven were not recognized as such and had little visibility; however, they did impact the development of new products. Staff efforts were split between daily operations, departmental "projects," and new products, with priorities fluctuating depending upon who had what power to influence those priorities and work schedules.

PROFITABILITY IMPACTS

Intuition Carries a High Cost

In the 1970s and 1980s, new product development was justified primarily on marketing intuition with little or no attention given to the cost of bringing the product to market. And some products introduced produced little or no business. In recent years, the need for rapid-fire introduction of new products forced the research, development, and implementation functions at the company to come under intense scrutiny. Restructuring and streamlining were needed, while, at the same time, improving the quality and delivery merited the same intense review. See Figure 1 for the general shape of the product life-cycle for most products (2).

Soaring Development and Administration Costs

The cost to research and develop the product was also running out of control, eating into the shrinking profit margins of the product. Pricing assumptions

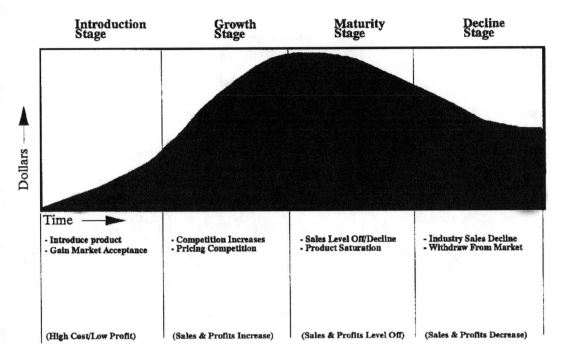

Introduction Stage	Growth Stage	Maturity Stage	Decline Stage
- Introduce product - Gain Market Acceptance	- Competition Increases - Pricing Competition	- Sales Level Off/Decline - Product Saturation	- Industry Sales Decline - Withdraw From Market
(High Cost/Low Profit)	(Sales & Profits Increase)	(Sales & Profits Level Off)	(Sales & Profits Decrease)

Dollars ↑

Time →

FIGURE 1   PRODUCT LIFE-CYCLE

used to design the product were outdated in relation to the time and effort needed to get the product to market. In between attempts to get products out the door loomed the day-to-day administration of sold products which needed to get accomplished. The day-to-day administration became more labor intensive, driving up the cost.

A typical insurance product, once sold, requires administration for twenty to forty years—until the death benefit is paid to the beneficiary. Over this lengthy period of time, there can be many changes in its administration including the typical changes in beneficiary, changes in face amount, premium mode payments, etc. (3). So the same outdated pricing assumptions on the product became more outdated, driving up the actual costs to administer business. Overly optimistic assumptions as to sales volumes and persistency also lead to non-recovery of expenses (4).

The investment of premiums by the company's asset managers was also affected. Risk identification is the first step in managing the investment process. Management made a conscious effort to define a general risk/return tradeoff for the company as a whole. Investment policy formulation was re-tailored to the company's risk management philosophy. Understanding the risk embodied in policyholder options and determining a company's tolerance for that risk is what drives investment policy (5) and, therefore, profitability. See Figure 2 for the relationships of liability and asset risk management.

Products which had been introduced years earlier still were being administered manually beyond initial issue of the policy. The levels of staff required to manually administer the policies continued to grow to take care of the ever-increasing number of products which were added but never fully implemented.

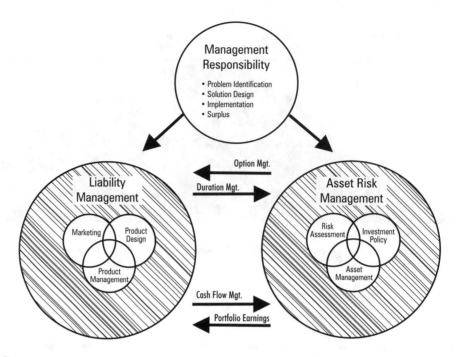

FIGURE 2

THE COMPANY EXAMINED ITS ENVIRONMENT

How could the company achieve a dramatic expansion of its product portfolio while maximizing the shrinking profit margins typical in the late 1980s and 1990s? What needed to happen in its typically bureaucratic organization to streamline research and development efforts? How could management take advantage of hidden skills of the highly specialized staff bound by functional organization fences? It examined its needs, developed goals, and cast a critical eye into its environment and culture. Its initial action was to set up a task force.

A traditional way of solving group problems, the task force approach was selected to get senior management and its related staffs to acknowledge that working within departmental fences and ignoring divisional opportunities was counterproductive.

An internal business consultant, new to the company with a general insurance background and specializing in project management, led the effort. Coupled with the senior management person who became the strongest proponent in making the changes that would later be identified, the first non-systems "project" was launched.

Cross-Functional Teams Emerge

A two-tier approach was used in working with this first cross-functional team. The purpose of this approach was to build a team spirit while delegating responsibilities at the group level for problem identification and resolution. The Tier 1 group was charged with policy issues while Tier 2 was charged with the "how" of implementing the policy decisions. Together the groups would form the first step in integrating the necessary changes.

Senior management formed the Tier 1 team and was given the purpose of determining why the current processes were not working, identifying what and who was needed to improve the research and development of new products, and identifying the critical steps and staff needed to implement new products. The team needed to develop a vision of a new process that was unencumbered by past thinking and approaches and which leveraged the enormous competitive potential of its staff and technology.

The group also needed to recognize working as a team had distinct advantages over working in their separate departments. Ownership for the problems and solving them collectively along with the Tier 2 team had to be recognized, truly believed, and accepted by the Tier 1 team.

The Tier 2 team was comprised of the subject matter experts—those individuals on the firing line each day servicing the policies, policyholders, plus the agent producers who sold the business. Focusing on the "how" of the issues at hand, without restrictions, gave them the freedom to act in retooling solutions to support the refined process with policy decisions supplied by the Tier 1 team.

The two teams worked together to meld back together the parts of the business that were split into unmanageable pieces when the business grew too large to handle the complexities. The old vision of labor principles required abandonment to make way for the new changes.

FACTS EMERGE

Reluctant Leadership

The actuarial department, responsible for the pricing and future profitability of the product, was seen as the "leader" in introducing the product. Since it carries the largest responsibility for the product during its lifetime, it was viewed as having the primary responsibility for getting the product to market. This finding was confirmed by looking at other insurance companies; however, at Pacific Mutual, the actuaries were not equipped with the necessary skills to lead large groups to complete the process they initiated. Nor were they especially interested in leading a large group, preferring instead to spend their time on mathematical equations and interpretation of product financial specifications.

The marketing department, which usually introduced the product idea to the actuary, was also reluctant to lead such efforts. It considered its time better spent with the various field offices marketing and promoting the products. The marketing group gathers intelligence on competition and market opportunities that must be translated into product design. It was not sensitized to the administrative side and preferred to remain in its area of expertise.

Leadership beyond the initial pricing of the product remained fractured and fragmented when it came to the product's actual implementation. This portion of the process—implementation—was where the Tier 1 and 2 teams focused their energies.

Lack of Ownership

The other twelve departments at that time had no overpowering ownership in a new product when they were wrestling with current product administration—products which were not fully administrable on the company's computers.

The result of the non-ownership by the departments was the continuing rise of manual processes being performed by increasing levels of additional staff to support what should have been a fully automated process. They were often unsympathetic to the importance of underwriting and issuing a new product because they were sensitive to the insurance producer and the policyholder. "Customer satisfaction" had yet to be defined and understood.

Defining the Steps

No one department really knew all the steps involved in researching, developing, and implementing a product because each department interpreted the product requirements individually and implemented what it thought was adequate. The staff members which had worked on one product didn't necessarily remain on as product experts. They went on to other responsibilities or other divisions of the company or left and went to other companies, taking their knowledge and expertise with them. No process was in place to preserve and continue the long-term implementation and product administrative support.

Documentation, beyond what was required from a regulatory standpoint, didn't exist in one place. What existed was not uniform and was subject to interpretation by those who read it. Staff had nowhere to go for answers on new or old products.

The Solution: A New Process

It was determined that the current process (if it could be called that) was too fragmented, multidirectional, and unmanaged. It was also determined that a separate management group was needed to assure that the process was implemented smoothly as well as the first new product efforts. A major reorganization focusing on both servicing policies as well as researching and developing them emerged.

The "new product implementation" process was the end product of the six months spent by the two teams. The team approach used in the early stages of identifying the process which emerged was critical to begin building the teamwork concept which has become and continues to be the base framework of the process. Without commitment from top management and its ripple effects on the staff, the process could not be successful. The process has since that time been replicated in other insurance companies (6).

This emphasis on accelerating the product research and development process is not new; however, it has acquired greater importance due to the increasing costs of slow product development. Davidson and Birnbaum found that firms with short product development cycles outperform firms with long development cycles (7).

The process, once identified, required restructuring of the organization, and a support staff was put into place to put theory into practice. Matrix management became known, and training was conducted to begin acclimating the organization to the matrixed environment consisting of responsibilities for 1) day-to-day functional service work, and 2) project work (including new products). Figure 3 shows how the organization looks today along with several types of projects currently under way (8).

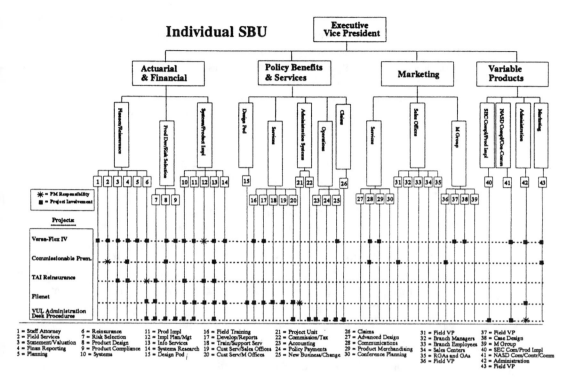

Individual SBU

Legend:
- ✳ = PM Responsibility
- ■ = Project Involvement

Projects:
- Versa-Flex IV
- Commissionable Prem.
- TAI Reinsurance
- Filenet
- VUL Administration Desk Procedures

1 = Staff Attorney	6 = Reinsurance
2 = Field Services	7 = Risk Selection
3 = Statement/Valuation	8 = Product Design
4 = Finan Reporting	9 = Product Compliance
5 = Planning	10 = Systems

11 = Prod Impl	16 = Field Training
12 = Impl Plan/Mgt	17 = Develop/Reports
13 = Info Services	18 = Train/Support Serv
14 = Systems Research	19 = Cust Serv/Sales Offices
15 = Design Pod	20 = Cust Serv/M Offices

21 = Project Unit	26 = Claims
22 = Commission/Tax	27 = Advanced Design
23 = Accounting	28 = Communications
24 = Policy Payments	29 = Product Merchandising
25 = New Business/Change	30 = Conference Planning

31 = Field VP	37 = Field VP
32 = Branch Managers	38 = Case Design
33 = Branch Employees	39 = M Group
34 = Sales Centers	40 = SEC Com/Prod Impl
35 = RGAs and GAs	41 = NASD Com/Contr/Comm
36 = Field VP	42 = Administration
	43 = Field VP

FIGURE 3

Design and Apply

As the process was being designed and laid out, a further level of difficulty was introduced—that of actually applying the concepts of the process as it was being designed. Several new products were in early research stages, so it was imperative to begin the new process on a positive footing while putting in place the methodology and practices which continue today. Phrases like "teamwork," "work smarter," "work in parallel," "cooperation," and "innovate—go outside the 9 dots" soon began cropping up.

A new variable product line was being established which required an increased need for involvement of external organizations to Pacific Mutual. One product had already been implemented, so there were fresh history, feelings, and perceptions to examine and question, and it reinforced the fact that a process with structure was critical. The second product employed the new process.

That first project team was staffed by senior management members still a bit reluctant that this new process would work smoothly given the level of situational complexity. They had as their assistants members of the Tier 2 team, the subject matter experts. Nine months later, they were pleasantly surprised that this new process not only got designed, but the interactive "design-and-apply" techniques were embraced by the team members and had a positive effect for the product being introduced. It was administrable on the system, and everyone felt he played a major role in making this happen. Overall, good feelings were prevalent about how the product got out the door.

It was a highly focused project, and its visibility at the highest levels of the company reinforced the sense of ownership—that the entire team shared the responsibility for success or failure. The introduction of the new product took less time than past efforts had, even though the team was dealing with a lot of unknowns for a fairly new product concept in a newly established product line. It also was obvious that the teamwork environment was going to work given time, further training, and practical experience. One of the keys to implementing this new process was its flexibility—anyone could suggest change, and the team collaborated in decision-making.

For the next two products, senior management members once again held principle positions on the team, testing and refining the new process with their subject matter experts as "backups." This unusual approach provided time in which everyone grew more comfortable with the process, the new teaming environment, and integrative practices. Senior management members realized that they didn't really need to get involved in the day-to-day project work—that their staffs were educated and willing to take on the additional work outside their daily operational duties. So they delegated authority for the next product effort down to the next levels of the organization. Management was pleased with the staff's ability to work together, quickly identify policy issues, and bring them to management's attention for quick discussion and resolution.

New Product Implementation Process Methodology

The underlying base for this process is teaming and project management. Interwoven are the company's core values of openness, change, risk taking, accountability, and goal orientation. The project life-cycle methodology from the systems department was reengineered to be more flexible and contemporary while not sacrificing necessary auditing controls for the new process.

Representatives from all departments directly or indirectly are involved with all product implementation efforts. Information is widely available and accessible. Kickoff meetings are held to inform and establish communications networks. The project team meets weekly or bimonthly to share progress, problems, and decision-making. The team resolves its day-to-day problems pulling in policymakers as needed.

The immediate team members stay on until the product reaches the market. Depending upon their level of involvement, their functional responsibilities are reduced or reassigned to others in their work group so that they can focus their efforts on the higher priority effort. Project work is now recognized and reviewed in yearly performance appraisals.

A permanent, functional department provides project management leadership, cost and scheduling, management for large projects on a day-to-day basis, communications, and project documentation, along with other situational needs of projects.

The permanent yet flexible life-cycle methodology adapted from the systems department exists within the process. Six distinct phases are involved in researching, developing, and implementing a product (or other projects) at Pacific Mutual. See Figure 4 for a graphic representation and high-level deliverables. Brief explanations of the life-cycle phases follow.

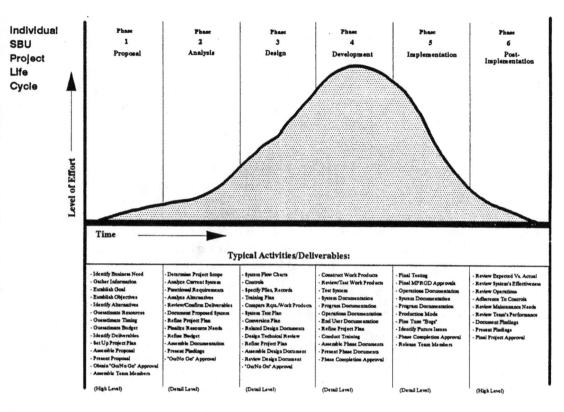

Individual SBU Project Life Cycle

| Phase 1 Proposal | Phase 2 Analysis | Phase 3 Design | Phase 4 Development | Phase 5 Implementation | Phase 6 Post-Implementation |

Level of Effort

Time

Typical Activities/Deliverables:

Phase 1	Phase 2	Phase 3	Phase 4	Phase 5	Phase 6
- Identify Business Need	- Determine Project Scope	- System Flow Charts	- Construct Work Products	- Final Testing	- Review Expected Vs. Actual
- Gather Information	- Analyze Current System	- Controls	- Review/Test Work Products	- Final M'PROD Approvals	- Review System's Effectiveness
- Establish Goal	- Functional Requirements	- Specify Files, Records	- Test System	- Operations Documentation	- Review Operations
- Establish Objectives	- Analyze Alternatives	- Training Plan	- System Documentation	- System Documentation	- Adherence To Controls
- Identify Alternatives	- Review/Confirm Deliverables	- Compare Rqts./Work Products	- Program Documentation	- Program Documentation	- Review Maintenance Needs
- Guesstimate Resources	- Document Proposed System	- System Test Plan	- Operations Documentation	- Production Mode	- Review Team's Performance
- Guesstimate Timing	- Refine Project Plan	- Conversion Plan	- End User Documentation	- Fine Tune "Bugs"	- Document Findings
- Guesstimate Budget	- Finalize Resource Needs	- Related Design Documents	- Refine Project Plan	- Identify Future Issues	- Present Findings
- Identify Deliverables	- Refine Budget	- Design Technical Review	- Conduct Training	- Phase Completion Approval	- Final Project Approval
- Set Up Project Plan	- Assemble Documentation	- Refine Project Plan	- Assemble Phase Documents	- Release Team Members	
- Assemble Proposal	- Present Findings	- Assemble Design Document	- Present Phase Documents		
- Present Proposal	- "Go/No Go" Approval	- Review Design Document	- Phase Completion Approval		
- Obtain "Go/No Go" Approval		- "Go/No Go" Approval			
- Assemble Team Members					
(High Level)	(Detail Level)	(Detail Level)	(Detail Level)	(Detail Level)	(High Level)

FIGURE 4

Concept Phase

This is where the initial research is performed by the actuary and her staff. They look at the market to see what is being sold against the company's product portfolio. Sometimes an idea comes from policyholders, but most often the ideas come from insurance agent producers. Initial research findings are shared with the producers and the newly formed marketing committee. If the idea is still sound, initial product specifications are developed and reviewed by a core project group, signed off on, and the next phase is undertaken.

Analysis Phase

In this phase, the project manager is appointed, if he hasn't already been involved at the concept phase, and brought up to date. The project manager identifies the core group of team members who will be needed and gets them into position to begin reviewing the initial product specifications. The project manager also begins preparing the product approval package for senior management by providing a description of the product, how it will be sold and to what segment of the market, what an average policy looks like, and what the financials are on investment and its return. The initial product specifications are published to all members of the team, and work begins to blend the specifications into business change requirements, minimizing disruption to the level of service in operations.

Development Phase

The largest phase in terms of overall time and cost across the organization, the development phase sees upgrading of administrative systems to handle the new product, generation and submission of the policy contract and its provisions to the proper regulatory bodies, review of initial competition information on similar products, generation of sales promotions, and tightening of marketing plans.

Implementation Phase

This is the culmination of the previous phases. All major tasks and milestones critical for the product's market introduction are completed in this phase. Those items necessary for the long-term administration of the product are identified and listed and logged into a tracking system to be implemented at a later date. The administrative system becomes operational. The home office announces the product to its agent producers and awaits the first insurance applications and underwriting materials to come in.

Post-Implementation Phase

A review is usually conducted informally within thirty days of the product's introduction, to assure no vital tasks have been missed, however small, for the first year's administration of the product. It is usually during this period that initial business begins to increase, and the staff and systems become accustomed to the additional product—fitting it into the current environment.

CONCLUSION

Because reengineering doesn't happen overnight, and because competitive conditions are increasing, now is the time for insurers to overhaul their business processes. Changes in the industry are accelerating and will continue to do so as less competitive companies are acquired by larger, more nimble companies.

Pacific Mutual is one of those nimble companies demonstrating its ability to blend people, processes, and technology together successfully. It continues to move on all fronts—strategic, organizational, and technological—in a coordinated fashion.

Pacific Mutual has responded to the ever-present need for new products in its highly segmented markets by specifically addressing the whole team concept, a phased approach in research and development, organizational tools, and project management techniques. It is moving toward a more open, innovative culture. Evidence of this is its new entrance into self-directed work teams for the day-to-day functional administrative service work.

Pacific Mutual respects the flexibility and fluidity of its "new product implementation process" as evidenced by the high level of ownership to keep the process contemporary and innovative. Each time a product is implemented, mechanics of the process are examined for appropriateness and changed as needed.

Pacific Mutual has also favorably impressed its insurance agents with its ability to deliver a quality product in less time, resulting in earlier sales than ever before following a product introduction. The products themselves continue to be highly successful with no product undergoing this process being discontinued due to fragmented, ineffective research and development. In fact, the company in 1990 and 1991 enjoyed its highest sales volume in its history since its formation in 1868.

Project management has arrived—again. Its principles and practices are spreading throughout the company. What makes it successful this time around is the project management support staff's ability to reintroduce it in a way that has been acceptable to the entire organization while retaining the basic principles' effectiveness. Each division of the company has its project management experts who have collaborated on various project management efforts including a generic project management guide, review of project management computer software, and other related endeavors. The company's first in-house project management course previewed this year.

REFERENCES

1. Long, D. L., and G. A. Morton. 1988. "Principles of Life and Health Insurance, Second Edition." Life Office Management Association, Inc.

2. Goodwin, K. W. 1989. "Life and Health Insurance Marketing." Life Office Management Association, Inc.

3. Huggins, K. 1986. "Operations of Life and Health Insurance Companies." Life Management Association, Inc.

4. Forbes, S. 1987. "Financial Issues Critical To Industry." *Resource*. Mar./Apr.

5. King, D. A. 1991. "The Invisible Dynamics of a Life Insurer." *Best's Review*. July.

6. Metz, J. "Product Implementation at Life of Virginia." *Resource* 16, no. 10.

7. Gupta, A. K., and D. L. Wilemon. 1990. "Accelerating the Development of Technology-Based New Products." *California Management Review*. Winter.

8. Hezzelwood, W.; F. Simon; W. Tachiki; M. Urbina; J. M. Wilson. 1992. "Project and Systems Reference Guide." Pacific Mutual Life.

9. Lawrence, Philip J. 1991. "Reengineering the Insurance Industry." *Best's Review*. May.

Study Questions

R&D in the Insurance Industry—PM Makes the Difference

1. In Figure 4, the author depicts the new project life-cycle. This life-cycle has six different phases, including an "implementation phase." Do you perceive this phase as having a clearly defined beginning and end, or do you think that this phase is occurring throughout the entire project?

2. The general life-cycle for most products in the life and health insurance market is depicted in Figure 1. Do you see any resemblance between this life-cycle and a generic project life-cycle?

3. The case mentions that previously the term "on-time" meant differing things to different groups of workers. Therefore, groups completed tasks based on their own interpretation of what was necessary to complete that task. How is this problem addressed and solved through the new methodology?

4. The author states, "Because reengineering doesn't happen overnight, and because competitive conditions are increasing, now is the time for insurers to overhaul their business processes. Changes in the industry are accelerating and will continue to do so as less competitive companies are acquired by larger, more nimble companies." Do either of these statements (or both) apply to other industries with which you are familiar? Explain.

5. The author mentions Pacific Mutual's core values of "openness, change, risk taking, accountability, and goal orientation." What barriers would the lack of these values present to a company trying to introduce project management teams?

Implementing Integrated Product Development: A Case Study of Bosma Machine and Tool Corporation

F. Paul Khuri, United States Air Force, Brooks AFB

Howard M. Plevyak, Jr., Air Force Institute of Technology, Wright-Patterson AFB

Project Management Journal, September 1994, pp. 10–15

In 1986, the President's Blue-Ribbon Commission on Defense Management noted that weapon systems take too long to develop, cost too much to produce, and often do not perform as promised or expected (1). At the same time, private industry was attributing its success in the competitive global market to its use of new initiatives such as integrated product development (IPD) (1). The United States Air Force defines IPD as:

> A philosophy that systematically employs a teaming of functional disciplines to integrate and concurrently apply all necessary processes to produce an effective and efficient product that satisfies customers' needs (2).

This research focuses on one company's implementation of IPD—Bosma Machine and Tool Corporation (Bosma). The research investigated six areas:

- changes to the work environment resulting from implementation
- team organization
- training used
- group dynamics of the new team
- rewards, incentives, and other sources of motivation used
- measures used to assess the success of the team.

This study is not intended to provide a definitive implementation guide, but rather to provide a series of IPD lessons learned from private industry.

According to Dr. W. Edwards Deming, a pioneer in the field of quality, one of the obstacles to implementation of a quality program such as IPD is the "search for examples" that companies undertake to find a procedure they can follow instead of planning their own route (3). Lessons learned from the case study may be used to educate organizations starting or continuing their transition to IPD. It is essential that case studies of companies that have implemented IPD concepts be included as examples of its application. Case studies increase the database of applications, and provide a source for an IPD curriculum essential to further the understanding of its principles. The universal understanding of these principles is the key to overcoming the barriers to implementing IPD.

BACKGROUND

The concept is not a new idea. It evolved from previous definitions and practices of systems engineering. The use of IPD in commercial industry has resulted in successful and efficient product development. Bosma was chosen for its experience and publicized success in IPD, as well as for its understanding of the problems of implementing IPD. Bosma is a small machine shop company that generates some $6 million in annual revenues. Marinus Bosma, a Dutch immigrant, started the business in 1973 in a barn behind his home. He wanted to fabricate machine bases, frames, weldments, and other specialty products. It was a typical job shop, and Mr. Bosma was the sole manager over twelve employees. The company grew rapidly to about seventy employees today, and is now run by President and Chief Executive Officer Lee Bosma and Vice President of Engineering Ben Bosma, both sons of Marinus. Marinus Bosma now works as a consultant in company research and development.

IPD IN BOSMA

The principles of IPD, with its concept of teaming, represent a general framework that may be tailored to the specific needs of an organization. It may be helpful to draw an analogy to manufacturing a car. All cars have the same basic purpose—to provide transportation. They share several common features, such as wheels, doors, seats, and an engine. Each car manufacturer takes the basic idea of "car" and determines design, performance, features, and color. In the same way, Bosma Corporation used the basic principles of IPD to implement a teaming approach to product development. Within Bosma, the teams are referred to as self-directed work teams (SDWTs). A self-directed work team integrates personnel from all areas involved in manufacturing a product to address problems, work together, and exchange ideas. SDWTs also empower employees to take on more responsibility and make decisions in areas previously reserved for management, such as subcontractor qualification, inventory management, and customer relations. This study focused on Bosma's M-1 tank ammunition door SDWT which manufactures 300-pound steel doors for the Army's M-1 tank. Interviewees were divided into upper management and team members. Upper management consisted of the vice president for engineering, the chief executive officer, the plant manager, and the team leader. Team members included two computer numerical control (CNC) operators, two edge work machine and mill operators, and two coating specialists.

WORK ENVIRONMENT

The M-1 tank ammunition door project was Bosma's first venture into a long-term production contract. Previously, the company operated mainly as a small-volume job shop. At first, Bosma assigned a program manager to the M-1 tank ammunition door contract. As the project evolved, upper management found that the existing organizational structure had become unproductive. The program manager was soon overwhelmed by the level of detail associated with the project, including government requirements for schedule, cost, and assembly detail. Foremen were running machines while supervising other employees. A marked morale problem developed, employee turnover and absenteeism increased, and a general air of apathy settled on the employees. Management decided that a change was needed. Upper management learned about SDWTs from a consultant and conducted further research by visiting other companies. Management wanted to concentrate on improving job satisfaction as well as productivity. It concluded that a production contract lent itself to a teaming environment and decided to try SDWTs. The transition to SDWTs was not easy. Team members reported a major barrier to SDWTs was accepting the idea of making decisions without prior management approval. The team members were not certain that they were fully empowered to make decisions which impacted the project, and only through encouragement from management were team members finally convinced that they were empowered. Another major barrier reported by team members was lack of communication within the team. Team members were initially hesitant to voice their opinions for fear of retaliation. Some team members tended to dominate the early team meetings, while others were withdrawn. Team members solved this problem by encouraging individual input in an atmosphere of non-attribution.

A third barrier involved willingness to change the process. Team members were accustomed to following specific procedures from a foreman, and consequently were not motivated to improve the process. SDWTs instilled ownership of the process within the team members, who concentrated on improving, rather than simply repeating, established procedures. Management found the transition no easier than the team. Upper management reported a major barrier to SDWTs was releasing traditional management control over the workers. Under SDWTs, management no longer dictated procedures to workers. Management's lack of detailed knowledge of team member activities was difficult to accept at first. As productivity and processes improved, however, management gained confidence in the abilities of team members to manage themselves.

Another barrier was convincing team members they were truly empowered. Management overcame this barrier by encouraging team members to take responsibility and by supporting team decisions. Both team members and upper management reported the problem of foremen's roles during team initiation. Team members were unsure of who supervised them, the team leader or shop foreman. In addition, shop foremen believed they still controlled team members. To tackle this problem, management defined clearly the roles of both team members and non-members within the new framework.

TEAM ORGANIZATION

To set up the team, management identified all steps in manufacturing the ammunition doors and identified those workers qualified to accomplish each step. Team members were chosen both for technical expertise and ability to work with others, with an emphasis on the latter. At the first team meeting, management presented the SDWT framework and information on project schedule and cost to the team members. Members were then asked for inputs to management's ideas. The team members decided whether any features of the existing manufacturing process needed improvement. Management and team members then collaborated to establish the team focus and set quality and productivity goals.

Team Members' Views of Team Leader

Team members defined the roles of the team leader as team motivator, troubleshooter, team representative to outside vendors and customers, goal setter, and facilitator. As motivator, the team leader encouraged members to improve their processes continuously and maintained the team focus. As troubleshooter, the leader worked with team members to solve any problems beyond members' control that might degrade team performance. The team leader also represented the team to the customer to address customer requirements and product concerns. As the contact to outside vendors, the team leader ensured timely delivery of materials and parts required by the team. Finally, the team leader established goals for the team and facilitated the team's progress toward those goals.

Management's View of Team Leader

Management described the team leader's roles as communicator, facilitator, problem solver, and motivator. As communicator, the team leader relayed ideas between team members and management. As facilitator, the team leader tackled any obstacles outside the team members' direct control. The team leader was also a problem solver beyond the scope of the project, addressing personnel issues and conducting performance reviews. Finally, as motivator, the team leader encouraged team members to deal directly with vendors and suppliers whenever possible.

Team Members' Views of Themselves

Team members held themselves responsible for all aspects of their jobs, including product quality and machine maintenance. They were responsible for bringing process and product innovations to management's attention. Team members took the initiative to set the schedule, meet goals set by upper management, and increase proficiency by cross-training. Finally, team members were committed to satisfying their customer, defined as the next person receiving their product.

Management's View of Team Members

Management's definition of the role of team members paralleled the members'. These roles included cross-training within sections and communication among members. Management also believed team members should consider all suggestions equally, regardless of the suggester's status. To encourage such open communication, the team should re-emphasize the role of the individual. Both management and team members believed they could be part of more than one team if each member's primary team schedule was not impacted.

Interactions

Though not official team members, consultants, suppliers, and customers were an important part of team activity. Consultants acted as independent evaluators of team progress and as team trainers. Suppliers were made aware of the SDWT and their responsibilities to team members, including supplying detailed information about their products to team members to enhance quality control. Customers were in contact with each team member on a one-to-one basis, and were fully aware of each team member's responsibilities.

The customer quality inspector was considered an informal team member. Team members reported project planning requirements were simplified because of decreased middle management direction and more open communication between team members. Some members reported more planning was required because they were responsible for more aspects of their jobs under SDWTs. Upper management reported more advanced planning was required under SDWTs, since all aspects of the project were considered up-front, rather than incrementally as work progressed. Planning in advance decreased the amount of planning required at later stages. Some management personnel reported less planning was required, because under SDWTs more responsibility was being delegated to team members.

TRAINING AND EDUCATION

Team members received their technical training on the job. Of all their courses, members reported that training in statistical process control (SPC) was most valuable. To expand their proficiency, members were cross-trained whenever possible. To gain insight and encourage innovation, team members toured both customer and vendor plants. Both upper management and team members considered plant trips significant in encouraging innovation. Training evolved from being process-centered to team-centered, focusing on environmental issues such as conflict resolution, positive attitudes, and communication of ideas to the company. Upper management first attended training in total quality management and leadership principles. Management then researched SDWTs in literature and attended seminars on teaming. Finally, management visited other companies to observe examples of SDWTs in the workplace.

GROUP DYNAMICS AND COMMUNICATION

Upper management established several guidelines for team interaction, including how to run a meeting, length of a meeting, and confidentiality within a meeting. Management stressed participation from all, and mandated that all ideas receive equal consideration. All issues, both personal and technical, were to be addressed and resolved before the end of each meeting.

Management stressed the need for open communication within the team. Team members were taught the responsibilities they had to each other, and the importance of continuous flow of information. Status boards were developed to allow any team member to track the ammunition doors and parts. To ensure communication in the early stages of team building, management declared weekly meetings mandatory. Team members were also encouraged to learn about each other's jobs and fill in when needed.

Before SDWTs, there was no open communication between employees and management. The forced use of the chain of command filtered worker inputs to upper management, causing mistakes from misinterpretation and delaying decisions. Many workers complained that concerns and suggestions were not addressed in a timely manner, lost in paperwork, or ignored altogether. The previous autocratic management style also inhibited feedback from workers fearing retaliation.

SDWTs overcame many of these barriers. Although upper management mandated open lines of communication, some team members were unwilling to make decisions for fear of retribution. With the transfer of responsibility to team members, management knew less about the daily activities of team members; however, management believed such detailed knowledge was no longer necessary. Management considered formal suggestion procedures disempowering; workers would not submit suggestions unless they had reasons to believe they would be incorporated. By opening direct lines of communication, management overcame this problem.

Team progress was reported to company personnel in several ways. Team information was publicized in company-level meetings and through a monthly company newsletter. The company's monthly suggestion rewards were also publicized.

MOTIVATION, REWARDS, AND INCENTIVES

When SDWTs were first introduced, there were mixed reactions from team members. Some members were highly motivated about employee empowerment and the opportunity to express themselves, while others were skeptical of the new approach. As implementation progressed and positive results were realized, team members gained more confidence in the new structure, and maintained a consistently high level of motivation. They cited experience as the key to overcoming early skepticism toward SDWTs. The demanding production schedule made each member dependent on another; any deficiencies in a specific area were quickly brought to the attention of all. Most team members felt confident that any deficiencies could be remedied by direct confrontation at the team level, while a few still felt hesitant to approach others personally. Some team members reported that the company-wide profit sharing policy motivated them to meet the delivery schedule with a quality product. Others were motivated by more simple compensation, such as a pat on the back or satisfaction in meeting a goal.

According to upper management, early team attitudes toward SDWTs were mixed. Some members were highly motivated by the novelty of the concept; others resisted due to fear and unfamiliarity with SDWTs. Team members soon overcame their hesitation as the new concept proved itself. Positive feedback from customers and results of the new process placed motivation quite high. Most importantly, upper management's consistent support of team members silenced any skepticism and proved company commitment to SDWTs. Upper management did not intervene in cases of below standard performance of team members, allowing problems to be solved at the team level.

Although no formal rewards were established at the team level, management had several ways of motivating team members. These included a pay scale indexed to proficiency level and cross-training, updates of sales figures in the company newsletter, and a sales thermometer in the shop. The best motivator of all, according to management, were the team members themselves. Team members were self-motivated to do a good job, and demanded much more of themselves than management had.

Team members reported that SDWTs, despite their emphasis on the team rather than the individual, did not diminish promotion opportunities.

Promotions and raises within the company were still tied to individual performance. Additionally, team members felt that there were more opportunities for recognition and advancement within SDWTs, since it is easier to be recognized in a smaller group.

Upper management stated that promotions within SDWTs would only be a concern if all members were paid equally and pay raises were tied to team performance. Rather than being viewed as a threat to personal authority, SDWTs were credited with freeing the team leader to conduct strategic planning and support activities.

Team members were convinced that SDWTs renewed their commitment to quality and continuous improvement. All team members understood that they were responsible for their own work as well as the whole team's product. Members' names were placed on each completed item, and pride of ownership ensured the high quality of the final product.

Upper management believed that SDWTs emphasized quality to team members and resulted in significantly improved products. There were no quality control inspectors on the team; team members were held personally responsible for the quality of their product.

The change to SDWTs resulted in several personnel reassignments. Some skeptical workers quit, stating that the level of responsibility required of them was too great. Others were transferred off the team but remained within the company. New workers were hired for the team as a result of expansion and increased workload. The new hires were excited about empowerment, and displayed positive attitudes about working in a team environment.

MEASUREMENTS

To measure the success of SDWTs, upper management began with the company vision and mission statements. The vision statement was a long-term goal for the company, The mission statement explained how the vision would be achieved. Management then quantified the mission statement by setting long- and short-term goals and specified the measurements used to track each goal. After graphically flowcharting the manufacturing process, management chose several measures to track progress. These measures were later reevaluated to determine their usefulness. Measures determined not useful by team members and management were checked only periodically or discarded altogether.

Team members were responsible for tracking the measurements on a daily basis. Items tracked included number of rejects, productivity, quality, cost, and schedule compliance. Team members' reported success of SDWTs was evident by a decrease in the number of rejects, increased productivity, and improved quality. Schedules were met and exceeded, and costs decreased significantly.

Team members used SPC extensively to track part tolerances at each work station. Management reviewed SPC charts to ensure continuous quality improvement, monitoring deviations from established standards. When management decided the deviations were no longer significant, they were measured only periodically. Other tools used by management included long-term schedule charts and accounting reports. Long-term schedule charts tracked compliance to the delivery schedule and forecasted the likelihood of meeting future deliveries. Accounting reports were used to show time spent on the job as well as cost and repairs. Productivity measures, such as dollars per person per year, were provided as part of the financial audit.

The team measured customer satisfaction through direct customer feedback, and established an unwritten rule to meet any customer need. Team members considered product acceptability the ultimate measure of customer satisfaction and visited the M-1 tank plant to discuss expectations of their customer regarding the quality of the ammunition doors. Upper management maintained open lines of communication with customer personnel in contact with team members and measured customer satisfaction through quality surveys. The surveys were independently constructed by a consultant to avoid bias.

Since implementation of SDWTs, survey results have been extremely positive; however, such positive feedback, although encouraging, seldom identifies areas needing improvement.

CONCLUSIONS AND RECOMMENDATIONS

Teaming Framework

We have used the results of the case study to compile a generic sequence of steps for implementing an integrated product team:

1. *Develop vision and mission statements.* Management must establish clear vision and mission statements to give the company a strategic goal.

2. *Learn about teaming concept.* Management must research literature, attend seminars, and visit other companies to learn specific details of teaming.

3. *Conduct feasibility study.* Management must assess the practicality of implementing teaming within the organization.

4. *Commit fully to teaming.* Once the decision is made to implement teams, management must commit fully or teaming will fail.

5. *Sell the teaming approach.* Management must sell the teaming approach to company members. The company culture must change to accommodate the new approach.

6. *Identify pilot product team.* Select one product to demonstrate the advantages of teaming to the company and to highlight weaknesses.

7. *Chart process to identify team members.* The process used to manufacture the product must be flowcharted to identify all personnel involved.

8. *Recruit team players.* Team players must be chosen based on technical competence and personality, with an emphasis on the latter.

9. *Identify team leader and define the roles.* A team leader must be chosen from within the organization and the role clearly understood by all team members.

10. *Define roles of team members.* All team members should be identified to each other and their relationship to the overall process should be defined clearly.

11. *Define roles of all other personnel.* Roles of all personnel within the company who may have an impact on the team must be clearly defined.

12. *Set guidelines for team interaction.* Establish and reinforce open communication among team members and management. Eliminate any barriers to communication.

13. *Train team members.* Team members should be trained in the methods used for successful teaming. This includes technical training, particularly in SPC, and human relations training.

14. *Establish motivation, rewards, and incentives program.* Identify rewards and incentives, both internal and external, that are to be used to motivate the team.

15. *Set team goals and begin project.* Goals related to the company vision and mission must be established by all team members prior to project initiation.

16. *Cross-train team members.* Team members should be cross-trained as soon as team confidence is established.

17. *Seek continuous improvement.* Management must encourage continuous improvement of the processes and products developed by the team. This includes developing measurements to track progress of improvements.

LESSONS LEARNED

The case study provided several lessons learned on the implementation of integrated teams. These lessons are categorized under management policies and general policies. Management policies describe recommendations specific to management, as reported by upper management in the case study. General policies describe recommendations not specific to any one group, and represent inputs from both management and team members in the study.

Management Policies

1. Management must fully commit to teaming. Anything less than full commitment by management will result in failure of the team.

2. Management can only empower team members by example. Upper management is reluctant to allow team members to be autonomous. Management must accept the fact that those closest to the work know how to accomplish it.

3. The transition of management style is difficult but essential for integrated teams to work. Under teams, management's job is to lead more and manage less. Roles of former supervisors and foremen must be redefined to avoid conflicts.

4. Executives should conduct self and peer evaluations to measure their effectiveness.

5. Flatten the organization. Management layers increase the probability of operator error. Communication through a chain of command filters out valuable information from both ends of the chain.

General Policies

1. Communication between all levels is a top priority. Direct communication between management, team members, and customers encourages innovation. Management and the team must consider all suggestions from team members.

2. Train all company members in teaming and human relations. Jealousy of non-team members can be avoided by management defining roles in the teaming plan.

3. Training should mix members from different teams to increase organization cohesiveness.

4. A baseline series of measures must be established, against which the success of the teams may be gauged.

5. Choice of team members is crucial to team success. Members should be chosen based on technical expertise and ability to work in a group. Teams should be allowed to hire and fire members to maintain team effectiveness.

6. Assemble teams as early as possible. Ideally, teams should be set up prior to contract award.

7. Allow time for employees to adjust to the teaming approach. Responsibilities should be given to team members incrementally. Teaming is not for everyone. Some workers are not comfortable without direct supervision.

8. Pride of ownership improves motivation and product quality. Management should present strategic goals to workers and let them determine how to meet them.

9. Responsibilities and priorities must be defined for those who support multiple teams.

SUMMARY

This study provided a detailed report of the implementation of an integrated product team. The purpose of this research was to enhance understanding of the IPT concept and to facilitate implementation. The areas addressed in the study were work environment, team organization, training, group dynamics, motivation, and measurement. The most significant findings on work environment were that the organization's leadership should commit to the teaming idea and sell it to the organization's members.

REFERENCES

1. President's Blue-Ribbon Commission on Defense Management. 1986. *A Quest for Excellence, Final Report to the President by the President's Blue-Ribbon Commission on Defense Management.* June. Washington: GPO.

2. HQ AFMC/EN. 1992. "Integrated Product Development and Supporting Initiatives." Paper. July 20.

3. Walton, M. P. 1990. *Deming Management at Work.* New York: Putnam Publishing Group.

Study Questions

IMPLEMENTING INTEGRATED PRODUCT DEVELOPMENT: A CASE STUDY OF BOSMA MACHINE AND TOOL CORPORATION

1. The Bosma Machine and Tool Corporation experienced a number of barriers during the transition to self-directed work teams (SDWTs) from its previous organization. What were some of those barriers?

2. When a new team is put together to run a project, anxiety among members can run very high. As a project manager said, "Moving a team member's desk from one side of the room to the other can sometimes be just about as traumatic as moving someone from Chicago to Manila." What can the project manager do in order to reduce the initial stress among team members?

3. What are the characteristics of an effective team? Do you think these characteristics are present in less effective groups?

4. There are numerous examples in the literature of companies using self-directed work teams. Review the literature to find another example of the use of these kinds of teams. Discuss the organization of the teams and the benefits gained from their use.

5. Some opponents of the team approach might argue that the culture of the United States is too individualistic to support this kind of organizational design and that Americans are not predisposed to work as part of a team. Defend or refute this position.

How ICL Used Project Management Techniques to Introduce a New Product Range

Peter Kayes, School of Technology and Information Studies, Thames Valley University, U.K.

International Journal of Project Management, October 1995, pp. 321–28

ICL was a product of the United Kingdom (U.K.) merger mania of the 1960s, when the Labor government endeavored to create strong U.K. companies to protect the U.K.'s technological base from United States (U.S.) domination. However, within a few years of its formation, the U.K.'s leading computer supplier was in trouble. A new managing director was brought in from one of the major U.S. computer suppliers, and he brought a new management style with him. This paper looks at how project management techniques were used at ICL in the 1970s and how they helped the company to cope with organizational challenges and to manage the risks of introducing a new product range of mainframe computers into the market. Examples of successful projects that were undertaken during this period are provided. The paper also speculates on the extent to which this has helped ICL survive through the late 1980s and early 1990s, during which time the industry has undergone major structural changes. The experiences and project management techniques described are still relevant to ICL and the information technology industry as a whole today.

I worked in the U.K. computer industry from 1967 to 1982, before moving into higher education to teach. For most of this time I was with ICL, where I witnessed the transformation of a traditionally run U.K. company into a project-driven organization. This resulted from the appointment of a new managing director and his perception of how the company needed to operate to stay in business.

I spent some eight years as a project manager in the remodeled company, working in a variety of situations with different project structures. This paper looks at the impact of the introduction of a project management approach in the company.

BACKGROUND

ICL was created in 1968 as a result of a merger between ICT (International Computers and Tabulators) and English Electric Computers; it was to be the mainstay of the U.K. computer industry. The merger brought together the major U.K. suppliers of commercial computer systems at that time; they had between them some 50 percent of the U.K. mainframe market.

The merger was encouraged by the U.K. Labor government, which took office in 1964, and believed that the indigenous U.K. computer industry was on the point of extinction [1]. This recognized the realities of the investment costs of competing in the international computer market. ICT had a highly successful range of computers, the 1900 series, and some 2000 of these systems had been sold. Its architecture was based on 6 bit characters and was viewed by some as dated. English Electric was marketing a range of computers known as the System 4 range, which was IBM 360 compatible and was made in the U.K. under license from the RCA Corporation. Only 200 systems had been sold, but the architecture was competitive and used 8 bit bytes. These two ranges of computers were incompatible with each other.

A decision was taken to develop a new range of computers as a result of a study of various options. The technical case for the choice was based on competitive comparisons and research and development work worldwide. It drew strongly on work being carried out at Manchester University, U.K., where the MU5 was the latest in a line of developments which had led to other major advances in their time, such as the Atlas computer. It also drew on research at the Massachusetts Institute of Technology, U.S., and the University of Eindhoven, Netherlands, where Dijkstra had been developing concepts for structuring operating systems (2).

The marketing decision carried risks. The justifications given for the decision included technical and internal political factors and not simply commercial reasons. It was thought that a new ICL product would help to build the new corporate identity, and this case was advanced as a break with the past. The strategy was high risk because of the usual need for customers to be able to transfer their programs onto a new machine. Lack of forward compatibility removed the competitive advantage normally enjoyed by a supplier in terms of its existing customers. To try to sell customers machines which were incompatible with their present ones increased the risk of losing them to competitors. A customer who had been tied to ICL for years by the proprietary design of the software would have a free choice of supplier when considering a move to the "new range." However, on the other hand, there were the technical issues of the two existing incompatible ranges and the outdated design of the majority of the company's systems.

The development of the "new range" (the 2900 series as it became known) took five years from the initial design documents to the early prototype systems. Some 200 programmers worked on the operating system alone, and this cost 1,000 staff years of development effort before the first version was released for limited field use in 1974/75. The cost of this development had been budgeted for, but the work took longer than expected, and it was toward the end of this period that the managing director of ICL, Geoff Cross, turned his attention to the development side of the company.

Geoff Cross was recruited from Univac in the early 1970s to rescue ICL, which was losing money in a stagnant market; there was also increasing competition from minicomputer manufacturers such as Digital Equipment Corporation and Data General. His first priority was to address the sales situation, which he did with considerable success, increasing sales volume by sharpening up the sales force, introducing new products such as the 2903/4 minicomputers, and developing new ways of selling, such as the creation of customer centers offering bureau services.

By 1974, time was running out for the older models as the customer base was being won over to the new 2900 systems. The sales volume of the old systems was declining, and the first 2900 systems were due to be shipped at the beginning of 1975. The business plan required that they be delivered on time to maintain the revenue stream. The director of the systems programming division (SPD) was having difficulty holding development work to deadlines.

MANAGEMENT OF LARGE DEVELOPMENTAL PROJECTS

CADES Approach to Software Development

For some years, the SPD had used project management techniques, such as PERT, to help monitor and control development work. From the beginning, the VME/B operating system development work was supported by the use of a database system, CADES (computer-aided design and evaluation system), and modular design techniques. CADES was used as both a management tool and a design aid.

A structured approach to software development was becoming fashionable at this time, after years of anarchy when it was unusual for a computer programmer to stick to deadlines. Folklore indicated that any program would take twice as long to produce as planned, regardless of whatever forecast was made. The computer industry's version of Parkinson's Law was that work expanded to fill twice the time available! In an attempt to bring more professionalism to software development, engineering techniques were adopted. This is one facet of what is now referred to as "software engineering."

As in network analysis, structured software design and modular programming techniques require a problem to be broken down into a series of small manageable tasks. A module of code is then written to perform each task. A sound design will identify how many modules are required and how they interrelate. It is possible to design each task to require a similar amount of code. On the basis of experience, it is possible to estimate how much testing is required to get a module working. This makes it possible to estimate fairly accurately how much work is required to complete the overall job and to monitor progress. CADES was used to support this management approach.

A team of 200 systems staff was involved in the development of VME/B for a period of five years through to the early releases. This amounted to a huge project that comprised in excess of 1,000 staff years of effort. This was a massive investment, which cost some £50M in today's terms, that had to be managed.

A central design team of twenty people was responsible for the development of the operating system, which was divided into subsystems, as shown in Figure 1. Each designer had responsibility for one subsystem. The designer monitored the production of the subsystem under the direction of the chief designer. The production was undertaken by programmers in teams of ten to twenty, under a line manager. Each of these was responsible for writing the modules of a subsystem, and one member of the design team was responsible for the work of each programming team. A central support team of twenty was responsible for running the CADEs database, which was an overhead of 10 percent of development costs.

As modules were written, their specifications were coded and entered into the CADES database, which performed certain checks, eliminating some syntax and logic errors. Software interfaces were checked for correctness and access permission. Procedure calls and data definitions were generated, thus reducing the risk of errors as well as capturing design and usage data.

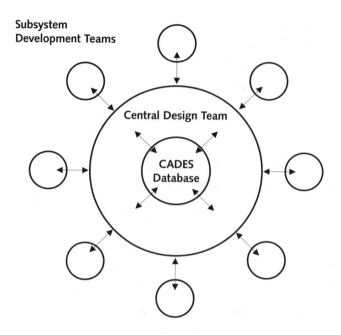

Subsystem Development Teams

Central Design Team

CADES Database

FIGURE 1   VME DEVELOPMENT TEAM

Modules were expected to consist of no more than 150 lines of code, to avoid the problems associated with long unstructured programs. It was expected that each module would take one programmer one week to write. The logical structure defining which modules were required was produced at an early design stage for "sign-off" by the designers. It was thus possible to estimate the total time required to write the software and to monitor progress. Problems not addressed at this stage were those of system testing and the need to rewrite or "enhance" modules as developments progressed.

The benefits of CADES can only be estimated, as it was used on a unique project on the basis of faith and experience of previous similar developments. The rationale was that 80 percent of the costs associated with software are incurred by maintenance work post release. The objective of CADES was to provide a discipline and databank that might be capable of halving these costs. Whether this was ever realized cannot be measured. There were many other benefits, some more tangible than others:

• The database provided mechanisms for change control, and version numbers for each module.

• The number of bugs created during development was expected to be significantly lower than for a conventional process, because of the code generation and automated checking. It was thought that the number of these was at least 50 percent less than the typical number in conventional software development at that time.

• The database provided lists of modules that used items of data and other similar cross-references. These could be used by the designers to identify the impact of any design change (how many and which modules would be affected), thus helping in the evaluation of a proposal and in the estimation of the cost of implementing it.

• The database was used to produce microfiche listings of the code of the system and, ultimately, online diagnostic access for support staff dealing with customer problems. These processes would have been more expensive to provide separately.

The management approach used up to this point combined features of a functional hierarchy and features of a coordinated matrix (4). It had limited success while all the developments were within the area of responsibility of the senior manager in charge of VME/B; but, as soon as other software teams such as the compiler writers team became involved, there were disputes about who was responsible for what, where the causes of bugs lay, and so on. Further measures had to be taken.

Project Managing the System Releases

The SPD had always relied on a traditional hierarchical management structure, and it had no experience of coping with the challenges it now faced. A secondary matrix structure was introduced as part of the new management style by the team of U.S. project managers that Geoff Cross had recruited. Their brief was to make sure that the delivery dates were met. Their direct line to the top meant that when they wanted something done, it got done. Their approach was never to accept that something could not be done, but to ask, "What do you need to get it done?"

This simple question was central to their success. It enabled people to ask for additional resources to meet targets, rather than allowing them to use the lack of them as an excuse for missing targets. If someone asked and was convincing, he got what was asked for. The direct line to the top meant that budget provision could be found, resources transferred, or savings made elsewhere, in less critical areas if necessary. The provision of short-term resources in selected areas is relatively inexpensive in a company with 30,000 staff. In some cases, staff members were transferred or seconded from other parts of the company, with very little adverse impact in the short term. In some cases, secondees were people who needed training in the new products and so there was a direct benefit.

This approach illustrates the advantages of overriding normal line structure, in which managers can be reluctant to release people because of their focus on short-term service and operational needs, despite the long-term strategic advantage of investing in staff training. If a line manager does not have any direct responsibility for a new product, releasing people is seen as a problem.

In a highly technical area of development such as this, throwing resources at the problem does not necessarily solve it. When particularly difficult problems were encountered, the question became, "Who do you need to solve this?" and the key specialists were enlisted. In other cases, the decision was to go without a feature until it could be fixed and to release the product with "known shortfalls" rather than delay the release. The justification for this was that it enabled progress to be made along the critical path in all the areas which worked satisfactorily while the problem was investigated.

The approach of finding additional resources concentrated the minds of those responsible for the new products. It made them take responsibility for their actions as they had no excuse for doing otherwise. The blame culture was banished, and this contrasted with the previous management style of shouting at people to do things without providing any additional resources.

For me, this was a very positive introduction to a different form of project management.

Other structures were established to reinforce a project management style throughout the organization and to short-circuit line decision-making:

• A national network of experienced project managers was set up to communicate via project manager bulletin sheets.

• Quarterly meetings were organized to identify common matters of process, expose specific successes and failures, and identify mechanisms to overcome corporate bureaucracy.

• Monthly meetings, latterly called "troikas," brought together the three key operational players from across the organization at a tactical level (from the manufacturing, hardware/software validation, and customer services departments) who had the opportunity to fix anything, allocating materials and skills directly to a given task anywhere in the world.

Multidisciplinary teams were brought together to build, test, and then support the early releases of the software. Through direct reporting to a control center established by the "mafia," the traditional management blocks inherent in the SPD hierarchy were bypassed. When a resource was needed, the director of the SPD was instructed to find it. The cost in relation to the total SPD budget was tiny, but when someone is buried in a hierarchy, it is difficult to get a cry for help heard.

The team responsible for these system tests used milestones to measure success. Standardized estimates of the number of "test shots" needed per module were used during alpha and beta testing. These were based on experience and were related to the complexity of the module. They were often low, perhaps consisting of one or two shots only, and they provided good progress monitoring information weekly.

Milestones were created on the path to the first delivery dates, and they were immovable. Resources had to be deployed to ensure that activities did not jeopardize the achievement of a milestone. Concern that the system was not ready was not allowed to delay delivery, although most people thought that they would be given more time to get it "working" right up until the last minute. The software was shipped on the due dates.

One of the challenges posed by high-technology products, especially during the early stages of a new project introduction, is that hardware and software innovation is a regular if not weekly phenomenon. It is quite impossible for a hardware and software configuration to be system tested in a cloned validation or test environment. Local and network cabling can only be tested on-site. Real workloads always test a system in ways different from a simulation. These and other local environmental conditions mean that only a test on-site is a conclusive confidence test. Even then, ongoing developments such as new releases of software or changes in the customer workload create major continuing challenges for project management.

Establishing a Support Structure

ICL had to find a way to ensure that the staff members out in the field preparing customers' systems received the support that they needed. These customer support teams had to work with a very fragile system that was delivered on time but had a great many bugs and was largely untested in the live environment. They also had little relevant first-hand technical experience.

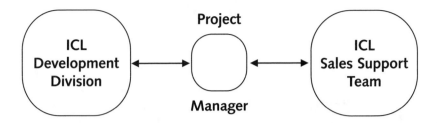

FIGURE 2   PROJECT MANAGER AS INTERFACE BETWEEN SALES AND DEVELOPMENT STAFF

The novelty of the new product was such that a project approach was needed to create an initial support structure. This had three facets:

- a central support team to which staff were seconded
- project managers appointed for key accounts to negotiate with and share responsibility with operational managers
- dedicated project teams responsible for working with early customers to help ensure the installations were successful.

The central support team was a natural development of the functions carried out during the final systems tests. New staff were drafted into the team from other areas of the company, such as field engineering support, to help train people for later work on customer sites. A four-shift operation was established to ensure twenty-four-hour support for the customer support teams, who were working under enormous time pressures. The specialist technical knowledge required was to be found in this support unit, and the team acted as a means to spread this expertise through cross-training while the staff were on shift. Large shift bonuses were offered to compensate for the twenty-four hour seven-day-week pattern. The overall cost was again low in the context of the SPD budget, but the arrangement broke all the rules in terms of demands on staff and the level of rewards paid to compensate them. The combination worked because sufficient numbers of able people came forward to join the unit. Good management of people issues was essential in making the package successful once the most technically appropriate approach had been identified.

The SPD was then asked to appoint project managers to take responsibility for supporting key customer project teams. The purpose of this was to provide a mechanism for a sales support team to obtain specific support for its project from the development staff (see Figure 2). The SPD project manager was responsible for serving as liaison between sales and development staff to ensure that the technical specification required to meet customer needs was met by agreed dates. The sales staff knew what the customer wanted, and the development staff knew what was going to be available and by when; these did not always match up.

The project managers appointed by the SPD knew who to talk to, and they were technically competent to understand the issues and options. This often meant adjusting the sales team's expectations about what was realistically possible within a reasonable budget. In some cases, prices were negotiated to bring developments forward by providing additional effort for which the sales teams were prepared to pay; in other cases, the availability dates of key facilities were adjusted and some brought forward when other facilities

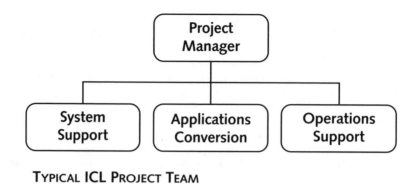

FIGURE 3   TYPICAL ICL PROJECT TEAM

could be traded out. On this occasion, the members of the sales team had to concentrate on what they really wanted, rather than demand everything. The key question was, "What will it cost?" By now, the development staff had learned not to say that something could not be done. Instead, they estimated the cost and impact of responding to a request. The project manager also had the job of ensuring that any agreement was then fulfilled by monitoring the delivery of the items negotiated.

Once the system was ready, responsibility was then transferred to the dedicated customer project team. This was a relatively small-scale implementation project.

DEDICATED PROJECT TEAMS

The major issue for both ICL and its customers in relation to the introduction of the new computer systems was the containment of risk. To this end, ICL used elaborate procedures to ensure that all sales proposals had been signed off by senior managers across the company before orders were sanctioned: the so-called "Blue Border" procedure. This constituted a detailed project plan describing the configuration, applications, finances, and support proposals.

For the introduction of the early 2900 systems into customer sites, the company adopted a policy of creating a dedicated project team headed by a senior project manager for each customer. This was part of the sales proposal, and the cost of the project team was taken into account in the profit and loss calculations included in the Blue Border. The early appointments of project managers were all made by the senior support manager, one of the "mafia."

The first fifty installations had such project teams. Their sizes varied according to the value and complexity of the installation. There was a relatively larger size and company contribution for the earlier systems of these fifty. The sales force had been particularly effective in convincing these customers of the need to protect their major investments through sound project control to minimize the shared risk of failure. The company also made a major contribution by providing scarce specialist technical skills to help the customers through these early development days.

A typical project comprised around ten staff years of support over a two-year period, although some were much larger. The team offered specialist skills to help each customer prepare for her new installation, as shown in

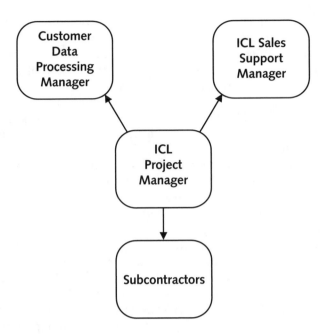

RELATIONSHIPS TO BE MANAGED BY PROJECT MANAGER

Figure 3. Delivery of the system was midway through this period, and much of the preparatory work consisted of conversion of programs to run on the new machine. Either the customer resourced this (in some cases, this amounted to fifty or more staff years of work), or it was subcontracted.

My job as project manager for one of these installations in the local government market had many facets. I had to recruit a suitable team to support the customer. I had to clarify the customer requirements and match these to the availability of hardware and software. I also had to negotiate with subcontractors, acting as a go-between for the customer and contractor when these were within the ICL group (see Figure 4). This inevitably entailed some renegotiation, both with the customer and within the company. Each project pioneered something. My site was the first site to be required to run a full-production workload for the customer and replace an existing system. Most installations up to that point had been used for development purposes only. The cost justification to the customer hinged around the old system being removed within one year. From the company's point of view, future orders from other customers in this sector of the market depended upon this installation being seen to be a success. I was in a strong position to get agreement for what was needed within the company and to obtain customer agreement to proposals that were realistic if it helped it to stay within budget. This was achieved by adjusting its expectations to what was possible within the time-scale and agreeing to standards by which success could be measured.

A project definition was drawn up by the project team, in consultation with customer staff, as a detailed statement of our mutual understanding of its requirements, taking into account the state of development of the product. This differed from the original sales proposal but was a negotiated and more detailed derivative of it. Arrangements were agreed upon for monitoring the work of project team members so that the customer would be willing to accept invoices for this as agreed in the sales terms.

Within the company, I was required to report monthly to a project review meeting held by a senior support manager. There was thus internal accountability to someone with relevant experience who was able to monitor the risks, test my knowledge of the current state of developments in the company and on-site, and explore my contingency plans. This review was important as there was no previous experience in this sales area of installing a 2900 system. The local support staff and managers needed to learn fast and were able to do this through involvement with the project and attendance at the meetings.

Part of the reporting included an update on the project milestones that had been drawn up. These were derived from the agreed project definition and our view of what was needed to meet this. Milestones were recorded and monitored centrally for all the 2900 projects at this time, along with project status reports indicating whether things were under control or going wrong. A green-amber-red system was used.

I used a combination of PERT networks and bar (Gantt) charts to monitor the state of the project and the resourcing needs. This was all done manually, largely because of the relatively small scale of the project, which involved no more than six ICL people over a two-year period. I had previously used a computerized PERT system on a project when I had to report progress to partners in the U.S. every two weeks. Although this project was of a similar size, the computer-produced output added credibility to our progress reports!

Performance standards that were agreed included serviceability and usability statistics measured in terms of the mean time between failures (MTBF) and the percentage of computer time that was used on productive work. The customer had not bothered with any such statistics on his previous system, knowing what it could do, and it was essential that we defined procedures for monitoring the system performance in addition to agreeing what would be acceptable. This was essential, not only to test whether we were meeting the agreed levels, but also to monitor improvements over time as a result of actions we took, especially if we fell below the required level. Being cynical, a statistic of 98 percent serviceability also sounds quite impressive, while a period of downtime of three hours a week sounds bad, although the two are equivalent. In reality, actual measurements often present a more favorable picture than impressions. Otherwise, it is only the bad news that is reported. The statistics are essential for objectivity and as a means of measuring progress.

The project was a success. The old 1900 system was switched off in 1978, twelve months after the 2900 system was delivered. All the application programs were running on the new system, and reasonable levels of reliability were being achieved. Fifteen years later, ICL is still the supplier of computer equipment to the site. Two 3900 mainframe processors run many of the applications under VME, although there has latterly been a trend toward the use of Unix boxes, also supplied by ICL. The site heralded considerable success for ICL in the local government market, with many other 2900 systems being ordered and installed after 1977. There were other residual technical problems that had been anticipated and which took several more years to resolve, but the long-term success of the site illustrates that this was considered acceptable by the customer.

The project approach was highly appropriate and very successful for these projects. It gave the project managers high status and considerable power and autonomy to get things done, while there was still accountability to the center. It gave both the company and its customers a significant boost in coming to terms with a major technical and organization challenge. The projects were successful because project staff were able to develop a positive relationship with the customers, were seen to be there to help, and gained the confidence of the customers. The ability of the project managers to cut through the bureaucracy of the company was a key element of this. We were "close to the customer" (5).

In any matrix and express escalation project management system, there have to be some rules. Within ICL, these operated as follows:

• At critical customer system review meetings (CCSRMs), any customer or system problem could be placed on the weekly agenda by almost anyone.

• Inclusion in a CCSRM meant that all faxes were responded to within the first hour, and progress was monitored every four hours, twenty-four hours a day, 365 days a year.

• Special investigation report (SIR) meetings took place every two weeks in the corporate boardroom (attended only by corporate and divisional directors) to monitor any CCSRM actions that had been outstanding for more than one day without a solution or at least a time-framed plan to achieve a satisfactory solution.

Anyone who caused a senior manager or director to take urgent action over a weekend or at night needed the confidence that such escalation was warranted. Equally, woe betide anyone who did not apply enough priority or corrective action, or who over exaggerated minor local issues into priorities. These measures did ensure that serious issues were addressed, and they provided support for the project management structures.

During the second phase of the introduction of the 2900 system (the installation of the next fifty systems), a streamlined structure was used, often with one experienced project manager looking after several sites, each with much smaller project teams. By then, the risks were lower, less was new, and more people who had relevant experience were available. The customers were still exposed to risk because of the scale of the change they were undertaking, and therefore they still needed support, but the risk was by then more one-sided. Customer support became more of a mainstream support responsibility, and the structure gradually changed back to a balanced matrix approach.

PROJECT MANAGERS AS CHAMPIONS

Project management is the natural way to work in the computer industry because of the high degree of novelty of most projects, the dependence on technology, and the high rate of change of this technology. Notwithstanding this, many of the issues faced by project managers are people based, requiring good interpersonal skills and a sound grasp of general management concepts, as I hope I have illustrated by my examples. Ideally, a project manager will have a combination of relevant technical and managerial skills, this being more essential on a small project where the project manager needs to provide technical leadership. On a large project, it is more possible to rely on other members of the team for the technical skills, as long as the project manager is able to exercise good judgment when necessary.

Reference 6 reflects much of the ICL project management style. The ICL project teams were empowered and were forces for innovation. The project manager was the "customer champion" within the company who protected the customers' needs. There was also an element of the project manager being a product champion within the company, helping to identify and resolve problems, some of which were unique to the project at that time.

The role was antibureaucratic, cutting through the lethargy of existing hierarchies. There were exceptions when resistance could still be found, but an empowered project manager does not give up! This is illustrated by a later example when we were developing a performance improvement package (PIP) to help customers get more work through their 2900 systems, addressing a major concern of the customer base about poor performance.

A project team was brought together to pool expertise on how to address the problem. A set of fixes was developed and tested on pilot sites, showing a significant overall improvement in system throughput of about 20 percent for relatively little implementation effort. We wanted to release this package to all sites, and we approached the software distribution center for help. It refused to put our performance manual out with its next mailing because it did not conform to its standards of presentation and editing. The fact that it was addressing an urgent need made no difference. To use the distribution center's system would have caused a delay of at least six months. Instead, we found an alternative source of distribution and support and got it out into the field within one month.

This may appear to be an example of a line operational manager not understanding the dynamic nature of the business, but this is an unfair analysis. It was actually an example of conflicting standards, where two parts of the organization had different objectives. In our view, it was as important for the company to be seen to be responding quickly to concerns as it was to come up with technical solutions. A six-month delay would have rendered the package irrelevant, as the next major software release was planned in that time-scale to incorporate many of the enhancements we had developed.

This final point also illustrates the need to maintain a link between operations and projects. It serves no long-term purpose for project managers to solve problems on a one-off basis and for the organization as a whole not to benefit from this. Solutions must be fed back to ensure that there is no unnecessary reinventing of wheels.

There is not much that I would change if I were applying project management principles today. ICL has delayered, like many other organizations, creating more autonomy, and empowering staff members to determine their own objectives and be accountable accordingly. This was the way we worked in our project teams, and it was a recipe for success, although this can never be guaranteed.

Potential conflicts can sometimes be resolved by reference to the corporate mission (something we did not have in 1979). I would also want to ensure there were mechanisms to share experience without constraining people to do things a particular way.

The "project" culture relates to the management of change, which is something that has always been a feature of the computer industry. Increasingly, this is becoming relevant to other industries and sectors of employment, even the U.K. Civil Service, which is experiencing unprecedented change.

Relevance to ICL Today

The project management approach introduced by Geoff Cross did much to enable ICL to survive the 1970s and the major challenges faced by the company at that time. Many people learned new skills during this period.

When Geoff Cross left the company after five years to return to North America, the company went through a period of uncertainty. The senior managers who took over did not have as sound a grasp of the project management approach, and there was a partial return to the previous hierarchical style of working. Many of us found this period frustrating, being unable to get messages through to the senior levels of the company about what needed to be done.

By 1980, the company was again in difficulty. Robb Wilmot was recruited from Texas Instruments to take over as managing director, and he set about restructuring the finances of the company and reducing the cost base, shedding over 5,000 jobs. Opportunities for partnerships were sought, and in 1981 this resulted in an agreement with Fujitsu to supply technology and components. The company became profitable, propping up its subsequent parent organization STC, which, having taken over ICL, itself got into trouble (7). By the end of the 1980s, Fujitsu had acquired an 80 percent stake in ICL, and the company has remained profitable and successful since, despite the severe impact of the world recession and the rapid technological and commercial developments in the industry which have affected most of ICL's competitors.

An account of the U.K. government PAYE project describes how ICL evolved during this period (8). The PAYE contract was won toward the end of 1980 by a consortium comprising ICL, Computer Sciences Corporation, and PACTEL. The project was based on 2900 series computers, and project management techniques were used to ensure that the project was successful. The features considered key to the success of the project were good planning and the preparation of a secure software environment, careful documentation of requirements, change control, commitment to success by senior management, and no attitude of "it cannot be done," but rather "yes, but this is what it will cost."

Many of the senior managers at ICL today experienced the cultural shift in the company during the 1970s. The lessons of that period were the importance of focusing on customer need, working single-mindedly to achieve goals, deploying resources accordingly, not accepting excuses for things not being done or being late, and empowering managers to use the organization to achieve their goals.

The current chairman and chief executive, Peter Bonfield, was brought into ICL by Robb Wilmot, and became managing director after the STC takeover in 1984. He describes his managers as entrepreneurs. They have a free hand to do as they want as long as it is profitable and in their target area. He believes in delegating, and he likes winners (9). This has a strong resonance with the project management style introduced in the 1970s. The lessons of that period will have been a valuable preparation for many in the company who have helped ICL to remain profitable in a hostile climate.

The techniques of project management are as relevant today as they have ever been, because of the need to minimize risk and achieve project deadlines. Thirty-five percent of new products launched fail commercially, and 45 percent of total new product expenditures are on unsuccessful projects (10). Meeting deadlines is one of the two top issues faced by IT executives (11).

Conservatism is still to be found among managers in traditional hierarchical organizations (12), and the introduction of project managers is seen as a threat to their status. However, increasingly, these traditional hierarchies are being transformed into dynamic structures as businesses are reengineered.

Dedicated project teams need to be located where the main risks need to be managed (13), which was the approach adopted by ICL with the introduction of the 2900 series. The client as the project champion, committed to its success, brings together the concepts of the need for senior management commitment (8) with the effective supplier-customer relationship ICL fostered with its dedicated project teams working to help the customers achieve their objectives.

In all these situations, the project manager needs a combination of technical and people management skills in order to anticipate problems and risks while developing the working relationships needed to resolve or avoid them. The need for an effective relationship with the customer is as important as the relationships within the project team and with other colleagues or superiors in the manager's organization. Roman (14) in summarizing the characteristics of an effective project manager, cites the ability to bring out the best in people as one such people management skill. Action-centered leadership combines meeting the needs of individuals and the needs of the team in achieving the goals (8).

A project manager is involved with innovation and managing change. The conventional operations manager is involved with managing continuity and existing processes effectively. Peters (6) suggests that change is on the increase, and that there is a shift away from mass production towards variety. This is confirmed as the view of IT managers (11). Bonfield encourages entrepreneurship and initiative. As the pace of change continues to increase, project management will play an increasingly important part in all organizations as they endeavor to manage the activities going on around them. While the parts played by Robb Wilmot and Peter Bonfield in rescuing ICL in the 1980s were essential elements that enabled ICL to survive, the project management skills learned under Geoff Cross prepared people to survive in the increasingly competitive environment of the 1990s.

Acknowledgments

The author would like to thank Ed Sampson, previously a fellow project and support manager at ICL and latterly a colleague at Thames Valley University, U.K., for a number of specific suggestions and reminders of approaches used at ICL which have been included in the text. Thanks are also due to Dennis Ramsay, marketing director for the National Accounts Division at ICL, for confirming the accuracy of the account.

REFERENCES

1. Wilson, H. 1974. *The Labor Government, 1964–70*. U.K.: Penguin.

2. Dijkstra, E. W. 1968. "The Structure of the T.H.E. Multiprogramming System." *Communications of the ACM*. 11, 341–46.

3. Buckle, J.K. 1978. *The ICL 2900 Series*. U.K.: Macmillan.

4. Turner, J.R. 1993. *The Handbook of Project Management.* U.K.: McGraw-Hill.

5. Peters, T.J., and R.H. Waterman, Jr., 1982. *In Search of Excellence.* U.K.: Harper and Row.

6. Peters, T.J. 1987. *Thriving on Chaos.* U.K.: Pan.

7. Marwood, D.C. 1985. "ICL: Crisis and Swift Recovery." *Long Range Planning* 18 no. 2, pp. 10–21.

8. Morris, P.W.G., and G.H. Hough. 1987. *The Anatomy of Major Projects.* U.K.: John Wiley.

9. 1992. "A Profile of Peter Bonfield." *Management Today.* Jan.

10. Halman, J.I.M., and J.A. Keizer. 1994. "Diagnosing Risks in Product-Innovation Projects." *International Journal of Project Management* 12, no. 2, pp. 75–80.

11. *Information Technology Review.* 1994/95. Price Waterhouse.

12. Payne, J.H. 1993. "Introducing Formal Project Management into a Traditional Functionally Structured Organization." *International Journal of Project Management* 11 no. 4, pp. 239–44.

13. Bames, N.M., and S.H. Wearne. 1993. "The Future of Major Project Management." *International Journal of Project Management* 11 no. 3, pp. 135–42.

14. Roman, D.D. 1986. *Managing Projects: A Systems Approach.* U.K.: Elsevier Science.

Study Questions

How ICL Used Project Management Techniques to Introduce a New Product Range

1. This case illustrates how a traditional company was transformed into a project-driven organization. Describe the characteristics of a classic functional organization. What are some of the strengths and weaknesses of a functional organization?

2. Through the case, the author describes how the company, its products, and the relationships with its customers were transformed. What are some of the lessons of the cultural shift the company underwent during the 1970s?

3. The author states that, "In a highly technical area of development such as this, throwing resources at the problem does not necessarily solve it." Is this only true for technical areas?

4. The author focuses on the importance of being "close to the customer." What is meant by this phrase and how is it accomplished?

5. The author notes that an effective project manager must have a combination of technical and managerial skills. What other specific skills are critical for an effective project manager?

MOTIVATING

3
MOTIVATING

Communication Strategies for Major Public Works Projects: The Los Angeles Metro Rail Program under Siege

Rodney J. Dawson, Los Angeles County Metropolitan Transportation Authority

PMI *Proceedings*, 1995, pp. 56–61

INTRODUCTION

In 1993, the Los Angeles Metro Red Line project won PMI's prestigious International Project of the Year award. By 1994, it was a project under siege. These are some headlines from *The Los Angeles Times*:

"Mistakes, Woes Add Millions to Subway Cost," "Misalignments Found in New Subway Tunnels," "MTA Delayed Response to Tunnel Warnings," "MTA Chief Seeks to Revamp Construction Arm," "Funds Cutoff Gives MTA Chief Biggest Challenge," "L.A. Subway Construction Chief Ousted."

What happened? Should PMI ask for its award back? Project veterans will tell you that in construction, "stuff" happens. When problems arise, should major public works projects automatically come under siege from the media, politicians, and the public?

William Glaberson writes in *The New York Times* that the media has gone beyond skepticism and adopted a new cynical brand of journalism. Using the construction of tunnels beneath Hollywood Boulevard and a localized surface settlement problem as a case study, this paper presents winning strategies for responding to the media. The paper also discusses how to effectively communicate with public officials and affected communities, emphasizing how to mitigate the adverse impacts of urban construction on local business and private citizens.

The Los Angeles Rail Program

The Los Angeles Metro Rail system is the largest public works program currently under way in North America. This multi-year, multi-billion dollar design and construction program is bringing urban heavy and light rail transit to Los Angeles. This high-profile construction program receives continuous scrutiny from the media, elected officials, businesses, and the public.

Metro Rail is part of the transportation strategy to reshape Los Angeles into a more efficient, productive, and healthier urban area. Each line in the system, shown in Figure 2, is a separate project.

Metro Blue Line and Pasadena Blue Line use conventional light rail technology. Metro Green Line is designed to use fully automated light rail technology, and Metro Red Line is a heavy rail subway being constructed in separate project segments. Figure 3 presents the cost, schedule, and status of

"Mistakes, Woes Add Millions to Subway Cost"
"Misalignments Found in New Subway Tunnels"
"MTA Delayed Response to Tunnel Warnings"
"MTA Chief Seeks to Revamp Construction Arm"
"Funds Cutoff Gives MTA Chief Biggest Challenge"
"L.A. Subway Construction Chief Ousted"

FIGURE 1   **THE *LOS ANGELES TIMES* HEADLINES**

these projects. Future projects may be built along alternative candidate corridors now under evaluation.

Good Work Overshadowed by Bad Publicity

Unfortunately, the kinds of problems experienced on all large construction programs have overshadowed the rail program's contributions to Los Angeles' transportation strategy. As a result, individual rail projects and the program as a whole have been subject to frequent criticism and attack from the media, the public, and elected officials.

What brought this about? The magnitude of the rail construction effort and the associated level of disruption the construction causes in communities instantly makes the rail program "big news." Investigative journalists sell newspapers by revealing problems, and the multi-billion dollar taxpayer-funded rail program provided ample opportunity for negative headlines. The political agendas of elected officials were not always aligned with the rail program, particularly at times when officials faced reelection and wanted to avoid any association with negative issues.

Hollywood/Hudson Intersection Settlement: A Case Study

In reviewing the events surrounding tunnel construction beneath Hollywood Boulevard and a problem of localized settlement at the Hudson Street intersection, we can see how the incident became fertile ground for the media and how the public reacted more to what was reported than to the actual incident.

The Events

During the summer of 1994, settlement of Hollywood Boulevard occurred at the Hudson Street intersection along the route being tunneled. A four-inch settlement occurred above the tunnel on the north side of the boulevard. Three weeks later, a five-inch settlement occurred above the tunnel on the south side of the boulevard. Street-surface settlement above the north tunnel increased to nine inches, and on August 20 distress was observed along 200 feet of the north tunnel. Immediate steps were taken to support the distressed tunnel area and further tunneling was halted until long-term remedial action could be taken.

The 9 inches of settlement were limited to approximately 15 feet of the generalized 200 feet of settlement area above the distressed tunnel. The actions taken by the project staff successfully prevented street or tunnel collapse.

1. Blue Line
2. Green Line
3. Pasadena Blue Line
4. Red Line Seg. 1
5. Red Line Seg. 2
6. Red Line Seg. 3/North Hollywood
7. Red Line Seg. 3/East Side
8. Red Line Seg. 3/Mid-City

FIGURE 2   METRO RAIL SYSTEM

However, the localized settlement was more than the 1–2 inches experienced during tunneling of the previous 8 miles of the alignment.

Media Reporting and Its Results

In reporting events along Hollywood Boulevard, the media practiced the cynical brand of journalism noted by Glaberson. News coverage failed to place the settlement event in a proper context, thus making the problem appear worse than it was. The media did not report on the construction process to the extent that the public could make an informed judgment about the events. The public's attention would have been less fixated on the 9 inches of settlement if the media had done two things: reported the localized nature of the settlement compared with previous experience along the tunnel alignment; and noted that swift and competent action prevented collapse of the tunnel or Hollywood Boulevard. This would have presented the public with a balanced report of the problem and the solution.

Not to understate the construction problems involved, the fact is that anyone driving along Hollywood Boulevard cannot see the settlement with the naked eye. Despite the headlines neither television cameras nor newspaper photographs were able to capture the settlement.

Figure 4 shows how some of the headlines reported settlement on Hollywood Boulevard.

The relative seriousness of the settlement on Hollywood Boulevard pales in comparison to recent problems encountered on similar, large urban tunneling projects, such as the sink hole in Munich, Germany, and the collapsed office building in London, England (Figure 5).

	Blue Line	Green Line	Pasadena Blue Line	Red Line Seg. 1
Route	7th St/ Metro Ctr. to Long Beach	Norwalk to El Segundo	Union Station to Pasadena	Union Station to West Lake
Length (miles)	22	20	14	5
Stations	22	14	14	5
Open Date	1990	1995	2002	1993
Design Status	100%	100%	78%	100%
Const. Status	100%	96%	2%	100%
Cost $ millions	$877	$718	$998	$1,450

	Red Line Seg. 2	Red Line Seg. 3 North Hollywood	Red Line Seg. 3 East Side	Red Line Seg. 3 Mid-City
Route	West Lake to Western/ Vermont to Hollywood	Hollywood to North Hollywood	Union Station to Whittier	Western to Pico/ Olympic
Length (miles)	7	6	4	2
Stations	8	3	4	2
Open Date	1998	2000	2002	TBD
Design Status	98%	86%	30%	0%
Const. Status	55%	7%	0%	0%
Cost $ millions	$1,517	$1,324	$980	$491

FIGURE 3   METRO RAIL PROGRAM STATUS (MARCH 1995)

"Subway tunneling halted because of sinkage"

"MTA delayed response to warning on tunnels"
"... tunneling undermined street"

"MTA hunts for (cause of) buckling Hollywood Boulevard"
"Soil settling ... force(s) closure of Boulevard"

FIGURE 4   HOLLYWOOD BOULEVARD HEADLINES

Furthermore, the media transformed reporting of events into personal attacks against project staff. High profile criticism of those in leadership positions on controversial public works projects often results in their removal. This happened to highly skilled leaders in Los Angeles following the Hollywood Boulevard incident, as it has happened elsewhere.

The kinds of reporting discussed above can be mitigated. As a result of our experiences with the media, we have devised several strategies for mitigating the effects of cynical journalism. These strategies may be used for any major construction project and are presented below.

Communication Strategies for Projects under Siege

There are several ways to handle communications when working on a highly visible, controversial project. Knowing how the media uses information is the first line of defense for any project or agency and learning how to communicate with the media greatly improves the chances for fair reporting. Two other key elements of a full communications program include keeping public officials and the public informed.

Know How the Media Uses Information

According to Glaberson in *The New York Times*, news is the enemy of hope. Cynicism has replaced healthy skepticism; with the media convincing us that everything is a scam, everyone is looking out for his own interests, and it is the reporter's job to reveal the "truth."

Consequently, anyone in the news is immediately suspect and journalists readily accuse politicians of being manipulative in pursuit of their narrow political agendas. Contractors, consultants, and business people are assumed to be venal and public sector staff inept, corrupt, or both.

Therefore, tactical communication with the media is essential. Without a communications strategy, when a single projects comes under siege it may place the whole program in jeopardy. The preferred strategy for communicating with the media is described below.

Communicating with the Media

The media is in the business of meeting daily deadlines. So, despite its focus on cynical revelation, editors need new news product each day. According to Robert Behn in *Governing* magazine, in order to generate this product, editors and reporters are biased towards stories that are simple, personal, and symbolic. He outlines how to present information, as follows:

"(Munich) Bus falls into hole caused by collapsed excavation"

"Land-slip office near collapse—
railway tunneling halted (London Heathrow Airport)"

"New tunnel woe could add $500 million, 2 years to job
(Boston Central Artery)"

FIGURE 5   **EXAMPLES OF OTHER CONSTRUCTION PROBLEMS**

- **Present a simple story**. Simple stories take less time and effort to report and are easier to read and understand. Consequently, they sell better.
- **Personalize the story**. Personal stories also sell better. Human interest at the beginning of a story is the best way to capture attention. It is easier for the media to report what is said at news conferences and personal interviews rather than to work through technical reports. Where possible, articulate and appealing individuals from the projects should be used as the center of a story.
- **Use symbolism to make the point**. Finally, journalists like stories that are symbolic and reflect some accepted truth or enduring theme. This gives the story an aura of credibility and respectability.

Lessons learned from the Hollywood Boulevard settlement taught us that we could have presented a simple, personal, and symbolic story by outlining the swift measures taken to stabilize the tunnel. A simple illustration showing the bracing put in place might have resulted in a positive headline, such as *"Fast action by project staff saves Hollywood Boulevard."* This would automatically have placed the emphasis on the personal endeavors of courageous staff working tirelessly to protect historic Hollywood Boulevard and its prominent "stars" inlaid into the sidewalk. Certainly a more sympathetic viewpoint would have at least been entertained by both the media and the public had we communicated this message instead of presenting a complex technical defense of our tunneling techniques.

Accordingly, considerable effort has now been put into finding good news construction stories of a symbolic nature such as job creation, support of minority businesses, and project benefits to the community. Figure 6 shows some of the positive headlines that could be generated about the program.

Keep Your Public Officials Informed

Elected officials have very little time to devote to a construction program, being only one of a wide range of issues competing for their attention. Their enthusiastic support for any public works project is most apparent when the project is launched, when funding is announced, and when the ribbon is cut at the start of operations. Between the announcement and the ribbon cutting there is little upside reward for backing the project and lots of downside political risk due to media attacks, community issues, construction problems, and aggressive lobbying from contractors competing for work.

Based on the Los Angeles experience, three factors make for an effective communication strategy with elected officials:
- "no surprises" to embarrass officials
- professional trust of project staff
- ownership of the project by elected officials.

Elected officials hate being surprised, particularly by bad news. When this was allowed to happen on the rail program, the typical reaction of the elected officials was to express outrage, ask why they were not informed, and search for whom to blame. Since there is no substitute for familiarity to build professional trust, senior members of the rail program invested significant time to brief elected officials who serve on the program's governing board. By keeping elected officials informed in a timely fashion, there are no surprises which can come back to haunt either them or the staff.

Much of this briefing effort has to be with the staff of the elected officials. Demands on elected officials' time usually make it impractical to brief them directly on a regular basis. However, regular access to their staff is possible, and good relations with staff translate into good relations with elected officials.

Technical briefings were done directly by project staff and not delegated to so-called government affairs staff. It is not efficient to provide government affairs staff with the depth and breadth of project knowledge to take on the technical briefing responsibility. Secondly, and of equal importance, exclusive use of government affairs staff is a barrier to developing the personal relationships and trust between project staff and public officials.

The Los Angeles experience shows that elected officials display more project ownership when they serve directly on the construction program's board and committees rather than when they delegate that responsibility to appointed representatives.

Until recently, the construction staff of the Los Angeles rail program was organized as a public-benefit, nonprofit corporation responsible to a board of private sector engineering and construction experts appointed by the elected officials. Staff recommendations passed by the appointed board were forwarded to the elected official governing board for final approval. As construction problems including the Hollywood/Hudson settlement arose, and the program came under increasing media and community attack, the elected officials distanced themselves from the program and lost confidence in the appointed board and project staff. Although relationships and professional trust existed between the *appointed* board and the project staff, an "us and them" attitude developed between the appointed board and the elected officials. This, in turn, caused the elected officials to distrust the project staff.

The appointed board was ultimately disbanded and the project staff reorganized as a division of the Los Angeles MTA. Recommendations for actions to the governing board now came from a construction committee made up of a subset of the governing board's elected officials. The elected officials began to assume ownership of the program and regain confidence in the project staff.

Given the fast-paced environment of capital construction projects, setting up the relationships and fostering ownership are critical in establishing the free-flowing communication channels required to keep officials informed of events (good and bad) in a timely manner. It is also helpful to acknowledge problems, lessons learned, and improvements sought.

"Rail program invests $525 million in the economy"

"98 percent of rail program investments for USA products and services"

"Rail program creates 15,000 jobs"

"Rail program contracts $65 million to minority and women owned firms"

*"Rail program leverages $12 million for community road,
park and utility improvements"*

"Rail program's accident rate 1/2 national average"

"Rail program provides $215 million for local vehicle manufacturing industry"

FIGURE 6   SYMBOLIC GOOD NEWS

Reach Out Far and Wide into the Community

"Not in my backyard" (NIMBY), says any neighbor to a construction project. Unfortunately, inconvenience to the residences and businesses along the rail project alignment is inevitable during construction. Compounding this disruption is its long duration, with construction of an underground tunnel or station taking up to three years. Moreover, on a multi-project rail program there is construction impact to some part of the community throughout a ten to twenty year period. With this amount of impact, a well thought-out community construction mitigation program is essential to the success of a rail program.

The strategy for the Los Angeles rail program is to assign community affairs specialists to each project team and assure that their time is spent working in the field. In this way they maintain a firsthand knowledge of construction progress and the issues impacting the community. Secondly, they get to know and be known by the local residents and businesses. Operating out of storefront offices that are easily accessible, community affairs staff provide a place for the public to drop in and ask questions or voice concerns about the construction. Emphasis is on being a good neighbor in the community. Special events are planned for the community, particularly to mark significant construction milestones, such as a tunnel breakthrough. Where schools are adjacent to construction areas, special events are planned to teach students about safe behavior around construction sites.

Regular community meetings are a key component of the rail program's community communication strategy. In these meetings, project staff is available to answer current issues of concern. Open and forthright disclosure is used to maintain the confidence and support of the community. Additionally, the meetings provide a forum for opponents to the construction program. This can be challenging but provides the opportunity to respond to program opponents in a managed setting.

SAFETY
MATTERS
MOST!

FIGURE 7   MTA SAFETY MASCOT—TRAVIS THE OWL

The last element of our community outreach program is the component designed to reach out to our youth. We developed our mascot, Travis the Owl (Figure 7), to capture the attention of our school children. With many schools close to the railroad tracks, it is important to teach our youngsters caution around the tracks and construction sites. Travis is a well-accepted symbol which carries our message to the youth in communities affected by the rail program.

CONCLUSION

Constructing a large, high-profile public works project is not for the faint-hearted. In construction, "stuff happens," and the public has a right to scrutinize and be told what is going on. Our challenge is to tell the accurate construction story with all its positive and negative aspects rather than allowing the media to tell it for us with a skewed perspective.

Intense scrutiny by the media, public, and elected officials does not have to undermine the long-term positive effects of a major urban construction project. Using communications strategies which consider the public's right to know, elected officials' need for accurate information, and the media's inclination toward cynical reporting can overcome the downside consequences of modern-day public works construction.

Study Questions

COMMUNICATION STRATEGIES FOR MAJOR PUBLIC WORKS PROJECTS: THE LOS ANGELES METRO RAIL PROGRAM UNDER SIEGE

1. This case describes both the media and political figures as possibly detrimental to this project. Describe the importance of properly communicating with the project stakeholders.

2. Stakeholder management can be the key to the success of many projects. Develop a model which can be useful for any project for proper stakeholder management.

3. How would you handle the morale of workers and others on the project given the criticism aimed at the project?

4. The case suggests three conditions for success when communicating with the media. What are these? Can you think of any additional conditions?

5. The author gives advice on handling communication with three different stakeholders. What are the common characteristics of the strategies?

Learning the Lessons of Apollo 13

Michael S. Lines, PMP

PM Network, May 1996, pp. 25–27

R on Howard's epic movie *Apollo 13* recounts the ill-fated Apollo 13 mission to the moon, a mission that came close to causing the first loss of life in space for a United States astronaut. The astronauts were only a third of the way into the mission when one of the oxygen tanks in the command ship Odyssey exploded, crippling the spacecraft, and endangering the lives of the crew.

The story of Apollo 13 is one of hope, inspiration, and perseverance, and one that holds many useful parallels for those in the field of information system (IS) project management. What are these parallels? Consider the factors that contributed to the success of the Apollo program.

Have a clear objective. More than anything else, having a clear objective helps to ensure a successful project. With the Apollo program, that objective was to land a man on the moon and return him safely to earth, a goal that was achieved just seven short years after President Kennedy first issued the challenge to the nation and the world.

To be successful, IS projects must also have clear goals and objectives. A complete statement of a project's objectives, milestones, and requirements, embodied in a statement of work or similar contractual document, helps to ensure that everyone agrees on the purpose and deliverables of the project. This also keeps everyone focused on the business reason for doing the project in the first place.

Pick the best people. The Apollo astronauts were the best of the best. Selected from the top test and military pilots, they were the most highly qualified and capable people available. That level of excellence showed when it came to overcoming obstacles and achieving the impossible, as was often required to complete the Apollo missions.

To achieve success in IS projects, we must also seek to employ the best people available, especially for the project manager and lead technical staff. We should seek to hire industry specialists with broad experience drawn from diverse assignments—people who can overcome the unexpected problems that occur in even the best planned project. By hiring the best, you acquire people who have already been tempered by the fires of adversity and have overcome them.

Support them with the best team. No matter how good the astronauts were, they would never have been successful without the team that supported them and their mission. From the scientists and engineers who built the rockets, to the programmers who wrote the navigation programs, to the seamstress who sewed the spacesuits, the success of the Apollo missions resulted from thousands of people pulling together to achieve something that once seemed impossible.

In IS projects, it's not the project manager but the project team that achieves the project objectives. Team leaders, programmers, testers, tech writers: the typical large IS project needs all these people and more to pull together diverse technology to meet a customer's business objectives. The project manager melds this diverse group of people into the effective team needed to meet the project objectives.

Support them with the best equipment and technology. The Apollo program achieved its objective by employing the best technology available at the time. In many cases, that technology was created specifically for the Apollo program and in turn led to advances in commercial industry.

IS projects don't have the luxury of the "blank checkbook" that the managers of the Apollo program did. Nevertheless, technology can be used in numerous ways to boost the productivity of the project team and help to ensure its success. From personal development systems, to CASE and design tools, to project management software and even E-mail to facilitate communication, the improvements in productivity and quality that technology brings are well worth the initial capital costs to the project.

Train constantly. The Apollo astronauts trained constantly and kept training until the last moment. A backup crew trained beside them so that someone would be available to carry out the mission if for any reason the primary team was unable to.

For IS project teams, training is also essential. Whether it is training to understand and use the technology being deployed (such as client/server), training in the use of tools, or training in project management or some other facet of project implementation, training is better done beforehand rather than in the heat of project implementation. All too often team members are expected to just "read the manual" to bring themselves up to speed with a new system or tool, and management expresses surprise when the quality and productivity gains expected are not realized. This attitude toward training would have been unacceptable for the Apollo program and should be unacceptable for IS projects as well.

Prepare for the unexpected. For the astronauts and mission planners, preparing for the unexpected was a crucial part of the program. They knew they were exploring unknown territory and, therefore, had to prepare contingencies for situations they might encounter. Their training for the unexpected, along with the redundancies and engineering of their spacecraft for those contingencies, enabled the Apollo 13 astronauts to survive.

For IS projects, preparing for the unknown starts with the initial project planning, when allowances should be built into the plan to account for both known and unknown possibilities. An active risk management program should be in place from the beginning of the project and updated throughout the project life-cycle to ensure that the project is as prepared as possible for whatever problems, either technological or otherwise, may arise.

For the Apollo astronauts, these factors were not only instrumental in their success, they were also integral to ensuring their survival. However, even when all precautions are taken and all the planning, training, and engineering has been done to the best of everyone's ability, "Murphy" can still strike.

Never consider defeat. When this disaster struck, the mission controllers, mission team, and crew of Apollo 13 never allowed themselves to consider the possibility that the crew would not make it back. Whether it

"Houston, we've had a problem."

Fifty-five hours into the Apollo 13 mission an oxygen tank exploded, severely crippling the ship about 200,000 miles from Earth. Loss of oxygen meant loss of power, and the undamaged, self-contained lunar module became the crew's lifeboat. The emergency measures this forced included cobbling together a higher capacity CO_2 scrubber using on-board materials (top). On the ground, mission control teams worked around the clock to solve new technical challenges (middle). The team's efforts paid off, and the crew of Apollo 13 splashed down safely on April 17, 1970.

was the initial objective of getting to the moon, or the revised objective of bringing the astronauts home safely, they knew they could not fail, and therefore they made sure they didn't.

While human lives are not at stake for most IS projects, the principle remains the same. When disaster strikes on a project, as long as you proceed from the standpoint that the project *can* succeed and *must* succeed, you'll find you have the drive to see that it *will* succeed.

Improvise. When the Apollo 13 ship was crippled, the mission team members had to use their ingenuity to solve their problems. Hundreds of thousands of miles from Earth, with no way to replace the failed CO_2 scrubbers, they had to make new ones from what they had available. Likewise, when the oxygen and power on the command ship Odyssey failed, the team improvised and made use of the lunar lander Aquarius.

For IS projects, when disaster strikes—the project is late, over budget, or delivering poor quality products—improvising with what you have available

Art Imitates Life

When he watched *Apollo 13*, PMI member Frank Saladis of Applied Business Technologies in New York heard those cinematic project managers make a lot of familiar statements. He compiled them to share with his organization and *PM Network* readers:

"Work the problem, people. Let's not make things worse by guessing."

"Start replanning—improvise."

"Failure is not an option!"

"Skip things that are not absolutely needed."

"Identify contingencies."

"Here is what you need to make, and here is what you have to work with."

"We are no strangers to emergencies."

"This was a successful failure!"

For Saladis, the movie brought home how the smallest detail can have a major impact on your project. "When they calculated the return trajectory," he notes, "they forgot to compensate for the fact that they did not have the weight of the moon rocks on the capsule. This slight change in the return path almost caused the capsule to burn up."

For further inspiration, Saladis suggests *The Bridge on the River Kwai.* "There is a 30-minute segment in this film that depicts a classic project management planning session, complete with agenda, resource planning, risk management, material requirements, schedule, site planning, etc."

So zip down to the video store for a little project management education!

can provide a solution. This often means redefining the parameters of the project, whether the schedule, budget, or deliverables, so that you can turn certain failure for the entire project back into success for a modified project that still meets the fundamental business objectives.

Take risks. The crew and mission team of Apollo 13 knew that they had to cut corners and take chances if the astronauts were going to survive. From piloting the spacecraft manually to cutting checklists to a minimum, with certain death the alternative, the mission team took calculated risks to ensure survival.

When an IS project is in trouble, the project manager must also take calculated risks to help ensure its survival—a gamble with new technologies, new people, or new processes. When faced with a choice between certain failure or possible success, the project manager must have the guts to take the risks and to face the consequences if failures occur.

Turn failure into success. Success can be found even in failure. For the Apollo 13 mission, that success was the achievement of bringing the crew back safely against all odds. The interest this generated revived the flagging public support for the Apollo program (for a time) and helped renew the commitment to safety within the space program (until it flagged again, leading to the Challenger disaster).

In IS projects, even when we fail and the project is canceled, there is always a lesson to be learned. Whatever the reason for the failure or cancellation, it should be looked on as an opportunity to learn and improve so that future failures can be prevented. The adage "unless we learn from history, we are doomed to repeat it" is as true for IS projects as it is for missions to the moon.

Study Questions

LEARNING THE LESSONS OF APOLLO 13

1. List and discuss three parallels between the Apollo 13 mission and project management that the author points out.

2. Describe a project or even an everyday activity in which the unexpected happened. How did you handle it, and did it work out? How does this ability to deal with the unexpected play a part in project management? What are the major processes identified by the *PMBOK Guide* intended to deal with the unexpected?

3. If you have seen the movie *Apollo 13* you have become familiar with the personalities of some of the people who played a part in the mission. List some of their attributes which make them good members of a project team. Do you see any resemblance between these management skills and those identified by the *PMBOK Guide*?

4. The Apollo 13 project was an example of an effective team. What are the key characteristics of an effective team?

Taxol®: An Example of "Fast-Track" Drug Development

Gerald W. Crabtree, Bristol-Myers Squibb Company

PMI *Proceedings*, 1993, pp. 616–21

INTRODUCTION

Following the signing of a cooperative research and development agreement (CRADA) between the National Cancer Institute (NCI) and Bristol-Myers Squibb (BMS) in January, 1991, Taxol® (paclitaxel) was made a top priority for development by BMS, with the commitment that a new drug application (NDA) would be submitted within four years. As a consequence of this commitment, it was necessary for BMS to undertake a major effort to develop Taxol®—an anticancer agent that had been called the most important new drug to come along in fifteen years—and necessitated that the drug be developed on a "fast track."

The so-called fast track included not only accelerated time of development, but also accelerated review by the FDA of the NDA. From the signing of the CRADA to submission of the NDA, little more than fifteen months elapsed. Five months after submission of the NDA, the application was reviewed by the Oncology Drugs Advisory Committee and recommended for approval. One month later, in December of 1992, Taxol® was approved for use in patients with metastatic ovarian cancer who had failed first-line or subsequent chemotherapy. First commercial Taxol® shipments began one week after formal approval of the drug.

This presentation will review some of the background for the interest in Taxol®, discuss aspects related to the fast-track development of this agent, and discuss the role played by project management in this overall development process.

BACKGROUND AND EARLY HISTORY

Between 1958 and 1980, the NCI sponsored a program in which extracts of more than 35,000 plant species were evaluated for their ability to terminate the growth of cancer cells in culture. In 1963, as part of this effort, samples of the Pacific yew tree *(Taxus brevifolia)*, a scarce and slow-growing evergreen tree found in the old-growth forests of the Pacific northwest, were shown to have significant cell-killing activity. Later that same year, Monroe Wall of the Research Triangle Institute, who was under contract to the NCI, expanded these initial observations to show that an extract of yew bark also killed leukemia cells in culture. Three years later, Wall's group was successful in isolating the active ingredient from the bark and named it "taxol." It was not until 1971, however, that Wall and his colleague, M. Wani, together with H.

Taylor, published the structure of the compound (1). Taxol® was shown to have a very complex molecular structure in which the basic taxane ring system is linked to a rare four-membered oxetan ring and has a side chain esterified at position C-13; this ester side chain is essential for the mechanism of action of Taxol® and for its cytotoxicity (2).

These early accomplishments notwithstanding, the development of Taxol® essentially ceased for a decade. Reasons for this delay included 1) as compared to other agents under development at the time, Taxol® did not appear to have superior antitumor activity; 2) significant problems in developing a suitable clinical formulation were encountered because of the poor water-solubility of Taxol®; 3) great difficulty in obtaining, extracting, and preparing a natural product for large-scale clinical use was anticipated (3).

Interest in Taxol® was renewed in 1979 when Susan Horwitz and colleagues at the Albert Einstein College of Medicine demonstrated that the cytotoxicity of Taxol® was due to unique disruptive effects on microtubule structure and function (4, 5).

Microtubules are cellular components whose principal function is the formation of the "spindle" apparatus which cells must have to undergo mitosis (cell division, the process by which most mammalian cells propagate). In addition, microtubules are used by cells to maintain shape, for motility, for anchorage, and for intracellular transport of various substances (6). Microtubules may also play a pivotal role in the interactions of growth factors with cell-surface receptors and in signal transduction whereby cells are directed to turn off or turn on cell division processes, and thus regulate growth (7–10).

Microtubules are polymers (many molecules bound together) of the protein tubulin that exist in equilibrium with tubulin dimers (two molecules bound together). Taxol® binds preferentially to intact microtubules rather than to the dimers (11). As a consequence, the polymer-dimer equilibrium is shifted toward microtubule formation. This shift towards microtubule formation caused by Taxol® is very unique; other drugs, such as colchicine and the *Vinca* alkaloids that affect microtubules, induce microtubule disassembly (5, 11–14). As a consequence, Taxol®-treated microtubules are very stable (4, 5, 15); this unusual stability inhibits the normal dynamic reorganization of the microtubule network. Cells treated with Taxol® form unusual bundles of tubulin, and although such cells can enter mitosis, they lack the normal mitotic spindle apparatus (16, 17) and cannot complete cell division.

FURTHER PRECLINICAL DEVELOPMENT OF TAXOL®

The decision by the NCI to develop Taxol® further in the late 1970s was based on the new knowledge about its unique mechanism of action (see above) and its broad activity in both mouse tumor and human xenograft (human tumor tissues grafted into mice lacking a functional immune system; thus, the "foreign" human tissue is not rejected) model systems used in the NCI's tumor screening panel (18). Taxol® showed excellent activity against the B16 mouse melanoma, a very resistant model system, and good activity against human mammary, human lung, and human colon xenografts, and against two mouse leukemias.

In addition to the NCI studies, independent investigators showed that Taxol® had substantial activity against human breast cancer xenografts in that it actually caused tumor shrinkage (19, 20). Activity was also seen against xenografts of human endometrial, brain, ovarian, tongue, and lung tumors.

At the NCI, the preclinical toxicology of Taxol® was evaluated in rodents and dogs (18). As is the case with many anticancer agents, the toxic effects caused by Taxol® were most apparent in tissues with rapid turnover such as bone marrow, lymphatic, gastrointestinal, and reproductive tissues. Damage to nerve, liver, cardiovascular, and kidney tissues was minimal.

Because of the inherent lack of water-volubility of Taxol®, it has been necessary to formulate this agent with Cremophor EL® (polyoxyethylated castor oil). In the dog, administration of this vehicle caused severe hypersensitivity reactions (21). Hypersensitivity reactions were also observed when Taxol® formulated in Cremophor EL® was used in the clinic; these reactions have been attributed to the presence of the Cremophor EL® and have necessitated that the patients receive premedication with antihistamines and steroids.

PHASE I STUDIES

NCI-sponsored Phase I trials of Taxol® using many doses and schedules of administration were begun in 1983 (22–30). Early trials were often discontinued because of a high incidence of hypersensitivity reactions; these discontinuations, in fact, threatened the future development of Taxol®.

In spite of the observed hypersensitivity reactions, in the Phase I studies, the major dose-limiting toxicity was shown to be neutropenia (profound depression of the numbers of a type of white cells in the blood). With cumulative therapy, neurotoxicity became particularly evident (25, 26). In leukemia patients treated with high doses of Taxol®, mucositis was seen as the dose-limiting toxicity (22).

In the Phase I trials, Taxol® exhibited activity in patients with melanoma, non-small cell lung cancer, and heavily pretreated drug-resistant ovarian cancer (31). Despite these observations, however, broad Phase II development was not undertaken because of the severe shortages of the drug, the high frequency of hypersensitivity reactions seen in the Phase I trials, and the concern that Taxol® would be difficult to develop due to the problems anticipated in developing a suitable clinical formulation. Rather, Phase II studies with Taxol® were performed in a limited number of types of cancer patients including those with melanoma, renal, or ovarian cancer.

EARLY PHASE II TRIAL RESULTS

By far the most exciting aspect of the first Phase II trials was the marked activity of Taxol® in patients with advanced ovarian cancer. In a study at the Johns Hopkins Oncology Center, eleven partial responses (PR) and one complete response (CR) were observed out of forty-four assessable patients treated (32). Seven minor responses (MR) were also seen; these patients whose tumors shrank 40–49 percent did not meet the criteria for a PR. In this study, the response rate (CR + PR) of 30 percent was deemed to be high. Noteworthy, along with the high activity of Taxol®, is the fact that most patients had been heavily treated with chemotherapy and/or radiation previously; usually such patients are markedly resistant to chemotherapy. In addition, many responses occurred in patients who were overtly resistant to treatment with platinum compounds, the recognized agents for use against ovarian cancer. Also, the doses of Taxol® that were used were much lower than those previously shown to be safe for minimally previously treated or new untreated patients; this was necessary because previously treated patients have a much reduced hematologic tolerance to most agents. At the doses used, Taxol® had a very acceptable toxicity profile.

Similar activity was seen in studies done by the Gynecologic Oncology Group (GOG) and at Albert Einstein (33, 34). Complete response rates of 12 percent and overall response (CR + PR) rates of 36 percent were seen in the GOG trial (33); these were in patients who had previously received one platinum-based therapy. In patients who were not considered resistant to platinum therapy, the corresponding figures were 21 percent and 50 percent. In the Albert Einstein study, one CR and five PRs were seen in thirty previously treated patients (34); responders had a median duration of survival of twenty-seven months.

Many patients in the above studies suffered treatment-limiting neutropenia. Accordingly, the ability of granulocyte-colony stimulating factor (G-CSF, an agent that stimulates the production of white blood cells) to ameliorate neutropenia and to allow for increased doses of Taxol® to be used was studied in trials carried out by the NCI Medicine Branch (35–37). In patients treated with the combination of Taxol® and G-CSF, neutropenia was no longer dose limiting; rather, it was peripheral neurotoxicity. However, through the use of G-CSF, significantly greater doses of Taxol® could be administered. Out of fourteen evaluable patients, one CR and four PRs were observed, all of whom were unresponsive to treatment with platinum compounds; five other patients experienced MRs.

In summary, it was this marked activity of Taxol® in patients with ovarian cancer, especially those whose tumors were no longer responding to treatment with platinum-based chemotherapy, that was a major factor in NCI's decision to accelerate the development of Taxol®. Accordingly, NCI decided that Taxol® should be developed via the CRADA mechanism whereby NCI and the development partner share data and coordinate future development efforts. The major initial objectives of the CRADA would be to increase drug supplies in order to allow the NCI to expand greatly the clinical usage of Taxol®, to assure wide commercial distribution of the approved product, and to establish alternative sources of supply (38). In a competitive process, BMS was selected as the CRADA partner, largely based on its experience and success in developing oncologic drugs, its past experience with natural products, and its submission of an aggressive Taxol® development plan. In return for devoting financial and scientific resources and for supplying the drug, BMS was to get exclusive rights to the NCI's clinical trial data. This exclusivity was needed because Taxol® was part of the public domain, and as such was not patentable. The clock started ticking in January of 1991 with the signing of the CRADA between NCI and BMS; the NDA was to be filed by the end of 1995.

INITIAL EFFORTS AT BMS

A major initial goal was to increase the supply of Taxol® so that the NCI could establish treatment referral centers to provide Taxol® therapy for appropriate ovarian cancer patients until the NDA was approved. The factors to be overcome in increasing the supply of Taxol® stemmed from the fact that the bark of the Pacific yew was the only readily available source of Taxol®. This fact, coupled with the knowledge that about 12,000 women die from ovarian cancer each year in the United States, and the fact that the bark from approximately three trees would be required to treat one patient, emphasized the enormity of the task. Furthermore, at about the same time that the CRADA was signed, data began to appear that showed that Taxol® had excellent activity against breast cancer; thus, the requirements for Taxol® could explode to where more than 300 kilograms of the drug would be needed each year.

Unfortunately, because of the complexity of the Taxol® molecule, complete laboratory synthesis of the drug was not an option at the time; in fact, even now, total synthesis of Taxol® has not been achieved, and it is problematic that such will ever be the case.

In order to increase the supply of Taxol®, agreements were signed between BMS and Hauser Chemical Research of Boulder, Colorado. Hauser and BMS forged agreements with the United States Bureau of Land Management to oversee collection and processing of Pacific yew bark. Even with this agreement, no federally owned lands could be logged beyond those that would normally be slated for logging.

During this collaboration, BMS supplied scientific expertise to Hauser that enabled the partners 1) to double the yield of Taxol® from bark extraction, 2) to exceed NCI's requests and needs for drug supplies by 1991, permitting the establishment of ovarian cancer treatment referral centers, and 3) to increase deliveries to NCI of the drug from 5,000 vials of clinical material per month to 50,000 vials per month in 1992. This permitted the NCI to establish treatment referral centers for patients who have breast cancer (38), a much more common tumor than ovarian cancer.

ROLE OF THE PROJECT DEVELOPMENT TEAM

Given the demand for Taxol® and the high profile of this agent in the oncology community at large, as well as the degree of coverage of the Taxol® story in the lay press, the project development team (PDT) for Taxol® was formally established immediately after the signing of the CRADA. Within BMS, Taxol® was designated as the number one priority agent for drug development. This designation allowed for work on Taxol® to progress at an accelerated pace. Extensive resources were reassigned to the project, and upper management made it known that, above all else, the development of Taxol® would proceed with the greatest possible speed. In fact, rather than a target date for an NDA filing of 1995, this was shortened to 1992. Even though speed was of the essence, however, quality could not be, and was not, sacrificed.

It was the purpose and mandate of the PDT to optimize development of Taxol® and, to do so, lines of communication among the various line functions were opened as well as lines of communication to, and from, upper management. PDT meetings were much more than "review of progress" sessions; members of the team became "problem solvers."

Being a member of the PDT for the number-one agent in the company had both "pros" and "cons." On the positive side, some members of the team found a certain degree of recognition within the company, and hence, a sense of pride developed, not only from a personal point of view, but also from a team aspect. Within their line functions, no major difficulties were encountered in obtaining the resources necessary to perform the required duties; i.e., work on no other project was allowed to supercede work on the Taxol® project. At the same time, there were negative aspects to being a member of the Taxol® PDT. The pressure was intense to get the work done in a timely fashion, but to "do it right the first time." Tempers became short at times because of this; project management played a major role in resolving many of the conflicts that arose (see below).

THE PROJECT MANAGER'S ROLE

As mentioned above, an important role for the project manager on the Taxol® PDT was that of arbitrator. As is often the case with a high profile project, stress management becomes a major issue. No time could be wasted by pointing fingers and blaming others. This fact was emphasized as the project progressed in complexity and the target date for the filing of the NDA came ever closer.

On occasion, differences of opinion among team members could not be resolved at the PDT meetings since such problems usually were between just two or three line function representatives. In such cases, with the assistance of the project manager, problems could be resolved via teleconference calls. In other more difficult cases, the project manager would arrange sub-team meetings to discuss the issues in detail. In addition, in the case of Taxol®, face-to-face discussions between the project manager and the various affected team representatives took place. This latter strategy proved to be very effective since PDT members were scattered among various sites within BMS, including research and development sites in New Jersey, New York, and Connecticut. At such face-to-face encounters, the importance of the representative's contributions to the development strategy were reiterated, thus rekindling the "sense of pride" alluded to above.

As the time for the NDA submission drew closer, the project manager's interaction with members of the Regulatory Affairs Department became increasingly frequent. Through this interaction, report submission dates, and so on could be readily monitored, and if major problems were foreseen that could not be resolved at the team level, upper management could be informed without delay, and the solutions could be found at that level.

The project manager's roles during the development of Taxol® were those of project monitor, facilitator, communicator, and peacemaker. Given the high priority of the Taxol® project, these roles were supported by management. In essence, the project manager was given the opportunity to do what had to be done to get the project accomplished.

REGULATORY AFFAIRS AND THE "FAST-TRACK"

A significant factor in the ability to get a rapid review of the Taxol® dossier by the FDA was the fact that regulatory affairs personnel established a good rapport with agency personnel through regular communication throughout the development of Taxol®. This communication not only included BMS personnel, but also those from NCI. As part of the CRADA agreement, a joint NCI-BMS steering committee for Taxol® was established. This committee met on a regular basis to discuss all aspects of the drug's development. This committee is still functioning at the present time, and there are no plans to disband it. The close collaboration between the NCI and BMS was best revealed when the NDA was reviewed at the FDA; both NCI and BMS personnel participated in the presentations before the reviewing body. Perhaps the best example of the successes of this collaboration and of the close communications with the FDA was that at the NDA review meeting, it was stated that the Taxol® dossier was the best organized application that the reviewing body had seen, and that it could serve as a "model" for other oncologic drug applications.

It is also apparent, however, that no matter the degree of FDA-company communication, the application would not have been reviewed with the alacrity that it was if Taxol® were not in such great demand, especially by the thousands of patients suffering from essentially untreatable ovarian cancer. The political pressures existing at the time surely played a major role in the agency's rapid review of the Taxol® NDA. However, the application was one of high quality (see above), so the review was no less complete than would have been the usual case.

LIFE AFTER THE NDA APPROVAL

Although Taxol® has been approved for use against ovarian cancer in the United States, Canada, and other countries, much more remains to be done. In addition, to the usual supplementary submissions for other indications, most notably breast cancer, a significant effort is being expended to establish alternative sources (to Pacific yew bark) of Taxol®. Given the concern regarding environmental implications of logging in general, reliance on a single species as a source for the drug would be imprudent. BMS and others are actively engaged in pursuing other avenues for obtaining Taxol®; these include using other yew species where the drug may be obtained from "renewable" parts of the plant, e.g., the needles, and thus the plant would not need to be destroyed. Ornamental cultivars and plant cell cultures are also being examined as possible sources for commercial quantities of the drug. Most promising, however, is the production of Taxol® by semi-synthesis. Here, a precursor of Taxol®, 10-desacetyl-baccatin, which has no antitumor activity in its own right, is chemically converted into Taxol®. The precursor is found in the needles of many yew species worldwide, and since needles are a renewable source, the supplies of 10-desacetyl-baccatin appear inexhaustible. Lastly, a major effort is being directed within BMS and elsewhere towards the discovery of analogs of Taxol® that may not require formulation in Cremophor EL®. Such analogs would not require the pretreatment of patients with antihistamines and steroids, and could prove more advantageous than Taxol® in that they might be more readily administered on an outpatient basis. However, any Taxol® analog would be classified as a new chemical entity distinct from Taxol® and, as such, would require a complete development effort of its own.

All of the projects mentioned above are ongoing, and all require relatively constant monitoring. The sense of urgency felt by the Taxol® PDT at BMS prior to the submission of the original NDA has not abated to any great degree. In concert with this, the role of the project manager in the overall development of Taxol® has not diminished. In fact, the diversity of Taxol®-related issues appears certain to make the project manager's role ever more interesting and challenging in the years to come.

REFERENCES

1. Wani, M.C., et al. 1971. "Plant Antitumor Agents VI. The Isolation and Structure of Taxol, a Novel Antileukemic and Antitumor Agent from Taxus Brevifolia." *Journal of the American Chemical Society* 893, pp. 2325–27.

2. Kingston, D.G.I., G. Samaranayake, and C.A. Ivey. 1990. "The Chemistry of Taxol, a Clinically Useful Anticancer Agent." *Journal of Natural Products* 53, pp. 1–12.

3. Borman, S. 1991. "Scientists Mobilize to Increase Supply of Anticancer Drug Taxol." *Chemical and Engineering News* 69, pp. 11–18.

4. Schiff, P.B., J. Fant, and S.B. Horwitz. 1979. "Promotion of Microtubule Assembly In Vitro by Taxol." *Nature* 22, pp. 665–67.

5. Schiff, P.B., and S.B. Horwitz. 1980. "Taxol Stabilizes Microtubules in Mouse Fibroblast Cells." *Proceedings of the National Academy of Sciences (USA)* 77, pp. 1561–65.

6. Dustin, P. 1980. "Microtubules." *Scientific American* 243, pp. 66–76.

7. Crossin, K.L., and D.H. Carney. 1981. "Evidence that Microtubule Depolymerization Early in the Cell Cycle is Sufficient to Initiate DNA Synthesis." *Cell* 23, pp. 61–71.

8. Carney, D.H., et al. 1986. "Changes in the Extent of Microtubule Assembly Can Regulate Initiation of DNA Synthesis." *Annals of the New York Academy of Sciences* 466, pp. 191–232.

9. Otto, A., et al. 1979. "Cytoskeletal-disrupting Drugs Enhance Effect of Growth Factors and Hormones on Initiation of DNA Synthesis." *Proceedings of the National Academy of Sciences (USA)* 76, pp. 6435–38.

10. Edelman, G. 1976. "Surface Modulation in Cell Recognition and Cell Growth." *Science* 192, pp. 218–26.

11. Parness, J., and S.B. Horwitz. 1981. "Taxol Binds to Polymerized Microtubules In Vitro." *Journal of Cell Biology* 91, pp. 479–87.

12. Schiff, P.B., and S.B. Horwitz. 1981. "Taxol Assembles Tubulin in the Absence of Exogenous Guanosine 5'-triphosphate or Microtubule-associated Protein." *Biochemistry* 20, pp. 3247–52.

13. Manfredi, J.J., and S.B. Horwitz. 1984. "Taxol: An Antimitotic Agent with a New Mechanism of Action." *Pharmacology & Therapeutics* 25, pp. 83–125.

14. Kumar, N. 1981. "Taxol-induced Polymerization of Purified Tubulin: Mechanism of Action." *Journal of Biological Chemistry* 256, pp. 10435–41.

15. Thompson, W.C., L. Wilson, and D.L. Purich. 1981. "Taxol Induces Microtubule Assembly at Low Temperatures." *Cell Motility* 1, pp. 445–54.

16. Roberts, J.R., et al. 1989. "Demonstration of the Cell Cycle Positions for Taxol-induced 'Asters' and 'Bundles' by Measurement of Fluorescence, Feulgen-DNA Content, and Autoradiographic Labeling of the Same Cells." *Journal of Histochemistry and Cytochemistry* 37, pp. 1659–65.

17. Roberts, J.R., et al. 1990. "Effects of Taxol on Cell Cycle Traverse: Taxol-induced Polypolidization as a Marker for Drug Resistance." *Cancer Research* 50, pp. 710–16.

18. National Cancer Institute. 1983. "Taxol (NSC 125973)." Clinical Brochure. Bethesda, MD: Division of Cancer Treatment, NCI, pp. 6–12.

19. Riondel, J., et al. 1986. "Therapeutic Response to Taxol of Six Human Tumors Xenografted into Nude Mice." *Cancer Chemotherapy and Pharmacology* 17, pp. 137–42.

20. Jacrot, A.U., et al. 1983. "Action of Taxol on Human Tumors Transplanted into Athymic Mice." *CR Seances Academie de Sciences* 297, pp. 597–600.

21. Lorenz, W., et al. 1977. "Histamine Release in Dogs in Cremophor EL and Its Derivatives: Oxylated Oleic Acid is the Most Effective Constituent." *Agents and Actions*, pp. 63–67.

22. Rowinsky, E. K., et al. 1989. "Phase I and Pharmacodynamic Study of Taxol in Refractory Adult Acute Leukemia." *Cancer Research* 49, pp. 4640–47.

23. Donehower, R.C., et al. 1987. "Phase I Trial of Taxol in Patients with Advanced Malignancies." *Cancer Treatment Reports* 71, pp. 1171–77.

24. Brown, T., et al. 1991. "A Phase I Trial of Taxol. Given by a 6-hour Intravenous Infusion." *Journal of Clinical Oncology* 9, pp. 1261–67.

25. Wiernik, P. H., et al. 1987. "Phase I Clinical and Pharmacokinetic Study of Taxol." *Cancer Research* 47, pp. 2486–93.

26. Wiernik, P.H., et al. 1987. "Phase I Trial of Taxol Given as a 24-hour Infusion Every 21 Days: Responses Observed in Metastatic Melanoma." *Journal of Clinical Oncology* 5, pp. 1232–39.

27. Grem, J.L. 1987. "Phase I Study of Taxol Administered as a Short IV Infusion Daily for 5 Days." *Cancer Treatment Reports* 71, pp. 1179–84.

28. Legha, S.S., D.M. Tenney, and I.R. Krakoff. 1986. "Phase I Study of Taxol Using a 5-day Intermittent Schedule." *Journal of Clinical Oncology* 4, pp. 762–66.

29. Kris, M.G., et al. 1986. "Phase I Trial of Taxol Given as a 3-hour Infusion Every 21 Days." *Cancer Treatment Reports* 70, pp. 605–607.

30. Ohnuma, T., et al. 1985. "Phase I Study of Taxol in a 24-Hour Infusion Schedule (Abstract)." *Proceedings of the American Association for Cancer Research* 26, p. 662.

31. Rowinsky, E.K., et al. 1990. "Taxol: A Novel Investigational Agent." *Journal of the National Cancer Institute* 82, pp. 1247–59.

32. McGuire, W. P., et al. 1989. "Taxol: A Unique Antineoplastic Agent with Significant Activity in Advanced Ovarian Epithelial Neoplasm." *Annals of Internal Medicine* 111, pp. 273–79.

33. Thigpen, T., et al. 1990. "Phase II Trial of Taxol as Second-line Therapy for Ovarian Carcinoma. A Gynecologic Oncology Group Study (Abstract)." *Proceedings of the American Society of Clinical Oncology* 9, p. 604.

34. Einzig, A., et al. 1992. "Phase II Study and Long-term Follow-up of Patients Treated with Taxol for Advanced Ovarian Adenocarcinoma." *Journal of Clinical Oncology* 10, pp. 1748–53.

35. Sarosy, G., et al. 1992. "Phase I Study of Taxol and Granulocyte Colony-stimulating Factor in Patients with Refractory Ovarian Cancer." *Journal of Clinical Oncology* 10, pp. 1165–70.

36. Sarosy, G. 1992. "Taxol Dose Intensification in Patients with Recurrent Ovarian Cancer (Abstract)." *Proceedings of the American Society for Cancer Research* 11, p. 226.

37. Sarosy, G., et al. 1992. "Dose Intensity: Is There a Dose-response Relationship for Taxol? (Abstract)." *Second National Cancer Institute Workshop on Taxol and Taxus*, Alexandria, VA., Sept.

38. DeFuria, D. 1992. "Taxol Commercial Supply Strategy (Abstract)." *Second National Cancer Institute Workshop on Taxol and Taxus*, Alexandria, VA., Sept.

Study Questions

Taxol®: An Example of "Fast-Track" Drug Development

1. What was the initial objective(s) of the project? What were the main reasons for the achievement of this objective(s)?

2. BMS and the NCI worked together to get Taxol accepted quickly. How is this stakeholder relationship going to affect the long-term aspects of other related projects?

3. List a few characteristics of the described project manager's role which you would consider important.

4. After the NDA had been passed, how would the project manager's job change?

5. When working on the development of Taxol, how should the project manager have managed and motivated project team members?

Privatization in Patagonia: The Selling of Argentina's Largest Hydroelectric Plant

H. Fred Smith, TransAlta Energy Corporation

PMI Canada *Proceedings*, 1994, pp. 34–40

When the bids were opened in Buenos Aires at an international public tender on November 19, 1993, for the concession rights for Argentina's largest hydroelectric plant, a newly formed consortium of three utility companies from Canada, the United States, and Chile submitted the winning bid—a financial obligation approaching $1 billion.

The sheer size of the bid alone was enough to daunt even a seasoned project manager. Dealing with four countries, three partners, and two languages in the short bidding cycle compounded the task. Moreover, the Piedra del Aguila (Stone of the Eagle) hydro plant itself came with some unique challenges.

Unfinished Construction

Construction was not complete, and the new concessionaire would have to take over the existing construction contracts. When the tender documents were issued in July 1993, only one of the four turbine generators was operating, and the other three were in various stages of fabrication and assembly in Argentina and Russia. Construction, which began in 1985, had been suspended in 1989 when funding had dried up. Construction had resumed in 1991, but the contractors' claims for schedule extensions and escalation had not been settled. Management of the construction effort and coordination of the some eighteen contractors on-site was being handled by Hidroeléctrica Norpatagónica S.A. (Hidronor), an Argentine government organization that was being rapidly dissolved with the progression of privatization.

Remote Site

The plant was located in a remote part of the country in the Patagonian desert near the Andes mountains. A large *Villa Temporaria* for 10,000 people had been constructed at the site to house the workers and their families, but it was being dismantled as construction progressed. No provisions had been made for housing the permanent plant workers once the temporary camp was removed. The nearest towns of any size were a three- to four-hour drive away, too far for daily commuting.

... And, It May Leak!

Finally, the dam had a couple of technical quirks. Cold water from the Andes mountains had filled the reservoir much more rapidly than expected. This caused thermal cracking in the concrete dam despite a number of preventive measures (1). Also, the reservoir was partially contained by one of the few "Paleocauces" in the world. The Paleocauce was an ancient river channel that abutted the reservoir next to the concrete gravity dam. Over geological history it had been filled in with porous layers of alluvia and basalt, gradually shifting the course of the Río Limay. While the river was shifting, water continued to seep through the filled materials. This in turn caused considerable back-erosion, which added to the fill's instability (2).

During construction, the Paleocauce had been reinforced extensively with grout curtains and drainage systems to try to prevent the Río Limay from resuming its ancient course, but a bevy of international experts had not concluded yet whether the efforts at reinforcement had been successful.

This paper addresses the due diligence evaluation of the 1,400 MW Piedra del Aguila plant, the challenges of preparing an international bid for a complex plant still under construction, the effort required to coordinate the activities of three separate technical teams with different languages and cultures, and the lessons learned from takeover of the plant in late 1993.

But first, a brief discussion of the Argentine electrical system and the government's privatization program is in order, followed by an overview of the features of its largest hydro plant.

ARGENTINA AND ITS ELECTRICITY MARKET

Argentina's electrical system has recently changed from a government monopoly to a privately owned market-based system of generation, dispatching, transmission, and distribution. Its restructuring, prompted by Argentina's economic crisis, presages trends sweeping utility systems around the world.

Debt Crisis Sparks Privatization

To counter spiraling inflation and a debt crisis, the Argentine government embarked on a major fiscal restructuring of the country's economy in 1989. The program included privatization of most government-owned enterprises, including airlines, the telephone system, the national oil and gas company, and the electricity sector.

Results of the economic restructuring have been significant. Inflation, which was over 200 percent per month when President Menem took office in July 1989, dropped to 8.4 percent annually by June of 1993. GDP growth was 8.7 percent in 1992 compared to a contraction of 6.2 percent in 1989, and a deficit of 3.3 percent of GDP in 1990 improved to a surplus of 0.8 percent of GDP in 1992 (3, 4).

Restructuring the Country's Electrical System

Modeled to some extent on the privatization of the British and Chilean electrical utility industries, the Argentine government restructured the country's electrical system into a market-based system. Radical revisions were made to the way electrical energy was sold and purchased.

A wholesale electricity market (WEM) was established, administered by the Secretary of Energy, generators, transmitters, distributors, and large users. Under the WEM, electricity distributors and generators can buy and sell electricity on a spot market, and spot-market transactions may be complemented by long-term contracts. Pricing is based on the marginal hourly cost of electricity.

Achieving Low Cost Electricity

The primary objective of the administrators of the wholesale electricity market is to ensure that electricity demand is met at the lowest possible cost, while also meeting principal service requirements.

In order to maximize the economic benefit of hydroelectric capacity, the WEM system deploys a series of models covering time horizons ranging from one day to three years.

Daily scheduling is carried out with a system-wide hydrothermal dispatch model that produces the most efficient scheduling of the hydroelectric energy available. All generators participate in the functioning of the WEM. They have opportunity to influence decisions regarding modifications to the models and to assure that the models have been implemented to serve the best interests of the country's electrical system

Selling the Electricity Concession

For privatization, Argentina's electricity sector was divided into three sub-sectors: generation, transmission, and distribution. Business units were formed to hold the operating concession for each facility or system, such as a generating plant or portion of a distribution system. Controlling interest in the respective business units was then sold in international public tenders. Transfer of the concession rights from the government-owned business unit to private investors was thus achieved.

The Piedra del Aguila Business Unit

Five business units were formed for the hydroelectric generation business of Hidronor, including one for the Piedra del Aguila hydro complex. The privatization of the Piedra del Aguila business unit was effected through the sale of shares representing 59 percent of the voting rights of the unit in an international public tender, the terms of which were stipulated in the "Pliego" (the tender documents). The purchaser of the 59 percent interest in the Piedra del Aguila business unit (the "concessionaire") has the right to appoint a majority of the board of directors of the unit, and otherwise direct and manage the business unit.

THE PIEDRA DEL AGUILA HYDRO PLANT

Located approximately 1,200 km southwest of Buenos Aires on the Limay River, the Piedra del Aguila hydroelectric plant is some 20 km from the village of the same name off National Highway 237. The plant is approximately equidistant (230 km) from the cities of Neuquen and San Carlos de Bariloche.

The Piedra del Aguila hydroelectric facility has a nominal capacity of 1,400 MW with an annual production in the order of 5.400 GWh.

Dam and Reservoir

A concrete gravity dam containing approximately 2.8 million cubic meters of concrete closes off the Limay River, creating a reservoir 100 kilometers long with a surface area of 292 square kilometers. The dam is 860 m long with an average height of 170 m. The reservoir is also contained on its left side by a natural sediment dam consisting of alluvial and basalt deposits on top of an ancient river bed (Paleocauce). An extensive system of grouting the Paleocauce has been deployed to seal the buried river channel including a grout curtain. The spillway is located on the left side of the dam and is controlled by four radial gates. The intakes for each of the four turbines are controlled by vertical gates; the water flows to the turbines through pen stocks 9 m in diameter.

Electromechanical Equipment

The turbines are located in the power plant at the foot of the dam. The turbines are Francis type with a vertical axis and a steel spiral case. Each turbine has a nominal capacity of 356 MW.

Each generator has three single-phase transformers to increase the voltage from 15.75 kV to 500 kV (50 Hz). A 500 kV substation is located just outside the powerhouse at the foot of the dam. The substation utilizes SF-6 insulated bus bar and switch gear with a double bus, single circuit breaker arrangement.

The plant is completely automated and uses a Bailey distributed control system (DCS) which allows run-up of the unit and synchronizing from the DCS control panel.

Construction Progress

After construction resumed in 1991, considerable progress was achieved. By the time the Pliego was issued in July of 1993 for the privatization bids, the civil works had been substantially completed. Assembly of the first turbine generator on-site had been completed and was being started up. Completion of Unit No. 2 was scheduled for later in 1993.

Population of the *Villa Temporaria* had been reduced to 3,500, and the civil works contractor had begun dismantling the housing units.

THE BIDDING CONSORTIUM

Three utility companies comprised the Hidroneuquén S.A. consortium: Chilgener S.A. of Santiago, Chile; Duke Energy Corp. of Charlotte, North Carolina, United States; and TransAlta Energy Corporation of Calgary, Alberta, Canada. The companies had never really worked together before except in the preparation of one round of unsuccessful bids for three hydroelectric plants in Argentina that had closed in June 1993.

TransAlta Energy had no assets in South America. Duke Energy's parent company, Duke Power Corp., had only recently acquired interests in TRANSENER, the Argentine electrical transmission system, and in Central Guemes, a 245 MW thermal power plant. Chilgener had led a consortium that had recently acquired the sprawling 1,000 MW Central Puerto thermal plant in downtown Buenos Aires.

Three Companies—Six Teams

Each company had an executive/financial team, responsible for organizing and structuring the funding required to support the bid, providing revenue forecasts, and developing the economic model. The financial teams assumed the lead role, organized the legal aspects of the bid, and assumed executive responsibility for assessing the final risks and fixing the bid price.

Each company also had a technical contingent who was charged with evaluating the engineering, construction, operational, and environmental aspects of the bid. The technical teams prepared the cost estimates for completing construction, providing the mandatory works stipulated in the Pliego, operating and maintaining the plant for the thirty-year life of the concession, and corporate management of the business unit. They also provided assessments of the risks associated with these activities.

¡Hola!—Four Cultures—Two Languages

Bid preparation under even the best of circumstances is usually hectic. Operating in four countries—Canada, the United States, Chile, and Argentina—with three equal partners and six teams complicates communications exponentially.

None of the people on the Duke and TransAlta teams spoke any Spanish—at least at the start of the bidding process. Outside the major hotels in Buenos Aires, few Argentines speak English; only a few of the Chileans were fluent in English. The Pliego and all the contract documents at the plant site were in Spanish.

Besides the language barriers, there were *cultural differences*, particularly among the technical teams. The Duke people were from the Carolinas—Southerners—who said "y'all," and wore funny hats. The Southerners had difficulty understanding the Canadians and vice versa. The North Americans were driven by a sense of urgency that simply lacked contagion in South America. The Chileans took long lunches, ate dinner late, and spoke a language the North Americans did not understand. The Chileans and Argentineans were outwardly polite to one another, masking old political animosities. The Argentineans seemed temperamentally indifferent to the vast economic and social changes sweeping their country.

Preparing the Bid

Bid preparation started in a panic. Traveling on vacation the last week in July, I received a call from my secretary. My boss wanted me to go to Argentina—something about "due diligence." Due diligence? Is this for a bank? What kind of power plant?

"I'll try to find out some more ... he's in a meeting ... can you leave Saturday at noon? Can you call me from a pay phone in a few hours?"

Let's see ... flying from Rhode Island to Calgary ... arrive Friday afternoon, need to pack, find some pesos (be nice to have a map and some information on the plant). Do I need a visa? Isn't it winter down there?

"Andes Mountains ... there may be snow. You'll need boots ... road's not that good in winter. Richard thinks you may be able to buy pesos in the Miami airport ... but you will be arriving there pretty late, the exchange booth may be closed. Nobody here seems to know much ... trying to set up a meeting Friday afternoon ...."

Snow? How cold? Who else is going? People from Duke? How will I know them?

"You're now flying on Sunday, depart at noon ... arrive Neuquén Monday night 9 P.M. Eight hour layover in Buenos Aires ... it's the only connection. I checked—it is Spanish ... not Portuguese. I can fax you some Spanish phrases ... call me when you're near a fax. It's a hydro plant ... I think we're going to bid on it ... like the others."

"Oh yes, I almost forgot, Richard said he has a few pesos. He'll give them to you—I don't think he's going back. There were bullet holes in the tail of the plane. I'm serious! It was in the northern part, though, on that coal plant. You're going south. Richard says not to worry."

Journey to Patagonia

When the plane left Calgary on Sunday, the trio from TransAlta—a pressed-into-service consultant from Newfoundland, a young electrical/mechanical engineer, and I—was still reading the bits and pieces of an unbound partial copy of the Pliego we had been given in a hasty briefing Friday afternoon. It was a bit like "Mission Impossible." We were almost expecting the packets of information to self-destruct after we had read them. We checked our tickets—for return fare.

We were supposed to meet the Duke team members in Miami on Sunday but could not find them. We linked up in the Buenos Aires municipal airport Monday evening. Duke had brought a whole contingent—specialists, consultants, translators, interpreters, environmentalists, and managers. The weather was wonderful, clear and 15° C. The parkas, boots, and survival gear became very heavy.

After a sleepless night for all in Neuquén (thanks to overheated rooms and a dog that barked all night), we had an early meeting with Hidronor at its main office in Cipolletti.

Does Anyone Know What's Going On?

Duke had set up the meetings with Hidronor to review the available documents and to inspect the hydro plant. Chilgener had already met with Hidronor on its own. Although TransAlta participated in the meetings with Duke, the utility companies had not decided to form a bidding consortium yet. Indeed, Chilgener, Duke, and TransAlta could well have ended up being competitors.

The first meeting with Hidronor was chaotic and frustrating. We were a large group (15) who had only met one another the night before. We crowded into a tiny conference room. Everyone seemed to have a different agenda. The translators and interpreters were having difficulty with the technical terminology. There was a constant babble of English and Spanish, and Spanish that sounded like English, and English that sounded like Spanish. The three telephones in the conference room rang constantly, and people entered and left the room at will. The Pliego was incomplete, and we did not have enough information to ask intelligent questions. Whatever we asked for did not seem to be kept in the Cipolletti office—we were told to ask for it at the site.

The tender closing date was just three weeks away. As the Duke and TransAlta technical teams dug into the complexity of the bid, a consensus was quickly reached that this date would be nearly impossible to meet.

On to Piedra del Aguila

The terrain outside Neuquén on the highway to Piedra del Aguila rapidly turned desolate—scrub brush, sand, and an occasional dusty village with a petrol station and roadside restaurant.

Fortunately, the staff members at the site were more hospitable than the terrain. After some initial frustrations, information proved to be plentiful. There was concern, however, that much was verbal, or transmitted "unofficially." Would the other bidders have the same information? Could we rely on it?

The teams took copies of everything that was available, took copious notes, and photographed every aspect of the dam and power plant.

The first turbine-generator unit had only operated for 800 hours at the time of the teams' visit—and was shut down for repairs. This did not bode well for the reliability of the plant. We discovered, however, that the shutdown had been planned—to allow some tie-ins at the 500 kV switching station—and the repairs were minor.

There was considerable discussion about the construction management personnel. What would happen to the Hidronor staff currently running the site? With privatization, Hidronor was being dissolved. Would the staff disappear? Could the new concessionaire hire the staff?

Hidronor was worried that the contractors on-site might try to take advantage of the change in ownership, which could significantly increase the risk to the bidders (and lower the price offered to the government for the plant). Hidronor initially said it would provide a list of personnel and salaries for us. They later said that the Hidronor professional staff might form a company and contract services back to Hidronor before the tender closing. The services contract would then be assigned to the successful bidder, like the construction contracts.

After some initial skepticism, the technical teams responded favorably to the latter suggestion. Ultimately, the Hidronor professionals formed two companies, and contracted their services to Hidronor as a joint venture (5).

Are We a Team?

By the time the technical teams drove back to Neuquén from the site, it had become official—Duke and TransAlta would work together, with Chilgener, as the Hidroneuquén S.A. consortium. There was also some welcome news from Hidronor. The tender closing date had been extended, the first of several extensions to be granted.

The teams returned to their respective home offices to prepare independent assessments of the plant.

Hammering Out a Consensus

After assessments had been prepared, the six teams met in Buenos Aires in mid-September to reach consensus. The technical groups and financial/executive groups met separately at first, then jointly.

The first technical consensus was reached when Chilgener and TransAlta agreed to use Duke's spreadsheet model to review the estimated costs. The remaining differences were not as easy to resolve. After several days, the teams had to agree to disagree on a few issues and compromise on many more. At the conclusion, though, a revised spreadsheet was produced that all three technical teams could accept and initial.

This revised spreadsheet became the basis for evaluating subsequent *Circulars* (changes to the *Pliego*) that were issued by Hidronor (6). It also seemed to provide an important structure to the bidding process, and helped the technical team members to start to work together.

Getting *Lean*—the Winner's Edge

An urgency about the bid seemed to develop around the first of November. The tender closing date had finally settled at November 19 and probably would not be extended; the Argentine government wanted to complete the transaction before year's end. The pre-qualifications were in, and three bidders had qualified to submit financial bids. (There had been rumors that the Hidroneuquén consortium might be the only bidder.)

The three technical team leaders decided that another trip to the site was necessary. The second turbine generator had been started up, and the first unit had been reportedly running well since September. The reservoir level had increased throughout September and October, subjecting a crucial upper alluvium/basalt joint in the Paleocauce to additional pressure and further testing repairs to the concrete dam. Finally, TransAlta and Duke had visited the Mendoza shop of IMPSA, one of the key electromechanical contractors, in September. We wanted to see if the Unit No. 3 materials we saw being fabricated had actually been delivered to the site and installed.

Chilgener also decided to send a team to have another look at the contracts. There were discrepancies in the certificates and progress payments that had never been resolved satisfactorily, and we felt we were carrying too much contingency for claims and uncertainties.

The site visit proved crucial—and positive—for two reasons. First, as expected, visiting the site a second time was a confidence builder. Both turbine-generators were running well and progress was evident on the third unit. The Paleocauce was performing better than had been projected with the additional head. Leaks in the concrete dam had been repaired cheaply. The Tecnor-Red joint venture was in place to manage construction, and site personnel seemed more committed with this uncertainty resolved.

More importantly, the technical people started to work together as a team. We started coming up with low-cost solutions to problems rather than compromising on contingency estimates. The long drives to the site, and then to Bariloche to redo the spreadsheets, provided time to informally discuss some outstanding issues.

The revised numbers that were faxed to our financial advisers in New York reflected our new confidence.

Grabbing the Prize!

The week before submission of the bid was anticlimatic for the technical teams. Emphasis shifted to the financial and executive side, assembling the funding, and fine-tuning return-on-investment calculations.

The bids were opened publicly in Buenos Aires on Friday, November 19, and word quickly reached Charlotte, Santiago, and Calgary—the Hidroneuquén S.A. bid was the winner, and by a slim margin!

A meeting in Santiago was quickly called for team leaders and key players to review a previously prepared takeover plan. Nominated members of the takeover team were confirmed, and the plan was updated and expanded. Team members returned to their respective countries to assemble additional staff, and the entire takeover team met in Neuquén on Monday, December 6. The official takeover date was December 29, 1993.

Chaos Reigns Supreme

Despite having a fairly detailed plan, the first few days in Neuquén were chaotic. Events continually conspired to keep everyone off balance.

The plan had been to set up temporary offices in a hotel while investigating permanent space. Part of the team would work in Neuquén and part would move to the site a few days later. An "advance" team had started looking for office space and had booked the hotel and transportation.

The newly nominated general manager of the newly registered operating company was the first to arrive in Neuquén, and he was unexpectedly met by a barrage of media people at the airport. The privatization was big news in the provinces of Neuquén and Río Negro, and the television and press all wanted the story. He spent the rest of the day giving interviews and setting up appointments.

The hotel did not have enough rooms to accommodate the entire takeover team, so part had to be berthed at another hotel on the outskirts of town. The vehicles picking people up at the airport did not have enough room for luggage, so more vehicles had to be found. The kick-off meeting the next morning had barely kicked off when the team leader announced that there was a group of insurance people going to the site right away, so part of the team had to leave as well.

After the kickoff meeting broke up, a telephone call came through—Hidronor was not happy about reading of Hidroneuquén's arrival in the local press. Did the new owners intend to meet with Hidronor? Another call. President Menem had not signed the decree authorizing the takeover yet. There were rumors he was on holiday and would not return until after the new year.

And so it went. Chaotic meetings, panic reactions. Each company had brought new members to Neuquén for the takeover, and they were unfamiliar with the plant, the complex deal, and the four months of intense work that had gone into the bid. A number of the North American personnel had never been to Argentina before and spoke no Spanish. Some of the Chileans spoke no English. The Argentine telephone system worked intermittently, making communication with the site difficult. More panic—there were really only ten days to set everything up because people were leaving for Christmas on December 16, and would not return until two days before takeover.

Terrorists Topple the Transmission Towers

Ten days of intense work—surprising progress—a week off for Christmas—and the team returned the evening of December 27. President Menem had still not signed the decree. The reception in Neuquén for 200 people had to be canceled. The reception at the site was still on for noon, but why was it at noon? The meters had to be read then, and they were spread all over the site. It would be at least one o'clock before anyone could attend. The reception was postponed, but the invitations had already been printed.

Then, the evening of December 28, the electricity went out in much of Argentina. Terrorists blew up two 500 kV transmission towers, taking out the power lines to Buenos Aires, the major load center.

The morning of the takeover, the Piedra del Aguila plant had been cut back from 700 MW to 250 MW and was spilling water. Output had been "0" the night before.

At twelve noon, the meters were read. The contracts and assets were transferred at the site, and the legal documents were executed in Buenos Aires. President Menem had appeared after all, and the decree had been duly signed.

The privatization of Argentina's largest hydroelectric plant, supplying 10 percent of the nation's power, was complete.

LESSONS LEARNED

The bid and takeover of the Piedra del Aguila hydroelectric plant had all the classic elements of a project. It was a temporary undertaking, staffed by personnel taken from different organizations, had a high uncertainty of outcome, and was dissolved once the project was complete.

The problems inherent in project management were exaggerated during the bid and takeover—by language barriers, cultural differences, technical communication difficulties, and great distances. These magnified the problems created by the very nature of project management and drove home some important principles.

There were many lessons learned during this project, and some old lessons were revisited. Some of the more significant ones are outlined below.
- *Team building exercises are synergistic and well worth the effort expended.* Significant breakthroughs for the technical staff members occurred when they worked together as a team. Chaos resulted when the teams broke down.
- *If two teams were better than six, one team would be better than two.* The financial/executive team should have been integrated with the technical team for a further breakthrough.
- *Partnering for foreign investment is essential.* Each of the three companies of Hidroneuquén S.A. brought unique experience and talent to the consortium in addition to investment capital.

... And Some Challenges Remaining

Besides the necessity of meeting the return-on-investment hurdle, and the risks posed to those returns by a government economy (and political system) in transition, the following issues may well define the ultimate success of the Piedra del Aguila venture.
- *Maintaining good relations with the host country;* this is manifest in a number of important ways. Many of the mandatory works involve community interaction—an archeological museum, maintaining area roads, and reforestation must be handled properly.
- *De-mobilizing the* Villa Temporaria; removing a town that has taken root over ten years may well be a greater challenge than completing the remaining turbine units.
- *Solving the housing dilemma;* once the *Villa Temporaria* is dismantled, the permanent plant staff members and their families must be housed. The solution has a long-term impact on plant economics and staff members' satisfaction with their workplace.
- *Maintaining a true partnership among the three partners;* the equal partnership will not be maintained if the partners do not, or are not, allowed to contribute equally. The partnership can easily lapse into a managed investment if management decisions and authority are unequally shared.

REFERENCES

1. Tovar, M.S., O. Navarro, and A. Giovambattista. 1991. "Preventive Measures to Limit the Aging Process of Piedra del Aguila Dam." International Commission on Large Dams (ICOLD), Vienna, Q.65 R.66.

2. Bustinza, Juan. (For a more complete discussion of the geological arrangement and morphology of the site). 1988. Piedra Del Aguila Development Geological Report, Foundation Characteristics, Cipolletti, Argentina.

3. 1993. "Confidence Man." *The Economist,* June 24, p. 6.

4. Secretary of Energy, Ministry of Economy, Public Works and Utilities of the Republic of Argentina. 1993. "Selling Memorandum for the Privatization of Hidroeléctrica Piedra del Aguila." S.A. Buenos Aires, Aug.

5. Agreement No. 757 was executed on September 29, 1993, between Hidronor and TECNOR-RED INGENIERIA UTE for "Direction and Inspection of Electromechanical and Civil Works of Piedra del Aguila Hydroelectrical Development."

6. In total, fifty-six circulars were issued—the last four on November 16, three days before the tender closing. The volume of the circulars exceeded the original volume of the Pliego.

Study Questions

PRIVATIZATION IN PATAGONIA:
THE SELLING OF ARGENTINA'S LARGEST HYDROELECTRIC PLANT

1. What was the primary objective of this project as described in the case?

2. According to the author, the bidding and takeover process described in this case "had all the classic elements of a project": a temporary undertaking, staff from different organizations, uncertain outcome, and dissolution upon project termination. Are there other elements to a project?

3. List some of the risks to this project. How can they be handled?

4. From the case it can be inferred that at the beginning of the project many of the actions in the project were not adequately planned. Most of the activities seemed to be reactive instead of proactive, and uncertainty was a constant, as shown through the terrorist attack on the transmission towers. Is this common for all projects?

5. Can uncertainty such as that caused by the multinational relationships described in this project be planned for? At what stage in the project can the project management identify and consider risks such as these?

Project Personnel Roles Changed

From the perspective of project management in the two federal departments, the Quesnel ATB project had significant impacts on the traditional roles of the project personnel.

In the traditional delivery process, in-house or contracted design specialists would develop a proposed facility based on preliminary operational requirements, and the developing concept would be subjected to numerous in-depth reviews for both operational and technical suitability, usually with reference to the "standards" for design. In the design/build delivery process, the project manager prepared a simple sketch reflecting the client's space requirements incorporated into a modular building layout.

The project manager had to ensure that client requirements were met in terms of performance expectations, rather than the specific technical data of the traditionally used standards. Likewise, the evaluation team had to be sensitized to compare each bidder's concept on the basis of performance expectations.

On a traditional delivered project, once the contract is awarded the role of Public Works Canada's project managers is to enforce the time, cost, and quality of work stipulated in the contracts. With the design/build method, the project manager becomes more of a pilot steering the contractor through the final design and construction activities to ensure the client's expectations of scope, time, cost, and quality are met.

This change in role was demanding since policies and procedures had not been developed to aid this form of project delivery. Yet, in this context of seemingly incompatible or restrictive procedures, one of the most important lessons of the project emerged. It is easier to gain support for changing procedures when a project under implementation clearly requires an adjusted process. Once a change has been made, it is far easier to follow the path a second time. This can be an effective means project managers can use to change process systems to meet their needs.

The method adopted for delivering the Quesnel air terminal is being followed to deliver another larger-scale terminal for the Sandspit airport. The Pacific Region has adopted the proposal package used for Quesnel as a general package. It was edited to meet the specific performance criteria required for the Sandspit Airport air terminal building.

Client Role and Relationships Changed

The client also has many role adjustments to make. Transport Canada's Airports Group in the Pacific Region partners with engineers and architects at Public Works Canada (PWC). Each year, PWC project managers implement twenty or more projects together with their Transport Canada client.

Notwithstanding the excellent working rapport between the joint staff, traditional ways of doing business did change. Transport Canada usually assigns a technical specialist as project leader on behalf of the airport manager. In addition, support staff review project designs and specifications to ensure they meet client needs.

The Transport Canada project leader on the Quesnel ATB project found that communication requirements expand significantly when traditional processes are changed. Staff members responsible for detailing the client's operational and technical requirements had to redefine their relationship with the project manager and all other parties. Instead of scripting long lists of specific requirements, which in-house or consultant designers traditionally use, they focused on describing the performance characteristics required for the building. Instead of reviewing designs, selected technical staff members were assigned to the committee reviewing proposals for design and construction. Once a developer/contractor was selected, a new discipline came into force: the client was under greater pressure to complete design reviews quickly and minimize changes to the project scope. The emphasis was to get project requirements agreed to up front.

This need to define project requirements up front is not new to management. However, it did take a new process operating under time constraints to shake the requirements providers into adopting the idea. The management directive, that any requirements not provided up front would not be included later, played a key role in the success of the new project delivery method.

Transport Canada's senior management also found its role changed. Senior management members' interest and involvement in a different project delivery method meant they had to evaluate and manage new risks. How can quality be assured when you don't specify materials and construction methods? Could the project be delayed if the best overall bid is not the lowest bid, thus requiring application for the authority to skip the lowest bidder? Since the process is different, do we have the requisite knowledge and skills available to manage it?

Government agencies try to avoid taking risks. Government departments look differently at the risks taken in delivering a project by design/build, compared with how private sector firms regard those risks. Operating in the "fish bowl" of public scrutiny, government officials are very sensitive to the concerns and opinions of a broad constituency of interested parties. Ensuring continued support for a different approach to project delivery required greater than normal emphasis on consultation and communications. Key people were kept informed by steering committees, technical committees, airport site advisory committees, special meetings, briefing notes, and frequent one-on-one meetings and phone calls. All these techniques apply in normal project delivery but the frequency of meetings and the range of expertise among participants expanded with this project.

LESSONS LEARNED

When a public enterprise takes on a design/ build project that is a significant departure from how business is usually done, new relationships form, old relationships are enhanced, and processes change. If the process is successful, it can change how the players view their jobs and their capabilities. This type of initiative in a public sector environment can trigger further empowerment and system change. The project team became committed to solving problems aggressively; they wanted success and, individually and collectively, they sought opportunities to further improve the project delivery processes.

Listening to customers and addressing their concerns directly can have a revolutionary impact on an organization that traditionally defines project requirements for others.

Although design/build is not a guaranteed way of reducing project costs, it does offer an alternative method of delivery that can gain momentum as government departments continue to look for ways to deliver programs more cost effectively.

The design/builder can often provide innovations that are transferable to new projects. The design/build team has strong incentives to find ways of reducing costs and expediting the project. The approach can deliver cost-efficient innovations from the developer. For example, speed in project design and delivery is often cited as a primary reason to seek a developer who is a design/builder. In the case of the Quesnel ATB, although speed of delivery was not a driving priority, the project proceeded eight weeks ahead of original schedules. The obvious lesson is that the process can accelerate schedules, and the project manager should be prepared to respond and exploit the opportunity.

Since the developer's schedule created the requirement for the project manager and the client to assess their proposals more quickly, decisions were made and implemented fast. Decision-makers and reviewers not only made the effort to meet the shorter turnaround times, but they recognized that responsiveness was a key element in maintaining the quality of the relationship between the developer, project manager, and the client.

This broad-based understanding of the importance of working cooperatively has been instrumental in setting up the correct environment for implementing the next design/build project.

The cooperative relationship required frequent and open communication. The emphasis placed on developing communication plans, setting up work groups and committees, and holding more frequent meetings supported the collaborative effort.

In the early stages of the project, the communications requirement was even more of a challenge because the project team did not have a building design to show interested parties. It was also necessary to explain how the design/build process varies from the design/bid/build process that many people understand.

On the other hand the increased need for communications was offset by the project manager having a "single point of contact" with the designer/builder.

For future projects, additional consideration will be given to allowing for contingencies in setting the project budget. The client must evaluate risks and be prepared to consider that components of the project budget are targets to be met within reasonable tolerances, as opposed to fixed amounts. To this end, the public sector project manager would be wise to increase the contingency budget on design/build projects.

Applying new techniques in the public service environment can deliver collateral benefits. Public enterprise project managers can use design/build as a tool, not only for delivering projects for clients in a new way, but as a means of demonstrating that they are capable and willing to innovate. In a world that demands innovation and flexibility from public servants, this change in attitude can deliver the biggest benefit of all.

Study Questions

QUESNAL AIR TERMINAL: DESIGN/BUILD WORKS IN THE PUBLIC SECTOR

1. This case illustrates how, due to the pressure from a group of stakeholders, the project found a creative way of achieving the desired result. Stakeholders are a very important element of any project. Develop a generic set of stakeholders for any project.

2. Who were the specific stakeholders for this project, and what was their stake in the project?

3. This project worked with the public sector and thus existed in the "fish bowl" of public scrutiny described. In order to continue funding for the project, the project management must be sensitive to its relationship with the public. How did project management deal with this concern successfully?

4. The use of the design/build method for the contractor allows the fulfillment of many goals and requirements of the stakeholders in an innovative manner. What are some of the advantages of this method that are mentioned in the case?

5. The design/build method resembles an interdisciplinary team made up of members from engineering, design, and manufacturing. Due to the development of such a team, many positive effects are felt in the project. This type of team is also know as a product-process team or the concurrent engineering process. What are the advantages to this type of team or process?

6. It is stated in the case that "listening to customers and addressing their concerns directly can have a revolutionary impact on an organization that traditionally defines project requirements for others." Compare this statement to the well-known Hawthorne effect, which shows that attention paid to employees impacts the conscientiousness of employees in their work.

The National Aero-Space Plane Program: A Revolutionary Concept

Robert R. Barthelemy, Director, National Aero-Space Plane Joint Program Office
Capt. Helmut H. Reda, USAF, Plans Directorate, National Aero-Space Plane Joint Program Office

PMI *Proceedings*, 1992, pp. 490–93

INTRODUCTION

The National Aero-Space Plane (NASP) is a look into the future. It is a vision of the ultimate airplane, one capable of flying at speeds greater than 17,000 miles per hour which is twenty-five times the speed of sound (Mach 25). It is the attainment of a vehicle that can routinely fly from Earth to space and back, from conventional airfields, in affordable ways. It represents the achievement of major technological breakthroughs that will have an enormous impact on the future growth of this nation. Most of all, it is a projection of America at its best, as its boldest, at its most creative. It is more than a national aircraft development program, more than the synergy of revolutionary technologies, more than a capability that may change the way we move through the world and the aerospace around it. NASP is a revolutionary technical, managerial, and programmatic concept; it is a possibility of what can be in America.

The NASP program can be described from a technological, programmatic, and environmental perspective. In each case, NASP has departed from the traditional evolutionary path. To achieve the NASP vision, innovative and revolutionary approaches are required. The technical challenges require the synergism of several major technology breakthroughs. The programmatic and environmental challenges require a fundamental change in the development, management, and implementation of this strategic, high-tech program.

The Technical Challenge

The goal of the NASP program is to develop and demonstrate the feasibility of horizontal takeoff and landing aircraft that use conventional airfields; accelerate to hypersonic speeds; achieve orbit in a single stage; deliver useful payloads to space; return to Earth with propulsive capability; and have the operability, flexibility, supportability, and economic potential of airplanes. To achieve this goal, technology must be developed and demonstrated that is clearly a quantum leap from the current approaches being used in today's aircraft and spacecraft.

The NASP demonstration aircraft, the X-30, will reach speeds eight times faster than any other air-breathing aircraft. As it flies through the atmosphere from subsonic speeds to orbital velocities (Mach 25), its structure will be subjected to average temperatures well beyond anything ever achieved in aircraft. While rocket-powered space vehicles, like the Space Shuttle, minimize their trajectory through the atmosphere, the X-30 will linger in the atmosphere to use the air as the oxidizer for its ramjet and scramjet engines. The NASP aircraft must use liquid or slush hydrogen as its fuel, which presents new challenges in aircraft fueling, storage, and fuel management. To survive the thermal and aerodynamic environment, the X-30 will be fabricated from a combination of highly advanced materials: refractory composites, metal matrix composites, and extremely high-temperature super alloys. Because no large-scale test facilities exist to validate aerodynamic and propulsion operation above Mach 8, the design and operability of NASP aircraft must be carried out in "numerical wind tunnels" that use supercomputer-aided computational fluid dynamics (CFD). Propulsion systems based on subsonic and supersonic ramjet combustion will propel the X-30, and although these types of engines have been investigated in laboratories, there have been no significant flight tests. In the areas of aerodynamic design, flight control, thermal management, cooling systems, man-machine interface, and many other subsystems, NASP requires a major increase in capability to reach its objectives. The technical and system integration necessary to achieve single-stage-to-orbit (SSTO) aircraft operations will be more difficult than any yet attempted and will require a fundamentally new approach to aircraft design. In essence, NASP depends not on a single advance in technology, but on the synergism of breakthroughs in a number of major technical areas associated with aerospace vehicles.

The Technical Response

The NASP program is carefully orchestrated to achieve the technological advances and integration necessary to attain X-30 goals. There are five key areas of technology that are the focus of the NASP development program: engines, aerodynamics, airframe/propulsion integration, materials, and subsystems. Significant development activities are under way, and major advances have resulted. In the first three areas, approaches that were initiated at the start of the NASP program in 1986 are beginning to pay off. The work in materials and subsystems development was substantially accelerated in 1988, and there have been major breakthroughs since then in these critical technologies.

The feasibility and operability of a high-speed propulsion system are the key developments required in the NASP program, and those activities are receiving the greatest attention. The basic engine-approach NASP is a combined ramjet/scramjet air-breathing propulsion system which will provide high-efficiency thrust for much of the region between takeoff and orbit. Various low-speed systems and the use of rocket systems at very high Mach numbers and for orbital insertion are being investigated. Several key materials were identified as being critical to the feasibility of an air-breathing, SSTO aerospace vehicle.

Because of the high-temperature, high-strength requirements of the NASP airframe and engine systems, most of the interesting configurations employed combinations of high temperature titanium aluminum alloys, carbon-carbon or ceramic composites, metal matrix composites, high creep strength materials, and high conductivity composites. Although the development of these material systems has been under way for several decades, the progress being made was insufficient to meet NASP requirements. Development of all five material systems was accelerated through the formation of a national materials consortium focused on the five material types, with a greatly enhanced resource commitment. The consortium fabricated, characterized, tested, and developed materials in each category, and significant progress had been achieved in the arena of super alpha 2 titanium aluminide, titanium-aluminide-silicon carbide metal matrix composites, and oxidation resistance-coated carbon-carbon composites.

The aerodynamics of hypersonic aircraft and aerospace vehicles has been the subject of considerable government, university, and industry attention for the past thirty years. Much is known about this subject, and the NASP program is taking advantage of the wealth of information available in the United States. The aerodynamic requirements of NASP vehicles, however, are extremely stressful and sensitive to small changes in vehicle configuration and performance. In addition, the specific flight regime of the X-30 has not been extensively examined through ground experimentation or flight testing. Because the X-30 itself will examine the aerodynamics of air-breathing aerospace vehicles, effort on the current development program has focused on developing detailed CFD models and on verifying them using several experimental tests. A massive CFD effort, using a significant fraction of the total United States supercomputer capability, is under way to develop experimentally valid models to predict the inlet, combustion, and nozzle operation of the NASP. Three-dimensional, full Navier-Stokes codes that account for real-gas effects, chemical kinetics, and turbulent flow are being refined using shock tunnel, wind tunnel, and archival flight data to predict the critical NASP aerodynamic parameters to well within 1 percent of the desired values.

Because the airframe and engine systems development for the NASP has been pursued by separate organizations, the level of airframe-engine integration required of hypersonic aircraft necessitated a major emphasis in this area. Since the program began, this integration has commanded great attention and has received an enormous amount of government and contractor resources.

Although the previous four areas have demanded most of NASP resources, every subsystem of a hypersonic aircraft will be developed to the point when it will support the testing of an experimental vehicle. Major efforts are required to develop slush and liquid hydrogen systems, cryogenic tankage, fuel delivery systems, heat exchangers, turbopumps, avionics, cockpit systems, flight controls, and the instrumentation required to conduct X-30 research.

The Programmatic Challenge

It has been over eighty years since man first flew and over forty years since aircraft flew supersonically. For the past forty years, airplane speeds have advanced from Mach 1 to Mach 2 with only a few notable exceptions: the SR-71 was capable of Mach 3+ flight, and the rocket-powered X-15 achieved speeds around Mach 6. In general, however, it has taken us eighty years to go from Mach 0 to Mach 2. In contrast, NASP is attempting to increase the speed range of air-breathing airplanes to Mach 25 by means of a ten-year development and demonstration program. During the 1950s and 1960s, much activity was aimed at the exploration of hypersonic vehicles and their possible configurations. Wind tunnels, shock tunnels, and experimental aircraft were fabricated and used to examine the key parameters of hypersonic flight. Unfortunately, that activity ended prematurely in the 1960s, and the development of hypersonic aircraft virtually ceased until the NASP program began. A few government researchers and even fewer university and industry scientists kept the vision alive during those years, but progress in hypersonic has been extremely slow. Although research in the critical areas of materials, CFD, and combustion has progressed because of other demands, the national capability at the beginning of the NASP program was extremely limited, dispersed, and disorganized.

To conduct a challenging program like NASP, an extensive, competent, well-integrated, and focused national team from industry, government, and academia had to be developed. A prime task of the development phase of the NASP program is not only to bring the key technologies to a point that will allow an X-30 airplane, but to form the team required to do the job. In 1990, there were over 5000 professionals working on the NASP program, as contrasted to 250 in 1985. Although the principal goal of the NASP program is to demonstrate an aerospace vehicle capable of aircraft-like operations while achieving single-stage-to-orbit, the program has also become the basis for all hypersonic technology in the United States. Although the program must be focused on the goals of the NASP X-30 demonstrator, it must also generate the technology that will allow a broad basis for future hypersonic vehicles and derivatives of the NASP demonstrator.

The Programmatic Response

Management of the NASP program has emphasized collaborative, participative approaches because the goal of the program is so develop a national team that can lead us into the aerospace era of the Twenty-first Century. From the onset, the government laboratories and centers have been an integral part of the NASP team. Much of the initial expertise on the NASP program resided with government researchers, who continue to play vital roles as consultants, contributors, and evaluators for the program. When the program began, only a few industrial companies and academic institutions had substantial ongoing efforts in hypersonics. These few not only had to be supplemented, but some of the leading aerospace companies had to be added to the field. Five major airframe companies (General Dynamics, Rockwell International, McDonnell Douglas, Lockheed, and Boeing) and three leading engine companies (Pratt & Whitney, General Electric, and Rocketdyne) received firm fixed-priced contracts and were all heavily involved in the initial stages of NASP. Firm fixed-price contracts are rarely used for research and development efforts, but the Joint Program Office (JPO) realized intense competition existed between contractors regarding who would become the industrial leader for developing future hypersonic aircraft. The contractor selected to design, build, and test the X-30 would have a virtual monopoly on the research data and a tremendous lead to design future hypersonic vehicles. In 1987, McDonnell Douglas, General Dynamics, Rockwell, Pratt & Whitney, and Rocketdyne were selected to continue with the program.

Since the beginning of NASP, significant efforts to manage the program using innovative management concepts were made. Joint government/industry decision-making has been a norm for the program. Consortia formation and generic government/industry technology development has been fostered, and very strong associate contractor agreements between all appropriate parties have been affected. In 1988, a materials consortium of the five major companies was formed to accelerate the development of NASP airframe and engine materials. The program was a complete success with major materials advances and excellent cooperation between the companies. The materials consortium success, coupled with the need to develop a strong national industrial base for future hypersonic aerospace systems development, led in late 1989 to the consideration of a single NASP team. Progress and corporate contributions by the three airframe companies and both engine companies had been excellent, and a single team comprised of all five leading contractors seemed highly desirable. Although each company had pursued its own unique configuration approach, a national NASP team would allow a single, synergistic configuration to emerge, and all development efforts could focus on that concept. Another major advantage of a single team would be the guarantee of a broad yet competitive industrial base in the United States for future operational hypersonic and aerospace vehicles. Early attempts to foster such a national team paid off when the program schedule was extended in 1989 by two and a half years. With increased time for research and development, and a spending rate which was essentially constant from 1988 through 1993, the idea of a single, national NASP team took hold. In late 1989, the NASP JPO began procedures to form such a team. The five contractors were most responsive and agreed to form a joint venture partnership through a cost-plus-fixed-fee letter contract. This novel programmatic response was highly beneficial to the successful execution of the NASP Phase 2 research and development (R&D) program.

On the government side, innovative and integrated management has been the program standard. The NASP program actually began in 1981 when Mr. Anthony duPont, an aerospace engineer, convinced Dr. Robert Williams at DARPA that an air-breathing hypersonic aircraft could fly all the way into a low Earth orbit and return. Initial research supported duPont's claims, and in 1984, DARPA conducted a larger study called "Copper Canyon" to validate duPont's concept. The Copper Canyon study agreed with duPont's concept and identified key technological challenges to be overcome. Realizing a long-term financial commitment was required to achieve breakthroughs in multiple, unproven, high risk technologies, DARPA enlisted the participation from potential beneficiaries through a unique five-part memorandum of understanding (MOU) between the Air Force, Navy, SDIO, NASA, and DARPA. Each agency and service branch pledged funding, and with the exception of SDIO, assigned people to create a single government program office, the NASP Joint Program Office at Wright-Patterson Air Force Base. The five-part MOU also created a NASP steering group composed of high-level DoD and NASA experts, as well as other experts on aerospace, defense, and science. The steering group advised, provided program direction, and served as a source of advocacy to the Congress and administration.

To minimize bureaucratic aspects of a government-funded program, the NASP JPO maintained a manning level of approximately seventy-five people, used streamlined management principles, and operated under specialized management practices authorized by Air Force Regulation 800-29. Several hundred government technical experts throughout the United States assist the contractors to accelerate technology maturation. About 20 percent of the program resources have been, and will be, spent in government R&D efforts. The JPO's principal role has been to focus the efforts of the thousands of personnel in hundreds of companies and universities toward the program goals. Executive direction is provided by a steering group of senior-level DoD and NASA officials, which meets biannually to guide the program. The Joint Program Office is manned with program and technical managers from the Air

Force, Navy, and NASA, and operates as a unified government organization with a strong total quality and high-performing team culture. The common vision for both government and industry partners is the X-30 and the experimental demonstration of the aerospace plane. It is this vision which drives the program and allows this unique programmatic response to be successful.

The Environmental Challenge

The National Environment Policy Act of 1969 requires all major federal programs to consider consequences of their proposed actions that may significantly affect the quality of our environment. Before proceeding to Phase 3 of the NASP program, the public, key decision-makers, and all interested groups will be informed of potential environmental impacts. The NASP program will make gigantic leaps in technology, creating unique environmental challenges. These challenges are being addressed in the NASP environmental impact statement (EIS).

The Environmental Response

The NASP program is very conscious and committed toward protecting the environment. All impacts described in the EIS will be addressed and pro-actively mitigated prior to program implementation. The country's top environmental scientists are investigating all potentially significant impacts of the NASP. They will report their findings in the EIS and respond to questions through public hearings. Their findings, along with lessons learned from the Space Shuttle and other high-technology programs, will directly influence the X-30 vehicle design and ground support system. Actual environmental data gathered during the X-30 flight test program will be incorporated into the design process for follow-on NASP-derived vehicles. Lessons learned from the NASP EIS will lay the basic foundation for future environmental assessments of hypersonic vehicles.

The X-30 environmental program began in 1988 when the Air Force Center for Environmental Excellence Environmental Directorate at Norton AFB accepted the task to develop the NASP EIS. In 1989, the Air Force Flight Test Center at Edwards AFB wrote the initial, "Description of Proposed Action and Alternatives," which describes the NASP Phase 3 program. In 1990, The Earth Technology Corporation, located in San Bernardino, California, United States, was awarded a task-order contract to develop the EIS. The public was first informed of the NASP environmental program in January 1991 when a notice of intent was issued in the Federal Register and major newspapers in the Washington, D.C., and Edwards AFB areas. Public scoping meetings were held in February 1991 at Washington, D.C., and Lancaster, California. At these meetings, the general public and news media were given a one-hour overview of the NASP program followed by a public comment period. Twenty-four people responded with written and oral comments. The public will again have an opportunity to comment on the program when the draft EIS is made available. Comments on the draft EIS will be studied and addressed in the final EIS and then forwarded to the Environmental Protection Agency (EPA). The EPA's Environmental Record of Decision will be an input used by key government officials to decide whether to preceed with Phase 3 of the NASP program.

To assess the environmental impact for Phase 3 of the NASP program, a baseline description was developed. The foundation of this baseline plan follows:

• Final design of the X-30 will occur at the home sites of all five primary contractors and will be integrated by the contractors' National Program Office (NPO) through an electronic telecommunications network. Approximately 100 to 200 people will be assigned to the NPO for program integration, while the majority of the effort and personnel remain at their contractor home sites.

• Final assembly will occur near the flight test complex at Edwards AFB. Approximately 300 to 600 people will assemble, check out, and ramp test the X-30. Component manufacturing and subassembly will occur throughout the United States. Subassembly, integration, and checkout will occur at the primary contractor sites and the final assembly site.

• Ground testing will occur throughout the United States to take maximum advantage of existing and future ground-seat facilities. New technologies and flight hardware must be appropriately ground seated prior to flight certification.

• The NASP ground support system and flight test complex will be located at Edwards AFB, California, utilizing the test infrastructure from the Air Force Flight Test Center and NASA's Dryden Flight Research Facility. Approximately 1,000 to 3,000 people will be involved in the flight test effort. Flight testing will occur over portions of the continental United States, with each flight's exact geometry dependent on the desired test conditions, weather conditions at Edwards and abort landing sites, X-30 turn radius, availability of instrumented ranges, and noise constraints. Up to 150 missions may be flown to achieve SSTO and gather specific research data.

The existing environmental database for hypersonic vehicles is small and resides primarily within NASA and several DoD laboratories. To maximize quality of the EIS with minimum cost, a national environmental team was formed to take advantage of unique government resources. The team is structured around ten environmental resource areas: physical features, air quality, biological/wilderness, cultural resources, infrastructure, land use, airspace, health and safety, socioeconomic, and noise.

Over forty other environmental topics are also being studied, including: encroachment on threatened and endangered species; disturbance to plants, wildlife, and their habitats; airspace congestion; noise and visual intrusions; socioeconomics; population changes; impact on public services; disturbance of archaeological and historical sites; impact on Native American activities; etc. Although the EIS is still being developed, preliminary results indicate only minor impacts exist. The top three environmental topics are: 1) sonic booms, 2) stratospheric ozone depletion, and 3) hazardous materials. These topics are being thoroughly investigated by the NASP Environmental Team through the USAF environmental impact and analysis process and will be documented in the EIS and Environmental Record of Decision.

Initial estimates from two independent studies confirm the X-30 will have a negligible impact on the concentration of stratospheric ozone. (Since the X-30 will use cryogenic hydrogen for fuel and air from the atmosphere as its oxidizer source, water is the primary combustion product.)

NASP has studied the impact of sonic booms since 1989. The NASP design team used these studies to optimize the X-30 ascent profile to minimize the sonic boom impact on the Antelope Valley. As the X-30 accelerates to supersonic speeds, it will remain within specially assigned supersonic corridors which were located in sparsely populated areas to minimize the environmental impact below the flight track. The sonic boom signature within these corridors will be similar to the Space Shuttle's re-entry over-pressures. Beyond those corridors, a combination of flight-path optimization and simple operational constraints will essentially eliminate the perceptibility of a sonic boom on the ground.

NASP designers are also striving to eliminate hazardous materials on the airplane and within the ground support system. However, if they cannot completely avoid such materials, the NASP program will take all the necessary environmental precautions to make sure they are handled and disposed of properly.

SUMMARY

The NASP program is an experiment that tests the ability of the United States to work together to achieve revolutionary technology development and effectively translate that technology into viable products. Because it is succeeding in meeting that goal, it has become an example of government-industry collaboration, effective technology utilization, long-range visioning, and focused national commitment. These are the very principles that were at the core of the outstanding progress the nation achieved earlier in this century. They are the same principles that have been so successfully used by our economic competitors during the latter part of this century to capture a significant share of the markets and capabilities that once were ours exclusively. These are the principles for our nation's future growth, and NASP is the foundation for our aerospace leadership in the Twenty-first Century.

Study Questions

THE NATIONAL AERO-SPACE PLANE PROGRAM: A REVOLUTIONARY CONCEPT

1. The authors state: "Although the program must be focused on the goals of the NASP X-30 demonstrator, it must also generate the technology that will allow a broad basis for future hypersonic vehicles and derivatives of the NASP demonstrator." These two objectives are complementary but could potentially become conflicting. Discuss some of the key characteristics of the objectives of a project.

2. By its characteristics, this project can be called a mega-project. This type of project requires special attention on certain issues. List some of the strategic issues you consider important for this kind of project. Do you think the managers of this project have addressed these issues? How would you define a mega-project?

3. Discuss some of the project benefits that can be highlighted when communicating with the general public about this project.

4. There have been cases of mega-projects (such as the superconducting super-collider project) that have been terminated after several years of work. Discuss the importance of knowing when to terminate an unsuccessful project. Is there a possibility that the NASP project might have the same fate?

5. Identify the stakeholders in this case and discuss their roles in the project.

DIRECTING

4

DIRECTING

Quality Management Works

Tony Yep, Project Manager, Bantrel Inc.

PMI Canada *Proceedings*, 1996, pp. 40–45

INTRODUCTION

I remember sitting at my desk one day halfway through the project. It wasn't a particularly busy day, and things were going well. As usual, the project team was busily working away on its tasks and meeting its commitments. The members were very focused and self motivated on what they had to do, and they seemed to be enjoying their work, judging by the smiling faces passing by the open door of my office. A thought flashed by. "The project team didn't need me!" It was a strange feeling, but I distinctly remember that it felt good. As the project manager, I knew that I would only be as good as the people who worked for me, and that they were the key to making this project a success. I also knew that this quality management stuff works!

As project managers, how often do we get to apply the many quality theories we have been exposed to in the execution of our projects? More importantly, how do we know that they will work? On this particular project, I had the opportunity to apply and test many of the theories on total quality management, and I found, not surprisingly, that the theories work fine!

A quality management approach was used, and various management techniques were implemented, to accommodate this approach on the project. This called for an open, democratic management style, fully supportive of team-based activities with empowerment filtered down to the people who took ownership and commitment to execute the work and to meet the project objectives. People were encouraged to feel good about their work and their participation as part of the team. The theory works fine when all the elements are put in place, and everyone wants to make it work.

This paper will deal with *specific* management techniques which were done on a practical level, and the principles which were followed to make this project a very successful and satisfying experience. Although many of these techniques relate to the execution of engineering work, they can apply to the execution of any project, as the theories on quality management remain the same. The important thing is to recognize that the benefits are there for the taking if you try them out. You, too, can be pleasantly surprised at the outcome.

THE PROJECT BACKGROUND

ARCO is an industry leader in the United States in the development of cleaner burning fuels. This project was part of its current initiatives with its California Air Resources Board (CARB) Clean Fuels Projects for a major upgrading of its Los Angeles Refinery to meet the stringent air emission standards for the State of California. The CARB project totalled over $400 million in installed cost, and the CARB gasoline had to be in production by March 1, 1996. ARCO is also a strong proponent of total quality management on its projects, and it supported many quality improvement initiatives. The project had a significant performance incentive to encourage and promote the use of quality management in the engineering work.

Cross-discipline engineering was required to complete the design and drawings for the installation of four new pentane storage spheres and a new flare stack system. This work was initially started by Bechtel in the United States and the balance of the work was transferred to Bantrel Inc., Bechtel's Calgary office, to complete the detailed engineering work. This project was schedule driven, totaling about 33,000 hours, over a seven-month period, with manpower peaking at about forty people. The engineering disciplines involved were systems/mechanical, civil/structural, piping, instrumentation, and electrical.

Bantrel was the first engineering company in Canada to be registered to ISO-9001 back in 1993. This meant that the company had in place established procedures on how it does its work, quality control and quality assurance programs to ensure that the work is done correctly, a procedure to identify and correct deficiencies to achieve continuous improvement, and adequate training programs supporting these procedures. Call these the hard measures of quality management, as all these items can be physically measured.

However, a true quality management system must include more than just the hard measures of a quality system. The soft measures such as teamwork, empowerment of the people, management style, and working environment become critically important if the full benefits of any quality program are to be achieved. With the full support of Bantrel management, it was decided to implement as many of the soft aspects of quality management on this project so that its results and benefits could be assessed.

Quality Issues

Quality management is a term used interchangeably with "total quality" in our company to describe an organization's system for continual improvement and its commitment to the quality process. Quality management challenges the two paradigms common in our business:
• Errors and rework are inevitable.
• Workers have only their labor to contribute.
• Today's methods will be adequate to meet tomorrow's challenges.
    Quality gurus such as Deming, Juran, and Crosby agree that:
• *Quality improvement requires a shift in management philosophy.*
• *True improvement results from a focus on the quality of the work process (i.e., the system and not blaming individuals for problems).*
• *A culture conducive to continuous improvement is required.*
• *All functions and departments must be included.*
• *Training is critically important.*
• *Recognition of achievements is necessary.*
• *Improving quality leads to improved productivity.*
• *The person doing the job is generally the most knowledgeable about that job.*
• *People want to be involved and to do their jobs well.*
• *More can be accomplished working together (teamwork) to improve the system than individuals working around the system.*

- *The adversarial relationship between the workers and management is counterproductive and outmoded.*
- *Everyone must be involved to improve the way things are done.*

The quality theories derived from these authors are shown in italics throughout the rest of this article.

People and Trust

Quality theory states that "management must recognize that people are the organization's most valuable and long-term resource. Management must help their people through training which will result in quality improvement. Management must not blame workers for problems in the system, and it must remove barriers that rob the people of their pride of workmanship. People want to work for the overall good of the organization and to share in its success."

People are not dumb, and they don't give away their trust freely just because you are the project manager. Trust needs to be earned, as reflected by actions supporting the words. The strange thing about trust is that you have to give it first before you have any hope of getting it back in return. People need to be trusted as much as they inherently want to do a good job. To promote an atmosphere of trust and cooperation, an open and democratic management style was used and along with it an "open door" policy. In other words, the project manager's office was always open for anyone on the project team to discuss any issues, work related or otherwise.

Early in the project, the discipline leads were told that they would not be blamed if anything went wrong with their work, and that if they failed, then, collectively as a team, we all failed. Furthermore, the project manager would ultimately be responsible, and he would accept the blame for all the work done by the team. It took a long time for the leads to believe this, as they were so used to being blamed for the failings of the project. Still, after two months, written memos from various disciplines would be sent explaining why they couldn't do certain things, sort of covering their backsides. And each time no one blamed them, even when they knew they were at fault, and the problem was resolved together. In time, they realized that the project manager's actions were indeed consistent with his words, and that he trusted them to do the right job, and they could trust him to support and help them when they needed it. The biggest benefit to all this was that whenever a potential problem arose on the project, the leads were no longer afraid to bring it up, and there was always enough time to implement corrective measures to prevent the issue from becoming a real problem.

The Quality Plan

A specific quality plan was implemented to train the project team on the various aspects of quality and continuous improvement. The basic quality requirements were covered in the company's corporate quality manual. Client and employee questionnaires were used as a feedback mechanism to identify areas where quality improvements could be made. Quality training sessions on "What is quality?" and the "need for quality" were conducted to help the team understand the theories behind quality improvement and why we need to work as a team and how to focus our services to both internal and external customers. Team-building exercises were implemented, such as the survival "Alaskan Adventure" test, to meld the team together and to have a bit of "fun" on the project. The project team reacted very well to these training initiatives, as it showed that the company was serious about quality.

Team Concepts

When the project team was assembled, a specific request was made not to stack the team with high performers or "superstars." People who were available at the time were assigned to the project, and it was left to the project manager to apply the quality theories and to put the team together. The initial group was quite diverse—this was the first big project for the piping lead, the project secretary was a recent hire, and the instrument lead was an agency (contract) person. Actually, 30 percent of the project team was comprised of agency personnel, which is not unusual.

Quality theory states that *if a team to be molded into a cohesive unit, all team members must be treated equally. If they contribute to the success of the project, they must all share in its benefits.* Typically, one quarter of the team will be the high performers. These individuals are generally self motivated, committed, and highly competent. The next half can be considered the competent middle group who will usually do a good job and work well in a team environment. The last group is the one that can make or break the project. If this group does not believe in teamwork and produces lower quality work with less effort and commitment, then it will drag the total team performance down. A team will consist of performers of all levels, and to be effective, every participant must be committed to contribute to the best of her ability and to try to continuously improve. That is what makes a team.

To show how strong a bond teamwork can be, there was a time on the ARCO project that the civil/structural group had to work overtime to meet their scheduled commitments. As the project manager, I didn't ask them to work overtime, I only authorized it after the lead indicated that they needed to do so. When the lead asked his group how many would work Saturday, all twelve said that they would come. Can you imagine what the feeling would be on this team if only half showed up and the other half didn't care? They all cared. They were a team.

The agency people were a bit surprised that they were treated like the staff personnel. Like the rest of their team members, they shared the same team luncheons, they participated in the same quality training sessions and team-building exercises, they received the ARCO recognition awards along with everyone else, and they were involved in key decisions affecting their work. On the project, there was no distinction. The agency people responded as if they were part of the team, with the same commitment and desire to see this project a success.

Team Buy-in and Empowerment

Quality theory states that *teams should take ownership of their decisions. They should be empowered to implement their recommendations and alter the system within the approved boundaries of their mandate. Management should not tamper with the team decisions, but should create the right environment to facilitate this process. All individuals on the team should be empowered in their accountabilities to the extent they become self-managing. And they should be empowered to fully communicate their concerns and know that they are being heard.*

Empowerment; it is such a powerful word ... a cure-all to all our ills, like a magic pill. Speak the words "the people shall be empowered," and poof, it happens. If it were that easy, then everyone could be project managers! True empowerment takes work and time to make it happen.

On the ARCO project, the discipline leads were expected to take full responsibility for their schedule commitments and their manhours. This is no different than for any other project, but, here, a more integrated team approach was tried. The project controls person is generally responsible for schedules and for the measurement of the engineering progress based on job hours expended and physical progress achieved. Traditionally, this individual was viewed by the disciplines as a "stoolie." In other words, his job was to find out what the disciplines weren't doing on schedule, or that were spending too many manhours, and report it to the project manager who would then put pressure on the disciplines to get things back on track. The disciplines disliked the time spent helping the project controls person status the schedule and work progress, as they were, in fact, supplying information being used against themselves. Usually, there would be regularly scheduled formal status review meetings where all the leads attended, and while it may benefit project management, the disciplines felt that this was a waste of their time.

To change this situation, the formal status meetings were eliminated. In their place, the project controls person was asked to work one-on-one on a regular basis with each discipline lead to help her plan her work, to define her deliverables, to establish her manpower requirements, and to come up with realistic schedules the disciplines would accept. The schedules maintained the overall milestone targets required by the project, and it was the scheduler's responsibility to ensure the collective activities of all the disciplines were in a logical work progression to minimize rework as a result of out-of-phase interdisciplinary work. It was the discipline leads' responsibility to identify their manpower and resource requirements based on the defined schedule and work progress and to advise project management of any deficiencies.

A simplified work progress measurement system was implemented to show the discipline leads on a biweekly basis how the job hours were being expended and what progress, by defined deliverables (e.g., drawings, data sheets, etc.), was achieved. The discipline leads were shown how to decipher and use the information on their progress. There was a standing order that overtime work would be authorized whenever the discipline leads felt it was necessary; it was their responsibility. Furthermore, if a certain deliverable was slipping schedule, the delay in completing that task was not to take longer than one working week to complete. This put some flexibility in the schedule to account for unforeseen delays.

This arrangement worked very well. In time, the discipline leads considered project controls as part of their own groups. They were getting timely information which they now actively sought as it helped them better execute their work and identify problem areas. There never was a problem on the project which wasn't known at least two weeks in advance and resolved on schedule. The discipline leads truly took ownership of their work, management supported their efforts, and they became empowered as a result.

Effective Communications

Open and honest communication is essential to build up trust and this type of communication must be encouraged at both the project level and the discipline levels.

Quality theory states that *people must be treated with dignity, trained and supervised properly, and they must know what their job is so that their performance can improve. They must understand the process, the project expectations and where they fit in.*

To achieve this objective, a project orientation was given to every person working on the project, either full time or part time. This was done personally by the project manager, as it gave the people a chance to meet the project manager directly, to ask him questions, and to hear what the expectations were for the project, how it was going to be executed, and why its success was important to the company. Project orientations were conducted throughout the duration of the project as long as new people came aboard. On the ARCO project, sixty-eight people were oriented even though the project only peaked at forty full-time personnel.

The project execution plan was reviewed as part of the project orientation. Typically in the past, this document tended to be very voluminous, filled with lengthy project procedures and other boilerplate descriptions of the various discipline functions. It was not a very user-friendly document, and as such, people tended not to read it—even the project managers! The revised format of this document is now typically no more than a 1/4" thick, and it has been rewritten to be very "readable," with the project team being the primary user. Task, work, scope, and responsibilities are covered, along with the method of execution by discipline, the key players and points of contact for the client and the project team, the project reporting requirements, the objectives of the quality plan, and listings only of the applicable project procedures, specifications, and standards. Everyone on the project team was encouraged to read and use this document, which everyone did.

To achieve tighter communications among the disciplines, the physical layout of the project team members was made in such a way as to shorten the actual distance between those disciplines which had to work closely together. For example, all the project leads were put together with the piping lead sitting next to the civil/structural lead and the instrumentation and electrical leads adjoining. The systems/mechanical lead and the project controls lead were close by. In this way, there was no valid reason why they wouldn't be talking to each other.

Project communications were also optimized. The project files, which included the relevant discipline and quality files, were centralized, as were the vendor print files. Project team members were encouraged to use these files for the latest data as opposed to keeping a separate set of files for their own use. The master mark-up of the piping and instrument diagrams (P&IDs) were kept on a centrally located roller board. The disciplines were still responsible for keeping an up-to-date set of their drawings on stick files, but available for all disciplines to access for review. This worked well, and it reduced the amount of rework needed because of wrong or outdated information being used.

A different approach was also tried for internal meetings which traditionally meant a formal status meeting of a sort once a week where the disciplines reviewed their progress for that period. As this project was schedule driven with many interrelated activities happening immediately at the start, a daily meeting was convened first thing every morning, and it lasted no more than one half to three-quarters of an hour. The discipline leads attended as did the project secretary and the document control representative. Each participant was asked to identify what information or help he needed from the others in the team to help him complete his work.

The project control lead kept the group informed of the schedule and estimating commitments and the input required for the various change orders. As project manager, I used this opportunity to keep the project team fully appraised of any developments with clients and the latest company news. The discipline leads in turn were responsible for filtering this information down to the rank and file. Formal meeting notes were not necessary because if the person didn't get some information needed that day, the same question would be raised the next day. These meetings were kept light and informal even though serious topics may have been discussed.

This worked very well as the information was always current and relevant. It also freed the leads from having to attend too many meetings which in turn permitted them to spend more time in planning their work and supervising their groups. As the project progressed, the frequency of these meetings decreased from daily to three times a week to once a week. Weekly status reports were still prepared for the client, but these were easily done by the project controls lead since the work status was always known. The only formal meeting involving the discipline leads was for the monthly status review meeting with the client in our office.

The project bulletin board was also a constant source of information. The project roster and organization chart were posted and updated as changes were made. In addition, the latest project news and results of client and employee questionnaires, along with a weekly office safety tip, were posted. People awarded the ARCO Recognition Award were notified and recognized on the bulletin board. Humor was introduced by weekly cartoons or philosophical sayings to draw the project team to the bulletin board and to keep the team atmosphere light and less stressful. People were always curious to see what was new on the board, as the humor material was unpredictable.

The ARCO Recognition Program

The ARCO Recognition Program was set up to recognize individuals and groups who make outstanding contributions to the project in terms of costs savings, dedication, schedule adherence, etc. People were recognized with plaques and prizes ranging from mugs, pens, caps, T-shirts, tote bags, and clocks, all the way up to cash awards, dependent on the level of the award.

When I first saw the program, I questioned its value as I couldn't see why people should be rewarded "for simply doing what was supposed to be their jobs." Apparently in Canada, such programs are rare among engineering companies. However, this recognition program had an impact. People liked receiving the plaques, which they proudly displayed, and the gift, however minor it was, seemed to be appreciated. All awards were made in the presence of all the team members.

Quality theory states that *all team members must share in project awards.* Along this line, discipline groups were recognized en masse as their major work hurdles were achieved. First came everyone in the civil/structural group, then the piping group, followed by electrical and instrumentation. Even the secretary and document control personnel were recognized. In all, almost everyone on the project team was eventually recognized. ARCO initially thought it was very unusual to recognize such massive groupings since it didn't give awards to everyone. But ARCO agreed, as that's what was needed to reinforce teamwork. It was a positive experience for everyone.

A Lunch for No Particular Reason

As part of the quality plan and team-building program, a project luncheon or training session was scheduled once a month without fail. Normally, project luncheons or celebrations would be held only after certain milestones were achieved, and then the "rewards" would be given. In this case, there were no strings attached. Sometimes the lunch was held just as part of team building and to get the project team out together socially. And this included everyone—full time, part time, and agency members.

Every month there would be a luncheon, sometimes combined with a quality training session or a team-building exercise, but more often than not, for no particular reason other than you were a member of the project team, and you were sharing some of the benefits. After all, a happy worker will be a very productive one—so the quality theory says. In addition to these luncheons, the project team was treated to donuts at least once a month. So if nothing else, the project team was well fed! Everyone associated with the project was appreciative of this special type of treatment, as it was unexpected.

Management Style: Autocratic versus Democratic

Quality theory states that *management style will be greatly influenced by the management approach adopted—either traditional or quality. The traditional management approach is considered to be an outdated style of running organizations, unable to use the full potential of their workers. Whereas a quality management approach focuses on creating a workplace that encourages everyone to contribute to the company.* Following are some attributes of these approaches.

Traditional Management	Quality Management
Expecting people to know	Emphasis on education and training
Reactive	Preventative
Schedules/goals independent of reality	Goals based on system/resource capabilities
Communications oppressed by fear	Breaking down barriers through trust and reduction of fear
Short-term gains	Long-term focus
Management by objectives	Long-term relationships
Recognition of individuals best at fighting fires and problem solving	Team based focus; people made to feel good about their work and contributions; recognition of improving processes

The traditional management style can be considered to be autocratic, demanding, and uncompromising. On the other hand, the quality management style can be open, democrative, and people oriented. The question here is that if teamwork and people are to be very important variables toward the success of any project, then what management style will best foster teamwork and trust? Adopting an open, democratic, and participative management style does not mean that the project manager will lose control and be less effective. On the contrary, she will have more control and be more effective because she will have the whole team supporting her throughout.

The Benefits

Corporate management is always interested in return on investment. This is no different for any quality management initiative. Is it worth it? What tangible benefits we will get using a quality management approach? The argument here is that there are many examples of projects done the traditional way which met schedule and cost and which made the company money, so why change? The counter argument to this is: How much more profitable would this project be if quality management is used? The best way to settle this would be to take two identical projects and execute them both ways and see the results. But this is not practical.

We should look at the long-term benefits. Quality theory states that *there is too much emphasis on short term profits. Most North American executives think they are in the business to make money, rather than products and services. If you become the world's most efficient provider of whatever product and service you offer, the profits will follow.*

There are a lot of intangibles which do not readily convert themselves to cold hard cash. A happy worker is a more productive worker. How do you measure the productivity gains? Companies which are successful and people oriented will attract better people and, more importantly, keep their good people from leaving. What's the cost for training and personnel turnover? Quality management will minimize rework, and that is measurable. On the ARCO project, the actual rework attributed to design/drawing errors, late vendor data, poor interdiscipline coordination, and computer system downtime totalled less than 3.4 percent of the total engineering manhours.

The ARCO project was very successful. It met the manhour targets even allowing for some major design changes requested by the client. It met all schedule commitments; the team was flexible enough to accommodate a two-month acceleration of the underground works. The amount of rework required in the field was negligible with only some slight problems encountered with the underground works due to unforeseen obstructions. The field installation costs came well below the budgeted costs, attributed in large part to the quality and completeness of the engineering work. This resulted in achieving 90 percent of the performance incentive, making this project exceed its financial projections. And the people? They said it was the best project they'd ever worked on! They felt good about their achievements, and it was the closest they came to having "fun" at work. They looked forward to the next project like this. So how do you measure all this? The benefits are there when you put all the quality theories into practice.

The Project Manager's Responsibility

On any project, the project manager has the leadership and the ultimate responsibility for quality. He should be a firm believer of the quality principles and be willing to adapt them to his projects. He must be a coach and a motivator to all project personnel. His actions must lead by example and demonstrate total commitment to participative management and customer satisfaction. Quality management will not happen if the project manager does not make it happen.

Quality management cannot be delegated. The project manager must be a hands-on quality champion on the project. He must be fully involved and must "walk the talk." He must lead, guide, and coach. He must facilitate, listen, trust, and be trusted with a highly involved work team. To improve his project management skills, he must be willing to change.

Which brings us to the saying, "If you always do what you've always done, you'll always get what you've always gotten ..." which implies that improvements cannot be achieved without change. Think about it. If you believe that the quality theories are correct, then quality management works! The choice is yours.

Study Questions

QUALITY MANAGEMENT WORKS

1. In order to facilitate communications on the project, team members with different responsibilities were seated next to each other. How would this affect diverse team members, such as those in production and design?

2. This project used a creative method for dealing with status review meetings. Why was it possible and useful to use this type of control system?

3. The author of the case made reference to several total quality theories of Deming, Juran, and Crosby. Which of these points do you consider most important to the success of the project? Discuss.

4. What are the benefits of the recognition programs, free luncheons, and teamwork training sessions? As a project manager, is it your responsibility to coordinate efforts such as these?

5. Do the concepts presented in this case match all that you have read, heard, and learned concerning project management? Given what you have read in this case, is a project manager also a total quality manager?

Destroying the Old Hierarchies

Seth Lubove

Forbes, June 3, 1996, pp. 62–70

Aircraft are no longer gee-whiz products—just machines for moving people and goods cheaply over long distances. As it struggles to adapt, Boeing has a new boss with a new mission.

At a recent charity event, Boeing Co.'s new chief executive officer, Philip Condit, donned a cowboy hat and belted out a rendition of the country and western classic "Could I Have This Dance?" A karaoke machine provided the accompaniment.

No one could imagine Condit's predecessor, Frank Shrontz, 64, a lawyer by training and a former Pentagon deputy, singing in the shower much less in front of strangers. The change in personalities at the top of the world's largest aircraft manufacturer is rich in symbolism.

The seventh man to run Boeing since its founding by timberman William Boeing in 1916, fifty-four year-old Condit is a Boeing lifer who faces the tough task of redefining Boeing's often confrontational relationship with its 108,000-employee work force, tightly unionized by the militant International Association of Machinists & Aerospace Workers. Nobody states the problem better than Ronald Woodard, the blunt-spoken president of Boeing's Commercial Airplane Group: "We have to understand that we are a manufacturing enterprise. We aren't an engineering, technology development enterprise." There's a world of meaning in that seemingly bland statement.

Booming on the surface, Boeing is in fact a company in transition. Much as they are technological marvels, today's passenger jets are basically commodities to Boeing's customers, the world's airlines. Their job is to move people and goods from point A to point B at minimum cost consistent with safety. Boeing makes great airplanes, but so do Airbus and McDonnell Douglas. Who gets the sale depends to a large degree on price, terms, and availability.

That's what Boeing's Woodard means when he talks about making people understand that Boeing is a manufacturing company, not a high technology company.

Boeing jets represented two-thirds of the dollar value of all commercial airplanes ordered in 1995. Boeing's defense division, already the prime contractor on NASA's space station, is competing on the Joint Strike Fighter jet project, a potential $160 billion contract. Wall Street expects per share earnings to rise by 20 percent this year (before charges in 1995), to $2.75, on sales of $22 billion. The Street expects earnings to go on rising through the decade.

But that will happen in what is now a commodity business only if Boeing can do what companies like General Electric do so successfully: take costs out of the product and continue to take out.

Condit made his mark when he oversaw development of Boeing's latest-generation airplane, the 777, known internally as the "triple seven." Smaller than Boeing's humpbacked 747, the 777 is more distinctive for what you don't see than for its profile. It's a pilot-friendly and airline-friendly product. For the first time, the pilot's commands to the rudder and flaps are communicated electronically, rather than by cables and levers. Airlines can internally reconfigure such areas as galleys and lavatories within as few as seventy-two hours, compared with two to three weeks on older aircraft. No marketing detail was too small; even the toilet seats gently sink onto the toilet bowls, instead of loudly smacking. First put into service by United Airlines last June, the 777 is Boeing's first plane designed entirely on computers.

But for Boeing, Condit's biggest change was in the organization of the program. Adopting the theme of "Working Together," Condit broke down the old-fashioned procedural walls within the company. In the past, design engineers worked independently of the production and operations people who actually built the plane. Here it is, the designers would say; now, go build it.

Condit instead organized hundreds of integrated "design-build" teams, composed of members of all these groups. Each consults the other, so that production people aren't stuck with overly costly, hard-to-build design specifications, for example. This sort of reform, common now in manufacturing, came late to Boeing. "None of us is as smart as all of us," Condit says, explaining his new integrated design strategy. He wants to reorganize the whole company along these lines. Explains Ron Woodard: "We're trying to destroy all the old functional hierarchies."

This is where the job gets tough. Any significant changes involving the workforce still have to get past the machinists local, Boeing's largest union, with about 33,000 members. (Boeing's engineers are represented by another, less combative union, the Seattle Professional Engineering Employees Association.)

Say what you may about the shrinking clout of private-sector unions in this country, the fact is that the Machinists can still bring Boeing to its knees, as they proved during last fall's sixty-nine-day strike. "The thing that's different is ten years ago we could have had a strike and delivered airplanes late to customers, and they didn't care," says Woodard. But today a strike means lost sales.

Frank Shrontz hammered at reducing cycle times and cutting costs, to the point when Boeing now delivers an airplane within ten months of the order, compared with eighteen months previously. He pushed toward greater standardization of parts and shrank the workforce from 161,700 in 1990 to 108,000.

But Condit knows that making further gains in reducing costs and improving delivery time depends on making improvement in that amorphous area known as human relations. In naming Condit as his successor, Shrontz cited Condit's interpersonal skills—not necessarily his engineering abilities—as the characteristic he considered most important for the next leader of the company. "We can make pronouncements up here all day long," says Shrontz, sitting in his orderly office overlooking historic Boeing Field. "Phil is motivational. We need to motivate the people to understand the importance of the change and to help make it happen."

Unlike Shrontz, who was rarely seen on the shop floor, Condit frequently pops into plants unannounced, usually tie-less and dressed casually.

Recently he walked unescorted onto a 777 undergoing final assembly in Boeing's Everett, Washington, plant and asked the supervisor to leave the plane so the workers could speak without feeling intimidated.

During the strike last fall, when most Boeing executives kept a low profile, Condit walked over to a group of picketers outside his Seattle office and chatted amiably about the proposed contract for forty minutes, He even signed striking union member Tony Russell's picket sign. Addressing the message to Russell's wife, another Boeing employee, Condit wrote: "We all need to work together."

Back at work now, Russell, a tool builder, is already seeing some differences in his job. Under the old, military style of management, if Russell detected something wrong in his engineering plans, he'd have to go through his supervisor and the problem would move through the chain of command until it eventually reached the engineer.

Now Russell speaks with the engineer directly. When he was building the scaffolding for the 777 line, for instance, Russell noticed that the metal deck he received was bigger than the deck on the blueprints. Russell called the engineer and quickly fixed the problem.

Multiply this sort of shortcut throughout a company as large as Boeing and you can see how much expensive time was wasted before. You can see, too, why it used to take the company eighteen months to deliver a product as complex as a giant jet.

When Phil Condit chats up workers on the factory floor, he's not just going through a public relations exercise. He is obviously sincere when he talks about making the workers partners rather than just a factor of production. Traditionally, when Boeing needed additional hands, it would run a classified ad in the newspaper for, say, qualified assembly mechanics. It would get maybe 2,500 applicants and hire perhaps 1,500, just so many bodies in the machine.

In keeping with the new attitude, Boeing is putting more time and effort into the hiring process. In April, announcing that it would hire 8,200 new hands, Boeing also said it would put applicants through extensive aptitude tests.

A cynic might say that Boeing wants to weed out potential malcontents, but that misses the point: Boeing is also recognizing that an efficient work force is one that genuinely believes in what it is doing and gets along well as a team. Thus such questions as: How does a worker respond in a confrontation with a supervisor? None of this is new in manufacturing circles (*Forbes*, Oct. 9, 1995), but it's a big change for Boeing.

Selection of supervisors and managers, too, will change. Rather than promoting a person who is good at, say, riveting, and making him a supervisor of rivets, the company will look for managers who can motivate, rather than intimidate, the workforce.

To underscore the emphasis on communications, at least symbolically, Boeing now sends annual reports to all its employees, not just shareholders. The company also put 75,000 employees through a program that discussed the realities of a tough market. The message: We no longer have it made just because we're Boeing; the customers tell us our planes cost too much and take too long to deliver.

"It has been a cultural change, a fundamental change in the way we think, act, and do," says C. Gerald King, president of Boeing's Defense & Space Group.

The machinists union is responding—cautiously. It says it is willing to relax job specifications to allow cross-training of workers. But William Johnson, president of the local that represents the Boeing workers, is hard-nosed about subcontracting, or what the union calls "off-loading" work, now done in-house. Boeing makes 52 percent of its planes' parts in-house and wants to shrink that down to 48 percent. Management thinks it can save an estimated $600 million annually by such outsourcing. More important: outsourcing is a way to win favor from foreign airlines by agreeing to let factories on their home turf do some of the work.

In settling the latest strike, union and management compromised on outsourcing. Boeing agreed to give the union warning on any major subcontracting deals and to retrain surplus workers for other jobs in the company. "In the old days we would have fired them," says Larry McKean, senior vice president of human resources.

But what is perhaps the biggest current irritant in management/labor relations at Boeing remains the constant pressure on the workforce to meet constantly shrinking delivery schedules. Front-line managers—and the workers below them—are evaluated on how fast they can get the planes out the door. If the work falls behind, the teams must go on overtime. "They're trying to get into cross-training, but we don't really have time," says a frantic Robert Boudreau, a lead mechanic on the 777 wing line, as he motions to a schedule that indicates his team is days behind on its work.

Many workers are cynical about the new togetherness the company tries to foster—"buzzers" is their slang for the buzzword phrases like "total quality management" and "world class competitiveness."

Daniel Mahoney, general counsel of the engineers union, sums up the dilemma neatly: "You just can't have peer democracy in the workplace. We have these extraordinary leaders in management who are willing to treat the rank and file with great respect and listen to their ideas. But at the same time they have a responsibility to get the best product out on time."

But Mahoney doesn't deny that Phil Condit is doing his best to reconcile those seemingly irreconcilable objectives. Condit plans incentive pay and rewards for achieving individual performance goals. To make his point, he banishes Boeing's model airplanes to a display case outside of his office and in their place displays his mother's black and white photos of children from around the world. He says he wants his employees to think, "Gosh, the company is really interested in my welfare." And there can be no doubt: Condit really means it.

He rightly says that many new ideas are just old ideas the people forgot. Visit the restored converted barn where William Boeing first began building planes, he says. Designers were on the top floor; production was downstairs. If production people had a problem with a blueprint, they just walked upstairs for an answer. Can Boeing get back to that as an employer of over 100,000 people spread over 76 million square feet of factory floor. No, but Condit is determined to show that at the new Boeing, while aircraft are now a commodity, people no longer are.

No Experience Necessary

Want to work at Boeing? Be prepared to sit through at least four hours of tests. The company wants workers who will fit into cross-functional teams and show initiative.

Experience? It counts less than aptitude. As a recent Boeing want ad stated, even if you've never touched an airplane, you may have what Boeing is looking for. When testing prospective assembly mechanics in February, the first tests asked seventy-five questions involving skills such as mathematics, spatial understanding, and mechanical abilities. The point is to get workers who can move easily among jobs.

Applicants were then shown a dozen videos of possible workplace situations. One portrayed a confrontation between a worker and a supervisor. The supervisor asks the worker to cut corners to meet a schedule. The worker objects. The boss tells the worker to leave if he doesn't like it. What would you do: 1) Quit? 2) Do the job, but report the incident to a higher supervisor? 3) Do the work, but talk to the supervisor later? 4) Complain behind the boss' back?

"Quit" is the wrong answer. So is "complain." These suggest you are not a team player. The right answers are: Do the job but talk it over later either with the supervisor or a higher authority.

Of the applicants, 73 percent passed. Broken down by sexes, 65 percent of the women passed. Broken down by race, 57 percent of "minorities" passed.

Study Questions

DESTROYING THE OLD HIERARCHIES

1. The article mentions that former CEO Frank Shrontz considered interpersonal skills as one of the most important characteristics of his successor. What are some of the key management skills needed to run a project or enterprise? Support your answers with information from the *PMBOK Guide.*

2. The labor union-management relationship at Boeing had been very antagonistic in the past and remains tense. How is Boeing's new CEO Philip Condit attempting to ameliorate these relations?

3. The biggest change made by Condit on the 777 project from previous Boeing endeavors was the organizational design. "Working Together" challenged all the former ways of doing things and brought together the design and production areas of Boeing. The undertaking of this endeavor was supported by teams. Does this management approach have any resemblance to the work organization utilized in project management?

4. Boeing is one of the three major players in the airline production industry, with AirBus and McDonnell Douglas as the other two major companies. How does this small amount of competition affect the selection and management of projects?

5. Why is the use of interdisciplinary teams for product design, also known as concurrent engineering, a key element of projects and of regular management activities?

6. How does the title of this case, "Destroying the Old Hierarchies," describe what is going on at Boeing?

Saturn's Vision for Program Management: A Different Kind of Approach

Lisa W. Churitch, Saturn Corporation
Denis P. Couture, Integrated Management Systems, Inc.
Clement L. Valot, Integrated Management Systems, Inc.

PMI *Proceedings*, 1992, pp. 74–80

INTRODUCTION

In 1985 Saturn Corporation was founded to produce an American-made car to compete head-on with Japanese vehicles in the areas of cost, quality, function, and service. General Motors (GM) knew it needed, "a different kind of company" with a different kind of approach to the business of developing and manufacturing cars.

Saturn team members came from all corners of the GM organization. They adopted and adapted business processes that would help them meet Saturn's objectives, recognizing that improving how the product was developed would improve the product itself.

Like other domestic car makers, Saturn is organized into functional teams, including powertrain, body systems, marketing, and finance. Management of product development programs is coordinated by functional managers *and* by cross-functional teams—Saturn corporate and program management teams—who accommodate planning and coordination of activity within and between functional groups respectively (see Figure 1).

Individual development teams translate concepts into cars. Saturn's ability to provide these teams with clear direction based on integrated plans is important. Making them accountable for success is essential.

All Saturn team members share program objectives for product quality, cost, and timing. While the matrix organization structure can be an effective mean to manage these objectives, it often presents special challenges in developing plans and resolving problems when "local" and program-wide objectives are in conflict.

Saturn needs a program management approach that will accommodate the complementary roles of program and functional management teams. The approach will be successful only if it supports:
- planning integration within and between functional teams
- providing clear direction to development teams
- rapid, effective problem identification and resolution
- practical use of project management methods and systems.

The challenges associated with developing and implementing any idea in a large, disparate organization are considerable. Introducing a program management approach at Saturn is no different. After several years and as many attempts at standardizing an approach, a strategy was put in place based on

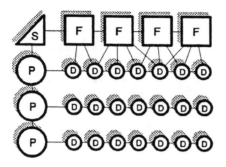

F=functional teams
S=Saturn corporate teams
P=program management teams
D=individual development teams

FIGURE 1

long-term vision. The strategy described the construction of an approach from the ground up, one block at a time. Saturn is implementing the strategy and, in the process, fine-tuning the vision itself.

This paper provides a snapshot of Saturn's vision for program management: its organization and how work breakdown structures and schedules will serve its needs. The paper will also describe the implementation strategy, progress to date, and some challenges faced. And what makes this approach different.

ORGANIZATION

Saturn's product development activities are in Troy, Michigan; its manufacturing facility is in Spring Hill, Tennessee. Between these two operations, Saturn has constructed an organization focused on a single mission:

> Market vehicles developed and manufactured in the United States that are world leaders in quality, cost, and customer satisfaction through the integration of people, technology, and business systems and to transfer knowledge, technology, and experience throughout General Motors.

All Saturn members are assigned to functional teams. Functional teams assign members to various cross-functional teams.

Functional Teams

Functional teams are either business or resource teams.

Business	Resource
Body systems	Marketing
Interior systems	People systems
Electrical	Materials
HVAC	Finance
Powertrain	Program planning
Chassis	Proto build and test

Business teams are primarily responsible for product development and manufacturing, resource teams for supporting business team and corporate operations.

Functional teams serve several roles:
- participate on cross-functional teams to plan and implement product development programs
- provide technical resources and direction to product development teams through part and tool engineering, prototype builds and tests, and model changeover
- manage and implement nonprogram-related team-specific activities such as technology assessment, training, and budgeting.

Cross-Functional Teams

Functional team members are assigned to cross-functional management and development teams.

Action councils are composed of top company and functional managers. They set program objectives, allocate resources to teams, and resolve high-level conflicts. Each action council has a specific business focus, and some oversee product development programs.

Program management teams (PMTs, also called work groups) coordinate high-level program planning and management activities. Teams include members from most functional teams and the United Auto Workers (UAW). Teams are led by marketing during the development phase and by engineering and manufacturing during the implementation phases.

The PMTs establish *project centers* to coordinate detailed design, design releases, and prototype builds and tests. They include members from engineering, manufacturing, and program planning dedicated to one program.

Development Teams

Development teams can be single- or cross-functional depending on technical requirements.

Product development teams and design teams develop specific product systems (functional or vehicle—see work breakdown structure), components, or parts, and closely coordinate activities with other teams. They are responsible for meeting the objectives established by the program management teams and their functional teams.

WORK BREAKDOWN STRUCTURES

Development work is organized two ways to accommodate various planning and management requirements:
- by vehicle systems, organizing the product into areas with content crossing multiple functional teams
- by functional systems, organizing the product into functional content crossing multiple vehicle systems.

For example, a door is a vehicle system that contains electronics, body panels, interior trim, and coatings, each developed by and coordinated between different functional teams. The electric locks contained in the door are part of a functional system that must be coordinated with other electronics in the vehicle.

Two work breakdown structures allow program plans to be "sliced" both ways, to view requirements from both perspectives.

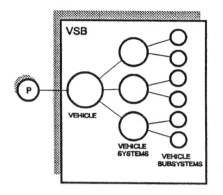

Code	VEH SYSTEM/Subsystem
A	FRONT OF VEHICLE
A1	FRONT COMPARTMENT
A11	Structure, Exterior, Lighting
A12	Hood
A13	Front Bumper
A2	ENGINE COMPARTMENT
B	CENTER OF VEHICLE
B1	PASSENGER COMPARTMENT
B2	INSTRUMENT PANEL
B3	DOORS
B4	GREENHOUSE
C	REAR OF VEHICLE
C1	REAR COMPARTMENT
D	UNDERSIDE OF VEHICLE
D1	UNDERSIDE OF VEHICLE

FIGURE 2

Vehicle System Breakdown

The vehicle system breakdown (VSB) structure organizes the vehicle into four areas. Within each area there are vehicle systems and subsystems. Multiple functional teams are involved in the work associated with a given subsystem.

A coding structure provides a way to uniquely identify elements within the VSB (see Figure 2).

Functional System Breakdown

The functional system breakdown (FSB) structure organizes the vehicle according to functional, or technical, systems. Within each functional system, there are assemblies and subassemblies comprised of parts. And how these are actually defined can vary widely between functional teams. Because each functional system is designed by the same functional team across all vehicle programs, the FSB is similar to an organizational breakdown structure and is used to assign responsibility.

A coding structure provides a way to uniquely identify elements within the FSB (see Figure 3).

Component Definition

The VSB and FSB as described are product breakdowns. Converting these to work breakdown structures is done by defining vehicle components and the steps required to develop each. A component, for this purpose, is defined as one part or a group of parts, subassemblies, or assemblies which:
- are developed as a unit by a single functional team
- are associated with a single vehicle system or subsystem
- contain parts not included in other components.

For each program, the FSB and VSB are used to develop a list of up to 200 components used for vehicle and functional planning. Component definitions vary from program to program depending on content and extent of changes from the current product (see Figure 4). Each component is developed using the GM product development process, "4-Phase Process," which was adapted to Saturn's own approach and organization.

The process describes discrete activities and events that must be completed during each development phase:

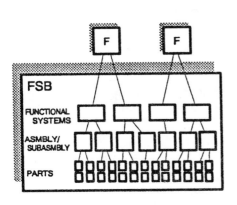

Code	FUNCT'L SYSTEM/ Assembly/Subassembly
01.	STRUCTURAL
.01	Spaceframe
.01	Body Side
.02	Framing
.03	Underbody
.02	Cockpit/FOD
.03	Door Structures
.04	Coatings, Sealants, Raw Mtls
02	EXTERIOR PANELS
03	BODY
04	-open-
05	ELECTRICAL
06	HVAC
07	INTERIOR
06	POWERTRAIN
09	CHASSIS

FIGURE 3

- Phase 0—technology and concept development
- Phase 1—product and process development
- Phase 2—product confirmation and process validation
- Phase 3—production and continuous improvement.

Each component development is defined with a standard list of twenty-three activities and events detailing Phases 0, 1, and 2. Because each component is uniquely associated with an FSB and a VSB element, the activities represent the lowest level of work breakdown for each of these structures.

SCHEDULES

Saturn has guided each new vehicle development to production using a variety of schedules maintained at different levels of detail by different parts of the organization. In the beginning, planning coordination was done informally—that is, by affected teams sitting with others to resolve specific interfaces. Because of the large number of interfaces, the need for a more formal means to coordinate schedules earlier was apparent.

This section describes the vision of how planning integration will be done at Saturn: how it will use the FSB and VSB structures to help teams plan their work and coordinate it with others'. While the schedules described exist in some form, the full vision has not yet been realized. The Implementation section of this paper describes the strategy being used; the Progress section describes where it currently stands.

Vehicle development planning is done with a schedule hierarchy based on the VSB (see Figure 5).

Vehicle Schedule

Saturn uses a vehicle schedule to plan and track major program milestone dates. The schedule consists of approximately 200 activities and twenty to forty milestones. It is structured according to major vehicle systems and reflects the relative timing of these. Critical path method (CPM) scheduling is

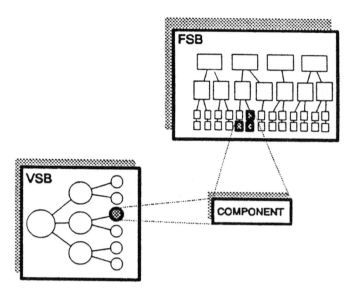

Figure 4

not typically used because of the complex relationship between macro-level activities.

The vehicle schedule is used during program planning to:
- establish key program milestones, based on program content and objectives and past performance
- do strategic what-if analysis
- do macro-level budget and staff planning
- provide a framework for the development of the system schedule.

It is used during program implementation to:
- provide a hammock for updated system schedules
- use as a management reporting tool
- assess program status
- assess impacts of changes.

Vehicle System Schedules

Vehicle system schedules are used to plan and integrate all aspects of vehicle development activity and to coordinate systems and subsystems activity. Major components are included when their specific visibility is required.

A summary four-phase subnetwork for the work within each system, subsystem, and component is created. Constraints between these subnetworks reflect the general relationships between development teams based on experience and trust. No attempt is made to articulate detailed interfaces between teams. These are either defined in other Saturn business processes or too complex to capture effectively.

Vehicle system schedules consist of 500 to 1000 activities and events, each coded according to the VSB. The schedule reflects a viable means to achieve the milestones established in the vehicle schedule.

The vehicle system schedule is used during program planning to:
- validate vehicle schedule
- coordinate systems, subsystem, and selected component schedules

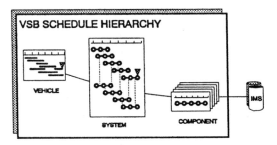

FIGURE 5

- do tactical what-if analyses
- provide a framework for component schedule development.
    It is used during program implementation to:
- provide a hammock for updated component schedules
- assess program status
- assess impacts of changes.

Component Schedules

Component schedules are developed based on dates in the vehicle systems schedule. They are constructed using the twenty-three activities described in the Component Definition section. This provides a framework, not a replacement, for detailed planning. Development teams are responsible for planning their work within this framework, coordinating technical interface, and advising when the framework is untenable.

Component schedules also provide a means to establish part-level target dates prior to detailed planning. These are loaded in the information management system (IMS) in which parts readiness dates are maintained. (Data are transferred via an upload from the project management software to IMS on the corporate mainframe.) Standard CPM network models were developed for the eight major functional systems. These models enable the rapid, consistent development of these schedules. As indicated earlier, a new program may have up to 200 components. Models are selected and adapted to component-specific requirements.

Because planning integration was done in the vehicle system schedule, component schedules are maintained independently. No constraints between component schedules are formally maintained.

Component schedules are used during program planning to:
- validate the system schedule
- provide specific direction to development teams
- provide target dates to the IMS.
    They are used during program implementation to:
- provide a hammock for updated design schedules
- assess component status
- assess "local" impacts of detailed changes
- provide updates to the IMS.

Component schedules also provide the basis for functional team planning. Another schedule hierarchy is developed using the FSB (see Figure 6).

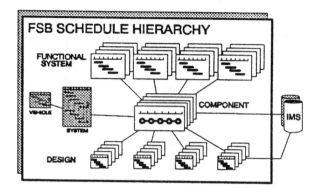

FIGURE 6

Functional System Schedules

Functional system schedules are developed by functional teams to coordinate the activity across vehicle systems. While the vehicle system schedule was used to coordinate different functional teams' activities for a given subsystem, the functional system schedule is used to coordinate activity for a given functional system across multiple vehicle systems. The functional and vehicle systems schedules are developed in parallel, since changes to one may cause a conflict in the other.

To return to an earlier example, the electric door lock development may be delayed to coordinate it with other door design activities in the vehicle system schedule; however, it may result in a problem for the team developing the security and electronics systems, whose activities are coordinated in a functional system schedule.

Functional system schedules may also contain activities not covered by supporting component schedules. As a result, a resorting or summarization of component schedule activity is not adequate.

Functional system schedules are used during program planning to:
- validate the vehicle system schedule via the component schedules
- coordinate work between component schedules and other functional team activity, including other programs
- aggregate resource requirements within and across programs.
They are used during program implementation to:
- assess component and functional team status
- assess impacts of changes.

Design Schedules

Design schedules are when "the rubber meets the road," where plans are turned into action. Component schedules normally describe the development of groups of parts, each of which must be designed and engineered, each requiring specific tooling.

Standard component networks are often inadequate to plan and track these activities in detail. Design schedules are developed to provide this detail, based on component schedule requirements. The detailed design process varies widely between functional systems. They are developed to meet the "local" needs of the design leaders and designers.

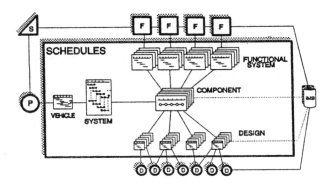

FIGURE 7

Design schedules are used during program planning to:
- validate component schedules
- provide specific targets to development teams and members.
    They are used during program implementation to:
- assess pert and component status
- assess local impacts of detailed changes
- provide updated promise dates to the IMS.

SCHEDULE ADMINISTRATION

Management and development teams develop and use schedules to serve their complementary roles. Individual schedules are not created or maintained in a vacuum (see Figure 7).
- System-level schedules provide a framework for component and design schedules.
- Design and component schedules are used to validate system-level and vehicle schedules.
- Vehicle system and functional system schedules are used to coordinate the same work from two perspectives.

As a result, how they are administered is important to their consistency and integration throughout program planning and implementation.

Schedule Ownership

Schedules are owned by teams who are responsible for their development and maintenance, and tacitly for their completeness and correctness. The following matrix outlines ownership responsibilities.

Schedule	Owner (P) – Primary (O) – Operational
Vehicle	Saturn action councils (P)
	Program management team (O)
Vehicle system	Program management team (P)
	Project center (O)
Functional system	Functional teams
Component	Development teams
Design	Development teams
IMS (each part)	Development teams

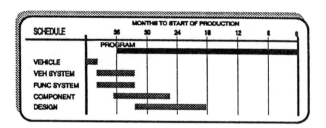

FIGURE 8

Schedule Development

New program schedules are developed "top-down," with the vehicle schedules providing the basis for vehicle system and functional system schedules. These are developed concurrently to enable coordination between them before component and design schedule development (see Figure 8).

As successive levels of schedules are developed, they are used to validate more summary schedules. Changes may result to any schedule if:
- inadequate time has been allotted for design work
- critical development team interfaces have been omitted
- resources are unavailable
- the scope of work or milestone dates have changed.

Schedule Updating

Schedules are updated "bottom-up" based on progress against design schedules. Design and component schedules are updated biweekly; vehicle and functional systems schedules, bi-weekly; and vehicle schedules, bi-weekly. A comprehensive updating cycle will be completed as in Figure 9.

Each schedule owner is responsible for providing input to others. Like the schedules themselves, updates are only approximations that need to be evaluated and adjusted to reflect as nearly as possible the owner's current status and intent to complete.

IMPLEMENTATION

During the early stages of Saturn's start-up, several planning approaches were tried with local success, but none was widely accepted. In 1990, a strategy was developed to construct the approach according to the vision one block at a time as described in the Schedules section. It was designed to roll-out the approach no faster than the organization could reasonably absorb it, given the numerous other challenges that it faced on other fronts.

Strategy

The strategy consists of three phases. During each phase at least one type of standard schedule is developed and implemented; meanwhile, existing planning methods are maintained on current vehicle programs.

Phases contain the following goals:

Phase 1
- Develop the FSB and VSB structure.

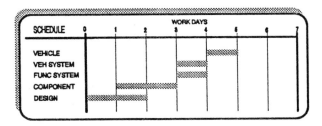

FIGURE 9

- Develop standard component schedule format and content.
- Develop generic network models and applications based on development team input.

Phase 2
- Develop standard design schedule format and content.
- Develop generic network models and applications based on development team input.
- Develop interfaces between IMS, component schedules, and design schedules.

Phase 3
- Develop standard functional system schedule format and content.
- Develop standard vehicle system schedule and vehicle schedule format and content.
- Develop generic network models for the above, based on functional manager and program management team input.
- Develop interfaces between these and component schedules.

Progress and Challenges

After two years into the implementation of the strategy, Phase 2 was complete, and Phase 3 is under way. Detailed planning, by way of the component and design schedules, is being done consistently by most development teams. The dates in the IMS database are being maintained based on this level of planning.

The integration of component schedules continues to be done informally through the experience of functional managers. Phase 3 will embed much of this experience in the vehicle and functional systems schedules. It is recognized, however, that the approach will *never* be able to capture the full experience of these managers and that the approach needs to accommodate this experience on each new program.

Various challenges faced during this process are highlighted below.
- **Resistance to change.** Development teams have seen it all before and are rightfully skeptical about the value of the latest approach to anything. Saturn team members have come from many parts of the corporation which have implemented project management methods in some fashion. If previous experiences were positive, they expected the same approach applicable or not; if negative, they needed encouragement and active support. In either case, the need to show early success, albeit local, was important.
- **Systems.** Large mainframe systems were tried before 1990 and failed for reasons related more to lack of a clear approach and strategy than the systems

themselves. The current approach uses PC-based software because it is easie to "sell," adapt, and use "in-the-trenches" and it avoids the high cost of large systems. Too much early standardization and cost can unduly burden the im plementation of ideas and crush them before they can take root.

The current level of system use can be expanded as the ability of the or ganization to use it cost-effectively increases. With the completion of Phase 3, system requirements will be reviewed.

• **Nature of product development work.** Application of CPM to plan thi work is sometimes a forced fit. Design work is not as linear as planners wan it to be. A-B-C is often, in reality, A-B-A-B-C-B-C depending on the genera evolution of the product itself. Saturn's program management approach had to be structured to accommodate the dynamic nature of the design process— that is, to be flexible enough to respond to change, but specific enough to provide targets and direction. The disconnection of systems schedules and component schedules will provide this compromise.

What's the Difference?

Saturn is committed to the concept of team-member participation. Its func tional and cross-functional teams play important, complementary roles that all contribute to program success. The intent of Saturn's program manage ment approach is not to be different, but to meet the needs of a different kind of organization.

When finally put in place, there will be differences that simply support Saturn's mission.

Organizational

• **Distributed planning.** Plans and schedules are developed by teams for work under their purview. Each successive level of detail is developed locally, within the framework created by overall program schedules, not dictated specifically in detail.

• **Development team responsibility.** Development teams are provided with timing objectives for their "piece." They are responsible for detailed plan ning, validation of program plans, and identification of technical interfaces with other teams. This avoids the "Big Brother" syndrome which removes control and responsibility from the front lines.

• **Two hats.** Because each functional team is represented on relevant cross- functional management teams, technical issues cannot be "lobbed" over the wall. There is no wall. The team is responsible for seeing each issue from a Saturn *and* functional team perspective.

• **Technical coordination.** Technical coordination is done by vehicle sys tem and by functional system. These two views of work activity are comple mentary and decrease the risk of errors and omissions.

Technical

• **Component definition.** Components can be defined flexibly allowing large variations in program content and approaches.

• **Schedule integration.** Program planning is integrated at the systems lev el, allowing the technical relationships between vehicle subsystems and be tween components to be expressed generally. This avoids the nightmare of massive networks that are too complex for anyone to understand. Detailed constraints are managed between development teams.

- **Work breakdown structures.** The ability to associate a component schedule to both functional schedules and vehicle schedules through the FSB and VSB allows faster turnaround in updating and less risk of inconsistent date.
- **Systems use.** Because schedules are kept smaller and more localized, systems can be smaller and less expansive. They can be increased incrementally in size and complexity based on need and the ability to add value.
- **Evaluation of change impacts.** Changes to program requirements can occur at a part level or program level. The functional and vehicle systems schedules provide a "middle level" of detail for assessing overall impact to program milestones and to component level targets.

SUMMARY

Saturn's approach to program management is intended to make program planning the responsibility of each development team and manager. The approach recognizes that program and functional management teams have complementary roles in providing direction to and coordinating the activities of development teams.

The schedule hierarchies support this approach. By distributing the planning process, each part of the organization develops and maintains the schedules it uses. By integrating plans across vehicle systems and functional systems, schedule conflicts can be resolved before detailed design work is started.

The implementation plan reflects a practical method to embed the approach into the way Saturn does business.

Study Questions

SATURN'S VISION FOR PROGRAM MANAGEMENT: A DIFFERENT KIND OF APPROACH

1. The case mentions some of the shortcomings of a matrix organization structure including troubles in developing plans and resolving problems when "local" and program-wide objectives are in conflict. Define the meaning of a matrix organization structure and list its disadvantages.

2. This case defines Saturn's program management, but seems to focus on scheduling. How are Saturn's cross-functional teams used in the development of schedules?

3. The matrix organization structure emerged in the early 1960s as an alternative to the functional structure. This organizational form enjoyed popularity in the 1970s and early 1980s. What are its main advantages?

4. The description of program management teams in the case describes teams being led by marketing during the development phase and engineering and manufacturing during the implementation phase. How might this varying leadership affect the performance of the teams?

5. The processes required to develop a Saturn vehicle are organized through the use of two work breakdown structures. Describe those two breakdown structures. What kind of organizational structure does their creation resemble?

Using Project Management to Create an Entrepreneurial Environment in Czechoslovakia

John Tuman, Jr., Institute for Management Technologies, Inc.
Moses Thompson, Team Technologies, Inc.

PMI *Proceedings*, 1992, pp. 405–9

INTRODUCTION

Democratization of Eastern Europe will succeed only when countries like Czechoslovakia can compete in the global marketplace. To be competitive, Czech and Slovak managers must not only learn modern management techniques, but they must also develop a leadership and management style that is tailored to their cultures and their economic and legal infrastructures. Experience to date demonstrates that project management can provide the framework for building a Czech and Slovak management prototype.

OBJECTIVES

Six months after the change in government in Czechoslovakia the authors were in Prague conducting a seminar on project management. More than 800 executives and managers of state-owned companies were eager to learn how to function in a free-market economy.

This paper presents the results of more than two years of work in Czechoslovakia. The focus of this paper is on how to use project management to change a management environment spawned by more than forty years of state-centralized planning.

The paper discusses how Czech and Slovak executives and managers are using project management to transition their organizations into the global marketplace.

This paper will:
• give an overview of the major problems confronting Czech and Slovak managers as they try to transition their organizations into a free market economy
• describe the techniques and tools that are being used to help Czech and Slovak managers plan the future of their companies
• delineate how project management is being used to control and direct environmental projects, joint ventures, and privatization programs.

The aim of this paper is to demonstrate how project management can be used to plan entrepreneurial ventures and change entrenched attitudes and values.

BACKGROUND

In 1939 Czechoslovakia ranked tenth in the world in per-capita income ahead of Austria and Belgium. Since that time the destiny of the two nation of the Czech and Slovak Federative Republic has been shaped by turbulen events: nationalism, war, and political change. The "velvet revolution abruptly swept aside the more than forty-year experiment with socialism.

Today, Czechoslovakia stands on the threshold of major change. Th country is being split into two separate nations, one Czech and one Slovak It is a time of great uncertainty for the ten million Czechs and five millio Slovaks. Both countries must deal with enormous social, environmenta and economic problems. The process of transitioning from a centrall planned economy to a free-market economy is painful and difficult.

To make the transition to a free-market economy, some 13,000 sma businesses and some 4,500 large industrial enterprises are being privatized In some circles the economic transformation process is described as "shoc therapy." By the end of 1991 Czechoslovakia had a 22 percent decline in in dustrial output, an increase in the unemployment rate from 2.5 to 8.5 per cent, an inflation rate of 58 percent, a 33 percent decline in domestic de mand, and a 14 percent decline in gross domestic product. To compoun this problem the country has perhaps the most adversely affected environ ment in Europe. In addition the western industrialized region of the Czec Republic is one of Europe's largest exporters of pollution.

Despite the present grim state of affairs, the Czechs and Slovaks are i the best position of any of the former East Block nations to succeed. Both re publics can boast of a well-educated and highly skilled workforce, highly de veloped industries, sound infrastructure, and a relatively small foreign debt

However, many experts fear that the biggest stumbling block to progres is not the enormity of the problems but the lack of individual initiativ brought about by forty years of centralized government planning. As on western expert put it, "Former Eastern Block bureaucracies will never mee the challenge. They just don't have the vision, the motivation, or the flexi bility to re-orient overstuffed and overcentralized government agencies."

Our experience was just the opposite. After more than two years' work i Czechoslovakia we find a vitality and a drive and an intense desire to change Moreover we find the willingness and the spirit to try approaches which de part significantly from the past. In this environment, project management i being used to develop processes, procedures, systems, and the managemen culture that will help the Czechs and Slovaks build their future.

DEVELOPING A PROJECT MANAGEMENT PHILOSOPHY FOR CZECHOSLOVAKIA

In Prague, Czechoslovakia, we discovered government ministries staffed b middle-aged managers caught in an unexpected midlife crisis that would un nerve the best of us. Past policies, programs, and standard operating proce dures dissolved before their eyes, and their positions in the ministries wer no longer secure.

The "velvet revolution" of 1989 confronted managers with a new set o challenges. Centrally planned programs administered by hierarchical, bu reaucratic organizations oriented towards job generation and resource uti lization were being eliminated. State-owned companies were being priva tized, and the focus was on restructuring, downsizing, decentralized planning, and increased use of autonomous working groups.

For more than two years we have worked with more than 1,200 Czech and Slovak managers and their project teams in seminars and workshops. During this period we discovered a strong demand for creative use of project management technologies. At first the interventions were in the form of large presentations to 300–600 mid-level managers when we spoke to them on project management philosophy, methods, and techniques to address the turbulent economic and management issues of the immediate future.

In March 1990 we conducted a major seminar for 600 senior Czech and Slovak managers on the theme of "Project Management for Turbulent Times." Again in October of the same year at the CECIOS International Management Conference in Prague, we made presentations on team-based project management methods for more than 400 mid-level managers from the metallurgy industry.

These general seminars were followed by intensive applications-driven workshops for organizations and industries with particular needs and problems. Most of this training and consulting centered on project design and implementation management. Since then, we have conducted project-launch workshops for more than forty project teams.

Our experiences in Czechoslovakia in 1990 enabled us to identify a number of specific problems and needs that were characteristic of the Czech-Slovak environment. By carefully analyzing management needs, we were able to formulate development and intervention programs that utilized the full potential of project management.

Need for Widespread Project Planning and Design Skills

After decades of dependency on central ministries for planning, managers found themselves faced with the responsibility for project design as well as implementation. While there is broad familiarity with traditional project scheduling technology, at least in theory if not in practice, there is a widespread dearth of project planning expertise. For this reason, our subsequent programs and interventions placed strong emphasis on the planning function and its relationship to project implementation and evaluation.

For example, at the very outset we reviewed the quality of project designs from several sectors and organizations and found that they:
- lacked a clear statement of purpose or impact
- lacked clear performance measures
- lacked cause-and-effect logic between outcomes and impact
- lacked linkage between project and program goals
- were overambitious in scheduling (unrealistic time frames)
- had unrealistic budget/resource estimates
- failed to identify risks
- had no plans for sustainable benefit continuation
- lacked monitoring or evaluation plans for improvement
- failed to define the team planning/implementation process.

It was clear that these weaknesses needed to be addressed during the project design phase when the cost of planning is significantly less than during implementation. However, these were precisely the areas where most of the Czech and Slovak managers felt they were weakest in their management skills. As a result, we focused subsequent programs and workshops on the up-front project design process. As it turned out, this strategy produced a strong positive response, and our early project management interventions set the stage for a long-term involvement in Czechoslovakia.

Demands for Leadership in Project Management

Many of the Czech and Slovak managers expressed their anxiety about having to fulfill a leadership role. In the former structure, direction came from the top so there was no need to exercise leadership. One Czech manager said, "I read this book, *In Search of Excellence*, and I thought I was reading about another planet. How would we create these kinds of organizations and how was I supposed to become this kind of leader?"

As it turned out, leadership became the essential element in applying project management. We found that tools and methods were irrelevant unless we could address the fundamental behavioral changes required for effective leadership and teaming around project objectives.

Need for Team-Based Project Organization

A related need was the managers' concern about teamwork. As one said, "We never work in teams. I don't even know if I trust teams. You tell me teamwork will produce better outcomes, and I find this very hard to believe." And another, "... based on this workshop experience, I am convinced that teams are a necessary part of my future as a leader, but I am troubled by how I am going to do this. Where will we learn these skills, and will there be any support for them from my supervisors?"

Need to Constantly Define the Customer

It will not come as a surprise that most Czech and Slovak project managers had very little interest in customer satisfaction. At a large meeting of the senior managers for one government ministry, we asked the question, "Can someone please tell us who the Ministry's customers are?" The question was met with a long silence and then several off-line discussions. It was clear that we would have to help project teams to define their customers and focus project outcomes on satisfying customer needs.

APPLYING PROJECT MANAGEMENT TECHNIQUES

Our initial experience in Czechoslovakia revealed that the needs of Czech and Slovak managers were considerably different than that of their European and American counterparts. It was clear that more emphasis had to be given to project design and team development than to the mechanics of project planning and scheduling techniques.

Project Design

We decided to use the logical framework approach for project design and planning. The logical framework is a proven method for addressing the key design issues needed for quality project planning. It treats the project as an experiment in cause and effect and structures the design with the same rigor one would approach testing a hypothesis under uncertain conditions.

The logical framework methodology was initially developed in the 1970s for the United States Agency for International Development (USAID). It is also related to the 1981 development of the Zeil Orientierte Projekts Plannungs in collaboration with the German Technical Cooperation Agency. Since then a number of other development agencies, among them the United Nations Development Program and the Canadian, British, Irish, Belgian, and Norwegian aid agencies, have adopted it as a design and planning tool.

The logical framework methodology guides a team through identification of the causal linkages between the project deliverables, the impact they have on the customer, and the relationship between project-level and program-level impacts. In addition, the logical framework lays out the performance measures and the means of verification at each level of project accomplishment. The methodology also helps the team to identify the external conditions and risks on which each level of project achievement depends.

In addition to the up-front project planning methodology we also used more traditional planning and scheduling methods for organizing at the activity and task level. These tools included:

- the work breakdown structure (WBS)
- network diagramming (CPM)
- stakeholder analysis
- performance matrix (for deliverables)
- Gantt chart schedules (team and individual)
- performance budget matrix.

A series of workshops and training programs were implemented to show Czech and Slovak managers how to use the state-of-the-art PC-based project management packages. Most of these managers were acquainted with network theory, scheduling, and resource optimization. As the PC computer became more accessible, many of these managers became quite proficient in using the latest project management software package. However, learning to use project management tools is easy; learning to develop and manage a project team is a more complex problem.

Team Development

Through a collaborative effort between the World Bank's Economic Development Institute (EDI) and Team Technologies, Inc., tools were developed to facilitate the creation of high-performance project management teams. One tool known as "TeamUp" is used by EDI and other agencies for accelerating the formation of project teams in the field. The TeamUp methodology is intended to bring diverse professional, ethnical, national, and organizational team members together for the purposes of project appraisal, implementation, and evaluation. Most often these teams are expected to accomplish untested project designs under risky and uncertain conditions. TeamUp was a most appropriate tool for the Czech-Slovak environment. It is interesting to note that the joint development efforts by the World Bank's EDI and Team Technologies have resulted in three software packages (PC/Log FRAME, PC/TeamUp, and PC/PIP) that are now commercially available to all project practitioners.

These tools were used extensively in specific project interventions directed at privatization and environmental cleanup projects. Our experiences in these areas are described in the next section.

New leadership roles of mid-level managers
- Taking responsibility for the planning function
- Learning how to provide vision and define mission
- Taking responsibility for the team and yourself

Primacy of project design before project scheduling
- Getting the causal logic of the objectives clear before WBS

Collaborative planning
- Getting the stakeholders involved
- Role of commitment in setting objectives
- Using public involvement methods to build support

Managing uncertainty, risk, and external variables
- Responsibility for influencing the outside
- Managing conflicts and dealing with differences

Creating the team-based organization
- Fundamental value and use of teams
- Leader's responsibility for designing the organization
- Teams and hierarchies

Discovering the customer (as not yourself)
- Defining impact on the customer as the purpose of your work
- Defining sustainable benefit continuation in the project design
- Establishing an output rather than an input orientation
- Making performance measurement a part of planning

Future versus past orientation
- Work possibilities before problems

FIGURE 1   CZECH-SLOVAK PROJECT MANAGEMENT TRAINING PROGRAMS

DESIGN OF PROJECT MANAGEMENT INTERVENTIONS

To address the needs of the Czech and Slovak teams and their leaders, we crafted a series of seminars and workshops to address the problems and needs described earlier. A summary of these programs is given in Figure 1.

Standard Project Planning Methodology

By 1991, Prague was awash with seminars, workshops, and training programs. The government staff was inundated with a flood of demonstration videos, brochures, product descriptions, and overhead transparencies. However, the Czech and Slovak managers were interested in proven, pragmatic methods and techniques that they could use to move their organizations into the global competitive environment. As an example, after exploring a wide variety of alternatives, three Ministry officers who had attended one of our seminars, decided that logical framework method was what they needed for planning the government's privatization projects. Within twenty-four hours of completion of one of our seminars, they called us at our hotel requesting that we come to the Ministry for a discussion. We walked into a room filled with senior officers from the key ministries involved, where one of them said, "We know a lot about project scheduling theory. We have studied it and know the case studies. We have listened to a lot of seminars. We have decided that we need to learn how to design a project first, before we plan and schedule it. Your methodology can help us do this. Therefore, we have decided that the logical framework method is the best for us, so we have decided to make it a Ministry standard."

Within a three-month period we went on to train 120 officers and eighty customers, put twenty-five projects on the new system, translated the software into Czech language, established a training site in the Ministry headquarters, and formally standardized the method. This is a good example of how a formerly rigid bureaucracy can transform itself into a highly flexible and dynamic project-oriented organization.

Privatization Projects. Several thousand state corporations will privatize before the nationwide process is complete. While the accomplishment of this objective is daunting enough, the real issue for many of these corporations is "what do we do after privatization?" Project management methods worked extremely well in assisting the privatizing company to plan the reorganization and restructuring of its company after the privatization process was complete.

One area which remains extremely fertile for project management interventions is the management of those elements of a company not of interest to domestic or foreign investors. For example, one company in the process of privatization will discard an entire maintenance and support services division of approximately 4,000 employees. Converting this resource into a set of small businesses and avoiding the social stress this degree of unemployment can cause in a community is not only economically but politically relevant. Our team used project management methods to work with one large corporation to do just this, and the result was a proliferation of small, but successful businesses which leased corporation equipment and sold services and products back to the region at large. The most proactive entrepreneurs were the employees of these organizations, rather than corporate management.

Portfolio Management Projects. One federal ministry found our project management planning methodology essential for getting order into its portfolio of projects. Using our methodology it could establish program level goals and integrate approximately twenty-five projects per annum. The logical framework and TeamUP method provided the structure for negotiating agreements with their clients and a means of communicating among themselves the internal logic of their project efforts. The Czech & Moravian Development Bank found this kind of project approach useful for managing the loan appraisal process. By making the distinction between deliverables and impact, the logical framework makes the identification of project benefits transparent and thereby facilitates benefit/cost and internal rate of return analysis. It also clarifies the risk at each level of the project, a concern for every banker. When this kind of design document is expanded with a set of project implementation tools, it provides a more rational basis for assessing and communicating the quality of a bank loan. At the Czech & Moravian Development Bank we are in the process of training all staff to use the logical framework project planning and appraisal method as the standard loan application document.

Also, at the Ministry of Economy we are training more than one-hundred staff people and have established our logical framework approach to project design as a standard for submitting loan and grant applications.

Industrial Projects. At the Kaucuk Petroleum Refinery, the general manager decided to introduce our team planning method called TeamUP for installing a team-based project management and organization development strategy. One engineering team used TeamUP to organize itself around air quality objectives established in the Joint Environment Report (World Bank). Within a two-month period team members planned out their project to desulphurize diesel fuel, implemented it, and put the new "clean" fuel on the market at competitive prices. All this was accomplished at the cost of one workshop and the team's time.

Environmental Projects. The project management method is being applied to the public involvement process for organizing large-scale environmental cleanup projects. Contrary to how things were done in the recent past, these projects now require broad participation from special interest groups, municipalities, religious leaders, corporations, government agencies, and international donors. A great deal of up-front project planning is required to reflect the needs and concerns of these diverse participants.

Our local team is currently initiating the regional environmental cleanup project design to mitigate damage in a four-city area. What is unique about this effort is that it is not driven by compliance to a federal or state regulatory framework. Instead a project management approach was used to organize the stakeholders and develop a corporate and community-driven program based on the ability to establish common values and share objectives. Tools like trees analysis (cause and effect diagramming) and logical framework, supported with environmental assessment data, accelerated the process of developing consensus. Our project management unit will use this up-front project planning as input to the more traditional planning and scheduling tools to develop the detailed project implementation plans.

THE FUTURE OF PROJECT MANAGEMENT IN CZECHOSLOVAKIA

The break up of Czechoslovakia into two independent nations will only intensify the need to organize, plan, and implement a host of government, business, and industry projects. The equitable distribution of the nation's industrial capability, infrastructure assets, and power generation and distributions systems are just a few of the issues to be dealt with. If the transition to separate Czech and Slovak nations can be managed effectively and efficiently, there is a strong possibility that both can be successfully integrated into the global economy. If the process is not managed successfully, then both nations face the possibility of slipping into Third World status.

Having worked closely with Czech and Slovak managers since 1989, we are betting that the future will be difficult but prosperous. The Czechs and Slovaks are industrious people with a heritage for prevailing through the most difficult of situations. Based on our experience and our understanding of the people we have been involved with, we have made a long-term commitment to the Czech and Slovak future. Team Technologies has opened an office in Prague and has staffed it with highly qualified Czech and Slovak professionals.

To ensure that the Prague office (and future Bratislava office) represents state-of-the-art management capability, we have instituted an aggressive technology transfer program. Our staff of Czech and Slovak professionals have work assignments in various American and European companies.

These assignments broaden their bases of experience and education and enable them to focus on specific management issues in their own countries.

We are committed to this venture because we firmly believe that the quality of life everywhere can be improved by effectively and creatively managing human and natural resources. To this end, we believe project management will play a significant role the future of the Czech and Slovak nations.

REFERENCES

1. Komarek, V. 1992. "Shock Therapy and Its Victims." *The New York Times*, Jan. 5.

2. 1992. "Computer-assisted project management." *EDI Review*, Jan.

3. Moldan, B., and J.L. Schnoor. 1992. "Czechoslovakia, Restoring an Ill Environment." *Environmental Science Technology*, Jan.

4. Tuman, J., Jr. 1990. "Project Management In Different Organizational Cultures: A Tool for Creating Competitive Advantage." *Proceedings* INTERNET 90, Vienna Austria.

5. Peters, T. 1987. *Thriving on Chaos.* New York: Alfred A. Knopf.

6. Bovard, J. 1987. "Eastern Europe, The New Third World." *The New York Times*, Dec. 20.

7. Foreman, C. 1990. "East Block Legal Overhaul Lures Investors." *The Wall Street Journal*, Mar. 16.

Study Questions

USING PROJECT MANAGEMENT TO CREATE AN ENTREPRENEURIAL ENVIRONMENT IN CZECHOSLOVAKIA

1. The authors state that they found Czech and Slovak managers familiar with traditional scheduling technology, but without project management expertise. Therefore, they aimed their training programs towards the planning function and its relationship with project implementation and evaluation. Discuss the importance of project planning.

2. The case describes several weaknesses found on project designs such as: lacked clear statement of purpose or impact, lacked clear performance measures, etc. The authors state: "These weaknesses needed to be addressed during the project design phase when the cost of planning is significantly less than during implementation." Do you agree with this statement? Why?

3. The Czech and Slovak managers were anxious to learn about being a leader. What it is the difference between a manager and a leader?

4. Discuss the importance of recognizing cultural differences when implementing project management and list examples of cultural features relevant to this case.

The Channel Tunnel: Larger Than Life, and Late

Virginia Fairweather

Civil Engineering, May 1994, pp. 42–46

The Channel Tunnel is finally open for business. Cheers are in order, but the project is more than a year late, with its original cost estimate doubled to $14.9 billion, and it led to a $2.25 billion claim that was settled last month. Project veterans suggest there are lessons to be learned.

The Channel Tunnel linking Great Britain and France is an engineering achievement and a symbol of man's imagination and daring. But it is also the world's largest privatized project with implications for other such financial arrangements. Along with engineers and contractors, bankers and the governments of France and England were trying something unprecedented and there are lessons to be learned from their experiences. As one project executive says with some irony, the project of the century had the "claim of the century." (This claim for $2.25 billion was resolved in early April, with the final contract value fixed at approximately $1.7 billion. Under the settlement, project owner Eurotunnel will pay the contracting organization, Transmanche Link (TML), approximately $105 million–$127 million, in addition to payments already made under an earlier agreement.)

The privatization payback will come long after the ribbons have been cut and the champagne has been drunk. About 600,000 shareholders as well as banks and other governments looking at privatization will wait until the next century for the promised returns. The list of obstacles to that payback is a long one. The final cost of the system is $14.9 billion, about double the original estimate. The high-speed rail link on the United Kingdom (U.K.) side to London is only on the drawing boards, the fares for the Channel crossing are higher than hoped ($325 to $465), and ticket sales are lower than expected. The existing ferries cost less and have the attraction of duty-free shops, absent on the train system because duty-free sales were supposed to end with the advent of the European Economic Community.

Some of the payback pressure was eased when the two governments agreed to extend the concession to Eurotunnel for another ten years, until the middle of the next century. The extension is conditional on Eurotunnel's next public offering (this summer) raising about $750 million.

But even with the delays, cost overruns, and the bureaucracy, many of those involved look back at the job as the adventure of a lifetime. If its lessons are heeded, the Channel Tunnel will point the way for future international privatization projects. Some participants look back at the project and touch on a few of the problems.

John Noulton, a Eurotunnel executive, has been with the project since the mid-1980s and helped draft the concession documents the French and British governments signed off on in 1986. He says the original government white paper relied on tried, and tested, technology, but that costs had "ratcheted up" nonetheless.

Noulton describes just one hitch in the original plans. In a classic underground construction scenario, the state-of-art tunnel-boring machine bit bad ground in spite of decades of soil investigations. The tunnel-boring machine with its sophisticated computer controls was designed for compact chalk, he says, as was the tunnel-lining system. The precast concrete lining segments were supposed to lock together by compression. When they hit the bad patch, water affected the electronic system, says Noulton, and worse, the designed-for-compression could not take place in the hollows in the outside ground. At one point, he recalls men were standing on top of the lining segments, trying to hold them together with a belt. We had to inject grout to solidify the ground, a costly endeavor, he says, but "once you've got the machinery down there your main cost is manpower."

Noulton says these problems were encountered in the service tunnel, the first of the three running tunnels. By the time they proceeded to the rail tunnels, engineers knew what to expect. In the end, the tunneling was finished on schedule, he says.

As to the claim, Noulton joins a general chorus second guessing whether the project's fixed equipment should have been contracted on a lump-sum basis. The fixed equipment, in this case, means the mechanical and electrical work, catenaries, signaling, and telecommunications. That contract resulted in the $2.25 billion claim against Eurotunnel by the contracting organization, TML. The claim winded its way through the project appeals system until a protocol was reached in July 1993. Under that arrangement, Eurotunnel advanced $75 million each month to TML to complete the job.

Nonetheless, this was an "unstoppable project," says Noulton, ticking off what he sees as the high points. First was the "tremendous elation and momentum" created when both nations signed the treaty approving the project in 1987. Raising the money was the next high point. The public offering of shares in the project was made right after the United States stock market's Black Friday, in October 1987. Even under those inauspicious circumstances, "overnight" we had more than 100,000 shareholders, says Noulton, which he calls "a miracle."

The third phase was construction. In spite of delays, the job was "pretty well" on time, he says. Now the project is in the "make it work, make it pay" phase. That task looks daunting, but payoff wasn't expected until the next century, he says.

John Neerhout Jr. was project chief executive at Eurotunnel from early 1990 to 1993. Neerhout came from the Bechtel Co., San Francisco, to which he has since returned. Neerhout made some sharp comments on the $2.25 billion claim and its origin in a speech to the Project Management Institute last fall, and a portion of that speech follows:

> Managing the construction contract was complicated by numerous factors, but perhaps the central problem was the banks' early involvement in the renegotiation of the contract, and the multiple methods of compensation for differ-

ent parts of the works. Tunneling was done on a cost-plus fixed-fee basis with a target cost above or below which there would be a sharing of the difference. Rolling stock was procured on a cost-plus-percentage-fee basis. The banks insisted on the least defined portions, the terminals and the mechanical and electrical (M&E) equipment, to be done on a lump-sum turnkey basis.

As difficult as some of the earlier technical and commercial problems were, it was the fixed equipment that caused the most intractable problems ....

As fitting for the project of the century, TML made the claim of the century demanding an additional amount equal to 150 percent of the original lump-sum price for the M&E (i.e., from $930 million to $2.25 billion at 1985 prices!).

They maintained that all of the cost overruns were due to Eurotunnel's interference and disruption. From our perspective this was nonsense. Their organization was not adequately set up for M&E work. They subcontracted design to 46 contractors. TML's attention had been devoted primarily to tunneling in the early years. So, when subcontractors' bids came in and commitments were made, TML's cost forecasts kept increasing.

Their reaction was to make a claim for recovery of all costs on the basis that Eurotunnel had caused such delay and disruption that the contract lump sum was no longer valid, and did this without any substantiation of their claim, as required by the contract.

That was in July 1991. Eurotunnel referred this claim immediately to the disputes panel as per the contract. In March 1992, to Eurotunnel's and the banks' horror, the panel ruled in TML's favor, ordering Eurotunnel to pay $75 million per month until a negotiated settlement was reached.

Eurotunnel had to pay, but filed for arbitration with the International Chamber of Commerce, asking for an urgent award to stop the interim payments. The arbitrators made two interim awards, both in Eurotunnel's favor. In September 1992 they ruled that the payments were incorrect. In March 1993 they ruled TML had to reformulate its claim into individual claims for variations and/or breach of contract.

Several high-level negotiations resulted in agreements and contract amendments while others got nowhere. The first of these agreements was made in late 1988 and again in late 1989. The major tunneling claims were settled, and the rolling stock fee was capped. But on fixed equipment, TML rejected offers to settle made in December 1991 and in May 1992. We tried again for a settlement in the second half of 1992, going through very detailed and lengthy negotiations, but could not reach agreement.

Parallel negotiations during mid-1992 did settle new claims for the tunnels and old claims for the terminals.

No serious negotiations were held in the first half of 1993 as TML adopted an "economic" slowdown.

Several overtures were made through various channels and finally, again under the auspices of the Bank of England, agreement was reached on a protocol to secure the transfer of control (from TML) and phased opening. It was signed by Eurotunnel, TML, the Agent Banks and the Bank of England on July 27, 1993. Under the protocol, Eurotunnel took early control of the sites and conducted the final testing with TML's assistance.

That's the good news. The bad news is that Eurotunnel has to advance additional money against the fixed equipment claims not settled. TML must still substantiate their entitlement [This was done in December 1993.] We estimate the process to resolution will last well into 1995!

Peter Middleton is an executive with the Maitre D'Oeuvre (MDO). This oversight group was, like just about everything on the project, a scrupulously even combination of French and British firms, SETEC and Atkins, respectively. Every three months, Middleton says, the group prepared a "hefty" status report for the owners, the contractors, and the banks.

Looking back to the beginning of the project, Middleton says the banks and the contractors who put the deal together in the mid-1980s were a daring lot, but "had no idea how to be owners." As a result, they went ahead with what is regarded by many as the "disastrous" lump-sum contract for the fixed equipment. While there have been delays and unanticipated costs elsewhere, this aspect of the entire project possibly caused the greatest cost overruns and resulted in the claim.

Middleton says the civil work contract definitions and the contract terms were "reasonable," and the scope familiar to the parties. This part of the contract was written on a cost-plus-fixed-fee basis, with overruns to be shared by the owner and the contractor. The lump-sum contract was inappropriate for work "imperfectly understood" by the banks and the contractors, says Middleton. But there was a lot of pressure to go forward, he says. The contractors wanted the work, the bankers wanted certainty, says Middleton, and so the lump sum prevailed.

Frank Cain, senior vice-president, Bechtel Power, Europe, Africa, and the Middle East, spent a year as Eurotunnel's project chief executive, succeeding colleague Neerhout.

On the claim on the fixed equipment, Cain thinks the lump-sum contract was inevitable: "Banks always want lump sums and certainty." Cain has tried to "particularize" the claim—break it down. "It's easier to pick up pieces to agree on," he says. Parties came close to an agreement in early 1993, but the banks would not buy in, he says. At that point, the current protocol took effect, in which Eurotunnel paid TML each month against a final settlement.

The Intergovernmental Commission (IGC), the oversight body made up of civil servants from France and the U.K., mandated that where there were differences in the two countries' standards, the higher of the two should prevail. In theory this was a great idea, he says, but contractors couldn't easily interpret this when differences related to items such as a concrete pour.

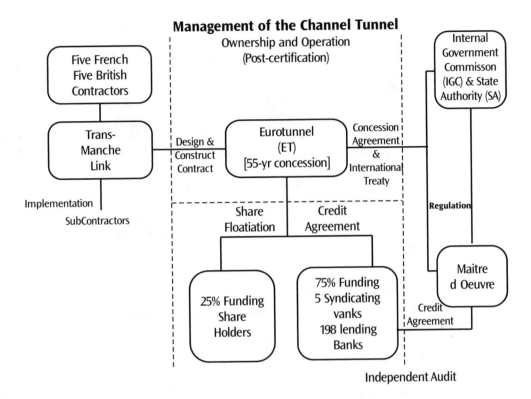

Management of the Channel Tunnel

Ownership and Operation (Post-certification)

FIGURE 1 A VASTLY SIMPLIFIED CHART OF THE PROJECT'S MANAGEMENT. IN ADDITION, MANY OF THE GROUPS NOTED HAD THEIR OWN LEGAL AND ENGINEERING CONSULTANTS. IN DECEMBER 1993, THE PROJECT WAS HANDED OVER TO THE OWNER, EUROTUNNEL, TO COMPLETE TESTING OF THE RAIL SYSTEM AND EQUIPMENT AND TO BEGIN SYSTEM OPERATION.

Cain takes the construction veteran's view that "delays and cost overruns are not unusual in a large project." Nonetheless, he faults IGC for both. Under its safety charge, it instituted an "arbitrary" and last-minute requirement for Euroscan at both terminals. This first-of-its-kind electronic antiterrorist device will check trucks at random before they enter the tunnel. Design and installation of Euroscan caused delays and higher costs, says Cain.

Jack Lemley is another American asked to help salvage the troubled project on the contractor side as chief executive for TML. Lemley, a heavy-construction veteran who had set up his own niche consulting firm out of Boise, Idaho, was troubleshooting in Nepal when he was asked to take charge for TML. Reluctant at first, Lemley decided to take on his "European adventure." He talks about the organizational challenge and government interference, with quite a different point of view than that of John Neerhout.

Lemley says his greatest initial challenge was to meld what were two operations: Translink (the five English contractors who were part of the original proposal in the mid-1980s) and Transmanche (the five French counterpart contractors). Each had its own managing director. The Translink director had responsibility for commercial and business affairs, the Transmanche director, for coordination of all engineering. Lemley changed this to two managing directors, one for all engineering and one for all construction. Lemley thinks this and other changes made for a more efficient operation and got the project back on schedule.

Safety on this project was "far ahead of the rest of the industry," says Lemley, and this is the other achievement he likes to point to. The safety record improved during his tenure, Lemley adds. "We were running half the national average of accidents for the French or the British."

Lemley's regrets about the project loom larger than his satisfactions, but they stem from matters out of his control. The tunnel concession, in his opinion, gave the governments "free rein to change physical criteria without providing the money to do so." The government in this case is IGC. Parties to future concessions and, by implication, other privatization projects, must understand that if requirements are upgraded, someone must pay, he warns. Eurotunnel, the owner of this transportation system, could have been a "tremendously rich utility," says Lemley, but IGC has taken away every margin for error.

Lemley remains rankled about IGC'S escalating safety requirements. While safety on the job was a Lemley priority, the safety of the system became a growing concern with IGC, and costly changes were dictated to TML at every step of the way. IGC dragged its collective feet until costs for some modifications skyrocketed, according to Lemley. One example cited by others involved a series of safety-related options that included the widening of pedestrian doors in a passenger car train, from 600 mm to 700 mm. When final approvals were not forthcoming, TML went ahead with the manufacturing phase to keep on schedule. The change would have cost about $9 million before manufacturing. When the IGC finally decided they would not accept the 600 mm door, the change cost almost $70 million plus a nine-month delay.

Lemley says TML used seismic design criteria that were used for nuclear power plants in both countries. Nonetheless, midway through design, IGC decided to increase these by a factor of four, says Lemley. "We found that the tunnel was over designed, but we had to upgrade the mechanical and electrical systems to conform to new criteria."

The approval process went through several steps, first TML, then Eurotunnel, then MDO, and finally IGC, too many, in Lemley's estimation. But his greatest grievance is the fact that IGC could ask for anything "hiding behind the concept of the public welfare and safety," and someone else had to pay for it. The concession agreement did not and could not provide for these unforeseen and costly changes. It's unfair, he says, to the developer to change the rules midstream. Finally, Lemley, who left the project last fall to resume his own consulting, sees "great merit" in the $2.25 billion claim.

CHANNEL CROSSING HISTORY

In 1751, the Amiens Academy in France conducted a competition on "better ways" than by ship to cross the English Channel. Since then, and possibly before, there have been several attempts to circumvent nature and geography, and several false starts. In 1974, the idea got as far as the tunneling stage, but the effort was abandoned. What follows are some important dates and statistics about the last and successful effort.
• 1978: British and French contractors decide to resume the failed 1974 efforts.

- 1983: Five French banks and contractors, and five British banks and contractors propose the tunnel scheme.
- 1985: The French and British governments ask for proposals for the fixed link.
- 1986: The Anglo-French treaty was signed. Transmanche Link (TML), made up of five British and five French contractors, won the contract and Eurotunnel was declared the owner of the fifty-five year concession for the link.
- 1990: The service tunnel, running from both sides of the channel, breaks through.
- 1991: In May, the north tunnel is completed and in June, the south tunnel is completed.
- 1993: The first shuttle locomotive goes through the tunnel. In December TML hands the project over to owner Eurotunnel.

    Some Channel Tunnel trivia:
- The two running rail tunnels have 7.6 m inner diameters.
- A service tunnel has 4.8 m inner diameter.
- The tunnels are 38 km long, linked by 150 cross passages of 3.3 m for equipment.
- The project required eleven tunnel-boring machines.
- Tunnel linings are interlocking concrete rings, cast on sites on both sides of the channel.
- Larger crossover chambers are 164 m long, 21 m wide and 15 m high. The French used a mini-Mount Baker method to tunnel their side; the British used the new Austrian tunneling method.
- The construction access shaft on the French side was 55 m in diameter and 75 m deep; on the British side, the shaft was 110 m deep and 10 m in diameter.
- About 15,000 workers were employed on the project.
- The project also included terminals on each side of the channel and the creation of a park below Shakespeare Cliff on the British side, where tunnel muck formed 30 ha of new land behind a seawall.
- The trip takes three hours from Paris to London and the cost ranges from $325 to $465.

Study Questions

THE CHANNEL TUNNEL: LARGER THAN LIFE, AND LATE

1. Despite facing many management failures, the channel tunnel is certainly one of the world's engineering wonders. The author concentrates her analysis on the conflict between Transmanche Link (TML) and Eurotunnel. Suggest a course of action that should have been taken to prevent this conflict.

2. Some of the Intergovernmental Commission (ICG) decisions caused a portion of the cost overrun on the project. As a project manager, what could you have done to minimize the impact of these decisions?

3. In an interview in the article, one executive, in referring to the bank and contractor who put the project together, said that they "had no idea how to be owners." What is the role of the owner of the project? Where did the owners of this project fail?

4. List some of the other factors that might have contributed to the cost overruns and schedule delays on this project.

Minimizing Construction Claims under the Project Management Concept

Regula A. Brunies, Revay and Associates Limited
Ross Brophy, Public Works and Services, Government of Newfoundland and Labrador St. John's

PMI Canada *Proceedings*, 1986, pp. 198–212

INTRODUCTION

Fast-track projects, in recent years, have developed the dubious reputation of being incubators for claims. Although the project management concept is not necessarily synonymous with fast-tracking, nevertheless the two notions are so frequently associated that the project management method of construction has acquired the same stigma.

The classical justification of the project management concept in construction and its usual application is when the type, size, or complexity of the project demands early participation of various relatively unrelated disciplines. The early formation of the complete project team can offer potential savings, not the least of which derive from construction expertise with all its ramifications, such as knowledge of constructibility, efficient procurement, and contractor-type estimating of construction costs. This expertise will assist in the correction of user-client's unreasonably high expectations, or design decisions, which might have yielded costs beyond the authorized funds available or late delivery/occupancy of the project.

Such a project team can be likened to a newly founded company whose sole objective is to go out of business as rapidly and as economically as possible, while still reaching a given goal of accomplishment—project completion within budget and on schedule. Often, the team has neither the time nor the inclination to spend much effort on the optimization of administrative procedures. Traditionally, the members of the team are relative strangers and know very little about the modus operandi of each other. Unfortunately, these apparently unimportant or simply insufficiently developed administrative features often create missing links in the chain of command and give rise to contradictory instructions, all of which ultimately produce delays and/or interfere with the orderly progress of construction. In other words, they will invite claims.

An analysis of recent projects reveals that the above scenario is more often the rule than the exception; therefore, the search for preventive measures is not only justified but outright essential. Genuine claims have simply become far too frequent and of such magnitude, particularly under the project/construction management concept, that they cannot be brushed aside anymore as an unnecessary nuisance originating from money-hungry contractors, a view so often displayed by owners and/or their representatives. However, there are also other owners who have undergone a metamorphosis

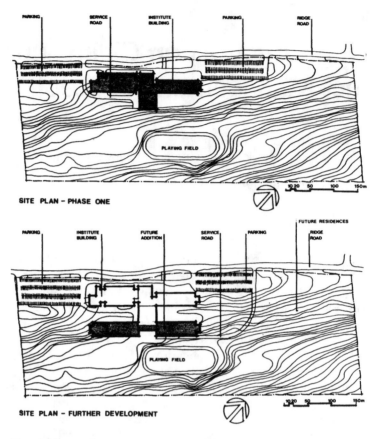

PARKING SERVICE ROAD INSTITUTE BUILDING PARKING RIDGE ROAD

PLAYING FIELD

10 20 50 100 150m

SITE PLAN – PHASE ONE

FUTURE RESIDENCES

PARKING INSTITUTE BUILDING FUTURE ADDITION SERVICE ROAD PARKING RIDGE ROAD

PLAYING FIELD

10 20 50 100 150m

SITE PLAN – FURTHER DEVELOPMENT

FIGURE 1   THE MASTER PLAN

of thinking with regard to claims and attacked the problem at its roots, namely, day one of the project.

This paper will examine how a prudent owner was able to successfully complete a $42 million project within budget and on time, without claims, and last but not least, with content contractors.

THE PROJECT

The project discussed is a major education facility located in St. John's, Newfoundland, called "Institute of Fisheries and Marine Technology." The institute was previously housed in inadequate, old university buildings and other scattered locations which no longer satisfied its needs. The institute offers instruction in the design, construction, operation maintenance, and navigation of vessels of all kinds, to those who may be involved in fishing at the Grand Banks of Newfoundland, or in the exploitation of the vast oil resources off the Northeastern coast of Canada. In addition to the three-year, full-time program, the college offers short courses in such areas as fishing techniques and equipment maintenance. Graduates of the college are found on all oceans and enjoy an international reputation.

PROGRAM	NO. OF STUDENTS	SECTION SIZE	NO. OF SECTIONS	SUBJECT	SUBJECT NUMBER	HOURS/ WEEK	SECTION HOURS
Food Technology I	30	30	1	Biology	121	3	3
Food Technolgy III	16	30	1	Processing Biology Food Engineering	321 321	2 4	2 4
Food Technology I	30	30	1	Processing Technology	121	3	3
New Courses	54	30	2	Biology	-	3	6

Total Section Hours 18

Area Requirements	m²
30-station instructional area	78
Storage and preparation room	27
Total Area	105

FIGURE 2   ROLE STUDY REQUIREMENTS BIOLOGY LABS AND SHOPS

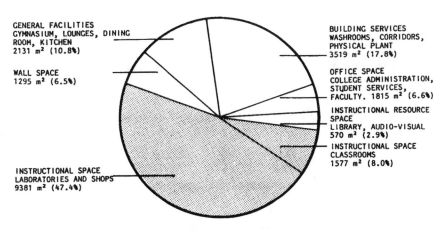

FIGURE 3   SUMMARY OF BUILDING SPACE CATEGORIES

During the early planning phase, the Department of Public Works and Services of the Government of Newfoundland and Labrador (owner) commissioned a role study which included educational specifications, a design brief, and preliminary studies, while negotiations between federal and provincial governments were progressing with the objective of arriving at a mutually satisfactory cost-sharing agreement. The preliminary studies were completed by the time the agreements were signed.

The Master Plan

A site (comprising 17 hectares/142 acres; see Figure 1) had been designated by the provincial government for the new Institute which overlooks the city of St. John's. The master plan reflected the need for flexibility; that is, the new building must be able to accept additions with minimal disruption to the institute's activities. This was achieved by providing for additional wings coming off a central spine parallel to the existing wings.

During the first phase, the existing student dormitories will be used. However, if residences are required in the future, they can be located on institute

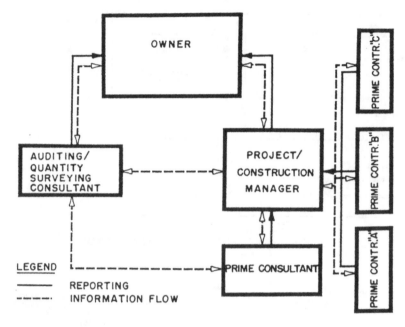

FIGURE 4   ORGANIGRAMME

property east of the main building and parking lot. These structures can con
nect into existing site service facilities such as parking. The role study includ
ed detailed space requirements for a projected student enrollment of 987 (FTE
students based on the curriculum of the programs.

The method used involved a tabulation of section hours for each kind o
instructional space needed. The instructional spaces were adjusted until there
were enough section hours to ensure a good utilization of space and efficien
scheduling. To determine the necessary number of classrooms, thirty-fou
hours of instruction per week per classroom was decided upon, representing
75 percent utilization factor, based on a maximum of forty-five hours of use
per week.

To estimate capital costs for construction of the new building, a prelim
inary building design was prepared based on the agreed-upon requirement
outlined in the role study, which recommended specifics with regards to
wind, snow, and other climatic conditions; internal circulation; location o
rooms; and site services.

The Project Environment

Newfoundland is an island separated from the mainland and, therefore, its
communications must be via water or air. Winters are cold, and there may
well be frost on the ground as late as May. With a population of only 550,000
many of the construction ingredients must, of necessity, be purchased off
shore and transported long distances, which may add to the project duration
if not carefully planned. Also, some of the more sophisticated tradesmen may
still have to be flown in from the mainland, even though local resources
would always be given priority. While some local firms have started to spe
cialize in project/construction management, most of their previous experi
ence has been limited to either design or general contracting, mainly on the

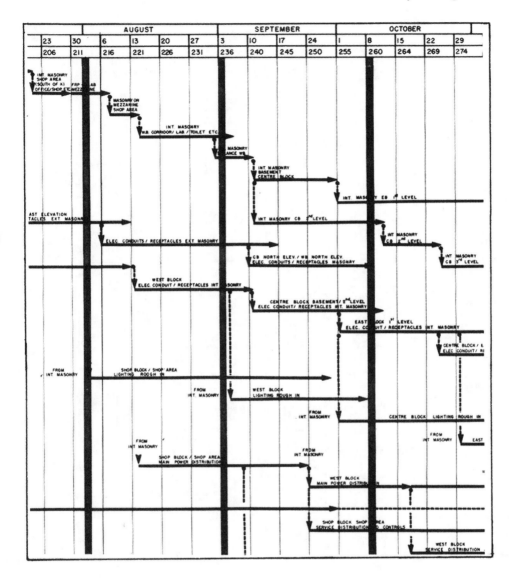

FIGURE 5   MASTER SCHEDULE FORMAT

island. Generally, large firms from the mainland have had difficulties in understanding the local environment and thus have not been able to compete successfully with the local specialists.

The provincial government will nevertheless hire offshore consultants if deemed advantageous to the success of the project, but usually on a single-project basis and with the understanding that the consultants will work closely with local firms. Additionally, the consultants are expected not only to perform their duties but at the same time act as importers of more advanced technology for the future benefit of the local specialists and the island.

If some of the newer project management buzzwords do not form part of the standard vocabulary of a Newfoundland project manager, those must initially be avoided or else they only cause embarrassment or antagonism. However, this ought not to hinder application of modern techniques. Once

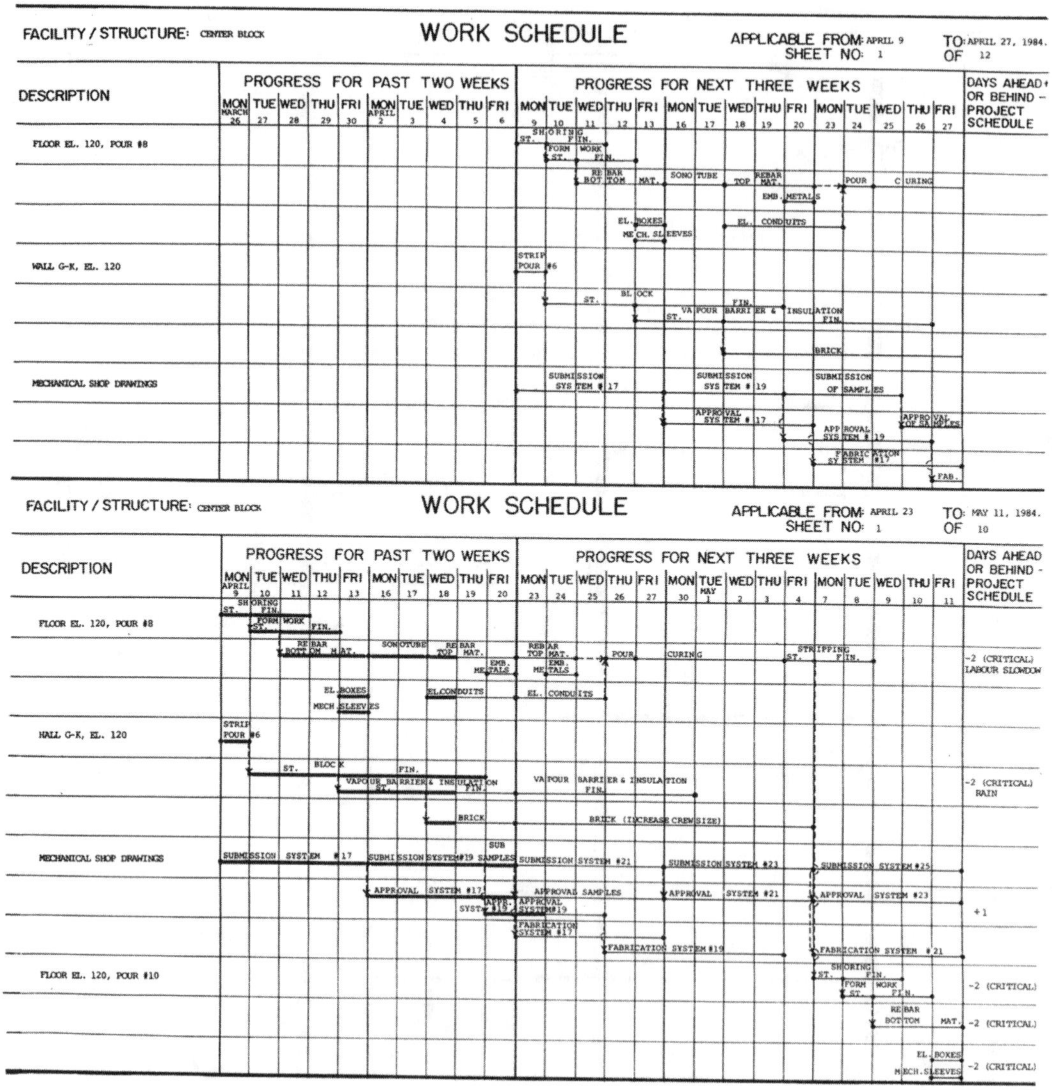

FACILITY / STRUCTURE: CENTER BLOCK   WORK SCHEDULE   APPLICABLE FROM: APRIL 9   TO: APRIL 27, 1984.   SHEET NO: 1   OF 12

(Work schedule chart: Center Block, applicable April 9 to April 27, 1984, Sheet No. 1 of 12. Descriptions include FLOOR EL. 120, POUR #8; WALL G-K, EL. 120; MECHANICAL SHOP DRAWINGS.)

FACILITY / STRUCTURE: CENTER BLOCK   WORK SCHEDULE   APPLICABLE FROM: APRIL 23   TO: MAY 11, 1984.   SHEET NO: 1   OF 10

(Work schedule chart: Center Block, applicable April 23 to May 11, 1984, Sheet No. 1 of 10. Descriptions include FLOOR EL. 120, POUR #8; HALL G-K, EL. 120; MECHANICAL SHOP DRAWINGS; FLOOR EL. 120, POUR #10.)

FIGURE 6   SHORT-CYCLE SCHEDULING FORMAT

everybody understands and is enthused by the results, such techniques may even be called by their names, and the objective of improving project management techniques will have been accomplished.

The provincial government's understanding of the uniqueness of the local situation and its guidance in optimizing local resources have been highly successful in improving the local project management scene, an important step towards minimizing claims under the project management concept.

Owner's Pre-Project Experience

The Department of Public Works and Services in the Province of Newfoundland is responsible for implementing construction of the major buildings that are erected for the provincial government. These buildings include hospitals, large adult and post-secondary education facilities, and similar projects.

ACCT CODE NO.	DESCRIPTION	BUDGET				CONTRACT VALUE			ACTUAL COSTS			TOTAL FORECAST COST			VARIANCE CHANGE FROM PREVIOUS REPORT	REMARKS
		A	B	C	D=B+C	E	F	G=E+F	H	I	J=H+I	K	L=G+K	M=D-L	N=N*-M	
		ORIGINAL BUDGET	REVISED BUDGET AGREED BY OWNER APR. 18/84	*OWNER'S REVISIONS	CURRENT BUDGET	ORIGINAL CONTRACT VALUE	CONTRACT CHANGES TO DATE	CURRENT CONTRACT VALUE	PREVIOUSLY APPROVED	APPROVED THIS MONTH	TOTAL APPROVED TO DATE	ESTIMATED COST OF CHANGES TO COMPLETE	FORECAST OF FINAL COST	VARIANCE		
800	Site Security	90,000	90,000	-	90,000	84,641	-	84,641	53,333	4,318	57,651	5,359	90,000	-	-	
1800	Site Grading	525,000	496,366	-	496,366	419,174	77,192	496,366	496,366	-	496,366	-	496,366	-	-	
2000	Site Services #1	500,000	402,400	-	402,400	403,280	(22,547)	380,733	380,733	-	380,733	-	380,733	21,667		
2200	Services to Site Office	45,000	35,117	-	35,117	34,400	717	35,117	35,117	-	35,117	-	35,117	-	-	
2400	Excavations & Foundations	1,150,000	905,571	-	905,571	929,100	(25,309)	903,791	903,791	-	903,791	-	903,791	1,780	-	
2600	Structural Concrete	2,300,000	2,235,984	15,698	2,251,682	2,190,176	14,631	2,204,807	2,204,807	-	2,204,807	-	2,204,807	46,875	-	
2800	Structural Steel	1,100,000	1,142,768	-	1,142,768	1,129,696	(10,000)	1,119,696	1,109,616	-	1,109,616	7,807	1,127,503	15,265	-	
3000	Mechanical	3,600,000	3,428,800	65,714	3,494,514	3,306,000	94,049	3,400,049	3,146,712	128,219	3,274,931	98,131	3,498,180	(3,666)	18,435	
3200	Electrical	3,120,000	2,832,624	70,553	2,903,177	2,713,400	51,120	2,764,520	2,355,702	109,185	2,464,887	78,432	2,842,952	60,225	9,769	
3400	Sprinkler & Fire Protection	435,000	451,000	920	451,920	454,000	(26,221)	427,779	339,865	51,454	391,319	12,500	440,279	11,641	920	
3600	Architectural	6,210,000	7,970,600	11,866	7,982,466	7,695,748	(133,359)	7,562,389	6,797,556	294,330	7,091,886	189,035	7,751,424	231,042	3,701	
3800	Kitchen Equipment	550,000	550,000	34,913	584,913	508,920	-	508,920	199,123	124,996	324,119	41,080	550,000	34,913	-	
4000	Site Services #2	380,000	400,000	27,767	427,767	373,675	2,850	376,525	328,683	22,701	351,384	23,475	400,000	27,767	-	
4200	Siteworks/ Landscaping	970,000	1,200,000	72,600	1,272,600	1,197,796	-	1,197,796	-	43,718	43,718	74,804	1,272,600	-	-	
4400	Laboratory/Library Furniture	770,000	790,000	-	790,000	814,407	1,931	816,338	423,006	248,737	671,743	21,663	838,001	(48,001)	(774)	
	Contingency	1,087,000	-	-	-	-	-	-	-	-	-	-	-	-	-	
4600	General Conditions	435,000	435,000	-	435,000	435,000	-	435,000	73,138	18,584	91,722	(95,000)	340,000	95,000	73,000	
	Building Permit	-	140,000	-	140,000	140,000	-	140,000	-	-	-	(10,000)	130,000	10,000	10,000	
	TOTALS	23,267,000	23,506,230	300,031	23,806,261	22,829,413	25,054	22,854,467	18,847,548	1,046,242	19,893,790	447,286	23,301,753	504,508	115,051	

FIGURE 7   PROJECT STATUS REPORT

The department has been responsible for the design and construction of facilities up to 640,000 square feet of floor area, and as certain institutions are planned to be integrated, larger and more complex buildings will come under the responsibility of the department. Over the years the department utilized various methods of construction, including the conventional general contracting, the classical project management, and the modified construction management system. Experiences have ranged from very good to very bad on each of the methods chosen.

GENERAL CONTRACTOR CONCEPT

The department generally favors the use of general contractors under the supervision of the project's architect. From the department's point of view, these projects are controlled by senior, in-house project managers whose responsibility is project direction from inception until commissioning, including financial control and scheduling. This method has proven successful for smaller projects up to the size of $15,000,000.

These projects were not built under "fast-track" or "phased-construction" programs, and the entire design was completed before public tenders were called for the complete project. At times separate tenders were called during the planning stage for site preparation to enable the general contractor to move on-site without the uncertainties of clearing, grubbing, and excavation, thus resulting in earlier start of main building construction and lower prices. Under this method some claims had to be dealt with, normally caused by lateness in decision-making on the part of the user-client. Generally, these were delay claims and posed little problems for settlement.

Another minor source of claims arose from certain inaccuracies in drawings or misinterpretation of drawings. Most of these claims were settled out of court to both the contractor's and client's mutual satisfaction.

				O	P	Q	R	K=O+P+Q+R
Accounts Code No.	Description	Current Contract Value	Includes Last CO No.	Approved COs Not Included In Current Contract Value	Estimate of Known Changes	Unidentified Changes to Complete	Allowance for Additional Anticipated Costs	Estimated Cost of Changes to Completion
800	Site Security	84,641	-	-	-	5,359	-	5,359
1800	Site Grading	496,366	1	-	-	-	-	-
2000	Site Services No. 1	380,733	4	-	-	-	-	-
2200	Services to Site Office	35,117	1	-	-	-	-	-
2400	Excavations & Foundations	903,791	7	-	-	-	-	-
2600	Structural Concrete	2,204,807	6	-	-	-	-	-
2800	Structural Steel	1,119,696	1	-	7,807	-	-	7,807
3000	Mechanical	3,400,049	29	-	53,131	45,000	-	98,131
3200	Electrical	2,764,520	18	-	8,432	70,000	-	78,432
3400	Sprinkler s & Fire Protection	427,779	3	-	500	12,000	-	12,500
3600	Architectural	7,562,389	51	-	121,035	68,000	-	189,035
3800	Kitchen Equipment	508,920	-	-	-	41,080	-	41,080
4000	Site Services No. 1	376,525	2	-	-	23,475	-	23,475
4200	Paving, Landscaping & Site Lighting	1,197,796	-	-	-	74,804	-	74,804
4400	Wood/Metal Cabinetwork & Specialties	816,338	4	-	21,663	-	-	21,663
4600	General Conditions	435,000	-	-	(95,000)	-	-	(95,000)
	Building Permit	140,000	-	-	(10,000)	-	-	(10,000)
	TOTALS	22,854,467		-	107,568	339,718	-	447,286

FIGURE 8   SUBSIDIARY COST REPORT

PROJECT MANAGEMENT CONCEPT

The department, on larger and more complex projects, has utilized the project management method of construction. However, recent experience with this method has yielded lengthy delays, high cost overruns, and large claims caused by a certain over-enthusiasm and overoptimism by project managers.

Moreover, the conclusion derived from a study of these projects was that 1) the risks of fast-tracking were far too great and unpredictable, and 2) "phased construction" was the alternative to minimize those risks.

"FAST-TRACK" VERSUS "PHASED CONSTRUCTION"

Project managers, as well as literature on the subject, all too often refer to the terms "phased construction" and "fast-track" interchangeably, without any distinction. Although similar in some respects, the two methods differ in the type of design/construction overlap. The design of an individual work package in "phased construction" is substantially complete when construction starts. With "fast-tracking," work packages are rushed to the field, with the design being completed after construction has begun. In short, fast tracking is an accelerated "phased construction" method with design/construction overlap within the individual work packages.

The two methods only resemble each other to the extent that construction starts before the entire project design is 100 percent complete. The analysis of fast-tracking projects indicates that inherent risks include:

- loss of the planned benefits due to schedule delays

		To March 31	April	May	June	July	Aug.	Sept.	Oct.	Nov.	Dec.	Jan.	Feb.	March	April	May	June	July	Aug.
800 SITE SECURITY	Mthly		3,275	3,275	3,275	3,275	3,275	3,275	3,275	3,275	5,000	4,300	3,275	3,275	3,275	3,275	3,275	3,275	3,275
	Cum.	22,100	25,375	28,650	31,925	35,200	38,475	41,750	45,025	48,300	53,300	57,600	60,875	64,150	67,425	70,700	73,975	77,250	80,525
1800 SITE GRADING	Mthly																		
	Cum.	419,174	419,174	419,174	419,174	419,174	419,174	419,174	419,174	419,174	419,174	419,174	419,174	419,174	419,174	419,174	419,174	419,174	419,174
2000 SITE SERVICES No. 1	Mthly		86,815	47,866	34,467														
	Cum.	234,132	320,947	368,813	403,280	403,280	403,280	403,280	403,280	403,280	403,280	403,280	403,280	403,280	403,280	403,280	403,280	403,280	403,280
2200 SERVICES TO SITE OFFICE	Mthly																		
	Cum.	34,400	34,400	34,400	34,400	34,400	34,400	34,400	34,400	34,400	34,400	34,400	34,400	34,400	34,400	34,400	34,400	34,400	34,400
2400 EXCAVATIONS & FOUNDATIONS	Mthly		45,455																
	Cum.	863,645	909,100	909,100	909,100	909,100	909,100	909,100	909,100	909,100	909,100	909,100	909,100	909,100	909,100	909,100	909,100	909,100	909,100
2600 STRUCTURAL CONCRETE	Mthly		323,040	585,471	660,027	552,121	53,517												
	Cum.		323,040	908,511	1,568,538	2,120,659	2,174,176	2,174,176	2,174,176	2,174,176	2,174,176	2,174,176	2,174,176	2,174,176	2,174,176	2,174,176	2,174,176	2,174,176	2,174,176
2800 STRUCTURAL STEEL	Mthly		82,509	709		497,240	166,653												
	Cum.	372,585	455,094	455,803	455,803	953,043	1,119,696	1,119,696	1,119,696	1,119,696	1,119,696	1,119,696	1,119,696	1,119,696	1,119,696	1,119,696	1,119,696	1,119,696	1,119,696
3000 MECHANICAL	Mthly			89,660	98,820	60,540	13,235	48,890	312,957	423,238	396,673	590,011	427,582	383,860	265,624	147,293	27,417		
	Cum.	0		89,660	188,480	249,020	262,255	311,145	624,102	1,047,340	1,444,213	2,034,224	2,461,806	2,845,666	3,111,290	3,258,583	3,286,000	3,286,000	3,286,000
3200 ELECTRICAL	Mthly			400	14,642	17,864	30,074	113,944	175,007	243,633	302,381	715,878	344,673	270,283	243,340	118,786	92,495		
	Cum.	0	400	15,042	32,906	62,980	176,924	351,931	595,564	897,945	1,613,823	1,958,496	2,228,779	2,472,119	2,472,119	2,590,905	2,683,400	2,683,400	2,683,400
3400 SPRINKLER & FIRE PROTECTION	Mthly							17,830	81,130	75,552	111,830	106,131	41,527						
	Cum.							17,830	98,960	174,512	286,342	392,473	434,000	434,000	434,000	434,000	434,000	434,000	434,000
3600 ARCHITECTURAL	Mthly		36,846	190,940	392,172	623,148	1,149,320	1,089,109	643,338	488,745	548,562	751,899	329,938	311,476	227,491	418,404	94,154	35,205	
	Cum.	40,000	76,846	267,786	659,958	1,283,106	2,432,426	3,521,535	4,164,873	4,653,618	5,202,180	5,954,079	6,484,017	6,795,493	7,022,984	7,441,388	7,535,542	7,570,747	7,570,747
3800 KITCHEN EQUIPMENT	Mthly												87,636			411,480	9,804		
	Cum.	0											87,636	87,636	87,636	499,116	508,920	508,920	508,920
4000 SITE SERVICES No. 2	Mthly								130,000	150,000	93,675								
	Cum.	0							130,000	280,000	373,675	373,675	373,675	373,675	373,675	373,675	373,675	373,675	373,675
4200 SITEWORKS/LANDSCAPING	Mthly						8,000	123,000	184,790	27,139						300,000	300,000	254,867	
	Cum.	0					8,000	131,000	315,790	342,929	342,929	342,929	342,929	342,929	342,929	642,929	942,929	1,197,796	1,197,796
4400 LABORATORY/LIBRARY FURNITURE	Mthly															350,000	350,000	114,407	
	Cum.	0														350,000	700,000	814,407	814,407
4600 GENERAL CONDITIONS	Mthly		15,000	15,000	15,000	15,000	15,000	15,000	15,000	20,000	27,000	40,000	40,000	35,000	32,000	27,000	20,000	20,000	30,000
	Cum.	39,000	54,000	69,000	84,000	99,000	114,000	129,000	144,000	164,000	191,000	231,000	271,000	306,000	338,000	365,000	385,000	405,000	435,000
TOTAL MONTHLY ($)			593,340	947,563	1,221,625	1,781,398	1,540,774	1,665,411	1,628,545	1,470,283	1,799,444	1,772,410	1,358,714	976,951	528,390	1,776,238	897,145	427,754	33,275
TOTAL CUMULATIVE ($)		2,025,036	2,618,376	3,565,939	4,787,564	6,568,962	8,109,736	9,775,147	11,403,692	12,873,975	14,673,419	16,445,829	17,804,543	18,781,494	19,309,884	21,086,122	21,983,267	22,411,021	22,444,296

FIGURE 9   BUDGET CURVE DATA—ORIGINAL CONTRACT

- loss of financial benefits due to the cost of claims and litigation
- intentionally low bids and unrealistic schedules by contractors because of incomplete tender specifications, resulting in artificially high pricing of extra work and change orders as well as claims
- far-reaching effects of mistakes during the early design/engineering phase.

Evolution of a Modified Concept

With regard to the Institute of Fisheries, the department carefully evaluated its options. Because of the size of the project ($42.3 million), the complexity and the user-client's early occupancy requirements, the department decided to use the project management concept.

However, because of the recent negative results with respect to delays, cost overruns, and claim situations, the traditional concept was modified through the introduction of an independent auditing/quantity surveying consultant with responsibility for preparation of detailed contractor-type construction estimates, master scheduling, and for monitoring of project expenditures and financial/schedule projections.

Rationale

The rationale for the introduction of this new team player was based on the fact that historically project/construction managers, with respect to schedule and budget, tend to lean toward either one of two extreme directions:
- PM/CM creates an extremely tight budget and schedule to secure approval of the project and/or mandate.

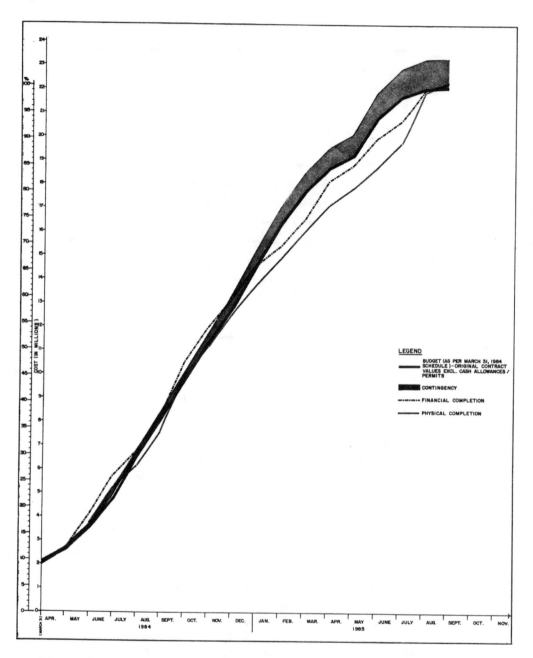

FIGURE 10   PERFORMANCE TEST—TOTAL PROJECT

- PM/CM creates an unnecessarily high budget and extended project duration to minimize his liabilities towards the owner.

The department concluded that the introduction of an independent third party will circumvent those desires which are understandable and human, but seldom justified.

While the tasks of scheduling, estimating, and monitoring are traditionally carried out by the PM/CM, the independent third party can perform the same tasks without any conflict of interest.

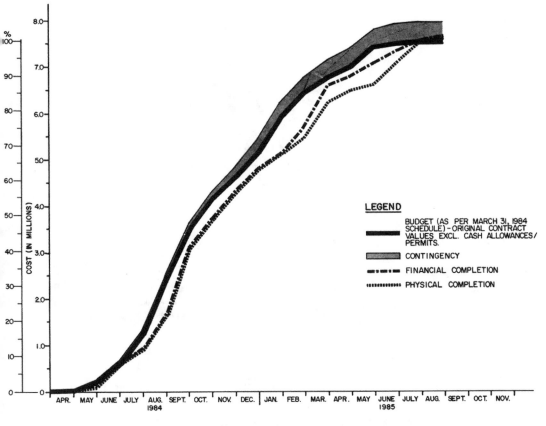

FIGURE 11   PERFORMANCE TEST—ARCHITECTURAL PACKAGE

In light of most recent court decisions in the United States, the importance of unbiased monitoring by a party without any financial interest, ensuring quick reaction time, is even more significant. In the eyes of the law, the scheduling and coordinating responsibilities under the project management concept rest with the owner in her capacity as the principal of her agent, the PM/CM. In the past, owners have tried to escape this risk by making prime contractors responsible for coordination, but with little success, as courts consider such responsibility unenforceable (i.e., prime contractor "A" has absolutely no means to force prime contractor "B" to do anything he would not do voluntarily). This was stated very clearly by the GSA Board of Contract Appeals in the case of Jacobson & Co., GS BSA No. 5606, 80-2 BCA (CCH) 1980.

> The Government can decide on whatever method of construction and contracting it chooses, but in doing so it also assumes the responsibilities inherent in its choice. With phased construction, it is obvious that the contracting officer has the obligation and duty to demand that the various contractors cooperate with the construction schedule and not interfere with the work of other contractors.

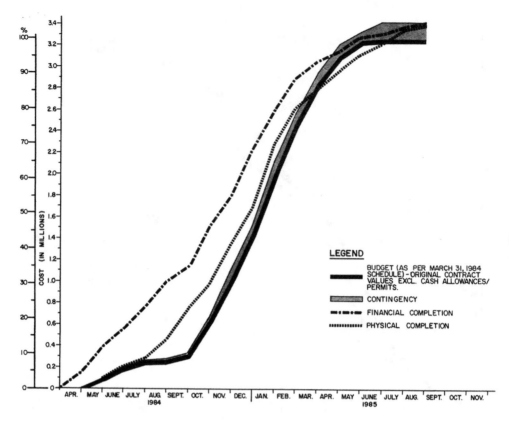

FIGURE 12   PERFORMANCE TEST—MECHANICAL PACKAGE

While the owner may always have legal recourse against the PM/CM, responsibility for payment of a justified prime contractor's claim resulting from the action, neglect, or delay on the part of his agent (i.e., PM/CM) rests in first instance with the owner.

It is evident that preventive measures are less costly than lengthy legal battles extending years beyond project completion.

The New Project Team

The department, in order of priority, appointed a project manager, prime consultant (design), and an auditing/quantity surveyor consultant. The organizational structure was such that the prime consultant reported to the project manager, whereas the auditing/quantity surveying consultant reported independently to the department to ensure that objectivity was maintained, and that it would not become overly familiar with the needs of the construction and design groups.

The department, through past experience, had learned the vital importance of ensuring that all participants had clear definitions of their responsibilities and the roles they were to play on the project. The department further insisted that detailed administrative procedures with regard to equipment procurement, progress payments, change orders, and so on be drawn up and in place before the start of construction to ensure that there would be no misinterpretation or misunderstanding of what had to be done by each member of the project team.

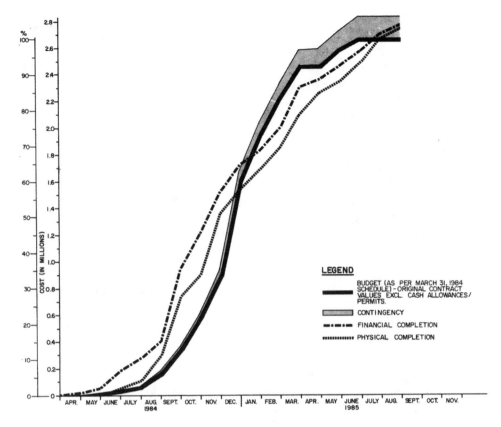

FIGURE 13   **PERFORMANCE TEST—ELECTRICAL PACKAGE**

There was some initial concern on the part of the project manager that such detailed procedures were too onerous and would slow down the project, but subsequent advantages voided that concern.

The Project Manager

The firm chosen to perform the functions of project manager was a local firm specializing in this field and was planning to do its own construction management. The senior representatives designated to be responsible for the execution of this project had either a strong background in design or in general contracting in the Newfoundland environment. The project manager reported to the owner on a monthly basis on tendering, costs, on-site construction activities, and scheduling, as well as problems and key activities. The initial reaction to the introduction of an additional consultant was not overly enthusiastic and governed by a typical reaction to anything new: "We've always gotten by before; why should this time be any different?"

The Prime Consultant

The design firm chosen by the owner was a major local architectural/engineering firm with experience in working under the project management concept. This firm reported to the project manager. An offshore firm assisted in the preparation of the mechanical and electrical design.

Total Project

Budget	74.1 %	73.8%*
Financial Completion	69.6%	70.3%*
Physical Completion	66.8%	67.4%*

Architectural Package

Budget	78.6%
Financial Completion	67.7 %
Physical Completion	67.7 %

Electrical Package

Budget	73.0%
Financial Completion	68.1%
Physical Completion	61.8%

Mechanical Package

Budget	61.9%
Financial Completion	78.9%
Physical Completion	68.5%

*Corrected for current savings of $210,000 in General Conditions.

FIGURE 14   STATUS OF COMPLETION—JAN. 31, 1985

The Auditing/Quantity Surveying Consultant

The newcomer to the traditional project management concept, selected from several invited bidders, was made up of:
• the local branch of a major international audit/management consulting firm (assisted by its in-house, mainland management experts)
• a mainland construction management consulting firm specializing in estimating, planning, and cost control, as well as preparation and/or evaluation of construction claims.

Throughout this paper, the auditing/quantity surveying consultant will be referred to as the "consultant."

Scope of the Consultant's Mandate

Following several discussions with the owner, the mandate of this consultant was agreed upon to include:
Start-Up Phase
• setting-up of code of accounts
• assistance in the preparation of administrative procedures
• preparation of independent detailed contractor-type estimate in addition to estimates prepared by project manager and prime consultant
• preparation of realistic master schedule for design, procurement, and construction, in collaboration with project/construction manager
• design of cost and change order control system, in collaboration with project/construction manager.
Monitoring Phase
• monthly audit of expenditures to date, as well as projection of the final costs
• independent reporting on progress
• design and subsequent application of performance test (quantity surveying system) to advise owner of status of progress versus expenditures, and to

serve as an early warning system to either prevent or minimize claims or detect potential claims early
- report to department on regular intervals and meet with project team on the construction site.

The consultant was officially appointed in late summer 1983, when site clearing had been completed and design was approximately 60 percent complete, tenders for the packages "excavation and foundation" and "site services no. 1" were about to be received, and tender for the structural steel package was to be called shortly. However, above-grade site construction was not to start before spring 1984.

Start-Up Phase

Preparation of the independent detailed contractor-type estimate and master schedule commenced immediately after a familiarization meeting with all members of the project team, receipt of master schedule in force (bar chart), and drawings and specifications available at that time.

Within two weeks, the preliminary evaluation of the available information had advanced to the point when certain important questions required clarification. The most important and pressing question to be dealt with was the completion date of the project.

Completion of the project was scheduled for spring 1986 with the complex relocation of existing equipment, furniture, etc., to take place during the summer months, all to be completed prior to the September start of the 1986/87 academic year.

From its preliminary analysis, the consultant concluded that the project could be completed about ten months earlier than planned, barring a possible construction strike in May 1985, when all current labor agreements were to expire.

Thus, the following two questions were asked:
- Is the spring 1986 completion date the result of budgetary/cash-flow constraints imposed by the Federal/Provincial Funding Agreement?
- Is the college physically able to move one year earlier?

Additionally, the preliminary status of the tender package breakdown, as well as the wisdom of calling any further tenders in the absence of an approved master schedule, were questioned. More specifically, the consultant cautioned the inclusion of any vague dates in the tender documents as long as there was no approved master schedule, thereby making specific reference to contractual clause 1.2 in the structural steel contract package (out for tender at this time), which reads, in part:

> .4 Caution—The owner will not be responsible for any delay claim resulting from late completion of structural concrete work, or other circumstances, which prevent start-up by these target dates.

In clear terms, the consultant stated at this point, in writing:

> Exculpatory clauses such as 1.2.4 should not be used as an excuse for the absence of an agreed-upon schedule.

The owner's reply with regard to the 1986 completion date clarified that none of the reasons suspected applied. Nevertheless, it was the owner who had advised the project manager that under the project management concept

it had seen too many forecasted completion dates which, in fact, could not b
met, all resulting in ramifications much worse than a realistic completio:
date at the outset of the project. The owner, however, fully agreed that:

- an early decision with regard to the tender package breakdown was essentia
- no further tenders were to be called without an approved master schedul
- the use of contractual exculpatory clauses was no answer to a self-inflict
  ed avoidable claim situation.

This first quick exchange of correspondence, copies of which were trans
mitted to the PM/CM, resulted in a three-day working session on-site betwee:
the consultant and PM/CM, in part also attended by the prime consultant.

Concerning the completion date, the entire team agreed that construc
tion could be substantially completed by summer 1985, and with an earnes
effort by all parties, the college could be opened in September 1985.

The tender packages breakdown was agreed upon, with the exception c
architectural work which remained to be resolved at a later date.

The tender call for the structural concrete was to be issued in late No
vember 1983, with mechanical, electrical, and fire protection packages to fol
low around mid-December 1983.

Admittedly, the road was bumpy in the beginning, but smoothed ou
once it was established that the objectives of the outside consultant were n:
different from those of the PM/CM, namely, to successfully complete th:
project within budget and on time.

THE CONSTRUCTION COST ESTIMATE

The preparation of a detailed contractor-type estimate normally require:
drawings and specifications that are reasonably complete (i.e., 85 percent t:
90 percent).

In the fall of 1983, the drawings and specifications were at varying stage:
of completion ranging from practically nil to 100 percent (structural stee
package out for tender). With regard to architectural work, it was found tha:
there were many conflicts between drawings and finishing schedules. All con
flicts were immediately reported to the prime consultant. Certain speci
fications were obtained verbally; others were not available yet. While prepar
ing the estimate, drawings were continuously revised, and corresponding
adjustments had to be made to the estimate, and every attempt was made t:
incorporate the intent of the design into the estimate. The consultant's esti
mating team relied heavily on one of its member's specific knowledge o:
Newfoundland conditions which, being a native Newfoundlander, had gaine:
from his fifteen years of contracting experience in Newfoundland.

The consultant, in the preparation of the estimate, went far beyond th:
standard contractor's approach.

The consultant first established a common work breakdown structur:
for estimate and master schedule activities, which would later facilitate th:
cost loading of the master schedule designed to serve as the basis for moni
toring progress and expenditures.

1. The difference between financial and physical completion, i.e., $1,6222,483, is the estimated amount paid for materials delivered to site but not installed yet. Approximately 50% of this amount is related to the Mechanical Contract, approximately 25% to the Electrical Contract, and the remaining 25% to the Sprinkler and Fire Protection, Kitchen Equipment Laboratory/Library Furniture and Site Services No. 2 combined.

2. The negative status of physical completion versus budget, i.e., –7.3%, is made up of a combination of several factors, as follows:

   a) Savings in General Conditions   –1.0 %
   b) Postponement of Site Works/
      Landscaping Contract   –1.7 %
   c) Delay in Site Services No. 2 Contract   –0.2 %
   d) Delay in Architectural Contract   –3.7 %
   e) Delay in Electrical Contract   –1.2 %
   f) Delay in Sprinkler Contract   –1.1 %
   g) Advance in Mechanical Contract   +1.0 %
   h) Extra Work Performed   +0.5 %

   The combined shortfall of the Architectural, Electrical, and Sprinkler Contracts amounts to a substantial 6%, or $1.3 million. Moreover, progress recorded on the Sprinkler Contract is either too optimistic, or Contractor was underpaid.

3. The budget projection of Jan. 31, 1985, included $580,000 for contingencies allocated to the individual contract packages. Approximately 28% are expended to date. Additionally, out of the $231,000 allocated to General Conditions, only $20,724 were actually expended. However, permanent heating commenced on Jan. 25, 1985, and monthly expenditures will increase accordingly.

4. The Architectural package, and more specifically, installation of drywall and ceilings, have seriously fallen behind schedule, resulting in a corresponding delay on electrical work. Low performance was further aggravated by the non-availability of permanent heating until Jan. 25, 1985, and the delay in enclosure of the atrium. Progress of drywall and ceiling installations is now improving in the east block and west block, while the center block is still slowed down because of the atrium.

   Notwithstanding this improvement, the completion date will be extended by one month, i.e., to early September 1985, without implementation of an acceleration program. Nevertheless, it is anticipated that the project will be completed within budget.

FIGURE 15   CONCLUSIONS—JAN. 31, 1985 PERFORMANCE TEST

The Master Schedule

The master schedule, although prepared by the consultant, nevertheless clearly reflected the intents of the PM/CM, who was ultimately responsible for the supervision and coordination of the work.

The initial run resulted in a September 1985 completion date. Subsequent compression of the interior finishing yielded the desired early August 1985 completion date. The latter schedule was to serve as a yardstick for all future evaluations of performance.

In order to achieve the accelerated completion date, the consultant recommended that detailed schedules for the interfacing of the electrical, mechanical, fire protection, interior masonry, and drywall trades be prepared, to avoid claims which often arise from lack of coordination between these trades. To counteract these problems, it was further recommended that interference drawings be prepared by the mechanical contractor. For the purpose of the detailed scheduling, the consultant supplied the CM with an easy-to-follow format for short-cycle scheduling.

The Cost and Change Order Control System

The cost reporting and change order control system designed for this project include the following:
- cost summary
- project status report
- subsidiary cost report
- contract assessment for each contract package
- monthly cash-flow comparison.

The monthly cost summary and cash-flow comparison included expenditures for the entire project, while the other three reports included construction costs only.

The project status report was developed as an executive summary, providing all information on budget, contract value, actual costs, total forecasted cost, and variances. The main headings were subdivided as follows:

Budget:	Original budget (PM/CM)
	Revised budget
	Owner's revisions (scope changes)
	Current budget
Contract value:	Original contract value
	Changes to date
	Current contract value
Actual costs:	Previously approved
	Approved this month
	Total approved to date
Forecasted costs:	Estimated cost of changes to complete
	Forecast of final cost
Variance:	Total variance
	Variance change from previous report

The column "Revised Budget" was introduced in April 1984 as a result of the tenders received for the architectural package, which were substantially higher than the PM's original budget. At the same time, the general contingency carried in the estimate was allocated to the individual work packages to reflect the cost of anticipated changes to the work, as well as anticipated costs of acceleration to meet the critical completion date.

The column "Owner's Revisions" reflected change orders originating from owner's scope changes. These were kept separate, since the PM/CM carried no responsibility for these changes. Hence, they had to be excluded for measuring his performance.

For the purpose of "controlling costs," the most important column of the project status report is found under the heading "Estimated Cost of Changes to Complete." The consultant insisted that the CM was to identify monthly for each contract package what kind of additional costs it expected to incur until completion of the work. A subsidiary cost report was designed to separate:
• changes approved and included in current contract value, indicating the last change included
• change orders approved by CM but not approved by owner
• estimate of known changes
• unidentified changes to complete
• allowance for additional anticipated costs.

The introduction of this level of detail forced the PM/CM and the prime consultant to analyze, explain, and justify monthly forthcoming changes and issue them in a timely manner, so as not to interfere with the progress of the work which otherwise could result in claims for delays and/or loss of productivity.

Additional reasons for this monthly justification of estimated cost of changes to complete were:
• to seek remedial action if the final cost was forecasted to exceed the budget
• to free unused monies for allocation to other items such as owner's budget for new equipment, furniture, etc., which otherwise could not be purchased.

Monitoring Phase

A performance test was designed with the objective of accurately measuring progress and expenditures against budget and master schedule and to immediately signal problems which may jeopardize completion within time and budget. At the same time, this test, coupled with the cost reporting system, was to serve as an early warning system for discovery of potential claim situations which, if known at the incipient stage, could effectively be minimized or remedied. It is evident that for this purpose, time and cost have to be measured on an integrated basis, a concept not always understood and/or applied.

The performance test measures financial and physical completion of the project at any given stage against the budget as follows:
• Physical completion is the value of work accomplished and expressed as a percentage of the estimated value as of the date the analysis is prepared.
• Financial completion is the total amount of money spent (or committed) as of the date of the analysis, expressed as a percentage of the total estimated cost.
• The budget curve reflects the progress as depicted on the master schedule and corresponding expenditures thereof, or in other words, it indicates the earned percentage of the elapsed time of the project.

A detailed S-curve was prepared based on the cost-loaded master schedule and the estimate, adjusted for actual tender prices, received. The common work breakdown structure established for the construction cost estimate and the master schedule facilitated this task. Particular attention was paid to the labor/material breakdown of each activity, since material on-site, but not installed, was not considered progress. Time-oriented activities only—such as labor, approvals, lead-time for deliveries—were to be considered for the determination of physical completion.

A second budget curve was established which included contingencies allocated to each contract package within the timeframe they were most likely to be incurred.

Budget curves were translated into graphics for the entire project, as well as for the electrical, mechanical, and architectural packages. The reason for also controlling these three packages on an individual basis was based on the fact that the majority of building construction claims originate from one of these trades because of the close coordination required between them.

APPLICATION OF PERFORMANCE TEST

The 75 percent completion stage has been selected for a demonstration of the application of the performance test.

CONCLUSIONS

The owner's choice of the "phased construction" method, coupled with the modified project management concept whereby an independent third party without any direct financial involvement was added to the traditional project team, undoubtedly were the two key factors responsible for the successful completion of this project.

The third party preparation of a contractor-type construction cost estimate and the master schedule, both based on a common work breakdown structure, allowed for the design of an accurate performance test/early warning system. Simplicity of presentation instead of voluminous computer printouts resulted in usage rather than storage in drawers.

This system, combined with the independence of the consultant, allowed for totally objective and timely evaluation of progress and cost. The latter facility, in turn, assured early reaction time. Independence proved equally successful for:
- the unbiased adjudication of scope changes
- constructive communications between all parties
- acceleration of reaction time on all aspects of the project, notwithstanding time-consuming governmental procedures.

Hence, claims were not only minimized but, in fact, completely avoided. A word of caution, however: only "man-made" claims are controllable. Extended project durations and corresponding increases in cost cannot be prevented in case of strikes, changed soil conditions, or similar "non-man-made" causes. However, in any claim situation, early reaction time and an unbiased adjudication process will reduce the cost of claims.

Study Questions

MINIMIZING CONSTRUCTION CLAIMS UNDER THE PROJECT MANAGEMENT CONCEPT

1. What are some of the key management skills needed to run a project or enterprise? Support your answers with information from the *PMBOK Guide*.

2. What problems were encountered under the project management concept in this case?

3. Describe the "risky" practice that was leading to some of these problems, including some of the overriding factors that negated any projected benefits.

4. Describe the modified project management approach used to reduce some of these risks.

5. What risks was the Department of Public Works and Services trying to reduce by adding another consultant to the project management team?

6. What were some of the contributions made by the auditing/quantity surveying consultant? How did these contributions minimize project risk?

7. What actions can be taken by project managers to minimize some of the associated risks before starting to monitor a project?

CONTROLLING

5

CONTROLLING

Giving Mother Nature a Helping Hand

C. Lewis Penland, C. Lewis Penland Inc.

PM Network, July 1994, pp. 14–22

Designing and building a golf course is different from many construction projects. The typical construction project follows a definite pattern of determining the client's requirements, developing specifications, designing (from concept to detail), and executing those plans as closely as possible to the drawings and specifications. Designing and building a golf course is more of an evolutionary process. While some of the usual steps are followed as in the typical construction project, those steps are repeated over and over, generally on the site as construction progresses.

While decisions on details are required at the site on a typical construction project, those decisions are more technical than aesthetic. Constructing a golf course is just the opposite, and therein hangs a tale.

A HISTORICAL PERSPECTIVE

Games similar to our present-day golf have been played since the Middle Ages. But it was in Scotland that the game of golf evolved into a form recognizable to us. The earliest golf courses were found on the Linksland, which was publicly owned and which allowed the common person as well as the royalty the opportunity to participate in the game. Golf thus became a democratic tradition in Scotland.

The original Linksland course evolved on sandy deposits left hundreds of years ago by the receding ocean. The rich soil found on these early courses was deposited by rivers running from inland and leaving fertile soil here. The first rivers that contributed to these original courses were the Eden, Tay, and Forth. True Linksland golf courses evolved from God's hand, with very little influence from man.

A typical links course consisted of high sand dunes shared by the wind, and grassy hollows if the soil was fertile enough. The dominant grasses were bentgrass and fescue, which are naturally occurring in Scotland's salt water areas. These courses were without trees or ponds, but that didn't eliminate the hazards encountered on a typical round of golf. Certain areas would be grazed barren by livestock. Sheep seeking shelter in the hollows would wear away the turf. Nesting holes of small game would collapse and the fertile topsoil erode away, leaving sand wastelands and pot bunkers. These areas are still dreaded and avoided by today's golfer.

Tees, fairways, and greens as we know them did not exist. It is speculated that the early greens were of the same bristly grass that grew everywhere else. The earliest golfers used rabbit holes for putting cups. The tee area for

Before this hole was ready for play, a lot of work and forethought were put into it. For the author, project management is one of the most important tools in managing the design and construction processes for a hole like this one.

the next hole was one club's length from the cup. A well-manicured putting surface was not found on early courses.

The original courses did not require a superintendent and crew for maintenance. Bird droppings provided the needed fertilizer and rain, the irrigation, thus providing a healthy turf. The sandy soil beneath the surface provided for excellent drainage. Grazing sheep and wild game kept the grass clipped. If the turf got too lush and long, the golfer simply did not play. The sandy wastelands and pot bunkers were raked only by the wind.

The earliest courses had no set number of holes: the early links at Leith and Musselburgh had five holes each; North Berwick had seven; Prestwick, twelve; and Montrose, twenty-five. The most recognized golf course in this early period was St. Andrews. Records indicate that St. Andrews existed in a primitive form as early as 1414 A.D. The original course probably differs greatly from today's because of the rapid recession of the sea in the last century. The layout of St. Andrews resembles that of a shepherd's crook. The course consisted of twelve putting areas. Ten of these were used by the player going outward and back homeward, thus the terms "out" and "in" to designate which of the common holes a player was playing. The two remaining holes were only used once apiece, as the eleventh and home holes. Therefore, a round of golf at St. Andrews consisted of twenty-two holes.

During the middle of the eighteenth century, innovations were added to the existing game of golf. One was the creation of private golf clubs; these members continued to play on the public links courses. The earliest private clubs were The Honorable Company of Edinburgh Golfers, established in 1744; The Society of the St. Andrews Golfers, established in 1754; and The Honorable Company of Golfers at Blackheath, in 1766. (The latter was the first golf club established outside of Scotland.) This growth continued into the 1800s and created the demand for golf course designers. It was during this time that man started to change some of nature's influence on the course at St. Andrews. Many of the changes had an impact far into the future, when designers began to search for some basic principles for golf course architecture.

Beginning of the renovation of the fourteenth hole of Highlands Falls Country Club, Highlands, NC, showing the installation of a retaining wall around the green.

The first notable change was in the putting green. More attention was paid to the need to keep a healthy turf in this area. In 1764 The Society of St. Andrews Golfers felt that the first four holes were not challenging enough. It consolidated them into two long holes, eliminating two greens and two holes. Each hole was played twice in a round, nine holes "out" and nine holes "in." This created a course with eighteen holes. Scottish legend disagrees with this explanation and contends instead that a bottle of Scotch whiskey contains eighteen jiggers and that the rate of consumption was that of a jigger a hole. The Society of St. Andrews Golfers contends that a round of golf should conclude with an empty bottle of Scotch.

Around 1833 the practice began of cutting two cups into the common greens. Two years later King William IV recognized the St. Andrews links to be "Royal and Ancient." The Society seized the opportunity to recognize St. Andrews as the "Home of Golf" and itself as the authority on the game. Prior to this the links of Leith had generally been considered the home of golf. The Honorable Company of Edinburgh Golfers disbanded at Leith in 1831. It was re-established at Musselburgh in 1836 and again at Muirfield in 1891. With continued deterioration of Leith, the original members could do little to dispute the St. Andrews claim.

St. Andrews thus became the Royal and Ancient Golf Club of St. Andrews. From then on, the standard number of holes on a golf course was eighteen, and any new courses were compared to St. Andrews. The original course was not altered by man until sometime around 1849. Until that time the average course was only 40 yards wide, bordered by heather. Today most golfers complain that the landing area is too narrow if it's 50 yards wide and the roughs are mowed to a height of three-quarters of an inch.

At this time, the heather, overseen by Allan Robertson, the long-time professional and clubmaker at St. Andrews, was widened out and replaced with turf. These changes enabled the course to be played as either a right-hand course or a left-hand course. Also around this time a new seventeenth green was constructed, which was the first recorded introduction of some artificially created hazards. When Mr. Robertson died in 1859, he was the first recognized designer of golf courses.

The early architects laid their courses out on the spot, and most took only a couple of days. They found natural green sites and then plotted the course from these. Little earth moving was undertaken, as the natural contour of the land was incorporated into the design. Existing turf was used and very little attention to future maintenance was considered. The only concern was for a readily available supply of sand for topdressing the greens.

These minor changes have had far-reaching effects on the game of golf. Strategy was introduced: a player was no longer required to play the ball over every hazard, but could choose a much safer route, with a penalty of one or two strokes. Prior to this, St. Andrews, like most links courses, required forced carries over hazards and severely punished any stray shots out of the tight fairways.

Thus, at two different time periods, St. Andrews exemplified two different schools of architecture. The original design by today's standard would be considered a "penal design," where the golfer isn't given the choice of a safer route to the green and is severely penalized for anything less than a perfect shot. After 1849 the course changes demonstrated the "strategic design," which allows the player the opportunity to test the given hazards and be rewarded with less strokes or choose the longer, safer route to the green. Anyone who practices the art of golf course architecture realizes the profound influence that St. Andrews has had on the game of golf now and forever. With the growth in the popularity of the game, construction of courses was required in areas other than Linksland.

GOLF COURSES IN AMERICA

Wherever the Scots traveled, they took the game with them. The first known export of golf from Scotland was to England, when a group of Scots constructed a seven-hole course at Blackheath in 1608. Another excellent layout was constructed around 1618 at Old Manchester on Kersal Moor. Around 1786 golf was introduced into Charleston, South Carolina, in the United States. Scottish soldiers and engineers introduced the game to France in 1856, and constructed the Pau Golf Club.

The title of "Father of American Golf" was bestowed upon John Reid, a Scot who settled in Yonkers, New York. In 1888, Reid, with several associates, staked out a rough three-hole course near his house. Later that same year they staked out a six-hole course in a nearby pasture. A golf organization was formed and named St. Andrews Golf Club. Over the years, St. Andrews Golf Club has considered itself the oldest golf club in America. This self-proclaimed title is disputed by many. The Foxburg (Pennsylvania) Country Club contends that a nine-hole course was constructed on its site in 1887. It is also evident that the Dorset (Vermont) Field Club was in existence by 1886. J. Hamilton Gillespie, a transplanted Scot, played golf in 1883 in what is today downtown Sarasota, Florida.

Charles Blair McDonald studied as a youth at the University of St. Andrews in Scotland. While attending the university, he was introduced to the

In an area where annual rainfall averages 100–130 inches, berms and drains are crucial in preventing as much stormwater as possible from ever getting onto the green.

game of golf. Upon returning to his home in Chicago in 1875, he constructed a homemade course on the deserted Douglas Field. McDonald constructed a seven-hole course at Lake Forest, Illinois, in 1892. In 1895 he constructed the nation's first eighteen-hole course for the Chicago Golf Club at Wheaton, Illinois. By 1896 there were over eighty known courses in the United States, and in 1900 there were approximately 982. At least one course was found in each of the forty-five states.

The first professional brought to the United States to design a course was Willie Dunn, of the Musselburgh Dunns. He was fondly called "Young Willie" to separate him from his father, "Old Willie." Young Willie was commissioned to design and construct a golf course for the newly organized Shinnecock Hills Golf Club. The course was constructed on a links-style site at Southampton, New York, and was completed in 1891. The final creation was anything but perfect; however, given the inexperience of his crew and the primitive equipment he had, it was a miracle it turned out as well as it did. Dunn remained at the course as pro/greenskeeper. At first the course consisted of twelve holes. Dunn then added a women's six-hole course, which was later integrated with the other course, making it a full eighteen-hole course. The Shinnecock Hills course should have served as an example for other courses being constructed at that time; however, its inaccessible location prevented many developers from studying this excellent example.

The biggest contribution Willie Dunn made to golf in America was that of importing golf-related talent from his homeland of Scotland. He sent word back to Scotland that America was a ripe plum waiting to be picked. Some friends and acquaintances were lent travel fare. Some of these talented men were clubmakers, others greenskeepers. They came here because Young Willie Dunn was convinced that the real future of golf was not in Scotland, Britain, or Europe, but in America.

ANATOMY OF A GOLF COURSE

When you tee your ball up on the No. 1 hole of your favorite course, you probably don't realize the artificial environment that exists there. With proper design and construction, the golf course will blend with its surrounding environment.

The chosen turf grass can vary from bentgrass to Bermuda grass, and will dictate the mowing heights. Tee areas are mowed at a closer height than are the roughs. The greens are the most manicured area of the golf course. The mowing heights on bentgrass greens can vary from 5/32" to 1/4".

Another important area of the golf course not noticed by most golfers is the natural appearing swales, designed to remove surface stormwater from the course. If properly constructed, these swales enable courses to more quickly open for play after a rainstorm.

Below the surface there is an irrigation system that has miles of PVC pipe and wires. The irrigation system is probably one of the most important items in the everyday maintenance of a golf course. Without it, modern golf courses could not be maintained to the manicured degree they are today.

Computer and radio technology have made great advances in the efficiency of the irrigation systems. Sensors in the field gather data on humidity, soil temperature, and weather conditions, and transmit the data to a desktop PC. The data is analyzed and appropriate action taken as needed. The data is usually transmitted using radio signals. The golf course superintendent can monitor and control irrigation from a computer and modem or over a standard phone line utilizing voice-activated commands.

GOLF COURSE DESIGNERS

There are many notable golf course designers; some are credited with designing and constructing many courses, while others have only one or two to their credit. The first course designers were in Scotland. Old Tom Morris was the most recognized. Tom was a native of St. Andrews, where he apprenticed under Allan Robertson, the greenskeeper at the old course at St. Andrews. After Robertson's death, Tom Morris became greenskeeper.

Morris' most recognized contribution to golf course design was the use of the "double loop system." This layout consisted of two nines with opposite rotations. Seldom did three successive holes play in the same direction. A golfer was required to contend with the wind in several different directions. The double-loop system is still utilized today.

A young Scot, Donald Ross, apprenticed under Tom Morris at St. Andrews. Ross designed an awesome number of monumental courses in his time, including Pinehurst No. 2 in Pinehurst, North Carolina; Seminole Golf Club in North Palm Beach, Florida; and Oakland Hills Country Club in Birmingham, Michigan, to name a few. In all, over 600 golf courses were either redesigned or constructed by Donald Ross in the early part of this century. Anyone who has had the pleasure to play a Donald Ross course will agree that he was one of the finest golf course designers. The courses that were constructed at that time were done with horses and manpower, not the modern earthmoving equipment of today.

The sole purpose of the golf course designer is to imitate nature. Anyone who practices this art form develops his own philosophies and style. My

Equally important is an extensive drainage system beneath the surface of the green, assuring healthy turf and fast return-to-play times after stroms.

preferences are more toward the natural and the classic design style. I believe that people today have enough frustrations and aggravations in everyday life; when they play golf the experience should be both challenging and enjoyable, and the hazards should be visible from the tee boxes so that the player can choose the route best suited for her skill level.

Before ground can be broken on a new golf course, many hours of careful planning are required. The course designer requires a topographic map of the area being considered. Usually a site engineering plan is developed and any wetlands or critical areas are identified and taken into consideration during the planning process. The designer will then digitize the topographic map into a computer.

Once the data is in the computer the designer can begin to route the golf holes on the map. The routing plan will usually place the golf holes in areas not suitable for the housing that typically surround today's golf courses. Most of these areas are usually in flood plains. The contour information of the entire development enables the golf course designer to estimate the storm runoff volumes and specify the proper storm runoff systems to protect the course when the development is fully constructed. The designers also can estimate cubic yards of material that will be moved to create the golf course. The amount of material that is moved can vary from as little as 250,000 to 1 million cubic yards. In some cases, where the terrain is very flat, large lakes are excavated to create the contours of the finished golf course. The final shaping is overseen on-site.

The permitting process for golf courses can vary from a few months to several years. The modern golf industry is constantly striving to be good stewards of the environment. Most golf course designers are incorporating wildlife areas into their overall designs. Storm runoff from the course can be reclaimed and recirculated through the irrigation system. Effluent water from the development can be used for irrigating the golf course. The golf turf helps filter the effluent water. Wetlands are protected and in some cases artificial wetlands are created. The golf course lakes constructed in Western

Finishing grading completed; ready for sod.

North Carolina are stocked with trout, which are good indicators of the aquatic environment.

A properly designed and constructed golf course is an optical illusion. We golf course designers work with shadows and different varieties of grasses to create different moods and feelings. When you step onto a tee box to play a hole, the designer's strategy for the hole should be made obvious to you. We place mounds, sand traps, water, etc., in an attempt to give the golfer the ideal route to the green. I have taken traps and placed them 25–30 yards away from the green, but from the golfer's point of view from the fairway, the traps appear to be only inches away from the green.

The tee boxes are another important area where we deal with the golfer's subconscious. If the tee boxes are aimed in the proper direction, the golfers seem to hit their balls that way. If the tee boxes aren't, they seem to have more difficulty achieving the proper shot.

Water is another way we work with the golfer's subconscious. If we can construct a hole with the tee boxes near a waterfall, the effect is very calming and relaxing for the golfer.

GOLF COURSE CONSTRUCTION

Golf course construction can be separated into two distinct categories: new construction and renovation. New construction involves taking approximately 150 acres of land and constructing an eighteen-hole championship course. Renovation can involve one or a few greens, or involve reshaping an entire hole from tee to green. The actual building of the golf course starts in the imagination of the designer and must be communicated to the builder.

Once the overall layout of the golf course is decided, the staking of the golf holes is started. The staking of the new course is very critical. The potential site is walked to get a feel for the lay of the land prior to actually

or any golf course renovation project, the design and construction phases are necessarily intertwined. The designer, with input from the course pro and maintenance superintendent, tries to discover the perfect hole, one the player will be challenged by, yet want to play again and again. Overall, project management is a very important tool in striking that perfect balance.

drawing the plans. During the staking process in the field, we are able to see how the golf holes will be positioned on the existing ground. I personally prefer the method described by Donald Ross. He would always find the naturally suitable green sites and then work back to the tees. The staking process is the last opportunity to locate specimen trees, and to correct any design conflicts not revealed on the contour map. The yardage of each hole is measured and the clearing limits established. The first clearing limits will be narrow, approximately 50 yards. This initial narrow clearing limit will allow us to open up the hole slightly, and thus provide for better visibility.

The land clearing process is very important. Brush, stumps, and debris should not be buried anywhere on the course. I have encountered many situations on existing golf courses where buried brush has caused problems many years later. Some of these burial areas were placed under green sites, cart paths, and fairways. These areas have sunken and caused extensive subsurface water retention problems. In most cases where the timber and wood is suitable, we recommend having it logged, with an on-site supervisor. After logging, the remaining debris is either burned or ground and chipped into mulch.

The erosion control systems are installed during the land clearing process. These systems provide protection from any off-site erosion. They will be constantly monitored and redesigned until the course is properly "grown in," usually two years after play has started.

The rough grading involves moving of the majority of the material. This material can vary from sand, coral, clay, or rock. During the rough grading stage of the project, great care must be taken to preserve certain natural-occurring contours and to create new contours that appear to be natural. We take what the land gives us and integrate it into the design process. For example, if large boulders or rocks are discovered during grading, they are moved aside and used to build retaining walls around greens, tees, or lakes.

It is very important to have a contractor who has experience in golf course construction, or someone on-site to oversee the contractor. Many contractors have experience in road building, where all slopes are symmetrical and uniform and the finished elevations are on a grade stake. On a golf course, the slopes are shaped more to resemble a natural-occurring contour. The final grades are determined in the field, and few survey stakes are installed.

The finish shaping of a golf course is a very specialized field. All final grades and shapes will be constructed at this time. The shape of the tees, fairways, traps, and greens will be completed during this process. If the rough grading was done precisely, the final shaping is very easy to complete. It is for this reason that we require our rough grading crews also to be involved in the finish shaping. When we hear a comment like, "Leave it, the farm tractors will get it," the next morning that operator will be doing the final shaping on the area he had rough-graded the day before!

The finish grading involves some specialized equipment. Most of the finish shaping is done with farm tractors with specialized attachments. Everyone has his own method for preparing the golf course for seeding or sodding. We have developed our own implements for finish grading, and fabricate and install them on four-wheel-drive tractors.

The greens are the areas given the most attention during construction. The greens consist of an area from 5,000 to 10,000 square feet. This area will be excavated to a depth of 18 inches. The final contour of the greens surface will be determined at this time. All material installed will maintain a constant depth over the varying contours. Grade stakes are installed, and the material graded to the correct elevations.

The bottom of the green will have 4-inch drain pipe installed at 10-foot intervals. Four inches of pea gravel will then be installed on top of the drain-pipe. At this point it is optional to install a 4-inch layer of coarse sand. The newly revised United States Golf Association specifications have made this layer of sand an option. The next layer of material is the actual greens mix.

There are many different opinions concerning the proper mix. Some designers will utilize pure sand, blending soil amendments in. The blended amendments are usually naturally occurring microorganisms needed for proper root zone performance. Other designers will follow the USGA recommendations of a mixture of 80 percent sand and 20 percent peat moss. I have found the USGA recommendations to result in excellent performing greens.

Sand traps found on modern golf courses can vary from a few inches deep to 20-feet deep. These depressions have a drainage system installed and covered with sand. The sand traps should be shaped so that they are proportional to their surroundings. Surface runoff water should be bermed away from the trap. Traps should also be constructed with the thought of future maintenance in mind.

The introduction of the golf cart has caused a new obstacle for the modern designer. Now we must incorporate a continuous pathway into the landscape. These paths can be constructed of several different materials. Concrete and asphalt are the most commonly chosen materials. The cart trails should be a minimum of 8-feet wide, and installed following the contours of the golf hole. Whenever possible, the cart trail should not be visible from the tee boxes. We are usually able to hide cart trails in feature mounds created around the course.

Once the golf holes are finish-graded, the seeding and sodding start. At this time it is important to have the soil tested. The test results will indicate the necessary soil amendments needed for the type of turf grass to be grown there. After the seeding process, the golf course superintendent will constantly monitor the project until 100 percent of the proper turf grass is established. The golf course superintendents are very important people to have on-site in the early planning stages. The superintendents that I've had the pleasure to work with have been very knowledgeable and were tremendous assets during the construction and design process.

Opening day is the hardest day of a golf course project. I usually go to the course at 6:30 A.M. and look at a perfectly manicured piece of work, knowing that in a few hours the first divots will dot the landscape. We have taken a raw piece of land and found the golf holes that were hidden there. For many months your life is deeply intertwined in the land and its hidden character. After opening day, the course is no longer yours and you move on to another project, with a whole new set of problems.

MANAGING THE PROJECT

I manage these complex projects with many modern tools, the most important of which is my Macintosh laptop computer. I am able to take a lot of valuable information into the field now. I use Claris' MacProject for my project scheduling. The program allows me to use project networks and Gantt charts. My first exposure to these was at Western Carolina University; however, at that time we were required to do them by hand. With MacProject, I am able to do a lot of "what if" situations in minutes.

The project schedule is very useful when making presentations to clients. I once spent three hours organizing a project with a client. When I finished and packed up the computer, I thanked the client for the opportunity to bid on her project. The client told me that there wasn't any need to bid on the project; I had been awarded the job when I unpacked the computer.

Before we start a project, we estimate the optimum time to seed or sod the turf grass. Once this is determined, we figure back to our latest starting date. Many factors can influence a golf course project, of which the most influential is the weather. We keep a close watch on the weather channel and plan accordingly. The weather is very hard to factor into an overall project schedule.

I use the computer to keep drawings and field notes. The greens are all drawn and grided on the Macintosh. The green is then staked on-site using a Spectra-Physics laser tower instrument. This laser level is capable of accurate measurement of contours to the degree of $1/8"$ in a quarter of a mile. This enables us to construct greens with some very exacting sizes and contours. In the past, the irregular shapes and features made it difficult to estimate square footage of greens (I use MacDraft to grid and size greens). The laser also has an attachment for equipment. We use the laser to level tees and grade storm runoff pipe.

The billing is also done within a database, and is allowing us to organize data into valuable information that is used during the bidding process. The database is very useful for budget and actual cost comparison. I am working on a database for inventory now. The newest modern tool available to the golf course builder is the cellular telephone. In the past, much of my time was wasted going to phones and returning calls. I can now place a call on site while sitting on a piece of equipment. With an attachment, I can plug the cellular phone into my Macintosh and send or receive faxes in the field.

Conclusion

Golf course designers are continuously adjusting the design to create the most pleasurable experience for the golfer, both consciously and subconsciously. We are trying to see the next green just as the golfer sees it, complete with fairway, flag, sand traps, and water hazards. Without that element of design, golf becomes a purely mechanical process. With proper design, each golfer has the opportunity to exercise not only physical skills, but also mental skills of strategy and tactics that best fit his own skills—actual as well as perceived—as a golfer. If each play of the course is a challenge that makes the player want to try it again and again, then we can truly call this a successful project.

The Making of a Golf Course Designer/Builder

Winston Churchill said that "Before we can know where we are going we have to know where we came from." Before the Revolutionary War, my ancestors settled in the mountains of Western North Carolina. They migrated here from Scotland and settled into an area very similar to their homes in the northern highlands of Scotland. These early settlers were rugged and resourceful people, bringing with them a strong sense of the family or clan.

My work involves a lot of time away from home. However, I have always placed my family above my work. Without understanding and constant support from my wife, Cindy, I would not continue with this career. We have a six-year-old son, Seth, who works with me on projects when he is not in school. His earliest designs have been in his sandbox at home. Our other son, Patrick, is two-years old. I look forward to the time when he also joins us on projects.

I grew up in the construction business; my father had a grading and land clearing company. Some of his earliest projects were on the Blue Ridge Parkway in Western North Carolina, which at the time was the largest landscape architectural project ever undertaken. My father then went into the land clearing business. Most of our projects included interstate highways, airports, and power lines. In 1968 Penland Contracting started clearing for major transmission lines for Duke Power. Today Penland Contracting is responsible for construction of a major transmission line through some of the most rugged and scenic terrain in Western North Carolina. Japanese managers have toured the projects to study some of the techniques implemented in this rugged terrain.

After graduating from college, I was given a gift of a one-way ticket to Ketchikan, Alaska. E.J. Whitmire, the friend who gave me the ticket, said, "Get home the best way you can." It was an adventure I will never forget. I was employed by the Louisiana-Pacific Lumber Company. The logging method we utilized was high line, which is best suited to rugged terrain where roads are not feasible. While employed in Alaska I had the opportunity to work with some of the best people in this field.

I returned to Franklin, North Carolina, with my newly acquired skill. While logging in the Cashiers area, our services were retained by Sapphire Lakes Country Club to log the land where they were constructing a new golf course. Tom Jackson was the golf course architect designing the golf course. After logging, he requested us to start land clearing and working with the other two grading contractors there. Winter in the Cashiers area is very wet and not conducive to construction, so the decision was made to stop work until the spring.

When we returned the next spring, we were the only contractors working on the golf course. Tom Jackson wanted us to build the course for him. During this time I became very interested in golf course design and entertained thoughts of returning to school to study it. Tom asked me to work on a course at his home in Taylors, South Carolina, and assured me that I would receive a thorough indoctrination into the business of golf course construction and design while working with him in the field. If I still wanted to pursue a degree, he would write a letter of recommendation for me. I received an education in the field that cannot be taught in a classroom. He taught me lessons that he had learned while working with two great architects, Robert Trent Jones and George Cobb. As Tom would say, "My eyes were trained that summer." I have had the pleasure to work with some renowned golf course architects, but I still enjoy working with Tom the most.

The earliest lessons involved laying out a golf course on a raw piece of land. We would always walk the land several times and then start to determine the ideal green sites. While walking the land, we would look for the natural existing contours and integrate the golf holes in them. Tom taught me how to close my eyes and use my imagination to see the finished product. Some designers I have worked with have a detailed set of grading plans and literally force their designs on the terrain. The finished products appear artificial to me. The good designers today use general layout plans and do the final designing on-site, very similar to the earlier designers. The land is our canvas and the bulldozer, the paintbrush.

Study Questions

GIVING MOTHER NATURE A HELPING HAND

1. List at least three stakeholders in a golf course design project and what they might have at stake in the project.

2. The *PMBOK Guide* established five phases of a project: initiating, planning, executing, controlling, and closing. In this case, most of the activities required for the development of a golf course are mentioned. Define each of the processes and identify at least two tasks for each of these process groups in golf course development.

3. As an USGA course evaluator and stakeholder, what should your primary concern be?

4. As the project manager on the renovation of the eighteenth hole at the famed Pebble Beach Golf Course, what is the most important aspect of your project from a personal standpoint?

Students are encouraged to do some research concerning the management and technology implications involved in the design, construction, and management of a golf course. A few references that provide useful insight into these matters include: *Golf Course Architecture: Design, Construction and Restoration Planning,* by Michael Hurdzan, Sleeping Bear Press, Chelsea February, 1996; *Golf Course Management and Construction,* by Balogh Lewis Publishers, June 1992; and *The Golf Course: Planning, Design, Construction and Management,* by F. W. Hawtree, Routledge, Chapman & Hall Incorporated, New York, April 1983.

Managing Environmental Regulatory Approval Durations

Edward W. Ionata, PMP, Parsons Brinckerhoff

PMI *Proceedings*, 1993, pp. 152–56

INTRODUCTION

The success of many projects requires gaining approvals from outside agencies. Project progress is often impaired while permits, approvals, or licenses are processed, an activity which is not directly controlled by the project. A series of techniques were used in managing regulatory approval durations for two mega-projects located in Boston, Massachusetts. The techniques are being used to manage acquisition of more than 400 environmental permits required for the construction of massive public infrastructure projects, but can be applied to any situation when approval from outside agencies is necessary.

PROJECT DESCRIPTIONS

The techniques described were developed and utilized to support acquisition of environmental permits for two major projects presently under construction: the Boston Harbor project and the Central Artery/Third Harbor Tunnel project.

The Boston Harbor project involves constructing a new wastewater treatment facility for the metropolitan Boston, Massachusetts area. Construction for this ten-year project started in 1989 and will treat an average flow of 500 million gallons of wastewater per day from forty-three cities and towns. Original cost estimates for the project exceeded six billion United States dollars.

The Boston Harbor project treatment facility is being constructed on Deer Island in Boston Harbor. More than forty separate construction contracts will take place on a relatively constrained site in order to complete the facility. Additionally, boat terminals were built to provide transportation for workers and materials, and construction support areas on the mainland and on the island were set up to provide laydown space, fabrication areas, and offices. The major elements of the project include a three-mile-long deep-rock tunnel to deliver wastewater to the treatment plant; primary, secondary, and residuals treatment facilities; and a nine-mile-long outfall tunnel which discharges treated effluent. Permitting for the project is essentially complete, and construction is well under way.

The Central Artery/Third Harbor Tunnel project involves redesigning and rebuilding the interstate highway system which runs through Boston. The project will eliminate extensive traffic backups which occur for up to

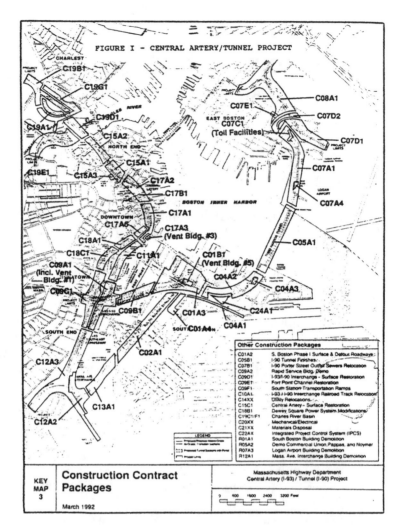

FIGURE 1   CENTRAL ARTERY/TUNNEL PROJECT

fourteen-hours per day. A four lane, 3,800-foot-long highway tunnel is being constructed under Boston Harbor connecting major interstate highways to Logan International Airport. The project will also replace the existing elevated highway running through downtown Boston, Route I-93, with a new road that will be below the surface in tunnel for most of its length. Construction of this new underground central artery will create vast areas of open space on the surface presently covered by elevated highway. A new bridge will be built to carry Route I-93 over the Charles River.

The project requires more than fifty separate construction contracts. Project costs are presently estimated at 6.4 billion United States dollars. Permitting for the harbor tunnel portion of the project is complete, and construction of the harbor tunnel is well under way, while design and permitting for the rest of the project is being completed. The project, like the Boston Harbor project, will require approximately ten years of construction. Figure 1 shows the extent of the project and delineates geographic limits of the various construction contracts.

REGULATORY FRAMEWORK

Construction of the two projects involves a complex, interrelated series of regulatory approvals focusing primarily on coastal land use and the protection of air quality, water quality, and wetlands. A variety of local, state, and federal regulatory programs apply to both projects. Construction of the Boston Harbor project requires more than 150 individual permits and licenses, and the geographically larger Central Artery project requires more than 250.

Three major conditions cause the acquisition of permits and licenses for these projects to be particularly challenging. They are described in the next three sections.

Complexity of the Projects

Applications filed with the regulatory agencies must capture the complicated nature of the facilities to be built for these projects and of the innovative construction techniques required. Both projects involve multiple structures and buildings spread over large geographic areas and overlapping several regulatory jurisdictions. The application processing systems and procedures at the regulatory agencies are set up to process straightforward applications (usually a single building or facility on a relatively small site). Developing strategies which provide the necessary information to the agencies without overwhelming the application processing system is a crucial element of successful permitting management.

Complexity of the Regulatory Programs

The permits required for these two projects involve more than thirty local, state, and federal agencies and regulatory programs. In many cases, there are procedural links among the various agencies and programs, even to the extent where formal ties exist between state and federal programs and between local and state programs. In addition to the number of agencies involved, regulatory complexity was compounded by the necessity to build and operate facilities requiring:
- filling and replicating wetlands
- ocean dredging and dredged material disposal
- harbor and open ocean marine heavy construction
- hazardous waste site remediation
- creation of air pollution sources
- creation and capping of landfills
- construction in densely populated urban areas.

Project Schedules

Both projects are heavily schedule driven. The Boston Harbor project is controlled by a strict, court-ordered schedule which aims to complete construction of facilities needed to comply with federal Clean Water Act standards by 1999 [1].

The Central Artery project schedule is driven by the need to complete the project quickly to alleviate traffic problems in Boston and so improve air quality, minimize disruption of Boston during construction, and eliminate costs associated with delay.

Permit acquisition is a critical path component of both projects. Both projects have divided construction into a series of construction contracts. Funding agencies for both projects require acquiring applicable permits prior to awarding each contract.

MANAGEMENT TECHNIQUES

The following management techniques were used on both projects in orde to minimize potential negative impacts created by the regulatory framework

Development of Detailed Schedule

The key element in managing permitting on both projects was the develop ment of detailed schedule logic, and integrating that logic with the projec master schedules. The permitting function was treated as a project sub-plar on both projects. A detailed work breakdown structure was developed fo permitting, with the same level of importance as such other critical patl sub-plans as design development or construction contract procurement (2).

Permitting logic development began by developing a list of all of the per mits and licenses that could possibly apply to the projects. A thorough liter ature search was then performed to gather detailed information for each per mit identified regarding data needs for preparing applications, procedure and durations for filing and processing applications, potential delays and av enues of appeal, and the relationship to other regulatory programs.

Using the information gathered, and in consultation with the various reg ulatory agencies, generic permitting logic and durations were established Research and discussion with agencies indicated that, although in some case the granting of particular permits had to precede the granting of others, no ad vantage would be created by filing applications in any particular order. Botl projects adopted the practice of filing all of the permits for an individual phase of construction at the same time. This allowed all agencies to begin processing at the earliest possible date, and allowed as much time as possible to solve any problems identified by the agencies. At worst, a permit could be essentially complete, with official completion being restrained by the granting of a prece dent permit. Permits restrained by other permits were often officially grantec immediately upon completion of the precedent permit, or were conditionally granted pending completion of the precedent permit.

The generic permitting schedules were distributed to all of the applicable agencies for review and comment. The goal of this distribution was to verify that the durations ascribed to permit application processing were realistic and achievable. Comments from the various agencies were used to adjust the generic schedules, and then specific permitting schedules for each con struction package were developed, reflecting the permits required for the types of work included in each package.

The construction package schedules were then integrated with the pro ject master schedules to determine the impact of scheduling on design award of construction contracts, and construction. When possible, contin gency plans were developed to allow construction progress to continue if per mits were delayed.

Development of first generic and then specific permitting schedules con tributed to a realistic, integrated master schedule. The master schedule was used by both the project and the regulatory agencies to assess staffing level required to prepare and process permits. The detailed nature of the sched ules developed allowed close tracking of permit progress, not the typical guesswork start/finish tracking often used for project aspects not directly controlled by project management.

Utilizing the same generic schedule as a starting point for each element of construction facilitated fine-tuning the schedule logic and durations based upon experience gained with earlier construction elements.

Coordination of Permitting and Design

Permit applications for both projects were filed prior to completion of final design for each individual construction contract. This allowed permit applications to begin being processed while design was being completed, shortening the total time required. This also allowed additional efficiency by incorporating any design changes required by the agencies as a part of the normal disposition of review comments for a construction element, rather that having to go back and modify completed plans and specifications.

Coordination of permitting and design on both projects included review of preliminary and developmental design plans by the permitting group, and regular participation in design progress review meetings. This resulted in permitting staff having acquired a working knowledge of the element of construction to be described in permit applications well in advance of having to prepare applications. Coordination of permitting and design allowed filing of permit applications at the 50 to 75 percent design level, accelerating the start of the permitting process. The decision regarding what level of design permit applications would be used as a basis was controlled by the complexity of the design, the level of detail required by permit applications for that design, and a judgment of the likelihood of the design changing significantly during its final stages.

Filing permit applications prior to completing design carries the risk that applications will have to be modified or even changed to reflect major design changes made late in the design process. Experience on both projects has shown that the delay encountered when applications must be modified is insignificant when compared to the time savings resulting from filing early.

Coordination with Regulators

The regulatory agencies that will process permit applications must understand the overall purpose of the project and how that purpose will be accomplished. Both projects utilized extensive outreach programs targeted to keep all management levels within the agencies informed about the goals and progress of the projects.

A single point of contact for all environmental permits was established on both projects, avoiding the confusion and misunderstanding which could result from a different person contacting agencies regarding permits for each construction package. Some agencies responded by providing a liaison to the projects to help manage multiple applications to a single agency or to many departments or programs within an umbrella agency. The Massachusetts Department of Environmental Protection provided a coordinator for both projects to facilitate processing of permit applications through a variety of divisions within the agency and to provide input to design and planning prior to preparing applications. Several other state, federal, and local agencies named liaisons to the projects to coordinate the large number of permit applications filed to each agency.

The detailed permitting information included in the project schedules was used by project staff and the agency liaison to predict and control workloads for both project and agency staff. The Central Artery project also provided

funding for additional staff at the Department of Environmental Protection t
assist in the timely processing of project applications.

Regular progress briefings and planning sessions were held with both th
management and staff levels of the regulatory agencies. These briefing
demonstrated how all of the individual construction packages' correspondin
permits fit into the projects as a whole. The briefings also allowed agenc
staff to gain knowledge of what future applications would entail and to ider
tify concerns prior to applications being filed. This resulted in many prob
lems being rectified prior to filing and avoided subsequent delays.

The Central Artery project developed a formal group of cooperatin
agencies that meets regularly to review project progress and future plan:
More than thirty separate agencies and divisions participate. Subgroups hav
also been formed for more intensive coordination on such specialized env:
ronmental permitting issues as wetlands, water quality, and air quality.

Both projects have also held regular briefings for senior executives of th
various regulatory agencies. The benefit of all of the coordination efforts is t
provide a clear vision of what the projects seek to accomplish, and to pas
this vision on to the regulators so that permit applications are placed in cor
text and hopefully are more clearly understood.

Centralized Control of Permitting Activities

A project-wide environmental permitting group was established by each pre
ject. All environmental and permitting functions were coordinated by thes
groups working as a service group supporting both the design and constructio
functions. Establishing project-wide environmental permitting groups allowe
specialized staff to prepare similar applications and shepherd those applic;
tions through approval for a number of construction packages. This enhance
applying lessons learned and improving the quality and effectiveness of the e1
fort, while building familiarity and trust among the agencies.

Decentralizing the permitting function by placing generalist permittin
personnel within each construction package staff would not foster a uni
form, controlled approach and would result in a common problem raised b
agencies: that the agency has to "teach" inexperienced project staff each tim
an application is filed, and that the project as a whole never seems to "learn
by applying lessons from earlier applications. This situation can be particu
larly frustrating to agencies when numerous applications for elements of
project, all prepared by different people, are reviewed by the same regulatoi

Controlling Quality of Permit Applications

Centralizing the permitting function in a project-wide service group, as wa
done on both projects, leads to effective control of the quality of permit ap
plications. The format of permit applications is largely dictated by the regu
latory agencies. Both projects sought, within the dictated formats, to stan
dardize the descriptions, schedules, and other information included in th
applications.

The number of related construction packages and the number of permit
required for each package create a potentially confusing situation whic
could be made unmanageable by slightly differing descriptions of the sam
work. Many of the regulatory programs are interrelated, and regulatory sta1
collaborated to review related applications. In addition, the public has th
opportunity to review and comment upon many applications. Application

were carefully prepared to use identical language to describe the proposed work wherever possible, and supplemental information was provided to explain how the application and the construction it describes relates to other project applications and the project in its entirety.

Controlling the Number of Permits

An obvious way to reduce the permitting effort and to better control the project schedule would be to reduce the number of permits required. Since each time a permit application is filed a lengthy and sometimes unpredictable processing pathway begins, risk can be reduced substantially by decreasing the number of permits needed. Two major approaches were used by the projects to attempt to reduce the number of permits needed:

• **Design consultation:** Experienced specialized permitting staff members reviewed the design of each construction package at the conceptual stage and at later developmental stages. These reviews focused primarily upon identifying the regulatory jurisdictions affected by each package and consulting with designers to determine if modifications could be made to eliminate the need to file for a particular permit, or reduce the difficulty of acquiring that permit. Since both projects are adjacent to water bodies, this approach was extremely successful when facilities could be relocated (sometimes only a few feet) out of established buffer areas near the shore, eliminating the need to file some permits. The locations of numerous structures on the Boston Harbor project were moved in order to stay out of regulatory jurisdictions.

• **Permit "packaging":** Wherever possible, permits for groups of construction packages were lumped together and covered by single permit applications, or project-wide permits were sought. The major consideration in creating permit packages has been schedule. The number of applications could be kept to a minimum if no filings occurred until design of the entire project was complete; but the schedule-driven nature of both projects, and of most other large infrastructure projects, would not allow waiting for design to be completed. Permit packages were created for the Central Artery project when possible when design for a number of geographically linked construction packages was completed at approximately the same time. The Boston Harbor project took place mostly on a constrained site where everything was geographically linked, so permits were packaged into several time periods corresponding to construction phases.

Ensuring Environmental Compliance

Complying with the permits already issued is an essential element of managing and controlling the permitting process. If the agencies involved with a project are dissatisfied with compliance of the earlier permits issued, acquiring the later permits will undoubtedly be more difficult, complicated, and time consuming. Formal, continuous compliance monitoring occurs on both projects by project staff, along with occasional site inspections by agency staff. Assuring compliance in the field is essential in maintaining the credibility with the agencies that is necessary for efficient application processing (3).

CONCLUSION

The elements of a successful management system for regulatory approvals are simply applications of basic project management techniques to a complicated and frustrating problem. Identifying and defining the permitting tasks and breaking them down into basic operations allows developing a detailed schedule and plan which serve as a basis to predict and control the effort and to develop contingencies. Communicating internally with other project functional areas, and externally with the agencies involved, realistic milestones can be set, and the actions required to meet those milestones can be clearly identified. Improvement through design consultation and reorganizing permits into packages can streamline the effort. Controlling the quality of the permit applications when they are prepared avoids rework. Controlling the quality of construction, from a permit compliance standpoint, avoids enforcement delays and enhances success of ongoing permitting efforts. Treating permitting as an important sub-plan of the project and including permitting as an integral part of the project master plan results in a project with realistic milestones, ability to develop contingencies, and a greater chance of success.

REFERENCES

1. Armstrong, W. G. 1989. "Organizational Structure: Management of the Boston Harbor Cleanup Project." *Proceedings*. Upper Darby, Penn.: Project Management Institute.

2. Michael, S.B., and L.C. Struckenbruck. 1981. "Project Planning." *The Implementation of Project Management*. Reading, Mass.: Addison Wesley, pp. 94–117.

3. Ionata, E. W. 1991. "Environmental Compliance: A Quality Management Approach." *Proceedings*. Upper Darby, Penn.: Project Management Institute.

Study Questions

MANAGING ENVIRONMENTAL REGULATORY APPROVAL DURATIONS

1. What efforts were made to decrease complexity in the permitting process? How did these methods reduce the risk involved in the project?

2. Project time management is a key factor on any project. The projects described in the case were especially sensitive to any delay or any disapproval of permits. In section 6, Project Time Management, the *PMBOK Guide* identifies five major activities to be carried out to ensure a prompt completion of the project. One of these factors is schedule development. Define the concept of schedule development and how it was carried out in this project.

3. Another important activity in project time management is schedule control. Document the description of this activity and how it was undertaken in this project.

4. How did this project incorporate project integration management (*PMBOK Guide*, Chapter 4) in its process?

5. Given that the governmental agencies all have an interest in the timely completion of this project, how can the project managers exploit this strategic issue in the completion of the project?

6. How important did project management consider the permitting process? Was this level of attention and concern appropriate?

Pittsburgh International Airport Midfield Terminal Energy Facility

Philip J. Damiani, Manager, Mechanical Engineering; SE Technologies, Inc.
Robert J. Teachout, Senior Engineer, Mechanical Engineering; SE Technologies, Inc.

PMI *Proceedings* 1992, pp. 44–50

PROJECT ABSTRACT

The purpose of this paper is to present the conceptual thought process and the project management methodology that facilitated in producing the Pittsburgh International Airport Midfield Terminal Energy Facility (see Figure 1). The primary objectives were to design a facility that was of first-class quality, on schedule, within budget parameters, and in compliance with all environmental regulations. The energy facility was subcontracted by Allegheny County to a third-party developer. This developer would provide the conceptual engineering, detailed design, construction management, operations, and maintenance to produce thermal (heating/cooling) energy and electric power for the new Midfield Terminal.

The conceptual engineering analyses that precedes full-scale preparation of engineering design drawings and specifications are fundamental to the long-term financial objectives of any new facility project, particularly those that involve energy-intensive processes. This basis of design phase planning often requires close scrutiny of fuel options and long-term fuel availability, major equipment, alternate selections, environmental concerns, and operations/maintenance requirements over the expected life of the facility.

When the basis of design is complete, the owner/engineer project management strategies play a major role in the success of the project. Key elements of the project management program include proper budgeting/scheduling of the engineering design, construction, and start-up phases; proper communication between all parties interfacing with the facility; availability of certified information during the design phase; and the engineer's degree of detail in the contract documents to minimize cost contingencies from the contractor.

INTRODUCTION

The Midfield Terminal Energy Facility was designed to meet the 9,100 tons of ultimate cooling load and 113×10^6 Btuh ultimate heating load of the new Midfield Terminal Complex (see Figure 2). All thermal energy loads are weather dependent type, space heating/cooling for the terminals and aircraft. No process type (i.e., deicing, base load domestic hot water, etc.) thermal energy loads are tied to the energy facility. The energy facility also provides electric power to the Midfield Terminal from the new substation located between the energy facility and the field-erected concrete cooling tower. The substation will

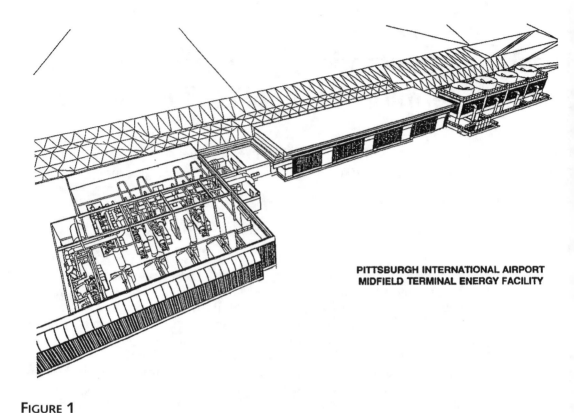

PITTSBURGH INTERNATIONAL AIRPORT
MIDFIELD TERMINAL ENERGY FACILITY

FIGURE 1

initially have three 22.9 kV/4.16 kV, 10,000 kVA (12,500 kVA FA) delta-wye transformers rated at a 55° F temperature rise. Each substation vault also contains a 4,160 V, 1,800 kVAR capacitor bank to optimize power factor. Space is reserved for a future fourth transformer. The ultimate projected peak electric demand on the substation is 24 MW. The Pittsburgh International Airport is owned and operated by the Allegheny County Department of Aviation. The new Midfield Terminal includes a 500,000 square-foot landside/central services building and a 1,200,000 square-foot airside building having a present seventy-five aircraft gate capacity with provisions to expand to an ultimate 100-gate terminal. These two terminal buildings are situated nearly 0.5 miles apart, and are connected by an underground people mover to shuttle passengers between the two buildings, and a utility tunnel with several miles of piping, cable, and conduit. Due to the nature and proximity of the buildings at the Midfield Terminal, a formidable engineering challenge was presented for designing a central energy facility (see Figure 2).

PROJECT OBJECTIVES

The Midfield Terminal and Central Facility is projected to be a long-term operation and major consumer of electric power and natural gas. The facility must be capable of providing energy deliverables 365 days per year and requires staffing twenty-four hours a day. An airport application is especially sensitive to issues concerning reliability of equipment safety, combustion and

Ultimate Cooling Load:	9100 Tons
Chilled Water Supply/Return Temp:	42° F/58° F
Chilled Water Flow Rate:	13,650 gpm
Chilled Water Distribution Pressure Loss:	200 feet TDH
Ultimate Heating Load:	113×10^6 Btuh
HTW Supply/Return Temperature:	350° F/250° F
HTW Flow Rate:	2,425 gpm
HTW Distribution Pressure Loss:	190 feet TDH
Ultimate Electric Demand:	24 MW
Substation Electrical:	23 kV/4.16 kV
Substation Transformers:	3 each @ 10.0 MVA (12.5 MVA FA)
Substation Capacitors:	3-4160 V banks each @ 1800 kVAR

FIGURE 2   FACILITY ULTIMATE DESIGN CRITERIA

---

cooling tower emissions, and other environmental-related concerns. The key objective of the energy facility equipment systems review was to maintain focus on reliability criteria. The Pittsburgh International Airport has an excellent record of minimizing the number of days that the airport has been forced to shut down aircraft operations due to equipment malfunctions or weather conditions. The basis objectives incorporated in the conceptual study process were ultimately to specify an energy facility that met the following owner/engineer primary criteria:

- long-term availability of energy/fuels
- reliable equipment system selections
- state-of-the art centralized control
- optimum equipment systems efficiencies
- environmentally safe emissions
- low maintenance operations.

PROJECT MANAGEMENT

The key to successful project management on any major facility is to have a well-defined plan that is realistic, obtainable, and properly monitored throughout the project. Project management is able to balance successfully the following:

- quality
- costs/budget
- schedule.

It is relatively easy to balance two of those three factors, but the project will not be successful without meeting the objectives of all three. The first objective—quality—was stressed not only by Allegheny County but also by the owner of the energy facility. This energy facility was to be a first class facility with the best equipment available to produce reliable energy over a long-term contract. The quality in a project is controlled by staffing the project with the proper technical personnel and ensuring that they have the information and tools needed to study and analyze the technical requirements and make recommendations to the project manager for equipment and systems.

Project cost is equally important but is directly proportional to the level of quality required. Many owners try to "save money" by minimizing engineering costs, and this often results in poor construction documents and excessive contingencies in the form of additional construction change orders to a project. Good quality engineering can be cost effective. If the owner/engineer team understands the objectives and the long-term benefit that can result from value engineering. The third objective, project schedule, must be realistic so that all tasks, purchasing, interface with other entities, and other contingencies are properly factored into the schedule.

The owner/engineer negotiated a realistic engineering and construction budget that would ensure the level of quality required and sufficient monies to implement the project once the conceptual design was completed. A complete project schedule was prepared covering three years that included performing various studies to select the best equipment, prepare major equipment coordination with other engineers and contractors, pre-purchase major equipment, detail design with required review phases, prepare construction bidding, award contract, develop facility construction, start up end testing, and conduct demonstration phase testing. These major tasks covered a period of three years and were carefully monitored to ensure that the project did not get off schedule. If realistic budget and quality are established, the project is properly controlled by controlling the schedule, not the budget. This appears to be contrary to many project managers who are always concerned about budget, budget, budget. If the plan is correct and the budget sufficient, the schedule is the key element in controlling all project costs and achieving project success.

The energy facility met all of the quality, budgets, and schedule objectives as defined earlier in this paper. Major equipment was pre-purchased, design documents were developed, and the project was bid on time in September of 1990. The construction contract was awarded in mid-November of 1990 (one-year schedule), and in the first week of December major equipment started to be delivered to the energy facility as planned. All major equipment was in the facility by March 1991 and facilitated the contractor in finalizing the fabrication piping drawings. The construction for the project continued and was completed on time; however, start-up and testing were delayed due to some minor problems beyond the control of the owner/engineer. The start-up and testing, as well as the demonstration phase testing, began later than scheduled. However, because of contingencies built into the schedule, we were able to complete the project six weeks ahead of schedule.

HEATING EQUIPMENT ALTERNATIVES

During the proposal phase, the County RFP required the energy developer to provide a high-pressure steam heating system that would provide sufficient high pressure steam and spare capacity to meet the heating load of the Midfield Terminal complex. Since there was no opportunity during this phase to recommend alternative heating systems, the project was bid-based on a steam heating system. As the conceptual design developed, SE Technologies, Inc. (SET) began to put together a very strong case for a high-temperature water (HTW) system in lieu of a high-pressure steam (HPS) heating system. The high-temperature water system would provide 350° F water to the Midfield Terminal

- Total of Four High Temperature Water Generators (HTWG)—(Three) Operating and (One) Standby
- HTWG Key Design Features (typical of each unit @ 100 percent firing)

Manufacturer:	Cleaver Brooks
Model Number:	DLW-60; Packaged Water Tube 400 Psig Design
Heat Input Rating:	49,534,000 Btuh
Heat Output Rating:	39,300,000 Btuh
HTW Water Flow Rate:	808 gpm
Water Inlet/Outlet Temperatures:	250° F–350° F
Primary Fuel:	Natural Gas
Emergency Fuel:	No. 2 Fuel Oil

FIGURE 3   HEATING PLANT DESIGN CRITERIA

complex, with a 250° F minimum return temperature (see Figure 3). It has always been SET's opinion that hot water heating is a more economical and lower maintenance system for heating buildings versus steam; however, to convince Allegheny County, a formal study and presentation had to be prepared. The heavy commercial, institutional, and industrial sectors seem to have overlooked many of the benefits of high-temperature water systems for space heating since steam heating systems have been used for so many years in many facilities. Steam heating systems have been the work horse for many years and many engineering and design consultants who are used to designing steam systems continue to design them since it is basically what they have done in the past. Obviously there are economies of scale for the engineering firm that is familiar with a certain type of system and comfortable with the concept. The consultant can draw on previous designs and thus minimize the efforts in preparing a package for another client. The end-user, or owner, may also be used to a steam system and, therefore, feels comfortable with this type of design. The owner for the Midfield Terminal Energy Facility was open to investigating other types of heating systems in an effort not only to reduce his operation and maintenance costs but also to provide a safe and more reliable system and product to Allegheny County. SET then proceeded to do an in-depth study and analysis of HTW heating systems versus HPS heating systems.

The first criteria that SET evaluated in comparing the two types of systems was the capital cost for the two plants. SET laid out the equipment and piping arrangement that would be required for both the HTW and HPS system and did a construction cost estimate for both systems. Initial estimates indicated that the construction cost for the HPS system may be slightly less than the cost for a HTW system. However, the cost difference would be so minor (less than 5 percent) that during a competitive bidding environment this cost advantage for high-pressure steam may disappear. Aside from the minor first cost advantage, SET was unable to find any other major advantages for HPS systems relative to the Midfield Terminal's weather-dependent heating loads. Therefore, the following are the advantages that were discovered for the HTW system versus the HPS system.

Better Reliability

One of the key issues in designing any part of a new airport is the reliability of the facility. The county made it very clear to all the engineers, designers, and contractors involved with the Midfield project that reliability was of utmost importance in the design of our system to ensure the continued operation of the airport under all possible environmental conditions. The HTW system is a much less complex system compared to a steam heating system. There is less equipment and equipment of a simpler design in the HTW heating system, and also since it is a closed system, ancillary equipment for deaeration and complex chemical treatment is not required. Although distribution pumping is required for HTW systems, all the pumping systems to the energy facility have standby pumps to ensure reliability of pumping systems.

Improved Safety

Another concern in the construction of the new Midfield Terminal was the safety of the systems, since this will be a public facility used by virtually anyone in Allegheny County as well as throughout the nation and the world. There is a perception among some engineering consultants and owners that a HTW system is more dangerous than steam. A practical test was performed by a United States military agency with a high-temperature water system operating at 370° F in a 2,800-cubic-foot closed area. A blind flange was knocked off the end of a 1-inch pipe. At first a slug of water escaped followed by a fog that spread across the ceilings. In all, it took four and a half minutes before the heat became overwhelming and enough oxygen had been displaced to cause evacuation of all personnel from the space. An identical test was conducted with 150 psi steam system. The evacuation time for this test was only one minute. When a high-temperature water system is relieved to atmosphere, only about 25 percent of the relieved quantity of water will flash to steam. The balance remains in its liquid state.

Greater System Efficiency

In general, the HTW system does not have the parasitic steam and heat losses that are common with standard high-pressure steam systems and no consequent waste of energy and efficiency. Also, the minimal requirement for chemical treatment on a HTW system greatly improves the overall operating cost for high temperature water.

Lower O & M Costs

SET calculated that the net energy savings of steam losses versus pumping energy was significant. Also, the elimination of distribution system trap maintenance as well as minimal chemical treatment costs greatly contributed to overall lower O & M costs.

System Start-Up Simplification

The HTW system maintained in a liquid state by anti-flash pressure protection as compared to the liquid/vapor/liquid cycle inherent with HPS. Therefore, the initial start-up and cyclic control requirements that exist for spring/fall transition weather are easier with HTW. The longer start-up requirements and potential for water hammer associated with the steam system are eliminated.

Closed System

Since the high-temperature water system is a closed system, makeup water requirements become minimal. The closed system also provides a relatively corrosion-free environment once the initial chemical treatment has been made.

Smaller Piping

The design for the energy facility, using high-temperature water, reduced the size of the distribution supply and return piping compared to the steam supply and condensate return system. Since there are many miles of piping in an airport facility, this was a great economic benefit in favor of high-temperature water. The smaller diameter piping required for high-temperature water systems also attributed to lower pipe heat loss throughout the system.

Pipe Installation Simplified

Since the high-temperature water system is a forced-circulation or pumped system the piping is not required to be installed with critical slopes toward drip legs or traps as required for a steam system.

Closer Temperature Control

The large volume of water in the high-temperature water system provides a tremendous amount of heat storage. Heating loads in airports can change suddenly due to many planes landing at a peak period of time. Because of this heat storage capability, or "flywheel effect," high-temperature water can meet a sudden increase in load without measurable drop in supply temperature. If there is a sudden load increase, the supply temperature is held constant, and the return temperature will diminish without affecting other heating systems. A sudden load increase on a steam system causes the drum pressure to drop with a corresponding slight decay of supply temperature.

There are obvious disadvantages for a HTW system, such as, if steam is required for a process, or to move a turbine for power generation. However, these were not required for the Midfield Energy Facility and, therefore, could not help support a case for the HPS system.

HEATING EQUIPMENT EVALUATION RESULTS

The capital cost for the high-temperature water systems estimated and bid for the Midfield Terminal Energy Facility was within project budget and competitive with the high-pressure steam system. Reviewing the annual operating costs for each system type, a high-pressure steam plant would incur higher fuel costs despite having a slightly higher thermal efficiency. The high pressure steam plant lower system efficiency (i.e., fuel to useful thermal output) is due to:
- parasitic steam to preheat/deaerate boiler feedwater
- continuous blowdown
- flash steam (heat) and mass losses from condensate holding tank and deaerator, respectively
- steam and trap losses in the system.

The high-pressure steam higher electric costs result from greater horsepower for forced draft fan and boiler feedwater pumping. For a high-temperature water system, although electric costs are required to pump the water throughout the facility, the savings in steam losses from receiver tanks, traps, and leaks far exceeded the low pumping energy required. The water/sewage charges for high-pressure steam would also be higher due to great system losses, and, in turn, would require more chemical treatment. SET performed a life-cycle cost summary based on the capital and operating costs. The HTW system was determined to have a lower life-cycle (present worth, cost).

The emergence of modern (forced circulation) HTW systems for district space heating applications began early in the 1950s. The most common users of HTW plants have been airports, military bases, universities, and other institutional settings where multiple buildings are spread over long distances. SET recommended to the owner and to Allegheny County that the HTW heating system was the best system with advantages to both the energy facility owner as well as the energy user. From the perspective of a conventional arrangement, when the purchaser is also owner/operator, a HTW system has an operating cost advantage. The owner of the energy facility benefits from reduced maintenance and operating coats. The energy user also benefits with reduced distribution losses versus pumping energy required and also lower maintenance costs of many miles of piping with steam traps and drip legs as well as chemical treatment.

COOLING EQUIPMENT ALTERNATIVES

A variety of commercially available cooling system prime equipment options were given a conceptual phase evaluation. These included electric-driven, centrifugal, and rotary screw-type chillers; factory packaged chillers versus field-erected chillers; open drive versus hermetic, CFC versus HCFC/HFC refrigerants; and steel packaged PVC fill towers versus field-erected non-PVC fill towers. The initial screening eliminated large capacity (>2,000 ton) field erected chillers due to comparatively large purchase costs, larger space and maintenance clearance requirements that infringed on other major equipment arrangements, and potentially greater ancillary equipment requirements. The county required a low-connected horsepower, field-erected cooling tower with a long-life ceramic-tile fill housed in a special concrete architectural finish. After the initial screening, a cooling plant optimization study was completed by the engineer to define some key design parameters as the basis of the bid specification. The optimization study highlighted an 8,225-ton cooling plant (present design), evaluated cost based on ten-year/fifteen-year terms, 85° F entering condenser water temperature (ECWT) versus 90° F ECWT; cooling tower fan horsepower and 75° F wb versus 78° F wb design; condenser water pump horsepower end variable flow rates; condenser water pipe sizing; end chiller compressor kW/ton. The county requirement for the chilled water supply temperature was fixed at 42° F.

The engineer modeled and furnished to chiller manufacturers an annual cooling load profile datasheet in order to obtain kW/ton performance at the varying tonnage and entering condenser water temperature for different outdoor air wet bulb ranges. The optimization study evaluation considered packaged electric-driven centrifugal and rotary screw, both open drive and hermetic. The chiller pricing included options for 5 kV reduced motor starters, motor surge protection, marine boxes, and sound attenuation. A number of chiller performance selections was obtained by chiller manufacturers based on the above scenarios. The manufacturers were encouraged to model different evaporator and condenser selections (one pass through three pass), compressor options (single or multi-stage), and any worthy unspecified selections within the electric-driven chiller category. The engineer provided the building layout drawings to the bidders to give them the opportunity to provide the optimum chiller arrangement based on number of units and kW/ton efficiency, while ensuring the required maintenance space clearances for their proposed arrangements.

In general, conditions that optimize the economics of the cooling tower/condenser pumps/condenser piping distribution have an adverse impact on chiller kW/ton efficiency and vice versa. For example, the chiller rated kW/ton performance is optimum for conditions of low entering condenser water temperature and low temperature rise across condenser. These chiller processes often result in higher operating costs for the cooling tower fans and condenser water pumps and higher installed costs for this ancillary equipment. The key to evaluating each of the cooling plant scenarios evaluated cost is to compare chiller installed cost and kW/ton performance with the balance of the cooling plant auxiliary equipment installed costs and electric operating costs.

COOLING EQUIPMENT EVALUATION RESULTS

The optimization study concluded that a cooling plant utilizing 85° F ECWT, a 10° F rise across the chiller condenser, 75° F wb cooling tower design, and a condenser water flow rate of 3.0 gpm/ton was the most cost effective. The optimization study cost model was driven by the disproportionate chiller compressor kW draw total of 5,100 kW nominal versus only 750 kW nominal for the cooling tower fans/condenser water pumps. Thus, the chiller kW/ton selection weighed heavier than condenser water pump/piping costs and cooling tower price considerations.

This key performance data was written into the chiller specification. All chiller bid proposal data was modeled in spreadsheet form to compare total evaluated cost among the different chiller manufacturers and associated ancillary equipment cost data. The lowest evaluated costs became the "baseline" to compare the cost difference with higher cooling plant evaluated total cost. The differential evaluated cost represented the owner's cash for parity to make all total evaluated costs equivalent. Similar to the optimization study, the final chiller selection evaluation results focused on cooling plant major kW consumption (chiller compressors, cooling tower fans, and condenser water pumps) based on the specification cooling load profile and chiller f.o.b. factory price quotations. In addition, the engineer interjected some balance of plant installation cost adjustments to the evaluation to compare each chiller bid on even terms. For example, a minor HVAC cost penalty was assessed to open drive-type chillers because of their much greater ambient heat rejection compared to hermetic chillers. Adjustments were also made for any separate electric power feeds, auxiliary cooling water requirements, and additional condenser water piping, depending on location of pipe flanges on the condenser bundle.

There were alternate evaluation cost scenarios that considered extended warranty coverage and substitution of HCFC/HFC refrigerants. All shortlisted

- Total of seven Electric-Driven Centrifugal Chillers
- Centrifugal Chiller Key Design Features (present)
- Manufacturer: Trane Company
- Model Number: CVHE113
- Cooling Output: 1,175 tons of refrigeration
- Chilled Water: 1710 gpm; 42° F supply, 58° F Return; three pass
- Condenser Water: 3525 gpm; 85° F entering; 95° F leaving; two pass
- Refrigerent: R-11 (Compatible with R-123)
- Chiller Motor Size: 1100 hp nominal; 4160 V
- Chiller Full Load Performance: 0.62 kW/ton
- ARI Certified Performance: 0.64 kW/ton (APLV)

FIGURE 4   COOLING PLANT DESIGN CRITERIA

chiller proposals were predicated on chillers that would presently utilize an HCFC refrigerant (R-22) or be completely compatible with a future HCFC conversion (R-11 to R-123).

The Trane company proposal, with seven 1,175-ton hermetic R-11 chillers, was the successful bid proposal (see Figure 4).

Several benefits to the owner were identified as a result of the evaluation results and Trane chiller selection:

- lowest five-year and ten-year evaluated cost, based on a total evaluated equipment bid quotation
- simple installation involving a single 4160 V feed to each chiller and less chilled water/condenser water piping requirements (no separate low voltage electric feeds or auxiliary city water cooling piping required for packaged chiller components)
- chiller construction and all components completely compatible with substitute refrigerant R-123 (unit to be equipped with a high efficiency air-cooled purge unit)
- local Trane office has a large factory-trained maintenance service department within ten miles of the project
- Trane can offer an EMS/DDC system to simplify cooling plant centralized control communication with its chiller control panels.

CONCLUSION

The Midfield Terminal Energy Facility project culminates nearly five years of conceptual engineering analyses, design, construction management, and start-up activities. The strategic project management plan developed by the owner/engineer with the proper emphasis given to scheduling, budgeting, and quality resulted in a highly successful project. The project was engineered, designed, constructed, tested, and demonstrated all within schedule (six weeks early) and under budget. The owner's commitment to realistic scheduling, budgeting for comprehensive preliminary engineering studies to select optimum equipment system, and detailed bid documents resulted in very competitive construction bids and minimized construction contingencies.

The project management strategies implemented by owner/engineer will also benefit the owner with long-term operating cost savings.

Study Questions

PITTSBURGH INTERNATIONAL AIRPORT MIDFIELD TERMINAL ENERGY FACILITY

1. The design team was concerned with developing "real" quotations and selecting the best energy system. Which of the nine project management body of knowledge areas was used most? Describe this process.

2. The authors state that project cost is directly proportional to the level of quality required. Comment on this statement.

3. Something which was not mentioned by the authors of this case was that the airport was created using public funds and thus faced the problems associated with dealing with the government and, consequently, the public as stakeholders. How did the owner/engineers of this project deal with this challenge?

4. The authors state that if realistic budget and quality are established, the project is properly controlled by controlling the schedule. They later state that the schedule is the key controlling mechanism. What are the key assumptions of this statement?

5. The authors mention the importance of negotiating the quality, budgeting, and scheduling with the project's owner. Elements of every project and even every activity of life involve negotiation. Project managers always have to conduct negotiations in a project. What are some strategies for negotiating as a project manager?

Environmental Mega-Project under Way: Sludge Management in New York City

Itzhak Wirth, St. John's University

PMI *Proceedings*, 1993, pp. 666–80

BACKGROUND

The city of New York is conducting a program to implement land-based alternatives to ocean disposal of sludge from its Water Pollution Control Plants (WPCPs). The city owns and operates fourteen WPCPs located throughout the five city boroughs, and sludge is the final product of these plants. Currently the city of New York produces about 17,900 wet-tons of sludge at about 2 percent solids on a daily basis.

For over fifty years, New York City's sludge was dumped into the Atlantic Ocean. In November 1988, United States congressional legislation, the Ocean Dumping Ban Act, was signed into law. This presented to the city of New York a forceful incentive to act most effectively.

OCEAN DUMPING BAN ACT OF 1988

For existing dumpers, such as the city of New York, the Ocean Dumping Ban Act prohibited the dumping of sewage, sludge, and industrial waste within nine months of the bill's enactment, August 1989, unless the dumper had received a permit that included an agreement to end the dumping. The act made it unlawful to ocean dump sewage, sludge, and industrial waste after December 31, 1991. It required the governors of New York and New Jersey to report to the United States Environmental Protection Agency (EPA) annually on the progress being made in implementing the schedules to end ocean dumping, and the EPA had to report to Congress on the progress.

The Ocean Dumping Ban Act of 1988 established fees for ocean dumping prior to the 1991 deadline. Dumpers who continued dumping after the 1991 deadline would be subject to sharply escalating civil penalties. The penalties increase by an amount every year. Eighty-five percent of the fees and a portion of the penalties, beginning with 90 percent in 1992 and declining by 5 percent every year thereafter, must be deposited in the dumper's trust account. Portions of the remaining funds go to EPA, the Coast Guard, and the National Oceanic and Atmospheric Administration to cover the costs of administering the Act, or to the states for specified activities.

The trust accounts can be used by dumpers, with EPA's approval, to implement alternatives to dumping. Funds remaining in the trust account after the dumper has ended its dumping are returned to the dumper to be used for compliance with the Clean Water Act and for reducing debt incurred for compliance, including operations and maintenance costs, with this act and the Clean Water Act.

PROGRAM OBJECTIVE AND CURRENT STATUS

Intensified activity with the sludge management program began by New York City's Department of Environmental Protection (DEP) in April 1988. The program is expected to cost in excess of $1.7 billion by the time it is completed in 1998.

Construction of eight dewatering facilities has been recently completed at the expected cost of about $700 million. Employing mechanical dewatering processes (including centrifuges, polymer mixing equipment, dewatering equipment, and material handling systems), these facilities convert the entire WPCPs output of sludge at 2 percent solids into a 20–30 percent solids mixture.

THE LIFE-CYCLE CONCEPT

In light of the Ocean Dumping Ban Act, the city of New York has entered into a Consent Decree and Enforcement Agreement with the United States government for phasing out ocean dumping and providing for the development and implementation of a land-based sludge management plan. The agreement provided for three major plan components or phases, referred to as immediate phase, intermediate phase, and long-range phase.

THE IMMEDIATE RANGE PHASE

The Consent Decree and Enforcement Agreement entered into by the city required the implementation of dewatering measures for land-based management of sewage-sludge. Because of the significance of dewatering to various aspects of the intermediate and long-range phases, the New York City DEP initiated the development of dewatering facilities in 1988.

Alternative evaluations were made during the development of the proposed dewatering approach. The evaluations included a technology assessment (i.e., type of dewatering equipment) and a site assessment (i.e., the number and location of sites). As part of the immediate range phase, eight dewatering facilities were constructed at existing WPCPs. These facilities dewater sludge from the fourteen WPCPs using centrifuges to dewater the sludge from 2 percent solids into a 20–30 percent solids mixture. The selected dewatering sites and the WPCPs they serve under the long-range phase are shown in Figure 1.

Existing sludge pipelines or barges from existing barge facilities transport sludge from the WPCPs without dewatering facilities to the dewatering facilities. Construction of the dewatering facilities, which is necessary for both the intermediate and the long-range phases, has been fully completed and operational in 1992. The total cost amounted to about $700 million.

Legend

WI	Wards Island
HP	Hunts Point
26	26th Ward
RH	Red Hook
TI	Tallman Island
JA	Jamica Bay
BB	Bowery Bay
OB	Oakwood Beach
NR	North River
NC	Newtown Creek
CI	Coney Island
OH	Owls Head
RO	Rockaway Beach
PR	Port Richmond
◯	Dewatering Facility

FIGURE 1   NYC SLUDGE DEWATERING LOCATIONS (IMMEDIATE RANGE PHASE)

THE INTERMEDIATE RANGE PHASE

Under the intermediate range phase, the city had contracted private firms for land-base sludge management services beginning in 1992 and ending in 1998, when the long-range phase is implemented. The selection of private firms (contractors) to handle and beneficially use or dispose of the city's sludge started with a request for proposal (RFP) selection process. Using a host of planning, cost, and environmental factors, the city had selected four contractors to thermally dry, chemically stabilize, land apply, and landfill the city's sludge.

During the intermediate range phase, an approximate total of 330 dry-tons per day (DTPD) of sludge at about 30 percent solids is produced on the average. This is extracted from the daily average of some 17,900 wet-tons of sludge at 2 percent solids produced by the city's WPCPs as mentioned earlier.

The intermediate range phase was formulated based on the assumption that peak levels would be 1.6 times as high as average levels. To provide flexibility and redundancy in the planning for the intermediate range phase, the city had negotiated with the contractors to provide a capacity to process a larger quantity of dewatered sludge than the amounts produced at the

Site		Technology	Throughput (DTD)		
			Average	Peak	Installed Capacity
Manhattan:	Wards Island North	Chemical Stabilization	103	165	184
	Wards Island South	Composting	22	35	40
Bronx:	NYOFCO	Thermal Drying	106	169	300
	North Brother Island	Composting	36	58	88
Brooklyn:	Sunset Park	Composting	68	108	128
	Revere Sugar	Composting	34	54	64
Queens:	Phelps Dodge	Composting	57	91	152
	Maspeth	Composting	39	62	64
Staten Island:	Newark Bay	Composting	34	54	70

FIGURE 2   NYC SLUDGE PROCESSING PLAN (LONG-RANGE PHASE)

WPCPs that were initially planned to be allocated to each contractor, as well as the ability to process sludge from any WPCP. This scheme provides for two alternative plans (or their combination) for the intermediate range phase: an operational plan and an installed capacity plan. The operational plan represents the expected sludge quantities and sludge sources that would be allocated to each contractor. The installed capacity plan represents the capacities that the contractors would provide under their contracts with the city, allowing sludge to come from any source. The aggregate of the capacities under the installed capacity plan is greater than the city's expected peak sludge generation. This excess capacity and the source flexibility reflect the need to have redundancy in the event that one of the contractors is unable to process its allocation of sludge as a result of a breakdown or other problem. The anticipated average and peak dewatered sludge quantities along with the installed capacities provided are summarized in Figure 2.

THE LONG-RANGE PHASE

The long-range phase sets up a land-based sludge management system that would enable the city to ensure long-term beneficial use of its sludge beginning in 1998. The selection of the long-range phase plan resulted from a systematic evaluation of many possible alternatives. Among the factors considered in this evaluation are legislative and regulatory requirements, sludge quantity and quality, sludge processing technologies, sludge product markets, and setting options. Based on the anticipated life of the mechanical equipment for the proposed facilities and the project's financial period, the year 2020 was selected as the program's planning horizon. The long-range phase includes a preferred plan with nine processing facilities throughout the city to compost, chemically stabilize, and thermally dry sludge for beneficial use (see Figure 2). The plan also considers potential backup options that could be used in the event that any part of the preferred plan cannot be implemented. The backup options include additional sites (other than the nine preferred plan sites) and/or increasing the capacity at preferred plan sites.

The preferred plan was designed with the intent of implementing beneficial use processing facilities in each borough that on the whole are consistent with an identified market demand, accommodate peak sludge production (1.6

	Compost	Thermally Dried Sludge	Chemically Stabilized Sludge
New York City Public Demand	210	70	500
Private Demand	190	80	large potential
Total Demand	400	150	500+
Long-range Plan Average Processing Level	290	106	103

FIGURE 3   **TOTAL PROJECTED PUBLIC AND PRIVATE MARKET DEMAND AND LONG-RANGE PLAN CAPACITIES (DTPD)**

times the average), and provide for adequate capacity redundancy. All quantities are based on projections of sludge production in the year 2020, and represent annual average daily quantities. Total sludge production in 2020 is estimated at 500 DTPD on average and 800 DTPD at peak. With a total installed capacity of 1090 DTPD, the long-range phase plan would provide about 35 percent redundancy during peak production periods. The total cost associated with the long-range phase, construction and equipment, is expected to amount to $1 billion.

SLUDGE PRODUCT MARKET ASSESSMENT

The city intends to promote the beneficial use of all sludge produced under the long-range plan. The quantities of each of the three sludge products under the long-range plan are based on a market assessment of potential uses for compost, chemically stabilized sludge, and thermally dried sludge products, focusing on in-city public agencies as the preferred users. The largest component of the plan, 290 DTPD of about 58 percent of the 500 DTPD projected average sludge production in 2020, is dedicated to composting (see Figure 3). Major potential end-users of this product are New York City agencies, including but not limited to the Department of Parks and Recreation, Department of Transportation, Department of Sanitation, the Port Authority of New York and New Jersey, and private marketers. The remaining 42 percent of the expected dewatered sludge is about evenly split between chemical stabilization and thermal drying. The chemically stabilized sludge is intended for use as cover material at landfills in the area or for agricultural uses. The thermally dried product is intended for market as a fertilizer amendment.

THE WORK BREAKDOWN STRUCTURE

The work breakdown structure (WBS) divides the engineering effort into successively smaller units of work, with each step of the subdivision identified as a level.

Tasks comprise Level 3 of the WBS and subtasks comprise Level 4. The work in each subtask includes the specific documents produced, e.g., reports, design drawings, specifications. At the subtask and task levels, man-hours expended can be meaningfully compared to percentage completion of these documents. These are the levels, therefore, on which the project is managed and controlled.

Man-hours are estimated at the activity level. Time is charged at the subtask level (Level 4). Control of man-hours and schedule is accomplished primarily through direct communication with the responsible sub-consultants and engineers who are performing the work at the subtask level.

Level 1—Project

- Project end-product: the sludge management plan.

Level 2—Categories

- Lump sum services: This category includes the task whose scope can be defined at project initiation and includes reviews and evaluations and assessments of various alternatives.
- Cost reimbursable services: This category includes the supervisory effort of the project manager and deputy project manager and administrative support, as well as the tasks whose scope can only be approximated at project initiation. This includes interim and preliminary facility design, testing, and work associated with environmental licensing and permitting.

Level 3—Tasks

- Evaluation of Existing Conditions
- Projection of Future Conditions
- Regulatory Evaluations
- Technology Search and Assessment
- Transport Assessments
- Site Assessments
- Evaluation of Alternatives
- Environmental Assessment
- Review and Complete DEP Dewatering Plan
- Comparison of Recommended Land-Based Alternatives with Ocean Disposal
- Preliminary Facility Design
- Implementation Program
- Regulatory Liaison
- Environmental Impact Statement and Other Permitting Documents
- Public Participation
- Uniform Land Use Review Procedure
- Project Management and Control
- Training and Technology Transfer to DEP
- Sludge Analysis
- Phase I Dewatering Final Design
- Assist with Fast-Track Privatization
- Pilot Testing
- Demonstration Projects
- Other Direct Costs.

The units of work on Level 3 are designated tasks. Each task is identified by a two-digit number.

At Level 4, each task is divided into a number of subtasks. Each subtask is of a size to be meaningfully monitored by one responsible engineer. Each subtask is identified by the task number followed by sequential sub-numbers.

The subtasks are the working units of the WBS. The tasks are the primary summary units.

Subtask products (reports, drawings, specifications, etc.) may be modified from those listed to better suit the work; in general, the project schedule, which will be updated from time to time, will reflect a current listing of these products.

Level 4—Subtasks

Task	Subtask	Title
01		EVALUATION OF EXISTING CONDITION
	1.1	Evaluation of Landfill and Existing Transportation Systems
	1.2	Sludge, Residuals, and Digester Cleanout Quantities Characteristics
	1.3	Review of Prior NYC Assessments and Sludge Management Planning by Others
	1.4	Facilities Evaluation
02		PROJECTION OF FUTURE CONDITIONS
	2.1	Projection of Future Conditions
03		REGULATORY EVALUATIONS
	3.1	Research of Environmental Licensing, Land-Use, and Health Regulations
	3.2	Research of Federal Regulations Relative to Sludge Management
	3.3	Research of State Regulations Relative to Sludge Management
04		TECHNOLOGY SEARCH AND ASSESSMENT
	4.1	Technology Search
	4.2	Sludge Dewatering Technology Assessment
	4.3	Residuals Disposal Technology Assessment
	4.4	Thermal Reduction Technology Assessment
	4.5	Composting Technology Assessment
	4.6	Land-based Technology Assessment
	4.7	Miscellaneous Other Sludge Disposal Technologies
05		TRANSPORT ASSESSMENT
	5.1	Sludge Transport Assessment—Non-Pipeline
	5.2	Sludge Pipeline, Residuals, and Digester Cleanout Transport Assessment
06		SITE ASSESSMENTS
	6.1	Site Assessments—Local and Independent or Remote Sites
	6.2	Assessment of Sites at Existing WPCPs
07		EVALUATION OF ALTERNATIVES
	7.1	Framing and Screening of Alternatives
	7.2	Human Health Risk Assessment/Preliminary
08		ENVIRONMENTAL ASSESSMENT
	8.1	Environmental Assessment
09		REVIEW AND COMPLETE DEP DEWATERING PLAN
	9.1	Review and Complete DEP Dewatering Plan
10		COMPARISON OF RECOMMENDED LAND-BASED ALTERNATIVES WITH OCEAN DISPOSAL
	10.1	Comparison of Recommended Land-based Alternatives with Ocean Disposal
11		PRELIMINARY FACILITY DESIGN
	11.1	Preliminary Facility Design
12		IMPLEMENTATION PROGRAM
	12.1	Financing Considerations
	12.2	Permitting and Scheduling
	12.3	Management and Staffing Considerations
	12.4	Risk Management

THE SITE SELECTION PROCESS

The purpose of the site selection process is to identify sites suitable for the processing and/or end-use of sludge in conjunction with the long-range phase of the sludge management program. The intent is to enable the identification of an adequate number of sites and areas that could accommodate a range of sludge processing and/or end-use technologies for the sludge quantities being produced. The following technologies are considered:

- processing technologies
  - biological conversion (composting)
  - chemical stabilization
  - thermal drying (pelletizing)
  - thermal conversion (incineration)

- chemical conversion
- end-use technologies
  - distribution and marketing
  - land application (silviculture)
  - land reclamation (abandoned mines)
  - land fill (final cover or daily cover).

The site selection process is divided into three categories: 1) local site assessment, 2) remote site assessment, and 3) nomination assessment. They are described below.

LOCAL SITE ASSESSMENT

The local site assessment process is confined to identifying potential sites for sludge processing and/or end-use within the city of New York. It was decided to develop a coarse ranking of potential sites based on three screening criteria rank-ordered by weight as follows: first, site size (confined to 3 acres or more); second, site zoning (M3—heavy industrial uses, M2—medium industrial uses, M1—light industrial uses); third, site ownership (public, private, other). Subsequent to this ranking, consideration would be given to environmental and demographic factors including the appropriate distribution of facilities across the five boroughs of New York City. As a result of this procedure, seventy-three sites were identified within New York City. The list, rank ordered, is presented in Figure 4, and the breakdown by size and borough is introduced in Figure 5.

REMOTE SITE ASSESSMENT

New York City's objective of managing both the processing and end-use of its sludge within its five boroughs is restricted by insufficient large vacant industrial sites. End-use technologies require land areas in orders of magnitude that simply do not exist within New York City. Thus, it is necessary to look for sites in New York State beyond the city's boundaries. Furthermore, New York State requirements to the siting of landfills, an end-use option, are more restrictive. Also, landfills require significantly larger land acreage than sludge processing facilities. This precipitated a screening of the entire state, not merely the counties adjacent to New York City. Concomitantly, any area suitable for landfill would also be suitable for the siting of processing facilities.

In the case of remote siting, transportation represents a primary cost and, consequently, transportation criteria are considered prior to any other criteria in the process of site identification. Thus, routes and corridors were identified with respect to three common transportation modes, namely, track, train, and barge. Considering economic and feasibility factors governing the transportation system (including travel time, load size, labor costs, and others) the study area has been restricted to a "one-truck-trip" zone (i.e., a 120-mile distance) covering nine counties, and further, a "two-truck-trip" zone (i.e., a 285-mile distance) covering twenty-nine counties. This is shown in Figure 6.

Upon the establishment of the transportation system zones, preferred sites are selected from among candidate areas within the transportation

rough	Site No.**	Size (Acres)	Zone	Type	Ownership
Bronx	12	52	M3	Public	Ports & Trade
Bronx	11	5	M3	Public	Ports & Trade
Bronx	13	5	M3	Public	Ports & Trade
Bronx	18	5	M3	Public	Ports & Trade
Bronx	2	4	M3	Public	NYC PDC
Bronx	14	4	M3	Public	Real Property
Bronx	19	4	M3	Public	Ports & Trade
Bronx	7	27	M3	Private	
Bronx	5	6	M2	Public	NYC PDC
Bronx	16	3	M2	Public	Real Property
Bronx	9	2	M2	Public	Ports & Trade
Bronx	6	10	M1	Public	NYC PDC
Bronx	15	10	M1	Public	Real Property
Bronx	10	8	M1	Public	Ports & Trade
Bronx	1	4	M1	Private	
Bronx	17	3	M1	Private	
Total 16		**152**			
Brooklyn	11	17	M3	Public	Ports & Trade
Brooklyn	10	5	M3	Public	NYC
Brooklyn	7	3	M3	Public	Ports & Trade
Brooklyn	15	3	M3	Public	NYC PDC
Brooklyn	2	20	M3	Private	
Brooklyn	1	18	M3	Private	
Brooklyn	4	16	Ml	Public	Ports & Trade
Brooklyn	5	6	Ml	Public	Ports & Trade
Brooklyn	16	3	Ml	Public	NYC PDC
Total 9		**91**			
Manhattan	1	3	M3	Public	Real property
Manhattan	3	3	Ml	Public	Ports & Trade
Total 2		**6**			
Queens	4	7	M3	Public	NYC PDC
Queens	2	5	M3	Public	NYC PDC
Queens	5	24	M3	Private	
Queens	3	5	M3	Private	LIRR
Queens	6	3	M3	Private	
Queens	14	3	M3	Private	
Queens	8	16	Ml	Public	NYC
Queens	9	7	Ml	Public	NYC
Queens	1	4	Ml	Public	NYC PDC
Queens	10	4	Ml	Public	Ports & Trade
Queens	11	3	Ml	Public	Ports & Trade
Queens	12	3	Ml	Public	Ports & Trade
Queens	13	3	Ml	Public	Ports & Trade
Total 13		**12**			
Staten Island	26	37	M3	Public	Ports & Trade
Staten Island	22	35	M3	Public	Ports & Trade
Staten Island	29	31	M3	Public	NYC Parks
Staten Island	12	26	M3	Public	Ports & Trade
Staten Island	21	19	M3	Public	NYC PDC
Staten Island	20	14	M3	Public	Ports & Trade
Staten Island	18	12	M3	Public	Ports & Trade
Staten Island	19	10	M3	Public	Ports & Trade
Staten Island	2	9	M3	Public	NYC PDC
Staten Island	1	7	M3	Public	NYC PDC
Staten Island	27	4	M3	Public	Ports & Trade
Staten Island	34	4	M3	Public	Ports & Trade
Staten Island	17	65	M3	Private	
Staten Island	8	40	M3	Private	
Staten Island	10	40	M3	Private	
Staten Island	28	115	M2	Public	Ports & Trade
Staten Island	6	45	M2	Private	
Staten Island	15	10	M2	Private	
Staten Island	16	4	M2	Private	
Staten Island	4	100	M1	Public	NYC PDC
Staten Island	25	36	M1	Public	Ports & Trade
Staten Island	32	15	M1	Public	Real Property
Staten Island	23	12	M1	Public	Ports & Trade
Staten Island	24	12	M1	Public	Ports & Trade
Staten Island	31	4	M1	Public	Real Property
Staten Island	30	3	M1	Public	Real Property
Staten Island	33	3	M1	Public	Real Property
Staten Island	7	12	M1	Private	
Staten Island	5	8	M1	Private	
Staten Island	13	7	M1	Private	
Staten Island	14	7	M1	Private	
Staten Island	9	3	M1	Private	
Total 33		**749**			
Grand Total 73		**1085**			

ote: Sort Order—M Zone, Ownership Type, Size-Acreage   **Corresponds to site numbers in Figures 2 and 6.

IGURE 4   RANKING OF LOCAL SITES

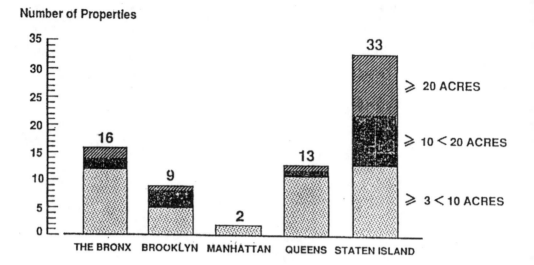

Number of Properties

Sources: NYC Department of General Services, Division of Real Property
NYC Department of Ports and Trade
NYC Public Development Corporation
NYC Office of Business Development, Real Estate Assistance Unit

FIGURE 5   SEVENTY-THREE VACANT INDUSTRIAL PROPERTIES IN NEW YORK CITY LOCAL SITE ASSESSMENT

system boundaries. Screening criteria were developed for this purpose and they are introduced in Figure 7. These criteria were incorporated in a screening process using first a 1:250,000 USGS map, followed by an enhanced level of detail using a 1:24,000 USGS map. This yielded a total of twelve preferred sites. Intensive demographic data gathering was conducted with respect to these sites including site visits and projections to the year 2010. The twelve preferred sites are shown in Figure 6.

SITE NOMINATION ASSESSMENT

In the site nomination assessment process, potential sites or opportunities for setting of sludge management facilities are solicited from other agencies, citizen groups, and institutions.

In an effort to obtain local site nominations, New York City DEP developed a list of representatives from city agencies who have an interest in, jurisdiction over, or knowledge of appropriate properties for siting sludge management facilities. DEP initiated an invitation requesting their involvement in the city's sludge management site selection process. It provided all representatives with the list of seventy-three sites under consideration throughout the city. This list was the outcome of the earlier local assessment process. Fourteen agencies were contacted including NYC Department of General Services, NYC Department of Ports and Trade, New York Telephone Co., Metropolitan Transportation Authority, and others.

The remote site nominations process included a conference of representatives from interested state agencies. These included NYS Department of

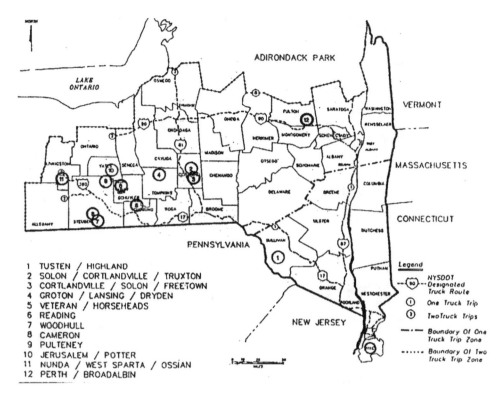

1 TUSTEN / HIGHLAND
2 SOLON / CORTLANDVILLE / TRUXTON
3 CORTLANDVILLE / SOLON / FREETOWN
4 GROTON / LANSING / DRYDEN
5 VETERAN / HORSEHEADS
6 READING
7 WOODHULL
8 CAMERON
9 PULTENEY
10 JERUSALEM / POTTER
11 NUNDA / WEST SPARTA / OSSIAN
12 PERTH / BROADALBIN

FIGURE 6   **TWELVE CANDIDATE AREA TOWNSITES REMOTE SITE ASSESSMENT**

Environmental Conservation; NYS Department of Agriculture and Markets; NYS Office of Parks, Recreation, and Historic Preservation; and others. The conference was followed by a written questionnaire addressed to these agencies and their local branches. The suggestions offered in response to the questionnaires, along with comments recorded during the conference and follow-up discussions, were researched to the extent necessary in order to determine the potential for use of areas suggested by the results of the remote site assessment process.

IMPLICATIONS WITH RESPECT TO PROJECT MANAGEMENT BODY OF KNOWLEDGE

In the United States and Canada, the Project Management Institute (PMI) had published in 1987 *The Project Management Body of Knowledge (PMBOK)*, and has continued to update the original document since then. [The most recent update, published in 1996 is referred to as the *PMBOK Guide*.] The objective was to establish project management as a unique discipline and independent profession. Consequently, the *PMBOK* strived to represent a set of generic (across industries) project management standards.

Here we attempt to examine selected practices of New York City's sludge management program against concepts and definitions within the *PMBOK*.

Sensitive Land Uses

Populated Areas
Airports
Government Land
Parks
Mineral/Energy Resources

Hydrology

Primary Water Supply
Principal Aquifers
Surface Water

Geology

Bedrock

Soils

Agricultural Districts
Prime Agricultural Soils
Soil Characteristics

Wetlands

Endangered Species

FIGURE 7   PREFERRED SITES SELECTION SCREENING CRITERIA

ON PROJECT LIFE CYCLE

According to the 1987 *PMBOK* edition, in the framework of time and level of effort as variables, project life-cycle is represented graphically as a bell-shaped curve skewed towards the direction of passing time. Further, the 1987 *PMBOK* edition prescribed for the project life-cycle "four sequential phases in time through which any project passes, namely, concept; development; execution; and finishing. ... These phases may be further broken down into stages depending on the area of project application."

In a significant departure, a 1993 *PMBOK* revision would define the project life-cycle as a "collection of phases whose number and names are determined by the control needs of the performing organization."

New York City's sludge management program is frequently described as three sequential phases and inconsistent with the 1987 *PMBOK* edition prescriptions. The 1993 revision eliminated the inconsistencies between the sludge management program and *PMBOK* with respect to project life-cycle.

ON WORK BREAKDOWN STRUCTURE

According to the 1987 *PMBOK* edition, work breakdown structure (WBS) is a task-oriented "family tree" of activities which organizes, defines, and graphically displays the total work to be accomplished in order to achieve the final objectives of a project. Each descending level represents an increasingly detailed definition of the project objective. It is a system for subdividing a project into manageable work packages, components, or elements to provide a common framework for scope/cost/schedule communications, allocation of responsibility, monitoring, and management.

Consistent with *PMBOK* guidelines, New York City's sludge management program utilizes a four-level WBS. A terminology difference is noted, namely, "Project/Categories/Tasks/Subtasks," as opposed to "Project/Work Packages/Components/Elements." Further investigation is called for to identify a preferred number of task hierarchy levels as a function of project size. Also, it seems within reach to give more rigorous task-level definitions, including a uniform numerical code system.

On Marketing

We failed to identify within *PMBOK* a direct reference to marketing in project management or marketing derivatives such as demand identification and demand forecasting, areas of significant preoccupation by project management personnel in the sludge management program.

On-Site Selection Process

We were able to identify elements of the massive site selection process conducted in the sludge management program with *PMBOK* definitions of feasibility studies and economic evaluation associated with the cost management area. However, such definitions appeared to be too general to support a performance evaluation attempt of the site selection process.

References

1. City of New York, Department of Environmental Protection. 1989. New York City's Sludge Disposal Management Plans, Tuesday, May 16.

2. City of New York, Department of Environmental Protection. 1990. "Environmental Mega-Project Underway." *NYC Sludge News*, Fall.

3. City of New York, Department of Environmental Protection, Bureau of Wastewater Treatment. *Facilities Planning Project for Development of a Land-Based Municipal Sewage Sludge Management Plan*. Executive Summary, Capital Project No. WP-284.

4. Duncan, W. R., 1993. "Toward A Revised PMBOK Document." *Project Management Journal* 24, no. 2, June.

5. House of Representatives, 100th Congress Second Session. 1988. Report 100-109. *Ocean Dumping Ban Act, Committee of Conference Reports*. Oct. 18.

6. Lutzic, G. N., 1990. "Land-Based Sludge Management in the Big Apple: A Status Report." Department of Environmental Protection, New York City. Paper presented at the WPCF Specialty Conference on Residuals Management, New Orleans, LA, Dec. 2–5.

7. PMI Standards Committee. 1987. *Project Management Body of Knowledge (PMBOK)*. Drexel Hill, PA.: Project Management Institute, Sept.

8. Stone & Webster Engineering Corporation, Hazen and Sawyer, P. C., Engineers, E & A Environmental Consultants, Inc., and EA Engineering, Science and Technology. 1991. *New York City Long Range Sludge Management Plan*. Published by City of New York Department of Environmental Protection, Bureau of Wastewater Treatment, May.

9. U.S. Environmental Protection Agency, Intra-Agency Sludge Task Force. 1984. Washington, D.C.: *Environmental Regulations and Technology Use and Disposal of Municipal Wastewater Sludge*. Sept.

Study Questions

ENVIRONMENTAL MEGA-PROJECT UNDER WAY: SLUDGE MANAGEMENT IN NEW YORK CITY

1. The author presents the work breakdown structure of the project in detail and explains the process followed in its development. *PMBOK Guide*, section 5.3.2, Tools and Techniques for Scope Definition, discusses methods used to develop a work breakdown structure. Which of those methods listed were used in the case?

2. Would you consider this case the description of one or three projects, given the three distinct phases described and the extended time frame for the phases described?

3. The team work package is mentioned near the end of the case. It seems to be a synonym of the work categories described in the case. Define a work package and describe any similarities between the two terms.

4. This project doesn't mention cost management, aside from estimating costs for each phase and describing the costing elements in the work breakdown structure. In light of the described penalties for noncompliance with the dumping bans, how important is cost management?

5. The case states that there is not a section in the *PMBOK Guide* which directly addresses the site selection process. Is it possible that all of the sections of the *PMBOK Guide* at least generally describe this process? Go through each section and describe how it might affect the site selection process.

Gaining Project Acceptance

Larry Martin, Vice President and Director of Transportation Environmental Analysis, CH2M Hill
Paula Green, Environmental Coordinator, District IV Illinois DOT

Civil Engineering, August 1995, pp. 51–53

Involving every constituency early in the development of public-works projects can build acceptance even when parties don't get exactly what they want. Two Illinois transportation projects illustrate the five essential elements of a public/agency involvement process.

First there was public education, then public participation. The latest stage in the evolving process of gaining approval of a public-works project is public/agency involvement—a comprehensive program that provides avenues for receiving and responding to input from all project stakeholders including the general public; organized community groups; business interests; historic societies; environmental groups; and local, state, and federal agencies. Hearing and addressing all stakeholder concerns early in project development can avoid many pitfalls and adversities in the long run, even when the final plan contains aspects that some stakeholders find disagreeable.

Comprehensive public/agency involvement programs cleared the way for unimpeded approval of two recent transportation projects in Illinois: a feasibility study for improvement of Interstate 74 through Peoria, one of the oldest freeways in Illinois, with parts designed in the mid-1950s before design standards were established for interstate highways; and a feasibility study of a new highway connection between Peoria and Chicago, known as the Heart of Illinois Project. CH2M Hill, Chicago, was consultant to Illinois DOT on both projects.

Public/agency involvement programs include five essential elements: identification of stakeholders; tiered approach to involvement: active investigation to identify issues of concern or conflict; resolution of concerns and conflict to an acceptable solution; and formal approval.

IDENTIFYING STAKEHOLDERS

Some stakeholders in a public-works project are obvious: city and county councils, chambers of commerce, and agencies that have regulatory oversight. Others, such as some environmental interest groups, neighborhood and historic associations, and business organizations, are vocal and visible enough to be quickly identified. However, nearly any project will affect groups that are unknown at the beginning of the process. Efforts to identify these stakeholders might include drives through the area; visits to adjacent businesses, institutions, and residences; and consultations with local representatives. The questions to ask are, "Who cares about this project?" and "What groups represent the interests of those individuals?"

The most significant challenge in identifying Heart of Illinois stake holders was the size of the potentially affected region—a 3,000-square-mile area encompassing ten counties with a population of 700,000. Besides identifying as many stakeholders as possible, the project team put extra effort into publicity efforts and paid special attention to the formation of a technical group to ensure representation of geographic and special interests.

Remaining flexible as the project unfolds may be the most important aspect of stakeholder identification. Several months after start-up of I-74/Peoria project development, some neighborhood groups surfaced that felt they weren't being involved. We added representatives from these groups to the technical group and held meetings with them. These neighborhood groups could have proved more contentious had we not veered from the original membership or meeting schedule.

TIERING APPROACH

It would be impossible to conduct an input meeting that allows every stakeholder to speak. Tiering can make the input/reporting process less daunting.

One method is to solicit input or approval from various categories of stakeholders at different times. In the I-74/Peoria project, we conducted meetings with various tiers of participants, including:
• executive briefings for senior Illinois DOT officials, Federal Highway Association (FHWA) representatives, and key technical support staff (An on site briefing and field trip was also provided for FHWA and Illinois DOT representatives.)
• presentations and working sessions for Illinois DOT technical leads
• meetings of the technical group which consisted of technical representatives of the local governments, institutions, industries, and various other agencies
• presentations for city councils and the regional planning agency
• more than twenty meetings with representatives of two area hospitals affected by the project, the local chamber of commerce, the Salvation Army, the region's largest employer (Caterpillar, Inc.), organized neighborhood and business area groups, and others
• one formal public information hearing and one local public hearing.

All told, about sixty-five meetings were held with all tiers of project stakeholders. By meeting individually with the various tiers, the study team was able to address the specific concerns of each group.

We used another method of tiering, in which various constituencies are reached through an advisory or other representative group. In the Heart of Illinois project, a technical group composed of representatives from every stakeholder group in a 3,000-square-mile area would have been unwieldy. Instead, the technical group was limited to about thirty members, composed to ensure representation of each geographic region and special interest. The group included elected officials from each geographic region (selected so that the group did not weigh too heavily with representatives from the Peoria area), agricultural and rural quality-of-life concerns, industrial/economic interests, and nature-conservancy groups. The technical group was supplemented by a mailing list of several hundred interested parties who received regular newsletters and project updates.

Technical-group members arranged, publicized, and cohosted project meetings in their communities, helping ensure that all stakeholders had an opportunity to have their say about the project Also, the group members were already informed about the project. Having familiar faces at public meetings to discuss the project significantly increased the comfort levels of local participants and decreased the workload for project team members.

Heavy reliance on technical-group members does have drawbacks. The project team assumed, incorrectly in a few cases, members were getting information back to their local government bodies. We recommend confirming important communications to avoid such potential failures.

IDENTIFYING ISSUES

By seeking out potentially contentious issues and addressing them promptly, the study team will not be blind-sided at the formal hearings. For the Heart of Illinois project, instead of trying to gather stakeholders from far and wide to voice their concerns, the project team developed a "road show."

We set up a series of local drop-in centers to present basic project information and solicit comments. They were most successful when a technical-group member made the arrangements and took responsibility for involving local constituents. We also responded to requests from service groups, city councils, and other organizations by arranging additional meetings, again through local technical-group members.

An important aspect of issue identification for the Heart of Illinois project was to define clearly the scope of the project for the stakeholders. Nearly all of the public information about the project emphasized that the study would not "select a preferred corridor, but only determine if any corridors are physically, environmentally and economically feasible."

Because the project established only finalist corridors, the remaining steps in the public/agency involvement process—resolution and approval—were relatively small parts of the process. Issue identification did not lead to conflicts to be resolved; instead, it added to the list of corridor candidates and considerations. Through public/agency input, the project team learned of proposed developments and recreational areas that it had not previously known about and found out about an underground natural-gas storage area within one proposed corridor.

In contrast, issue identification for the I-74/Peoria project led directly to points of contention that required resolution. One divisive issue that could have seriously impeded project approval involved I-74 through-trips. Many stakeholders believed that existing traffic problems resulted from through-trips (particularly trucks) clogging the freeway at peak periods. If through-traffic used the I-474 bypass, they contended, traffic congestion would disappear.

Illinois DOT authorized a survey that showed that about 75 percent of all through-trips (and 98 percent of through-truck trips) already use I-474. In fact, through-trips account for only 2 percent of peak-period traffic on I-74 at the Illinois River. These statistics were exceptionally valuable in dispelling further doubts about the need for the project as final recommendations were developed.

In addition to identifying contentious issues, we also used meetings to revisit stakeholders once the issues were resolved. Even if the solutions ran contrary to their position, stakeholders' antagonism toward the final plan was tempered by the knowledge that their concerns were heard and addressed.

RESOLUTION

Resolution involves: 1) an effort to refine project plans to address stakeholder concerns; and 2) a commitment to meet with stakeholder groups as needed to assure them that their concerns have been addressed in the plans.

Just west of the Peoria central business district, two large, prestigious health-care institutions, St. Francis and Methodist hospitals, border I-74 on the north and south sides of the freeway, respectively. Two historic neighborhoods are also in the area: the West Bluff Historic District and the East Bluff Neighborhood Improvement Association.

At present, I-74 access to and from the medical centers needs to be improved. Master planning projects undertaken by the two hospitals also had to be integrated with any I-74 modifications in the area. CH2M Hill brought in the consultants working on the hospital plans, and the hospitals formed a subcommittee to address the I-74 study.

Based on input from about twenty special meetings with the hospitals and interest groups, the preliminary improvement alternatives were modified. In the recommended plan, left-hand ramps will be eliminated, hospital access will improve with a half-diamond interchange, and access ramps and turn restrictions will direct traffic away from the West Bluff Historic District. Input from West Bluff residents led to a proposed bike/pedestrian path across I-74 for local access through neighborhoods split by the highway.

In downtown Peoria, the existing I-74 runs through the North Side Historic District and abuts various structures and properties of historical significance. Again through a series of meetings, we were able to develop an acceptable alternative in which ramps are located outside of the historic district, preserving its character while enhancing access to the downtown business district.

FORMAL APPROVAL

The first four steps in the public/agency involvement program benefit the final stage, formal approval, in several ways. The project team is not likely to be taken by surprise by any new issues or concerns, nor will the public be surprised about any project elements. The process also helps dispel any feelings that a project is being forced on the community. The fact that agencies have had the opportunity to provide feedback on the project along the way also aids the formal agency approval process.

The I-74/Peoria corridor study resulted in adoption of $180 million in highway improvements with almost complete acceptance by the affected agencies and the general public. The project has now moved into preliminary engineering. As a subcontractor to Alfred Benesch & Company, Chicago, CH2M Hill will reconstitute the technical group to provide continuity of public/agency involvement during this phase.

Funding has been earmarked in the state highway program for the next phase of the Heart of Illinois Highway. A decision on corridor feasibility is expected soon. The feasibility study has laid the groundwork for public communication and involvement in future phases of the work.

Study Questions

GAINING PROJECT ACCEPTANCE

1. What is a "stakeholder?"

2. Regardless of the size of the endeavor, every project has to deal with stakeholders. Develop a list of the most common stakeholders on any project.

3. The method used by the Heart of Illinois Project to gain project acceptance has five key elements. List and define those elements.

4. Consider any of the other cases found in this casebook. Identify all the internal and external stakeholders for the project and briefly discuss their stakes. List any strategic issues that could inhibit the progress on the project.

5. Define a generic procedure for stakeholder analysis.

The Power of Politics:
The Fourth Dimension of
Managing the Large Public Project

Bud Baker, Wright State University
Raj Menon, Wright State University

PMI Canada *Proceedings*, 1994, pp. 830–33

INTRODUCTION

It is generally accepted that there exist three dimensions that determine the success or failure of a project: cost, schedule, and technical performance. In his book, *Successful Project Management*, Milton Rosenau calls this the "Triple Constraint," which requires "... accomplishing the performance specifications on or before the time limit and within the budgeted cost" (1).

Some authors have indicated that the conventional three-part model is incomplete, that there can be more to successful project management than just cost, schedule, and technical issues. Dr. Harold Kerzner, in his popular book, *Project Management: A Systems Approach to Planning, Scheduling, and Controlling*, has this to say on the subject: "Time, cost, and performance are the constraints on the project. If the project is to be accomplished for an outside customer, then the project has a fourth constraint: good customer relations" (2).

Kerzner goes on to explain that it's possible for an otherwise successful project to have such bad customer relations that any future business is impaired, or even impossible.

It is the position of this paper that, for large public projects, a critical aspect of customer relations involves "managing" the political system. Further, it is our position that politics is, in many cases, the most critical aspect of managing the large publicly visible project. We will show that politically astute project management can save an otherwise unsuccessful project, and also that unsound political maneuvering can kill a project that might have otherwise survived.

Successfully Managing the Political Interface

Contemporary examples exist in which politics have played a key role in project success. The recently completed English Channel tunnel project was only the most recent attempt to successfully connect England and the rest of the continent. The primary difference between the successful tunnel of today and the failed efforts of yesteryear is in the area of politics. After all, the tunnel was first proposed in 1802, and the project was actually begun in earnest as early as 1876. Technologically, the tunnel was feasible even then: more than a mile of tunnel was bored at each end. But the project ended because of politics: the British feared that the tunnel posed a threat to national security (3). Subsequent attempts also ended in failure: in 1930, again several years later, and once again in 1975. Each time the cause was the same: lack of political support on the British side of the channel (4). It took until 1993—after nearly two centuries of political debate—for the tunnel to become a reality.

Here in North America the situation is no different. In the following pages we'll examine two public "mega-projects." One—monumentally successful—shaped the way Americans live, work, and play every day. The other—destined to be synonymous with project mismanagement—was recently terminated, largely because it had lost its political support.

President Eisenhower and the Interstate Highway System

Just forty years ago, on July 12, 1954, President Dwight David Eisenhower proposed a massive road-building plan, one which would bring a host of benefits to the American public. Among these benefits, Eisenhower mentioned increased national productivity, enhanced highway safety, and a strengthened defense establishment, necessary "should atomic war come" (5). Additionally, Eisenhower believed that the thousands of jobs created would help lift the United States out of the post-Korean War doldrums (6). The cost figure he used—$50 billion—was admittedly only "a good start on the highways the country will need for a population of 200,000,000" (7).

Despite Eisenhower's personal support, the project was quickly swamped with political problems, largely related to finances. Projected costs rose fast enough to shock even the most pessimistic observers. Within just four months, the cost estimates had grown 52 percent, to $76,000,000,000, and they further ballooned to $101,000,000,000 just two months after that (8).

But it wasn't the projected cost overrun that sidelined Eisenhower's first plan—it was politics. Truckers objected to increased taxes on tires and fuel. Western governors, faced with vast expanses of highways but few drivers, objected to the use of tolls as a financing source. Eisenhower's Democratic opponents wanted to keep road design standards at the county and state level and objected to the proposed financing methods as well. In the summer of 1955, Congress killed Eisenhower's plan and adjourned (9).

The setback, though, was only temporary. Early in 1956, Eisenhower adopted a more bipartisan approach. He reconciled with key Democrats, and the result was the Interstate Highway Act of 1956. The key principles behind the Act were these:
• There would be limited tax increases on the trucking industry.
• In return for federal design control, 90 percent of cost would be borne by the federal government.
• Urban areas—where the votes were—would receive most of the construction dollars.
• Contentious issues—e.g., the use of tolls as a financing tool—were intentionally avoided. Both sides agreed to postpone any decisions until the project was under way; not a sound concept for most projects, certainly, but necessary here (10).

In sum then, the Act offered something to everyone, and aroused the ire of almost no one. And therein lies the secret of political success. As Mark Rose, author of Interstate Express Highway Politics, 1941–1956, so eloquently put it:

> None of this agitated anyone … Americans … were optimistic about the natural congeniality of highway construction and economic growth. If traffic tangles were reduced, if

billions were spent for more roads, the economy would prosper. Truckers and contractors then could look forward to personal wealth; economists and government officials, to steady economic growth; and farmers and urban motorists alike, to faster trips to market, to jobs, and to recreation areas (11).

Certainly some tactics—e.g., the intentional postponement of critical decisions—aren't applicable to every project. But politics is, as they say, "the art of the possible," and the rules are, of necessity, different. Following is another example, one in which the concepts of political project management were ignored, with predictably disastrous results.

The Superconducting Supercollider (SSC)

When questioned in the British Parliament about the usefulness of experiments about the "thing" called electricity, scientist Michael Faraday was quoted to have said: "One day you will be able to tax it!" But, regardless of potential usefulness, science projects fall within the discretionary part of the United States federal budget—the portion that annually requires a yes or no from Congress—in contrast to social security, veteran benefits, and other entitlements. Science projects only rarely gather popular support and capture public imagination.

The superconducting supercollider (SSC) is a classic example of the above. The objective of the $11 billion SSC was to validate the existence of the "Higgs Boson." A British theorist named Peter Higgs proposed a mechanism—called a Higgs field—that invisibly pervades all of space. Physicists believe that particles acquire their mass and their individual properties from this field through the Boson (from the Indian Scientist S. N. Bose). The SSC was designed to conduct experiments within a 54-mile underground circular chamber, accelerating subatomic particles to 99.9999 percent the speed of light and smashing them together at combined energies of 40 trillion electron volts. The thought was that this would provide answers to fundamental questions about the formation of the universe. While it is dangerous to predict how much society stood to gain from this research, many believe that the benefits could have been enormous. In their view, past, pure science research, like that of the first atom splitting, led to the discovery of nuclear energy, quantum theory, and most of the electrical and computer technology we take for granted today (12).

But all that will need to remain forever as mere speculation. On Oct. 19, 1993, Congress—after spending $2 billion on the SSC project—unceremoniously pulled the plug, ending eleven years of effort and putting 2,000 people out of work (13). Certainly there were problems with the SSC. Cost had ballooned, largely due to increasing technical specifications, and schedule was slipping correspondingly. But the real problem facing SSC management was not technical, or budgetary, or schedule related. The real problem was politics. Whatever one's view of the merits of the SSC, the budget review process of Congress is a messy affair in which politicians tend to view scientific projects as a type of pork to be parceled around the country. But the SSC seems never to have been understood, either by the public or Congress. It is interesting to note that in the 280 to 150 vote in the House to ax the SSC, not more than 20 percent of Congress had any understanding whatsoever of the technical aspects of the project (14).

Another political problem facing the SSC was the lack of support from the Clinton Administration. As Congressman Joe Barton, R-Texas, described what killed the SSC: "If you boil it down to one word, Clinton" (15).

There was never more than a lukewarm acceptance of the SSC from the Clinton Administration, and when the going got tough there was only concern for the budget deficit.

Part of successful project management involves managing the pertinent political interfaces. In this regard, SSC management was somewhat less than successful. SSC managers campaigned for good will at universities, schools, scientific meetings, and the like. This "preaching to the choir" failed to convey the benefits of the project to the real decision-makers: the Clinton Administration and the members of Congress. Even the few well-conceived public relations efforts ran into bad luck. For example, a procession of SSC luminaries assembled in Washington, including several Nobel laureates, for one last major media offensive. But their presentation turned out to be at the same moment as the historic Rabin-Arafat handshake signaling the possibility of peace in the Middle East. Not a single television camera turned up to cover the scientists (16).

The project also suffered from an identity crisis. It was difficult to figure out if this big science project was to make America first in basic science, or if it was a world science project. In 1987–88, under President Reagan, United States international specialists led discussions with friends and allies that led to foreign commitments to contribute as much as $1 billion to the SSC. But in the Bush Administration, the importance of an international approach to the SSC was ignored, and foreign investors, not surprisingly, pulled out.

For a project that would have cost only 0.2 percent of the national research budget (17), the SSC assumed a symbolic importance way beyond its economic significance. It became, in fact, a symbol of fiscal irresponsibility. For all the billions spent, the truth was that the SSC produced very few jobs, at very high cost, most in a very limited geographical area. The SSC was situated south of Dallas in Waxahachie, Texas, and was to generate about 2000 jobs at the cost of $4.7 million per job (18). With limited economic importance beyond Texas, the SSC had few backers in Congress. Without former Texas senator Lloyd Bentsen in the Senate to champion it, the SSC became a prime target of budget cutters, concerned with a $4 trillion deficit and unmoved by the SSC's limited appeal as a "Texas project."

The project's negative press wasn't helped by news of millions being spent on parties at ritzy hotels, liquor, plants, and to ensure art work (19). The widespread dislike of the senior SSC officials in the Clinton administration didn't help either. Energy Secretary Hazel O'Leary commented on the high sense of self importance and arrogance among the top SSC officials who were denying access to confidential information to auditors from federal agencies (20). Other scientists—perhaps jealous of the SSC budget—claimed that the SSC was undermining the credibility of all science. Worse still, J. Peter Grace's Citizens Against Government Waste picked the SSC from a list of hundreds of government projects and recommended its cancellation. The Grace group also enlisted the support of Friends of the Earth, the Senior Coalition, and other groups, not to mention a few high-profile scientists (21).

LESSONS LEARNED

Projects can, and do, succeed because of politics. And they *fail* because of politics as well. The contrasting fates of the interstate highway system and the superconducting supercollider provide lessons that apply to any large publicly funded program. Among those lessons are:

1. The need to tell the story of the project in a way that's clear not only to the techno-wizards, but to the masses as well. We can all understand a highway system. We could even all understand President Kennedy's call to put a man on the moon. But the concept of a 54-mile donut-atom-smasher? One that could tell us the origins of the universe? And one that's underground, no less? Perhaps Congress can be forgiven its inability to understand all the technical aspects of the SSC—very few nonphysicists, in Congress or not, seem able to grasp the concepts involved.

2. The need for top management to be fully behind the project. Eisenhower staked the credibility of the American presidency on the interstate system. Four decades later, President Clinton—distracted perhaps by health care and the North American Free Trade Agreement—barely lifted a hand to save the SSC. As is so often the case in the private sector, the support of top management is crucial. Such support does not guarantee success, but the lack of it can go a long way toward ensuring failure.

3. The need for project managers to "sell" their project to non-believers. In some ways, the tendency of SSC managers to talk to scientific audiences and college campuses is understandable; it's a great deal easier to market to those we believe are predisposed to our point of view. But while it may be understandable, it's exactly the wrong thing to do. Project managers must communicate with all their constituencies, especially the contentious ones. Those audiences are the show-stoppers, and you ignore them at your peril.

4. Benefits must be widespread. Contrast the interstate system, which can truly be said to have shaped nearly every American life over the past forty years, with the SSC: only a relative handful of jobs provided at great cost to people who were, by and large, readily employable elsewhere. The successful public project draws its support from the masses, and that support can most readily come when the benefit is most broadly based.

FINAL THOUGHTS

People without a sense of history are proclaiming an end to war, and thus to large defense projects, and others see the death of the SSC as the end of "big science." But both views are surely short-sighted. Large public projects have existed since the time of the Pharaohs, and it's unlikely that they're suddenly finished for all time. But whether in defense, or science, or public works, the lessons are the same: successful project management means successful political management as well.

REFERENCES

1. Rosenau, Jr., M. D. 1992. *Successful Project Management* New York: Van Nostrand Reinhold, p. 15.

2. Kerzner, H. 1989. *Project Management: A Systems Approach to Planning, Scheduling and Controlling* (3rd Edition). New York: Van Nostrand Reinhold, pp. 5–6.

3. Morris, P. W. G., and G. H. Hough. 1987. *The Anatomy of Major Projects.* Chichester England: John Wiley & Sons, p. 21.

4. Ibid., pp. 21–22, 37–38.

5. "Eisenhower Bids States Join U.S. In Vast Road Plan," 1954. *New York Times*, July 13.

6. Rose, M. H. 1979. *Interstate Express Highway Politics, 1941–1956.* Lawrence, KS: The Regents Press of Kansas. p. 70.

7. "Eisenhower Bids States Join U.S. In Vast Road Plan." Op. cit.

8. "Clay Says Road Program Needs $26 Billion More Than Planned." 1954. *New York Times*, Nov. 12; also "Eisenhower Gets 101 Billion Federal-State Road Plan." 1955. *New York Times*, Jan. 12.

9. Rose, M. H. Op cit., pp. 80–83.

10. Ibid.

11. Ibid., pp. 91–93.

12. "Subatomic Secrets, Nobel Laureate Pens A Side-Splitting Physics, And The Planned Texas Supercollider." 1993. *San Jose Mercury News*, March 30.

13. "Smashing The Supercollider." 1993. *Newsweek*, Nov. 1.

14. "The Best Sitcom On TV: Congress And The Budget." 1993. *Detroit Free Press*, June 29.

15. "Lawmakers: Budget Cutting Mood, Scathing Criticism Brought Down Collider." 1993. Associated Press, Oct. 24.

16. "Superconducting Supercollider Project Hangs On Edge." 1993. *Boston Globe*, Sept. 27.

17. "Science's Newest Frontier." 1993. Lexington Herald (KY), Sept. 25.

18. "Texas Candidates Scramble In Race For U.S. Senate Seat." 1993. *Christian Science Monitor*, Mar. 31.

19. "Lawmakers: Budget Cutting Mood, Scathing Criticism Brought Down Collider." 1993. Associated Press, Oct. 24.

20. "Energy Secretary Says She's Planning Shakeup On Collider Project" 1993. *Fort-Worth Star-Telegram*, July 1.

21. "The Last Behemoth." 1993. *The Washington Post*, Aug. 4.

Study Questions

THE POWER OF POLITICS: THE FOURTH DIMENSION OF MANAGING THE LARGE PUBLIC PROJECT

1. Besides politics there are numerous other factors that play a role in the success or failure of a project. Identify five to six of those elements and discuss the most critical among them.

2. The paper states that the interstate highway system project was successful because, among other factors, "the act offered something to everyone, and aroused the ire of almost no one." The statement clearly refers to the project stakeholders. Develop a list of the common stakeholders of any project.

3. What does the author mean by "the fourth dimension of managing"?

4. Aside from the superconducting supercollider, there are other examples of large projects that were terminated primarily because of political considerations. From your own experience or the literature find and discuss another example with the class. What could have prevented the termination of the project?

The Environmental and Molecular Sciences Laboratory Project: Continuous Evolution in Leadership

D.E. Knutson, PMP

J.K. McClusky, Pacific Northwest Laboratory

PMI Canada *Proceedings*, 1994, pp. 923–29

INTRODUCTION

The Environmental and Molecular Sciences Laboratory (EMSL) construction project at Pacific Northwest Laboratory (PNL) in Richland, Washington, is a $230 million major systems acquisition for the U.S. Department of Energy (DOE). The completed laboratory will be a national user facility that provides unparalleled capabilities for scientists involved in environmental molecular science research. This project, approved for construction by the Secretary of Energy in October 1993, is under way. In this paper, PNL's role as the integrating contractor, the historical leadership challenges faced by the project, the significance of the project's location near the DOE's Hanford site, and a forecast of challenges for the future are discussed.

Background

The United States (U.S.) is embarking on an environmental cleanup effort that dwarfs previous scientific enterprise. Using current best available technology, the projected costs of cleaning up the tens of thousands of toxic waste sites, including DOE sites, is estimated to exceed one trillion dollars (1). That level of expenditure contains no guarantee that the sites can be restored to their original condition, and no consensus on "how clean is clean enough."

"Ultimately, the scientific challenge is to determine as accurately as possible each term in the path that links the source of the contaminant with the particular biological end points or health effects and to understand the mechanisms that connect them. However, the present state of scientific knowledge regarding the effects of exogenous chemicals on human biology is very limited. Understanding the connections at the molecular level is, at best, a blurred picture and often a black box" (2). Long-term environmental research at the molecular level is needed to resolve the concerns; and form the building blocks for a structure of cost-effective process improvement and regulatory reform.

The current definition of the EMSL project was initiated in 1990 to begin building the scientific base necessary to address some of the concerns identified above. Capabilities that have been implemented in the EMSL and will be brought to bear in developing cost effective solutions include:

Material Inventory (metric tons)

Nuclear Material	Uranium (4,100)	
	Irradiated Fuel (2,700)	
	Cs/Sr Capsules (15)	
	Special Nuclear Material (85)	
Tank Waste	Single Shell Tank Waste (230,000)	
	Double Shell Tank Waste (130,000)	
	Tank Structures (410,000)	
Environmental Contamination	Contaminated Soil and Overburden (125,000,000)	
	Contaminated Groundwater (1,100,000,000)	
Solid Waste	Stored Solid Waste (850)	
	Buried Solid Waste and Overburden (400,000)	
D&D	Facilities (430,000)	

FIGURE 1   MATERIAL INVENTORY

- surface chemistry to understand the interfaces and chemical interactions between solid/gas and solid/liquid surfaces in the environment
- materials and interphase chemistry to understand and expand epitaxial science and application of remote sensors in characterization and process control efforts
- molecular biology to understand the measurable health effects of radiation or hazardous chemical insult to the human and natural environment
- massively parallel computing to advance the capability of molecular modeling, rational enzyme design, plume interaction, very large data set manipulation, and rational process design
- advanced process engineering to speed the transfer of technology from the laboratory to field applications
- environmental dynamics capabilities to understand the scale up from nanoscale molecular to macroscale environmental solutions
- state-of-the-art communications, training, and interaction systems to provide the link for other researchers, national laboratories, industry, and academia to extend collaborative capabilities and bring EMSL to bear on their needs.

The background discussion above is provided to show the breadth and impact of EMSL. It is important to keep this complexity in mind during the following discussion of location, integration, planning, and future challenges.

Location

The Hanford nuclear site near Richland, Washington is a 560-square-mile reservation established in the 1940s to produce plutonium for the nuclear weapons programs of the United States. Approximately 5 percent of the Hanford site land area is occupied by facilities that contribute to the complex

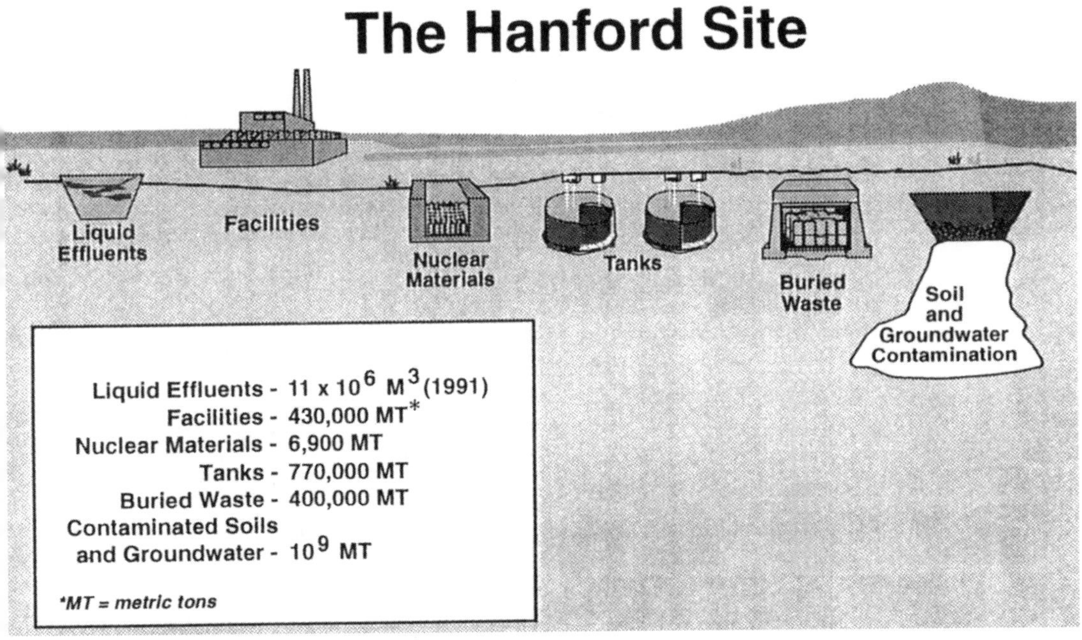
The Hanford Site
Liquid Effluents
Facilities
Nuclear Materials
Tanks
Buried Waste
Soil and Groundwater Contamination
Liquid Effluents - 11 x 10^6 M^3 (1991)
Facilities - 430,000 MT*
Nuclear Materials - 6,900 MT
Tanks - 770,000 MT
Buried Waste - 400,000 MT
Contaminated Soils and Groundwater - 10^9 MT
*MT = metric tons

FIGURE 2 SITE CONTAMINANTS

contaminant streams identified below. Due to disposal practices of the past and leaking storage facilities of the present, the Hanford site contains some of the DOE's most scientifically challenging waste cleanup problems:

- one-third of all DOE's inactive waste sites
- one-half of DOE's transuranic waste
- two-thirds of DOE's high-level waste volume
- one-third of DOE's high-level waste radioactivity.

Visualizations of this statement are provided in Figures 1 and 2. As shown, the quantities are defined in metric tons to illustrate the magnitude and complexity of the Hanford cleanup effort. Estimates of this remediation challenge alone range from $50 to $100 billion. The impact of the challenge is significant, and the hard work of the past several decades has led to development of technology applications that are sufficient to begin the characterization and remediation effort. Where appropriate, those efforts are under way (3). But, as obvious as it seems for getting on with restoration, it is equally obvious that existing technology will not be able accomplish the task in an acceptable time frame, or at a cost that is acceptable within current fiscal and legal constraints (4). A long-range focus is needed to provide an infusion of new technology, improvements in existing technology, and a scientific basis for regulatory change. These challenges must be met to bring efficiencies to the restoration effort and make the process "better, faster, and cheaper." The location of the EMSL, near the Hanford site, was driven by the potential ability of this facility to draw the scientific talent to the problem and use that talent in collaboration with other researchers to have an impact on these challenges (5, 6).

Integration

DOE Richland Operations (DOE-RL) manages multiple prime contracts responsible for various maintenance, operations, and technology functions at Hanford. Pacific Northwest Laboratory (PNL) was selected as the integrating contractor to pull responsible individuals and groups into a functioning team (7). The term used to describe that teaming effort is an "integrated management team (IMT)." Figure 3 illustrates the structure of that team. In this effort, PNL has specific responsibility to adequately bring cleanup efforts to closure for overall project management, development, design, and procurement of research and computer equipment, facility and interface design coordination, and business management functions. Facility design was provided by a fixed-price A/E contract with Zimmer Gunsul Frasca (ZGF) Partnership from Portland, Oregon. Facility construction is via fixed-price contract with the Grant/Apollo Joint Venture of Richland, Washington, and construction management services are provided by ICF Kaiser Hanford Company. Landlord functions, site services, and the site infrastructure systems are provided by Westinghouse Hanford Company. At the completion of the project, PNL will be responsible for start-up and long-term operation of the facility.

The external teaming between six corporate entities using PNL as the integrator to implement the EMSL project was significant and has been a challenge. Effective communication between and among contractors, as well as clear understanding of roles and responsibilities was imperative. Scope definition played a major part in achieving that understanding. The success of the EMSL project through the start of construction was due in part to the willingness of the IMT contractors to participate in the organizational structure and foster the teaming relationships that were required. Two important lessons for the future of IMT contracting are: early definition and acceptance of team responsibilities, and identification of leadership willing to accept those responsibilities. The integrating contractor must play a central role in information collection and dissemination, as well as in implementation of work scope. The IMT structure must efficiently provide that information and foster implementation. Without the teaming relationships and role acceptance in place, the management process of the IMT devolves to oversight functions, which draw resources away from the project's primary task, and add an unnecessary overhead to the project.

As significant as the IMT organizational structure was, the teaming and integration required within PNL was possibly the greatest challenge. A matrix organization consisting of personnel drawn from eleven research, technical, and support organizations was created to handle the myriad technical, regulatory, and documentation efforts of the project. The combinations of scientific need and project constraints were integrated through the design of eighty-four individual laboratories and seven research organizations that will occupy the facility. As the future unfolds, the integration of the EMSL into the broader capabilities of the National Laboratory system and specifically into the role and vision of the DOE and PNL will continue to challenge the leadership skills of management.

The integration of the EMSL extends beyond the confines of the Hanford site. The permitting process for the facility involves strong interaction with the state of Washington and the local government of the area known as

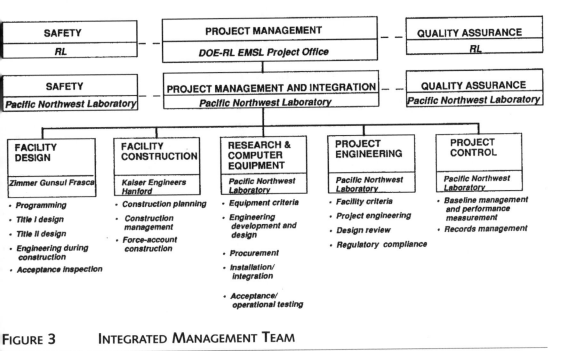

EMSL
Integrated Management Team

FIGURE 3   INTEGRATED MANAGEMENT TEAM

the Tri-Cities. Local and state regulations were taken into consideration in the design and planning of the EMSL and, as a result, the permitting process proceeded effectively. An awareness for cultural resource preservation resulted in interactive involvement between the State Department of Ecology, the regional Native American tribes, and the IMT.

As an example, the formal groundbreaking ceremony for the EMSL was held Friday, April 8, 1994. Heavy equipment was moved to the site Monday, April 11, to begin clearing and excavation. On Tuesday, April 12, a Native American burial ground was uncovered. Existing plans required the presence of an archaeologist during site excavation and included plans for dealing with cultural resources. These were immediately implemented, and the heavy equipment was moved to another portion of the site. On April 13, another burial site was uncovered, and the site excavation process was halted. This included a suspension of all contractor activities at the site. From April 13–18 planning was implemented to identify the actions required to move the EMSL construction site away from the burial ground. The list of actions included three key events: first, the selection of a new site which required transfer of private property donated by Battelle Memorial Institute to the U.S. Department of Energy, with approval by the U.S. Department of Justice; second, a revised Environmental Assessment (EA) and Finding of No Significant Impact (FONSI) reviewed by the state of Washington and the regional Native American tribes; third, a site and foundation redesign to move a tri-level building from a sloping river site to a flat farm land site. To minimize construction costs, construction had to be re-initiated by mid July and all of the above actions had to be completed within ninety days. Needless to say, the approval process had to be streamlined.

The U.S. Department of Justice approved the land transfer within ten working days following a strong teaming effort between the legal staffs of Battelle, DOE-RL, and DOE-HQ that cut the overall preparation time for this transfer to thirty days. The land transfer action was completed June 16, pending a FONSI determination, when the Secretary of Energy accepted the donation of the property.

The EA and FONSI actions were completed in record time by having approval authority for both the EA determination and FONSI delegated from DOE-HQ in Washington D.C. to the local Richland Field Office. The review processes in place with the state of Washington and the regional Native American tribes, as well as face-to-face meetings and follow-up, cut the EA process from the usual eight to sixteen months to two months.

Finally, the building redesign was initiated in parallel with the land transfer and EA approval process. Once the decision was made by the Department of Energy to move the building site, on April 22, the A/E contract was modified and redesign began. Most of the existing building design was utilized, which allowed the construction contractor to resume work and restart the construction submittal process. The remainder of the redesign was completed quickly, and a site package was issued in mid-July. The three key actions were completed in ninety-one days, and the construction contractor was shut down for less than one week in that period. The cost of this relocation was minimized by the efforts above and resulted in a total impact of about 2 percent of project cost.

Integration and cooperation between the IMT, DOE-HQ, DOE-RL, the state of Washington, the regional Native American tribes, and the U.S. Department of Justice were critical to successful recovery from a situation that could have easily stopped the EMSL project completely. A lesson for the future is that integration of management and review processes is necessary and not easy. Yet, effective integration can start with as simple a teaming step as inviting a concerned stakeholder to witness key events, such as clearing and foundation excavation, to ensure that her interests are protected.

The process of integration for the EMSL project is not complete. The fabric representing the collaborative nature of the facility is only now beginning to take shape. Ties to DOE's Hanford environmental management programs, industry, academic, and national laboratory collaborations have been instituted and must now be broadened and strengthened. In its function as a national user facility, the EMSL will support interests from around the world. The IMT will change as the evolution of EMSL continues, and the integration processes in place now will set the stage for the future.

Planning and Controls

The EMSL has demonstrated a strong management control system that complies with the DOE orders governing major systems acquisitions (MSA) (8). There is a significant review history that resulted in making the management systems successful. Multiple reviews occurred on this project between conceptual design and approval of construction. Within this review process and evolution of the project, the project scope was managed to cost and the total project cost (TPC) maintained at $218 million. It has only been at the Key Decision No. 3 date, when approval and funding delays threatened the entire functional capability of the project, that the TPC was increased to $230 million. A consistent approach to scope management, and cost estimate maintenance, is a continually reinforced lesson learned for future major projects.

A logical question would be how scope could be managed in a research environment to accommodate this consistency. A unique occurrence in the research environment at PNL was the initiation of a scope definition process for the EMSL called the research work plan. This process was initiated in 1992 at the request of the DOE to reach agreement on the baselines, methods for equipment development, and other activities that would be provided as part of the EMSL project.

It is unique to this project that all technical activities are governed by a work plan. For developmental activities, the document is written by the individual scientist and describes the boundaries to be placed on creative energy. These boundaries are described in terms of the scientific driver for the equipment development, technical and cost risks that would potentially impact completion, and a complete description of the thought process and decision points to be maintained during development. For the project manager, it is an opportunity to describe the baseline controls and performance measures to be implemented in gauging progress. The process is useful in allowing the project manager to visualize the "end state" of development, and the scientist to visualize the controls that will be used to demonstrate completion and success. In practice, the document is used to resolve differences between expectation and intention, and to implement the cost, schedule, and technical baselines for the project.

The DOE has been aggressive in its implementation of better business practices across the National Laboratory and Weapon Complex institutions. Within that implementation effort it is important to recognize that the scope definition process is the single greatest asset to successful project implementation. For the EMSL project, in a National Laboratory setting, the implementation of the work plans and baseline controls demonstrate a useful lesson learned.

Future Challenges

The future holds many unknowns, not the least of which is the vagaries of administration that govern the National Laboratory system. However, the realities of shrinking budgets, demand for quantifiable return on investments, and competition for resources will continue. The past provides insight into dealing with the future. The EMSL is one of only a handful of major projects providing research capabilities that were supported by the DOE through the mid-1990s. Why did EMSL succeed when other projects did not? As previously discussed, there were many reviews critical to the life of the EMSL project. There were shifts in DOE sponsorship from The Office of Energy Research to The Office of Environmental Restoration and Waste Management and back to Energy Research. There were critical action items to define the basic justification for EMSL and reflect the management practices of the sponsoring organization. Each review clarified the EMSL mission and validated the fundamental need for its capabilities. It is again unique to this project that the fundamental vision, identified in 1988, has not been significantly altered and has withstood the challenges mounted in the review process. In that process lies a lesson for the future. The definition and vision of our major projects must be clear. Major projects must be visionary in scope and realistic in application. The vision of EMSL forecasts a need for significant improvement in process efficiency, methods, characterization, and regulatory interpretation through the use of molecular science. This was realistic and necessary to effectively deal with restoration of sites with a complex mixture of contaminants such as exists at Hanford. To implement that vision required an expanded scientific base. Hindsight shows that the vision of EMSL was not in alignment with contemporary thinking in 1988. Legal requirements of the time, requiring application of existing technology and demonstrating progress utilizing that technology, reflect that fact. The challenge that the EMSL project met was to define the capabilities of EMSL in a way that identified its relevant application, fundamental need, and feasibility of completion in a way that could be understood and accepted.

The challenge for the future is to build on the EMSL capabilities without allowing ourselves or our customers to believe that EMSL will solve all the problems or do the job alone. The unique significance of EMSL is in its ability to focus talent on a relevant problem. Like the magnifying glass that focuses sunlight to create a flame, the future success of the EMSL, and the return on investment to the taxpayer, depends on the ability to funnel the collaborative interests of a broad range of scientific talent, much of it external to PNL. To achieve this focus, the processes of integration, business practices, and planning and controls that defined success for the EMSL project must evolve into the long-term future operation of the laboratory. They can not be discarded.

The EMSL Legacy

The EMSL project has been, by any quantitative measure, very successful. It has demonstrated innovation in management structure and creativity in problem resolution. The project has taken an aggressive stance by implementing baseline controls in a research setting and by demonstrating a visionary application for its capabilities. The project has minimized risk with most of the current or innovative state-of-the-art equipment under contract, the building construction under way, and the management systems in place to control the project outcome with reasonable accuracy. The completed laboratory will provide a comprehensive and unique capability that does not exist anywhere else in the world. If its full potential is achieved, the EMSL will form the foundation for a Department of Energy and National Laboratory mission that begins to address the outcome of years of nuclear weapons production. It can establish new meaning for "value science" and return on investment in the research arena. The EMSL legacy is one of hope and intellectual focus that can redirect and stimulate a new scientific discipline in environmental molecular science. Within that science is the capability to address many of the challenges faced by the DOE. The EMSL legacy is limited only by its ability to draw from the capabilities, and stimulate the interests, of the Department of Energy, industry, the National Laboratory system, and academia.

Acknowledgment

The EMSL Construction Project at PNL is being funded by the DOE Office of Energy Research. Pacific Northwest Laboratory is a multiprogram national laboratory operated for the DOE by Battelle Memorial Institute under Contract DE-AC06-76RL0 1830.

REFERENCES

1. "Remediation of Hazardous Waste Sites."1992. *Science* 255, no. 5047, Feb. 21, p. 901.

2. "Complex Cleanup: The Environmental Legacy of Nuclear Weapons Production." 1991. Congress of the United States, Office of Technology Assessment, Feb.

3. "Hanford Cleanup—New Technologies to Treat the Nation's Nuclear Waste." 1993. *Chemical and Engineering News*, June 21.

4. The Hanford Federal Facility Agreement and Consent Order, May 1989 as amended.

5. Site Evaluation, Environmental and Molecular Sciences Laboratory. 1991. Stone and Webster Engineering Company for the Department of Energy, Aug.

6. Record of EMSL Siting Meeting, Memorandum for Distribution, Office of Science and Technology for Civilian R&D, dated May 13, 1993.

7. Establishment of the Environmental and Molecular Sciences Laboratory (EMSL) at Pacific Northwest Laboratory, Memorandum from Eric J. Fygi, Acting General Counsel to Tom A. Hendrickson, Acting Under Secretary and Acquisition Executive, Dated June 5, 1992.

8. Independent Management Systems Review Report. 1993. MAC Technical Services Company for the Department of Energy.

Study Questions

THE ENVIRONMENTAL AND MOLECULAR SCIENCES LABORATORY PROJECT: CONTINUOUS EVOLUTION IN LEADERSHIP

1. The authors highlight the importance of having a clear mission and objectives in the project. What does it mean to have a project with a clear mission and objectives?

2. The case also mentions the importance of scope management in a research environment. Define scope management for any project.

3. The relocation process was carried out very successfully and only meant a 2 percent over-cost. To which factor do you attribute this accomplishment?

4. The authors state: "The challenge that the EMSL project met was to define the capabilities of EMSL in a way that identified their relevant application, fundamental need, and feasibility of completion in a way that could be understood and accepted." What would be some of the consequences of not defining the capabilities in this way?

5. The authors state: "A matrix organization consisting of personnel drawn from eleven research, technical, and support organizations was created to handle the myriad technical, regulatory, and documentation efforts of the project." Discuss the advantages and disadvantages of the matrix organization.

Chrysler and Artemis: Striking Back with the Viper

Stephen W.T. O'Keeffe

Industrial Engineering, December 1994, pp. 15–17

There is no room for complacency in today's supply-heavy automotive industry. Faced with offerings from a broad array of domestic and foreign suppliers, 1990s consumers are demanding greater functionality, reliability, performance, and fuel efficiency, as well as improved safety features. Only those manufacturers that meet consumers' expectations will survive. As Lee Iacocca put it, "in this market you either lead, follow, or get out of the way." Today's Chrysler is neither a follower nor a spectator.

Aware that the only way to succeed in this intense market is to deliver superior products at a competitive price, Chrysler has focused its attention on achieving that goal, completely reassessing established design and production methodologies and systems. In order to achieve its goal, it was imperative that Chrysler slash product introduction cycles—allowing it to incorporate technical advances in its vehicle's more quickly and rationalize production processes—to ensure price competitiveness. However, while expedition and streamlining were a major part of the task, they were by no means all of it. Employing its famous quality improvement process approach, Chrysler wanted speed and cost savings, but it was not prepared to sacrifice quality.

It was against this backdrop that Chrysler Corp. conceived the Dodge Viper, its high-performance sports car for the 1990s. When the concept car debuted at the North American International Auto Show in Detroit in January 1989, it was evident from the reaction of attendees, and from the sackloads of letters that arrived at Chrysler, that the corporation had developed a well-received product. But it was not until May 1990, when Iacocca gave the project the green light, that Chrysler focused on how to turn the Viper dream car into a reality.

Fashioned after the great roadsters of the 1960s and early 1970s, the Viper's designers envisioned it as the perfect marriage of yesterday's elegance and today's performance technologies and reliability. The team pictured the Viper as the ultimate beautiful muscle car, an eye-catching vehicle whose 0-to-100-to-0 mph, sub-fifteen-second performance would take your breath away.

However, the car was to be more than an exotic extravagance. Iacocca charged the Viper project with a critical role in reshaping the path of Chrysler's future. Nothing more than a beautiful shell in 1989, Iacocca gave the Viper team just three years to transform the concept into a production vehicle, involving the complete development of the vehicle—including the body, an all-new 8.0 liter V40 aluminum engine, and a six-speed high-performance transmission—a task that has traditionally taken five years. If the Viper team was successful, the project would set a precedent for all future vehicle development at Chrysler.

Facing such tight deadlines, a multitude of variables, and working with finite resources, Chrysler recognized that consistent, end-to-end project management would be quintessential for success. Therefore, the corporation was very selective about the components that went into the project. Working on such a high-stakes program, Chrysler could not afford to internalize any weaknesses. Personnel was hand picked for the project. Employing that same commitment to excellence after reviewing the project management systems on the market, Chrysler chose Artemis Prestige from Lucas Management Systems.

Roy Sjoberg, team Viper executive engineer, outlines Chrysler's functional project management systems requirements: "Front-end planning and subsequent process engineering and reengineering were an implicit part of the task that lay before us. We needed a sophisticated tool that was capable of handling multiple projects concurrently and interactively. We needed a tool that would allow us to see the big picture and to gauge the impact of each operation on that panoramic view."

Sjoberg points to his experience with earlier versions of Prestige as a significant factor in the project management system selection process. He had used the application to manage the design of vehicle interiors with great success. "Almost everything was new on the Viper program. In this uncertain environment, we knew that we could rely on Prestige to meet our project management requirements," he notes. "Viper represented a clean slate for Chrysler," said Sjoberg. "This was our chance to cut to the bone, ensuring the efficiency of all processes."

WHAT IF

Sjoberg explains that Chrysler recognized that significant process reengineering would be necessary if the project was to fulfill the corporation's goals. "Working with finite resources and within tight time parameters, we could not afford to target all processes for reengineering. We had to identify the significant obstacles that stood between us and our three-year development goal, targeting any problem processes on the front end," he says. "The software's powerful what-if capability, coupled with its multi-project vision, gave us the insight to do this."

Sjoberg goes on to explain how his team used the application's what-if capacity to project the impact of changes in resource allocations, or of process restructuring and reengineering, on the Viper's big picture or critical path plan. "It enabled us to gauge the effect of any change before committing to it," he says. "What-if helped us recognize those processes that most needed attention, and to identify where resource redistribution could have the greatest impact on net yield."

However, no matter how careful the front-end planning, no project—especially one involving a number of external suppliers—is ever totally free of unforeseeable problems. To prevent this, Chrysler made great use of the software's what-if capabilities in damage control.

"A glitch or delay in one critical area can undermine an otherwise trouble-free project," says Sjoberg. "Like every project, Viper had its teething problems. However, rather than letting the problem happen to us, we used the software to take a very proactive stance."

Sjoberg explains how, when a problem cropped up, the team would input the delay into the project management network, observing its impact on Viper's critical path plan. "We could see immediately whether the problem was significant and gauge precisely what action to take," he notes. "If the delay threatened other processes, and through them our total goal, we were able to reallocate resources to remove the obstacle. Hence, as we could see the impact of any process on the total scheme, we were able to anticipate any potential bottlenecks, and ensure that the total project never left the tracks."

Likening the development process to a journey, Sjoberg stresses that a diversion from a plotted route is only worthwhile if it reduces the total travel time. "Any discerning traveler would want to know precisely where an alternative route will lead, and what its impact will be on the total travel time before taking it. The new software has been our road map for success on the journey from inception to delivery of the Viper."

AN ECLECTIC UNDERTAKING

Involving total design and development from scratch, Viper would have presented a classic project management challenge, even if Chrysler had taken a traditional approach to the program. However, not content to develop each high-performance component in record time, Chrysler was determined to stretch the parameters of vehicle design and construction processes at the same time. Achieving the individual goals established for each component and simultaneously implementing innovative technologies heaped additional pressure on the project management function to ensure that all elements moved ahead in a coordinated fashion. The Viper team pioneered several automotive innovations for a mass market vehicle:

• **Engine.** Less than a year after the formation of the engine feasibility team, Chrysler had its first 8.0 liter V-10 test engine. Timely completion was essential for development of the transmission and other components.

• **Transmission.** Accomplishing a five- to six-year task in just eighteen months, the Viper team produced a Jekyll-and-Hyde six-speed manual box, capable of unleashing the full torque of the engine to achieve 0–60 acceleration in 4.5 seconds, or of smooth gear changes that permit the Viper to be classified as an "easy shifter."

• **Frame.** The team rejected conventional-stamped steel construction, selecting tubular steel which offered significant time savings without compromising strength.

• **Body.** In search of a better and less labor-intensive panel construction process, the Viper team developed Resin Transfer Molding (RTM) on the Viper. The first car in the United States market with the majority of its body panels, inner and outer, produced using the RTM process, the technology produces panels that are 40 percent tighter than conventional-stamped sheet metal parts, without sacrificing strength or safety. The RTM process offers significant quality improvement over established synthetic panel-forming processes, including greater durability and improved quality of finish.

RTM has slashed the retooling lead time associated with changes i body styling. This will allow Chrysler to respond more rapidly to emergin consumer tastes.

- **Brakes.** Slowing a vehicle from 100 mph to rest in less than five second would require an extraordinary braking system. The team developed a fou pot (piston) caliper front brake disc system—usually only seen on race cars— along with ventilated rear, single-piston slider brakes.

The project management software provided the communications net work that assured the program's success, working both on the micro leve within each component, and on the macro scale, to ensure that critical link ages between elements were made according to plan.

The first Vipers that were scheduled to arrive in May 1992 were all spo ken for before they even arrived at dealers. Beyond the glitz and sheen of new sports car roll-out, the Viper program established new standards for ex cellence at Chrysler. End-to-end, enterprise-wide project management ha proven itself as an essential ingredient in the corporation's recipe for suc cess. "At today's Chrysler, budgets are tight and adhered to," says Sjoberg "Though there was a learning curve associated with Prestige's logic and sys tems operations, consistent with our long run philosophy, the investmen has been well worth the pay off," he notes.

Study Questions

CHRYSLER AND ARTEMIS: STRIKING BACK WITH THE VIPER

1. Chrysler had to shorten its product introduction cycles in order to be com petitive in the automotive industry. What are the general characteristics of a project life-cycle?

2. Discuss the competitive advantages of reducing product development time in the automobile industry and other industries.

3. The management of the project was able to analyze various scenario through the use of the "what if" feature of the software. What are the key el ements to take into account in developing a project's schedule?

4. Explain the advantages that Artemis (the project management software brought to the Viper project. How did these advantages contribute to a short er product development time for Viper?

St Lucie Unit 2: A Nuclear Plant Built on Schedule

V. B. Derrickson, Director of Projects, Florida Power & Light Company

AMI *Proceedings*, 1983, pp. V-E-1–V-E-14

INTRODUCTION

Since the mid-1970s when nuclear power was the "energy source of the future" everything has seemed to go wrong for the ailing industry. From quality problems to financial problems, the entire industry has been shaken in one way or another. There have been no orders for nuclear plants in the United States since the mid-1970s.

Florida Power & Light Company (FPL) currently has four nuclear units in operation, with St. Lucie Unit 2 being the last to receive an operating license in June. Its sister Unit 1 received its license in 1976 and has, through 1982, compiled one of the best operating records in the United States.

The early days of Unit 2 were plagued with much of the same confusion and regulatory hassle that other units have experienced; but, upon receipt of the construction permit in June 1977, utilizing FPL and Ebasco experience gained during the construction and start-up of Unit 1, we were poised to attack the new project in a way that has enabled us to meet our objectives and complete the plant on schedule.

In the following pages, we describe what was accomplished and how it was done, utilizing a highly skilled project team with excellent tools, motivated to reach its goal.

WHAT WAS ACCOMPLISHED

The full power license for St. Lucie Unit 2 was received from the Nuclear Regulatory Commission (NRC) on June 10, 1983, just six years after construction began (see Figures 1 and 2). The industry average for construction of nuclear plants in this time period is about ten years (see Figure 3).

During the course of the project we were constantly on or near our schedule and always ahead of industry averages (see Figures 4 and 5). This was done despite issuance of numerous regulations by the NRC (TMI), a 1979 hurricane which did considerable damage to the Reactor Auxiliary Building, labor problems, and an NRC schedule review team that determined the best we could do was to complete the plant a year later.

The final price tag is about $1.42 billion, including allowance for funds used during construction (AFUDC). Many plants completed in this time frame are in the $2 to $5 billion range. By completing the plant on schedule our customers additionally benefit from the lower cost of nuclear fuel now. St. Lucie Unit 2 displaces about eight million barrels of imported oil annually.

FLORIDA POWER & LIGHT COMPANY

COMPARISON OF CONSTRUCTION START TO FUEL LOAD*

Plant	Fuel Load	Number of Months
MCGUIRE 1	1/81	117
LASALLE 1	4/82	103
GRAND GULF 1	5/82	92
SUSQUEHANNA	8/82	100
SUMMER 1	8/82	112
SHOREHAM 1	2/83	124
SAN ONOFRE 2	2/82	96
WATERFORD 3	5/83	102
ST. LUCIE 2	3/83	71
BYRON 1	8/83	100
ENRICO FERMI 2	6/83	169
COMANCHE PEAK 1	6/83	104
CALLAWAY 1	4/84	103
MIDLAND 2	7/83	124
WATTS BAR 1	8/83	127
PALO VERDE 1	8/83	87
WASHINGTON NUCLEAR 2	9/83	133
PERRY 1	11/83	109
SEABROOK 1	9/84	99
WOLF CREEK 1	10/84	93
LIMERICK 1	10/84	173
CATAWBA 1	10/84	125
HARRIS 1	12/84	131
BRAIDWOOD 1	4/85	116
RIVER BEND 1	4/85	72
BELLEFONTE 1	5/85	128
WASHINGTON NUCLEAR 3	6/85	98
MILLSTONE 3	12/85	139
BEAVER VALLEY2	12/85	140

*Source NRC Yellow Book —June 1982

FIGURE 1

In addition to the cost and schedule achievements, the performance of the plant operation to date indicates a quality technical effort as well. The hot functional test, for example, was completed in twenty-seven days versus an average of some two months for other plants. The fuel was loaded into the core in less than four days versus an industry average of eight to ten days.

In operation to date, the post core loading test program has been completed in less than two months, enabling us to put the plant into commercial operation only two months after its original scheduled date of May 28, 1983!

FLORIDA POWER & LIGHT COMPANY

COMPARISON OF CONSTRUCTION START TO COLD HYDRO

Plant	MWE	Number of Months
BYRON 1	1120	75
DIABLO CANYON 1	1084	84
FARLEY 2	829	82
McGUIRE 1	1180	88
NORTH ANNA 2	907	101
SALEM 2	870	125
SAN ONOFRE 2	1140	79
SEQUOYAH 1	1128	114
SEQUOYAH 2	1148	133
ST. LUCIE 2	**802**	**59**
SUMMER 1	900	79
WATTS BAR 1	1165	105
AVERAGE TIME (Months)		**95**

FIGURE 2

FLORIDA POWER & LIGHT COMPANY

PROGRESS VS. INDUSTRY PERFORMANCE

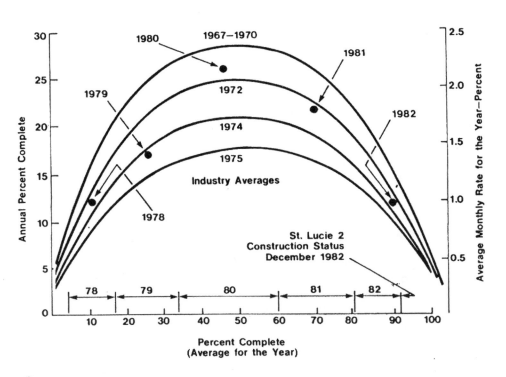

FIGURE 3

FLORIDA POWER & LIGHT COMPANY
COMPLETED MILESTONE ANALYSIS

ITEM	SCHEDULED	ACTUAL
CONSTRUCTION PERMIT	JUNE, 1977	
START RCB BASEMAT CONCRETE	07/06/77	07/07/77
START INTAKE STRUCT BASEMAT CONCRETE	10/15/77	10/01/77
START T.O. PEDESTAL MAT CONCRETE	12/15/77	10/15/77
START ERECT STEEL CONTAINMENT	1/18/78	12/21/77
START RAB BASEMENT CONCRETE	02/10/78	02/10/78
COMPLETE POST WELD HEAT TREATMENT	12/10/78	01/22/79
START M.S.T. STEEL ERECTION	12/28/78	02/12/79
START RCB INT. CONCRETE	01/17/79	11/07/78
START FHB BASEMAT CONCRETE	05/05/79	06/05/79
START PREOPERATIONAL TESTING	04/20/80	03/19/80
START SETTING NSSS MAJOR EQUIPMENT	06/18/80	06/22/80
COMPLETE RCB OPER FLOOR CONCRETE	09/23/80	10/17/80
SET CONTAINMENT VESSEL DOME	09/26/80	10/04/80
COMPLETE RAB EXT. CONCRETE	12/15/80	12/18/81
COMPLETE LOOP LARGE BORE PIPING	03/14/81	02/06/81
COMPLETE REFUELING WATER STORAGE TANK	04/30/81	04/28/81
COMPLETE RCB EXTERIOR SHIELD WALL CONCRETE	09/06/81	08/11/81
INTAKE COOLING WATER INT. MTR RUN	09/25/81	09/23/81
COMPLETE OCEAN DISCHARGE PPG (KIEWIT)	12/25/81	10/14/81
TURBINE ON TURNING GEAR	12/15/81	12/16/81

FIGURE 4

FLORIDA POWER & LIGHT COMPANY
COMPLETED MILESTONE ANALYSIS

ITEM	SCHEDULED	ACTUAL
ECCS FLOW TEST	01/04/82	01/13/82
SECONDARY HYDRO	02/04/82	02/04/82
COLD HYDRO	03/17/82	05/19/82
HOT FUNCTIONAL	07/03/82	10/21/82
ILRT	08/11/82	11/24/82
START SAFEGUARDS TEST	09/20/82	02/23/83
COMPLETE FUEL DELIVER	09/30/82	12/30/82
START CORE LOAD	10/28/82	04/06/83
HOT OPS II	11/30/82	05/07/83
START CRIT. & PERF TESTS	12/21/82	06/02/83
START PWR. ESCALATION (5% PWR)	01/05/83	06/13/83
COMMERCIAL OPERATION	05/28/83	08/08/83

FIGURE 5

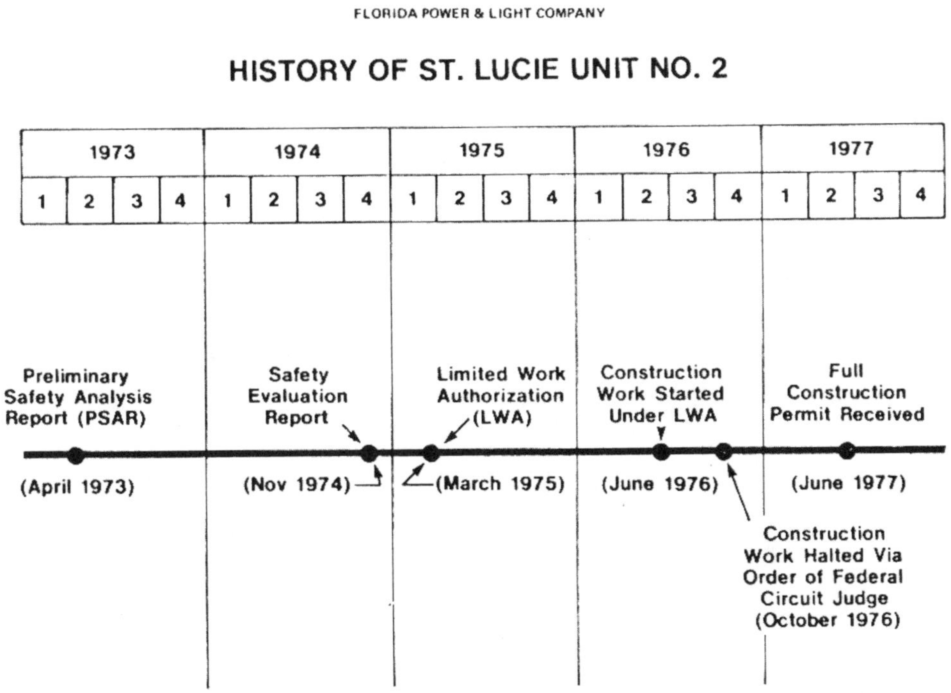

HISTORY OF ST. LUCIE UNIT NO. 2

FIGURE 6

How It Was Accomplished

History

Originally, construction of both St. Lucie 1 and 2 was planned to proceed concurrently, but then FPL decided to delay construction of the second unit due to a reduced load forecast. St. Lucie 1 started with construction forces moving on-site in late March 1969. The Atomic Energy Commission issued the construction permit on June 30, 1970, and first concrete placement for the Reactor Containment Building took place a week later. Installation of the nuclear steam supply system began in September 1973 and core loading, in March 1976. St. Lucie 1 began commercial operation in December 1976.

Work began on St. Lucie 2 in 1971, with initial efforts directed toward preparing the preliminary safety analysis report (PSAR), environmental report, and antitrust information required by the NRC before construction start. Although the PSAR was submitted for review in April 1973 (see Figure 6), subsequent meetings and site visits were conducted with the NRC staff to resolve such questions as site characteristics, radiological assessment, hydrology, geology, and seismology. Other discussions probed emergency planning, industrial security, and design features of the nuclear power plant. In response to these requests and discussions, an additional forty-four amendments were eventually docketed to the PSAR.

The NRC issued its safety evaluation report in November 1974, and in March 1975 awarded the limited work authorization. Construction work

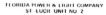

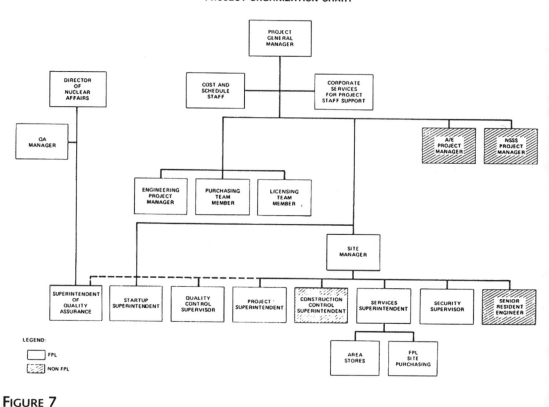

FIGURE 7

started in June 1976, after receiving state site certification, and was limited to excavation and foundation work up to existing grade level.

Four months later, however, construction work ceased and the work force was laid off. A regulation specified that the NRC study a number of potential sites before allowing any work to begin, whereas the staff of the licensing board had studied a hypothetical alternative to the St. Lucie site. After various appeals and site hearings the NRC eventually granted a construction permit in May 1977, but not before $60 million was added to the construction cost as a result of the work stoppage.

Management Commitment

In the early stages of the project, FPL established a project management organization to direct, inspect, survey, monitor, and audit the performance of all services performed by FPL contractor personnel and/or any subcontractors (see Figure 7). This organization is the contact with FPL on all contract-related matters and has the right of approval of all services and work performed.

A project general manager, through a project team organization, is FPL's designated representative having the responsibility and authority for the total management of the project.

In 1977, completion of St. Lucie 2 on schedule and within budget became one of FPL's corporate objectives. Thus, through the management by objectives program, all department objectives were required to support the project.

FIGURE 8

Project objectives were established annually to support completion of the project on schedule and within budget. Results were reported to management semiannually and corporate management assistance was provided when required.

Project Planning and Scheduling

During the period October 1976 to March 1977, a team of construction supervisors under FPL direction, developed what was to become the project master schedule. A sixty-five month schedule for the project (start of concrete to start of fuel loading) was established and major milestones were identified and fixed. This set the stage for all future planning. This schedule consisted of an integrated engineering and construction plan and included summary start-up logic.

The schedule philosophy adopted by the project was twofold: implement five levels of control and schedule development, and maintain key schedule indicators of project status.

A brief description of the five levels of schedule control can be seen in Figure 8.

Level I. The milestone schedule was developed by discipline by building. Approximately 200 activities were used to describe the total project with time indicated in months. It was updated quarterly for upper-level management information.

FLORIDA POWER & LIGHT COMPANY

IMPLEMENTATION SCHEDULE OF CONTROL TOOLS

ACTIVITY	YEAR							
	1976	1977	1978	1979	1980	1981	1982	1983
PROJECT MILESTONES	⇧ SHUTDOWN	⇧ RESTART			⇧ SET NSSS		⇧⇧ ECCS COLD HYDRO ⇧ HOT OPS I	⇧⇧ CORE LOAD POWER ESCALATION
PQMR (1)								
LEVEL II SCHEDULE		——————						
LEVEL III SCHEDULE			—————————————————————					
START-UP SCHEDULE					———————————————			
MATERIAL TRACKING				————————————————————				
PHYSICAL ACCOMPLISHMENT				————————————————				
EMS (2)								
REFORECASTING								
BULK COMMODITY CURVES					————————————			
BULK CONSTRUCTION		——————————————————————						
SYSTEM TURNOVER					———————————————			
TREND PROGRAM					———————————————————			
PCWL (3)								——

(1) PROJECT QUANTITY AND MANHOUR REPORT
(2) ELECTRICAL MANAGEMENT SYSTEM
(3) PROJECT COMPLETION WORK LIST

FIGURE 9

Level II. The master project schedule was broken down by system, build
ing, and area. Its purpose was to establish basic interfaces and schedule
parameters at a lower level of detail. The Level II integrated project schedule
had approximately 20,000 activities, including 10,000 construction activities

Level III. The detailed construction schedule depicted the way the pro
ject was actually to be carried out and monitored to the most current infor
mation. The Level III breakdown was by building, elevation, and cubic, and
included approximately 32,000 activities in total. Since it was developed on
a yearly look ahead, it replaced the old Level II logic.

Level IV. The work package level was a detailed planning tool designed
to capture all work within a predefined cubic. Fragnets were developed to
emphasize logic and construction sequencing. These manual fragnets were
then rolled up to form the Level III computer schedule. Work packages also
included bills of material and late material and engineering items.

Level V. "Two Week Look Ahead" was a manual bar chart reflecting daily
work schedules over a rolling two-week window. It was used for short internal
scheduling, manpower leveling, and requisitioning material from stores.

The second half of our scheduling philosophy was the use of indicators
i.e., control tools. An overview of most of our control tools and the timing of
their implementation can be seen in Figure 9. A few of the more visible in
dicators were productivity, schedule variance, physical accomplishment and
bulk quantity tables.

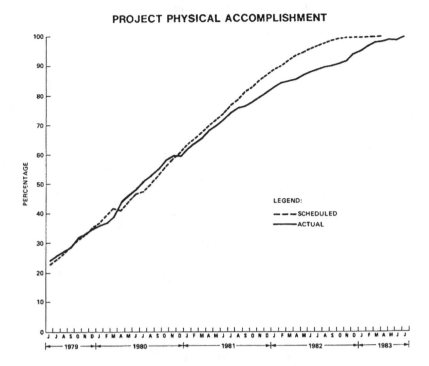

FLORIDA POWER & LIGHT COMPANY

PROJECT PHYSICAL ACCOMPLISHMENT

LEGEND:
- - - SCHEDULED
——— ACTUAL

FIGURE 10

Physical accomplishment was primarily developed through our cost reports and portrayed the percent complete of construction (see Figure 10). They were implemented for each major area (building) and total project, and were updated monthly. The percent complete was established by using actual craft man-hours expended based on installed quantities. An example would be reporting concrete complete the day it was placed.

Schedule variance was tracked using the construction critical path as shown in Figure 11. Each month the Level III computer schedule was statused, run, and analyzed to produce the monthly schedule variance. With the fuel load date maintained at October 28, 1982, the critical path varied from a high of fifteen weeks ahead of schedule to a low of twenty-one weeks behind schedule, due to the various major events as shown.

Productivity was used as an indicator both weekly and monthly to identify site management problem areas requiring corrective action (see Figure 12). Causes of poor productivity were analyzed and corrected to avoid major schedule impacts and cost overruns.

Constant reporting of installed and forecast quantity information provided management with an excellent trending tool to measure performance against estimates as well as against other nuclear site quantity performance (see Figure 13).

Special priority was placed on engineering, design, and delivery of piping and hangers. These were scheduled for delivery a full eighteen months prior to the "early start" dates. The result was that hanger installation preceded

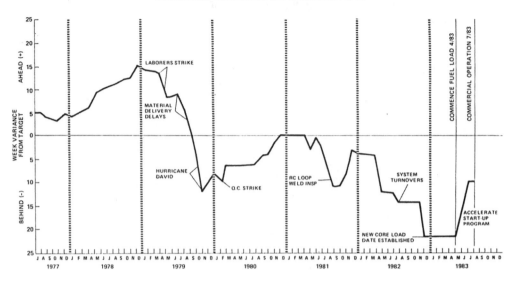

FLORIDA POWER & LIGHT COMPANY

SCHEDULE VARIANCE ON CRITICAL PATH

FIGURE 11

pipe erection and minimized the need for temporary pipe support devices to a large degree. This resulted in an orderly pipe installation program.

Although uncertainty existed about the future of St. Lucie 2 when the limited work authorization was withdrawn in October 1976, a decision was made to continue in accordance with previous established engineering, design, and procurement schedules. As a result, when the construction permit was granted in May 1977, approximately 75 percent of the original scope of engineering and design was completed, and 40 percent of the engineered materials were delivered. In retrospect, this decision typified the total commitment and support this project has received from its inception from FPL's executive management.

Another factor which contributed to the success of the construction effort at St. Lucie 2 was a detailed review of the design from St. Lucie 1. The objective of this review was to recommend areas where design enhancements could be made to improve construction productivity and costs. As a result, approximately 250 items were addressed and incorporated into the design. In addition, a design problem review (DPR) program was initiated. This was a comprehensive review by engineering of all St. Lucie 1 changes, i.e., backfit changes, operating plant enhancements, regulatory requirements, etc., in order to ensure their consideration and disposition for St. Lucie 2. Over 1,000 items were considered with approximately 350 incorporated into the St. Lucie 2 design.

Construction Site Organization

The construction site organization utilized an integrated approach which has proved quite effective (see Figure 14). It consisted of both FPL and Ebasco personnel integrated into one organization. In this organization, Ebasco's supervisory construction staff, under the overall direction of the FPL site manager, managed and directed construction activities of craft work forces and subcontractors according to the schedules established. The organiza-

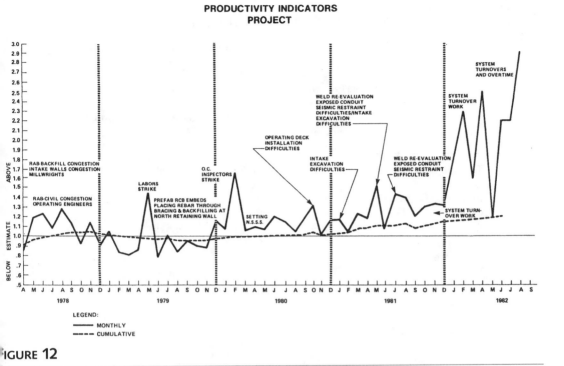

PRODUCTIVITY INDICATORS
PROJECT

LEGEND:
——— MONTHLY
- - - - CUMULATIVE

FIGURE 12

tional functions which FPL wanted to influence directly were under FPL supervisors reporting to the site manager. These functions included quality control and quality assurance; construction cost control planning and scheduling; and support services such as area stores, site purchasing, and contract and office administration.

Construction Site Management

There have been many major productivity and quality improvement efforts utilized in the construction effort (see Figure 15). Since 1978, St. Lucie Unit 2 maintained through the methods group of plant construction a periodic work sampling program including crafts and equipment utilization. St. Lucie Unit 2 showed a 37 percent increase in direct work and well exceeded the national average in four of the six samples. Operation analysis of areas such as steel erection, condenser tubing, pipe and hanger welding and cable pulling were also performed. Some work operations improved as much as 50 percent.

Time-lapse photography was used on over twenty work operations, and significant results were obtained. As an example, the condenser tubing production was doubled using the same manpower.

Management Assessment of Performance and Quality (MAPQ)

To enhance the ongoing quality improvement program at St. Lucie Unit 2, MAPQ was used in the following manner.
• Design and administer two survey instruments to top management involved in the project to determine the project objectives and possible indicators for these objectives (see Figure 16).
• Interview key personnel to determine other performance and quality indicators needed, and to develop goals or targets for each objective.

411

FLORIDA POWER & LIGHT COMPANY
SELECTED QUANTITY STATUS (For Core Load)

Commodity	Forecast Percent Complete by Industry Model	PSL No. 2 Actual Percent Complete As Of 2/13/83	Total Project Forecasted Quantities As Of 2/13/83	Quantities To Go As Of 2/13/83
Terminations	89.0	96.9	112,456	1,000
Cable	92.0	98.6	4,023,070	10,000
Small Bore Pipe	94.5	97.6	95,964	2,341
Cable Tray	100.0	100.0	40,463	0
Conduit	93.0	98.4	426,529	1,500
Large Bore Pipe	95.0	100.0	80,279	0
Lare Bore Pipe				
Hangers	—	98.6	4,404	60

FIGURE 13

- Have coordinated program that includes methods group (studies and work sampling) and management services activities that maximize productivity efforts.
- Establish management by objective/indicator charts with past data and future goals.
- Assign one individual responsible for progress of each chart and have a management review system in place using management by exception principles.
- Accomplish studies of problem areas and present findings to the site manager, PGM, and the site quality review board.

Start-up Planning and Implementation

One of the major contributing factors in the completion of St. Lucie 2 nearly on schedule has been the ability to turn over components and systems to our operating department in an orderly and timely manner. The success of this phase of the project was due to the early planning, scheduling, and implementation of a start-up program, and probably more importantly to FPL's overall philosophy concerning acceptance and testing of equipment and systems.

This overall philosophy had as its primary objective the earliest possible acceptance of equipment, components, and partial systems, in order to enable early testing and problem identification..

First, we developed an overall start-up program plan and schedule which required on-site presence of operating department personnel thirty-five months prior to the scheduled "start of fuel load" date. This was not just a token work force, but rather a sizable commitment of manpower numbering approximately sixty-four people.

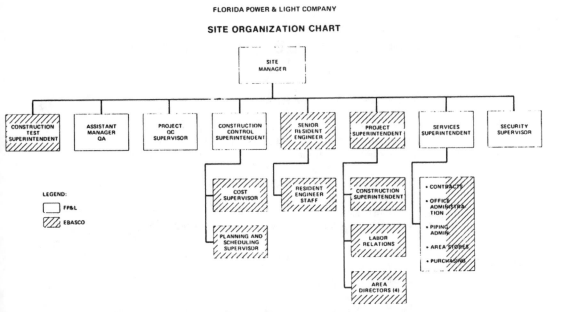

FLORIDA POWER & LIGHT COMPANY

SITE ORGANIZATION CHART

FIGURE 14

Their early work consisted of a number of tasks, the highlights being:
- define start-up system boundaries
- prepare preoperation test procedures
- establish construction turnover sequence
- establish preoperational test requirements
- determine start-up (construction and operations) manpower levels
- establish target milestone dates.

Construction/Start-up Schedule Integration

The detailed start-up schedule and logic was then integrated with the construction schedule to develop one combined schedule that the job site worked to and engineering and design supported.

IMPLEMENTATION

With the establishment of the target milestones for start-ups, the start-up/construction accelerated turnover (SCAT) program was initiated to expedite the turnover of systems from construction to operations. Essentially, this program identified portions of total systems partial turnover (PTOs) which are then completed and turned over to operations, allowing early testing and problem identification of system components. Approximately 488 "packages" were identified and scheduled for turnover in priority sequence to support established start-up milestones. In addition, a computerized listing of all system components was developed and used by the construction test group to "punch list" the systems for completeness. In addition to the PTOs, conditional turnovers (CTOs) were also established, whereby operations accepted systems on a conditional basis, with an agreed upon list of exceptions, but sufficiently complete such that testing and checkout could proceed. Again,

FLORIDA POWER & LIGHT COMPANY

PRODUCTIVITY AND QUALITY IMPROVEMENT

Past Efforts

- Periodic work sampling program
  - by craft and by areas
  - equipment (cranes and cherry pickers)
- Operations analysis of areas such as steel erection of the turbine generator building
- Supervisors utilization study
- Office engineering study
- Change reviews
- Productivity seminars
- Assessment of St. Lucie's work sampling results against industry standards
- Foreman/craftsmen delay survey
- Quality of working life improvements
- Material tracking system
- Newsletter
- Up-front planning in identifying systems turnover problems (assignment of construction personnel to system to preplan the work and review system punch lists)
- Project progress review report
- Safety actions
  - medical services enhanced
  - safety awards
- Schedule or risk analysis
- Change review boards
- Organizational changes, i.e., area to craft
- Tool control program
- Materials studies
- Establishment of quality review board

FIGURE 15

this was in keeping with the start-up philosophy, by which early acceptance of components and partial systems enabled sufficient time to identify and resolve equipment and start-up test performance problems with minimal impact to the overall scheduled core load objective for the project.

In the course of the start-up phase of the project, the construction organization objectives gradually shifted from a bulk quantity installation effort and area concept of control to total support of start-up turnover requirements and work performed on discipline basis.

ONGOING CRITIQUE OF THE PROJECT

Many times during the life of the project, independent groups were brought in to review various facets to ensure the project team was not overlooking problems. For example:

- FPL-QA Department checked all areas.

MAPQ PSL 2 INDICATORS

Efficiency Indicators	Effectiveness Indicators	Quality
Out/Input	**Goals**	• Rework Indicator
• Productivity Indicator	• Absenteeism	• QC holds
	• FCR performance	• NCRs performance
	• Budget performance	• Audit findings
	• System turnover performance	
		Impact Internal
Utilization Measures	• Tool cost/direct labor	
• Work sampling	• Overhead ratio	• Safety
• Delay indicators	• Total construction perf. budget	• Quality of working life
	• License schedule	• Attitude, motivation, and morale
	• Schedule performance	• Newsletters
	• Unit schedule performance	
	• Partial system turnover performance	**Impact External**
	• Field staffing performance	• PSC, NRC, customers fuel savings loss, and news media
	• Stores support	
	• RPA performance	
	• DCN performance	
	• Overtime percentage	

FIGURE 16

• Quality Task Force reviewed the project QA/QC program.
• Independent Engineering Verification Task Force evaluated the adequacy of the design and translation of design to field installation.
• Bechtel Power Corp. checked the welding program.
• Southeast Research Institute monitored Welding QC.
• Quadrex Corp. reviewed the containment cooling system.
• Bechtel Power Corp. studied the plant AC electrical systems.
• EDS reviewed the containment spray system.
• Theodore Barry & Associates audited the project management organization.
• Schedule Task Force continually reviewed the project schedule.

These teams operated on a task basis and reported results to the project team for review and corrective action if necessary.

EXAMPLES

Reactor Auxiliary Building "Stair Stepping" Concept

One of the innovative ideas that went into the initial plan and schedule was the "stair stepping" concept for the construction of the Reactor Auxiliary Building. In this plan, the building was constructed with emphasis placed on early completion of the west end of the building. The philosophy being that early completion of this end of the structure provided an early start to

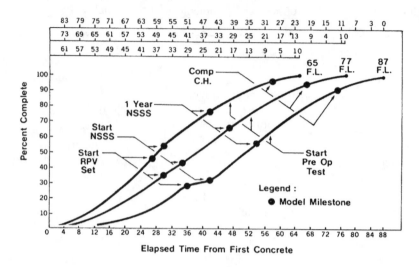

NRC NUCLEAR PLANT CONSTRUCTION SCHEDULE MODEL

Elapsed Time From First Concrete

FIGURE 17

installation of the more critical areas of equipment installation in the reactor auxiliary building; i.e., the control room and the reactor auxiliary control boards, the cable vault area, and NSSS auxiliary equipment.

As a result, the building during construction took on a "stair step" appearance, and as each elevation was completed, all major equipment and appurtenances were moved into that level prior to the roof being installed. Considerable amount of Q deck construction was also utilized in an effort to minimize forming and shoring requirements. The net result was that critical areas were completed earlier and key crafts could start their work sooner.

Reactor Containment Building

Foundation design considerations were finalized when plans called for both St. Lucie 1 and 2 to be built simultaneously. Subsurface exploration borings indicated poorly consolidated sand with thin layers of clay to a depth of 65 feet below existing grade. To meet seismic criteria, a plant island was constructed by excavating the unsuitable material, back-filling with well graded sand, and then compacting to required specifications. This plant island resulted in a compacted Class I fill measuring 780 to 920 feet and 78½ feet deep. The plant island was sized as small as possible by spacing the plant structures at minimum distances apart. When we decided to delay construction of St. Lucie 2, these plans were technically feasible, but subsequently they did require unique design and construction efforts for the second unit.

One of these special provisions, we believe, was the first nuclear safety Class 1 cofferdam ever to be engineered and constructed. It was necessary to protect the safe shutdown ability of St. Lucie 1 under all foreseeable circumstances, including earthquakes.

A circular sheetpile cofferdam for the reactor containment building was braced with internal compression beams and sized to allow excavation, con-

LICENSING TEAM ORGANIZATION

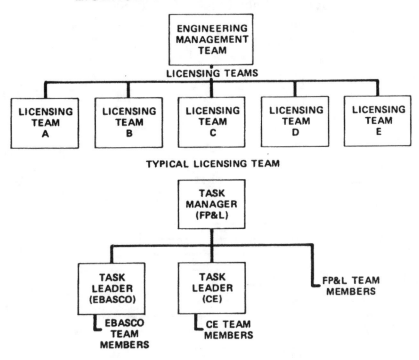

FIGURE 18

creting of the base mat and walls up to grade elevation, and subsequent back-fill operations.

The 180-foot-diameter circular cofferdam was constructed by driving 500 tons of sheetpiling in 72-foot lengths through compacted sand with electrical vibratory hammers. The 900 tons of horizontal bracing (walers) consisted of wideflange beams 36-inches deep and weighing 230 pounds to the foot, installed every 5-feet on vertical centers. To allow dewatering of the cofferdam, eighteen deep wells were installed along the periphery. Driving of the sheeting started in June 1976, and the mudmat (working surface) was placed in late September of that year.

Slipforming

Another innovative construction accomplishment at St. Lucie 2 was the "slipforming" of the concrete containment shield wall for the reactor containment building, in lieu of the traditional "jump" method. This concrete cylinder has a 3-foot-thick reinforced wall, approximately 190-feet high with an inside radius of 74 feet. It is supported by a ring wall (9-feet thick and 4-feet high) which, in turn, rests on a 10-foot-thick base mat. The shield wall contains more than 1,000 tons of reinforcing steel with another 23 tons of embedded materials such as electrical conduits, grounding cables, and anchor bolts.

Wall placement through slipforming of 10,000 cubic yards of concrete averaged 11½-feet per day, and the operation took place without interruption in only sixteen and a half days in November 1977. Manpower for slipforming

LICENSING SCHEDULE FOR SUPPORT OF
NOVEMBER 1982 OPERATING LICENSE (OL)

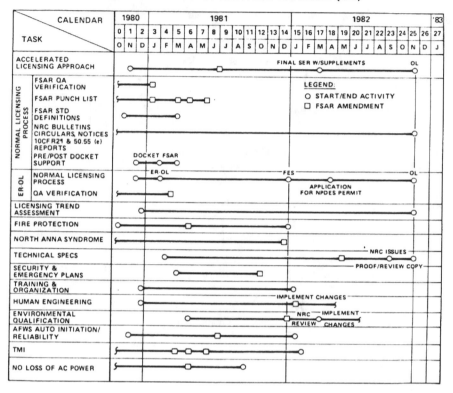

FIGURE 19

averaged 398 craft workers, and the crafts worked three shifts a day, seven days a week until completion. Immediately after completion of slipforming, construction on the steel containment vessel started inside the shield building.

Hurricane David

When the project was 26 percent completed, a severe storm seriously jeopardized our ability to meet objectives and be ready for start of fuel load in November 1982. The high winds of Hurricane David struck (on September 3, 1979) toppling a 150-ton construction derrick being used to supply materials into both the Reactor Containment Building and the Reactor Auxiliary Building. The storm completely destroyed the derrick, composed of an 180-foot tower with a 256-foot mast resting on top of the tower, and a 200-foot boom. More importantly, the falling derrick severely damaged the Reactor Auxiliary Building under initial construction. Lost schedule time to repair the damage and replace equipment was estimated at thirteen weeks.

Immediately engineering and construction supervisors formulated recovery plans. A task force of construction and site engineering personnel pinpointed all damage on design drawings. Engineers assessed this damage, developed repair procedures, and determined the extent of necessary nondestructive testing of adjoining areas. Consequently, equipment damage was

FLORIDA POWER & LIGHT COMPANY

DETAILED CONTROL ROOM DETAILED REVIEW PROGRAM ORGANIZATION

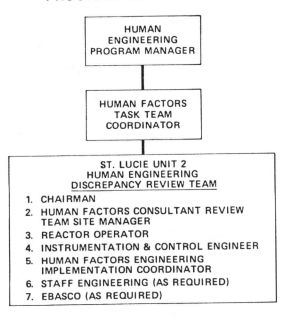

FIGURE 20

reviewed with vendor representatives, and orders were expedited for replacement equipment. Construction plans called for additional overtime of crafts and construction supervisors to make up the additional hours required for repairs. As the recovery operation proceeded, site activity maintained its previous schedule unaffected by the derrick collapse.

NSSS Installation

An important benchmark in the NRC's assessment of nuclear plant construction is the installation of the nuclear steam supply system's major equipment, i.e., reactor vessel, steam generators, and pressurizer. The project was able to meet this milestone on a progressive schedule by adopting two innovative ideas.

First was early planning and the decision to erect the containment steel vessel utilizing the "tops-off" approach. Basically, this method provides post-weld treatment of the vessel before setting the dome. Because of thinner plates, the dome did not require heat treatment and could be erected at a later time. As a result, interior concrete work started months earlier than otherwise possible and ensured that support structures were ready for NSSS installation.

Secondly, the interior concrete was not brought up to the operating level before setting the nuclear vessel. Instead, engineering and construction personnel, in conjunction with the heavy rigging subcontractor and the polar crane manufacturer, simplified the "posting" arrangement for utilizing the polar crane in setting the vessels. Using a two-shore (instead of six-shore)

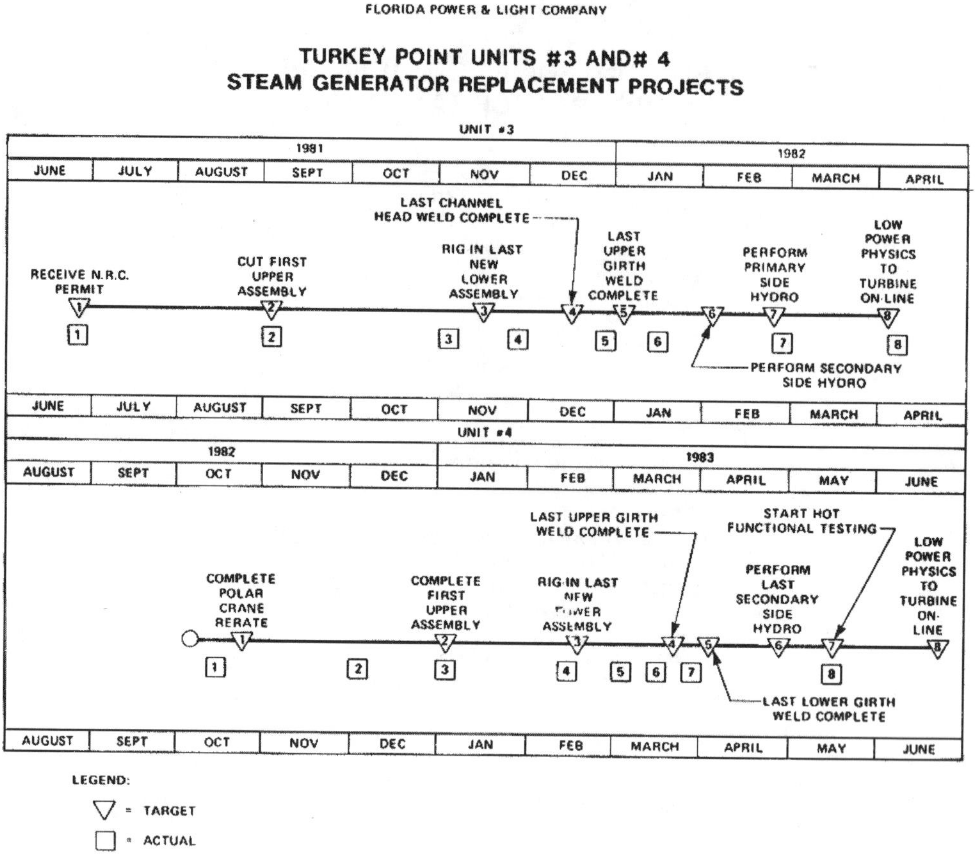

FLORIDA POWER & LIGHT COMPANY

TURKEY POINT UNITS #3 AND# 4
STEAM GENERATOR REPLACEMENT PROJECTS

LEGEND:

▽ = TARGET

☐ = ACTUAL

FIGURE 21

polar crane girder support system saved considerable schedule time and enabled construction forces to meet the target date of June–July 1980.

FSAR Preparation and Review Cycle by the NRC

A significant threat to the project schedule occurred in 1980 during the Nuclear Regulatory Commission's caseload forecast panel review of the site and project schedule. The NRC estimate of project completion generally follows a statistical schedule model shown in Figure 17. This model was developed prior to TMI and includes three curves showing the lower, medium, and upper quartile. Using the model and other data obtained during its on-site visits in February and September of 1980, the NRC projected a fuel load date of December 1983, which was thirteen months later than that established by the project. Since the NRC schedule for review of the final safety analysis report (FSAR) was based on this later date, it was necessary to convince its members that the project would meet our schedule. Through concerted FPL upper- management efforts, the NRC accepted the project schedule and completed the FSAR review in a record time of nine months.

The plan developed for the project called for the preparation of what was designated as the design defense/FSAR interface document. A well-known problem in meeting nuclear power plant schedules is the "ratcheting" that occurs

FLORIDA POWER & LIGHT COMPANY

INGREDIENTS FOR A SUCCESSFUL PROJECT

- Management commitment
- Financial resources
- Realistic and firm schedule
- Clear decision-making authority
- Flexible project control tools
- Teamwork—individual commitment
- Engineering ahead of construction
- Early start-up involvement
- Organizational flexibility
- Ongoing critique of the project
- Bethesda office for licensing
- Owner takes the project lead

FIGURE 22

FLORIDA POWER & LIGHT COMPANY

CORPORATE OBJECTIVE FOR QUALITY

"To involve employees in each functional area in the
implementation of the quality improvement program."

FIGURE 23

FLORIDA POWER & LIGHT COMPANY

FPL PROGRAM QUALITY POLICY

"It is the policy of the Florida Power & Light Company to
pursue and deserve a reputation for quality leadership
for all of its services and products offered; by providing
them in a reliable, timely, efficient, and economic
manner that will merit customer satisfaction."

FIGURE 24

---

during the licensing review cycle and results in additional unforeseen additions
to the project scope and an increase in schedule. To minimize that from occurring on St. Lucie 2, a documented three-party review (Ebasco, FPL, and Combustion Engineering) of the St. Lucie Unit No. 2 design against the NRC standard review plans was conducted to document the degree of compliance and
identify possible areas of contention. The design defense documents also served

FLORIDA POWER & LIGHT COMPANY

QUALITY IMPROVEMENT
TEAM ORGANIZATION

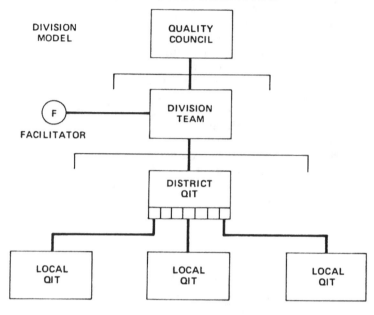

FIGURE 25

to organize and develop in a rational manner the final safety analysis report (FSAR) for the St. Lucie 2 Plant.

In conjunction with this effort, a detailed three-party (Ebasco, FPL, and Combustion Engineering) integrated schedule indicating preparation; and review, primary, and secondary responsibilities of all sections of the FSAR were prepared, with Ebasco responsible for the control and production of the document.

Also, an integrated Licensing Team Organization (see Figure 18) was established so that each identified licensing task had a three-party team assigned to handle all activities associated with the task in compliance with the established schedule (see Figure 19).

To ensure that the licensing effort was supportive of the project objectives, an overall plan was developed for this phase of the project.

As a result, licensing was removed from the critical path of the project by reducing the time span of "Docketing of FSAR" to ACRS letter recommending operating license to nine months versus nineteen to twenty-one months pre-TMI days.

Control Room Design Review

In response to an NRC requirement, a control room design review program organization was established (see Figure 20). The review was conducted, as delineated in four phases, as follows:

Phase 1   Project Planning

Detailed Control Room Design Review program plan was prepared.

FLORIDA POWER & LIGHT COMPANY

QUALITY IMPROVEMENT IMPLEMENTATION STEPS

1. Management commitment
2. Quality improvement team
3. Management orientation and training
4. Economic analysis
5. Root cause identification
6. Corrective action
7. Awareness
8. Recognition

FIGURE 26

FLORIDA POWER & LIGHT COMPANY

QIP PROGRAM ASSESMENT (AS OF MAY 25, 1983)

Program Status:
- Number of — team leaders trained   290
  - — facilitators trained   43
  - — managers trained   107
- Number of teams   192
- Number of solutions implemented   45
- Number of solutions prioritized   133
- Average savings/avoidance per solution $232,000*

*Only includes local savings and does not credit any system applications.

FIGURE 27

Phase 2   Control Room Review

This represents the period in which data collection, reduction, and analysis are conducted, resulting in human engineering discrepancy (HED) reports.

Phase 3   Enhancement and Design Solutions

Discrepancies are collated, alternative enhancements and design solutions are generated, and the results are considered in trade-offs.

Phase 4   Reporting

Results of detailed control room design review with plans for modifications are published.

The items identified and reported on in Phase 4 that required completion prior to the issuance of the operating license were turned over to the start-up department. Start-up handled the interface with construction and the integration into the overall construction schedule.

Turkey Point Units 3 and 4—Steam Generator Replacement

While not directly related to St. Lucie, another project was done at Florida Power & Light Company utilizing similar techniques.

FLORIDA POWER & LIGHT COMPANY

QIP PROGRAM ASSESMENT (AS OF MAY 25, 1983)

Cost Benefit of QIP:

Annual cost of program			$1.4M
Includes:	Quality assurance	$427K	
	Information central	$ 50K	
	Facilitators	$490K	
	Recognition	$263K	
	Awareness	$ 64K	
	Training	$107K	
Annual savings based on current average		$57 million	

FIGURE 28

The steam generator replacement at Turkey Point Units 3 and 4 became necessary due to continued degradation of the tubes caused by corrosion-induced stress cracking. The program consisted of replacement of the tube bundles by cutting the steam generators at the channel head immediately below the tube sheet and above the tube bundle U-bends in the transition cone area. During the outage, the upper assemblies (stamp domes) were refurbished by replacing the primary and secondary moisture separator packages and feedrings. The replacement outage on Unit 3 began June 24, 1981, and returned to power April 10, 1982. The Unit 4 outage began October 10, 1982, and the unit returned to service May 10, 1983.

When the problem became serious in 1976, FPL planned a phase approach to the steam generator replacement. In Phase 1 a model was built to aid in preparing a detailed scope document. Phase 2 was the awarding of the engineering contract to Bechtel Power Corporation and the establishment of an integrated project organization. Engineering was completed and, with the aid of the model, procurement of long lead-time items was started. Phase 3 was the actual replacement of the steam generator with engineering completed and all material on-site. This phased and integrated approach gave FPL the opportunity to stop the replacement of the steam generators, if a repair solution became feasible, without incurring a financial loss due to early engineering or procurement activities.

Upon completion of the Unit 3 replacement project, a critique was conducted from which improvements were made to the Unit 4 effort. As a result, the second project was accomplished in seven months versus nine months for the first (see Figure 21).

SUMMARY

The success of the St. Lucie Unit 2 project can be at least in part attributed to planning the work, accurate and timely reporting of results via valid indicators, well-trained and skilled personnel, and, most of all, teamwork.

There were many ingredients which also contributed to the success of the St. Lucie 2 project. These are summarized in Figure 22.

The ongoing critique was also a significant contributor. Utilizing task teams, numerous problems were identified and solved.

While we currently have no new nuclear projects on which to apply our skills, we have initiated a corporate quality improvement program which utilizes many of the ingredients that helped make the St. Lucie project a success.

The quality improvement program (QIP), for example, utilizes teams for problem solving, indicators, and incentives. This program is described in Figures 23, 24, 25, and 26. It is our intention to have every employee trained and involved in the QIP.

As you can see in Figures 27 and 28, many people have been trained, and we are well on our way toward achieving our objective, which is for all work: "Do it right the first time."

Study Questions

St. Lucie Unit 2: A Nuclear Plant Built On Schedule

1. Describe the project planning and scheduling system used on the St. Lucie Unit 2 project. Define schedule control.

2. What are some of the key issues to consider when evaluating the usefulness and effectiveness of a project control system?

3. Describe some of the scope management factors that contributed to the success of the project.

4. Describe how the management assessment of performance and quality (MAPQ) was performed.

5. How does the MAPQ process assist the scope management function?

Measuring Successful Technical Performance: A Cost/Schedule/Technical Control System

Robert H. Kohrs, Program Manager, Underwater Tests, Westinghouse Electric Corporation
Gordon C. Weingarten, Programs Business Manager, Westinghouse Electric Corporation

PMI Canada *Proceedings*, 1986, pp. 158–64

INTRODUCTION

It is well established that any successful project is determined by the appropriate balance of technical, schedule, and cost parameters. But that balance is often very difficult to achieve. Perhaps this problem is most simply illustrated by a sign once observed in a co-worker's office which read:

GOOD!

FAST!

CHEAP!

PICK ANY TWO.

Though meant to be humorous, it also illustrates a very common attitude about the difficulty in meeting all constraints imposed on typical projects. Obtaining a balanced output on a project is, in fact, a major responsibility of that individual charged with overall integration, the project manager.

For more than twenty years, project managers have utilized some form or other of a cost and schedule control system. Cost and schedule controls have been thoroughly discussed in the literature, and understood and used to varying degrees of sophistication by almost all project managers. Very extensively developed systems have been applied to projects involving power plants, chemical plants, and defense systems, all typically billion dollar projects. Frequently referred to as a C/SCS (cost/schedule control system), these systems are based on a set of criteria with a rigid structure in organization, systems, and procedures. Among the most sophisticated C/SCS systems are those based on the Department of Defense 7000.2 specification requirements.

Those individuals and agencies who have conceived and implemented these elaborate cost and schedule systems have done an excellent job; but, in most cases have failed to include the measurement of perhaps the key factor in the entire project ... technical performance! Will the project work? Will the pumping system pump enough fluid? Will the missile reach optimum speed? In other words, when the project is done on schedule and within budget, will the technical performance be grossly over designed or less than satisfactory?

The developers of these cost and schedule control systems considered two-thirds of the program management triangle and stopped. They had systems and organizations in place, disciplines established, and reports designed that could have been adopted to handle the entire problem, but did

427

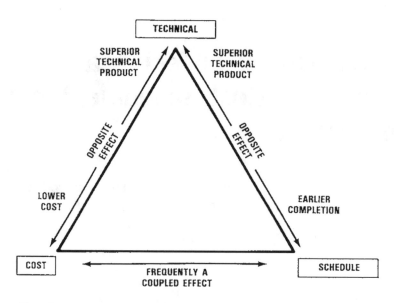

FIGURE 1   THE PROJECT MANAGER'S TRIANGLE

not complete the process. The project management process demands a balanced, coordinated effort between cost, schedule, and technical factors. This desired balanced output of a project can be diagramed as shown in Figure 1.

Note that moving toward the "superior technical product" typically can move the project away from "lower cost" and "earlier completion." How far up towards the "superior technical product" apex could, or more importantly, should, the project be driven? Furthermore, having made some implicit judgmental answer to that question, how are the three parameters measured and compared to assure that the proper positioning has, in fact, taken place?

In order to obtain a meaningful balance, factual information on each of the three key parameters must be obtained. Cost data and schedule information gathering methods have been developed over the years and are normally available to the project manager. But how can technical data be obtained on a summary basis without including all the complex information fully understood only by the technical specialist? How is this information to be transformed into parameters which permit comparison to the cost and schedule constraints of a project?

This paper discusses one way technical, schedule, and cost parameters and variances may be measured and compared on a common basis, so that the project manager may, in fact, make properly balanced decisions during the evolution of the project.

BACKGROUND

The approach discussed herein has evolved naturally from observations in a project management environment characterized by an incentive contract for a large defense-oriented project. This approach could, however, be applied to both smaller and commercially oriented applications. Simply stated, what has been observed is that when cost, schedule, and technical performance are all incentivized, an inherent and implicit system is fortuitously created which permits quantitative measurement of technical performance. For purposes of this discussion, incentivized means the addition of cash incentive awards to enhance contractor performance.

Cost is always measured in dollars. Although schedule is best measured in time, time is converted to dollars and schedule performance is measured in terms of dollars in these cost and schedule control systems. Therefore, if a measure of technical performance in terms of dollars could be made, then all three parts of the project manager's triangle would be expressed in a common denominator suitable for top management review and analysis. Therefore, balanced decisions in the inevitable compromises between cost, schedule, and technical performance may be made by the project manager and executive level management on the basis of this common parameter.

How do these components get measured to provide data to assure that the desired balance is, in fact, achieved? To answer these questions, it is constructive to go back to the beginning of a project and examine the steps followed in the formulation of a project plan.

Initially in a project, objectives are communicated to the team, and a plan for successful completion of those objectives is formulated, generally in the following order.

Step 1: What? Define technical tasks; what specific analysis, design, procurement, fabrication, assembly, and test will be performed to accomplish objectives of the project.

Step 2: When? Put the technical tasks into a framework; link together into a schedule; define dependencies; calculate a network; define dates for start and finish of individual tasks and for the project as a whole; adjust and define parallel efforts in order to meet project end date requirements.

Step 3: How Much? Define resources (manpower, machinery, space, etc.) for each task; add together using schedule data; examine resources constraints; adjust schedule and technical tasks to be consistent with available resources, and/or initiate action to provide additional resources as required.

At this stage, the project manager's planning role is well formulated, and his role in monitoring and measuring progress begins.

Cost Variance

Costs are readily summarized and reported back to project management via the financial community which exists in every company to take care of payroll, billing, subcontracts, etc. In a typical project management environment, the one extra step of comparing the planned budget to the actual expenditures on a periodic basis (weekly, monthly, etc.) is readily accomplished. This gives rise to the first measure of successful performance, the cost variance, defined herein as:

Cost Variance = Budget – Actual

This variance is evaluated on a periodic and project-cumulative basis. So, typically, the last of the three major evaluation parameters to be established in a project plan (cost) is the most readily measured, because a large accounting support function inherently exists in every company.

How does the cost data assist in measuring technical success, the subject being investigated herein? Obviously costs are one important part of the project triangle; but, costs are really an outgrowth or derivative of the two other parts of the triumvirate planning process, schedule and technical tasks, which preceded costs in the planning of the project. To get to that elusive measurement of technical success, the process must march backward along the path that created the project. The next step to be examined is the schedule, step two, in the planning process.

Schedule Variance

Measuring scheduler success is somewhat of a subjective departure from the hard, cold cost data in that special information must be set up in the plan to identify key milestones thought to be significant to the project. Furthermore, these milestones must be of sufficient quantity and small enough periodicity to provide management with a quantitative measure, i.e., the second variance in the project, defined herein as:

Schedule Variance = Milestones Completed – Milestones Planned

In a two-dimensional measurement system consisting of cost and schedule, the schedule parameter is typically "converted" to equivalent dollars by taking financial credit for work accomplished through an earned value, based on original planning. Although the transformation does tend to distort the pure scheduler nature of the measurement, useful information is created for management in that a measure of whether cost or schedule variances are more significant at any given time can be made on the same numerical basis.

Technical Variance

It is in the attempt to measure technical success that many problems arise for the project manager. Much more so than for schedule measurement, it is difficult to attempt to regiment to a common denominator the success or failure of a technical task. Not at all minor in this process is the prevalent attitude of the functional engineering analyst, designer, and manufacturing or production specialist that draws a protective barrier between the technical task and the project manager's inquiries. It is understandable for the project manager to track financial accounting data and status of defined milestones (as long as the milestones are major events and not too specific or personalized). But quantitative measurement of technical performance by a project group is simply not a well-accepted procedure.

Then how is a project manager to satisfy himself, upper management, and the customer that not only are the costs and schedule on track, but so is the technical job itself? This is especially significant when it is recalled that the technical job is, in reality, the driver for the schedule and the costs, and in that sense the foundation for the success (or failure) of the entire project.

Cost variances are measured in planned to actual dollars. Schedule variance is somewhat more subjectively measured in number of key milestones realized compared to planned, converted to dollars by earned value judgments. But what are the quantitative parameters to measure technical success?

Technical Variance = ?????

DISCUSSION

The organizational and contractual framework for the discussion to follow on a process for measuring technical performance is characterized by:

- a large group (1,000 people) of engineering and manufacturing personnel
- matrix project organization across multiple disciplines (see Figure 2)
- design and manufacturing effort, with major subcontractors for one half the work
- defense product contract of $100 million/year for several years
- contract in a cost plus incentive format, with incentives on cost, schedule, and technical performance.

It is this last characteristic—a fully incentivized contract, with all three parameters on the project manager's cost/schedule/technical triangle represented in the incentives—that has led to a straightforward way to provide measurement of technical status of the project.

The technical portion of the project incentive was fully negotiated with the customer and placed in the formal contract. The objective of the incentivization was to provide performance margins above the basic technical specification requirements to allow for future expansion of the system, lower maintenance, added reliability, and added manufacturing quality. To cover this range of goals, a multitude of technical parameters, appropriate to this product, were incentivized. Typical parameters used are listed below to illustrate the spectrum. Naturally, these parameters are system dependent, but the list gives a perspective on the kind of items to consider.

Typical incentive parameters could be:
- acceleration
- velocity
- time
- shock mitigation
- vibration
- temperature
- structural loads
- factors of safety
- bearing pressures
- burst pressures
- mean time between failure.

Many of these parameters were applied to several subsystems in the work breakdown structure (WBS) for the project. This particular combination of parameters for which the customer desired additional margin or greater assurance in meeting basic requirements was then incentivized proportional to the judged value to the customer. Dollar values for the incentives tended to be a few percent of the cost of that subsystem, (but the dollar values were substantial when compared to an individual's frame of reference).

This contractual format has been found to be a natural, inherent way to obtain a measurement of technical performance. Each cognizant technical manager is asked periodically to quantify the technical status of her component or subsystem by comparing whatever test and/or analytical information is currently available, to the incentivized goals. In making this evaluation, many technical factors are implicitly integrated into the rating, with the output being a technically based prediction of the expected incentive which would be realized if the product were made at the current level of development.

The results are obvious; each component or subsystem ends up being rated simply by the technical staff, but in terms of dollars. These units are, of course, the same as those available to the project manager for cost performance, and with an earned value system in place, also for schedule performance. At this

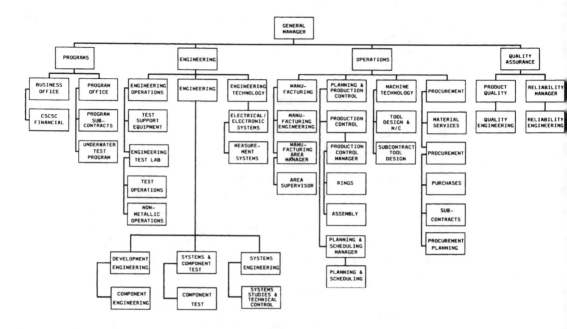

FIGURE 2   GENERALIZED MATRIX ORGANIZATION

point then, the project manager has available a definition of where the component or subsystem is currently positioned in the project manager's triangle. The technical variance may be defined as:

$$\text{Technical Variance} = \text{Attained or Predicted Performance} - \text{Performance Needed for Maximum Incentive}$$

Since the customer has predefined the precise utility or value of each component or subsystem in dollar magnitudes in the contract, the project manager and executive department managers can periodically review, on an overview basis, the status of all major items from a simultaneous cost, schedule, and technical basis. Any large variances out of preset thresholds can then be highlighted for detailed management action and corrective action.

The process is attractive in that it necessitates the development of certain project management items (which are generally advisable anyway). The items include:

• detailed planning in the beginning of the project to define components and subsystems

• quantification of the customer's requirements and goals in very clear (dollar) terms (The customer defines utility and value of each of these components and subsystems deemed especially important to the success of the project.)

• these technical performance parameters communicated in a very direct manner to the engineering manager personally responsible for the design and development of that product component or subsystem

• technical status, which is at times very difficult to communicate across the multitude of technology found in any large sophisticated project, readily collected in terms understood by all, regardless of technical background.

Even though the responsible technical manager integrates all current test and/or analytical data and arrives at a judgment on attained incentive, the process of coordinating these technical inputs still requires reasonable technical understanding and is best performed in a systems engineering functional group. That group coordinates with the project office by using the project WBS as a common database. The project office already has the organization, the procedures, and forms in place to take cost and schedule data. It is a natural evolution to modify these incentivized technical milestones.

The cost and schedule status culminates in a cost performance report (CPR). The report typically includes the dollar values for current, cumulative to date, and at-completion values by WBS element and functional element; a near-term forecast; and a narrative including an executive summary and a detailed discussion of variances exceeding a predetermined threshold.

The technical incentive status can now be included in the CPR. A financial format is included in the financial section and a narrative included in the executive summary and detailed section discussing reasons for variances to attainment of maximum technical performance. This technical variance discussion, combined with cost and schedule variance discussions, serves to highlight the interaction between cost, schedule, and technical parameters never visible before in a two-dimensional reporting system. An example of a summary sheet is shown in Figure 3.

The summary variance report indicates the monthly change in cost schedule and technical status, the cumulative change, and estimate of status expected at completion for all three parameters of interest.

For example, the assumption made in Figure 3 is a hypothetical program called the "diving system." One of the incentivized portions of the diving system is the diving chamber. The diving chamber is expected to be a spherical metal chamber capable of containing several oceanographic scientists and associated equipment. Eventually a quantity of twenty will be produced. It is expected to reach a depth of at least 3,000 feet, but never more than 10,000 feet. The weight of the chamber is limited by the strength of the umbilical and the design of the transporting surface craft. The lighter the structural skin, the larger the volume may be without exceeding maximum weight limits. Conversely, the thicker (stronger) the skin, the deeper the vessel can go within weight limits of the specification. Clearly, a balanced design is needed. Figure 4 illustrates the tradeoff ranges for this component.

In this example, the chamber is assumed to be contractually incentivized as follows:
- Each 1,000 feet depth below 3,000 feet earns the contractor $100,000 to a maximum of $700,000.
- Each 100 cubic feet of volume above 1,000 cubic feet earns the contractor $10,000 to a maximum of $400,000.
- The contract is firm fixed priced, at a value of $10 million, with an estimated profit of 10 percent.
- The project schedule is one year. Early delivery earns the contractor $1,000/day to a maximum of $30,000; late delivery penalty is $10,000/day to a limit of $300,000.

Among the options available to the contractor are:
- Design to minimum requirements; this is the easiest option to meet cost and schedule, but earning only the $1 million profit of the fixed price contract and possibly the $30,000 positive schedule incentive.

COST/SCHEDULE/TECHNICAL VARIANCE REPORT								
WBS No. 1.6.9.5			**Project Cognizance** A.B. Smith					
System Diving System			**Technical Cognizance** J.R. Jones					
Component Divers Chamber			**Report as of** 30 June 1986					

	Current Month			Cumulative			At Completion		
Cost	BCWP	ACWP	CVAR	BCWP	ACWP	CVAR	BUD	EAC	CVAR
Schedule	BCWS	BCWP	SVAR	BCWS	BCWP	SVAR	BUD	EAC	SVAR
Technical	Maximum Incentive	Forecast Incentive	TVAR	Maximum Incentive	Forecast Incentive	TVAR	TOT	EAC	TVAR
	1000	800	(300)	1100	550	(550)	1100	1000	(100)

FIGURE 3   COST, SCHEDULE, AND TECHNICAL SUMMARY VARIANCE REPORT

• Using exotic material, design to the maximum depth and volume, earning additional $1.1 million incentive, but risking profit on cost of $1 million and possible negative schedule incentive of $300,000.
• Some interim position, earning some incentive and profit.

Obviously, the goal of the project manager is to maximize profit at acceptable risk as well as provide the customer with a good product delivered on time. Because of the significant schedule penalties, technical status of the design must be assessed as the projects in progress.

It is assumed, in this hypothetical case, that the project has four phases: development, evaluation, qualification, and production. One unit is built for each of the first three phases, and twenty are built in production. This phasing is typical of most large-scale research, development, and production projects.

The cost, schedule, and technical summary variance report (Figure 3) may now be prepared on a periodic basis to permit the project manager to guide and direct the project.

Little explanation is needed for the cost and schedule sections of Figure 3, as they follow standard definitions:
• current month: measurement in dollars of reporting period performance
• cumulative: sum of all periods' performance from beginning of project to date
• at completion: estimated value expected at project completion
• BCWS: budgeted cost of work scheduled
• BCWP: budgeted cost of work performed
• ACWP: actual cost of work performed
• CVAR: cost variance = BCWP – BCWS
• SVAR: schedule variance = BCWP – BCWS
• BUD: budget at completion
• EAC: current estimate cost at completion
• TVAR: technical variance.

The technical portion of the variance report (Figure 3), although measured in dollars, does differ from the conventional cost and schedule parameters. As noted above, the hypothetical project has four phases. Contract incentives are assumed to be proven and earned on the qualification phase unit,

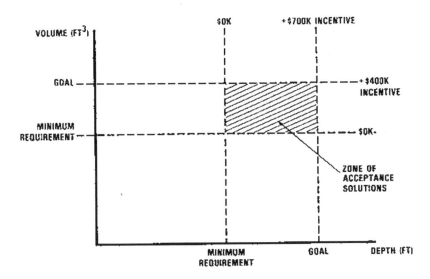

TRADEOFF CHART FOR TECHNICAL INCENTIVES

immediately preceding production. Therefore, the "At Completion" sections on the variance report would represent the incentive that the technical manager anticipates earning at the end of the project. The "TOT" column represents the total possible design incentive from technical sources on the diving chamber ($1.1 million in this example). The "EAC" column is the expected incentive on the qualification phase unit ($1 million in this example). This estimate is updated every reporting period as the design progresses. The "TVAR" is the quantification in dollars of the technical variance.

The "Cumulative" section contains the results of any phase that has actually been completed. The "Maximum Incentive" column shows what could possibly be earned through maximum technical performance. The "Forecast Incentive" column shows the amount that would have been earned had the completed unit been the final product.

The "Current Month" section data is based on that unit in progress at the time of the report. The project manager would require explanations of deviations from maximum technical incentives, TVAR, just as in the cases of cost and schedule variances.

The reasonableness of the "At Completion" estimates are assessed based on the trend of the design incentive to date, as the product goes through the various phases. For example, the report could show if the cost variances were showing $1 million negative variance at completion because exotic materials, with costs $1 million more than budget, were being used for the purpose of earning the $1.1 million performance incentive. This information would be clearly visible, comparable, and challengeable. The project manager may not want to risk the unknowns in use of the exotic material for essentially a break-even on total project profits.

Additionally, the project manager may very well question the credibility of the technical forecast of 91 percent incentive achievement in the "At Completion" unit with only 50 percent success achieved on the first unit and 73 percent success forecast on the current unit. The collected information gives some indication of technical progress along the development timeline to aid in those judgments. The variance discussion in this case may point to the fact that cost is being sacrificed in order to achieve the maximum technical incentive performance and that projected performance is still in question. Armed with that information, the project manager may need to evaluate that trade-off to assure a balance between cost, schedule, and "technical excellence."

Naturally, this reporting process is meant to be a supplementary overview of the day-to-day interactions and other formats for communications which include: engineering weekly meetings to review periodically all components and subsystem technical status; weekly and monthly status reports; and periodic project review meetings with the customer. The cost/schedule/technical variance report does, however, provide a formalized overview on a controlled, periodic basis to provide upper management with the assurance that the project is proceeding on a correctly balanced path, and that any technical variances are identified early for subsequent management action.

The examples used in this paper describe a method of measuring technical performance using technical incentives, resulting in contract-defined rewards—the "cost plus incentive" contract environment. In the fixed-price world, the measurement of technical performance, using incentives, is still possible. The process is more subtle and more powerful.

In a fixed-price contract, the customer is buying a product for a specified price that meets minimum specifications. When not incentivized by the customer, any performance in excess of the specification of the contract is, in essence, an investment paid for by the contractor. This product with enhanced capability may be or become of greater value to the contractor. It may make him more competitive in the future. It may broaden his market. In other words, it may result in making him more money. If that is the case, it would, of course, be worth it for him to invest something to exceed the original specification. On the other hand, it may be worth nothing to the contractor to exceed the contract specification, if he will realize no advantage. After all, he is being paid to just meet a specification and nothing more. The market may not be willing to pay any more in the future even for a superior product.

It is important to consider, at this point, the personality of the engineer. The realities of the world are that the bent of the engineer is to improve her design, to exceed the specification. Left unchecked, the engineer will tend to tinker with her design until it is "perfect."

It, therefore, behooves the owner/project manager, the engineering manager, and the marketing manager to decide early in the project what exceeding the minimum contract specification is worth to the company; what the added cost (or investment) of exceeding specifications is worth to the company; and then, set an incentive commensurate with that worth to measure technical performance. (Incentive money does not necessarily mean paid to performers" any more than they are paid on a cost-type contract.) If it is decided that no investment should be made to exceed the specification, then a negative incentive would be set. This means that if the design exceeds the contract specification, the designer has spent unnecessary money to achieve that result, and has unnecessarily cost the company profits on this fixed price job.

Figure 5 represents the concept of incentive award dollars from the customer versus incentive investment dollars from the company. To the performer—designers or manufacturers—the incentive dollars look the same. The measurement of performance, therefore, would be the same in either case (as described earlier in this paper).

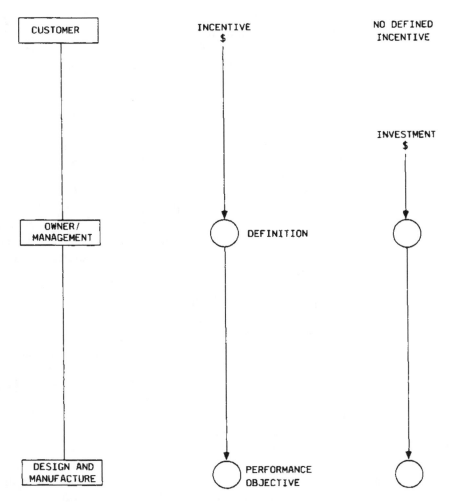

CUSTOMER

INCENTIVE
$

NO DEFINED
INCENTIVE

INVESTMENT
$

OWNER/
MANAGEMENT

DEFINITION

DESIGN AND
MANUFACTURE

PERFORMANCE
OBJECTIVE

FIGURE 5   **APPLICATION OF INCENTIVE MEASUREMENT TO GENERAL CASE**

The absence of such an incentive determination by the owner/program manager at the outset of a fixed price venture merely means that the determination of the investment of the company's funds is left solely to the discretion of the engineering manager at best, or the individual engineer at worst.

CONCLUSIONS

Cost and schedule measurements are well-established inputs to the project manager. Technical measurements, however, have historically been a more elusive subject. Very little formalization of this third part of the project manager's triangle of concerns has taken place.

Those few systems that have been developed typically require considerable manpower to implement and maintain; complexities of the system and the inability to tie to a common denominator have left many doubts about the benefits of technical performance measurement systems.

For the particular case of a fully incentivized contract, an inherent, readily implemented process of quantification has been realized. Technical managers report on their current technical progress towards a contractual goal. This goal is fully understood by the technical manager because it is the product of extensive communications and negotiations with the customer early in the project.

It would appear that the concept of an incentive environment for a project, with incentives placed on cost, schedule, and technical performance, provides a unique opportunity for a balanced project management approach to measure success on a rational, relatively simple basis. In other commercial applications it may be possible, for example, for a company to set up internal bonus awards for personnel instead of customer-supplied incentives. The process of implementation should remain the same. The challenge for the future is to apply this observed phenomena creatively to other industries with differing customer and marketplace situations, and yet retain the structure and motivational forces which permit the measurement of cost, schedule, and technical performance in a constructive and efficient manner on a common denominator basis.

Past experience shows that the formal, existing two-dimensional cost and schedule systems, with all their benefits, do not quite tell the total story. The one element missing (and the fundamental element of any project) is the technical performance. The project manager most often has no formalized process to balance the decisions, tradeoffs, and product decisions that must continually be made in any project. Personal judgment and experience will always be primary in all these decisions, but a formalized quantification of the impact of those decisions on the cost/schedule/technical balance within the project should add substantially to the success of the project.

Most project managers measure and predict the cost and schedule elements of a project. It is time to now quantitatively add the third element of technical performance to assure action when problems do arise and to promote a truly balanced end-product and successful project.

Study Questions

MEASURING SUCCESSFUL TECHNICAL PERFORMANCE: A COST/SCHEDULE/TECHNICAL CONTROL SYSTEM

1. Demonstrate your understanding of the project manager's triangle as presented in the case.

2. How can cost and schedule variances be measured? Discuss the difficulties in defining technical variance.

3. A successful project is one that not only fulfills the constraints of time, cost and technical performance, but fulfills other requirements such as minimal scope change and customer acceptance. Discuss some of these other requirements.

4. The case emphasizes the importance of measuring technical performance. What are the elements to consider in performance reporting in cost, schedule, or technical performance?

The Legal Standards for "Prudent" Project Management

Randall L. Speck, Rogovin, Huge & Lenzner, P.C.

PMI *Proceedings*, 1987, pp. 566–76

INTRODUCTION

In our increasingly disputatious society, the project manager has become the focus of ever closer scrutiny and occasional opprobrium. Although most projects are completed successfully to resounding kudos, some have suffered serious calamities — skyrocketing costs, repeated delays, and unreliable quality. The most notorious examples have occurred in utility companies' construction of state-of-the-art nuclear power plants where ten-fold cost increases, oft-postponed completion dates, and massive rework have been commonplace. In some of those cases, utility company stockholders have been penalized to the tune of several hundred million dollars for their project managers' apparent lapses.

Every project manager is vulnerable to censure, however, whenever the project falls short of its goals and in the process injures a third party (e.g., consumers, owners, contractors, the government, or even stockholders). This paper reviews the legal standards that have evolved over the last decade to measure project managers' performance and offers a few practical guidelines that may help to fend off unwarranted criticism.

This brief primer on the standards for prudent project management is not intended, however, as a substitute for legal advice that has been tailored to the circumstances of a particular project. The law varies by jurisdiction, and, as noted below, the touchstone for acceptable behavior is often elusive. Thus, it is advisable to solicit anticipatory counsel matched to a project's individual characteristics rather than waiting until the potential for misfortune has been realized.

In the legal vernacular, a project manager's conduct is usually acceptable if his performance is considered "prudent" and "reasonable." Obviously, such loosely worded directives make poor guideposts for the manager about to embark on a project that may be fraught with risks and uncertainties. These nebulous terms have been infused with a modicum of meaning, however, based on the very large, analogous body of negligence law. In its simplest terms, a person is negligent (i.e., imprudent or unreasonable) if she fails to act in a manner that is consistent with the standard of care that would normally be expected under the circumstances and thereby injures a third party.

Based on these hoary principles, unattainable perfection is not required. The law in most state and federal jurisdictions merely prescribes the actions that a "reasonable person" would take under similar conditions, but several states have recently adopted more rigorous criteria in specified regulatory contexts. Even though those standards are not yet well defined, they seem to demand project management techniques that will produce the most efficient performance possible. Project managers should certainly be aware of the tests that will be used to evaluate their actions and adjust their behavior accordingly.

Given an environment in which day-to-day decisions made under the pressures of a dynamic project may be strictly scrutinized, the project manager should be prepared to document the reasonableness of his choices. Managers are normally given substantial latitude in running a project, and regulatory commissions or courts are loathe to second-guess a supervisor's judgment. Nevertheless, the project manager may, as a practical matter, be forced to explain cost, schedule, or quality deviations in some detail, and the consequences of inadequate data could be extremely costly for the utility. Again, forewarned is forearmed. Thorough contemporaneous documentation (as opposed to explanations constructed after the fact) can provide a palpable defense to charges of mismanagement.

There is no facile recipe for prudent management. Presentations at this and other PMI symposia cover the range of issues that are likely to arise in any challenge to management's performance, and there are a myriad of sub-issues that could loom large in litigation or regulatory proceedings evaluating a major project. There are three critical aspects of the project manager's responsibilities, however, that are the most likely candidates for probing review: 1) planning, 2) organization, and 3) control. A brief case study of the New York Public Service Commission's evaluation of the construction of the Shoreham Nuclear Generating Facility provides a good framework for analyzing the substantive requirements for prudent project management.

Finally, claims of unreasonable management will inevitably be predicated on some form of monetary loss—e.g., excessive cost of the final product, inadequate performance that requires expensive repairs, or lost profit attributable to delays. If there is evidence of management shortcomings, the court or regulatory agency will be required to reconstruct the project as it would have unfolded if management had performed prudently. Of course, that exercise tempts the protagonists to flights of imagination and to hypotheses of an aerial project that has no relevance to reality. Commissioners and judges are commonly called upon, however, to weigh models or estimates of what would have happened if the facts had been different. Thus, with appropriate data derived from the project itself, the parties can formulate a reasonable assessment of the cost consequences of any alleged management dereliction.

Contexts for Challenges to the Reasonableness of Project Management

Almost any project may be subjected to a reasonableness review whenever a service or product is to be produced for a third party, based on a specified standard, with a specified time for completion, or for a specified price. If those expectations are frustrated, the injured party is likely to seek redress, particularly when the stakes are large. The most common form for examination of project management is in regulatory proceedings to set the rates that a utility will be allowed to charge. Very similar issues arise, however, in the execution of government contracts and in disputes between owners and contractors over performance under the terms of the contract.

Regulation as a Substitute for Competition

It is a basic premise of most regulatory policy in the United States that the regulator serves as a surrogate for competition. In theory, the marketplace and the profit motive provide the impetus for unregulated enterprises to operate efficiently, and no external controls are necessary or desirable. For certain natural monopolies (e.g., electric utilities), however, there is no realistic opportunity for competition. Thus, a governmental watchdog is designated to act on behalf of the ratepayer and the public interest to monitor the company's performance against the standards that would be expected in a competitive environment. As the Federal Energy Regulatory Commission (FERC) has held,

> management of unregulated business subject to the free interplay of competitive forces have no alternative to efficiency. If they are to remain competitive, they must constantly be on the lookout for cost economies and cost savings. Public utility management, on the other hand, does not have quite the same incentive. Regulation must make sure that the costs incurred in the rendition of service requested are necessary and prudent.

New England Power Company, 31 F.E.R.C. Para. 61,047, at 61,083 (1985) (quoting *Midwestern Gas Transmission Co.,* 36 F.P.C. 61, 70 (1966), *aff'd* 388 F.2d 444 (7th Cir.), *cert. denied,* 392 U.S. 928 (1968) (cited herein, as "NEPCO"). Similarly, the New York Public Service Commission concluded that "the prudence rule is a regulatory substitute for the discipline that would be imposed by a free, competitive market economy where the penalty for mismanagement and imprudent costs is a loss of jobs, profits or business failure." *Long Island Lighting Co.,* 71 P.U.R. 4th 262, 269 (1985) (cited herein as "LILCO"). Finally, the Iowa State Commerce Commission articulated its regulatory duty as follows:

> to maintain surveillance over costs associated with a particular decision, and in the absence of the kind of incentive provided by a competitor, the responsibility falls upon us to provide the requisite incentives. We do not believe we are unduly interfering with management prerogatives when we attempt to distinguish between reasonable and unreasonable management decisions. We believe such an inquiry is required of us by the legislature's directive that rates we allow be reasonable and just.

Iowa Public Service Co., 46 P.U.R 4th 339, 368 (1982).

The basic principle of regulatory review of utility expenditures is at least sixty years old. The United States (U.S.) Supreme Court in 1923 held that a regulated company is entitled to a return on its investment that is "adequate, under efficient and economical management," to enable the utility "to raise the money necessary for the proper discharge of its public duties." *Bluefield Waterworks & Improvement Co. v. Public Service Commission., 262 U.S. 679, 693 (1923).* Justice Brandeis elaborated on this precept in his oft-quoted definition of "prudent investment":

> The term prudent investment is not used in a critical sense.
> There should not be excluded from the finding of the [capi-
> tal] base [used to compute rates], investments which, under
> ordinary circumstances would be deemed reasonable. The
> term is applied for the purpose of excluding what might be
> found to be dishonest or obviously wasteful or imprudent
> expenditures. Every investment may be assumed to have
> been made in the exercise of reasonable judgment, unless
> the contrary is shown.

*Missouri ex rel. Southwestern Bell Telephone Co.v. Public Service Commis-
sion*, 262 U.S. 276, 289 (1923) (Brandeis, J. concurring).

In recent years, regulatory bodies have used these principles to deny
recovery to utilities for very significant portions of their capital expenditures related to major projects. The magnitude of these disallowances has
been staggering: the New York Public Service Commission excluded
$1.395 billion of the cost of the Shoreham Nuclear Project based on its
findings of unreasonable project management, *LILCO, supra,* and subsequently denied recovery of approximately $2 billion of the capital cost of
the Nine Mile Point 2 nuclear project, *Re Nine Mile Point 2 Nuclear Generating Facility,* 78 P.U.R. 4th 23, 41 (N.Y. 1986); the Missouri Public Service Commission disallowed $384 million for imprudent management in
constructing the Callaway Nuclear Plant, *Re Union Electric Co.,* 66 P.U.R.
4th 202, 228 (Mo. 1985), and the Iowa State Commerce Commission excluded $286 million of the costs for the same plant, *Re Union Electric Co.,*
72 P.U.R. 4th 444, 454 (Iowa 1986); the Michigan Public Service Commission rejected $397 million of the Fermi 2 capital expenditures as im-
prudent, *Re The Detroit Edison Company,* Case No. U-7660 (Mich. S.C.,
April 1, 1986); the New Jersey Board of Public Utilities reduced the rate
base for the Hope Creek nuclear plant by $432 million based on unreason-
able management, *Re Public Service Electric and Gas Co.,* No.
ER85121163 (N.J. Bd. of P.U., April 6, 1987); the Kansas State Corporation Commission denied recovery of $244 million of the costs of the Wolf
Creek Nuclear Generating Facility, *Re Wolf Creek Nuclear Generating Facility,* 70 P.U.R. 4th 475, 508 (Kan. 1985), and a Federal Energy Regulatory Commission judge followed suit by excluding $128 million in Wolf
Creek costs, *Kansas Gas and Electric Co.,* 39 F.E.R.C. Para. 63,013, at
65,065 (1987); the Illinois Commerce Commission disallowed $101 mil-
lion of the Byron 1 Nuclear plant costs, *Re Commonwealth Edison Co.,* 71
P.U.R. 4th 81, 98 (Ill. 1985); and the California Public Utilities Commission refused to permit Southern California Edison to include $344 mil-
lion of the plant costs for San Onofre-2 and -3 because it had been imprudently spent, *Re Southern California Edison CO.,* 80 P.U.R. 4th 148,
153 (Calif. 1986). Finally, in what may be a watershed case, the California
Commission is currently considering a staff recommendation to disallow
$4.37 billion—75 percent—of the $5.8 billion cost of the two-unit Diablo
Canyon nuclear generating station.

All of these dramatic deductions were related to the construction of nuclear power plants, but the same maxims have been used to deny cost recovery for projects involving traditional fossil fuel power plants, a synthetic

natural gas plant, and oil and gas pipelines. Because of the substantial re-placement fuel costs that can be incurred, utility watchdogs have also fo-cused increasing attention on the management of outages (both scheduled and unscheduled) for nuclear power plants, and disallowances have ranged as high as $34 million for the imprudent costs associated with a single out-age. Stivison, David V., "When the Big Plants Shut Down: State Commis-sions Respond to Nuclear Outages," *Public Utilities Fortnightly*, February 6, 1986.

As regulatory commissions become more comfortable with their role as sentinels against unreasonable costs, they are likely to expand their inquiries to include any significant utility expenditure that might have been controlled more effectively by management. Thus, the project manager for any regulat-ed entity or its contractors should expect her decisions to be subjected to microscopic attention.

The Prudent Management Standard for Contract Disputes

The measure of performance under many contracts is almost identical to the prudent management standard that has been applied in the regulatory con-text. In fact, by statute, contracts for some defense projects are subject to renegotiation if the contractor earns "excessive" profits; but

> in determining excessive profits, favorable recognition must be given to the efficiency of the contractor or subcontractor, with particular regard to attainment of quantity and quality production, reduction of costs, and economy in the use of materials, facilities and manpower.

50 U.S.C., App. See. 1213(e).

Thus, a project manager that can demonstrate his project's efficiency may be able to retain profits that would otherwise be returned to the gov-ernment.

Virtually any project-related contract could also be the subject of litiga-tion focusing on the manager's performance. In a very typical case, a sub-contractor may claim that she lost profits on a project when the prime con-tractor or the owner failed to integrate all of the project elements efficiently and caused a delay in the subcontractor's work. Similarly, an owner may sue his services contractor or vendor for failure to manage a project component prudently so that it would satisfy the owner's requirements. (For instance, the utility owners of the Nine Mile Point 2 Nuclear Generating Station re-cently filed suit against three suppliers seeking $500 million in damages for leakage problems in eight main steam isolation valves that allegedly delayed the plant's operating license. *Nuclear News*, June 1987, at 39.) Occasional-ly (and preferably) the performance standard is spelled out in sufficient detail in the contract itself, but much more frequently, the parties are relegated to presenting evidence on the reasonableness of project management under the particular circumstances of that contract.

STANDARDS FOR PRUDENT PROJECT MANAGEMENT

The Reasonable Project Manager

The reasonable person test. The Federal Energy Regulatory Commission concluded in its seminal *New England Power Co.* decision that "the most helpful test" in resolving issues of "prudent investment" is the "reasonable person" test, which the commission defined as follows:

> In performing our duty to determine the prudence of specific costs, the appropriate test to be used is whether they are costs which a reasonable utility management ... would have made, in good faith, under the same circumstances, and at the relevant point in time.

NEPCO, supra, at 61,084. This "reasonable person" test has been consistently applied by state public service commissions in evaluating the prudence of costs incurred by utilities under their jurisdictions (*e.g., Re Southern California Edison Co., supra,* at 168) and has been applied as well in other areas of law involving regulated companies, including occupational safety and health, banking, and government contracting.

The "reasonable person" is widely accepted as a standard in large part because it is an *objective* test that avoids the adverse policy implications of alternative legal criteria such as strict liability or "guilty knowledge." A strict liability approach would deem a project manager imprudent whenever a management decision produced harm significantly greater than its benefits. Under that analysis, however, regulatory bodies would undoubtedly be inundated with requests by public utilities for advance approval of projects before they undertake substantial capital investments. A "guilty knowledge" approach would consider management imprudent only when the manager acted with a conscious apprehension that his conduct was wrongful or otherwise faulty. That standard tends to exculpate irresponsible management, however, because it would be virtually impossible to prove that management acted with conscious knowledge of its wrongdoing. The "reasonable person" standard avoids these legal pitfalls and provides an appropriate level of regulatory or judicial scrutiny.

The "reasonable person" in the project management context draws its meaning from an extensive body of tort cases involving issues of negligence. It is clear from these well-established principles of tort law that the "reasonable person" standard is, above all, an objective standard, not dependent on individual judgment:

> The standard which the community demands must be an objective and external one, rather than that of the individual judgment, good or bad, of the particular individual.

Restatement (Second) of Torts Sec. 283 comment c at 12 (1965), Thus, the "reasonable person" standard does not depend on what a particular person considers reasonable under the circumstances, but rather on a standard of reasonableness imposed by the community. Indeed, the courts have gone to great lengths to emphasize the abstract and hypothetical character of the reasonable person:

> The reasonable man is a fictitious person, who is never negligent, and whose conduct is always up to standard. He is not to be identified with any real person...

Restatement, supra, See. 283 comment c at 13.

Community standards. Community standards as a measure of the reasonable person's behavior may be established in a variety of ways, not the least of which are published treatises by respected project managers such as those presented at this symposium. Professional codes such as the Project Management Institute Code of Ethics (e.g., requiring application of state-of-the-art project management tools and techniques to ensure that schedules are met and that the project is appropriately planned and coordinated) and the Canons of Ethics of the American Society of Civil Engineers may also help define the parameters of prudent project management.

In some cases there may even be a statute or regulation mandating a particular level of project management attention. For example, the Department of Interior stipulations that governed construction of the Trans Alaska Pipeline project dictated that the owners should "manage, supervise and implement the construction ... to the extent allowed by the state-of-the-art and development of technology." Agreement and Grant of Right-of-Way for Trans Alaska Pipeline, January 23, 1974.

The U.S. Department of Defense also established very clear community standards for high technology projects in its Cost/Schedule Control Systems Criteria, C/SCSC Joint Surveillance Guide, initially issued in the late 1960s and periodically updated. Courts and regulatory agencies have used these external measures to assess project managers' performance.

Internal project standards. In some instances, however, the most relevant criteria for evaluating project management's prudence may not be set by the community, but by the managers themselves. Certainly the most applicable estimates, schedules, or quality norms are those that were tailored to the particular project at issue. Project management presumptively considered all pertinent constraints when it set those benchmarks, and it may be reasonable to apply those standards to assess project execution. As the California Public Utilities Commission held in assessing schedule performance on the San Onofre project, "one is entitled to assume that the proponents of the project would devise a schedule that contains the least amount of 'float' or avoidable delay." *Re Southern California Edison Co., supra,* at 187.

The New York Public Service Commission followed this approach in evaluating Long Island Lighting's performance on the Shoreham project. The company argued that it would be more appropriate to compare the procurement cycle actually achieved at Shoreham with those attained at other nuclear construction projects. The commission concluded, however, that

> such a comparison would not be germane. This is because the cycles planned but unachieved at Shoreham were those that [the utility's] management considered essential if the procurement function was to succeed in supporting the engineering and construction schedules. A cycle short enough to support construction in some other plant's schedule might nevertheless have been too lengthy to achieve that same objective at Shoreham. Conversely, the failure of procurement to support

construction at another plant would not establish that Shoreham was prudently managed despite such failures.

LILCO, supra, at 286. Similarly, the Missouri Public Service Commission
used the definitive estimate for the Callaway project as "the proper starting
point for an investigation of cost overruns and a determination as [to]
whether costs incurred on the project are reasonable." *Re Union Electric Co.,
supra,* at 229.

Internally approved project standards have an initial attractiveness that
has seduced some fact finders to divine imprudence whenever project goals
are not met. That conclusion is clearly inappropriate. Project objectives may
be set for a variety of purposes — i.e., to provide an ambitious target that
will always be just beyond the reach of all but the most capable managers.
Moreover, the project managers may simply have erred and established standards or procedures that are impractical. Finally, circumstances may have
changed so that the norms conceived at the beginning of the project no
longer have any relevance. Thus, judges and commissioners should not
blithely adopt the project's standards as coincident with prudent management without first testing the objective reasonableness of those criteria within the framework of the conditions that actually existed.

Standards that exceed common practice. Even compliance with an established precedent—whether set by the community or by project management
internally—may not be sufficient, however, to demonstrate prudence. The
reasonable person standard applied by courts and juries reflects an observation made by Judge Learned Hand more than half a century ago in his opinion in *The T. J. Hooper:* "in most cases reasonable prudence is in fact common prudence." 60 F.2d 737, 740 (2d Cir.), *cert. denied,* 287 U.S. 662
(1932). Thus, evidence of the usual and customary conduct of others under
similar circumstances is normally relevant and admissible as an indication
of what the community of project managers regards as proper.

Proof that project management practices and organizational structures
consistently fell short of contemporaneous industry standards and practices
serves a particularly useful function for the trier of fact:

> Proof that the defendant took less than customary care has a
> use different from proof that the defendant followed business
> usages. Conformity evidence only raises questions, but sub-
> conformity evidence tends to answer questions. If virtually
> all other members of the defendant's craft follow safer [or
> more efficient] methods, then those methods are practical;
> the defendant has heedlessly overlooked or consciously failed
> to adopt common precautions.

Morris, *Custom and Negligence,* 42 Colum. L. Rev. 1147, 1161 (1942).

It should be emphasized that although failure to conform to industry
standards establishes imprudence, proof of limited conformity to the practices of others does not carry the same weight in establishing prudence. Consequently, even if one or more specifically identifiable "real world" project
managers would have acted in a particular fashion, such evidence of limited
conformity would not establish prudence. For unlike the fictional "reasonable manager" of the law, "real world" managers, even though they are gen-

erally considered "reasonable" by their peers, sometimes act unreasonably or imprudently.

Because even people who are generally reasonable may sometimes act negligently, it is not surprising that the law refuses to allow any one individual to set the standard of prudent behavior by her conduct alone. Indeed, the courts have consistently held that even adherence to an industry-wide custom or practice will not insulate a defendant from liability because an entire industry may be negligent. This principle was perhaps most eloquently articulated by Judge Hand in his oft-cited opinion in *The T.J. Hooper:*

> In most cases reasonable prudence is in fact common prudence; but strictly it is never its measure; a whole calling may have unduly lagged in the adoption of new and available devices. It never may set its own tests....Courts must in the end say what is required; there are precautions so imperative that even their universal disregard will not excuse their omission.

The T.J. Hooper, supra, 60 F.2d at 740.

The New York Public Service Commission applied a similar analysis to the Shoreham Nuclear project and found that "if gross inattention to cost and schedule control was typical of the industry, industry practices on their face would be unreasonable and could not excuse [the utility] from its responsibility to act reasonably." *LILCO* at 278. Indeed, commissions have also found that utilities are not necessarily prudent simply because they produced project results that were better than the norm. The Illinois Commerce Commission found that although the Byron Nuclear Power Plant was

> one of the cheaper plants to be built recently, that certainly does not preclude investigation into particular aspects of the project to determine whether there were reasonably avoidable diseconomies....The favorable plant cost comparisons do, however, help to prevent the Commission from inferring mismanagement simply from cost increases, increased project ratios, or other such simple arithmetical comparisons.

Re Commonwealth Edison Co., supra, at 101.

Requirement for expert project management. The common use by commissions and courts of a reasonable manager standard implies application of the qualifications required from a specialist, which differs substantially from the criteria applied to the ordinary person engaged in ordinary activities. This expert standard, again, is a familiar facet of negligence law, which has traditionally demanded more than ordinary care from those who undertake any work calling for unique skill. Specialists have always had a duty to display "that special form of competence which is not part of the ordinary equipment of the reasonable man, but which is the result of acquired learning and aptitude developed by special training and experience." *Restatement (Second) of Torts,* Sec. 299A comment a.

An expert generally is held to "the standard of skill and knowledge required of the actor who practices a profession or trade"—the "skill and knowledge," in other words, "which is commonly possessed by members of that profession or trade in good standing." *Id.* Sec. 299A comment e. Thus, as members of a particularly skilled group, project managers will normally be held to a standard based on the distinctive skill and knowledge commonly possessed by members of the profession they undertake to practice.

The level of expertise demanded by regulatory commissions or the courts will be commensurate with the complexity and challenge of the project. For instance, significantly greater talent and experience will be expected from the manager of a multi-billion dollar nuclear power plant project than from the project manager responsible for the addition to a residential home. In general, the greater the risk of calamitous outcomes (e.g., runaway costs or injury to the environment or populace from quality shortcomings), the greater the burden that will be imposed on the project manager.

Reasonable Project Management "Under the Circumstances"

Hindsight prohibited. Courts and regulatory agencies have uniformly applied the criteria for prudent project management applicable at the time decisions were made based on the facts that were available to the decision-maker at that time. For instance, in adopting a reasonable utility manager standard in *NEPCO*, the FERC remarked that

> while in hindsight it may be clear that a management decision was wrong, our task is to review the prudence of the utility's actions and the costs resulting therefrom based on the particular circumstances existing ... at the time the challenged costs were actually incurred.

NEPCO, supra, 31 F.E.R.C. Para. 61,047, at 61,084. Thus, the commission made it clear that the standard to be used is not one of perfection, that is, judging the reasonableness of management decisions with the benefit of hindsight. Instead, management conduct must be evaluated according to the circumstances that existed at the time the relevant decision was made.

Some project managers have attempted to invoke severe time constraints as a mitigating circumstance that might justify less than optimal procedures. The courts, however, have imposed two important limitations on the rule that an actor's conduct must be evaluated according to the circumstances (including "crisis circumstances") that existed at the time of the challenged conduct. First, crisis conditions are not considered as a mitigating circumstance when the manager's own negligence creates the crisis. "The fact that the actor is not negligent after the emergency has arisen does not preclude his liability for his tortious conduct which has produced the emergency." *Restatement, supra,* Sec. 296(2), at 64. Thus, a utility project manager may be held responsible for cost increases in a situation in which he acts "reasonably in [a] crisis which he has himself brought about." *Id.* Sec. 296 comment d at 65. Second, a person who engages in an activity in which crises arise frequently is required to anticipate and prepare for those situations. In particular, experts or professionals who perform work that is characterized by frequent crises (i.e., most project managers) are required to have particular skill and training to deal with those situations. *Restatement, supra,* Sec. 296 comment c at 65.

As part of the "reasonable person" standard, the FERC has expressly held that "management must operate its systems to avoid circumstances that give rise to emergencies." In *Texas Eastern Transmission Corp.*, 2 F.E.R.C. Para. 6l, 277 (1978), the FERC precluded the gas company from recovering the costs of emergency gas purchases because the commission found that the company imprudently operated its system so as to create a situation in which emergency purchases were necessary. The commission emphasized that it was not judging the company's behavior with the benefit of hindsight; rather it found that, based on information available to the company at the time, it was imprudent in failing to take steps early in the year that would have eliminated the need for later emergency gas purchases. *Id.* Para. 61,277, at 61,617–18.

The "large complex project." A few commentators have argued that some projects (which they dub "large complex projects" or "LCPs") are *sui generis* and that their peculiar circumstances (e.g., size, complexity, application of new technology) make it impossible to define meaningful management criteria for assessing performance. This position has been soundly rejected. In the proceeding before the New York Public Service Commission to establish the allowable costs for the Shoreham nuclear project, the utility advocated a "theory which suggests that large-scale complex projects are inherently unmanageable" and a standard of conduct that "would insulate [the utility's] management from a finding of imprudence short of outright fraud, self-dealing, blatant carelessness, or gross negligence." *LILCO, supra,* at 269. The commission disdained this approach because "the public is entitled to expect that such undertakings by public utilities are controllable." *Id.* The development of the project management discipline over the past twenty-five years would appear to confirm the Commission's judgment. Project managers are unlikely to be able to hide their failures behind rationalizations that their projects were somehow unique and not amenable to standard project management techniques.

Project Managers' Responsibility for Vendors' Actions

In most instances, the focus of any judicial inquiry will be on whether the project manager acted prudently. Of course, that investigation should include an examination of the project manager's role in selecting contractors, defining the scope of their work, supporting their efforts, and monitoring performance. Any dereliction in these duties would obviously be the project manager's direct responsibility.

According to some regulatory commissions, however, the project manager may also be vicariously liable for the imprudent conduct of her agents. For example, the Maine Public Utility Commission found that under its regulatory scheme, the ratepayers should "pay no more than the reasonably necessary costs to serve them. Any other reading [of the statute] is likely to lead to economic inefficiency, to excess costs, and sometimes to dubious practices between utilities and their suppliers." *Re Seabrook Involvements by Maine Utilities*, 67 P.U.R. 4th 161, 168–69 (Me. P.U.C. 1985). The Maine commission held explicitly that "a supplier's unreasonable charges, even when not found to have been imprudently incurred by the utility, cannot be passed on to the utility's ratepayers." *Id.*

Similarly, the Pennsylvania Public Utility Commission found that because the project manager, not the ratepayers, chose the contractor, the risk of performance failures should be borne by the stockholders.

> It must be recognized that the basic question is who should pay for the cost of the improper design and manufacture of the Salem 1 generator. ... Including these costs in [the utility's rates] means that all ratepayers are charged for [the contractor's] actions. This insulated both [the utility] and [the contractor] from responsibility for the generator failure. Conversely, denying ... recovery places the costs on the party most capable of pursuing legal remedies and negotiating future contractual protections, [the utility]. Only [the utility] can structure its operations in such a fashion as to minimize the costs of contractor error or pursue damages should errors occur.

Re Salem Nuclear Generating Station, 70 P.U.R. 4th 568, 606–607 (Pa. P.U.C. 1985).

The Michigan Public Service Commission has also held the utility strictly liable for the derelictions of its construction contractors and vendors.

> It is the responsibility of [the utility], and not its ratepayers, to ensure that the selected vendors perform the assigned work. The fact is that repair and rework were necessary regardless of how and when it was performed or whose fault it was. As a result, additional expenditures occurred which otherwise should not have. The Commission believes it is more appropriate that this expenditure becomes the responsibility of the company and not the ratepayers. To do otherwise might be detrimental to the ratepayers because utilities would be less inclined to be diligent in their supervision and negotiations with contractors in the resolution of problems such as this.

Re Detroit Edison Co., supra, at 8.

Although these cases ostensibly hold the project manager responsible for contractor negligence regardless of his own fault, good policy may not dictate so harsh a result. The fundamental premise underlying the commission's holdings is an expectation that the project manager can control the contractor's performance, either through negotiation of strict contract terms that make the contractor accountable for any mismanagement or through careful monitoring and direction of the contractor's work. If the utility can demonstrate that its project manager took reasonable steps to preclude contractor misfeasance, that evidence should provide an adequate defense, particularly if the contractor withheld material information about its failures from the project manager. The manager should be penalized only if there were steps that she could reasonably have taken to avoid or mitigate the contractor's imprudence.

An Alternative Standard: "Efficient" Project Management

In some jurisdictions, regulated companies should anticipate being held to a somewhat more rigorous performance standard if they expect to obtain full recovery for their project costs. In Texas, for instance, the legislature has determined that a utility seeking to include an allowance for construction work in process (CWIP) in its rate base must show that a project has been managed "prudently" and "efficiently." Texas Public Utility Regulatory Act, Sec. 41(a). Under the most likely interpretation of this statute, utilities will have to show more than the reasonableness of their conduct; they will have to show that the project used "the most effective and least wasteful means of doing a task or accomplishing a purpose" and performed in "the best possible manner." *Houston Lighting & Power*, Docket No. 5779, Examiner's Report (December 20, 1984) at 17, *aff'd* (January 11, 1985). Similarly, the Illinois Commerce Commission has held that its statute requires a demonstration of more than mere reasonableness before a utility can recover its project costs:

> In addition to prudency, considered narrowly, the act now directs the commission to consider efficiency, economy, and timeliness, so far as they affect costs.

Re Commonwealth Edison Co., supra, at 94.

These seemingly broader mandates for project review have not been fully tested in the courts, but they appear to imply a greater focus on the results that are actually achieved. All projects are plagued with niggling inefficiencies, and management's task is to minimize them to the extent possible. Rigid application of the efficiency standard, however, might mean that no project, no matter how well managed, would be able to demonstrate absolute efficiency and recover 100 percent of its costs, at least in the context of extraordinary rate relief such as CWIP. In these cases, there will be an even greater premium on the project manager's skill.

THE BURDEN OF PROVING IMPRUDENCE

A Utility's Burden

Courts and regulatory agencies have long recognized the importance of giving managers relatively free reign to run projects as they see fit and to avoid second-guessing managers' decisions. Thus, absent a significant showing to the contrary, they have presumed that managers act reasonably. The FERC has formulated the following general rule:

> Utilities seeking a rate increase are not required to demonstrate in their cases-in-chief that all expenditures were prudent. ...Where some other participant in the proceeding creates a *serious doubt* as to the prudence of an expenditure, then the applicant has the burden of dispelling these doubts and proving the questioned expenditure to have been prudent.

Minnesota Power and Light Co., 11 F.E.R.C. Para. 61,312 (1980) (emphasis added).

Several states have concluded that a "serious doubt" is raised about management's prudence whenever the final project costs materially exceed the originally estimated costs, thus shifting the burden to the company to show that it acted reasonably and that all costs were justified. *Re Union Electric Co., supra,* at 212; *Houston Lighting & Power Co.,* 50 P.U.R. 4th

157, 187 (Tex. P.U.C. 1982); *Consumers Power Co.,* No. U-4717, slip op. at 8 (Mich. P.S.C. 1978). Other factors that might create a "serious doubt" include performance that deviates significantly from the industry average, a major accident or component failure, or a fine imposed by a regulatory body for violation of statutes or regulations (e.g., an OSHA or Nuclear Regulatory Commission fine for safety infractions). If any of these tokens are present, the project manager may be called upon to marshall evidence to defend his administration.

This allocation of accountability is consistent with the basic legal maxim that the party having best access to the relevant information must normally carry the initial burden of proof. The project manager, with intimate knowledge of project planning, organization, and control, should be in the preeminent position to vindicate her prudence. Such proof should be straightforward for a meticulously run project that pays assiduous attention to documentation. Many managers have been rudely surprised, however, by their inability to demonstrate their project's good health to an outsider despite hale and hearty prognoses throughout the project's life. The project manager must be able to point to contemporaneous documentation (not "posthoc rationalizations") to confirm management's prudence.

The Importance of Contemporaneous Documentation

Two recent decisions illustrate the weight courts and commissions have given to data that was created as a routine part of the project. In *Long Island Lighting Co.,* the New York Public Service Commission was faced with a contradiction between a very critical report prepared by the architect/engineer during the project and the owners' later disclaimers. The commission found that

> the company's reconstructed version of the facts is not plausible. [The A/E's] report identified a significant problem in need of correction when the construction effort was under way and when [the A/E] was intimately familiar with the problem by virtue of its role as architect/engineer. The judges had a choice between [the A/E's] contemporaneous analysis or an analysis prepared by [the owner] in 1984 for purposes of this proceeding. Thus, they quite reasonably attached more credence to the former.... If the report was faulty, [the owner's] management failed to discern its alleged infirmities back in the 1970s when it was important that the design change process be carefully appraised and effectively managed.

LILCO, supra, at 290. Similarly, the Missouri Public Service Commission in *Re Union Electric Co., supra,* relied on reports generated by the utility, its consultants, and its contractors during the course of the project in finding that the utility imprudently managed the Callaway nuclear project.

In evaluating after-the-fact explanations of events, courts have long recognized "the familiar phenomenon of post-hoc reconstruction." This phenomenon refers not to deliberately false testimony, but rather to "the often-encountered tendency, though unintentional, to testify to what one believes 'must have happened' and not to what did happen." *United States ex rel. Crist v. Lane,* 577 F. Supp. 504, 511 n.11 (N.D. Ill. 1983), *rev'd on these grounds,* 745 F.2d 476 (7th Cir. 1984), *cert. denied,* 105 S. Ct. 2146 (1985).

Because "post-hoc reconstruction" is so familiar, courts traditionally give greater weight to contemporaneous statements or documents than to later explanations of events offered by witnesses at trial or hearing. Moreover, it is well established that business records have special indicia of reliability based on the fact that managers relied on them in making decisions in the ordinary course of the project.

The prudent project manager, anticipating the possibility of a subsequent challenge, should pay particular attention to documentation as the project progresses. Ordinarily, the same records that should be used to plan and control the project will also be most useful in championing it through later trials. One of the most glaring weaknesses in the utility company defenses mounted to date has been the project manager's inability to demonstrate the specific causes for major cost increases. The shibboleths of "regulatory interference" or "changed conditions" as justifications for broken budgets have not been adequate when millions of dollars are at stake.

As knowledgeable project managers are well aware, however, a rudimentary configuration management system enhances rational decision-making to accommodate change during the project and at the same time creates a concrete record that can justify cost increases in any later proceedings. Some companies (notably Southern California Edison) now prepare a "pedigree" for each design change that includes a definition of the source of the design requirements, an evaluation of alternatives, a cost/benefit analysis, and steps taken to monitor expenditures versus the estimate. This data will be invaluable for managing the project, but will also demonstrate the reasonableness of the design change should there be a future interrogation. The most crucial lesson of the last decade of prudence proceedings is the absolute necessity for comprehensive record-keeping.

SUBSTANTIVE STANDARDS FOR PRUDENT PROJECT MANAGEMENT

It is impossible to prescribe the unassailable tenets of project management that, if followed, will always invoke the imprimatur of prudence. Standards will evolve as the discipline develops, and courts may be more or less tolerant of shortcomings based on the need to meet other societal goals (e.g., an energy crisis may cause a temporary relaxation of efficiency standards in order to meet the immediate demand). Nevertheless, a few basic principles can be adduced from recent cases. This section reviews some of the illustrative holdings from the New York Public Service Commission's Shoreham prudence proceeding in three critical areas: planning, organization, and control.

Planning

Planning is the essence of prudent management. Every element of a project demands foresight and a design for realizing goals. Planning is even more essential as the tasks become larger and more complex. Specialized expertise must be marshalled to anticipate technical specifications, lead times, potential impediments, and control requirements. Moreover, all of the parts must mesh to enable the owners and senior managers to assign priorities, assess risks, define the organization, and measure performance. Prudent planning minimizes foreseeable risks and, therefore, becomes more crucial as predictable risks increase.

Precautions that might arguably be optional become obligatory when the peril of inaction is grave.

The New York Commission identified planning as the lynchpin for a prudent project.

> Reasonable management would have foreseen the need for a systematic approach to this large-scale construction project and would, therefore, have exercised its responsibilities by formulating a plan to achieve its objectives. [The owner] failed to commence this project with a baseline plan defining what was to be built; how the work would be performed, and by whom; how changes would be incorporated into the plans if necessary; and, most critically, how the status of the project would be monitored and kept on schedule. This failure resulted in numerous problems throughout the project's history, including an inability to perform cost and schedule monitoring; confusion over roles and areas of responsibility among the project participants; low labor productivity; and the absence of a mechanism for providing the Board of Directors with sufficient, timely information to form a basis for providing guidance and making policy decisions. Accordingly, [the utility's] planning failure not only constituted imprudence,... but it also had direct and foreseeable adverse consequences on the course of the project....

LILCO, supra, at 275–276. Any prudence review will almost certainly focus first on the adequacy of project planning.

Organization

Four basic premises guide a prudent project organization: 1) clearly defined roles and responsibilities for all of the parties at the project's inception; 2) delegated responsibility and authority based on the project's plan; 3) a relatively stable organizational structure for the project's duration; and 4) experience as the basis for building an organization. Conversely, an imprudent project organization is typically characterized by duplication, poorly defined roles, antagonism among the parties, delayed decision-making, and instability.

Organizational flaws were at the heart of many of the problems pinpointed on the Shoreham project by the New York Commission.

> The Judges found that the lack of comprehensive, adequately explicit planning at the inception of the project laid the groundwork for serious conflicts and confusion over the respective roles of the various participants in the construction effort. They found that the failure to define discrete areas of responsibility led to a situation in which [the utility's] own project manager interfered with [the A/E's] managers,
>
> > producing friction, resentment, and antagonism between [sic] [the A/E, utility] and the major contractors. Because of these interferences and poorly defined authority, major tasks of planning, supervision

and coordination were not performed. Construction
was adversely affected.

... The record evidence establishes that in 1975 [the utility's project manager] began allowing contractors to submit
problems to him instead of to [the A/E]. This was interference with [the A/E's] construction management authority,
which undermined [the A/E's] control over contractors and
engendered antagonism between [the utility] and its archi-
tect/engineer. [The utility's] interference is also evidenced
by contemporaneous documentation describing confusion
over who, as between [the utility] and [the A/E], was in
charge of construction management.

LILCO, supra, at 276.

A common problem on many projects has been the absence of a clearly
designated project manager who could coordinate all elements of the project.
An astonishing number of major projects in the 1970s attempted to function
without a distinct focus for management authority. The result was predictable confusion and inattention to crucial problems.

Control

Prudent project controls must be commensurate with management's experience and the nature of the contractual relations. For instance, inexperienced
managers should be given a shorter reporting leash so that corrective action
can be taken at an appropriate stage before the project gets out of hand. Similarly, the owner's control under a cost-plus contract must be substantially
more stringent than with fixed-price contracts where the contractor has an
incentive to control its own costs. Fundamentally, controls must be tailored
to fit project conditions. Regulatory bodies have expressed a strong prefer-
ence, however, for formal controls over ad hoc, informal mechanisms, and
some form of network analysis has become virtually *de rigueur.*

The New York Commission found that controls on the Shoreham project were sadly deficient and that the utility "never instituted a reporting system adequate to enable management to discern problem areas and to make
well-informed decisions about possible corrective actions." *LILCO, supra,* at
293. The commission pointed to evidence that there were "no genuinely in-
formative field reports;" that due to understaffing, the reports to the project
manager on construction problems lacked substance and were frequently inaccurate; that reporting problems persisted; and "generally that the reporting
system was misleading and difficult to interpret." *Id.* The commission concluded that the utility "failed to establish a monitoring and reporting system
capable of providing the information that it needed for the purpose of making intelligent decisions about Shoreham's course and progress." *Id.* at 294.
Without these controls, the commission found that the project could not be
managed prudently.

CALCULATION OF IMPRUDENT PROJECT COSTS

Once there has been a determination that a project suffered from some imprudence, the court or regulatory agency must determine whether this imprudence

increased the project's costs, and if so, by how much. Causation is a factual question, and again there is no simple formula for whether particular consequences are sufficiently connected to the underlying management misconduct to warrant some form of penalty. Generally, courts and commissions have relied on expert testimony to establish a "clear causal connection" between management imprudence and resulting excess project costs. *LILCO, supra,* at 316; *Re Union Electric Co., supra,* at 228.

At first blush, the task of sorting prudent from imprudent project costs would seem quixotic. The courts have recognized, however, that reconstruction of the expenses that would have been incurred if management had acted differently is an extraordinarily imprecise art, and mathematical precision cannot be attained. This principle is not unique to the regulatory arena. Courts have long held in numerous substantive contexts that damages are, at best, approximations and can only be proved with whatever definiteness and accuracy the facts permit. One of the most frequently cited cases is the United States Supreme Court's decision in *Story Parchment Co. v. Paterson Parchment Paper Co.,* 282 U.S. 555, 563 (1931) (an antitrust case), in which the court held that

> where the tort itself is of such a nature as to preclude the ascertainment of the amount of damages with certainty, it would be a perversion of fundamental principles of justice to deny all relief to the injured person, and thereby relieve the wrongdoer from making any amend for his acts. In such case, while the damages may not be determined by mere speculation or guess, it will be enough if the evidence shows the extent of the damages as a matter of just and reasonable inference, although the result be only approximate. The wrongdoer is not entitled to complain that they cannot be measured with the exactness and precision that would be possible if the case, which he alone is responsible for making, were otherwise.

In four recent cases examining the prudence of nuclear power plant construction, state utility commissions have addressed the question of how to quantify the costs that should be disallowed as a result of imprudent management. In each, the commissions relied when possible on specific data tracing the cause of cost overruns. When this information was not available, the commissions adopted estimates (based on varying degrees of substantiation) to establish the cost of imprudence.

In *LILCO,* the New York Commission first concluded that the utility's management of the Shoreham nuclear project was imprudent in several respects. The commission rejected the utility's argument that the staff was required to quantify the effect of each discrete instance of imprudence in order to show that alleged acts of mismanagement directly caused specific costs. *LILCO, supra,* at 316–317. The commission concluded that the staff's methodology, which compared Shoreham cost data in four categories (engineering and construction manhours, schedule delay costs, and diesel generator problems) with cost data of other nuclear power plant construction projects was "logical and rational" and reached "a just and reasonable result." *Id.* at 317. Based on these approximations, the Commission disallowed $1.395 billion in costs. *Id.* at 326.

In *Re Union Electric Co.*, the Missouri Public Service Commission addressed the issue of whether the utility had prudently managed construction of the Callaway nuclear project. The Missouri commission concluded that, as a general matter, the utility "failed to meet the prudence standard," and that this imprudence "required significant disallowances in order to establish 'just and reasonable rates.'" *Re Union Electric Co., supra.*

To quantify the imprudent costs, the Missouri commission compared the actual cost of construction with a definitive cost estimate generated by the utility during the early stages of construction. The commission rejected the utility's argument that it should not be "held" to the definitive estimate, stating that "the definitive estimate is the proper starting point for an investigation of cost overruns and a determination as [to] whether costs incurred on the project are reasonable." *Id.* With respect to particular quantification methodologies, the commission acknowledged that the staff's calculation "represented an approximation," but concluded that the staff's model, "allowed a reasonable estimate of these costs." *Id.* at 243.

The Kansas State Corporation Commission in *Re Wolf Creek Nuclear Generating Facility*, found that

> lack of management attention coupled with the lack of efficient effective management on the part of the owners, resulted in schedule delays and increased costs that could have been mitigated by strong management action earlier in the project.

Re Wolf Creek Nuclear Generating Facility, supra, at 495. To quantify those increased costs, the Kansas Commission adopted two approaches. First, it relied on the owners' definitive estimate of costs, their reconciliation of those projections with final costs, and the staff's independent estimates of specific costs. *Id.* at 498–503. Second, the commission estimated the delay in the critical path that was caused by imprudent management and quantified the effect of that delay. *Id.* at 503–508.

Finally, in the absence of reliable contemporaneous data collected by the utility, the Michigan Public Service Commission resorted to admittedly imprecise approximations as a proxy for a more rigorous quantification of the effects of imprudence on productivity. The commission concluded that the utility "did not exercise good supervision and management" of piping installation on the Fermi 2 nuclear project, and that dereliction "resulted in unnecessary costs." It faced a dilemma, however, in attempting to specify the ascribable costs because the utility did not maintain separate accounts for repairs and rework. Nevertheless, it reasoned that

> ratepayers cannot and will not be forced to bear those costs. The Commission finds that an estimated 5 percent disallowance for low productivity is warranted. Furthermore, the Commission finds that a 10 percent disallowance both for excessive rework and repair and for poor supervision and management [of piping installation] is justified.

Re Detroit Edison Co., supra, at 29. The commission made similar approximations based on deficiencies in project engineering, *Id.* at 49–53, and delays caused "by inadequate attention, poor maintenance and inability to effectively manage problem resolutions." *Id.* at 53–58.

Each of these approaches to calculating the costs of a prudently man aged project has potential drawbacks or inequities. Great care must be exer cised, for instance, in choosing an appropriate baseline cost and schedule fo a particular project. As noted above, estimates and schedules may have bee devised for a variety of objectives and may not accurately reflect realistic pro ject goals. Comparisons with costs and schedules on other projects also pre sent significant pitfalls because no two projects are exactly comparable, an it is difficult to make fair adjustments between projects. The basic admoni tion to project managers, however, is a familiar refrain in this paper—be pre pared with contemporaneous data to justify the costs that were incurred. De viations from previous projections or from experience on other project should be explained. To the extent that there are justifications for cost in creases, a prudent project manager should be able to document them.

CONCLUSION

The last decade has been both the boon and the bane of the utility projec manager. The higher profile of mega-projects has generated intense post mortems that have focused on project managers' behavior. A shadowy profil of the "reasonable project manager" has emerged from these reviews, but i does not yet offer a model that can be easily emulated. In order to toe th line of prudence, managers must be constantly aware of the most sophisti cated techniques and alert to document their reasonable efforts to apply those strategies in their projects. The law should serve the salutary purpose of enhancing and improving project efficiency, and the growing body of lega precedent addressing prudent project management should have that effect.

REFERENCES

Speck, R. L. 1987. "The Legal Standard for Prudent and Efficient Project Management." In D.I. Cleland and W. R. King, eds. *Project Management Handbook, 2nd
Ed.* New York: Van Nostrand Reinhold.

Study Questions

THE LEGAL STANDARDS FOR "PRUDENT" PROJECT MANAGEMENT

1. This case illustrates the importance and difficulty of cost estimating. Wha are some ways of estimating costs?

2. What is meant by "prudent" project management? How does this concep relate to quality management? Why has it become so important?

3. Discuss the various standards, established in court cases, for prudent projec management. These include the reasonable project manager (reasonable per son, community, standards, etc.), reasonable project management "unde

the circumstances," project managers' responsibility for vendor's actions, and "efficient" project management. What are some of the advantages and disadvantages of each of these tests of prudence?

4. What can project managers do, up front, to ensure that proof of prudence can be given if need be? Discuss this in terms of the three critical areas: planning, organization, and control.

GENERAL

6

GENERAL

Communicating Constraints: Schedule Baseline and Recovery Measures on the Hong Kong Airport Projects

han Schmitz, International Bechtel Incorporated

MI *Proceedings*, 1995, pp. 121–28

INTRODUCTION

This paper presents the background, overall parameters, and current status of the complex $20.4 billion Hong Kong Airport Core Program (ACP). It describes scheduling, interface management, and conflict resolution techniques applied to meet the significant challenges and constraints of the ACP.

BACKGROUND

The existing Hong Kong airport at Kai Tak is a single-runway airport built on a finger of reclaimed land pointing into the sea, surrounded by hills and the dense urban development of Kowloon, and cannot be expanded. It is the third busiest international airport in the world, and Asia's busiest, with passenger volume growing at upwards of 10 percent per year. It will reach operational capacity as early as 1996. In addition to operational limitations, building height restrictions have been imposed along and adjacent to the urban-corridor flight path, and this has inhibited commercial and residential growth. Access between the western harbor container port area, prime commercial areas, and Kai Tak, which is also one of the world's busiest air cargo handling facilities, is constrained by a congested roadway system.

As part of an overall port and airport development strategy (PADS) to help assure Hong Kong's continued growth and position as the main commercial hub of Southeast Asia well into the Twenty-first Century, Hong Kong government approved development of a replacement airport in 1989. PADS also called for a five-fold expansion of Hong Kong's container port, already the world's busiest, with extensive transport links to connect the new port and airport with urban and industrial areas. The formal start of the new airport-related development of PADS occurred in September 1991, with signing of a memorandum of understanding (MOU) between Britain and the Peoples Republic of China. Under the MOU, it was agreed that the essential, or "core," scope of the new airport and transport links (airport core program—ACP) would be completed to the "maximum extent" possible by the midnight, June 30, 1997, transfer of sovereignty of Hong Kong to the Peoples Republic of China.

Notwithstanding the 1991 authorization to proceed with the ACP, major political issues related to debt financing of the new airport and its rail link;

creation of the airport authority as a statutory (public) corporation; and approval of contracts and franchises spanning the transfer of sovereignty were not substantially agreed between the British and Chinese sides until June 1995. Political delays had the effect of continually compressing the schedules for the airport and airport railway in regard to the June 30, 1997, target, until the point when this target was no longer physically realistic. This led to implementation of a multipath approach for the ACP, whereby sequential completion of the transport infrastructure projects remained targeted at not later than June 30, 1997, a target which ultimately became firm and fixed. However, the completion schedules for the airport and airport railway required reprogramming.

The first path included a control baseline of all project elements which were funded and in progress. Overall program objectives and key dates to meeting completion of these elements by June 1997 in accordance with the MOU were rigidly maintained. The second path included all unfunded project elements delayed due to external constraints. These elements were initially scheduled in terms of sequences and durations independent of the first path. As critical decisions were reached, the second path converged with the first path and was reintegrated with the overall ACP program plan and master schedule. The completion dates for such elements were then established using approved schedule sequences and durations from the points of political and funding approval, and contract award and commencement. This approach required a continuous cycle of baseline updating, including risk assessment and contingency planning; repackaging and resequencing of contract works and interfaces; and transfer of scope between projects. Communication of constraints, both internal and external; early identification of potential variances and conflicts; and proactive problem resolution have been essential to the success of the ACP.

SCOPE AND PARAMETERS OF THE ACP

The magnitude and complexity of the ACP are unprecedented in Hong Kong. Indeed, the ACP is one of the most extensive developments undertaken in the late Twentieth Century. The ACP comprises ten interrelated projects (over 200 contracts) being performed by four separate sponsors, each of which represents a large and complex development, which must be managed individually and in concert to meet the prime objective of completion within time, political, and budget constraints. The ACP projects include the first phase of the new airport and a new town adjacent to the airport; transport links extending between the airport and central Hong Kong; and extensive land reclamation to support these transportation facilities and to provide an attractive environment for commercial/residential development.

As of June 1995, progress on the ACP overall stood at approximately 35 percent complete. The seven government-sponsored transport infrastructure projects were at 62 percent complete, and the new harbor tunnel sponsored by a private franchisee, which connects the ACP expressway system to Hong Kong Island, also considered an essential part of the transport infrastructure, was approaching 50 percent complete. The transport infrastructure projects are on target for completion and commencement of operations before June 30, 1997. The operational targets for the airport and airport railway, being sponsored by government-owned public corporations, are now April 1998 and June 1998, respectively.

The New Airport at Chek Lap Kok

The site of the new international airport in Hong Kong is Chek Lap Kok, an island just off the village of Tung Chung on the northern coast of Lantau Island. Land for the airport was formed by leveling Chek Lap Kok and Lam Chau islands, and using the excavated materials along with marine-won sand to reclaim the additional land areas required.

The new airport, which is being developed and will be operated by a new statutory (public) corporation—the Airport Authority—owned by Hong Kong government, will initially have one runway in twenty-four-hour operation at opening, capable of handling a capacity of thirty-five million passengers and 1.5 million tons of cargo annually. The second runway, together with phased expansions of terminal and related facilities, will be operational according to air traffic demands. At ultimate capacity, planned for the year 2040, the airport will handle approximately eighty-seven million passengers and nine million tons of cargo annually.

Formation of the 1,248-hectare airport island and terminal foundation construction are now nearing final completion. The terminal construction contract and major systems contracts were awarded and commenced in 1994/1995. Overall, work on the airport was approximately 36 percent complete as of June 1995.

Physical construction of the airport is on track for completion in September 1997, to be followed by an extensive airport operational transition phase. The critical path to operations runs through privately financed franchise services such as air cargo, aircraft maintenance, and fuel supply. These services, which are essential for airport operations, have been significantly delayed in the political approval process.

The total budget for the airport is approximately $9.1 billion, including core airport facilities being constructed under sponsorship of the Airport Authority; government facilities such as the air traffic control center; and franchise services. Of this total, approximately $5.5 billion of funding has been approved, covering the government facilities and the maximum amount of equity that can be injected into the Airport Authority by Hong Kong government in accordance with prior political agreements. The remaining portion of the budget is to be financed by Airport Authority debt and pre-completion revenue, and private funding for franchises.

The political controversies to date have primarily centered on issues of funding and financing. These controversies have led to delays in the award of critical contracts and franchises, and have impacted the overall program. The revised opening date target, inclusive of minimum-capacity operating elements for franchise services, is now April 1, 1998, based on the results of re-programming and the recent agreement by the British and Chinese sides on airport financing and franchises.

Phase 1 Tung Chung New Town

The North Lantau development is a supporting community for the airport at Chek Lap Kok with a long-range target population of 260,000 by the year 2010. The Phase 1 Tung Chung New Town project is the initial part of this development and includes site formation and infrastructure for part of the new town. It will contain public and private high-density housing for approximately 20,000 residents by 1997 and local retail and commercial facilities.

Site development works have been completed, and housing and commerci‚ construction commenced in 1994. The Phase 1 Tung Chung New Town pr‹ ject was 46 percent complete as of June 1995.

North Lantau Expressway

The North Lantau Expressway (NLE) is a dual three-lane expressway, ap proximately 12.5 kilometers in length on earthwork formation of reclam‚ tion and cutting. It provides a connection from the western end of the La‚ tau Fixed Crossing along the Lantau Island coastline to the airport and th new town at Tung Chung. The scope of work for the NLE project includes utility reserve adjacent to the expressway alignment and site formation f‹ the airport railway along the expressway. Construction started in May 199‹ and is scheduled for completion in October 1996. The NLE project was 7 percent complete as of June 1995.

Lantau Fixed Crossing

The Lantau Fixed Crossing (LFC) project provides a fixed link accommoda‚ ing an expressway and a high-speed railway between northwest Tsing Yi I‚ land and the North Lantau Expressway at Tsing Chau Tsai on Lantau Islan on the west. The LFC represents the most critical ACP transport link. Th basic scheme includes a suspension bridge crossing the Ma Wan channel (th Tsing Ma bridge) with an overall length of 2,200 meters; viaduct structures t carry expressway traffic across Ma Wan Island; and a cable-stayed bridge ov‹ the Kap Shui Mun channel from Ma Wan to Lantau Island, linked by viaduct crossing Ma Wan Island. The Tsing Ma bridge will be the world's longest su‚ pension bridge carrying both road and rail traffic on the same structure.

This project includes a toll plaza, maintenance depot, automated traffi control center, and administration buildings at the junction with the Nort Lantau Expressway on the west and a major interchange with Route 3 o‹ the east. Although sponsored and funded by Hong Kong government, oper‚ tion of the bridges may eventually be privatized. Construction started i‚ May 1992, and LFC commissioning is scheduled for completion in Ma‹ 1997. As of June 1995, the LFC project was 66 percent complete.

Route 3 (Tsing Yi and Kwai Chung Sections)

Route 3 will ultimately provide a direct north to south link within the terr‚ tory, serving cross-border traffic with China. Development areas in th‹ North West New Territories, the expanding container port at Kwai Chung, a‹ well as growing traffic in West Kowloon and Hong Kong Island will also b‹ served. The Tsing Yi and Kwai Chung sections of Route 3, which link th‹ Lantau Fixed Crossing to the West Kowloon Expressway, form an importar section of the road access to the airport. ACP-related Route 3 constructio‹ started in February 1993, with completion targeted for December 199‹ The expansion of Route 3 from the LFC interchange to the Chinese bord‹ will be undertaken as a privately funded venture, starting in 1995. The ACI related Route 3 works were 53 percent complete as of June 1995.

West Kowloon Reclamation

The West Kowloon Reclamation (WKR) project reclaims approximately 33 hectares of land along the West Kowloon waterfront from Yau Ma Tei to L‚ Chi Kok to provide land for planned major transportation infrastructur works and other developments. The reclamation includes formation of new breakwaters and seawalls, and reprovisioning of all affected waterfront uses. The WKR project provides reclaimed land for transport links to the airport according to target dates required by various transport infrastructure projects. These links include the West Kowloon Expressway, the Route 3 highway facilities, the Western Harbor Crossing, and the airport railway and its associated Kowloon station. In addition, the WKR project seeks to form commercially attractive packages of land that will support early generation of development revenue. Reclamation works commenced in 1991, and land formation is being phased, with final completion by 1996. West Kowloon Reclamation works were 83 percent complete as of June 1995.

West Kowloon Expressway

The West Kowloon Expressway (WKE) project is a portion of Route 3 to be constructed on the West Kowloon Reclamation platform. It runs from the northern limit of the Western Harbor Crossing toll plaza to the southern limit of the Kwai Chung viaduct (Route 3 project) as a dual three-lane expressway. It is linked to the airport via the Lantau Fixed Crossing, the North Lantau Expressway, and Route 3 (Tsing Yi and Kwai Chung sections). Construction commenced in July 1993, with completion by October 1996. Progress as of June 1995 was 47 percent complete.

Western Harbor Crossing

The Western Harbor Crossing (WHC) project will provide a 2-kilometer-long (portal to portal), dual three-lane-immersed tube crossing of the western harbor, from the West Kowloon Expressway to the local road network on Hong Kong Island, and will allow direct expressway access between the airport and Hong Kong Island. This design/build project includes ventilation buildings at each end of the crossing, as well as a toll plaza, automated traffic control center, and administration buildings. The project is being implemented by a private franchisee who is financing, designing, constructing, operating, and eventually transfering the facility to Hong Kong government. The WHC franchise was approved by the Chinese side and construction started in mid-1993. Commissioning is scheduled for June 1997. As at June 1995, the Western Harbor Crossing was 48 percent complete.

Phase 1 Central Reclamation

A 20-hectare area on the harborside of the Central district of Hong Kong Island is to be reclaimed to provide a platform for construction of the Hong Kong terminus of the airport railway. This project also includes approach and overrun tunnels, together with efficient vehicle and pedestrian access routes to connect the terminus with existing transport infrastructure and other commercial developments. Central Reclamation works commenced in mid-1993, approximately one year later than planned due to delayed agreement by the Chinese side. The delay directly impacted the program for the airport railway.

Airport Railway

The airport railway is being sponsored by the Mass Transit Railway Corporation (MTRC), a statutory (public) corporation owned by Hong Kong government which operates the current subway system in Hong Kong. Two services will be operated. The airport express line is a dedicated airport service which will extend 34 kilometers in length from the airport at Chek Lap Kok via Tsing Yi and West Kowloon to the Central district of Hong Kong island. The airport express line, with a planned transit time of twenty-three minutes, is specifically designed to attract a high proportion of airport passengers. Four stations are planned at Central (with future provision for in-town airport check-in facilities), West Kowloon, Tsing Yi, and the airport where the station will be located in a separate ground transportation center complex adjacent to the terminal building. The Lantau line will provide a domestic service on the same route to the new airport support community at Tung Chung. This line will initially serve six stations, and will help relieve congestion from the existing system between Central and Kowloon, which is one of the world's heaviest-traveled subway sectors.

Along its route, the airport railway is dependent on all other ACP projects, with the exception of the Western Harbor Crossing, to provide essential infrastructure works which are necessary for the construction and operation of the railway, such as the lower rail deck and track form across the Tsing Ma bridge. In order to preserve the physical alignment of the airport railway and mitigate the impacts of schedule delay, a significant number of works items originally to have been undertaken by the Mass Transit Railway Corporation (MTRC) were transferred to government-sponsored transport infrastructure projects as "advance works."

The completion of the airport railway was originally targeted at June 30, 1997, per the MOU. However, award of critical contracts was delayed until late 1994 following initial approval of project financing by the Chinese side; final approval was not forthcoming until June 1995. While a significant amount of schedule delay had been absorbed through re-programming effort and transfer of scope, the ultimate effect of delay was a formal shift in the completion target for the airport railway by one year, to June 30, 1998.

All major contracts have now been awarded for the airport railway. A separate immersed tube tunnel is under construction for the airport express line from West Kowloon to the Hong Kong Central terminus, and construction of airport railway stations has commenced. Overall progress on the airport railway was 13 percent complete including "advance works" as of June 1995.

ACP Program Management Organization

Hong Kong government has established the New Airport Projects Coordination Office (NAPCO) to undertake overall program management and coordination of the multiproject ACP on its behalf. NAPCO is comprised of an integrated team of Hong Kong government personnel and International Bechtel Incorporated consultant staff. NAPCO reports directly to the Airport Development Steering Committee (ADSCOM), which is the executive decision-making body ultimately responsible for the ACP, and for coordinating policy issues with regard to the ACP projects.

ADSCOM is chaired by the chief secretary, whose executive authority is secondary only to the governor in Hong Kong, and membership includes government secretaries, such as the Secretary for Works and Financial Secretary, who are responsible for ACP matters in their respective policy areas.

The individual ACP projects are assigned to "works agents" for project level planning, execution, control, and management. Works agents are Hong

Kong government works departments and non-government ACP participants, such as the Airport Authority and MTRC, with direct responsibility for completing ACP projects within the framework of the baseline scope, master schedule, and budget developed and implemented by NAPCO, as approved by ADSCOM.

NAPCO's responsibilities are to ensure adherence by the works agents to the terms, conditions, and constraints dictated by the requirements of the approved baseline implementation plan for the ACP, and to act as a focal point for the management of project interdependencies and interfaces, and resolution of conflicts, changes, and claims which have a potential program-level impact.

ACP PROGRAM MANAGEMENT METHODOLOGY

A comprehensive integrated program/project control approach and system have been devised and implemented by NAPCO for the ACP. Details of the approach and system, including controls, administrative, and reporting requirements, are contained in a set of procedures and standards which all works agents must implement and adhere to under NAPCO guidance. Additionally, Hong Kong consultant agreement provisions and general conditions of contract for construction works have been revised to increase the level of schedule visibility and control, to ensure contractor participation, and to streamline decision-making processes in regard to dispute resolution, changes, and claims.

The overall management methodology is "top-down/ bottom-up," where ACP program-level objectives are established by NAPCO, endorsed by ADSCOM, and adopted as baseline targets at the project and contract levels through the works agents. Progress and status details are analyzed against the targets and progressively summarized upward through the works agent project offices to NAPCO.

BASELINE PLANNING AND IMPLEMENTATION

The basic control tool at the program level is the formal ACP baseline implementation plan approved by ADSCOM, which sets out a clear definition of the scope and budget of each ACP project as well as master milestone and interface schedules to execute them; project and contract scope, packaging, schedules, and budgets are developed by the works agents within the framework of the overall ACP baseline implementation plan, subject to NAPCO approval.

The ACP baseline implementation plan provides a comprehensive road map at the overall program level to point the projects toward their interim milestones, interface handover dates, and completion targets. It is the basic "original control" frame of reference by which NAPCO monitors the projects, detects and resolves problems, and is the prerequisite for program-level change control. The ACP baseline implementation plan is updated periodically to incorporate formally the effect of commitments and changes approved since the previous plan update, and to provide an opportunity for formal risk and contingency assessment, and reprogramming as necessary to meet ACP objectives.

A "current control" baseline is also maintained on a more contemporaneous basis by NAPCO, to reflect day-to-day contract variations and works schedule revisions as they are approved by the works agent project offices in accordance with ACP procedures. Where such revisions potentially impact program-level interfaces and milestones, prior review and concurrence by NAPCO is required. The "current control" baseline is then resolved into the overall ACP baseline implementation plan during the next following plan update cycle.

ACP Schedule Controls

Given the constraints, complexities, and interdependencies of the ACP, as well as the fact that interim delays will often have a cost implication, schedule control is the centerpiece of ACP program and project control. An integrated hierarchy of schedules has been developed by NAPCO for the ACP, in line with the "top-down/bottom-up" management methodology. This hierarchy, which has been implemented at all levels using a computerized critical path method (CPM) scheduling system, extends from detailed contract works schedules to project, interface, master program, and executive summary schedules. The ACP schedule hierarchy at the lowest level of detail will encompass upwards of 225 construction contracts and 350,000 activities at peak. Approximately 25,000 activities and 1,100 major interfaces will be maintained in the master program at peak.

Each schedule is statused monthly or more frequently as may be required by NAPCO against both the "original control" and "current control" baselines to indicate progress to date; report earned value, resource utilization and quantity completion; and forecast the work remaining in relation to milestones, targets, and key dates. Potential interface conflicts and program problem areas are flagged and addressed in critical item action reports for resolution via NAPCO.

Physical Progress Measurement

While concentration on monitoring of exceptions at control points such as interfaces is a primary program management technique, overall progress measurement has also been important for establishing acceptable parameters of progress and for schedule trending. However, an acceptable method is sometimes difficult to achieve consistently on an undertaking such as the ACP, given program complexities and multiple sponsors.

The physical progress measurement approach implemented by NAPCO at the integrated program level is somewhat unique. Each works element (or milestone with its attendant path of predecessor activities) within a construction contract schedule is summarized from its constituent detailed activities and weighted by its agreed dollar value (engineer estimate or original contract value for the "original control" baseline, and current contract value inclusive of executed changes for the "current control" baseline comparison). Actual physical progress for each works element is then determined monthly based on the duration from actual start through time-now, versus the total duration from actual start through the forecast finish date calculated from remaining duration, as reported in the latest status update of the contract schedule. The resulting duration-based percentage is then applied to the weighting for the given works element and divided by the total weighting for the element. Works element progress is aggregated to the contract level, contract progress to the project level, and project progress to the overall program level. Progress measurement results using this approach have a range of accuracy consistent with more conventional contract-level methods based on quantities or manhours.

Schedule-Based Risk Assessment

Within the "top-down" framework of fixed program completion objectives and constraints, schedule development has been iterative, and a significant amount of reprogramming has been necessary via NAPCO coordination, given political, administrative and technical delays, to keep the ACP on track.

Schedule-based risk assessment has been used to advantage by NAPCO and works agents in necessary reprogramming efforts. For example, a series of comprehensive risk assessments jointly conducted by NAPCO and the Airport Authority on the airport schedule, with a constrained June 30, 1997, opening date target, identified significant risks on paths through terminal building construction, testing, and commissioning. Based on the results of these assessments, risk mitigation plans were developed and implemented. Mitigation measures included repackaging of contracts for more effective sequencing; a further study of modular prefabrication and construction of terminal structural elements; development of a separate systems integration contract package for terminal specialist systems and equipment; and plans for authority-supplied construction support facilities and services to reduce mobilization periods and enhance construction efficiency by ensuring the supply and availability of construction commodities such as concrete.

INTERFACE MANAGEMENT AND CONFLICT RESOLUTION

NAPCO has the authority to direct program-level changes such as ordering acceleration for construction schedules to meet overall program objectives. The final decision in regard to acceleration and other program-related measures lies with NAPCO.

As a matter of policy, early notification of all matters likely to cause delay to the works is required so as to maximize the opportunity for early corrective action, given the degree of importance attached to the overall objective of timely completion of the ACP.

The obligation to notify includes all program, project, and contract participants, and is triggered by the event being foreseen or occurring rather than by delay actually being caused.

Acceleration measures are those actions to achieve completion of the works or a section of the works earlier than a key date or milestone stated in the contract, or to reduce an extension of time to which the contractor may be entitled. Typical reasons for acceleration include situations where an extension of time significantly increases the schedule risk on overall ACP completion objectives; the prolongation costs associated with an extension of time are greater than anticipated acceleration costs; an interfacing contract requires an earlier handover from the preceding contractor; and/or the end-user requires earlier access.

In cases when the contractor is in delay and not entitled to an extension of time, and the progress of the works appears insufficient to ensure timely completion of contractual key dates and milestones, the works agent is required to instruct the contractor to expedite progress and provide recovery schedules. The contractor is not entitled to additional payment under such an instruction, and indeed is subject to the disincentive of liquidated damages if contractual key dates are missed. If the contractor fails to properly implement the instruction to recover schedule, and the rate of progress remains insufficient, the works agent may suspend those works in delay and replace the contractor with another, to the account of the original contractor.

Except for relatively minor works, ordering of acceleration has not yet been required for the ACP. NAPCO has successfully worked with the works agents and contractors to recover from potential delay impacts, as exemplified by the following case.

The North Lantau Expressway (NLE) Tung Chung section contract includes 2.5 kilometers of dual three-lane expressway and 1.7 kilometers of two-lane utility service roadway. This section of the NLE project is constructed substantially upon reclamation formed under the Phase 1 Tung Chung New Town site formation contract. In addition, contract works include two major pre-stressed concrete bridges approximately 320 meters in length across the sea channel connecting Tung Chung and the new airport at Chek Lap Kok. The contract also incorporates works related to the airport railway, including the substructure of the airport railway's Tung Chung station.

NLE Tung Chung section contract works commenced on September 27, 1993. Completion of the works was contractually set at September 15, 1996, and subsequently revised to September 28, 1996, based on an extension of time claim granted by the works agent with NAPCO's concurrence. Although delays have been experienced for a number of works items, the contractor was instructed to recover such delays, and the contract is now forecast to complete per its revised schedule. From the perspective of the works agent sponsoring the NLE project, this is an apparently acceptable situation.

However, the commencement of construction of the airport railway Tung Chung station substructure, incorporated in the NLE Tung Chung section contract, was delayed. Although this delay did not have an adverse impact on the completion target for the NLE Tung Chung Section contract, there was a potential delay impact on the interface for installation of 132-kilovolt cables by a private utility provider, routed over the station box on the permanent power system alignment along North Lantau and across the sea channel bridges to the airport. From the NAPCO program management perspective, this is not acceptable.

Technical problems arising from the Phase 1 Tung Chung New Town site formation contract led to the late handover of site areas to the NLE Tung Chung section contractor, resulting in the contractor's successful extension of time claim. These technical problems, related to reclamation settlement and structural bearing capacity, forced the redesign of the station substructure by the Mass Transit Rail Corporation, in turn delaying construction commencement for the substructure. Additionally, the NLE Tung Chung section contractor's works progress fell significantly behind baseline schedule targets. Analysis of the contract and project schedules by NAPCO and the works agent, combined with joint planning reviews involving the utility provider, indicated a potentially critical schedule impact.

NAPCO developed a number of options to mitigate the effects of potential delay, so as to ensure that permanent power would be available to the airport in time for testing and commissioning to proceed. It was finally determined that re-routing the power cables around the station site to avoid the delayed substructure area offered the best option to recover from delays and mitigate risk.

NAPCO took a proactive approach with the project participants toward resolving a potential schedule variance problem before it became critical and impacted the overall program, providing an alternative solution which minimized cost and schedule impacts. If this action had not been taken, there could have been serious consequences to supplying permanent power to the airport.

CONCLUSION

The ACP is a complex undertaking requiring the application of enhanced program and project management. The methodologies and basic set of controls, including the schedule baseline and recovery measures described in this paper, have been implemented successfully, and are providing the tools to achieve the prime objective of ACP completion within time, political, and budget constraints.

Study Questions

COMMUNICATING CONSTRAINTS: SCHEDULE BASELINE AND RECOVERY MEASURES ON THE HONG KONG AIRPORT PROJECTS

1. What are the main objectives of this project?

2. The Hong Kong Airport Core Project (ACP) is one of the largest projects undertaken in the late Twentieth Century. It is made up of several segments, each of which could itself be considered a major project. What kind of organizational structure is used in this project? How does the job of project manager differ from that of the entire ACP project and one of the segments?

3. Explain the "top down/bottom up" management methodology described in the case. Relate this to the scope management of the project.

4. The method for physical progress measurement is detailed in the case. This method allows for all segments of the project to be aggregated for an overall project measurement of project completion. How does this method differ from the *PMBOK Guide* Chapter 6, Project Time Management, methods, and why do these differences exist?

5. Why must this project be managed from a change control/schedule perspective?

Can We Talk?: Communications Management for the Waste Isolation Pilot Plant, a Complex Nuclear Waste Management Project

Steven A. Goldstein, Sandia National Laboratories
Gwen M. Pullen, Sandia National Laboratories
Daniel R. Brewer, Sandia National Laboratories

PMI *Proceedings*, 1995, pp. 572–81

INTRODUCTION

The Sandia National Laboratories' (SNL) Nuclear Waste Management Program is pursuing for the United States (U.S.) Department of Energy (DOE) an option for permanently disposing radioactive waste in deep geologic repositories (1). Included in the program are the Waste Isolation Pilot Plant (WIPP) project for the U.S. defense program mixed waste (chemically hazardous materials and transuranic [TRU] radioactive waste—defined as elements heavier than Uranium containing more than 100 nanocuries/gram of alpha emitters with half-lives greater than twenty years), the Yucca Mountain project (YMP) for spent power reactor fuel and vitrified high-level waste, projects for other waste types, and development efforts in environmental decision support technologies.

WIPP and YMP are in the public arena, of a controversial nature, and provide significant management challenges. Both projects have large project teams, multiple organization participants, large budgets, and long durations; are very complex; have a high degree of programmatic risk; and operate in an extremely regulated environment requiring legal defensibility. For environmental projects like these to succeed, SNL's program is utilizing nearly all areas in PMI's *Project Management Body of Knowledge (PMBOK Guide)* to manage along multiple project dimensions such as the physical sciences (e.g., geophysics and geochemistry, performance assessment, decision analysis), management sciences (controlling the triple constraint of performance, cost, and schedule), and social sciences (belief systems, public participation, and institutional politics). This discussion will focus primarily on communication challenges active on WIPP. "How is the WIPP team meeting the challenges of managing communications?" and "How are you approaching similar challenges?" will be questions for a dialog with the audience.

479

WIPP as a Nuclear Waste Management Project

The Waste Isolation Pilot Plant is a multiphase project with an estimated duration approaching fifty years and a total project cost approaching $9 billion. The pursuit of a site for the repository culminated in 1975 with selection of underground bedded salt formations near Carlsbad, New Mexico. Public Law 96-164 (U.S. DOE National Security and Military Applications of Nuclear Energy Authorization Act of 1980) formally established the project. During siting, extensive surface-based testing was conducted to evaluate the site suitability, a repository appropriate to the conditions of the site was designed, and analyses were conducted to determine facility safety. This phase ended with the publication of an environmental impact statement in 1980 and a decision to proceed with the next phase, site and preliminary design validation, during which two vertical shafts were constructed, an underground testing area was excavated, and various geologic and hydrologic experiments were conducted. The design validation was followed by further collection of site data and by the construction of above-and below-ground facilities. The surface facilities necessary to receive waste and considerable underground excavation were completed, including rooms for further experimentation and some rooms designed for eventual permanent waste emplacement (2).

The project currently is in what is termed the "predisposal" phase and is completing experiments and modeling required to submit a compliance certification application to the U.S. Environmental Protection Agency (EPA) and other regulatory entities. Assuming WIPP is successfully certified, subsequent phases will involve transport and permanent emplacement of waste during the disposal phase (planned to begin in 1998), a closure phase for decontamination and decommissioning, and a post-closure phase during which the site will be actively monitored. WIPP's final completion date for sealing the waste-filled repository may approach the year 2025.

DOE's mission for WIPP is "to provide a technically, scientifically, and institutionally sound disposal decision recommendation to the Secretary of Energy based on a thorough evaluation of repository and system performance (including operational excellence, transportation, packaging, characterization, and certification), informed public participation, and institutional and regulatory acceptance" (2). An extended project team of over 900 people is comprised of DOE's Carlsbad Area Office (CAO) and several major contractor participants, including Sandia National Laboratories (as scientific advisor), Westinghouse Waste Isolation Division (as site management and operating contractor), and the WIPP technical assistance contractor, a consortium of companies providing administrative and management support. The team is split among three principal locations: the repository site (26 miles southeast of Carlsbad), the city of Carlsbad, and Albuquerque, New Mexico (285 miles from Carlsbad).

Major WIPP Communication Challenges

Communication challenges for a project of this size and complexity are extensive, including:
• establishing technical, cost, and schedule baselines which all project team participants endorse

- managing information for volumes of compliance-related documentation, (database linking, document control, records management, appropriately rigorous quality assurance)
- designing a full suite of project planning and status reporting systems and tools (e.g., work breakdown structure, work packages, logic-linked resource-loaded schedules, configuration management system)
- communicating within and between various "layers" of a geographically distributed project team (electronic networking, file transfers, video-teleconferencing, scheduling and management of a multitude of meetings and reviews)
- implementing DOE's public participation program to ensure that "public participation is a fundamental component in program operations, planning activities, and decision-making" (3) (The "public" includes technical oversight groups and the academic community, regulators, lay-level parties, and groups with a vested interest (either pro or con).)
- evaluating, executing, and communicating programmatic decision analysis methods which consider participants' viewpoints for work scope prioritization and decision-making
- communicating risk, managing perception and image, and controlling rumor mill and "damage" in a project regularly in the public limelight.

This paper focuses on three of these likely to be of common interest to other environmental projects, namely: "classical" project management communications (in the management science dimension), programmatic decision-making (physical science), and public group and regulator interactions (social science).

"CLASSICAL" PROJECT MANAGEMENT COMMUNICATION

Challenge: How do you share dynamically changing information among geographically separated team members?

Approach: Electronic networking within a distributed project team.

WIPP has over 100 work breakdown structure (WBS) elements. Until recently, the process of accumulating data related to scope, cost, and schedule for these elements was performed manually and has proven to be time consuming and labor intensive. Task leaders developed estimates in their individual formats (using tools like Microsoft Word, WordPerfect, Excel, etc.); budget specialists then input the submitted information into a database such as FoxPro.

With the introduction of local area networks and Windows-based applications, electronic networking has been used to alleviate much duplication of effort. Employing graphical user interface technology, a network tool was developed which used a "point-and-click" capability to enable a menu-driven, user-friendly system much more efficient in collecting and processing project planning information. This system allowed an easy and straightforward way of updating work scope, schedule, and cost baselines as different funding scenarios were being developed. The planning requirements Sandia faced were:

- short time fuses—four weeks for initial fiscal year budget scenario development and typically four days for responding to differing DOE budget cases
- system which interfaced with both IBM/PC and Macintosh platforms

- capability for real-time, online reporting
- capability for word processing features (spell checking, formatting, etc.).

The network planning tool provided a transparent interface wherein tas leaders in separate functional organizations and sites could make changes for di ferent planning scenarios quickly, with no subsequent rekeying or manipulatio of information required by project administrative staff. Without this networ planning tool, rapid-turnaround, multiple-scenario planning would have take much longer, cooperation of the technical staff would have been much lower, an quality of the plans would have been inferior.

In concert with network-based planning tools, SNL's WIPP project tean has implemented a common electronic calendar for scheduling project-leve events, video teleconferencing capabilities between the major project tean locations, and extensive E-mail and file transfer capabilities to reduce com munication transit time and rework of documentation.

PROGRAMMATIC DECISION-MAKING COMMUNICATION

Challenge: How do you explain waste repository behavior predicted fo 10,000 years in an understandable way?

Approach: Use performance assessment as a method of communicating safety and regulatory compliance.

Performance assessment (PA) is a quantitative, probabilistic process for as sessment of risks that is used in analyzing the ability of the WIPP disposa system to comply with select regulatory requirements related to long-term per formance. For WIPP, PA is used to estimate the cumulative releases of ra dionuclides and the associated uncertainties of the calculations. PA is also used to estimate releases of Resource and Conservation Recovery Act (RCRA)- regulated wastes.

Using laboratory and field data (and in some cases input from formal expert elicitations, published technical literature, and handbook values), computer models are formulated to estimate the behavior of and physical changes in the WIPP repository and the geologic features that surround it. These estimates are an assessment of the performance of the repository. A complete assessment:

- develops conceptual models of physical and chemical processes through interpretation of data and professional judgments by scientific staff, and communicates these models to PA numerical modelers and analysts
- identifies the features, events, and processes (FEPs) that might affect the disposal system
- examines the effects of these FEPs on the performance of the disposal system
- estimates the cumulative releases of contaminants, considering the asso- ciated uncertainties, caused by all significant FEPs
- compares the releases to the applicable EPA Code of Federal Regulations (CFR) to determine whether or not the predicted repository behavior violates the regulations.

Three parallel developmental stages are fundamental to the PA methodology for WIPP:
• identifying those future events that may have a significant effect on repository performance (and "screening out" defensibly all other scenarios that have little or no effect)
• acquiring a database and developing numerical models capable of simulating repository performance
• developing a procedure to assess compliance with the regulatory requirements (4).

For evaluating compliance with quantitative requirements of applicable long-term radioactive waste regulations, the results of performance assessment (PA) predictions are combined in a graphical form that can be compared with the release limits given in 40 CFR 191, Appendix A, Table 1. The graphical form of PA results is a complementary cumulative distribution function (CCDF). When a CCDF is graphed together with the normalized release limits, the probability that WIPP releases will exceed the regulatory release limits can be determined directly from the graph.

A CCDF typically includes uncertainty in both model parameter values and in future events and processes that may influence release from the repository (although at the WIPP site, human intrusion by drilling is considered the only future event that might lead to release). Uncertainty in future events is typically incorporated into WIPP CCDFs using random sampling. Parameter distributions are sampled by Latin Hypercube Sampling (LHS), and random (Monte Carlo) sampling is used to create possible drilling histories for the WIPP area.

CCDF plots typically are constructed as follows (4). Probabilistic distribution functions are assigned to important repository performance parameters, and those distributions are statistically sampled to ensure that all possible values, including extreme outliers, are properly represented. Performance is simulated using the selected parameter values, and for evaluating compliance, each resulting set of release values is weighted by the probability that the scenario simulated by that set will occur. Representative scenarios are simulated repeatedly, and the final composite plot reflects in a fairly easy-to-view graphical format the probabilistically predicted overall disposal system performance. Multiple plots can be superimposed to examine multiple conceptual models of repository behavior. While this modeling method is recommended by the EPA's Code of Federal Regulations for demonstrating regulatory compliance, it remains a continuing challenge for PA's practitioners to explain fully and credibly its subtleties, assumptions, uncertainties, and limitations to any but highly technically experienced public and oversight groups.

Challenge: How do you communicate to build consensus for making decisions on work scope priorities in a highly complex, coupled system?

Approach: Develop an analysis tool for aiding decision-making.

In March 1994, Sandia embarked on an effort to create a new decision-aiding analysis tool called the system prioritization method (SPM). Such a tool is useful and perhaps even necessary for balancing environmental (and other) project triple constraints, wherein:
• the schedule is aggressive
• resources are constrained

- work scope for completion is ill-defined
- linkage of WBS elements to compliance demonstration requirements are not rigorously mapped
- work scope prioritization and down-selection decisions are required to accommodate work scope changes (scope "creep"), and making these decisions based upon information (rather than intuition or seat-of-the-pants) requires processing of massive amounts of data, models, calculations, and "what-if" scenarios.

This tool is intended to define what might be the most viable combination of "activities," including scientific investigations, engineering alternatives (EA), and waste acceptance criteria (WAC), for supporting the final WIPP compliance application. Each activity has an associated cost, duration, two or more predicted outcomes, and a probability of occurrence for each predicted outcome.

A scientific investigation can be any logical combination of scientific subtasks and could, for example, include a number of field, lab, and modeling components. Scientific tasks can also include novel analyses, bounding calculations, or literature searches to document technical positions. Engineered alternatives represent specific engineering design modifications of either the WIPP facility or waste forms that could be implemented to improve the performance of the disposal system and help assure its ability to comply with regulatory performance requirements. Waste acceptance criteria represent constraints on the specific type, form, or quantity of radioactive, hazardous, or non-regulated material to be considered for disposal at WIPP. These constraints could be implemented to improve the performance of the disposal system.

The SPM process calculates the probabilities of certain sets of activities demonstrating compliance with portions of the regulations that apply to permanent disposal of radioactive wastes and RCRA-listed hazardous materials. SPM provides results in the form of a decision matrix to identify high likelihood of success, cost- and schedule-effective programmatic paths (5). For this particular WIPP application, SPM had eight key steps:
- development of a technical baseline
- specification of the SPM compliance indicator (CI), a binary measure (i.e., either 1 or 0) of whether the WIPP disposal system is predicted to succeed or fail in meeting the selected performance requirements (although some studies were performed to examine the effect of continuous rather than binary indicators)
- evaluation of the baseline CI for the WIPP disposal system using models and data from the technical baseline (4)
- Identification of activities available to the WIPP project that, if implemented, would have the potential to impact the system's CI
- elicitation of information from the project about what might evolve if specific activities are implemented (potential outcomes)
- evaluation of the performance of the disposal system using the potential outcomes of the activities and combinations of activities (activity sets)
- execution of a decision analysis and the creation of a decision matrix
- implementation of selected activities.

These steps are iterated as necessary until baseline calculations indicate compliance. Once this occurs, the preparation of a formal PA for regulatory compliance demonstration purposes can begin.

A prototype iteration of SPM (SPM-1) was completed in September 1994. It served as a benchmark and test bed for developing tools needed for a second iteration (SPM-2). SPM-2 was completed in March 1995 and is aiding in programmatic selection of efforts most closely linked to compliance demonstration.

As a starting point for establishing a baseline, SPM-2 developed position papers on technical and scientific issues or key modeling methods and presented them for review and comment to WIPP project public and oversight groups and regulators as part of WIPP's public participation program. Interdisciplinary teams that formed for both the technical position papers and for defining the SPM-2 baseline also provided a major portion of information on activities considered in SPM-2, and were elicited (by external facilitators) for the outcomes of those activities.

SPM uses performance assessment (PA) computer codes to generate mean CCDFs and RCRA contaminant concentrations to estimate the probability that an activity will contribute to the ability of the WIPP program to demonstrate compliance with regulatory criteria. This probability for demonstrating compliance (PDC) is the quantitative probability that, if the activity set is completed, the resulting design and information base for WIPP would be sufficient to demonstrate compliance with selected portions of the regulations. PDC, activity cost, and duration for each SPM programmatic option (activity) comprise an SPM decision matrix.

SPM-2 analyses looked at over 600,000 possible activity sets. Many of the analyzed activities had no impact on the CI, which subsequently allowed them to be removed from the decision matrix and reduced the number of activity sets to roughly 46,700. Because each activity set had multiple outcomes, the number of CCDFs needed to complete the SPM-2 analysis was roughly 1,350,000. A CD-ROM containing just under 200 megabytes of information, including the decision matrix and software tools for analysis, post-processing, and graphical display, was distributed to the DOE and public groups to assist them in understanding all SPM-2 information and the rationale for subsequent decisions. A key attribute of this CD-ROM is the capability of its software to search for and track terms, technical issues, assumptions, and concepts across all references supporting SPM-2 and in appropriate sections of the regulatory criteria (which are included on the CD-ROM).

SPM-2 successfully demonstrated a number of concepts. It:
- created a program element decision matrix that aids in the identification of lowest cost, lowest risk, and shortest paths towards compliance
- provided a single, high-information-density reference source (CD-ROM based) containing conceptual models, calculations, assumptions, compromises, sensitivities and uncertainties, and the leverage each program element has on the compliance demonstration argument
- brought project participants and public groups together in defining relevant issues to be addressed in a compliance application
- developed user-friendly visualization tools allowing public groups to study large decision matrices
- performed analyses showing the contribution of major WIPP activities, including EAs and WACs, toward a successful demonstration of compliance with selected EPA long-term performance regulations.

PUBLIC GROUP/REGULATOR COMMUNICATION

Challenge: How do public groups form opinions about safety and risk of environmental projects?

Approach: Research what opinions about technical credibility are based upon in various domains (6).

Successful performance assessment involves not only accumulation and organization of scientific information about how well a facility (like WIPP) will contain wastes, but requires that the credibility of the assessment be retained in the following "domains": scientific (e.g., National Academy of Sciences review panels, academic community technical experts), regulatory (EPA, state environment department), and public (both lay public and groups with a vested interest in nuclear waste). Failure to achieve and retain credibility in any of these domains results in a high probability of failure of the performance assessment effort.

Sandia has partnered with the Institute for Public Policy at the University of New Mexico to perform a series of studies of how technical information about WIPP's performance and regulatory compliance is understood and evaluated in various domains. These studies consider the roles of both the social and physical sciences in the regulatory compliance process. The focus of the study is on three major tasks:

1. Evaluation of how members of the public receive, understand, and utilize WIPP information. Assess:
- current sources and content of WIPP information
- effectiveness of alternative information sources
- effectiveness of alternative approaches to providing WIPP information.

2. Evaluation of Sandia patterns of communication with public groups:
- views of the public substantially affect Sandia's communication with those groups
- views of the public about safety can be understood as "implicit theories" that are often at substantial variance with those held by technical experts
- understanding how Sandia scientific staff and spokespersons view the public is necessary to develop training for more effective communication, and for critical examination of Sandia's own "implicit theories" of appropriate performance assessment.

3. Development of an understanding of how PA takes place in the regulatory and political process:
- develop an understanding of how scientific uncertainty is used in PAs conducted for controversial policy initiatives (like WIPP)
- understanding of ways in which regulatory agencies and public interest groups affect the conduct of PAs
- assess ways in which a scientific research organization can best respond to current and future PA needs.

From the public perspective, the WIPP PA amounts to a set of scientific claims about the acceptability of risks associated with the facility. Claims about the safety of WIPP are made by many sources and range from apocalyptic damage to perfect containment. When assessing such claims in a WIPP-specific survey that sampled 1,200 New Mexico citizens and another 600 U.S. citizens, a large fraction of the public (both NM and nationwide)

Scientist's Organization	Favor	Neutral	Against
National Academy of Sciences	24%	64%	12%
National Laboratory	54%	36%	10%
United States EPA	24%	28%	48%
United States DOE	66%	24%	10%
National Environmental Group	15%	23%	62%
Private Contractor	70%	21%	9%

IGURE 1 PERCEIVED BIAS TOWARD OPENING A NUCLEAR WASTE FACILITY BY TYPE OF SCIENTIFIC EXPERT

was found to be remarkably sophisticated at filtering and weighting the scientific and technical information that they receive.

Among the more important findings of the survey are that members of the public are able to make quite reasonable guesses about what kinds of positions on the risks of nuclear waste disposal will be taken by scientists from differing organizations. Respondents in the survey were asked to indicate whether statements made about opening a nuclear waste storage/disposal facility by a diverse set of "experts" would likely be: 1) biased in favor of opening the facility, 2) neutral and unbiased, or 3) biased against opening the facility.

As shown in Figure 1, National Academy scientists were expected to be the most "neutral," and private contractors the least neutral. (As used here, the term "private contractor" refers to a [typically] for-profit company hired by the DOE to perform the role of site owner-operator or managing and operating contractor.) Scientists working for private contractors, the DOE, and national laboratories (including Sandia) were perceived to be likely to make statements biased in favor of opening a nuclear waste facility, while those working for environmental groups and the EPA were seen to be likely to make statements biased against opening such a facility.

A second important finding is that, in assessing the credibility of scientific claims about the safety of a nuclear waste facility, members of the public place great emphasis on the independence of scientists from those who fund the research. For example, the survey respondents were asked whether they strongly agreed, agreed, disagreed, or strongly disagreed with the following statement: "For scientists to do unbiased work, they must have independence from whoever funds the research." The response pattern is shown in Figure 2.

Both the national and NM survey respondents tended to agree or agree strongly with the statement. In addition, majorities in both samples agreed or agreed strongly with the statement that "scientists are likely to give the answers that are preferred by whoever pays them." It is clear that there is significant skepticism about funded research, and that the credibility of PA results is likely to be affected by perceptions of the degree to which the funding agency (in the WIPP project's case, the DOE) is believed to interfere with the way in which the PA scientists and those providing technical inputs into PA go about their work.

A third finding of import for credibility of PA results concerns the ways in which prior expectations about the positions (or biases) of scientists from different organizations affect the ways in which members of the public weigh (and utilize) information that comes from these scientists. When lay citizens

Response	New Mexico	United States
Disagree Strongly	3%	1%
Disagree	13%	15%
Agree	48%	47%
Agree Strongly	36%	37%

FIGURE 2　　**"FOR SCIENTISTS TO DO UNBIASED WORK, THEY MUST HAVE INDEPENDENCE FROM WHOEVER FUNDS THE RESEARCH"**

hear scientific claims about the safety of WIPP, the credence given those claims is dependent on their perceptions of the biases of the scientist making the claim and the difference between the citizens' prior beliefs about safety and the claims made by the scientist. If the scientist is perceived to be biased in favor of opening WIPP, citizens tend to give greatest weight to scientific claims that suggest that risks are greater than they had previously believed (7). Thus, the stronger and more widespread the public perception that a scientist (or her organization) is biased in favor of opening a nuclear waste facility, the less likely it is that the public will believe claims from that scientist that the risks posed by the facility are smaller than had been previously believed.

What has historically made Sandia's PA different from other claims about WIPP safety is that the pubic has tended to perceive Sandia to have a relatively high degree of scientific independence and competence, and to be relatively unbiased on the matter of whether WIPP is sufficiently safe to open. As shown above in Figure 1, Sandia scientists rank second only to National Academy scientists in perceived neutrality. This gives Sandia scientists a greater base of credibility with the public than is true of other sources of scientific claims about the safety of WIPP, including scientists from DOE, environmental groups, private contractors, and even the EPA. Other survey results show that the relative credibility of Sandia scientists tends to be largest among those members of the public who are presently not committed for or against opening WIPP. How successful the WIPP project is at preserving this relative advantage for Sandia will depend, in part, on Sandia's ability to maintain a degree of credible scientific independence from federal sponsors in providing PA results.

A more general survey on beliefs associated with risks of nuclear waste management and WIPP (8) presents other concepts on how to communicate risk to various public group domains. Some conclusions are:

- Public groups who perceive themselves to be knowledgeable about WIPP tend to express greater support for opening the facility.
- When considering options for defense program transuranic waste disposal (i.e., leave it where it is now, ship it to WIPP, or find an alternative site), a plurality of survey respondents in Idaho and New Mexico support sending wastes to WIPP. In addition, the greater the self-rated knowledge about WIPP, the greater the support for shipping wastes to WIPP.
- While radioactive wastes are indeed seen as risky, members of the public can and do make distinctions among the relative levels of risk that result from different kinds of policies for managing those wastes.

In response to some of these observations, a modified method of measuring public group opinions is being developed. In the past, members of focus groups were asked to share their perceptions of a problem such as transportation, storage, or disposal of nuclear waste. At recent group sessions, at the conclusion of the formal session, participants were given the opportunity to ask questions of one or more technical experts on radiation, nuclear waste management, and the WIPP facility expressing topics of interest or concern to them. In part, the results of these sessions will permit Sandians to learn about concepts that members of the public deem important for understanding the safety of WIPP. This kind of learning is critical if the technical community is to conduct performance assessment that can bridge the gap between public and expert understandings of the risks associated with radioactive materials. At the same time, observations from these focus group sessions will be made on differing methods for providing scientific information to the public about issues which may have a significant non-technical component. Assessments will be made on the impacts of methods and information in changes that may occur in the public's opinions of risk.

Challenge: How do you manage involvement in your project of various public groups?

Approach: Base interactions upon an active public participation program.

There are upwards of a dozen oversight groups and another two dozen recognized local, national, tribal, institutional, and international public groups with interests in the process by which WIPP decisions are made and the impacts of those decisions. A Stakeholder Outreach Strategic Plan (9), written by the DOE/CAO, "supports a new paradigm of shifting from secrecy required by the nuclear weapons program to emphasis on gaining public trust in DOE's activities." A decision whether or not to open WIPP for permanent disposal of waste encompasses not only technical and scientific concerns but also a balance among technical, regulatory, and political and public policy issues and concerns raised by local, national, institutional, tribal, and international public groups. Some WIPP public group concerns and needs identified by the DOE include:

1. Public group issues might contribute to schedule delay or preclude WIPP's opening:
• concerns about the potential safety and environmental impacts that could result from geologic disposal of radioactive waste
• concerns about waste transportation accidents and the potential for release of radioactive and hazardous materials to the environment
• concerns that the DOE will evade regulations
• concerns that the DOE does not recognize tribal issues
• concerns about government inefficiency
• concerns about nuclear proliferation
• concerns about a highly aggressive project schedule.

2. Public officials require current, accurate information to participate effectively in decisions affecting WIPP activities. These key decision-makers must be responsive to the issues of their broad-based constituents.

Some potentially affected public groups have limited or no information about WIPP; others do not see its relevance to their needs. Issues include:
• lack of public knowledge about the project
• differing priorities.

Some public group outreach goals being pursued by DOE to address WIPP project concerns are to:

- develop and enhance relationships with other federal offices in New Mexico to improve coordination on shared issues, including land use management, transportation, waste management, public health and safety, and environmental protection
- encourage and facilitate broad public participation in planning and decision-making processes
- enhance awareness of concerns, needs, and cultural practices of the sovereign tribal nations
- foster international exchange and support.

SUMMARY

Guiding the multiyear, multibillion dollar, multiparticipant, somewhat contentious WIPP radioactive waste project to a successful conclusion provides the opportunity to experience nearly all aspects of communication planning, information distribution, progress reporting, and administrative closure elements as outlined in the *PMBOK Guide*. The project currently is preparing for its submittal of formal regulatory documents to the EPA and state of New Mexico, targeted for late 1996, and is planning and distributing information using a number of approaches, some of which are described in this paper.

While ongoing for some time, progress reporting will occur in earnest as feedback on the credibility and completeness of WIPP's compliance argument is generated by regulatory and public communities. Communications management in the legal arena of the regulator is a next major step on the horizon. Administrative closure will await the outcome of the regulators and public's assessments of what was communicated and how effectively it was delivered.

REFERENCES

1. Lynch, R. W., et. al. 1991. "Deep Geologic Disposal in the United States: The Waste Isolation Pilot Plant and Yucca Mountain Projects." Sandia Report SAND90-1656 UC-721, Sandia National Laboratories, May.

2. Department of Energy, WIPP: Strategy for the Waste Isolation Pilot Plant Test Phase. 1991. DOE/EM/48063-2 (Oct.); Department of Energy, Carlsbad Area Office Strategic Plan. 1995. DOE/WIPP93-025 Rev. 1, (Mar.).

3. O'Leary, H. R. 1994. Secretary of Energy memo to all DOE employees, Guidance on Implementation of the Department's Public Participation Policy, July

4. Bertram-Howery, S. G., and P. N. Swift. 1990. Status Report: Potential for Long-Term Isolation by the Waste Isolation Pilot Plant Disposal System. Sandia Report SAND90-0616 UC-721, Sandia National Laboratories. June.

5. Prindle, N. H., F. T. Mendenhall, Jr., and D. M. Boak. SPM-2 Final Report, Sandia National Laboratories (to be published).

6. Material in this section was provided by Hank Jenkins-Smith and Carol Silva, UNM Institute for Public Policy, University of New Mexico, Albuquerque, New Mexico.

7. For a general discussion of this relationship, see Jenkins-Smith, H. C., and G. Bassett. 1994. "Perceived Risk and Uncertainty of Nuclear Waste: Differences Among Science, Business, and Environmental Group Members." Risk Analysis 14, no. 5, pp. 851–56, Oct.

8. Jenkins-Smith, H. C., and A. Fromer. 1993. "Public Assessment of the Risks from Managing Transuranic Wastes: The View From Idaho and New Mexico." University of New Mexico, Institute for Public Policy, Department of Political Science. Dec.

9. Department of Energy, Carlsbad Area Office Stakeholder Outreach Strategic Plan. 1995. DOE/WIPP-95-1088, Apr. Also related is the Carlsbad Area Office Stakeholder Outreach Implementation Plan (under preparation).

ACKNOWLEDGMENT

This work was supported by the United States Department of Energy under Contract DE-AC04-94AL85000.

Study Questions

"CAN WE TALK?": COMMUNICATIONS MANAGEMENT FOR THE WASTE ISOLATION PILOT PLANT, A COMPLEX NUCLEAR WASTE MANAGEMENT PROJECT

1. Based on your project management knowledge, what would be an organized way of dealing with the different groups that have vested interests in the project?

2. The management of this case relies on the use of advanced techniques such as electronic networking, performance assessment, and a system prioritizing method. Describe one of these subprojects and comment on the feasibility of this project without the use of this tool.

3. Do you see any potential problems with the electronic networking system as it is described? What rules should be followed for the use of such a system?

4. The challenge described in explaining the behavior of the waste repository describes methods and models used but ends with a statement that the full explanation of the process is impossible except to those highly technically oriented. How should this communications problem be handled? Support your answer with reference to the project management literature.

5. In a project of this sort the two main challenges appear to be the use of new technology and the selling of this idea to the public. Would these two segments of the project be better handled as two distinct projects?

The Demise of the Superconducting Supercollider: Strong Politics or Weak Management?

Payson Willard, PMP, Willard & Associates, Incorporated

PMI Canada *Proceedings*, 1994, pp. 1–7

INTRODUCTION

The subject matter of this paper is a $10 plus billion United States (U.S.) Department of Energy (DOE) project called the superconducting supercollider (SSC). The SSC was to have been the world's largest scientific instrument but was terminated by the United States Congress in 1993. When the U.S. government approved the undertaking of this project in the 1980s, many states competed against one another to be the location of this prestigious project.

Locations in six states were selected as finalists before a location near Dallas, Texas, was announced as the winner. The Texas site was chosen mainly because of the subterranean conditions that existed there. During the five years that the SSC was under construction, no insurmountable technical barriers surfaced. Also, a highly publicized government audit in the summer of 1993 showed the project to be basically "on schedule and within budget." Over $2 billion had already been spent on this project, and it had been estimated that four years and $1 billion would be required to "close-down" this project. Despite all of the above, however, the SSC project was formally terminated on October 30, 1993! What caused this important scientific project to be suspended? Was the demise of the SSC due primarily to "strong politics" or to "weak management?" This paper highlights the complexity of the SSC project and addresses the key political and management factors that led to its demise.

WHAT IS THE SSC?

The SSC is a high-energy subatomic particle accelerator that was to be by far the most powerful particle accelerator in the world. The most powerful particle accelerator in existence at present is located at the Fermi National Accelerator Laboratory near Chicago, Illinois, and the SSC would have been twenty times more powerful than the Fermi accelerator! The SSC would have two beams of protons that would be propelled in opposite directions within two small tubes. These tubes would be located within a series of underground circular tunnels. The tubes would be cooled to –452 degrees Fahrenheit (4.35 Kelvin) by a river of liquid helium to eliminate electrical resistance.

The SSC would draw hydrogen atoms from a small container and remove the electrons, thereby leaving only the protons. These protons initially would be accelerated to successively higher levels of energy in four smaller "booster" rings, then they would be inserted into the main ring. The main ring would have a circumference of 54 miles and be located from 50 feet to 250 feet below ground. There would be perhaps as many as 130 trillion protons continuously circulating within each beam! Carefully synchronized bursts of radio frequency waves would energize the protons. The particles would be guided by 10,600 powerful superconducting magnets encompassing the tubes. After several hundred thousand revolutions around the 54-mile path, the particles within the beams would have velocities approaching the speed of light. Having obtained these velocities, the protons would then be directed to collide head on with one another in two interaction halls containing enormous detectors. This process is the rationale for the name, superconducting supercollider.

The rate of the proton collisions would be of a magnitude of perhaps 100 million times per second! These collisions would generate a shower of subnuclear particles. The SSC detectors must monitor these many collisions, decide if a particle of interest has been generated, then—if generated—collect data associated with that particular particle! The difficulty of performing this complicated process is magnified by the fact that the life-cycles of these particles are measured in microseconds! The data encompassed by this debris would be recorded and studied by scientists from countries around the world to gain more knowledge about the fundamental nature of matter and energy. The two detectors in which these collisions would take place would weigh in excess of 70 million pounds each!

What Are the Benefits of the SSC?

It is difficult to state what all of the ultimate benefits of the SSC would be because nobody really knows! Even President Clinton depicted this in a June 16, 1993, letter to Congress in which he expressed his support for the SSC and stated: "The most important benefits of the increased understanding gained from the SSC may not be known for a generation. We can, however, be certain that important benefits will result simply from making the effort" (1).

Hazel O'Leary, the U.S. Secretary of Energy, when appearing before Congress in August 1993, stated: "Although one would like to identify specific technological developments and economic returns on the investment that will flow from the SSC, such precision of foresight is not possible. However, if history is any guide, then we can predict with confidence that development of technologies necessary to build the SSC, and the understandings that emerge from experimentation at the facility, will provide major contributions to our economy" (2).

Management History of the SSC

In August 1988, DOE openly solicited proposals via a request for proposal (RFP) for the management of the construction and the subsequent operation of the SSC. The major criteria for the project management selection was expertise in high-energy physics research. Copies of this RFP were requested by

121 interested companies. However, DOE had received only one response by the November 4, 1988, deadline. This single proposal was submitted by the Universities Research Association (URA) team. URA had been formed in 1965 to construct and manage the Fermi National Accelerator Laboratory. Originally, URA was composed of thirty-four research universities but had grown to encompass seventy-eight universities when the SSC proposal was submitted. EG&G, Inc., and Sverdrup Corp. were part of the URA team. EG&G, Inc., was a company that had experience in providing technical services to DOE projects; whereas, Sverdrup Corp. was a small architect and engineering firm. On January 19, 1989, the URA team was selected as the management and operations contractor for the SSC. A professor of physics at Harvard University was designated as the SSC director and would have overall responsibility for all aspects of the project. Within a couple of years, however, Congress became concerned about the SSC management. This led to four congressional hearings on the SSC project management during the 1991–93 time frame!

MAGNITUDE OF THE SSC PROJECT

To better understand the magnitude of the SSC project management problems, one must first understand the magnitude of the SSC project itself. The SSC was a massive project that was to take in excess of a dozen years to build and eventually be estimated to cost in excess of $10 billion. The SSC and its facilities would require more than 16,700 acres of land. Also, over 2 million square feet of office and laboratory facilities would be constructed. As stated earlier, the main circular underground tunnel would be 54 miles in circumference and would vary from 50 feet to 250 feet below ground. The 10,600 superconducting magnets required to steer the beams of protons would need to be designed and manufactured. Each of the magnets would be 50 feet in length and would weigh 15 tons! The magnets would require the production of 625,000 miles of superconducting cable. Twelve refrigeration plants would be required to cool the magnets and would liquefy 2.4 million liters of helium. Approximately 10 million cubic feet of earth would be excavated. Over 10 million cubic feet of concrete would be required within the tunnel. In contrast to the massive size of the tunnel, the beams of protons would need to be focused into a collision area that would be only 2 ten millionths (2/10,000,000) of a square centimeter in size!

When the SSC was terminated in late 1993, the project was supporting over 7,000 full-time jobs in forty-eight states which were directly involved in the construction of the SSC facilities and equipment. In addition, over 1,000 scientists across the U.S. and another 1,000+ foreign scientists from twenty-two countries around the world were developing experiments for the SSC. Also, when Congress stopped funding for this project, over 12,000 acres of land had been acquired, over 14 miles of underground tunnel had been dug, over 7 million cubic yards of earth had been excavated, over 45,000 procurement contracts had been awarded, and over $2 billion had been spent!

THE DEMISE OF THE SSC

The SSC had been the focus of much attention since the commencement the project for several reasons. First, the SSC project was a multibillion-d lar project, Also, as stated earlier in this paper, it is very difficult to ident the benefits of the SSC—much less to quantify the impact of these benefi Because of the above, the SSC has been the recipient of much ridicule a scrutiny. There are, of course, many factors responsible for the demise of t SSC. Most of these factors, however, either are political in nature or are tributable to the SSC project management.

POLITICAL FACTORS

All large government-funded projects face political problems. Because of t high costs associated with the SSC project, however, this project was esp cially vulnerable. This vulnerability was magnified since the SSC was a co troversial, misunderstood project! Political factors were said to have played significant role in the termination of the SSC. The following are three k factors that impacted the SSC's demise:
- deficit reduction "feeding frenzy"
- SSC's Texas location
- absence of key pro-SSC Texas politicians.

The phrase "deficit reduction" was a key buzzword during 1993. Th phrase was brought to the forefront during the 1992 presidential electio Many of the new congressmen had been elected on deficit reduction pla forms. Since the SSC was a high-dollar, highly controversial, and not unde stood project, it was a good candidate for "reducing the nation's deficit" (3, 4

Ironically, the two largest science projects in the United States durin fiscal year 1993—the SSC and NASA's space station—resided in Texas. make matters even worse for the SSC, the House voted on June 23, 1993, continue funding NASA's space station. This was one day before the SS vote was cast, and the funding passed by a single vote—216 to 215! Aft the vote on the space station, some House members said the space station survival may have doomed the SSC since they were running out of big-tic et items to cut (5). Also, Texas elected its second Republican senator short before the funding process began for the SSC, making both Texas senato Republicans for the first time in history. Vengeance against Texas was said have played a role in the demise of the SSC since Congress is controlled l Democrats (6).

Two of Texas' most powerful politicians had been removed from th funding process during the past year—Lloyd Bentsen and George Bush. Ser ator Bentsen had been chairman of the powerful Senate Finance Committe before his current appointment as Secretary of the Treasury. President Bus was a staunch supporter of the SSC. President Clinton supported the SS and had included funding for the project in his budget. Bill Clinton didn' however, threaten to veto any bill that excluded the SSC as George Bush ha done the previous year!

PROJECT MANAGEMENT FACTORS

The SSC's management had been the focus of heated criticism from General Accounting Office (GAO) reports, congressional committees, and others throughout 1993. GAO (Congress' investigative agency), labeled the SSC project as "over budget and behind schedule." Immediately before the House vote, the Project on Government Oversight, a nonprofit group, released a "leaked" report that had been prepared by government auditors citing numerous inappropriate charges and excessive contractor charges which had been approved by SSC management. Also, many congressmen harshly criticized the SSC management. Representative John Dingell, chairman of the Energy and Water Investigations Subcommittee, stated he had seen many "dodgy" programs in his many years, "but the SSC ranks among the worst in terms of contract mismanagement and failed government oversight" (7).

This harsh criticism was directed at SSC management despite the very impressive accomplishments stated earlier. Successful management of any project must encompass more than simply the achievement of technical milestones. The criticisms had been focused mainly on the cost/schedule areas, but there were also other problem areas. The following deficiencies that hampered the SSC project will be addressed:

- failure to implement effective project management and control systems
- failure to "nail down" the scope of the project from its inception
- failure to promote the project to Congress and to the public
- ineffective DoD/SSC organizational structures.

It was a contractual requirement specified in the 1988 SSC RFP that the SSC must have a fully implemented cost and schedule control system (CSCS). Unfortunately, implementation of this CSCS system did not receive serious SSC management attention until late in fiscal year 1991. Despite repeated directives, no action was taken. In fact, a valid integrated cost/schedule system did not exist even when the project was terminated two years later!

Although many problems were encountered, most of these problems were problems that would be expected for a project of the magnitude and complexity of the SSC. The main reason that this contractual agreement was not met appeared to be a general lack of a strong commitment from project management to implement a valid system. Not only were the cost and schedule systems inadequate, but other project management systems were also incapable of providing management with accurate information in a timely manner. The procurement, inventory, and labor systems were observed by the author to be deficient.

When originally presented to Congress in 1988, the SSC project was to be a $4.4 billion project. In 1989, the projected SSC costs increased to $5.9 billion—then to $8.25 billion in 1991. A seventy-five-member Baseline Validation Committee established by DOE placed the projected costs at $10 billion in June 1993. Another government estimate of the SSC costs was $11 billion. Other unofficial but reputable estimates of the costs were as high as $16 billion! Part of these cost increases can be attributed to a costly design change and to a Clinton-mandated project stretch-out, but many of these increased costs were due to changes in the scope of the SSC project. For example, the SSC originally was to have had only one detector—then two detectors were approved. Since each detector costs $500+ million, why not build the second detector after the SSC was "up and running?" The scope of the SSC needed to be realistically "nailed down!"

As stated earlier in this paper, it is very difficult to identify the benefit of the SSC, much less quantify the impact of these benefits. It is even more difficult to describe the theoretical high-energy physics involved in the SSC. Although difficult to do, many people felt that the SSC External Affairs Department did a totally inadequate job of promoting the SSC (8). Many congressmen openly admitted that they did not really understand the SSC. Even Hazel O'Leary publicly stated she was "less than passionate" about the SSC shortly after being appointed the Secretary of Energy (9). During a later visit to the SSC site, however, Secretary O'Leary apologized for her earlier remarks. Most scientists and the SSC congressional backers felt that the SSC was an extremely worthwhile endeavor, but the project appeared to be a total mystery to most other outsiders. Since the SSC was totally dependent on congressional funding each year, SSC management should have done a better job of salesmanship!

There have been hundreds of articles written about the SSC and published in various magazines and the major newspapers across the nation. When describing what the SSC would do, it inevitably would be stated that the SSC would provide answers to questions such as:

- How did matter form?
- How did matter acquire mass?
- Is there a force more fundamental than presently known?
- What will eventually happen to the universe?
- What is the most elementary element?

Companies that worked with the SSC are currently exploring various practical applications for the superconducting technology which was developed for the SSC. Accelerated-generated proton beams are currently being used to treat certain types of cancer and other diseases. Superconducting magnet technology, like that developed for the SSC, is being used in prototype trains that levitate above the ground and travel at speeds up to 300 miles per hour. Other applications for the SSC technology are in the areas of computing, electronics, and the environmental sciences. Instead of emphasizing that the SSC would find answers to theoretical questions like those stated above, the impact on practical applications for the SSC technology should have been stressed. For example, the completed applied research associated with the SSC has already reduced the cost of superconducting cable from $100 per foot to $10 per foot, and the price is projected to soon be $1 per foot!

When the SSC project began, DOE decided that the SSC project required a unique oversight and management structure. DOE established a SSC project office near the SSC site in Texas. This office was headed by a DOE manager, who reported directly to the Secretary of Energy. This arrangement apparently was established to streamline and facilitate activities and to provide the Secretary of Energy with direct oversight of the project during the startup phase. In 1990, the SSC project office was given full delegation of authority for all aspects of the SSC. This combination of delegation of authority, along with the direct reporting relationship to the Secretary of Energy, shielded the SSC from the normal DOE oversight functions. All of the other DOE scientific construction projects were subjected to a series of normal reviews. These reviews, however, were not done for the SSC. Also, many key SSC managers were experimental physicists. Although they were excellent physicists, some evidently had had little or no project management experience— especially on large-scale projects!

In July 1993, an internal memo written by Joseph Cipriano was mysteriously "leaked" to the press. Cipriano was the associate director of energy research for DOE and responsible for the SSC project. The following is an excerpt from his memo:

> Replacing the lab director now may be the only way to keep the lab from falling apart. Morale is very low, confidence in existing management is practically nonexistent, and cost and schedule trends are worsening at an alarming rate (10).

In his memo, Cipriano recommended that DOE "take a year and fix SSC's management problems before going on." He recommended that the SSC issue no new contracts until the management problems were remedied. He also recommended that the Clinton administration's budget request be cut for fiscal year 1994 from $640 million to $400 million. Although this memo was not signed and apparently was obtained illegally from Cipriano's personal computer files, Cipriano acknowledged authorship!

It was common knowledge around the SSC that URA and the SSC director—Dr. Roy Schwitters—did not have the admiration of DOE and vice versa. According to SSC personnel, the relationship between Schwitters and Cipriano had deteriorated to the point that they communicated only by letter. Even when Cipriano began overseeing the SSC project in mid-1990, he then recommended firing URA because he felt the university group could not manage a massive construction project. In November 1993, the author personally heard Secretary O'Leary express her strong disapproval of the SSC director. Why did the government allow such an unhealthy situation to exist for three plus years—especially on a project as large and visible and important as the SSC?

FISCAL YEAR 1993—THE "ROLLER COASTER RIDE OF DEATH"

The SSC had experienced an intense funding battle with Congress during the 1993 fiscal year funding process. All of the "warning signs" existed that indicated another major funding battle would occur during the 1994 fiscal year funding process. In February 1993, GAO released a report stating that the SSC was millions of dollars over budget and construction was far behind schedule. This bad publicity—be it right or wrong—was released by the Associated Press for nationwide publication and independently reported by reputable newspapers such as *The Wall Street Journal* (11,12). Many members of Congress already felt that the SSC was a "boondoggle—an expensive boondoggle!"—and such adverse publicity was obviously detrimental to the project. In retrospect, the report accusations were probably incorrect.

SSC management, however, had been given ample opportunity to implement effective project controls and to vigorously dispute such erroneous charges in a defensible manner. The sad fact is that apparently nobody really knew the status of the project!

President Clinton asked Congress for $640 million for the SSC when he submitted his fiscal year 1994 budget. On June 18, 1993, the Appropriations Committee of the House of Representatives recommended that the SSC be funded for 1994 but be scaled back to $620 million. On June 24, 1993, however, the House

of Representatives voted by a 280 to 141 margin to permanently cancel t
SSC project! Since the Senate would be voting on the SSC several months l
er, DOE performed an in-depth investigation of the SSC during the summer
1993 in an attempt to save the project. Over 100 auditors were involved in th
investigation. Although numerous improprieties were found, DOE did co
clude that the SSC project was basically "on schedule and within budget!" UR
management was harshly criticized by DOE, however, for not having demo
strated full commitment to openness and accountability. This government a
dit produced approximately fifty specific findings and recommendations. T
key findings, however, were:

• SSC management had neither implemented an acceptable CSCS syste
nor established an acceptable "cost baseline."

• SSC/DOE organizations were incapable, as structured, of providing ad
quate control over the project.

As a result of these findings, Secretary O'Leary corrected the organiz
tion flaws stated earlier in this paper and instructed that the SSC project
subjected to the same oversight and programmatic reviews as other DC
projects. At a press conference, Secretary O'Leary told reporters: "We've g
to prove to the American people that we can better manage this project. V
can, and we will" (13)!

DOE announced in August 1993 that the SSC project managemei
would be restructured. As stated earlier in this paper, URA had initially bee
given total responsibility for the SSC project. In response to the audit's fine
ings, DOE stated that the URA team would no longer be the prime contra
tor for the SSC project. Instead, there would be two major contractors havi
complementary strengths—a "design/operate" contractor and a separate "e
ecute/integrate" contractor. URA was named as the design/operate contract
and would continue to be responsible for the scientific design and research a
pects of the SSC, the commissioning of the accelerator and scientific resear
equipment, and the operations of the facilities as they were completed. A ne
RFP would be generated to solicit proposals for a new execute/integrate co
tractor that would bring to the SSC world-class experience in managing larg
construction projects. The major responsibilities for this new execute/inte
grate contractor would include implementing the project management an
control systems and managing existing major subcontracts. Unfortunatel
all of these corrective actions by DOE were coming too late!

After several days of intense Senate hearings, the SSC project was ke
alive when the Senate voted on September 30, 1993, to fund the project. Th
vote was fifty-seven to forty-two. The hearings were broadcast live to T
monitors located throughout the SSC facilities. SSC employees were relieve
and jubilant at the conclusion of the voting! The Senate allocated $640M
for the SSC project for the fiscal year 1994. Since the House of Represent
tives had disapproved the SSC and the Senate had approved the SSC, a joi
conference committee of Congress was selected to make recommendation

The joint House/Senate conference subcommittee recommended th
the full $640 million be funded for the SSC. The House of Representative
however, later rebuffed the conference committee's recommendation an
again refused to fund the SSC by a vote of 264 to 159 on October 19, 199
After unsuccessful efforts to save the SSC by powerful SSC supporters, th
SSC was officially terminated on October 30, 1993, when President Clinto
signed the bill killing the project.

CONCLUSIONS

Although it is possible that the SSC might be revived in some future year at its present sight, the present demise of the SSC is very sad and perhaps could have been avoided! Although "strong politics" definitely were involved in the SSC's demise, "weak management" did severely hurt the SSC and made it vulnerable for termination. The following is an excerpt from an article published in *The New York Times*, following the congressional defeat which contains quotes from an interview with Roy Schwitters, the SSC director:

> Schwitters later admitted that perhaps his biggest mistake was that he had "failed to get strong enough, really experienced project management staff on board, who could do these accounting and scheduling things better," and that he had underestimated the importance and magnitude of that job (14).

The SSC project represented the marriage of world-class science and world-class construction. Missing was "world-class" management! Thousands of scientists around the world had devoted many years of their lives to the conceptual development of the SSC, and the results of their efforts were proving successful! No impassable technical barriers had been encountered that threatened the feasibility of the SSC performing successfully after its completion from a scientific standpoint. The SSC was to have been the largest hard rock tunnel in the world. The SSC construction crews digging the underground tunnels epitomized excellence while successfully performing their job. In fact, the construction crews set and reset world "rate of advance" tunneling for 5-meter hard-rock tunnel boring machines in all three categories—best day, best week, and best month (15, 16)!

The SSC was an exciting and prestigious project with which to be associated, and a strong spirit of dedication and excitement from workers throughout the project was observed by the author. SSC employees were totally devastated and expressed much sadness and extreme bitterness when the project was terminated. The employees felt that they had been betrayed by management.

The question as to whether this important scientific endeavor's "death" could have been prevented had there been more effective project management has been raised many times and will continue to be raised again and again.

It is unquestionable, however, that the management deficiencies discussed in this paper did severely hurt the SSC project. Was the "death" of the SSC due solely to its project management? Of course not, but the SSC might perhaps still be "alive and well" today had the SSC project had stronger leadership. While politics played a significant role in the termination of this project, project management (SSC and DOE) must assume the brunt of the responsibility for the SSC's demise because of the reasons stated in this paper.

Had the SSC had a strong project management team to complement its world-class scientific and construction teams, this project might not have been terminated! Perhaps the following excerpt from an editorial by Jim Slattery, the congressman who led the effort to kill the SSC, says it best: "My decision to push for cancellation of the project was not an easy one, because I recognize that the SSC had scientific merit. It was the management—not the science—that betrayed the SSC" (17).

REFERENCES

1. Letter from President Bill Clinton to The Honorable William H. Natcher, Chairman of the Committee on Appropriations, United States Congress, June 1 1993.

2. Statement of Hazel R. O'Leary, Secretary of Energy, before the Committee on Appropriations and Committee on Energy and Natural Resources, United Sta Congress, August 4, 1993.

3. "Supercollider in Political Spin." 1993. *USA Today*, June 9.

4. "Senate Vote Gives Supercollider Another Chance." 1993. *The New York Times*, Oct. 1.

5. "Intricacies of Budget Politics Exposed in Fight for Supercollider." 1993. *T New York Times*, March 31.

6. "Some Backers See Anti-Texas Bias in Plans to Kill SSC Project." 1993. *Ft Worth Star Telegram*, Oct. 22.

7. "Superconducting Supercollider: University Consortium Faulted on Mana ment and Accounting." 1993. *Science*, July 9.

8. "SSC's Fall Linked to its Complexity: Backers, Critics Cited Failed Salema ship." 1993. *The Dallas Morning News*, Oct. 24.

9. "O'Leary: Not Passionate About Supercollider." 1993. *USA Today*, Feb. 5.

10. "Energy Department Official Urges Firing Supercollider Chief." 1993. *Th Washington Post*, August 2.

11. "Investigators Say Supercollider is Way Over Budget." 1993. The Associa ed Press, Feb. 24.

12. "Supercollider Is Said to be Over Budget and Behind Schedule." 1993. *Th Wall Street Journal*, Feb. 25.

13. "SCC Management to be Overhauled." 1993. *The Dallas Morning News*, August 5.

14. "The Supercollider: How Big Science Lost Favor and Fell." 1993. *The Nev York Times*, Oct. 26.

15. "A Boring Record." 1993. *The Houston Post*, Apr. 27.

16. "SCC Sets World Tunnel Records." 1993. *Waxahachie Daily Light*, May 5

17. "Why I Stopped the Supercollider." 1993. Editorial by Jim Slattery, U.S. House of Representatives. *The Hutchinson News* (Kansas), Nov. 12.

Study Questions

THE DEMISE OF THE SUPERCONDUCTING SUPERCOLLIDER: STRONG POLITICS OR WEAK MANAGEMENT?

1. The superconducting supercollider (SSC) project did not deliver what was i tended. A successful project is one that not only fulfills the constraints time, cost, and technical performance, but fulfills other requirements suc as minimal scope change and customer acceptance. Research in Kerzne *Project Management: A Systems Approach to Planning, Scheduling, an Controlling* (1995), the definition of a project success and identify which fac tors were not achieved in the SSC endeavor.

2. Why did this project fail? Was the project's failure inevitable? If not, what could have prevented the failure of the SSC?

3. The case exposes many factors and reasons for the SSC failure. Which do you think were the real causes and problems not properly addressed by project management?

4. If Congress had voted to continue funding on the SSC, what would you have recommended as mandatory changes required to receive this funding?

5. Public relations were mismanaged with this project. Is this the fault of the project's management? How could the project have handled the public relations, given the uncertainty of the uses of the SSC?

6. Managing a project of this size requires the use of all areas of project management in order to guarantee the desired outcome. If you were in charge of a large project, on which of the nine identified processes of project management, *PMBOK Guide*, section 1.3.2, The Project Management Knowledge Areas, would you concentrate?

Boeing Spares Distribution Center: A World-Class Facility Achieved through Partnering

John R. McMichael, Lockwood Greene

PM Network, September 1994, pp. 9–19

BUSINESS OBJECTIVE

One of the main reasons airlines buy airplanes from Boeing Commercial Airplane Group (BCAG) is the quality and speed of Boeing's customer support. A key element of customer support is rapid response and distribution of replacement parts. Boeing's new Spares Distribution Center (SDC), located in SeaTac, Washington, is the key to the company's worldwide reputation for customer service. Its design and operation will allow the Customer Services Division to improve responsiveness and extend Boeing's existing global reputation for the highest quality of customer service.

BACKGROUND

In recent years, many Boeing customers have begun to use just-in-time inventory methods in their own operations to reduce the cost of storage space and inventory on hand. To achieve these goals, they have demanded faster turnaround on spare parts ordered from BCAG. By some estimates, it costs an airline approximately $50,000 in lost revenue per day when it has a plane on the ground waiting for a part.

As early as 1985, the Spares organization recognized that to be responsive to the changing demands of customers, it would have to change the way it was doing business. To accomplish that, it needed to identify areas for improvement.

One such area was that Spares operations occupied approximately 700,000 square feet in five buildings on three sites in the Puget Sound region. There was no opportunity to expand the operations at those locations. To accommodate a projected yearly growth rate in inventory and shipments, Spares would have had to fragment its operations even more by locating additional material storage and movement off-site.

Another opportunity for improvement was intra-region parts transportation logistics. Parts picked from one of four locations were transported to a single facility located in Auburn, Washington, and then processed and packaged for shipment to the customers. Travel time from there to SeaTac International Airport for shipping, which averaged forty-five minutes, was increasing due to worsening traffic congestion.

A 1989 study commissioned by Spares researched and documented these problems. The purpose of the study was to analyze existing operations and develop and evaluate alternatives. Facility, equipment, and operational solutions were based on a thorough understanding of current Spares business practices and how it intended to do business in the future.

The preferred alternative was to consolidate Spares operations into one facility on a site from which travel time to SeaTac International Airport in the year 2000 would be minimal. The recommendation approved purchasing a 27-acre site five minutes from the airport. An adjacent 10 acres were secured for future expansion. At that time it was concluded that the new SDC should achieve the following:

• create a cost-effective and integrated material handling system that was extremely reliable

• use employee input (through continuous quality improvement teams) to design work stations.

Most importantly, the new SDC had to improve the business and material flow for the distribution of parts.

PROJECT CHALLENGES

Siting Issues

Residential neighborhood. The new industrial facility is located on 27 acres, in a residential community immediately north of SeaTac Airport and south of the 175-acre North SeaTac Community Park. Sensitivity to the placement and appearance of this very large facility was critical to its acceptance by the community.

Noise mitigation. The close proximity of the project to the airport created unique design challenges requiring mitigation of outside noise transmission into the facility. Mitigation required the reduction of process noise transmitted into the surrounding neighborhood, such as those originating from exterior electrical generators and from the dust collection system. Conveyors were specified with cage roller bearings with a maximum noise generation level of 65 dB limits to reduce noise levels within the facility.

New municipality. The city of SeaTac incorporated as the project began. At the time the documentation for the State Environmental Protection Act (SEPA) was being prepared, it was not known whether the city or King County would perform this review. Furthermore, the fact that the city had never permitted a building project, let alone one as complex as the SDC, added to the complications in the permitting and building construction inspection processes.

The project team met with the city of SeaTac government and the community prior to the formal review process to discuss the scope of the project. Models of the building were developed to show how the new facility would look in the total context of the site and adjoining neighborhood. We listened to concerns throughout the program and explained what we were doing to answer them. On an ongoing basis, fliers and informational letters distributed among the community updated people on the progress of the project.

Specific examples of measures taken to ensure that the building would be as unobtrusive as possible and environmentally sensitive to the neighborhood were the lowering of the building in the site approximately 20 feet in the southeast corner; design of indirect lighting to prevent perimeter and parking lot lighting projecting into the neighborhood; and design of an attractive, yet functional, landscaping adjacent to the neighborhood featuring a meandering trail with interpretive signs identifying the plantings.

Technical challenges. Stored within the facility is a total of 400,000 stock-keeping units (SKU) and over 1.3 million parts. Not only is the number of parts daunting, they range in size from extremely small, e.g., rivets, to significantly large, e.g., 767 engine cowling. The challenges occurred in two general areas.

Material handling. Our goal was to identify, purchase, and install reliable material handling equipment to achieve a low-risk start-up within budget. To accomplish this, we realized the need for:
• operational reliability at both the equipment and systems level
• design for local control of equipment initially, but to include a system link-up capability allowing for future migration to an integrated system and a total warehouse management system
• design to accommodate year 2000 requirements for the receiving, warehousing, shipping, and support functions associated with operation of the SDC.

Design flexibility. From the very beginning, the driving element in the building criteria required a configuration totally driven by its function. In the past, many of Boeing's facilities were created by constructing the building shell first and then making necessary functional changes after the client moved in. On this project, all users were involved in the initial planning and their requirements dictated the design. From the inside out, the building was wrapped around the processes.

The material handling and workstation requirements were developed concurrently with the design of the facility. As such, area configurations and material selection decisions were made to maximize flexibility and to accommodate changes as they occurred. In order for the project to be completed within the scheduled time frame, the building construction drawings had to be completed before all the necessary equipment and user workstation requirements were fully defined. Design allowances were initially made using parametric and experiential data to complete the missing information. As detailed information became available, these design allowances were reviewed and refined as necessary.

DISTINCTIVE MANAGEMENT METHODS

From the beginning, the objective of the management team was to build and manage a team of people who would assume and share ownership in the process and the product of the SDC building program. Thus the program was driven by our mission, not by hierarchy or rules. The process differed substantially from normal Boeing procedures in these areas:

• A site-based management team provided the end users with a dedicated program team. This team provided the user with immediate access to the design process. End user input was proactively solicited to obtain an understanding of present operational processes.

• A different approach was used to move design changes further up in the design process. Traditionally, a scope of work is developed, an A&E designs it, and another company builds it. There is no continuity from start to finish as to why things happen. By the time you get to construction, the customer realizes that what he said (or meant to say) in the design meetings is not showing up in the building. Changes then occur during construction, significantly driving up costs.

• Lockwood Greene Engineering (LGE) established a project liaison office in Renton, Washington, consisting of a project manager, project architect, and project structural, civil, mechanical, and electrical engineers. These six people were transferred from Lockwood Greene's Oak Ridge, Tennessee, office to act as the focal point of coordination for all project design activities. Lockwood Greene's Oak Ridge office performed the actual detailed design for the facility.

• Boeing formed a teaming relationship with LGE in order to get away from the adversarial "us and them" approach of past projects. All major players were involved early in the project.

• The site-based user controlled the program budget. One of the program managers had signature authority.

• Keeping the program management team small enabled it to expedite consensus decision-making and utilize maximum flexibility.

• An extensive review of recently completed Boeing projects provided invaluable lessons-learned information related to material handling, control systems, contracting, and so forth.

• The new municipality of the city of SeaTac was brought in early in the project. This enabled its issues and concerns to be identified early in the design and made it a part of the project team. These agenda alignments of all parties greatly smoothed the planning and design processes.

PROJECT OVERVIEW

Purpose

The purpose of the Spares Distribution Center (SDC) is to receive, store, and deliver replacement parts to Boeing customers operating more than 7,250 Boeing airplanes worldwide. The facility stores 400,000 stockkeeping units (SKU) and ships more than 1.2 million parts annually, operating twenty-four hours per day, 365 days per year. Parts for priority orders are shipped within four hours of receipt of the order.

Mission

Provide a consolidated SDC that will facilitate the reliable achievement of customer response time goals on all Spares transactions.

Objectives

- Accommodate year 2000 requirements
- Be functionally and visually consistent with the mission and image of Customer Services Division
- Invest in the wellbeing of SDC employees
- Be sensitive to and compatible with the surrounding neighborhood and land uses.

Overview

- 700,000 square feet
- High-bay area (storage)—60 feet clear height
- Mid-bay area (receiving, packaging, storage, shipping, and other process areas)—30 feet clear height
- Offices and employee services (commons, cafeteria, classrooms, fitness center)—35,000 square feet
- 300,000 square feet of super flat floors
- Eight-hour fire separation
- Maximum foreseeable loss (MFL) walls
- Redundant voice data communications
- 10,000 feet of conveyor for conveyorable totes
- Nine hybrid vehicles
- Forty carousels, each 80-feet long, for small parts
- 1.6 million gallons on-site, underground water detention (two tanks)
- Extensive and redundant sprinkler coverage
- Removed 440,000 cubic yards of dirt
- 316 miles of fiber-optic cable for data communication.

PROJECT SCOPE

The original scope of work, developed by Boeing, contained a building design criteria document. This was primarily a macro-level overview of the facility, not a detailed requirement definition document. Extensive interviews and meetings over a year-long period determined the actual detailed requirements. However, many times throughout the criteria development phase,

the team was challenged to differentiate between real needs (hard requir
ments) and perceived needs, or wants (soft requirements).

Facility

The primary configuration control document became the coded layout: a d
tailed, to-scale architectural floor and equipment plan of all features of tl
facility and site, on which every item had an identifiable code. This was tl
primary document against which all other emerging changes were "teste
for compatibility and coordination.

All design issues were documented, tracked, and statused on an actic
item list. Individuals were assigned the accountability for the item with a sp
cific due date. Action item lists were reviewed and updated weekly at the re
ularly scheduled project team meetings. The appropriate resolution was pr
sented to the complete design team for review prior to its implementation.

It was intensely challenging to manage scope changes and still mainta
three major project milestone reviews. Extensive meeting minutes were mai
tained to document changes, in addition to updates of the coded layout. Sp
cific milestone reviews were based on change control as opposed to continuo
changes. In order to catalog the numerous design changes, design logs by di
cipline were initially maintained to provide visibility to the design team.

Material Handling

As the program got under way, a series of trade-off studies further refin
our understanding of the advantages of various kinds of material handlir
equipment. These studies were of critical importance to the entire SD
equipment program and exerted a ripple influence on most subsequent de
sions relating to building design and construction. These analyses include
• miniload automated storage and retrieval system (ASRS) versus carous
system
• hybrid vehicle versus narrow aisle man-up order picking vehicle
• two-level versus single-level carousels
• rack-supported storage versus self-supported building roof for high b
storage area
• vertical carousel versus horizontal carousel system
• bulk floor stacked versus rack storage
• carousel system automation
• column bay spacing for high-bay building columns.

Because the SDC building design wrapped around equipment requir
ments, processes were not constrained by predetermined space availabili
beyond the design goal of using space efficiently.

The scope of work for the material handling element of this project d
veloped through observation and review of present work practices ar
processes. The results of these efforts formed the foundation of understan
ing for Boeing's method of doing business. From this foundation began tl
identification of opportunities for improved methodologies that could be d
signed into the new facility.

Following the initial observation and orientation phase, extensive int
views and work sessions with the facility user representatives were held
"brainstorm" ideas for improving every aspect of their daily work lives. The
ideas were then subsequently organized by general category. With many of :
own ideas, the material handling team developed alternatives and options.

Process flow diagrams and dependency charts that were developed ensured the optimum layout of all process areas.

A detailed and comprehensive narrative describing each process center operation was developed. These documents described how each individual system operated, with particular emphasis on its interface with the material handling equipment.

As various material handling ideas were developed, freehand sketches, 3-D perspectives, floor plans, etc., were used to clearly illustrate concepts and ideas and to provide visual augmentation of the final product to the various lay users.

As mentioned above, the coded layout became the primary configuration control document for all team members. As the configuration of "bricks and mortar" and material handling features were merged with the facility requirements, they were documented on the coded layout. Any conflicts were promptly identified and addressed, and mutually beneficial solutions were developed.

As the material handling concept became more solidified, the systems were simulated using Automod 2e. This provided confirmation of the adequacy of each of the three subsystems as well as the entire integrated system to function to the desired performance criteria. The results from these simulation tests showed how quickly all the myriad parts and sizes could be moved through the system.

Cost or emerging functional requirements typically drove changes. Identified changes were discussed in weekly material handling team meetings. All team members were encouraged to participate in discussions on design alternatives, design concepts and approach, and selection of particular design options.

Material handling changes impacted the project in many different ways, including "brick and mortar," system functionality, cost, schedule, user acceptance, and system reliability.

In order to determine optimal design configuration, actual data was collected and summarized whenever possible.

Whenever conflicting requirements emerged, the project team always referred to the project's mission and objectives statements to provide the basis for compliance.

Examples of changes occurring during the design are adding five rows of high-bay racks and four hybrid vehicles; adding a tote take-away conveyor in the high bay to improve system response time; redesigning totes to be constructed of a fire resistance material to satisfy the fire inspector's requirements; reducing the size of the conveyor tote from 36 to 30 inches to improve ergonomics; and extensively evaluating and refining the conveyor/carousel workstations.

Control Systems

One of the fundamental project ground rules was that the project must be "low risk" on start-up. Boeing mandated that the performance of the new facility would not be dependent upon a very sophisticated control system that would take months to debug. However, the system had to have the flexibility to expand its automation capabilities as the needs of the facility dictated. In response to those needs, LGE implemented a successfully proven methodology to fully define immediate as well as long-term requirements:

Requirements definition specification (RDS). The specification was developed through extensive interviewing sessions with owner representatives from cross-functional groups. This document described in broad terms what the control system was to do. It also defined the migration path to add additional levels of warehouse automation as the needs arose.

Functional definition specification (FDS). This document described the architectural functionality of the control system. It defines how the system will be configured, organized, and modularized so that additional levels of automation may be conveniently integrated.

Customer requirements to standardize equipment across vendor boundaries and to increase the product-tracking capability of the systems drove scope changes. Changes were managed through the request for information (RFI) process from the owner to the vendor.

One of the material handling vendors was requested to change from this standard bar code scanner to another brand of scanner. This change allowed the owner to have a single brand of scanner, which reduced training and maintenance costs. This vendor experienced problems integrating the scanners into this product. Fortunately, these problems were identified during system prototyping and resolved during the site acceptance test.

Another change included adding additional fixed scanners to the conveyor system in order to track the tote to its final destination. This change will allow for the tracking of parts in the totes when future automation is implemented.

QUALITY MANAGEMENT

As previously mentioned, the philosophy of the management team was to build and manage a team of people who would assume and share ownership in the process and be accountable for the product of the SDC building program. Thus the program was driven by our mission, not by hierarchy or rules. This process differed substantially from normal Boeing procedures in these areas:

• The core design and user team was maintained throughout the entire project life-cycle, from conceptual development through start-up, commissioning, and post construction. This added not only to the stability of the project, but ensured that the owners' and designers' intentions were correctly interpreted, implemented by the contractors, and functionally validated as the process went into actual usage.

• The core design and user team supported directly and indirectly the users' quality improvement teams, meeting with them to develop work-station design, color schemes, and other aspects of the new facility that would influence the quality of their working environments.

• In order to achieve quality construction and procurement documents, formal user reviews were performed. Major design review milestones at 30, 60, and 90 percent were conducted on the facility construction documents both by peer reviews conducted by an independent consultant and review by Boeing facility engineers.

• The equipment procurement specifications likewise underwent thorough milestone reviews. The "brick and mortar" review team had input into the material handling specifications to ensure that all interface conditions were coordinated and had indeed been incorporated into the documents. In addition, comments were solicited from prequalified equipment suppliers and incorporated into the specifications prior to the actual bid release.

• User review comments were documented. Each comment had to be specifically addressed and satisfactorily resolved by the designer prior to the next milestone review. In cases when comments were in conflict, the designer met with the individuals or groups initiating the comment and facilitated the development of a consensus solution.

• A factory acceptance test for the integrated material control (IMCS) and graphics control system was required in the specifications and was a major factor in trouble-free installation and commissioning.

TIME MANAGEMENT

Time management for the project was implemented through an integrated critical path method (CPM) project schedule, an integrated action item list (with due dates) that was updated weekly, and required recovery plans for critical tasks that were behind schedule. Since the project schedule was integrated for all participants in the project, impacts on the material handling vendors from delays in construction were identified early and costs were minimized through advance notification and planning.

Facility

Major project milestones were:

Building conceptual design, design development, detailed design, issue for permit	3/90–4/91
Permitting, bid addendum	4/91–6/91
Building construction	9/91–3/93

Scope adjustments and their causes. As a strategy for managing planned changes, the coded layout was "frozen" at a particular date. This gave the design team a fixed target to work toward. Meanwhile, the liaison team continued to meet with Boeing to refine project requirements. These changes were documented and tracked to ensure incorporation at the next deliverable milestone. As a result, the completed building required very few user modifications to the final design.

In addition, the building configuration was designed to directly respon[d] to and be driven by the various material handling processes. This led to a[n] other major challenge. These processes were being defined and refined con[-] currently with the development of construction documents for the buildin[g.] By working closely together, the material handling team members were abl[e] to provide the facility designers with their "best guess" of the material han[-] dling equipment configurations at the various interface points. As a result, [a] significant amount of flexibility was designed into the facility to accommo[-] date installation and future operational changes.

Extremely late and evolving requirements imposed upon the project by [a] newly hired fire inspector for the city of SeaTac generated the primary con[-] struction delay challenges to the project. These requirements significantly im[-] pacted the fire protection and fire detection systems installations. Of the prob[-] lems encountered on the project, this one almost became the "show stopper.["] The requirements imposed were very stringent and very late in the construc[-] tion process. Extensive meetings with SeaTac officials were required to:
- fully disclose and understand the city's requirements
- negotiate whenever possible more realistic interpretation of code requirement[s]
- develop equivalences that would satisfy the intent of the code and eas[e] the safety concerns of the official while maintaining the integrity of the ori[g-] inal design and minimizing the cost to the owner.

This was done over a five-month period. In order to minimize disrup[-] tions to the contractor, it was done with an extreme sense of urgency by th[e] program team.

Material Handling Equipment

Major project milestones were:

Initial conceptual design	8/90–12/90
Finalize conceptual design	1/91–3/91
Generate bid specifications detail design	4/91–9/91
Bidding	10/91–12/91
Equipment manufacturing	1/92–7/92
Equipment installation	8/92–2/93

Major delays in equipment installation resulted when the building con[-] tractor was unable to complete and turn over for joint occupancy the re[-] quired building areas.

Control Systems

The schedule for control systems followed the material handling equipmen[t] schedule. There were no delays in the project due to control systems because o[f] the rigorous design, programming, and testing requirements on the vendors.

COST MANAGEMENT

In order to ensure compliance with the project's budget objective, a desig[n-] to-cost approach was taken for the entire project.

Facility

LGE developed a conceptual grade construction estimate using a parametri[c] approach as early as the 15 percent design development stage. Concurrentl[y]

Boeing's estimators prepared an independent cost estimate. These two estimates were subsequently compared and reconciled, with the resulting dollar value becoming the target number for the constructed costs.

At the conclusion of the 30 percent milestone, another construction estimate was prepared. At that time it appeared that the cost exceeded the budget. A value engineering analysis of the facility, prepared by the design team, resulted in the identification of approximately fifteen items for cost reduction consideration. This analysis included the values of probable construction costs. The advantages and disadvantages of eliminating each item were discussed. Through this process, the program eliminated approximately $2.5 million in additional construction costs without adversely affecting the building's functionality or appearance.

Material Handling

A very similar approach was taken with the material handling equipment. To add additional levels of confidence into the estimating process, input for installed costs provided by various vendors for conveyors, racks, hybrid vehicles, etc., were factored into the cost estimate.

At the end of concept development, the cost of the conveyor system had to be reduced by approximately $600,000. To accomplish this, the amount of conveyor equipment had to be reduced. To achieve this, it would be necessary to bring cultural changes to people that managed the operation. This required changing the process from a "batch" to a "continuous flow" operation. With cost reductions as our objective (and shield), we were able to drive the group to focus on improving the process. The material handling designers were now free to design a system that would improve the existing methods of warehousing and distribution.

Existing carousels, mid-bay racking, etc., were reused whenever feasible as an additional cost-saving strategy.

The entire team was aware of the budget status for each of the major elements, and was committed to achieving the objective.

RISK MANAGEMENT

External Risks

Permitting by a new municipality. As previously mentioned, the very first formal project document prepared to obtain project approval was the SEPA checklist. This document requires all governmental agencies to consider the environmental impacts of a proposal before making a decision. An environmental impact statement (EIS) must be prepared for all proposals with probable significant adverse impacts on the quality of the environment. The checklist is submitted to the agency having jurisdiction (AHJ) and describes in broad terms the scope and magnitude of the owner's planned development.

Because the city of SeaTac incorporated as a municipality only months prior to the start of the project, it was not known whether the city or King County would perform the checklist review. Furthermore, the city had never reviewed and issued a building permit, let alone one as complex as the SDC, and that created additional complications in the permitting and building construction inspection processes.

Acceptance by the local neighborhood. A facility this large was defi
nitely going to have an impact upon the character of the surrounding neigh
borhood, during construction as well as during the operational life of the fa
cility. The last thing the project needed was to alienate the community an
create opponents who would object to the project, possibly delaying it or per
haps canceling it altogether. It was imperative to make friends of the neigh
bors, be sensitive to their concerns, mitigate the impact of the facility upo.
the adjoining neighborhood, and to keep the neighbors well informed of th
project status and progress.

FAA approval. The project was extremely close to the flight line of th
eastern runway of SeaTac Airport. As such, many of the physical propertie
of the facility had to be in compliance with FAA guidelines. This include
such issues as the maximum height of the high bay, exterior building colo
site lighting, reflective characteristics of the building siding, and construc
tion crane height.

Internal Risks

Control system. As mentioned before, a low-risk start-up was one of th
fundamental ground rules of the project. Boeing project management cor
sidered the control system design and implementation as potentially hig
risk to the project. Custom software development with extensive sophistica
tion and complexity could have increased design costs and jeopardized th
overall schedule.

In order to mitigate this risk, a delicate balance was created between pro
ject team members and Boeing management and maintained through proac
tive communication and team-building skills. This balance required that th
pertinent people within the Boeing company be actively involved during th
initial development of the control system requirements, in order to obtai
their buy-in of the approach. The design and subsequent development of th
control systems were developed by the control systems suppliers, whic
minimized the project risk. These suppliers were managed by the projec
team's system specialists to enforce strict adherence to the performance re
quirements. Throughout the implementation phase, Boeing managers wer
statused frequently on project progress.

Material handling. The mechanical and control systems of the mater.
al handling equipment had to have an uptime of 98 percent in order to mee
the performance objectives of the project. Because of poor performance o
recently completed projects, there was a significant amount of skepticism.

The material handling system had to be 100 percent operational on th
day the facility opened. With a tight budget and construction schedule, thi
meant that there was little margin for error in the design process. All factor
had to be considered, everyone's needs had to be met, and on day one, all th
systems and processes had to function as designed.

Managing extensive user input. From the beginning, it seemed a
though the project was inundated with extensive user comments. Thes
comments were simultaneously late emerging, contradictory, and often cor
fusing. At almost anytime, it seemed as though these had the potential to e:
fect a major impact on the project schedule and budget.

Use of outside consultants. As with any new endeavors, the use of ou
side consultants was viewed with various degrees of acceptance from th
user groups (Boeing Facility), as well as from other support groups. Eac

LOCKWOOD GREENE

Lockwood Greene is a global business partner for the consulting, design, and construction management services.

We co-manage corporate business agendas to optimize financial return, operational performance, and competitive advantage through the accountable implementation of industrial facilities, processes, and systems.

For more than a century-and-a-half we have been providing consulting engineering, architectural, construction management, and industrial planning services to manufacturing and process industries across the nation and around the world. Building on a cadre of proven professionals with particular expertise in automated warehousing and distribution, environmental engineering and permitting, process control and instrumentation, and world-class manufacturing, our portfolio of experience has focused on the fields of aviation and aerospace, foods and beverages, metals, microelectronics, process, and port and marine facilities. Working together with our clients, we listen carefully to understand those needs and provide integrated and cost-effective design solutions.

Our business is to help our clients solve problems, reduce costs, be competitive, and be profitable by providing quality professional planning, design, and management service to them.

thought it had the capabilities to go it alone. Developing credibility, trust, and acceptance was challenging but critical to the success of the project. In all the cases cited above, the true key to defusing the situation was simply communication, communication, communication. Sure, there were technical problems to resolve and implement, but constant communications led to mutual understanding. Together with strong dedication to positive interpersonal skills, the walls were taken down brick by brick.

TEAM DEVELOPMENT AND HUMAN RESOURCES

Team Development

A partnering relationship must be created throughout the entire team. While this is the current "buzzword," the words and the music must be consistent for this truly to be effective. To do this, the deep adversarial relationships had to be significantly reduced, if not eliminated altogether. Meetings were conducted in a non-threatening atmosphere where everyone felt free to discuss problems and ask for help. Resources were assigned to address emerging problems based upon expertise, not along employment affiliations.

In addition to the formal weekly meetings, there was an informal weekly team-building breakfast meeting that brought together the Boeing management team, engineers, and contractors. The meeting was completely off the record, allowing all participants the opportunity to vent their feelings and frustrations, modify expectations, and so forth, with impunity.

Other team-building tools were:
- promotion of enthusiasm through planned and spontaneous recognition that was personal, specific and timely (The project developed a logo, which was applied to all manner of items—hats, cups, notebooks, key chains— and given to people to show that they were appreciated for the job they were doing.)
- instigating numerous planned and impromptu potlucks, coffee, and dough-nut breaks, working lunches, celebrating birthdays, celebrating project progress at every major milestone; e.g., groundbreaking, topping out, etc.
- off-hour award ceremonies sponsored for key participants and their fami-lies, including users, Boeing consultants, and representatives of jurisdiction-al authorities.

All of these activities were genuine and sincere, and collectively stated that each team member's efforts were recognized and appreciated.

Team Contribution to Project Success

By developing individuals into a motivated, focused work team, the entire team was dedicated to the success of the entire project, not just the specific areas for which they had specific responsibilities. Some examples are:
- The "brick and mortar" review team had input into the material handling specifications to ensure that all agreed that interface conditions had indeed been incorporated into the documents.
- Detailed equipment drawings were submitted to the facility design team for review at critical interface locations such as floor and ceiling supported equipment, electrical panel loads and location, and for final interface review
- The team collaborated to achieve mutually satisfactory solutions when ever constructed or installed conditions differed from the as-planned condi-tion. Specifically, the high bay take-away conveyor was a late addition to the project. The roofing system could not accept the additional equipment loads without significant structural modifications. After deliberation, it was decid-ed that a floor-supported system could be used without any detrimental ef-fects to the functionality or appearance of the building.
- Contractor questions or additional information requests were tracked and closely monitored; need dates were specifically established in order to elimi-nate or minimize any unplanned activities. Emerging situations were ag-gressively and proactively managed. To prevent contractor rework in the cas-es where the contractor installation deviated from design drawings, the engineer made every effort to make the installed condition work. Savings or credits to the owner were, however, aggressively pursued when appropriate.

CONTRACT AND PROCUREMENT MANAGEMENT

Material Handling Equipment

The material handling equipment (MHE) procurement and installation were managed by the program team. Prescriptive specifications were submitted to prequalified equipment vendors to solicit RFQs on the three major pieces of equipment; i.e., conveyors, high bay rack with hybrid vehicles, and carousels. Through a detailed bid evaluation process, the "best bid" was selected. The MHE integration team managed the design, fabrication, installation, and start-up by the MHE vendors. Contract management and control was streamlined with technical or contractual issues promptly addressed.

Facility Construction

The contractor was selected through a competitive bid process, after first pre-qualifying and developing a general contractors bid list. The contract was awarded to a general contractor based on the apparent low lump-sum bid and best schedule. The contractor self-performed general carpentry and concrete work, subcontracting all other work to local specialty contractors. The contractor was responsible for all coordination, scheduling, site supervision, etc., among all trades.

The contractor was responsible for the completion of specific building areas to achieve joint occupancy, allowing the installation of the material handling equipment in one area while building construction activities proceeded in others. This included coordinating with others to permit the transition and usage of the designated area.

This method provided the owner single-point responsibility for the coordination and construction of a very complicated facility, while at the same time providing the flexibility for early completion of specific building areas, allowing early starts on the MHE installation.

COMMUNICATION MANAGEMENT

Boeing was committed to involving all levels of the user's management and staff in this project. Because of the significance, complexity, and sophistication of the project to all its stakeholders, the level of owner, community, peer, and municipality review was rigorous and thorough. Furthermore, because these stakeholders represented a widely diversified understanding of many of the technical issues associated with this project, all means of communications were necessary to convey thoughts and ideas to the various audiences. This included three-dimensional perspectives and sketches, scale models, automation simulation of the material handling equipment, architectural renderings, newsletters, etc.

Communication—formal and informal, internal and external—was characterized by entrepreneurial enthusiasm. It was transactional and horizontal rather than directed and vertical. Roles and expectations of all participants were established early, identifying how they fit into the larger picture and what we wanted them to do.

SUMMARY

The successful execution of the Spares Distribution Center project can be directly attributed to the following factors:
• total project team commitment to the partnering concept in order to create a "win-win" relationship (Team members were held accountable for task assignments.)
• creation of "ownership in the project" by soliciting input from all stakeholders in the initial design stage
• effective communications with all project stakeholders (proven methodology for change control)

- true understanding of the functions and processes before designing a facility in order to correctly meet those needs
- provision of an integrated approach and solution to engineering- and business-related problems
- a "low risk" start-up approach for the material handling control systems.

Study Questions

BOEING SPARES DISTRIBUTION CENTER: A WORLD-CLASS FACILITY ACHIEVED THROUGH PARTNERING

1. Boeing's new Spares Distribution Center (SDC) project was very successful. From the case and your experience, what are the key elements that contributed to the project's success?

2. The case states: "As early as 1985, the Spares organization recognized that to be responsive to the changing demands of its customers, it would have to change the way it was doing business." Change is inherent in today's organizations and business environments. Discuss some of the major changes that companies are facing today.

3. The management of this project used a very effective method to deal with arising conflicts in the project. Describe the method.

4. This case discusses the use of "partnering" to manage relationships with customers. Describe what is meant by partnering and discuss its benefits.

5. The schedule on this project was managed using the critical path method (CPM). Define CPM and discuss its strengths and weaknesses.

Responding to the Northridge Earthquake

Jerry B. Baxter, California Department of Transportation

PM Network, November 1994, pp. 13–22

The world didn't come to an end last January 17th. But for about thirty seconds in Los Angeles (L.A.), it sure seemed like it. At 4:31 A.M., a forgotten earthquake fault awoke from a long slumber, triggering the most devastating seismic event in Los Angeles history.

The 6.8 magnitude Northridge earthquake was blamed for some sixty deaths, thousands of injuries, and billions in property damage. But nowhere was the destructive power of nature more evident than in the collapsed sections of four major freeways, including the nation's busiest, Interstate 10, and California's lifeline of commerce, Interstate 5. For an estimated one million commuters, getting around L.A. would not be the same for a long time.

The Northridge earthquake posed one of the greatest challenges to the California Department of Transportation in its nearly 100-year history. It also proved to be one of its greatest triumphs, testing the mettle and ingenuity of Caltrans employees in ways no one could have possibly foreseen. In an era of shrinking government budgets and eroding confidence in the public sector, Caltrans and the many other agencies involved rallied to the cause of earthquake recovery. It was this single-minded determination, along with some sound project management, that resulted in freeways being rebuilt in a fraction of the time originally predicted, with high quality, and at a reasonable price. As Governor Pete Wilson put it recently, this is the story of the great "California comeback."

CALTRANS AND FREEWAYS

Aside from its beaches and ubiquitous palm trees, perhaps the most prominent feature of the Los Angeles area is its freeway network. There are twenty-seven freeways totaling 615 miles within District 7, and the system was built around the concept that the automobile held the future of our mobility and that everyone should live within a few miles of a freeway. Each day, the freeways accommodate 102 million vehicle-miles of travel, or the equivalent of more than 200 round trips to the moon.

Designing, building, and maintaining this vast transportation grid is the responsibility of the California Department of Transportation, popularly known as Caltrans. It was established by the state legislature in 1972 and grew out of the former state Department of Public Works, Division of Highways. Other Caltrans responsibilities include mass transit system enhancement, railroad system development, seaport and waterway expansion, air

Motorists on the 5/14 interchange, just north of the epicenter of the Northridge earthquake, got an uncomfortably close-up view of the severity of the quake's damage.

transportation planning and assisting area governments and agencies in plan‐ning and developing local transportation improvements. Caltrans is divide into twelve regional districts. District 7, which includes Los Angeles and Ven‐tura counties, is the second largest of these districts and serves a populatio‐fast approaching ten million. District 7 employs approximately 2,800 people with the largest group—1,345—working in the construction and maintenanc‐area. The district's design department has 491 employees, and the traffic op‐erations department employs 325. The annual support budget is $162 mil‐lion for personnel and $101 million for operations.

During the next seven years, the district will manage a budget of ap‐proximately $2.3 billion, which includes all aspects of highway and inter‐city rail design and construction.

THE EARTHQUAKE

L.A. is often described as many small communities searching for a center. It i‐the freeway system that connects it all together. Several of those connection‐were broken on January 17, 1994. The ground shook for about thirty seconds and seismologists later put the quake's magnitude at 6.8 on the Richter Scale‐Even though it was not the much feared magnitude 8 earthquake expected t‐strike the San Andreas fault that runs up the spine of California, the North‐ridge quake nevertheless caused terrific shaking in the heavily populated Sa‐Fernando Valley. Seismologists later said the fault snapped in a spot 9 mile‐below ground, and caused a violent vertical thrust on the surface of up to 1‐feet. But, as those familiar with earthquakes have come to learn, the damag‐can be maddeningly capricious in where it strikes. For example, the Ventur‐Freeway, United States 101, which cuts through the heart of the San Fernan‐do Valley, was barely damaged and remained in service after the quake. Bu‐just to the north on the Simi Valley Freeway (Route 118), the 566-foot-lon‐bridge at San Fernando Mission Boulevard/Gothic Street collapsed when it‐ten concrete support columns gave way under intense shaking.

Stiff columns and not enough capacity on the expansion joints also were to blame 23 miles north of downtown on Interstate 5 at Gavin Canyon, where the northbound and southbound bridge decks collapsed. Just three miles to the south, bridge failures also occurred on the Antelope Valley Freeway (Route 14).

For many, however, L.A.'s quake devastation was exemplified by the Santa Monica Freeway. Concrete columns beneath the La Cienega and Fairfax bridges exploded, reinforcing steel bars 1 3/4 inches in diameter (about the thickness of your wrist) twisted out of shape like so much over-cooked spaghetti, and the bridges tumbled earthward. The nation's busiest freeway, which before the quake carried up to 341,000 vehicles a day, was suddenly, savagely, taken out of service.

THREE-PRONGED ATTACK

Caltrans didn't have time to stand around and mourn this potentially crippling damage to the freeway system. L.A. is car-dependent, and motorists don't tolerate even the slightest delay or inconvenience.

The Caltrans strategy of attack was on three fronts. First, there was the initial emergency response, followed by an interim traffic management strategy, and then longer-term rebuilding efforts. Each step was designed to ensure the quickest route to returning the transportation system to the way it was before the earthquake with the least amount of inconvenience to drivers. The process can be likened to how the wounded are attended during wartime. First there is the basic triage in the field, then interim treatment at a mobile army surgical hospital (M.A.S.H.), and then finally off to a regular hospital for long-term care and rehabilitation.

In the hours after the quake, most of Caltrans' 1,000 maintenance personnel fanned out to do visual inspections of the freeway system and to initiate closures on freeways that were collapsed or considered unsafe. These initial "windshield" inspections were followed up by more detailed inspections by structural engineers. Meanwhile, maintenance personnel, in coordination with the downtown Traffic Management Center, spent a grueling first day establishing detours around the closed freeways. This was no small feat, as information kept changing constantly. Strong after-shocks also complicated matters, forcing engineers to re-inspect bridges for signs of new damage. For the closed section of the Santa Monica (Interstate 10) and Simi Valley Freeway (Route 118), acceptable detours were available. Each area had surface city streets that paralleled the freeway. In fact, many motorists were already using these alternate routes before official detours were established.

In the case of the Santa Monica Freeway, mobility was helped by two important factors. The opening last year of the new Interstate 105 gave commuters another east-west freeway alternative to Interstate 10. Also, the Santa Monica Freeway is part of a traffic management demonstration project called the Smart Corridor, which links the freeway and key surface streets—primarily Olympic, Pico, Washington, and Adams boulevards—to better balance traffic flows on all corridor facilities. With Interstate 10 out of service, the Los Angeles City Department of Transportation's Automated Traffic Surveillance and Control (ATSAC) was able to adjust the timing on the surface-street traffic signals to accommodate the heavier traffic diverted

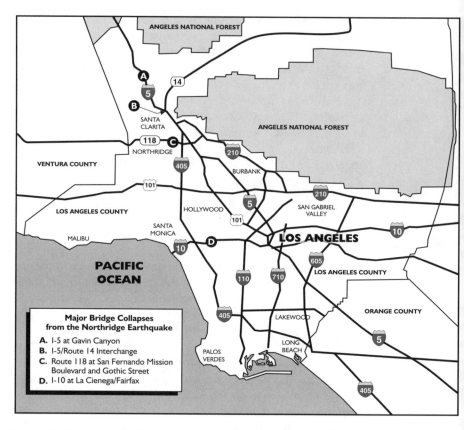

Major Bridge Collapses from the Northridge Earthquake

A. I-5 at Gavin Canyon
B. I-5/Route 14 Interchange
C. Route 118 at San Fernando Mission Boulevard and Gothic Street
D. I-10 at La Cienega/Fairfax

from the freeway. Caltrans also employed other traffic management techniques, including the use of closed circuit television cameras to identify trouble spots, and stationary changeable message signs to relay the latest road information to motorists.

The Traffic Management Center disseminated freeway and highway closures and suggested alternatives several times a day via fax and through Cityview Channel 35, the city's government cable access channel that is available in 500,000 households. Through the use of "freeway vision," viewers receive a version of Caltrans' realtime, computerized map of the freeway system that employs color-coded lights that display the latest traffic conditions. And as always, the Traffic Management Center worked closely with the news media, particularly radio traffic reporters, to help guide motorists around the closures.

It was a different story on Interstate 5, however. Truckers and commuters driving in from bedroom communities in the Antelope Valley to the north of the damage soon found there were no good alternatives. Some truckers ended up taking a 40-mile inland route to get to metropolitan Los Angeles. A truck heading to Los Angeles from Bakersfield, for example, was forced to take State Route 58 east to Interstate 395 south to Interstate 15 south to Interstate 10 westbound. Truckers also took the coastal route to Los Angeles, employing United States 101 to get into the San Fernando Valley. Faced with hours of delay, many postponed or canceled their trips. For a state struggling to pull out of the worst economic downturn since the Great Depression, everyone at Caltran knew it was essential to get L.A. moving again.

DEMOLITION AND DETOURS

Caltrans immediately went to work demolishing and removing the damaged structures, then creating temporary detours. At the I-5/Route14 interchange, Granite Construction Company of Watsonville, California, brought in forty people, who worked around the clock to remove about 5,000 yards of concrete and steel using trucks, loaders, and pavement breakers. When the bridge resisted traditional demolition efforts, explosives were brought in and sections were blown up. Meanwhile, just to the north on Interstate 5 at Gavin Canyon, Penhall International Co. of Anaheim, California, brought in fifty people to remove 15,000 cubic yards of concrete and steel.

At the same time, Caltrans maintenance forces, working alongside Chumo Construction of Baldwin Park, California, carved out a detour for Interstate 5 using a nearly forgotten frontage road called, appropriately, The Old Road. About seventy-five people worked around the clock to resurface the road with 20,000 tons of asphalt concrete, add signs, re-stripe, and add K-rail. In just eleven days after the earthquake, the $3.2 million detour around Interstate 5 opened to traffic, with a capacity of roughly 50 percent of the freeway. At about the same time, another important detour opened: two lanes of Route 14 opened for southbound traffic connecting to the southbound Interstate 5. Caltrans forces re-striped the southbound truck bypass to provide one mixed-flow lane and one high occupancy vehicle (HOV) lane. A few days later, a detour was created for the Santa Monica Freeway using the La Cienega and Fairfax on- and off-ramps for car-pools of two or more. The detour cut delay time to about three to four minutes for HOV traffic, and eighteen to twenty minutes for mixed-flow traffic.

An altogether different detour was put in place for the Simi Valley Freeway. The eastbound bridges had collapsed at San Fernando Mission Boulevard/Gothic Street, but the westbound bridges had just sagged. A $3.8 million contract was awarded to shore-up the former westbound bridges, re-pave to a smooth surface, and re-stripe the freeway to allow that structure to carry three lanes in each direction. The detour was completed February 20.

REBUILDING

Once the major detours were in place, traffic started to return to near normal levels. At the same time, ridership on transit services, which experienced a sharp spike immediately after the earthquake, headed back toward pre-quake levels. The most visible of the transit options was the new Metrolink commuter rail service. The Santa Clarita line, which carries Antelope Valley commuters into downtown, had a ridership of more than 21,000 passengers per day one week after the quake, but recently has been carrying less than 3,000 passengers a day. Ridership on special express bus service created after the quake has been light. However, a recent Metrolink survey found that half of the riders had started riding the train since the Northridge earthquake, and many of those cited quake damage as the reason they were no longer driving to work.

That's not to say that transit wasn't important after the quake. Expanding bus service and the rapid opening of new Metrolink stations gave thousands of Angelenos important options for getting to and from work. There was also resurgent interest in telecommuting—working from home or a

Reconstruction of the 5/14 interchange at about the halfway point.

Photo by Daniel Bayer ©1994

satellite location through the use of computers, fax machines, modems, and telephone lines. But the statistics show that given options, a vast majority of commuters prefer their own automobiles on their own freeway to other ways of getting around.

Meanwhile, Caltrans turned its attention to reconstruction of the freeways. Normally the process of awarding a contract to build a major structure takes many weeks. A contract is advertised and prospective contractors pick up bid packages and submit their proposals. At a scheduled date, the bids are opened and the lowest qualified bidder is selected for the job. Then a process of reviewing the winning bid, and finally approving it, takes place. But normal rules were thrown out the window for the Northridge earthquake. Governor Pete Wilson signed an emergency declaration allowing Caltrans to streamline its contracting procedures. Another important feature of the contracts was the incentive/disincentive. If the winning contractor finished the job early, a bonus was awarded for each day that the deadline was beaten. Conversely, for every day over the deadline, the contractor would be penalized the same amount. The amount varied depending upon the importance of the route. This proved to be a powerful motivation for contractors working on the job.

On January 29, a $14.8 million contract to rebuild the Gavin Canyon bridges on Interstate 5 was awarded to E.L. Yeager Inc., of Riverside, California, and the firm was given 130 calendar days to complete the work. The incentive/disincentive was $150,000 per day. The contractor finished the job thirty-three days early, earning a bonus of $4.95 million.

The incentive/disincentive clause created a stir on the Santa Monica Freeway when contractor C.C. Myers Inc., of Rancho Cordova, California, pulled out all the stops to complete the reconstruction of the Interstate 10 bridges in a blistering sixty-six days—a whopping seventy-four days ahead of the original contract, earning a $14.8 million bonus. Myers took every opportunity to save time and streamline his operation. He greatly expanded his work force. For example, he had 228 carpenters, laborers, and equipment operators on the job, when normally he would only have about sixty-five. This job employed 134 ironworkers, when it typically would employ only about fifteen. These dedicated people worked around the clock, even in the rain. The work was scheduled much like an assembly line. In that way, critical activities were followed by the next critical activity. Carpenters and ironworkers acted like teams competing against each other to see who could finish first.

Although Clint Myers received a substantial bonus for finishing early, he spent a lot of money on overtime, bonuses, and other premiums to keep the job rolling along. Complicating matters was the fact that beneath the freeway Caltrans had leased the airspace to a storage company, and many of the storage units were crushed by the collapse of the freeway. Needless to say, the owners of the belongings stored in now flattened storage units were clamoring for compensation. Also demanding attention were many residents who live alongside the freeway. With reconstruction work going on twenty-four hours a day, including jack-hammering and pile-driving, Caltrans temporarily housed many families in local motels. The agency even erected a temporary plastic soundwall to help reduce the construction noise traveling to a nearby apartment complex. The double-layer curtain, 450 feet long by 20 feet high, was designed to reduce construction noise by ten decibels.

Despite the difficulties and expense incurred by around-the-clock freeway building, most of Los Angeles cheered the Caltrans quake recovery efforts. The business community, too, was appreciative of the speed at which the Santa Monica Freeway took shape. And with good reason. The Governor's Office of Planning and Research released a report concluding that for every day the Santa Monica Freeway was closed, it cost the local economy more than $1 million. Damage to the infrastructure, the report noted, causes what economists refer to as "dead-weight loss;" that is, not a transfer from one party to another, but a loss to all society. Particularly hurt was the trucking industry; 4 percent of the Santa Monica Freeway traffic is trucks carrying merchandise.

PROJECT MANAGEMENT

Although there were initial estimates that it would take two years or more to restore the freeways to pre-quake service, all quake rebuilding jobs are scheduled to be completed by the end of this year. This was made possible because all resources of Caltrans and the Federal Highway Administration were made available to respond to this disaster. And FHWA officials were working side by side with Caltrans people to expedite the review process. Several other project management techniques were used to perform the restoration work in record time, as discussed below.

"Force Account" Contracts

This is a standard Caltrans tool available to respond to emergencies and disasters. It allows the immediate selection of a single contractor who is available, capable, and has resources to do certain work. The contractor begins immediately, with a minimum of plans, under the direction of a Caltrans resident engineer, and is paid for actual labor, equipment, and material costs

Crews worked around the clock to rebuild the 5/14 interchange. Shown here, a welder puts the finishing touches on the re-bar skeleton on one of many support columns.

plus overhead and profit. About sixty individual force account contracts totaling $20 million were awarded for such work as shoring salvageable bridges, demolishing damaged bridges, and constructing detours. Contractors were at work demolishing the most severely damaged freeway bridges within hours of the Northridge quake, often with little more than a hand shake and a signature on a piece of paper.

Informal Bid Contracts

Immediately after the earthquake, Governor Pete Wilson issued an executive order relaxing certain statutory requirements of the State Contract Act, allowing Caltrans to speed the process of designing, advertising, awarding, and beginning construction contracts. With this action, Caltrans was able to advertise with minimum plans, ask for bids within three to four days, open bids and award contracts the same day, and begin work the next day. This cut a normal four-month process to five days, but retained the advantage of competitive bidding. Sixty contracts of this type, totaling about $230 million, are being used to rebuild destroyed bridges, strengthen damaged bridges, and repave and repair buckled pavement and bridge approaches.

Incentive/Disincentive Contracts

In order to ensure early completion and opening to traffic of the critical, closed freeways, several informal bid contracts utilized an "A-plus-B" bid process and incentive/disincentives. An incentive/disincentive amount was determined, based on the daily cost of traffic disruption and detouring; and a maximum number of calendar days, working twenty-four hours a day, seven days a week, was determined. A pre-selected list of well-qualified contractors, usually five, were then asked to bid on an "A" amount for the normal contract quantities and a "B" amount based on a number of days they bid to complete the work, multiplied by the incentive/disincentive amount. The total of A-plus-B then became the basis for comparison of bids and award to the low bidder. If the contractor finished the work before the bid calendar days expired, a bonus was paid. If the contractor finished after the date, the contractor paid a penalty for each day after the deadline.

As of this writing, all incentive/disincentive contracts have resulted in early completions and bonuses for the contractors. While the $14.8 million bonus earned by the contractor on the Santa Monica Freeway, and the $4.95 million bonus earned by the Interstate 5 contractor, made headlines, other major projects returned much more modest bonuses and still achieved their objective of returning the freeway facilities to the motorists in the minimum possible time.

Special PM Processes

Program, project, and construction management for disaster response is provided by Caltrans staff personnel in much the same manner as with normal projects. In the case of the Northridge earthquake, an overall program manager is responsible for total coordination of projects. Individual project managers are responsible for delivery of plans, specifications, and estimates to the point of being ready to advertise for bids. Because of the critical traffic management involved in the multiple projects under construction at one time, a detour manager was designated to coordinate the flow of traffic through and around the work areas.

Immediately after the earthquake, Business, Transportation and Housing Agency Secretary Dean Dunphy was put in charge of an earthquake recovery taskforce that included top decision-makers in government, including Federal Highway Administrator Rodney Slater and Los Angeles Mayor Richard Riordan. The object of the task force was to remove roadblocks to quake recovery. Quake recovery proposals were brought to the taskforce for review and approval the same day. If an agency was not cooperating, there was a top person on the taskforce to resolve the conflict.

Within Caltrans, reporting to the district director, are division chiefs in charge of traffic, design, construction, maintenance, administration, right-of-way, etc. Each was responsible for deploying resources to accommodate earthquake recovery needs.

Financial Tracking

In the event of emergencies, Caltrans Director James W. van Loben Sels has the authority to release $4 million for emergency demolition contracts. Following the declaration of a state of emergency by President Clinton, an additional $100 million was made available for demolition and reconstruction from the federal highway fund. Eventually, Congress voted to authorize $1.4 billion for quake recovery, which included a $200 million contingency. For the first 180 days after the quake, federal Emergency Restoration (ER) funds paid for 100 percent of the completed restoration work. Thereafter, the normal federal participating share was available.

An important part of keeping track of costs associated with the Northridge earthquake was the establishment of special expenditure authorization (EA) numbers for each quake contract. The EAs are six digits and are similar

Caltrans was faced with not only the problem of restoring the freeway system, but of accommodating and detouring an enormous traffic flow. Shown here is the Old Road detour below the Gavin Canyon Bridge.

to an account number. The first five numbers are unique to the project, and the sixth number indicates the phase of the contract. If the last number is a 1, for example, that means the contract is in the design phase, while a 4 would mean the project is under construction. Employees, too, were assigned a specific Northridge earthquake EA to charge their time and overtime.

Quality Control

Although design and construction of these earthquake recovery projects are proceeding at a greatly accelerated pace, quality control remains high. Partial plans, sufficient for bidding purposes, were followed with more detailed plans as the work proceeded. Timing for delivery of additional plans was committed to in the bidding documents so that contractors could plan accordingly. The contractors' twenty-four-hour-a-day, seven-day-a-week operations, with no days off for inclement weather, were matched by shifts of Caltrans' inspectors, surveyors, and material testing personnel. Projects were "partnered" between Caltrans and the contractor, greatly facilitating the progress of the work, problem-solving, and quick decisions right on the job site. Contractor performance has been universally outstanding.

Minority Participation

Immediately after the earthquake, some in Los Angeles worried that in the rush to rebuild the freeways, minority- and women-owned construction firms would be left on the sidelines. To make sure that did not happen, Caltrans set a goal that 20 percent of the quake work would go to Disadvantaged Business Enterprises (DBE), but later upped that to 40 percent. To date, 39 percent of contracts have gone to minority- or women-owned companies, which is the highest DBE attainment in the entire state. By comparison, the model Century Freeway project hit only about 30 percent, while typical contracts usually reach 15 percent. A contract manager was responsible for tracking D/WBE usage.

Use of A&E Consultants

Much of the actual structure and roadway design, construction and engineering, and contract administration was done by Caltrans staff. However, to supplement Caltrans forces in the areas of structure design, surveying, materials testing, and design of traffic management systems, consultants were retained. The governor's order allowed Caltrans to go to sole-source selection, rather than competitive bidding. Contractors were selected based on professionalism, competency, and reliability, as well as previous experience, expertise, availability and proximity of resources, and ability to fulfill MBE/WBE requirements. A total of fifteen A&E contracts were awarded.

Key Decision-makers

Early on, Caltrans made a policy decision that once a repaired roadway was reopened, it was going to stay open. This was decided upon to avoid confusing motorists and to restore confidence in the safety of the transportation system. But this posed some logistical problems for our construction engineers. Key to resolving these conflicts was bringing in two experts from our Sacramento headquarters with experience in handling traffic detours and construction phasing. They were able to coordinate with all the contractors to make sure there were no disruptive road closures or conflicts between construction contracts. When it comes to opening or closing a freeway, all the decisions are major ones and had to be handled quickly on-site.

Delegation of Authority

Because of the fast pace of this type of natural disaster, a great emphasis was placed on individual initiative and problem-solving. Fortunately, Caltrans has already been in the freeway building business for a half-century. In the office, we already had as-built plans, aerial photographs, survey data, and engineers familiar with the structures. All that remained was to rebuild what was there, which also meant no cumbersome environmental review process was necessary. Engineers and traffic managers designed temporary traffic detours at the same time permanent bridge designs were being done. Within the design branches, certain staff was assigned to taskforces to work on particular projects with the goal of getting the plans, specifications, and estimates done as quickly as possible. To create emergency detours, a senior design engineer familiar with the area was teamed with a traffic engineer and asked to come up with the safest and most efficient routes around damaged structures. Using the as-built plans, often the designs were done by hand. The designer was then dispatched to the field to work with maintenance branch employees to implement the detour.

Management Structure

The existing hierarchy for decision-making was used, with the additional overlay of a quake recovery task force led by Business, Transportation and Housing Agency Secretary Dean Dunphy. The taskforce's main objective was to make sure all agencies were coordinating their efforts, and to remove any roadblocks to rapid rebuilding. After a few weeks, the taskforce realized that the recovery was on track and met only on an as-needed basis.

Beyond the task force, District 7 was pretty much in charge of quake recovery. The district director held daily meetings with his division chiefs, who then in turn often met with their branch chiefs to pass on instructions. After

about two weeks, Division Chief Jack Hallin, who had just finished oversee
ing the $2.2 billion completion of the Century Freeway, was made projec
manager of the quake recovery. Problems were sent up the ladder and quick
ly resolved by the project manager or, if necessary, the taskforce, which wa
represented by all the major agencies involved in the recovery effort.

Even when the normal chain of command was disrupted, work pro
gressed rapidly. The regional director for traffic operations, Chuck O'Con
nell, lived near the quake's epicenter, and his home sustained severe damage
He was unable to report to work for a week. The office chief for traffic sys
tems, likewise, was on a European vacation, and the office chief for traffic in
vestigations was also out of town.

The monumental task of managing virtually the entire earthquake from
a traffic management point of view was left to Raja Mitwasi, the energeti
branch chief of the District 7 High Occupancy Vehicle Lane Taskforce. H
performed admirably under extraordinary circumstances.

To augment our own personnel, District 7 drew upon maintenance, en
gineering, and administrative personnel from other neighboring districts a
well as from the Caltrans headquarters in Sacramento. Mitwasi usuall
fielded the offers of help from other districts, and put them in touch with th
branch chief of that functional area to make sure the additional people wer
needed and could be utilized properly.

From the outset, everyone at Caltrans was prioritizing. Earthquake re
covery was given top priority over everything else. Within the earthquake re
covery, structures engineers were making decisions on which bridges wer
damaged and which were not, which could support traffic and which shoul
be closed. Traffic was deciding which detours should be opened first, and en
gineers were deciding which bid packages to prepare first.

LESSONS LEARNED

The quake recovery effort was not without its problems, and communica
tion topped the list. The advent of beepers and, more importantly, cellula
phones was critical for the district office to get in touch with field personnel
Caltrans quickly discovered that it didn't have enough phones to go around
Fortunately, a local cellular telephone company loaned field personne
phones during the crisis.

Another bottleneck developed over bridge inspections. In the event of a
disaster, there are simply not enough structural engineers available to do im
mediate inspections of the thousands of bridges in the highway system. The
aftershocks also complicated inspection efforts, forcing engineers to visi
bridges more than once. Eventually, the quake zone was divided into subre
gions, and teams of engineers were sent to inspect bridges, soundwalls, and
other structures within the given subregions. The information was then
compiled into a quake damage database, which included a description of the
damage and cost estimate to repair.

Simple logistical matters also became irritants during the quake recovery
Our Traffic Management Center soon found out that they did not have ade
quate maps to work out the detours, and the list of home numbers for senio
traffic engineers was outdated, leading to delays in contacting key people im
mediately after the quake, which struck on the Martin Luther King, Jr. holiday

The 118 Freeway rebuilding nears completion.

Interestingly, one recurrent problem never manifested itself during the quake recovery: interagency rivalry. All agencies involved in the effort, including the California Highway Patrol, the City and County of Los Angeles, the Metropolitan Transportation Authority, and the City of Santa Clarita all cooperated fully.

Preventing Future Damage

The Northridge earthquake presented far more than a challenge to find ways around quake damage, and to see how quickly freeways could be rebuilt. It also placed renewed scrutiny on our ambitious seismic retrofit program that aims to strengthen hundreds of older freeway bridges to help them withstand the most powerful earthquakes. The Santa Monica Freeway was among the bridges identified for seismic retrofitting, and construction was scheduled to begin within a month of the Northridge earthquake. All 122 of the bridges that had been retrofitted in that way were not damaged in the Northridge earthquake, which is a real life testament to the value and integrity of those new designs. Everything Caltrans learned in the area of earthquake safety is going into these designs.

Currently the seismic retrofit program involves strengthening the columns of existing bridges by encircling certain columns with a steel casing or, in a few cases, an advanced woven fiber casing. In addition to the column casing, some of the bridge footings are made bigger and given additional support by placing additional pilings in the ground or by using steel tie-down rods to better anchor the footings to the ground. In a few cases bridge abutments are made larger and the past restrainer units are made stronger, as encasing the columns make them stiffer and can change the way forces are transmitted within the bridge.

Originally Caltrans had planned to retrofit 1,039 bridges with the column casing and footing strategy. After the Northridge quake, Caltrans launched a review of another 1,655 bridges statewide to determine if they needed retrofit work. In addition, Caltrans went back and reviewed another 700 bridges statewide that had been determined not to need any retrofit work as a check on the process and to make sure no possible bridges tha could need retrofitting had been overlooked.

As it stands now, there will be 2,403 bridges retrofitted statewide in phas one and phase two of the retrofitting program, out of 12,000 state-owne bridges. The goal for the entire seismic safety program is to have these com pleted by 1997. In District 7, Los Angeles and Ventura counties, there are a to tal of 701 bridges to be retrofitted out of a total of 2,566 bridges in the distric

Pulling Together

In the first hours and days after the Northridge earthquake, things looke pretty grim for Los Angeles. In the past two years we've endured a riot, rag ing wildfires, and drought punctuated by an occasional flood. Now there talk that killer bees are on the way. And then the earthquake. Some doom sayers predicted that it could be years before the freeways were restored. Bu as it always does, L.A. pulled together to respond to the earthquake crisis.

As it stands now, earthquake repair of the major freeways will be done b December—in less than a year—and our seismic retrofit program is well o its way to fortifying hundreds of other bridges in L.A. to help them with stand another great quake. Indeed, the Northridge earthquake wasn't the en of the world, or even the end of Los Angeles. But it did lay to rest the linger ing doubts about the resiliency of L.A. and its ability to rally behind a com mon cause. At least until the next earthquake.

Study Questions

RESPONDING TO THE NORTHRIDGE EARTHQUAKE

1. Natural disasters happen unexpectedly and cannot be scheduled. Howeve the reaction to a potential misfortune can be planned and managed. De scribe a method to manage these risks.

2. The case states: "It was this single-minded determination, along with som sound project management, that resulted in freeways being rebuilt in a frac tion of the time originally predicted, with high quality, and at a reasonabl price." What are the other reasons listed in the case that contributed to th success of the project?

3. The challenges faced in this project included the conflicts between som agencies. Conflicts are inherent to projects. What is meant by "conflict" in project and what are the possible courses of actions that a project manage can undertake to deal with them?

4. All organizations should have a crisis management plan in place to deal wit unexpected disasters. From the literature or your own experience, describe situation when an organization was successfully or unsuccessfully able t deal with a crisis. What led to the success or failure?

A Town Makes History by Rising to New Heights

Bruce Watson

Smithsonian, June 1996, pp. 110–20

The people of Valmeyer, Illinois, awash in water three years ago, have built a whole new hometown, this time above the flood line.

A few weeks after the Mississippi River drowned Valmeyer, Illinois, the town's entire population jammed into a community hall in nearby Columbia. Outside the hall, headlights of latecomers lit the parking lot. Inside, old friends shared coffee and rumors. The town where most of them had lived all their lives lay in the floodplain a few miles away, as lifeless as a model train set. With homes gutted and the community scattered to emergency trailers and shelters, a flock of weary neighbors had come to ask, what now?

As they jostled for seats, Darrell and Anna Glaenzer sheltered their own private questions. More than a month had passed since the couple loaded their children into the car and fled the coming deluge. A couple of days after the Glaenzers abandoned their place, the Mississippi rolled in, surging through downtown, pouring over porches, in some cases rising to rooftops. When the water rolled back, it left rotting walls and a moldy stench of raw sewage and fish. "We still thought, with the flood insurance, we could fix up that house and start again," Darrell recalls. "Then the town board passed out this paper with questions on it. I thought it was ludicrous at the time. Moving the entire town was the furthest thing from my mind."

Valmeyer (pop. 900), 30 miles south of St. Louis, was one of many towns drowned by the Mississippi in the summer of 1993. After the floods, the costliest in American history, some towns cleaned up; others split up. But Valmeyer has been making history by moving up. Taking advantage of a recent federal program in "hazard mitigation," a new Valmeyer has risen out of a 500-acre cornfield and woodland on a bluff just above the ruins of the old town. Citizens gathered the will and wherewithal to build a whole new town from scratch: hundreds of houses, a downtown, churches, a school, a fire station, and a post office. The new Valmeyer won't be quite finished until late this year. But after two cramped winters in a trailer city provided by FEMA (the Federal Emergency Management Administration), all but a few residents have moved in, staking their claims on porches fronting freshly seeded lawns.

Before the deluge, Valmeyer wasn't much different from any other small farmland town beside a two-lane blacktop. "It was the kind of town," handyman Mike Mueller says, "where you can be forty years old but everyone still sees you as your dad's son." Says Anna Glaenzer, "Our son would say, 'Mom,

I want to go to a friend's,' and I'd say, 'Be home by dark,' and I didn't worry. That meant a lot."

Flood years—1910, '43, '44, '47—were part of the town's lore, and residents shared the fatalism commonly found in harm's way. Many trusted the federal levee system, which had kept Valmeyer dry since the last flood. Darrell Glaenzer trusted his father. "My dad told me a long time ago there'd be another flood," Darrell says. "He said he might not live to see it, but if that levee broke we'd have water up to the ceiling. He died on July 9. Heart attack. That was the day after we began sandbagging."

For three weeks the TV news told townspeople that levees were being breached upriver, but Valmeyer stayed put. "You felt as soon as you moved out, you'd be giving up," Darrell recalls. "If you gave up, it would happen." On July 16, a week after doubling their flood insurance to $20,000, the Glaenzers moved baby books, jewelry, and their marriage license into their car but went on sleeping in their house. On July 31, everyone was ordered out; the river was on its way.

The main channel of the Mississippi usually stays a good four miles from the town's old site. This time the flood put Valmeyer under as much as 20 feet of water, a brown lake that stretched for miles. The water hung on in many places for two months. Then, in early September, as residents were digging out, it started to rain again. The river poured through the broken levee and flooded the place a second time. The first flood broke some hearts; the second broke spirits.

Suddenly crammed into emergency trailers, families put their belongings in storage and their lives in limbo. "There we were living the quote unquote American dream," Glaenzer says. "Both working, paying the mortgage, two kids in school. And like that, we're homeless. We'd wake up in the middle of the night and wonder, 'What's going to happen to us?'" In their first few weeks adrift, the Glaenzers returned to Valmeyer several times, remembering and grieving. "We'd go home and just sit on the porch," Anna Glaenzer recalls. "We always found something left behind, a toy or some junk to take back to the trailer. We couldn't just leave it lying there." It was not until the first town meeting in Columbia that the Glaenzers heard the term "hazard mitigation," bureaucratese for "keeping the hell out of nature's way."

Time was when FEMA would simply have paid to rebuild Valmeyer in the floodplain. But in 1988 the government at last got tired of throwing away taxpayers' money that way. It made plans to move people out of the path of "recurring natural disasters." Valmeyer, with 90 percent of its buildings ravaged, easily qualified for the new program. At the town meeting, residents learned the future according to FEMA. Anyone was welcome to rebuild in the old town, provided he used his own money and ran his own risks. But under the new laws, the town wouldn't receive a dime of government funds to rise again in the river's path—unless it chose to "elevate" all new structures above the latest flood level. Angry, confused, still numb from the nightmare, residents were asked whether they wanted to build a new Valmeyer and call it home.

The meeting lasted more than three hours. It took a second meeting the next night to handle everybody. Skeptics surfaced first, warning of endless bureaucracy and a "town" that would be, at best, little more than a subdivision. They'd never be able to build a whole town. Then a dash of pioneer spirit took hold. "Before they came up with the idea of moving, my mind was blank, my heart was just empty," says Jim Harget, a member of Valmeyer's town board. "I wanted to rebuild on our old site, but my wife said, 'Can you promise me a flood will never happen again?' I didn't know what to do." Pressed to decide, two-thirds of Valmeyer backed relocation. Still doubtful, the Glaenzers voted for it, too. Town officials promised to get moving. Then the Glaenzers went "home" to the trailer city that everyone called "FEMA-ville" to debate the matter all over again.

"Maybe we could borrow the money to rebuild," Anna suggested. "Sure, if we want to kiss the kids' college goodbye," Darrell responded. "We only got fifteen grand in equity down there. So we borrow thirty grand and rebuild. Then maybe get flooded again? My dad had it right."

They looked at real estate in neighboring towns, but with 50,000 houses flooded, some places once worth $75,000 were going for as much as $90,000. Even apartments were scarce, with rents rising like flood waters. A new Valmeyer began to seem like the only chance for a home.

And, bit by bit, townspeople learned how exacting a task they had taken on. This was not only a first for them; it was an enormous challenge for FEMA. The agency had helped to relocate other towns, but nothing on the scale of Valmeyer. Finance and construction involved twenty-two government agencies; costs were in the range of $28 million. Residents had to be warned that the project might take seven years. If it took that long, the Glaenzers figured, daughter Cari would have finished college and eight-year-old son Josh would be in high school. Many residents did buy homes nearby, but 200 families hung on to the idea that a new Valmeyer was worth waiting and working for.

Town leaders convinced a retired farmer to sell them a cornfield on the bluffs just above their wreckage. By December of that first fall, billboards on the empty cornfield announced "Valmeyer IL—A New Beginning." Renting a soda machine and some outhouses, the town opened its new Village Hall, a trailer just a dusty drive off Route 156 in the afternoon shadow of a water tower. Each week as winter winds rattled the Village Hall, seven committees of town residents met to plan a town. It proved a little like playing God, but without the hubris. Farmers found themselves plowing through state and federal building codes. Bank tellers and businessmen mastered blueprints. Secretaries and schoolteachers decided details from sewers to street lamps.

"Ordinances," recalls Jean Langsdorf, who chaired the town's design, parks, and commons committee. "We had to read through subdivision ordinances, sign control ordinances, soil erosion ordinances ..." Forced to become urban planners, committee members had to get familiar with infrastructure they'd taken for granted. "Who pays attention to streetlights?" Langsdorf asks. "Suddenly we were all making suggestions on lights, pavement, curb design, you name it. I'd get home after a meeting and wonder, what did we just do? Was it right? What am I doing heading a design committee? I'm an accountant!"

On high school gridirons where the Valmeyer Pirates play their archrivals, the Waterloo Bulldogs, Valmeyer was long belittled as a refuge for "river rats." It was a town in "the bottom," a place of high principles, work, and family, but low rents and rough edges. Now, while other flooded towns— Grafton, Illinois, and Rhineland and Pattonsburg, Missouri—were planning relocations through FEMA, the "river rats" began to feel proud about going whole hog for a new life. Valmeyer would rise again, no longer a town at the end of the road, but a community of 1,400 sporting the keyhole cul-de-sacs and golf course lawns of a modern suburb.

"What makes a town, anyway?" Jim Harget asks. "It's not just buildings. It's people. If we'd just sat around and bickered, we wouldn't have gotten anywhere."

On a blustery, sub-zero day in December, three months after voting to relocate, Valmeyer's families gathered in the cornfield where they hoped they would live someday. Streets had been mapped out by then. They used a lottery to determine the order in which residents picked individual house lots. Huddled together in tractor-drawn haywagons, the new pioneers learned that rebuilding might not take seven years. With luck and good weather, the story went, people might begin moving in by next Christmas. The only thing they really needed was houses, and some twenty-five local contractors stood ready to work. Each family, using insurance settlements, FEMA's buy-out money, and savings, had to plan for itself. So that winter, nearly an entire town went shopping.

"Every time you'd go to Wal-Mart, you'd see someone you knew," remembers Valmeyer policeman Rick Brewer. "People were pushing carts piled with light fixtures, ceiling fans, carpet samples. If anyone got a deal on faucets, they'd tell everyone else. We were all in this together."

"Choosing street names took longer than anything else to decide," Langsdorf recalls. "People get funny about such things. Did we want to bring up the same names from down below? Did we want to honor anybody?" The names chosen reflected a small town's talent for compromise. Empson Street was named after a doctor who delivered almost every baby in town. Other streets edged toward a new suburban flavor—Oak Court, Fox Pointe, Woodland Ridge. Then downtown, where a new Main Street might have been, there was Knobloch Boulevard.

As a street name, "Knobloch" (the K is not silent) may lack the panache of "Fox Pointe." But from the bottom to the bluffs, residents agree that without the street's namesake, Valmeyer would still be stuck in the mud. Since the flood, Mayor Dennis Knobloch was the quiet force holding Valmeyer together. A stoic, unflappable Midwesterner, known around town as a skilled artist and businessman, he had advanced from teller to chief executive officer of the Farmers State Bank on Main Street. In 1989 he easily won the $70-per-month job as the mayor; he was a few months into his second term when the floods hit. In the town's final hours, he was on the levee, sounding the emergency siren to make sure everyone had left, then giving the go-ahead to turn off the electricity. The clock on Valmeyer's old Village Hall stopped at 1:22 A.M. on August 2. As the waters rose, Knobloch stood with others in the cemetery on a small rise below the bluffs, close enough to hear the water rushing in.

"People were crying and hugging," Knobloch recalls. "We had worked around the clock for three weeks to prevent this, then had it go right through our fingers." Following the flood, while his wife, Elaine, and their three children tended the family's antique store in nearby Maeystown, Knobloch took up residence in his 1988 Chevy pickup, parked at the edge of Valmeyer. With a cellular phone and no shortage of grit, he began weaving the consensus to make a town grow from a bushel of promises. "I've never seen anyone work as hard to help a community," says FEMA director James Lee Witt.

A year after the decision to relocate, Knobloch drove me in his pickup through an empty field, seeing a town where others saw only dirt and sky. Pointing to a stretch of clods and corn husks, he said, "This is the light industrial area. The school is over there." In the new Valmeyer, that kind of foresight was important enough to have its own local acronym, VISIONS— Valmeyer Integrating Sustainably into Our New Setting. But even the most acute vision can't see the problems lying fallow in an open field, especially in this age of environmental impact reports and lingering litigation.

That farmer's cornfield had two owners, and when one died six months after the contracts were signed, the title got tangled in probate. After the town actually got possession, federal law required a survey for relics. A team of archaeologists from the University of Illinois at Urbana-Champaign finally salvaged a prehistoric campsite and a village. By then nearly a year had passed since the flood. At Valmeyer's annual Fourth of July picnic two years ago, hundreds of residents gathered in the ruined town for softball, a parade past empty buildings on Main Street, and fireworks spelling out "Valmeyer—A New Beginning." On the bluff above not much had been done.

Suddenly, it turned out that an adjacent quarry owned mineral rights under their new land. Before graded streets could be paved, townsfolk found they needed $3.2 million to settle that claim. Knobloch and committees began piecing together loans and bonds while everybody girded themselves to spend a second winter in trailers. "When we first moved into that trailer, it seemed so big," Darrell Glaenzer says. "Six months later, we had stuff piled all over. We couldn't stand to stay in it. When we were out, we kept looking for excuses not to go back."

Though the town was on hold, time and mortgages waited for nobody. As adjacent cornfields were cut and laid low for fall, FEMA officials called Valmeyer families one by one to the village trailer. Beneath a photograph of the old town up to its eaves in water, residents signed papers paying off their past, mortgaging their future. Under "hazard mitigation" guidelines, FEMA paid residents the difference between the market value of their old homes and their insurance. The Glaenzers' place was valued at $40,000. They collected $20,000 in insurance; FEMA paid them the other $20,000. But their old house was a shambles, and all but worthless now, though the Glaenzers had to pay off the full mortgage. This left them with $25,000—barely enough for a down payment on a new house.

Shortly after closing the mortgage deal, Anna Glaenzer had to sign a check in a local store to buy some jeans. The clerk noticed her Valmeyer address. "How nice of the government to buy you all new homes," she sniped. "Excuse me!" Anna shot back. "We're making payments on that new home!"

Darrell gently led his wife from the store before she could explain how the Mississippi had washed away not only their house but their savings. Before the flood, they were only ten years from owning their home. Now they were starting over with a thirty-year mortgage. They got a low-interest loan arranged for flood victims, but new homes don't sell for $40,000. Their new payments are nearly double the installments they paid before. "And I was perfectly happy where I was," Anna moaned. "I'd go home in a heartbeat."

But a home, old or new, was a place Valmeyer couldn't seem to find that fall. In December, as they had for decades, they lit the town's star on the bluffs. In FEMAville, Christmas came and went again. Not a single new house had been finished. Rumors of lawsuits and bureaucratic boondoggles made some wish they'd taken the money and run. Anna's brother, tired of waiting, sold his new Valmeyer lot before the house was built.

But late in 1994, with no guarantee that Valmeyer would ever be finished, Gordon Anderson bought a trailer and had it installed on his lot within walking distance of Village Hall. All winter, Anderson filled the trailer with furnishings. In April of last year, wading through mud carrying their six-month old son, Anderson and his wife, Joan, moved into the new Valmeyer, one of the first families to do so. Within days, the couple planted a dozen trees, tomatoes, and a mailbox out front. Other families soon joined them. "It was kind of fun, like camping out," Anderson remembers. By June 1995, Valmeyer was really changing from blueprint to boomtown.

All through summer, streets were paved a block at a time. Underground utilities went in, homes went up, and moving vans appeared on Fox Pointe and Oak Drive. By last fall, Valmeyer bloomed with the crocuses of suburban life—swing sets, barbecues, and bird feeders. The school went up. In hollow shells of churches, volunteer crews from dioceses in other states helped parishioners hammer nails and put up drywall. And on October 1, just two years and two months after they packed their lives in boxes, the Glaenzer family finally went home.

"Would you like to come in?" Anna asked me, standing in front of her dusty driveway. "Look, we actually have a place where people can come in and sit." She stepped around unpacked boxes, pointed out the site of a future patio, and beamed. "The day we moved in, I just lay on the sofa and said, 'I'm not getting up again. Please don't move me.'"

The new town looks nothing like the old, of course. Residents are taller than their new trees, and neither cul-de-sacs nor custom homes doth a hometown make. Many still fight tears when recalling the flood. But sitting on his front porch, Jim Harget explains how residents are turning a collection of houses into neighborhoods. "Simple," Harget says. "We're being neighborly." Every evening when the Glaenzers stroll down North Meyer Avenue, a new neighbor calls them in to show off the new house.

Meanwhile, most of Valmeyer in the bottom got torn down as bulldozers razed condemned buildings. Weeks before, its old residents made one last effort to salvage their past. Roaming the ruins, Valmeyer's Social Services Committee removed banisters and ornate trim from old houses and town buildings. These, along with photographs, news clippings, and restaurant menus will be featured in the town's museum, installed in an old log cabin that had been a home on the cornfield. Where a town of 900 once was, only a handful of houses still stand, restored by stubborn owners despite flood danger. The rest, clogged by weeds, flat as an ocean floor, is again what the river made it—a floodplain. "People say we've gotten new houses and everything will be wonderful," says resident Marietta Schneider. "But no matter what happens, the flood has taken something we'll never get back."

Every fall from now on, though, Darrell and Anna Glaenzer will have a rare view from their patio, built with bricks hauled up from his mother's old house. When cold weather strips the trees, they will gaze down on Valmeyer Road winding through the floodplain toward the old town. Then, turning around, they'll see new homes, the tops of new churches and the steady stream of neighbors being neighborly. Says Anna: "It still feels like we're living in somebody else's house, but give it a few years and maybe it'll seem like we've been here forever."

Study Questions

A Town Makes History by Rising to New Heights

1. Throughout the building of the new town, the mayor was the person who quietly held the town of Valmeyer together. He was the project leader even though there was not a formal project or a project manager. What are the characteristics of a project leader?

2. VISIONS—Valmeyer Integrating Sustainably into Our New Setting—besides being a creative acronym, was also the vision of the leader who helped to build the new town. Define the concept of vision and its importance in the project management context.

3. The case presents the feelings of the people affected by the flood, and some of the problems they had with neighboring towns. The author specifically discusses the situation Anna Glaenzer ran into at a local store, when buying some jeans. What could be done in order to reduce this kind of friction?

4. The case illustrates how people got involved in the different teams building the new town and how they handled those new challenges. Discuss these efforts from a project perspective of managing time, cost, and technical performance objectives.

Real-World Challenges to a Multinational Project Team: Building a Manufacturing Facility in India

Edward A. O'Connor, Bausch & Lomb, Inc.

PMI Canada *Proceedings*, 1994, pp. 377–80

INTRODUCTION

Bausch & Lomb Inc. chose to establish a $13 million joint venture in India for the purpose of producing and marketing high quality eye care and optical products in India and adjacent countries.

The Indian market was viewed by Bausch & Lomb as an opportunity to satisfy the demands of a large emerging middle class population in a country whose total population of 850 million people is the second largest in the world.

In recent years, India has been moving toward a more open economy encouraging multinationals to form joint ventures with local firms. To promote foreign investment, the Indian government has reduced tariffs on imported raw materials.

This was Bausch & Lomb's first venture into the Indian subcontinent. Supported by the staff of a prominent eye institute in Hyderabad and teamed with Bausch & Lomb eye care professionals, training of Indian eye care practitioners (ophthalmologists and optometrists) began immediately to support the development of the soft contact lens business there.

It was necessary to overcome major obstacles to complete the manufacturing facility. Bureaucratic paperwork, different management styles, high import duties, lack of available electric power, water, sewers, and limited communications networks created uncommon problems. These issues challenged the multinational project team in the Indian environment.

Bausch & Lomb's style of management is participatory with heavy emphasis on team work. This contrasts with the more autocratic style prevalent among many Indian firms. "There are clear demarcations between management and lower level employees. Discussions via labor unions are common; overtly expressed dissatisfaction is rare" [1].

While this presentation will describe project experiences in India, the lessons learned are applicable to most developing countries.

Unlike countries in the former Soviet Union, India has remained a closed economy for decades. This presented several unknowns to the team requiring mid-course corrections during the project.

Approved in early 1990, a multinational project team was quickly formed, and an Indian architectural and engineering firm (Tata) was selected. Actual production started in June 1992, seventeen months after groundbreaking. The project was completed under budget, meeting all of the deliverables for product cost and quality. Recent local press reports refer to this plant as the "jewel in the crown" for the state of Rajasthan, India.

SCOPE

For project objectives to be met, production needed to start within seventeen months from approval date, and total capital costs needed to be within the approved $13 million budget. All products produced needed to meet Bausch & Lomb's international quality standards.

Detailed construction drawings and specifications were developed by Tata to Bausch & Lomb's concept drawings and performance specifications. A complete detailed work breakdown structure was prepared by the project team for each product line with planned construction completion dates.

Reporting of cost, schedule, and technical performance status occurred monthly by each product line team member with key issues and action steps noted.

Team members were selected by the project manager for their expertise, their flexibility toward foreign cultures, and their ability to work as part of a multinational team.

Once the project team was formed in mid-1990, a successful four-day design conference was held in Europe to finalize technical details impacting the design of the 70,000-square-foot manufacturing facility. Fifteen technical representatives from Bausch & Lomb Inc., the joint venture (Bausch & Lomb India Ltd.) and Tata participated. Basic facility parameters were established including all utility capacities, space requirements, product work flow, plant expansion strategies, etc.

From this conference came the realization that the project was undercapitalized. Original assumptions needed revision. Equipment originally planned for India manufacture now needed to be imported at increased cost due to lack of Indian manufacturing capability for specialized equipment. Over $2 million in new costs were offset by selective reductions in optional equipment, favorable reductions in duty rates, and by subcontracting one product line (enzyme tablets).

Plant capacity plan was met and is capable of initially supporting sales for projected fifth-year volumes with designed-in expansion capability to double capacity in later years.

TIME MANAGEMENT

To meet the planned completion targets, a fast-track approach was implemented for building construction. The nearly $2 million in additional costs (noted above) for scope changes were required to compensate for the lack of available power, water, and effluent treatment as well as account for lack of locally available specialized equipment.

Importing special-purpose equipment proved to be not only costly in money (100+ percent duty), but also in time. In many cases, up to three months were required to clear India customs. Paperwork needed to be impeccable—otherwise a long delay could be expected.

Even though the team experienced custom clearance delays as well as delays in commercially available power for the plant, production still started seventeen months after groundbreaking. This was achieved by training at other Bausch & Lomb plants and by a phased production start-up utilizing imported semi-finished products.

QUALITY MANAGEMENT

We learned quickly that it was essential to import high precision, sophisticated special purpose equipment. Locally, the state-of-the-art for most equipment is 1940s technology. This is especially true in the machine tool sector. Much of our precision equipment was imported from Germany, Hong Kong, and the United States.

A key part of this project included designing and building the manufacturing facility to produce products to worldwide specifications and developing systems in accordance with ISO-9002. This international standard is aimed primarily at preventing and detecting any nonconformity during production and at implementing systems to prevent recurrence. While new to many Indian businesses, ISO-9002 is gradually becoming a goal—particularly for those who wish to export goods.

No less than forty government inspections are required annually for the new plant. Conformance to local codes and standards is expected—particularly from multinationals.

Legal contracts appear to be less important in India than in the United States. This is due largely to the cumbersome legal system at present. However, specific contracts were established for the architectural and engineering work and the civil contractor. Fortunately, no major problems arose during the execution of these contracts.

Prior to beginning production, each process was validated and each product was subjected to standard product qualification testing to ensure that all performance parameters were met. Once these validations and qualifications were successfully completed, a start-up audit was conducted, and approval was then given from Corporate Quality Assurance to begin production.

Quarterly product/process audits are performed for the facility by Bausch & Lomb representatives from the United States and Europe.

RISK MANAGEMENT

Producing a high-quality product in India is a risk in itself.

Facility construction techniques are highly manual, slow, and of poor quality. The only major piece of construction equipment at the site was a small concrete mixer. All other tasks were performed manually. Over 300 laborers were at site during the peak construction period. The joint venture acted as the general contractor, as is the custom in India.

External risks that were unpredictable were:
- changes in government regulations, such as duty rates, excise taxes, etc.
- unavailability of basic services such as water, electric power, telecommunications, and specialized vendors
- lack of skilled manpower—particularly in areas such as computer skills, mechanics, electricians, etc.

- bureaucratic serendipity—government approvals to import equipment took months with the prospect of rejection.

COMMUNICATION MANAGEMENT

Previous projects in the international sector were staffed with a project manager and technical support team based at its United States headquarters and a joint venture team at site.

Once the project was under way we learned that this would not be adequate for a project of this complexity in a Third-World environment where changes occur daily. We then stepped up our on-site support to maximize the number of technical personnel from Bausch & Lomb.

The plant is located 75 km from New Delhi. No fax communication is available, and local phone communications are unreliable. No international phone or communication is possible so all must be handled through the office in New Delhi. Couriers carry messages daily from the New Delhi office to the plant.

In response, the project team members spent up to three weeks per trip each quarter in India to meet the start-up schedule. Product line engineers from Bausch & Lomb worked on a rotating schedule to maintain technical coverage at the plant site. For each product line there was at least one engineer present to respond to immediate needs and to communicate with other team members via fax or phone from New Delhi. This worked well and avoided long stays in India.

The prize was the satisfaction of a very difficult job well done by a world-class multinational project team.

FACTORS FOR SUCCESS

- Hold a technical design conference to finalize design parameters and identify risks. Detailed engineering work can then begin.
- Select an in-country architectural and engineering firm that understands local culture and has experience with similar work.
- Select a good joint venture partner who knows local laws, understands the market and how to deal with the bureaucracy.
- Organize a competent, well-motivated team and recognize it for its contributions.
- Pick a good scheduling system that is user-friendly. While we chose Project Workbench, there are a number of good PC-based systems available on the market today.
- Select a good plant location, and design the facility for logical expansion.
- Get marketing to commit to a sales forecast. While easier said than done, this is critical to capacity planning.
- Know and test assumptions. Have a contingency plan. What will sink the project if an assumption is altered mid-stream?

LESSONS LEARNED

1. A separately funded three-to-six-month project planning phase is essential to:
- adequately define critical project assumptions
- fully develop accurate project costs
- understand the culture and environment of the plant location
- develop a realistic and achievable schedule.

Feedback from other multinational firms, local accounting organizations, and even the American Embassy is very helpful in preparing project assumptions.

2. To be successful with projects in developing countries we learned that it was necessary to have a full-time Bausch & Lomb project team on-site consisting of a project manager, financial controller, a facilities engineer, and at least one engineer from each product area. Daily decisions are required by the team involving approval of architectural drawings, meeting with contractors, and to ensure that design and construction standards are met. The potential loss of project control is too great without this day-to-day on-site support.

3. Effective and timely training of local plant management and manufacturing personnel is essential to project success. Even though we spent approximately 10 percent of the project budget on training, it wasn't sufficient. With the technology transfer of four product lines we should have budgeted closer to 20 percent—especially given the fact that many had to travel to plants in the United States and Europe to receive product-line training.

4. Plant capacity was designed to support projected business levels for the fifth year of operation. A better approach would have been to increment the capacity as market demand developed, thus improving plant utilization and lowering depreciation costs.

5. While a 10 percent contingency was budgeted, we learned that for developing countries such as India with several unknowns, a 20 percent contingency would not be unreasonable. Changes in government regulations impacting duty rates, regulated commodity pricing, etc., occur routinely and often have an adverse impact on project budgets.

CONCLUSION

This project proved that it is possible to produce high-quality products in India to international quality standards. Accomplishing this required significant training, high-quality equipment, a positive attitude, and support from our Indian joint venture partner.

With the support of the total project team, the project came in $400K under budget, despite equipment delays at customs and delays in commercially available power.

Today this plant manufactures products that meet worldwide quality standards.

REFERENCES

1. Craighead's International Executive Travel, Darien, Conn., USA.

Study Questions

REAL-WORLD CHALLENGES TO A MULTINATIONAL PROJECT TEAM: BUILDING A MANUFACTURING FACILITY IN INDIA

1. The author stresses the importance of designing and building the facility to produce products and systems in accordance with international quality standards. Project quality management is a key element in the success of any project. Define "project quality management" and the processes involved in it.

2. The case states: "Team members were selected by the project manager for their expertise, their flexibility toward foreign cultures, and their ability to work as part of a multinational team." Under what circumstances might a team member be removed from the project?

3. The author notes that Bausch & Lomb's style of management was quite different from the typical style in Indian firms. Discuss the importance of recognizing and managing cultural differences on large projects.

4. The author notes that a number of external risks were unpredictable. These became important strategic issues for the project. Define and discuss a process for managing "strategic issues."

5. Project managers are sometimes challenged with major bureaucratic obstacles in an endeavor. This fact can generate ethical dilemmas for the project manager (i.e., looking for shortcuts). Read the Project Management Institute's "Code of Ethics for the Project Management Profession" and discuss its impact on your own work.

Total Quality Management and Project Management

D.H. Stamatis, Contemporary Consultants

Project Management Journal, September 1994, pp. 48–54

Since the early 1970s, the United States (U.S.) has been under foreign attack. This attack has caused no obvious human casualties, nor has it employed the use of modern weaponry, but the results have drastically changed many lives. The attack is from the world markets, especially the Far East countries. The weapons have been superior quality products and customer satisfaction, and the casualties have been the many United States businesses that lost both market share and jobs. The United States' counterattack has been slow and fragmented. It has taken considerable time for many companies to realize that their competitive positions are in jeopardy, let alone to take steps to remedy the situation.

The methods used in countering this new competition have been many, each meeting with varying degrees of success. In the main, United States companies have merely mimicked what they felt was the Japanese formula for success, i.e., total quality management (TQM), statistical process control (SPC), supplier (as opposed to vendor) certification, quality function deployment (QFD), the Taguchi approach to design of experiments, and more. This mimicking has caused some major failures in the implementation process, with some sectors of industry claiming that TQM does not apply all across the board. (See endnote for detailed information on the subject.) The reason(s) for the failure of TQM to be a success may be due to several causes; however, the most critical appears to be the lack of identification with the focus of TQM, as well as a lack of an overall strategy for implementation (2, 4, 6, 7).

All this unfocused energy can be characterized by the old story of several blind men trying to describe an elephant. As the story goes, each man's description was dependent upon which part of the elephant he was touching, resulting in an inaccurate description of the animal. The blind men identified each part of the elephant as an independent part having nothing to do with the rest of the elephant. Lack of communication between the men and an inability to see the "whole" produced a result that had no resemblance to an elephant. As in the story of the blind men, companies have made the same mistake, i.e., failure to see the "whole" picture. As a consequence, we have companies that emphasize the Deming, Juran, Crosby, Q101, Targets for Excellence, Pentastar, Six Sigma, and many more individual routes to improvement. We have failed to recognize the concept of "quality" in its totality. Rather, we have focused on the individual program to get us through this improvement process, as well as satisfying the customer in the most expedient way.

Quality Management

The inability to define TQM as it relates to all functions within a company has resulted in the unsuccessful implementation of quality improvement programs. In what some would call a typical American style, quick fixes have been applied to the symptoms of problems instead of applying corrective action to root causes.

As opposed to viewing the process as an integrated whole, their failure has been in defining quality problems by looking at only portions of the implementation process: quality circles; worker involvement; employee empowerment; SPC; participative management; QFD; failure mode and effect analysis (FMEA); just in time (JIT); preventative maintenance; and many more.

Companies that have tried these individual programs have met with limited, if any, success. Success here is viewed as total improvement in any given organization. To be sure, many companies have very successful individual "programs," but they do not tie them together. Pockets of success are, therefore, the end result rather than a complete understanding of the overall goal of the organization.

Missing is the holistic approach (i.e., incorporation of all these programs throughout all disciplines and functions within the organization).

Where successes have been published, such as Ford Motor Company, Motorola, and Hewlett-Packard, it appears that multidimensional programs may have a greater chance of success if for no other reason than they involve more people. However, if these multidimensional programs are implemented only in the quality department, companies will still be frustrated with the lack of results. The lesson may be that a complete formula without a method for companywide implementation will not guarantee the desired final product.

Like a recipe for a cake without baking instructions, a quality improvement program without an implementation strategy is unlikely to produce the desired results.

It is, therefore, the method in which companies implement their strategies for improved quality that is more important than a complete list of ingredients. It is the author's contention that in order for a quality program to be implemented with the desired success, a project management approach must be instituted throughout the organization. Project management is recommended because it involves cross-functional and multidisciplined people for implementing the project. Quality here is viewed as just another project. (It is important to recognize that we are referring to *implementation* of quality, rather than the concept of quality itself, which is not a project but rather a philosophy of doing things.) The distinction between a project and philosophy is that the project has as one of its key ingredients a defined start and end date; in contrast, the philosophy has a definite start but no end date.

Implementation of TQM

The seven steps for implementing TQM are (8, 9):
1. Energize the organization with quality awareness.
2. Change the culture of the organization.
3. Define the scope of your commitment to the organization as a whole.
4. Identify key process and product variables.

**TOTAL
ORGANIZATION**

RESULTS

QUALITY
IMPLEMENTATION }

Marketing
Engineering
Purchasing
Scheduling
Production
Quality
Packaging
Shipping
Financial
Mgt. Info. Systems
Administration

}

TQM
Continuous Improvement
Employee Involvement
Customer Satisfaction
Cost Reduction
Best In Class
  Develop quality systems
  Develop value enhancements
  Develop synchronous manufacturing
  Develop manufacturing cells
  Promote employee empowerment

FIGURE 1   BURST FUNCTION OF QUALITY IMPLEMENTATION WITHIN AN
ORGANIZATION

5. Implement statistical process control.
6. Incorporate process improvement activities in the organization.
7. Assess the quality improvement in the organization.

Detailed discussion of the seven steps can be found in reference (9). However, in order for these steps to be effective, the organization must be willing to invest resources in high-performance teams. A high-performance team is a team that performs at levels of excellence far beyond those of comparable systems (the concept of synergy). Some of the ingredients of a high-performance team are:

• They produce high-quality and high-value products and services.
• They consistently perform well against known internal and external standards.
• They use significantly fewer resources than one would expect.
• They generate a sense of enthusiasm and excitement among their members and those who come in contact with them.

To get these ingredients, a company must be willing to change. One change must be in the area of employee empowerment. It is imperative that the organization communicate to its employees the concept of "what is in it for me" rather than "do it because it is good for the organization." This change can be facilitated through a project management approach, since this integration of change will involve everyone in an organization. This integration will help in the project planning.

Quality implementation is not a linear transformation, rather a burst function (matrix structure) crossing the entire organization. A pictorial view of this can be seen in Figure 1 (8). The idea of the "burst" is that it allows the whole organization to be actively working towards a common goal. However, the pace of the individual departments may be at different rates, as required.

TQM AND PM

The system is a dynamic one that constantly changes to connect people in different ways as the need arises for innovation and problem solving. This kind of flexibility will ensure that the organization remains adaptive to change. Furthermore, this matrix organization will speed up the cumbersome

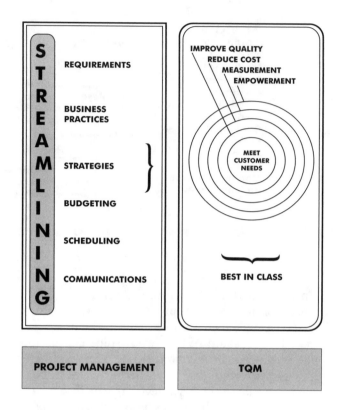

FIGURE 2   THE RELATIONSHIP OF PM AND TQM

communication paths of the typical hierarchical structure present in most organizations. The relationship of project management and TQM can be seen in Figures 2 and 3, respectively (9, 10, 11).

In Figure 2 one can see the overall relationship of project management and TQM. Specifically, the overall functions (the real essence) of both project management and TQM are shown in the figure. Figure 2 focuses on the goal of TQM, which is to be the "best in class" through meeting customer needs by improving overall quality, reducing cost, and providing measurement and empowerment. On the other hand, project management provides the streamlining of all requirements, business practices, strategies, budgeting, scheduling, and communications.

In Figure 3, one notices that the overlaps called TQM are, in fact, the connecting points for the levels in the organization. Precisely what are the characteristics that TQM provides and that project management facilitates? The following is only a sample:

1. *Shared visions, missions, goals, common purposes.* The executive, middle, and operating management are sharing the vision, mission, goal, and common purpose to the point of understanding their existence and as a consequence building a strong bond for a successful implementation.

2. *Visionary leadership.* The management of the organization acts as champion for the objectives set in 1. This championship is of paramount importance, since the champions are the ones who seek consensus and com-

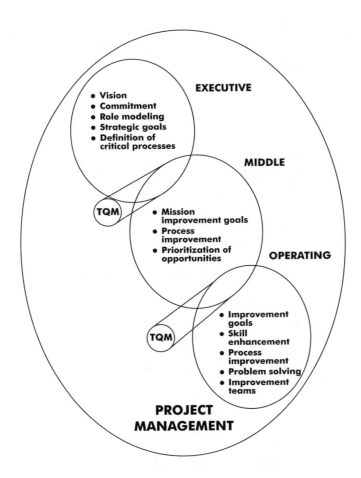

FIGURE 3 **PM AND THE RELATIONSHIPS OF TQM IN THE ORGANIZATION**

mitment among the entire organization as well as help in achieving the widespread clarity of the message.

3. *Efficient use of resources.* Management and all personnel must utilize all resources with high efficiency.

4. *Well-defined and -managed boundaries.* Management must recognize its limitations and stay within its own environment.

5. *Optimum flexibility.* Management must be stable enough to operate efficiently, yet flexible enough to respond quickly and effectively to changing conditions, demands, and opportunities not only in the horizontal mode of the organization but also in the vertical structure.

6. *Effective teamwork.* Management must encourage cooperation and teamwork and lead by example.

7. *Customer focus.* Management, in each of its levels, must be cognizant of customer needs, wants, and expectations. As a consequence, it gives high priority to items that will be of value to the customer.

8. *Effective renewal process.* Management must develop formal processes that enable it to readily adapt to changes in internal or external needs, demands and conditions.

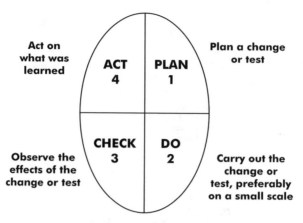

FIGURE 4   THE PLAN-DO-CHECK-ACT CYCLE FOR CONTINUOUS IMPROVEMENT

9. *Emphasis on learning, development, achievement, and support-oriented work cultures.* Management must recognize that learning is a continuous process and is essential for any organization. A balance between achievement and support orientation in the work environment is also essential.

10. *Effective performance and evaluation.* Management must focus on tasks and objectives rather than on personalities.

THE INFLUENCE OF PM IN THE IMPLEMENTATION PROCESS

At this point, one may wonder why we can't use the quality department to do all the above. The answer is very simple: quality departments do not produce quality products. Rather, they serve as the executioners and integrators of TQM in the organization. In fact, in some organizations the quality department serves as a "scorekeeper" of quality.

The execution and integration of TQM may indeed be facilitated with the quality department. However, unless the quality department utilizes the principles of project management, successful implementation may indeed be doubtful. Project management may be used, since project planning and project monitoring are the ingredients of true quality commitment in the organization.

How does PM fit into TQM? The answer is given in pictorial form in figures 4, 5, and 6 (3, 8, 12). Figure 4 identifies the Shewhart/Deming cycle and applies the basic principles of project management. Figure 5 identifies the plan-do-check (study)-act (PDC(S)A) cycle in process improvement, with even more detail of the expected functions. Figure 6 identifies the model for total quality management in relationship to the PDC(S)A cycle. In fact, it ties together the implementation steps of TQM and the phases of project management.

The modern thinking on quality is that work must be done through teams. But what is the purpose of the team? Its purpose is to improve

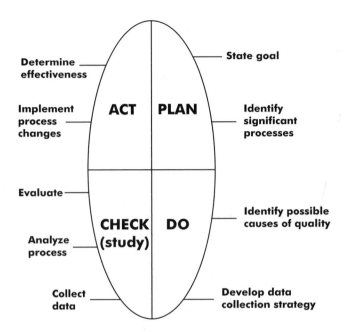

FIGURE 5

THE PLAN-DO-CHECK-ACT CYCLE DURING PROCESS IMPROVEMENT

processes through the use of the knowledge and skills of that team of individuals which has the greatest day-to-day knowledge of the process. The improvement, of course, is the decision of the team, based on consensus.

The team is always seeking to make the changes within its authority and responsibility that will improve the process. Why is it then that teams fail even though they work on opportunities, concerns, and/or problems within their process? Bradford identified a series of reasons (1), some of which are:

1. *Assignment too broad.* The project is too big for individual (specific) resolution.

2. *Responsibilities unclear.* No clear-cut authority and responsibility in the project.

3. *No measurability.* No mechanism for effective feedback.

4. *Lack of management support.* Everybody talks about the project, but nobody really does anything about it: the proverbial "lip service."

5. *Project irrelevant to the team members (no ownership).* Dictation of a problem from outside sources rather than development of the problem within the scope of the team.

6. *No appropriate skills for the team members.* Lack of fundamental knowledge in team dynamics and group dynamics and group behavior, as well as problem-solving techniques (basic to advanced).

7. *No clear-cut reporting relationships.* With no authority and responsibility, nobody really knows what is going on. The poor reporting facilitates poor-to-unacceptable feedback, resulting in a poor decision on the part of management.

How is project management going to help the implementation process? In order for us to answer that question, we must first address the issue of what project management is. Project management focuses on the project by definition

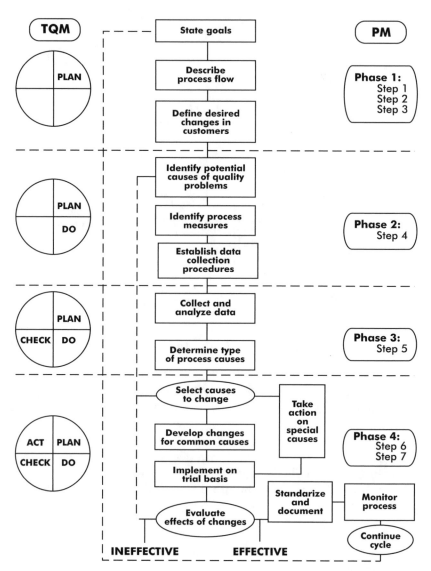

PROCESS IMPROVEMENT FOR TQM AND IMPLEMENTATION STRATEGY WITH PM

(5). A project, on the other hand, is an undertaking that has a beginning, an end and is carried out to meet established goals within specific costs, schedules, and quality objectives. Project management brings together and optimizes all variables (puts the focus on all resources) rather than maximizes any one single variable (going all out on time at the expense of something else). The resources that are optimized include skills, talents, cooperative efforts of teams, facilities, tools, information, money, techniques, systems, and equipment.

Since we defined the implementation process of TQM as a project, it follows that the allocation of the resources in any organization must be of importance and therefore the appropriate tool for such a task is indeed the project management approach.

How does project management differ from other management principles? There are at least two significant ways. First, project management focuses on a project with a finite life span, where other organizational units expect perpetuity. Second, projects need resources on a part-time and full-time basis whereas permanent organizations require resource utilization on a full-time basis. The sharing of resources may lead to conflict and requires skillful negotiation to see that projects get the necessary resources to meet objectives throughout the project life.

How and what will project management do to facilitate this implementation? Project management will ensure success of the implementation by following the four phases of a project's life (5):

1. *Define the project.* After management has made the decision to implement TQM, the first order of business is to clarify the project and arrive at an agreement among all concerned about the specific definition and scope as well as the basic strategy for carrying it out. Some of the activities that project management will address in this stage are:
- Study, discuss, and analyze the focus of the project and its relation to the organization.
- Write the project definition. This will develop confidence and understanding of the project. Of course, at this stage this definition may prove to be preliminary and may be revised as more information flows into the organization.
- Set an end-result objective. Using the preliminary definition, plan the end-result objective(s)—preferably on a milestone and/or critical path chart.
- List absolute and desirable needs. Plan or list outcomes that will define the success of the project.
- Generate alternatives. Since project management focuses on allocation of resources, it follows that the more alternatives we provide early on, the more likely we are to meet our objectives effectively.
- Evaluate alternatives. The focus here is on realistic expectations that reflect the end results rather than sheer optimism of "what we wish we could get."
- Choose a course of action. The evaluation of the previous step will help in the decision of an action plan that meets the project definition and objective.

2. *Plan the project.* Planning means listing in detail what is required to successfully complete the project along the critical dimensions of quality, cost, and time. Specifically, in this phase the following may be addressed:
- Establish the project objective. Review, and if needed, revise the objective to reflect the information.
- Choose the strategy for achieving the objective.
- Break down the project into small steps. The smaller the steps, the better the control and understanding. Remember, earlier we talked about failure(s) being attributed to projects that are too large.
- Determine the performance standards. Unless you take the time in this phase to define what your standards of success will be, you may have some problems later on in the evaluation phase.
- Determine time requirements. Be realistic. Time is very important, not only from a resource allocation perspective, but also from the morale of the participants. If you are too conservative on your time limits you are asking the impossible. On the other hand, if you are too loose, you portray a not-so-important project. This element of defining time is perhaps the most crucial in the entire implementation process.

- Determine the sequence of implementation. The who, where, what, wh and how of this sequence is relevant for a successful implementation.
- Design a cost budget. You must know how much this implementation i going to cost, not only for the satisfaction of the financial department bu also for planning purposes.
- Design the staff organization. You must know who is going to do wha and whether or not your organization has the available personnel to carr out the implementation.
- Determine the appropriate training. What is necessary as far as trainin needs are concerned? Who is going to do the training? Is it going to be inter nal or external? Are outside consultants going to play a major, minor, or n role in the implementation?
- Develop policies and procedures. What are the goals and the general vi sions of the implementation and how are you going to carry them out? Th policies and procedures are your guideposts in the entire implementatior process. However, they may be changing, as the implementation itself is dynamic process.

3. *Implement the plan.* The entire project is coordinated on an ongoing basis. Some of the responsibilities of this coordination are controlling and monitoring the work in process according to plan; negotiating changes to the plan, services, and supplies; and providing appropriate feedback to all con cerned. This feedback may be formal or informal and should resolve differ ences. Make sure that a corrective action plan exists and is being followed.

4. *Complete the project.* The goal of project management is to obtair client (in this case, management) acceptance of the project result. This means that management agrees that the quality specifications of the project parame ters have been met. For this agreement to take place as smoothly as possible, an objective evaluation must occur, based on measurable criteria defined ir the early stages of the implementation. As part of the completion phase, it is imperative that follow-up steps be defined. This will ensure that the TQM— now in place—will not fade away. The definition of this follow-up should be very specific so that the continuation of the TQM will be self-sustained.

Figure 6 summarizes the corresponding relationships of TQM via the PDCA model, the sequential steps or flowchart of the actual implementa tion process, and the PM contribution via the four phases. With each phase identified, the individual steps of the flowchart and the PDCA model are cross-referenced.

CONCLUSION

Project management principles are recommended as an optimum tool for im plementing total quality management in any organization. This recommen dation is based on the fact that TQM is people-dependent and, furthermore, the people are of cross-functional and multidisciplined backgrounds. To man age such diversity, project management is strongly recommended.

For further reading on the subject, see:

English, R., and E. Josh. 1987. "Teaching SP Using a Computer Simu lated Process Model." *TMI: Innovations in Quality, Concepts and Applica tions—Proceedings,* vol. 2. Detroit, Michigan (Sept. 21–24).

Griffiths, D.N. 1990. *Implementing Quality: With a Customer Focus.* Milwaukee, WI: Quality Press.

Hall, S.S. 1990. *Quality Assurance in the Hospitality Industry.* Milwaukee, WI: Quality Press.

Latzko, W.J. 1986. *Quality and Productivity for Bankers and Financial Managers.* Milwaukee, WI: Quality Press.

Nader, G.J. 1987. "Optimizing Quality Control, People, Performance and Profit." *TMI: Innovations in Quality, Concepts and Applications—Proceedings,* vol. 2. Detroit, Michigan (Sept. 21–24).

REFERENCES

1. Bradford, L.P. 1976. *Making Meetings Work: A Guide for Leaders and Group Members.* San Diego, CA: University Associates.

2. Clemens, R.R. 1987. "A Report Case on SPC: The Role of Management on Quality and Its Future." *TMI: Innovations in Quality, Concepts and Applications—Proceedings,* vol. 1. Detroit, Michigan (Sept. 21–24).

3. Deming, W. E. 1986. *Out of Crisis.* Cambridge, MA: Massachusetts Institute of Technology.

4. Hausmann, R.C. 1987. "Initiating Quality Management Systems in the Construction Industry." *TMI: Innovations in Quality, Concepts and Applications—Proceedings,* vol. 1. Detroit, Michigan (Sept. 21–24).

5. Kerzner, H. 1992. *Project Management: A Systems Approach to Planning, Scheduling and Controlling,* 4th Ed. New York: Van Nostrand Reinhold.

6. Lipscomb, J.R. 1991. "Managing the Transition to Continuous Improvement." *Quality Concepts: Conference Proceedings.* Detroit, MI: ESD, (Oct. 14–16).

7. Schein, E. 1985. *Organizational Culture and Leadership.* San Francisco, CA: Jossey-Bass.

8. Stamatis, D.H. 1992. *Total Quality Management: From Theory to Execution.* Southgate, MI: Contemporary Consultants Co.

9. ———. 1991. "TQM Implementation." *Concepts in Quality.* Detroit, MI: Detroit Engineering Society.

10. ———. 1992. "TQM and Project Management." Speech presented to the Detroit Chapter of the Project Management Institute. Detroit, Michigan.

11. Ibid.

12. Ibid.

Study Questions

TOTAL QUALITY MANAGEMENT AND PROJECT MANAGEMENT

1. The author recommends the implementation of TQM through project management (i.e., TQM implementation is considered a "project"). What are the key elements that define a project?

2. What is the difference between a project and a program? Is TQM a project or a program?

3. The author states that the matrix structure is part of the transformation of the organization towards TQM. What are the shortcomings of the matrix organization?

4. Teams are inherent to any TQM endeavor. What are the features that differentiate a team from just a group of people?

5. What project management tools and techniques can be applied to the implementation of TQM?

Organization and Management of a Multi-Organizational Single Responsibility Project

The James H. Campbell Power Plant Unit #3

M. P. Shrontz, Project Manager, Consumers Power Company

R. M. Porter, Vice President and Project Manager, Townsend and Bottum, Inc.

R. L. Scott, Senior Projects Manager, Gilbert/Commonwealth

AMI *Proceedings*, 1977, pp. 258–64.

INTRODUCTION

The James H. Campbell Plant Unit #3 is an 800 MW coal-fired power plant now being designed and constructed near Grand Haven, Michigan, for start-up in May 1980. Consumers Power Company (CPCo), the owner, has over the past several years established a practice of obtaining single responsibility type contracts for design, procurement, and construction of major projects. The primary objective of this type of contract is better coordination of engineering, manufacturing, and construction efforts. Specifically, the goal was to develop a project that would effectively incorporate the following:

- early completion of front-end engineering
- composite team action
- a comprehensive scheduling program
- a comprehensive estimating and cost monitoring program
- a value engineering program
- a meaningful and timely constructability program
- a productivity program
- a quality assurance program
- contract incentives.

Although CPCo was interested in the single responsibility-type contract and the desirable features this offered, the company also wanted to retain the capability of incorporating its own engineering, construction, operating, and maintenance experience into the project. In this manner, it hoped to obtain the most reliable plant possible.

Townsend & Bottum Engineers and Constructors (T&B), the constructor, and Gilbert/Commonwealth (G/C), the engineer, joined forces for this project in order to provide the single responsibility contract CPCo required.

Since T&B and G/C had previously worked on several projects in the more common separate engineer and constructor roles, they were well aware of many of the problems that must be resolved to achieve a successful project.

One of the most important objectives was to establish an integrated project team in one location with one manager being totally responsible to

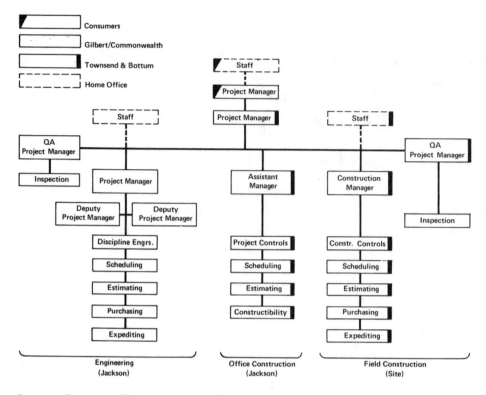

Consumers

Gilbert/Commonwealth

Townsend & Bottum

Home Office

FIGURE 1   PROJECT ORGANIZATION CHART

CPCo. Even single companies with total responsibility capabilities experience difficulties in performing in a totally cohesive manner. Only through determined efforts and dedication can two separate companies combine their resources to provide an efficient single responsibility effort.

Specific problem areas addressed in order to attain the specified goals were:

• establish better cooperation and team effort between engineering and construction

• development of common schedule budget and monitoring system

• development of complete and coordinated QA program involving engineering, manufacturing, and construction

• develop meaningful and timely constructability and productivity programs.

From Figure 1 it can be noted that the single project manager established residence in a the engineering office in Jackson in order to answer as directly as possible to CPCo.

The project manager has a manager of engineering and a construction manager who both report to him. Besides the usual discipline engineers shown reporting to the manager of engineering for a project such as this, there are many supporting services also, such as estimating, scheduling, purchasing, and expediting. From those positions, it is essential for a representative from both engineering and construction to work side by side in one location. The engineering scheduler provides most of the interface with the design engineers and the construction scheduler provides construction input and interface to the schedule. The resulting computerized schedule is issued by engineering until such time as construction becomes the major effort. At that time, the responsibility for issuing will shift to construction. However, all the participants remain the same.

In similar fashion, the estimating departments from both organizations have representatives located in the project office, and they are responsible for maintaining a constant interface. Construction is thus represented in the design office by seven or eight people including (in addition to those mentioned) an assistant manager, controls manager, and constructability engineer.

The spirit of cooperation as a team is cultivated by holding regular weekly meetings every Monday morning. The initial meeting involves all engineering discipline supervisors and service groups and the emphasis is on "what's critical to progress this coming week," and what must be accomplished to keep on schedule. This meeting is immediately followed by an overall project meeting including engineers, and office construction and field construction personnel. At this meeting the problems experienced and anticipated are discussed and resolved. Constructive criticism is necessary and welcome, and team members must learn to take this without getting "bent out of shape." Finger-pointing sessions, on the other hand, are not constructive. They destroy the team effort and are discouraged.

This type of operation does not, as one might expect, fit every individual's idea of the best method to accomplish the task. But, the importance of obtaining input that considers everything from lead time on technical specifications and engineering drawings to the number of pipe fitters that may be available in the local union hall during the fall of 1979 is necessary and requires meaningful information from engineers and constructors alike if the schedule is to be realistic.

TEAM-BUILDING SESSIONS

Getting a project group of design and construction engineers, schedulers, estimators, purchasers, and inspectors with their varying professional backgrounds to work together as a team was one of the major hurdles. Mastering the usual problems of distance, lack of communication, and appreciation or understanding among different groups and different companies required a concerted effort.

Besides the weekly meetings discussed previously, it was decided that "team-building sessions" should be conducted in an effort to promote better cooperation between all groups in all the various locations. The first of these involved G/C personnel and T&B personnel from Jackson, Ann Arbor, and the construction site. It was conducted in a hotel in Lansing rather than one of the offices so that participants would not be disturbed by telephone calls or other "urgent business." The use of a management consultant to act as the leader during these sessions not only provided an extra degree of expertise, but an unbiased viewpoint as well. Many methods were utilized to uncover hidden animosities and air these feelings. Some examples follow:

- List the things that are right with the project.
- List the things that are wrong with the project.
- In what three areas could engineering improve its effort so as to help construction the most?

- What are three of the most important contributions construction could make to engineering in order to improve the project?
- If everything was going perfectly, what would we be doing that we presently are not doing?

This type of program coupled with a social hour and followed by dinner together aided in providing the necessary stimulus for gaining an appreciation for the "other guy's" problems. Although it is difficult to define in detail the impact this had on the project, there was a noticeable improvement in the cooperative effort by most of the participants. A written critique at the end of the meeting revealed that almost all participants felt the session was very worthwhile to them. Further, they never really understood why certain things were a problem for other project team participants.

CPCo personnel did not attend the first team-building session, but did join the T&B-G/C team in a combined session in December 1976. This was a daylong conference involving sixty-five supervisory people from the three companies. With the help of the management consultant as moderator, each person was again encouraged to "lay all the cards on the table." By discussing these problems openly and objectively without referring to specific personalities, it was possible to group many specific comments into a few general categories. A somewhat surprising discovery resulting from the team-building sessions was the similarity of problems being experienced by all personnel regardless of company affiliation. Many of these were resolved by a single change in action or procedure by just one person or company. A report on these meetings was subsequently issued to all participants. It summarized the major problem areas and the action project management was taking to alleviate the problems. Noticeable improvement was again experienced in the team effort and cooperativeness among the individuals in all companies.

All three companies have retained the same management consultant independently to help their supervisory personnel gain a better understanding of how to deal with others within their own organizations. Of course, this helped in dealing with the team groups. Following are some of the problems uncovered along with their respective solutions.

Problem

"You engineers always have your minds made up before we have a chance to input our experience. You're unwilling to change."

Solution

Engineering was scheduled to issue system descriptions very early in design so that all parties could contribute their expertise before any detail design was performed. Informational meetings to discuss the comments were scheduled so differences of opinion could be aired and resolved before the final descriptions were published and the detail design started.

For future work it might be well to produce basic or mini-system descriptions prior to the detailed description so that major differences can be reconciled before the details are settled. Informational seminars to explain designs to all parties are a must and should be scheduled early.

Problem

"We're all done with the engineering before we get your comments back. If we change that now, we'll have to start all over again!"

Solution

The same solution as just mentioned is applicable to this, and in addition the appointment of special task groups (all involving owner, engineering, and construction) were formed to study and determine the specific requirements of particularly complex or controversial portions of the project. These task groups hold their own special meetings and resolve many details or lesser problems before project management becomes involved. In this way most of the "nitty gritty" has been taken care of, and only the major questions requiring management decisions remain.

Problem

"I know we commented on the drawings, but we didn't really know it was going to be like this until we saw it being constructed."

Solution

It has become obvious that the many complexities of a power plant cannot be visualized in their entirety by those working full time on the project. Thus, issuing the design and manufacturing drawings in vast quantities to the owner for approval does not, from a practical standpoint, provide a mechanism for obtaining his total contribution.

Therefore, a decision was made to build a 3/8" scale model of the facility. This not only helped the designers, but was a big aid in obtaining early and more meaningful input from the operating and maintenance personnel of the owner.

Formal review sessions covering all system layouts were conducted utilizing the scale model as the visual aid. Such things as maintenance clearance, laydown space, valve location, access to valves, and other possible discrepancies were thus reviewed. All questions at these sessions were recorded and formal replies provided to indicate if the suggested change was made, or if not, why not. This proved to be a very worthwhile method for obtaining and incorporating the owner's comments in a more realistic time frame.

Problem

"Engineering uses up all the float, and construction is stuck with a tight no-float construction schedule."

Solution

As indicated previously, the schedule was comprehensive and developed jointly by engineering, construction, and owner personnel. The basis for the project engineering, procurement and construction schedule was an optimized owner's start-up/checkout schedule which was developed and agreed to by all parties very early in the project. Decisions regarding any change in the schedule are likewise not unilateral decisions and must be based on the comprehensive schedule.

Individual supervisory engineers are reminded during the weekly project meeting of those items that are critical to them the following week. Considerable effort is expended in keeping this large (five or six people) scheduling group functioning, and it requires constant vigilance.

There is evidence that this effort is paying off. Among the housekeeping items that project management had to assure was that the discipline engineers cooperate with the schedulers to ensure that a meaningful schedule was bein developed.

When necessary, this included a scheduled time during the week whe the discipline engineer was required to meet with the scheduler and provic this input.

Problem

"Constructability is a second-guessing operation that is performed after eng neering is done."

Solution

The constructability engineer is assigned to the project in the design offic Thus, as the design is developed, her input is incorporated. In this mann the detail design has essentially received a constructability check before it finished and released to the field for construction. Constructability ideas a solicited from contractors, subcontractors, engineering, and owner personn and are evaluated through a formalized program. The program has been we received and utilized.

In keeping with the emphasis on the part of most utilities for more rel ability, evaluations included consideration for the "track record" of variou equipment. This somewhat stifles the innovative ideas of those connecte with the project, but was considered necessary in order to provide addition al assurance for a reliable plant. Although a formal reliability analysis wa not a part of this project, a failure mode analysis was made of certain critic equipment. It is planned that a more formal and detailed analysis will be ir cluded in the next project.

QUALITY ASSURANCE PROGRAM

CPCo had established the requirement for a QA program in the project. Thi was supplemented by its "red book," which outlines the essential require ments for this program and emphasizes the need for such a program to b "cost effective." There was concern that without some guidelines to follov the program developed might become out of balance or overly restrictive.

The formal quality assurance program instituted on this project wa engineering's first experience with such a comprehensive QA plan for a coa fired plant. The task was to trim a full-scale nuclear QA program with it inherent safety requirements into a meaningful program for the fossil pr ject. After considerable effort, a "new" program was implemented that wou meet the requirements of being "cost effective" without endangering the or going progress of the project.

To provide direction for this program a manufacturing QA program r quirements and surveillance list was developed (see Figure 2).

Basically, all structures and systems were assigned a reliability level (1 t 3). Depending on this level, the vendor program requirements and survei lance elements were charted. The content of equipment specifications an surveillance requirements are thus dictated by this matrix so that all proje personnel and manufacturers are tracking to the same consistency of effor on the same piece of equipment. In similar fashion, a program of qualit control was developed for construction. The same type listing was utilized a

JAMES H. CAMPBELL
UNIT 3
SYSTEMS AND COMPONENTS
Manufacturing QA Program Requirements List
Manufacturing Surveillance Requirements List

Item	Reliability Level	Vendor QA Program Elements Required 1 Quality Program	2 Design Control	3 Procurement Document Contr. (Instr. Specs. Proced. & Dwgs.)	4 Contr. of Purch. Matl. Eqt. & Serv. (Iden. & Contr. of)	13 Ship. & Pres.	14 Inspec. & Test Status	15 Nonconform Control	Purchasers Engr. Mfg. Surv. Program	Appendix A QP1/QP2 Revision LTR	Matrix Revision LTR	Mfg. Surveill. Plan 1	2 Insp. of Purch. Matl. Eqt. & Serv.	3 Insp. of Mfg. & Fab. Proc. & Tech.	4 Witn. of Test/ Rev. of Test Data	5 Final Inspection	6 Insp. of Eqt. Pres. & Prep. for Ship
III ELECTRICAL (Cont.)																	
C. Induced Draft Fan	1*	X	X	X	X	X	X	X	X	QP-1 D	B	X		X	X	X	X
Motors, 696 9P-00011 (SE-5)																	
D. Non-Segrated Phase	2	X		X	X	X			X	QP-1 G	B	X			X		
Bus 312, 9P-00139 (E-3)																	
E. Switchgear 3A & 3B	2	X		X	X	X			X	QP-1 G	B	X				X	X
351, 9P-00117 (E-6)																	
F. Station Power Trans-	2	X	X	X		X	X	X	X	QP-1 D	B	X		X	X	X	, X
formers 347,																	
9P-00038 (E-12)																	
G. Primary Air Fan Motors	2	X	X	X	X	X	X	X	X	QP-1 D	B	X			X	X	X
336, 9P-00042 (E-11)																	
11. DC POWER SYSTEM	1																
A. 125V DC & 250V DC	2*	X		X	X	X	X		X	QP-1 G	B	X			X	X	
Batteries & Chargers 301 (E-13)																	

FIGURE 2   FORM USED FOR QA PROGRAM AND MANUFACTURING SURVEILLANCE REQUIREMENTS

in the manufacturing list for continuity reasons. The construction program elements were also assigned in accordance with the level requirements for that portion of work.

Our team training sessions revealed what had been surmised: that the QA people did not feel like a part of the team. They have now been included in the weekly team meetings and have instilled confidence among the project personnel that they really can contribute. Their conceived image as "a company policeman" has now almost disappeared and further improvement in this aspect of the project is anticipated. As in so many cases the requirement for the "right" person to fill the lead position proved essential. Once he was located and put in charge, the interface problems cleared up and progress markedly improved.

PRODUCTIVITY PROGRAM

Recognizing the need for continuing efforts to improve productivity, severa programs were developed by T&B and are listed as follows:
• Design/construction interface: The process of getting construction experi ence into the design decision process
• Management, supervision, and craft information and planning system: the way information is exchanged between project participants
• Short cycle controls: control of lost time by craft labor due to lack of ma terial, tools, or waiting for answers
• Material control: control of material in storage, material handling, an ability to locate the material
• Supervisor development: on-the-job upgrading of the technical ability c field supervisory personnel
• Work performance improvement system: a performance review and goal setting process used for the nonmanual workforce
• Formal craft and supervisory training: involves on-the-job training an streamlining of job activities as well as rewards for good performance
• Action steps for improving overall employee involvement: improvement i motivation techniques by letting each person know where they are importan to getting the facility erected.

These programs are ongoing now and must await the conclusion of th project before their effectiveness can be completely evaluated. They requir considerable time and effort to implement, and we are confident that result will warrant this effort.

INCENTIVE FEE PROGRAM

An incentive fee program was established by CPCo to further encourage pro ject success. The single responsibility team will share in a bonus or penalt fee depending on the following factors:
• Beating the May 1980 schedule will provide a bonus, and missing tha schedule will result in a penalty. The size of the fees involves a percentage for mula for either side of the target date, and includes a "not to exceed" figure.
• Completing the project under the budget established by the project defin itive estimate will provide a bonus, and exceeding the budget will result in penalty. This includes a free zone on either side of the definitive estimat and includes a "not to exceed" figure.
• Achieving plant availability exceeding a fixed target for the first year of op eration will provide a bonus, and a penalty will result from availability belov the fixed target.

LICENSING AND PERMITS

Perhaps the most frustrating portion of the project is the inability to predic or control the schedule of licensing activities. A separate schedule is main tained on these activities, and a concerted effort is made to meet it, but th number of agencies that must either "approve" or "wait until another agenc signs-off before they can approve" makes it almost impossible. The apparen lack of concern for the cost and/or schedule of the alternatives suggested b some agencies and the lack in some cases of a "good rational reason" for these suggestions has been one of the project's most pressing bottlenecks. Interagency conflicts in which the project has been caught and has no means of resolving have also had an adverse impact on the project.

RESULTS AND CONCLUSIONS

There is little doubt that many projects have good programs for monitoring and controlling their activities, and there is little that is new in the programs developed for this project. The most important factor for the success to date is the emphasis placed on making the programs work. Some of the significant improvements which resulted from these programs are:
- substantial reduction of adversary attitudes
- greater pride in accomplishing tasks through team efforts
- more widespread recognition rather than suppression for contributions by the "super stars"
- better decisions through involvement of all available expertise
- improved ability to handle changes and meet schedule milestones
- much improved project control, schedules, and cost monitoring.

The success of this project to date is attributed in large measure to the cultivation and promotion of the team concept. Without this effort and the favorable response experienced from project management people in all three organizations, this progress would not have been possible.

Study Questions

ORGANIZATION AND MANAGEMENT OF A MULTI-ORGANIZATIONAL SINGLE RESPONSIBILITY PROJECT

1. What are the characteristics of an effective team? Do you think these characteristics are present in less effective groups?

2. How can funds allocation and top management support be solicited for team-building programs?

3. Demonstrate your understanding of the quality assurance program described in the case. What are some of the benefits and drawbacks of the program?

4. The teams formed out of the building sessions are interdisciplinary teams made up of members from design engineers, construction engineers, schedulers, estimators, purchasers, and inspectors. Due to the development of such a team, many positive effects are felt in the project. This type of team is also known as a product-process team or the concurrent engineering process. What are the advantages to this type of team or process?

Prudent and Reasonable Project Management

David I. Cleland, University of Pittsburgh

Project Management Journal, December 1985, pp. 90–97

Increasing attention has focused recently on the quality of project management in certain key energy-producing industries. *Forbes* magazine claims that the failure of the United States (U.S.) nuclear power program ranks as the largest managerial disaster in business history (1). *The Wall Street Journal* reported that two administrative law judges recently recommended that the Long Island Lighting Company be required to absorb $1.2 billion of the $4.2 billion cost of the Shoreham Nuclear Plant because of "company mismanagement" (2). But mismanagement is not limited to the nuclear power program. For the past eight years the state of Alaska has alleged before the federal Energy Regulatory Commission and the Alaska Public Utilities Commission that $1.6 billion in imprudent management costs were associated with the design, engineering, and construction of the $8 billion Trans-Alaska Pipeline System (TAPS).

The TAPS case is the largest analysis of management prudence ever undertaken. By the middle of December, 1984, when the record on TAPS was closed, an impressive array of documentation had been submitted by Alaska: 5,400 pages of prepared direct testimony from fifty-two witnesses whose cross examination required 12,900 pages. In total, the record consisted of 12,190 pages of direct testimony, 27,385 pages of cross examination, and 7,441 exhibits. Legal counsel is now preparing appropriate briefs for the judges—a preparation that will take all of 1985.

Although some people—such as David Davis—have concluded that while "… capital expenditure overruns and poor performance are symptoms of a widespread disease affecting pioneer projects" (3), some large projects have been successfully managed. For example, in the problem-beset nuclear power plant industry, a stellar performance was accomplished by Florida Power & Light when its St. Lucie 2 plant came online close to cost ($1.195 a kilowatt) and on schedule (six years). Since this plant went online in 1983, it has operated at 92 percent of capacity, well above the industry's 58 percent average (4). The Duke Power Company has successfully put five nuclear units into operation, which provide approximately 49 percent of its capacity as well as a comfortable 31 percent reserve capacity. Duke's labor costs have been lower than in the northeast, and it has been able to avoid any serious environmental opposition. But a large part of its success has been its competent in-house engineering and construction capability which eliminates the need to subcontract its plant design, engineering, procurement, construction, and start-up (5).

In spite of these successes, something is clearly wrong; there have been too many large construction projects that have not been prudently or reasonably managed. Too many problems at too many places in these projects can be attributed to management failures.

My purpose in this article is to present a general model for determining what constitutes "prudent and reasonable" project management, and I will use the TAPS experience as a case in point (6).

The TAPS, which stretched 800 miles across Alaska, was constructed between 1974 and 1976 at a cost of approximately $8 billion. TAPS started its life-cycle in 1968 following the discovery of oil at Prudhoe Bay, Alaska. The owner-builders of TAPS declared that it was the largest privately-financed project of all time. These owner-builders retained the Alyeska Pipeline Service Company as the project management contractor to plan for the project, and to oversee the project execution contractors engaged in on-site construction. The owners also established an owners' construction committee to administer the contract with Alyeska. In 1974, Bechtel was chosen as the construction management contractor for the pipeline and roads portion of TAPS.

PRUDENT AND REASONABLE PROJECT MANAGEMENT

In the utility industry the concept of "prudent" or "reasonable" management is applied at least in a "legal" sense, whenever owners of projects attempt to recover their investment through appropriate rate adjustments. In this context, government regulation provides opportunities for a "legal" interpretation of both prudence and reasonableness. I will not attempt to define these terms the way the courts and commissions have defined them; this task should be left to the lawyers. I will use a somewhat different notion of prudent and reasonable project management in assessing the management of the Trans-Alaska Pipeline System.

Prudent and reasonable project management is characterized by the judicious use of resources in an effective and efficient manner so that project objectives are accomplished on time and within budget. The prudent and reasonable management of projects includes:
• a demonstrated leadership by the project owner or sponsor through a management organizational form capable of providing effective strategic planning and management
• the use of a project management system as a model for strategy and management philosophy
• the use of proven, contemporary project management theory and practice in planning, organizing, leading, and controlling the use of project resources.

Prudent and reasonable project management starts with the judicious use of a project management system.

THE PROJECT MANAGEMENT SYSTEM

A project management system (PMS) is a set of six interrelated subsystems, each having a specific purpose in the total project management system. Figure 1 depicts such a PMS (7). This system and its relevancy to TAPS are discussed below.

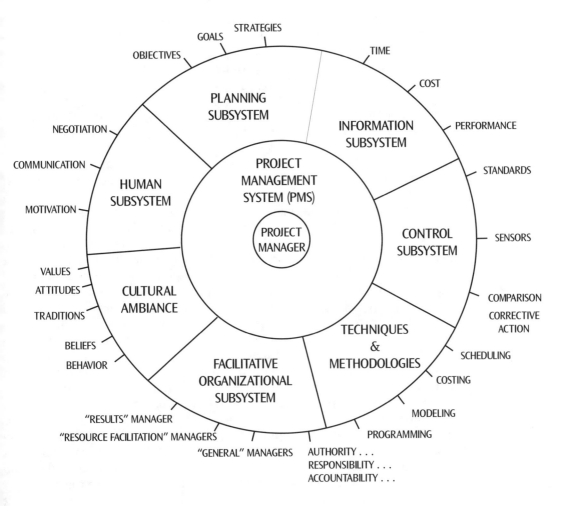

FIGURE 1 **THE PROJECT MANAGEMENT SYSTEM (7)**

Organizational Subsystem

The organizational subsystem that is used to manage the project includes an organizational design with appropriate authority, responsibility, and accountability relationships. It provides the basis for the use of resources in a systematic fashion by providing a functional focal point for starting and completing the project.

The type of project organization used depends on the nature of the project. Whatever type is used, there are two basic strategies that must be followed:

1. The relative authority, responsibility, and accountability of the project and supporting organizational elements must be clearly delineated and followed by key managers and professionals.

2. The organizational form used by the owners or client should permit the senior executives to maintain strategic surveillance of the project.

All too often, managers grossly oversimplify an organization as consisting primarily of structure. Within a project organizational design, which includes the organizational structure, there are individual and collective roles to be performed. These roles are the result of the development of a work breakdown structure, with its associated work packages, to which individuals can be assigned authority, responsibility, and accountability. Thus, rather than talking simply of an organizational structure, which tends to be static, we must consider not only the organizational structure, but also the roles within that structure. Selection of an organizational design requires analysis of such key concepts as authority, responsibility, and accountability to arrive at an orderly arrangement of the interdependencies and interactive parts of an organization.

TAPS owners established an owners' construction committee to administer the contract with Alyeska, the owners' agent, and the designated project manager.

Committees such as the owners' construction committee on TAPS are often called a plural executive. The plural executive is found in the field of policymaking in corporations at the office of the chief executive level. Such committees have been used and studied for more than thirty years. They are given the power to make decisions and to undertake one or all of the overall organizational managerial functions of planning, organizing, leading, and controlling. Typically, these plural executive groups do not become involved in short-range or tactical operations. They are more concerned with formulation and approval of broad strategy to include selection of overall organizational mission, objectives, and goals and then provide a strategic monitorship to determine if the organization is making progress toward accomplishment of its mission, objectives, and goals. Since it is a top decision-making and surveillance group, the plural executive also formulates the basic organization of the company.

But it is difficult for a committee, made up of multiple owners, to function as a plural executive. Successful operation of a plural executive requires a clear and unambiguous definition of roles and responsibilities and delegation of responsibility and authority for particular tasks within the context of an overall strategic plan. John Q. Anderson, a notable member of the project management profession, has studied the use of committees or plural executives in the organizational hierarchy in the management of large projects. He makes the following observations about the multicommittee approach [8]:

> The multiple committee approach is used when owners cannot or will not agree to delegate authority to a strong managing partner. The PMC (project management contractor) is left to deal with various committees directly, or through a weak managing partner (in terms of decision-making authority), indirectly. This relationship has two potential problems for the PMC:
>
> 1. The decision-making process will be slowed considerably by the committee approach; obtaining timely decisions, even in emergencies, can be next to impossible.
>
> 2. The PMC may receive mixed signals from the different committees, or even from different members on a single committee.
>
> In addition, a more subtle problem can be that the committees will not delegate sufficient authority to the PMC to allow optimum use of expertise and resources. The likelihood

of this occurring must be judged relatively high since delegation of authority by a committee to a managing partner was not accomplished in the first place (9).

The TAPS Owners' Construction Committee failed to define its strategic role in a charter that could have established its basic authority and responsibility. The problems Anderson delineates surfaced, and a review of the committee's actions on TAPS indicates that it did not focus on and resolve substantive strategic issues such as:
- the development of a master strategic plan
- early integrated life-cycle project planning
- the development of organizational strategy for Alyeska, the owners, and the construction management contractors
- the design and implementation of a comprehensive project management information system to facilitate organizing, planning, and controlling the attainment of technical performance objectives on time and within budget
- the development of an effective control system for TAPS
- the confusion of responsibilities between Alyeska and Bechtel resulting in overlap and duplication of people and functions
- the continued existence of Alyeska as a costly, redundant, time and resource-consuming layer in the TAPS project.

Key steps in defining the organizational design of TAPS were not taken during the early stages of the project life-cycle. The Owners Construction Committee never developed a strategic or master plan that could guide its organizational design (10). Without that strategy, it could not (or at least did not) define work packages and the roles of the parties that would be involved in the project: the owners, Alyeska, the construction management contractor, and the execution contractors. Without that strategy, it could not assign authority, responsibility, and accountability in a prudent manner. The result was a constantly evolving but always ineffective organizational design that lacked cohesiveness. While this lack of cohesiveness on TAPS is not endemic to all projects, it is characteristic of those projects that lack a strategic plan from which an organizational design can be developed.

The owners and contractors of large projects sometimes have parallel "counterpart organizations." When Bechtel was hired as the construction management contractor for the TAPS, it and Alyeska became counterpart organizations.

Unless authority and responsibility are well defined between the counterpart organizations, there is serious danger of costly duplication and inefficient decision-making. The authorities and responsibilities of Alyeska and Bechtel counterparts were not sufficiently defined to avoid these adverse consequences.

Although Alyeska's organization manual seemed to be the basic document that defined the roles along with the associated authority and responsibility of these parties, it had three fundamental flaws that lead to the conclusion that there was an absence of clearly defined roles and responsibilities on the TAPS project.

First, the organization manual's issuance by Alyeska on January 1, 1975, came far too late. Bechtel had already been on the job for fifteen months and had notified Alyeska repeatedly of its inability to obtain a clear definition of its role and responsibilities. The existing organization on TAPS was characterized by

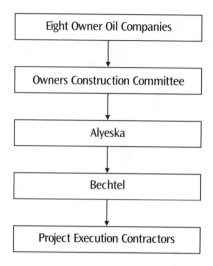

FIGURE 2   **TAPS ORGANIZATION (1974)**

"overlapping control, lack of defined responsibilities, a strong horizontal functional group superimposed on a weak vertical project organization, and a one-on-one relationship of Alyeska to Bechtel" (11). These are issues that should have been addressed and resolved at the very earliest stage of the Alyeska/construction management contractor relationship, not fifteen months after the counterpart organization had been in existence.

Second, the organization manual did little to clarify authority and responsibility. Although the manual did contain some "division of responsibility charts" (linear responsibility charts or LRCs), these charts were too vague and general to serve their intended purpose.

The organization manual failed to provide the type of definition of authority and responsibility that is a prerequisite of prudent use of a counterpart organization.

Third, the organization manual reinforced the preexisting excessive layering of managers in the hierarchy of the TAPS organization. Figure 2 depicts this hierarchy.

Alyeska constituted an intervening layer of managers and professionals in the hierarchy of the TAPS organization. This layering increased the distance between the top-level members of the Owners' Construction Committee and the "front-line" supervisors directly concerned with accomplishing project work package objectives.

These effects were compounded by the detailed day-to-day involvement of Alyeska staff in project affairs. In the absence of a clear specification of roles, responsibilities, and performance standards, Alyeska did not know the boundaries of its authority and consequently established its counterpart personnel who became actively involved in day-to-day management.

As a result of this layering and vague role definition, the TAPS project was plagued with violations of that most basic principle of management, unity of command, which assures that an individual receives orders from only one person. The contractors on TAPS unfortunately—and all too often—received orders from both Alyeska and Bechtel (12). This effect was highlighted in a report submitted to the Alaska Pipeline Commission:

The absence of adequate planning was exacerbated by a duplicate four-tiered management structure established by the owner companies (Owners' Committee, Alyeska, construction manager-Bechtel for the pipeline; and the Execution Contractors). Lines of management authority were confused; a "pass the buck" attitude prevailed, and all concerned—from Bechtel to the labor unions—were left distrustful and frustrated (13).

The lack of an adequate organizational design for TAPS can be attributed to an ineffective planning activity.

Planning Subsystem

The planning subsystem deals with the selection of project objectives and goals as well as the strategies for the use of resources to accomplish project ends. These strategies include plans of action, policies, procedures, resource allocation schemes, and the productive use of organizational resources.

Planning for all key aspects of the project must begin at the earliest stage of the life-cycle to define objectives, goals, and strategy. This conclusion is confirmed by a study conducted by Fluor Utah, Inc. During the early 1960s, after hundreds of projects had been completed, Fluor Utah reviewed the history of these projects to identify conditions and events common to successful projects vis-a-vis those conditions and events that occurred frequently on less successful projects. A senior Fluor vice-president concluded:

> A common identifiable element on most successful projects was the quality and depth of early planning by the project management group. Execution of the plan, bolstered by strong project management control of identifiable phases of the project, was another major reason why the project was successful (14).

Project planning on TAPS was not adequate. Archibald testified:

> The owners and Alyeska failed to require preparation of adequate, comprehensive plans at the owners' level, interrelating engineering, right-of-way, materials and equipment procurement, and construction activities ... the owners further ... failed to require the use of PERT/CPM network planning and scheduling method was widely known and used (15).

If planning is inadequate, then control will be impossible to accomplish.

Control Subsystem

The project control subsystem provides performance standards for the project schedule, budget, and technical objectives and uses information feedback to compare actual progress with planned progress. The project control subsystem also provides the means for comparing actual with planned progress and the required initiation of corrective action for better resource utilization.

Alyeska and the owners began construction before adequate, comprehensive planning had been performed. Consequently, adequate project control systems were not in place. This was contrary to practice in the construction industry.

More specific aspects of project planning, scheduling, and control which should have been properly used on the TAPS project included:

- identification of an appropriate work breakdown structure

- development of an overall project master schedule with supporting sched ules at each level of the work breakdown structure
- resource (labor, materials, machines, facilities, and funds) estimating and budgeting
- work authorization and control
- cost accounting and expenditure control
- materials and logistics management
- ongoing project evaluation and control (16).

The lack of adequate controls on TAPS was also noted in a report to the Alaska Pipeline System in the summer of 1977, viz.,

> ... the TAPS owners and Alyeska failed to establish sound internal controls prior to full-scale construction. This situation developed despite the fact that the owner companies' and Alyeska's auditors repeatedly emphasized the need for project controls. In sum, a combination of inadequate owner support and Alyeska's own ineptitude led the company into the most expensive privately financed project in United States history without sound internal controls in place (17).

Inadequate planning and organizing will be affected by the adequacy of the information system. The effect was apparent on TAPS.

The Management Information Subsystem

The project management information subsystem contains the intelligence essential to the effective planning and controlling of the project. Such information enables the principal managers of the project to plan for and track the use of supporting resources.

Inadequate information systems on the TAP project contributed to the lack of adequate controls. Crandall testified,

> ... there is little question that the control of TAPS required an adequate and well designed formal control environment to provide control information for senior managers. The volume of data to be processed indicated the need for computers in at least parts of this control environment (18).

The impact that the absence of cost controls had on the project are further noted:

> Thus, had cost controls been in place in early 1974, at the very start of the project, they would have allowed management to minimize costs while still attaining realistic schedule goals.... Thus, it is my opinion that if prudent cost controls, as part of a comprehensive control environment, had been installed at the start of construction, they would have helped assure completion of the project on or even before the scheduled date (19).

Cultural Subsystem

The cultural ambiance of a project is the synergistic set of managerial and professional shared ideas and beliefs associated with the way of life practiced in the project organization. The culture associated with the organization has distinctive characteristics that differentiate it from others; it reflects the composite leader and follower style, which sets the tone for individual and group attitude and behavior.

An organization's culture consists of shared agreements, explicit or implicit, among organizational members as to what is important in behavior and attitude in terms of values, beliefs, standards, and social and management practices. The culture that is developed and becomes characteristic of an organization affects strategic planning and implementation, project management, and all else.

Insights into the culture that existed on the TAP project are found in project documentation such as the following:

> ... I believe there is a more fundamental problem which must be addressed and resolved before it severely limits or even destroys the teamwork, coordination and communication needed by Alyeska organization in carrying out its assigned task, i.e., building the Alyeska Pipeline at the lowest possible cost. This fundamental problem is the aura of distrust and questionable credibility being attributed to key people in Alyeska and the major contractors (20).

A senior project manager in the Alyeska Pipeline Service Company noted in a letter:

> ... an attitude of "gold plating" has evolved. This attitude exists within both the Alyeska and the Bechtel organizations and comes about because of the unusual degree of public involvement, because of environmental and quality control demands, and because of the weather, terrain, and location. This attitude manifested itself in "slugging" the project with people, facilities, equipment, etc.... The results of the above are easy to see:
> • multiple and overlapping control
> • lack of defined responsibilities
> • a strong horizontal staff organization superimposed on a vertical project organization
> • one-on-one relationships
> • everyone (almost) requires a counterpart
> • staff assistants, coordinators, liaison men, etc. (21).

The foregoing examples provide insight into the culture on the TAPS project, i.e., those values and attitudes that really existed in the life of that project and affected its outcome.

An organization's culture is the social expression manifested by the people on the project. Prudent and reasonable management requires that close attention be paid to the project's "human subsystem."

The Human Subsystem

An evaluation of the efficacy of any project includes an evaluation of people. The outcome of a project is ultimately dependent on people—those professionals and managers who have a responsibility to make the project happen. Thus, project evaluation is people evaluation—an assessment of the quality of managerial and professional performance.

Because the final test of effective project management is the degree to which the project objective has been accomplished on time and within budget, project management means working with people to obtain results. Success or failure of a project depends on the artful and scientific management of a project's human resources. To determine this, management must be able to evaluate the performance and use of people.

Imprudent management of human resources for TAPS was claimed. For example:

> Management of the project resulted in pipeline productivity that was only 57 percent of what Alyeska itself estimated it should have been. Moreover, productivity declined significantly as the project progressed. The result was excess expenditures of nearly $1.3 billion on the pipeline portion of the project alone.
>
> Alyeska's poor labor management was a major contributor to the excesses (22).

When inadequate support is provided to people, mismanagement of a project's human resources can also occur. On TAPS:

> ... as a result of belated planning, the TAPS construction began without adequate housing, catering control, or communications facilities in place. The result was that not only did expenditures for these vital support functions far exceed expectations, but the housing and communications problems delayed construction progress. They also caused numerous adverse "ripple" impacts (23).

SUMMARY

Using the Trans-Alaska Pipeline System as an example, this article has presented a model for "prudent and reasonable" project management consisting of:
- owner strategic planning and management
- use of a project management system
- use of contemporaneous project management theory and practice in the management of a project.

Using this model as a philosophical base, I concluded that the management of TAPS was not prudent and reasonable.

First, the Owners Construction Committee failed to provide adequate leadership in assuring that certain actions were taken on the project. They did not:
- develop a master strategic plan for TAPS to include appropriate organizational missions, objectives, goals, and strategies
- establish management of the project from a *project management system* perspective
- design and operate an integrated formal information, planning, and control system to manage the TAPS project and to provide the basis for determining if project schedules, budgets, and technical performance objectives were being effectively attained
- define the key organizational roles of the Owners Construction Committee, Alyeska, Bechtel, and the execution contractors regarding relative authority,

responsibility, and accountability in the strategic and operational management of the TAPS project

- resolve conflict between the principal organizations during the TAPS project so that responsibility and accountability could be determined and monitoring of the project could be effectively carried out
- use the existing body of knowledge on the management of large projects.

Second, the involvement of Alyeska in the hierarchy of the TAPS organization created a redundant management layer which slowed decision-making and implementation as well as violated proven management principles.

During implementation of the TAPS project, the Owners' Construction Committee failed to exercise adequate control of the project. Alyeska and the Owners' Construction Committee became involved in the day-to-day management of the project by Bechtel and duplicated roles performed by that construction management contractor. This created confusion, inefficiencies, and increased costs on the project.

The United States nuclear power plant industry has been plagued with management problems. Many plants have been canceled, others are in various stages of construction. Rate proceedings are pending on many plants, and more are in the works. There will be rate challenges. Both public utility commissions and corporate managers require a general model for determining if projects have been prudently and reasonably managed. This article has proposed such a model.

REFERENCES

1. "Nuclear Follies." 1985. *Forbes*, Feb. 11.

2. *The Wall Street Journal*. 1985. Mar. 10.

3. "New Projects: Beware of False Economics." 1985. *Harvard Business Review*, Mar.–Apr., p. 95.

4. Ibid.

5. "Nuclear Follies." 1985. *Forbes*, Feb. 11.

6. The author of this paper, David I. Cleland, prepared direct closing testimony and exhibits, presented on behalf of the State of Alaska, Federal Regulatory Commission, Washington, D.C., Oct. 19, 1984. He is indebted to Eugene J. Comey, Terry F. Lenzner, and Randall Lee Speck of the law offices of Rogovin, Huge & Lenzner, Washington, D.C., for the opportunity to participate as an expert witness in the Trans-Alaska Pipeline System Case.

7. Adapted from Cleland, D.I. 1977. "Defining a Project Management System." *Project Management Quarterly* 8, no. 4, p. 39.

8. The TAPS organization consisted of a construction committee with several subcommittees. In actual practice the TAPS organization was a multi-committee operation.

9. Anderson, J. Q. 1978. "Organizing for Large Project Management—The Client's Needs." *Proceedings*. Project Management Institute, pp. II-13.2–II-13.9.

10. Archibald, R. D. 1984. *Prepared Direct Rebuttal Testimony and Exhibits*, Alaska Public Utilities Commission, Trans-Alaska Pipeline System. Washington, DC: Federal Energy Regulatory Commission, Jan. 10.

11. Moolin, Jr., F. P. *The Organization and Management of Large Projects... Realities vs. Theory*, Exhibit II-42-3, p. 75.

12. J.M. Leaver (Bechtel) to F.P. Moolin (Alyeska), "Alyeska/Bechtel Labor Relations Relationship," memo, dated Dec. 4, 1974; R.E. Johnston (Alyeska) to E.H. Belter (Bechtel), memo, "Bechtel Quality Control Nonconformances, Section 1, Alignment Sheet #16," Jan. 28, 1975.

13. Lenzner, T. F. 1977. *Report to the Alaska Pipeline Commission by the Commission's Special Counsel.* Washington, DC: Wald, Harkrader & Ross, August 1.

14. Duke, R. K., H. F. Wohlsen, and D. R. Mitchell. 1977. "Project Management at Fluor Utah, Inc.," *Project Management Quarterly* 8, no. 3, p. 33.

15. Archibald, R. D. 1984. *Prepared Direct Rebuttal Testimony and Exhibits.* Alaska Public Utilities Commission, Trans-Alaska Pipeline System. Washington, DC: Federal Energy Regulatory Commission, Jan. 20.

16. Archibald, pp. 16–20. See also K. C. Crandall. 1981. *Prepared Direct Testimony.* Alaska Public Utilities Commission, Trans-Alaska Pipeline System. Washington, DC: Federal Energy Regulatory Commission, Dec. 16.

17. Lenzner, p. 4.

18. Crandall, K. C. 1984. *Prepared Direct Rebuttal Testimony,* Alaska Public Utilities Commission, Trans-Alaska Pipeline System. Washington, DC: Federal Energy Regulatory Commission, Jan.10, p. 8.

19. Ibid., p. 9.

20. Atlantic Richfield Company internal correspondence dated August 6, 1974, from D.J. McCarthy, Jr., to R.G. Dulaney. Subject: Current Concerns in Alyeska Pipeline Project.

21. Letter from F.P. Moolin, Jr., to J.M. Leaver, Vice President, General Manager, Alaska, Alyeska Pipeline Service Co., Fairbanks, Alaska, Dec. 21, 1974.

22. Lenzner, pp. 6–7.

23. Ibid., p. 8.

Study Questions

PRUDENT AND REASONABLE PROJECT MANAGEMENT

1. What constitutes "reasonable and prudent" management? What are some specific traits of a prudent and reasonably managed project?

2. As a project manager what methods can be used to identify risks?

3. How does "prudent and reasonable" management relate to risk management?

4. What is the project management system? Briefly describe each of the six subsystems.

5. Considering each one of these subsystems, describe any problems resulting from the management of the Trans-Alaska Pipeline System (TAPS). In your discussion, be sure to point out any overlooked project risks.

The Space Shuttle Challenger Incident

Edited by Francis M. Webster, Jr.

Project Management Journal, June 1987, pp. 41–68

Second only to landing on the moon, the National Space Transportation System (NSTS), or shuttle, is one of the most ambitious and riskiest projects undertaken by man. On it depends the ability to exploit space, including building and servicing a permanent manned space station. On January 28, 1986, the NSTS program suffered the loss of the Challenger in Mission 51-L, a project of substantial magnitude in itself. The following is a condensation of the events leading up to and following this incident.

EXECUTIVE ORDER

- - - - - - -

PRESIDENTIAL COMMISSION ON THE
SPACE SHUTTLE CHALLENGER ACCIDENT

By the authority vested in me as President by the Constitution and statutes of the United States of America, including the Federal Advisory Committee Act, as amended (5 U.S.C. App. I), and in order to establish a commission of distinguished Americans to investigate the accident to the Space Shuttle Challenger, it is hereby ordered as follows:

Section 1. Establishment. (a) There is established the Presidential Commission on the Space Shuttle Challenger Accident. The Commission shall be composed of not more than 20 members appointed or designated by the President. The members shall be drawn from among distinguished leaders of the government, and the scientific, technical, and management communities.

(b) The President shall designate a Chairman and a Vice Chairman from among the members of the Commission.

Sec. 2. Functions. (a) The Commission shall investigate the accident to the Space Shuttle Challenger, which occurred on January 28, 1986.

(b) The Commission shall:

(1) Review the circumstances surrounding the accident to establish the probable cause or causes of the accident; and

(2) Develop recommendations for corrective or other action based upon the Commission's findings and determinations.

(c) The Commission shall submit its final report to the President and the Administrator of the National Aeronautics and Space Administration within one hundred and twenty days of the date of this Order.

2

Sec. 3. Administration. (a) The heads of Executive departments and agencies shall, to the extent permitted by law, provide the Commission with such information as it may require for purposes of carrying out its functions.

(b) Members of the Commission shall serve without compensation for their work on the Commission. However, members appointed from among private citizens of the United States may be allowed travel expenses, including per diem in lieu of subsistence, to the extent permitted by law for persons serving intermittently in the government service (5 U.S.C. 5701-5707).

(c) To the extent permitted by law, and subject to the availability of appropriations, the Administrator of the National Aeronautics and Space Administration shall provide the Commission with such administrative services, funds, facilities, staff, and other support services as may be necessary for the performance of its functions.

Sec. 4. General Provisions. (a) Notwithstanding the provisions of any other Executive Order, the functions of the President under the Federal Advisory Committee Act which are applicable to the Commission, except that of reporting annually to the Congress, shall be performed by the Administrator of the National Aeronautics and Space Administration, in accordance with guidelines and procedures established by the Administrator of General Services.

(b) The Commission shall terminate 60 days after submitting its final report.

Ronald Reagan

THE WHITE HOUSE,
February 3, 1986.

THE SPACE TRANSPORTATION SYSTEM (STS)

The space shuttle concept had its genesis in the 1960s, when the Apollo lunar landing spacecraft was in full development but had not yet flown. From the earliest days of the space program, it seemed logical that the goal of frequent, economical access to space might best be served by a reusable

Presidential Commission
on the
Space Shuttle Challenger Accident

June 6, 1986

Dear Mr. President:

On behalf of the Commission, it is my privilege to present the report of the Presidential Commission on the Space Shuttle Challenger Accident.

Since being sworn in on February 6, 1986, the Commission has been able to conduct a comprehensive investigation of the Challenger accident. This report documents our findings and makes recommendations for your consideration.

Our objective has been not only to prevent any recurrence of the failure related to this accident, but to the extent possible to reduce other risks in future flights. However, the Commission did not construe its mandate to require a detailed evaluation of the entire Shuttle system. It fully recognizes that the risk associated with space flight cannot be totally eliminated.

Each member of the Commission shared the pain and anguish the nation felt at the loss of seven brave Americans in the Challenger accident on January 28, 1986.

The nation's task now is to move ahead to return to safe space flight and to its recognized position of leadership in space. There could be no more fitting tribute to the Challenger crew than to do so.

Sincerely,

William P. Rogers
Chairman

The President of the United States
The White House
Washington, D. C. 20500

600 Maryland Avenue, S.W.   Washington, D.C. 20024   (202)453-1405

THE COMMISSION

William P. Rogers, Chairman—*Former Secretary of State under President Nixon (1969–1973), and Attorney General under President Eisenhower (1957–1961).*

Neil A. Armstrong, Vice Chairman—*Spacecraft commander for Apollo 11, July 16–24, 1969, the first manned lunar landing mission.*

David C. Acheson—*Former Senior Vice President and General Counsel, Communications Satellite Corporation (1967–1974).*

Dr. Eugene E. Covert—*Professor and Head, Department of Aeronautics and Astronautics, at Massachusetts Institute of Technology.*

Dr. Richard P. Feynman—*Professor of Theoretical Physics at California Institute of Technology. Nobel Prize winner in Physics, 1965.*

Robert B. Hotz—*Editor-in-chief of* Aviation Week & Space Technology *magazine (1953–1980).*

Major General Donald J. Kutyna, USAF—*Director Space Systems and Command, Control, Communications*

Dr. Sally K. Ride—*A mission specialist on STS-7, launched on June 18, 1983, becoming the first American woman in space.*

Robert W. Rummel—*Space expert and aerospace engineer. Holder of the NASA Distinguished Public Service Medal.*

Joseph F. Sutter—*Aeronautical engineer. Currently Executive Vice President of the Boeing Commercial Airplane Company.*

Dr. Arthur B.C. Walker, Jr.—*Formerly Associate Dean of the Graduate Division at Stanford University.*

Dr. Albert D. Wheelon—*Physicist. Currently Executive Vice President, Hughes Aircraft Company.*

Brigadier General Charles Yeager, USAF (Retired)—*Former experimental test pilot. Member of the National Commission on Space. He was the first person to penetrate the sound barrier and the first to fly at a speed of more than 1,600 miles an hour.*

Dr. Alton G. Keel, Jr., Executive Director—*Detailed to the Commission from his position in the Executive Office of the President, Office of Management and Budget, as Associate Director for National Security and International Affairs.*

launch system. In February 1967, the President's Science Advisory Committee lent weight to the idea of a reusable spacecraft by recommending that studies be made "of more economical ferrying systems, presumably involving partial or total recovery and use."

In September 1969, two months after the initial lunar landing, a space task group chaired by the vice president offered a choice of three long-range plans:

• an $8–$10 billion per year program involving a manned Mars expedition, a space station in lunar orbit and a fifty person Earth-orbiting station serviced by a reusable ferry, or space shuttle

• an intermediate program, costing less than $8 billion annually, that would include the Mars mission

• a relatively modest $4–$5.7 billion a year program that would embrace an Earth-orbiting space station and the space shuttle, as its link to Earth.

In March 1970, President Nixon made it clear that, while he favored a continuing active space program, funding on the order of Apollo was not in the cards. He opted for the shuttle-tended space base as a long-range goal but deferred going ahead with the space station pending development of the shuttle vehicle. Thus the reusable space shuttle, earlier considered only the transport element of a broad, multi-objective space plan, became the focus of NASA's near-term future.

The Space Shuttle Design

The embryo shuttle program faced a number of evolutionary design changes before it would become a system in being. The first design was based on a "fly back" concept in which two stages, each manned, would fly back to a horizontal, airplane-like landing. The first stage was a huge, winged, rocket-powered vehicle that would carry the smaller second stage piggyback; the

KENNEDY SPACE
CENTER, FL.—
With the space
shuttle Columbia
poised ready for
launch on Pad A
in the foreground,
the space shuttle
Challenger sits
atop the crawler
transporter on its
way to the newly
reconfigured Pad
B at Complex 39.

carrier would provide the thrust for liftoff and flight through the atmosphere, then release its passenger—the orbiting vehicle—and return to Earth. The orbiter, containing the crew and payload, would continue into space under its own rocket power, complete its mission and then fly back to Earth.

The second-stage craft, conceived prior to 1970 as a space station ferry, was a vehicle considerably larger than the later space shuttle orbiter. It carried its rocket propellants internally, had a flight deck sufficiently large to seat twelve space station-bound passengers and a cargo bay big enough to accommodate space station modules. The orbiter's size put enormous weight lifting and thrust generating demands on the first-stage design.

This two-stage, fully reusable design represented the optimum space shuttle in terms of "routine, economical access to space," the catch-phrase that was becoming the primary guideline for development of Earth-to-orbit systems. It was, however, less than optimum in terms of the development investment required: an estimated $10–13 billion, a figure that met with disfavor in both Congress and the Office of Management and Budget.

In 1971, NASA went back to the drawing board, aware that development cost rather than system capability would probably be the determining factor in getting a green light for shuttle development. Government and industry studies sought developmental economies in the configuration. One proposal found acceptance: eliminate the orbiter's internal tanks and carry

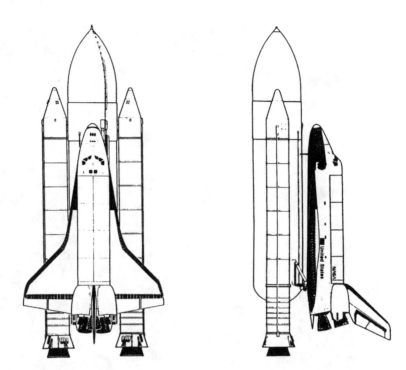

FIGURE 1   ARTIST'S DRAWING DEPICTS SPACE SHUTTLE STACKED FOR LAUNCH IN VIEW
FROM DORSAL SIDE OF ORBITER (LEFT) AND FROM THE LEFT SIDE OF STACK

the propellant in a single, disposable external tank. It provided a smaller,
cheaper orbiter without substantial performance loss.

For the launch system, NASA examined a number of possibilities. One
was a winged but unmanned recoverable liquid-fuel vehicle based on the em-
inently successful Saturn 5 rocket from the Apollo program. Other plans envisioned simpler but also recoverable liquid-fuel systems, expendable solid
rockets, and the reusable solid rocket booster. NASA had been using solid-
fuel vehicles for launching some small unmanned spacecraft, but solids as
boosters for manned flight was a technology new to the agency. Mercury,
Gemini, and Apollo astronauts had all been rocketed into space by liquid-
fuel systems. Nonetheless, the recoverable solid rocket booster won the nod,
even though the liquid rocket offered potentially lower operating costs. The
overriding reason was that pricing estimates indicated a lower cost of development for the solid booster.

Emerging from this round of design decision-making was the space shuttle: a three-element system composed of the orbiter, an expendable external
fuel tank carrying liquid propellants for the orbiter's engines, and two
recoverable solid rocket boosters. It would cost, NASA estimated early in
1972, $6.2 billion to develop and test a five-orbiter space shuttle system,
about half what the two-stage "fly back" design would have cost. To achieve
that reduction, NASA had to accept somewhat higher system operating costs
and sacrifice full reusability. The compromise design retained recoverability
and reuse of two of the three elements and still promised to trim substantially the cost of delivering payloads to orbit.

The final configuration was selected in March 1972.

THE SPACE SHUTTLE DEVELOPMENT

In August 1972, NASA awarded a contract to Rockwell International Corporation's Space Transportation Systems Division for design and development of the space shuttle orbiter. Martin Marietta Denver Aerospace was assigned development and fabrication of the external tank, Morton Thiokol Corporation was awarded the contract for the solid rocket boosters, and Rocketdyne, a division of Rockwell, was selected to develop the orbiter main engines.

NASA divided managerial responsibility for the program among three of its field centers. Johnson Space Center, Houston, Texas, was assigned management of the orbiter. Marshall Space Flight Center, Huntsville, Alabama, was made responsible for the orbiter's main engines, the external tank, and the solid rocket boosters. Kennedy Space Center, Merritt Island, Florida, was given the job of assembling the space shuttle components, checking them out, and conducting launches. Because these three centers will be mentioned repeatedly in this report, they will hereafter be identified simply as Johnson, Marshall, and Kennedy.

It was in an increasingly austere fiscal environment that NASA struggled through the shuttle development years of the 1970s. The planned five-orbiter fleet was reduced to four. Budgetary difficulties were compounded by engineering problems and, inevitably in a major new system whose development pushes the frontiers of technology, there was cost growth. This combination of factors induced schedule slippage. The initial orbital test flights were delayed by more than two years.

The first shuttle test flights were conducted at Dryden Flight Research Facility, California, in 1977. The test craft was the orbiter Enterprise, a full-sized vehicle that lacked engines and other systems needed for orbital flight. Tile purpose of these tests was to check out the aerodynamic and flight control characteristics of the orbiter in atmospheric flight. Mounted piggyback atop a modified Boeing 747, the Enterprise was carried to altitude and released for a gliding approach and landing at the Mojave Desert test center. Five such flights were made. The flights served to validate the orbiter's computers and other systems. The tests also demonstrated the craft's subsonic handling qualities, in particular its performance in the precise unpowered landings that would be required on all shuttle flights.

The Enterprise test flights were followed—in 1977–80—by extensive ground tests of shuttle systems, including vibration tests of the entire assembly—orbiter, external tank, and solid rocket boosters—at Marshall. Main engine test firings were conducted at National Space Technology Laboratories at Bay St. Louis, Mississippi, and on the launch pad at Kennedy.

By early 1981, the space shuttle was ready for an orbital flight test program. This was carefully crafted to include more than 1,000 tests and data collection procedures. All flights were to be launched from Kennedy and terminate at Edwards Air Force Base, where the Dryden Flight Research Facility is located (actually the third flight landed at White Sands Test Facility, New Mexico, because the normally dry lake bed at Edwards was flooded). Four test flights were conducted, using the orbiter Columbia, demonstrating the orbiter's ability to go into orbit and return safely, testing a remote manipulator system, and conducting several space experiments.

With the landing of STS-4, the orbital flight test program came to an end with 95 percent of its objectives accomplished. The interval between flights had been trimmed from seven months to four, then three. NASA declared the space shuttle "operational," a term that has encountered some criticism because it erroneously suggests that the shuttle has attained an airline-like degree of routine operation. In any event, NASA regarded all flights after STS-4 operational in the sense that payload requirements would take precedence over spacecraft testing, requiring larger crews.

After completing the orbital test in mid-1982, NASA began the "operational phase" of the space shuttle program, beginning with STS-5. The STS—for Space Transportation System—sequential numbering was still in effect at the time; after STS-9 NASA changed the method of numbering missions. Thereafter each flight was designated by two numbers and a letter, such as 41-B. The first digit indicates the fiscal year of the scheduled launch (4 for 1984). The second digit identifies the launch site (1 is Kennedy; 2, Vandenberg Air Force Base, California). The letter corresponds to the alphabetical sequence for the fiscal year, B being the second mission scheduled.

Including the initial orbital tests, the space shuttle flew twenty-four successful missions over a fifty-seven-month period. Columbia made seven trips into space; Discovery, six; and Atlantis, two. Challenger flew most frequently—nine times prior to its fateful last flight.

In those twenty-four flights, the shuttle demonstrated its ability to deliver a wide variety of payloads; its ability to serve as an orbital laboratory; its utility as a platform for erection of large structures; and its use for retrieval and repair of orbiting satellites.

ELEMENTS OF THE SPACE SHUTTLE

The space shuttle is the principal component of a national space transportation system designed to accommodate not only NASA's predictable needs but also those of the Department of Defense and commercial payload sponsors. Technically speaking, transportation system hardware embraces not only the shuttle but its Spacelab laboratory component, the upper stage propulsion units, contemplated heavy lift vehicles, and space tugs for moving payloads from one orbit to another. To provide for the broadest possible spectrum of civil/military missions, the space shuttle was designed to deliver 65,000 pounds of payload to an easterly low Earth orbit or 32,000 pounds to polar orbit. The following sections describe the main elements of the shuttle system.

The Orbiter

The orbiter is as large as a mid-sized airline transport and has a structure like that of an aircraft: an aluminum alloy skin stiffened with stringers to form a shell over frames and bulkheads of aluminum or aluminum alloy. The major structural sections of the orbiter are the forward fuselage, which encompasses the pressurized crew compartment; the mid fuselage, which contains the payload bay; the payload bay doors; the aft fuselage, from which the main engine nozzles project; and the vertical tail, which splits open along the trailing edge to provide a speed brake used during entry and landing.

The crew compartment is divided into two levels—the flight deck on top and the middeck below. Besides working space, the crew compartment contains the systems needed to provide a habitable environment (atmosphere, temperature, food, water, the crew sleep facilities, and waste management). It also houses the electronic, guidance, and navigation systems.

Cargoes up to 24 tons have been carried in the payload bay. Clamshell doors on the top of the orbiter meet along the craft's spine to enclose the bay, which is 15 feet wide and 60 feet long.

The payload bay is designed to hold securely a wide range of objects. The payload may include one or more communications satellites to be launched from orbit, an autonomous Spacelab for experiments in space, or cargo disposed on special pallets. To handle cargo in orbital flight, the payload bay has the 50-foot mechanical arm that is controlled from within the crew compartment. A television camera and lights mounted near the end of the arm enable the operator to see what the "hand" is doing.

Just as important as delivering cargo to orbit is recovering a satellite and bringing it back to Earth—retrieving a satellite in need of refurbishment, for example. The orbiter can carry 16 tons of cargo back from space.

The feasibility of a reusable space shuttle hinges on a particularly vital requirement: protecting the orbiter from the searing heat generated by friction with the atmosphere when the craft returns to Earth. Temperatures during entry may rise as high as 2,750 degrees Fahrenheit on the leading edge of the wing and 600 degrees on the upper fuselage, the "coolest" area. The thermal protection system devised for the orbiter must prevent the temperature of the aluminum skin from rising above 350 degrees during either ascent or entry. Insulation is of two basic types: silicon carbide, for the hottest areas, and ceramic tiles.

Space Shuttle Main Engines

The three high-performance rocket engines in the aft section of the orbiter fire for about the first 8½ minutes of flight after liftoff. At sea level, each engine generates 375,000 pounds of thrust at 100 percent throttle.

The propellants for the engines are the fuel (liquid hydrogen) and the oxidizer (liquid oxygen) carried in the external tank. Combustion takes place in two stages. First, the propellants are mixed and partly burned in pre-burners. Hot gases from the pre-burners drive the high-pressure turbopumps which deliver propellants to the main injector. Combustion, once initiated by electrical igniters, is self-sustaining. Before firing, the very cold liquid propellant is allowed to flow into the system as far as the pre-burners and combustion chamber to cool the pumps and ducts so that the hydrogen and oxygen in the system will remain liquid when the engine is started.

The main engines have been throttled over a range of 65 to 104 percent of the thrust at sea level. At liftoff, they are thrusting at 100 percent. Computers command engine thrust to 104 percent as soon as the shuttle clears the tower. They throttle to 65 percent to reduce the maximum aerodynamic loads that occur at an altitude of about 34,000 feet. Thereafter, the thrust is again increased to provide an acceleration of three times that of gravity in the last minute or so of powered flight.

External Tank

The external tank carries the propellants for the orbiter's main engines—143,000 gallons of liquid oxygen at -297° F and 383,000 gallons of liquid hydrogen at -423° F, which is much lighter than a comparable volume of oxygen. Together, the propellants weigh a little more than 790 tons. Martin

Marietta Denver Aerospace, Michoud, Louisiana, builds the tank, a welded aluminum alloy cylinder with an ogive nose and a hemispherical tail. It is 154 feet long and 27½ feet in diameter.

Because the orbiter and the two solid rocket boosters are attached to it at liftoff, the external tank absorbs the thrust of the combined propulsion system. It withstands complex load effects and pressures from the propellants.

The intertank structure or "intertank" connects the two propellant tanks. It is a cylindrical structural section that houses instruments and receives and distributes most of the thrust load from the solid rocket boosters. The front end of each booster is connected to the external tank at the intertank midsection.

Three other attachment points link each booster to the aft major ring frame of the external tank. The boosters are thus connected to the tank at four points, one forward and three aft.

Three structural elements link the orbiter to the external tank. A "wishbone" attachment beneath the crew compartment connects the forward end of the orbiter to the tank. The two aft connections are tripods at the base of the external tank.

A command from the orbiter computer jettisons the external tank eighteen seconds after main engine cutoff, about 8½ minutes after liftoff. To ensure that it will travel a predictable path, a tumble system rotates the tank end over end at a minimum rate of two resolutions per minute. The tank breaks up upon atmospheric entry, falling into the planned area of the Indian or Pacific Ocean about an hour after liftoff. The external tank is the only main component of the space shuttle that is not recovered and reused.

Solid Rocket Boosters

The two solid-propellant rocket boosters are almost as long as the external tank and attached to each side of it. The boosters contribute about 80 percent of the total thrust at liftoff; the rest comes from the orbiter's three main engines. Roughly two minutes after liftoff and 24 miles down range, the solid rockets have exhausted their fuel. Explosives separate the boosters from the external tank. Small rocket motors move them away from the external tank and the orbiter, which continue toward orbit under thrust of the shuttle's main engines.

The solid rocket booster is made up of several subassemblies: the nose cone, solid rocket motor, and the nozzle assembly. Marshall is responsible for the solid rocket booster; Morton Thiokol, Inc., Wasatch Division, Brigham City, Utah, is the contractor for the solid rocket motors. Each solid rocket motor case is made of eleven individual cylindrical weld-free steel sections about 12 feet in diameter. When assembled, a tube almost 116 feet long is created.

The eleven sections of the motor case are joined by tang-and-clevis joints held together by 177 steel pins around the circumference of each joint.

After the sections have been machined to fine tolerances and fitted, they are partly assembled at the factory into four casting segments. Those four cylindrical segments are the parts of the motor case into which the propellant is poured (or cast).

Joints assembled before the booster is shipped are known as factory joints. Joints between the four casting segments are called field joints; they are connected at Kennedy when the booster segments are stacked for final assembly.

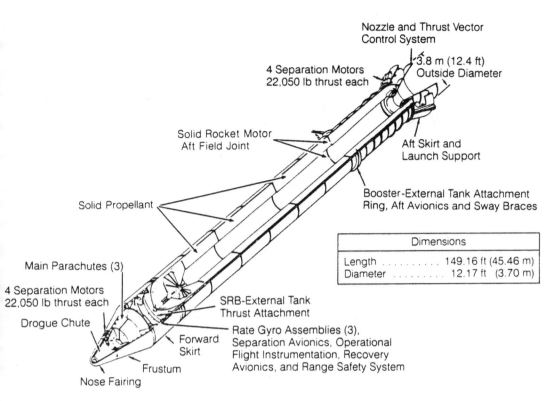

FIGURE 2   CUTAWAY VIEW OF THE SOLID ROCKET BOOSTER SHOWING SOLID ROCKET
MOTOR PROPELLANT AND AFT FIELD JOINT

Orbital Maneuvering System

The two engine pods on the aft fuselage of the orbiter contain maneuvering engines and their propellant—monomethyl hydrazine (the fuel) and nitrogen tetroxide (the oxidizer). Helium pressurizes the propellant tanks, and the fuel and the oxidizer ignite on contact.

Forty-four small rocket motors in the orbiter's nose and aft section maneuvering system pods allow adjustments of the vehicle's attitude in pitch, yaw, and roll axes. These rockets also may be used to make small changes of velocity along one of the orbiter's three axes.

Flight of a Shuttle

Except for ascent and entry, all of the shuttle's typical seven-day mission is in orbit. That is where the goals of a given mission are accomplished; scientific experiments carried out; satellites deployed into orbit, retrieved, or repaired; and observations made of the Earth and the solar system. The shuttle makes one revolution of the Earth approximately every ninety minutes during the satellite mission.

When it comes out of orbit, the shuttle is moving at about 17,500 miles an hour. Reaction engines position the orbiter nose forward again for entry into the atmosphere. Those thrusters continue to control the orbiter's attitude until the atmosphere becomes dense enough for the aerodynamic surfaces to take effect.

The shuttle enters the ever-thickening blanket of atmosphere at 400,000 feet of altitude and a speed of more than 17,000 miles an hour (about Mach 25). The orbiter's nose is positioned 40 degrees above its flight path. That attitude increases aerodynamic drag, thus helping to dissipate the tremendous amount of energy that the spacecraft has when it enters the atmosphere. Friction heats the surface of the orbiter, which is protected by thermal tiles, and ionizes the surrounding air, preventing radio communication with Earth for the next thirteen minutes.

The flight control system's computer program allows use of the reaction thrusters and aerodynamic surfaces in combination to control the spacecraft. At Mach 4.2, the rudder is activated, and the last reaction thrusters are deactivated at Mach 1. Thereafter, the craft is entirely maneuvered like an airplane by movement of the aerodynamic control surfaces: elevons, rudder, speed brake, and body flap.

In the landing approach, the orbiter has no propulsion. It has only its velocity and altitude. Its energy must be carefully managed to maneuver the shuttle aerodynamically to a safe landing. Beginning this terminal phase, the glide slope is steep—19 degrees—as the orbiter descends toward the runway. Half a minute before touchdown and two miles from the runway, the craft flares to a shallow, almost flat 1.5 degree glide slope. Touchdown occurs at 225 miles per hour. On the runway, the orbiter rolls to a stop, and the mission is complete.

FLIGHT 51-L OF THE CHALLENGER

Events Leading Up to the Challenger Mission

Preparations for the launch of mission 51-L were not unusual, although complicated by changes in the launch schedule. The sequence of complex interrelated steps involved in producing the detailed schedule and supporting logistics necessary for a successful mission always requires intense effort and close coordination.

Flight 51-L of the Challenger was originally scheduled for July 1985, but by the time the crew was assigned in January 1985, launch had been postponed to late November to accommodate changes in payloads. The launch was subsequently delayed further and finally rescheduled for late January 1986.

Preparations for Flight

Planning for mission 51-L began in 1984, but ten major change documents adding or deleting payload items caused some disruption in the preparation process. Because the twelve to eighteen month process is a series of repetitive cycles that define a flight design in progressively more specific detail, significant changes can require extensive time and effort to incorporate. The closer to the planned launch date the changes occur, the more difficult and disruptive it becomes to repeat the cycles necessary to complete a mission plan (see Figure 3: The mission 51-L milestone summary chart). Although there were several significant changes to the cargo manifest, most occurred early enough in the planning cycle to minimize their impact on the flight preparation.

The cargo integration review is one of the crucial coordination meetings in the flight preparation process. At that meeting, requirements for all pay

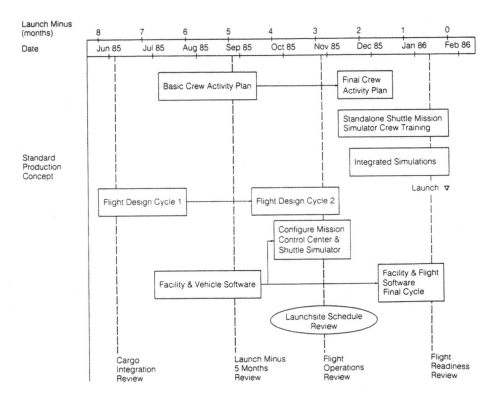

Launch Minus (months)

8 7 6 5 4 3 2 1 0

Date: Jun 85 | Jul 85 | Aug 85 | Sep 85 | Oct 85 | Nov 85 | Dec 85 | Jan 86 | Feb 86

Basic Crew Activity Plan

Final Crew Activity Plan

Standalone Shuttle Mission Simulator Crew Training

Standard Production Concept

Integrated Simulations

Launch ▽

Flight Design Cycle 1

Flight Design Cycle 2

Configure Mission Control Center & Shuttle Simulator

Facility & Vehicle Software

Facility & Flight Software Final Cycle

Launchsite Schedule Review

Cargo Integration Review

Launch Minus 5 Months Review

Flight Operations Review

Flight Readiness Review

FIGURE 3   DIAGRAM SHOWS THE SCHEDULING OF VARIOUS PREPARATORY MILESTONES IN THE MONTHS THAT PRECEDED THE LAUNCHING OF THE MISSION 51-L SHUTTLE

loads are examined to ensure that, collectively, they are within the capabilities of the vehicle and crew.

The launch minus five months flight planning and stowage review was conducted on August 20, 1985, to address any unresolved issues and any changes to the plan that had developed to that point.

There were changes to middeck payloads, resulting from the addition of Mr. Jarvis, that occurred less than three months before launch. Because the NASA communications satellite training requirements were quite similar to those for a previous flight, the crew training began using that existing crew activity plan and associated checklists. Considerable time was saved as a result.

Launch date delays for mission 61-C became a scheduling factor for the integrated simulations for mission 51-L. Originally scheduled for the third week in December, the 61-C launch was delayed until January 12, 1986. During the last six weeks before the Challenger launch, the 51-L schedule was changed several times as a result of launch delays of 61-C. The final impact on the Challenger crew training was reduced spacing between the ascent and entry simulations during the last two weeks before launch, but no training time was lost.

Flight Readiness Review

The Level I flight readiness review for mission 51-L took place on January 15, 1986. The flight readiness review should address all aspects of flight preparation about which any questions have arisen. In addition, attendees confirm that all equipment and operational plans have been certified ready by the responsible manager within NASA. Solid rocket booster joints were not discussed during the review on January 15.

The period during the day when a particular flight can be launched is determined by the requirements of the orbiter and the payloads. The launch period for mission 51-L was limited in order to provide the best lighting conditions for Spartan's observations of Halley's Comet. The resulting "launch window" was a topic of some discussion at the flight readiness review. The Challenger launch originally had been scheduled for a morning lift off. When Spartan was added to the mission, the launch window was changed to the afternoon. This change would have required a landing at night if a transatlantic abort landing had become necessary. Because the alternate transatlantic site, Casablanca, was not equipped for a night landing, the afternoon launch eliminated that back-up site. As January drew to a close, however, the conditions for optimum telescopic viewing of the comet could not be met. The launch window was shifted back to the morning hours so that the transatlantic abort site would be in daylight and a back-up site (Casablanca) would be available.

The results of the flight design process were summarized at the flight readiness review. The predicted ascent performance—including expected trajectory, main engine throttling profile, expected dynamic pressure, and the amount of propellant reserve expected at main engine cutoff—were presented and discussed. The expected landing parameters, weight, and center of gravity figures were also presented for a variety of contingencies. It should be noted that a waiver was required because the weight of the orbiter exceeded the allowable limits for an abort landing. No outstanding concerns were identified in the discussion of flight design.

Launch Delays

The launch of mission 51-L was postponed three times and scrubbed once from the planned date of January 22, 1986. The first postponement was announced on December 23, 1985. That change established the launch date as January 23, 1986, in order to accommodate the final integrated simulation schedule that resulted from the slip in the launch date of mission 61-C.

On January 22, 1986, the Program Requirements Change Board first slipped the launch from January 23 to January 25. That date subsequently was changed to January 26, 1986, primarily because of Kennedy work requirements produced by the late launch of mission 61-C.

The third postponement of the launch date occurred during an evening management conference on January 25, 1986, to review the weather forecast for the Kennedy area. Because the forecast was for unacceptable weather throughout the launch window on January 26, early countdown activities that had already started were terminated.

The launch attempt of January 27 began the day before as the complex sequence of events leading to lift off commenced. Fueling of the external tank began at 12:30 A.M. Eastern Standard Time. The crew was awakened at 05:07 A.M., and events proceeded normally with the crew strapped into the shuttle at 07:56 A.M. At 09:10, however, the countdown was halted when the ground crew reported a problem with an exterior hatch handle. By the time the hatch handle problem was solved at 10:30 A.M., winds at the Kennedy runway designated for a return-to-launchsite abort had increased and exceeded the allowable velocity for crosswinds. The launch attempt for January 27 was canceled at 12:35 P.M. Eastern Standard Time; the Challenger countdown was rescheduled for January 28.

The weather was forecast to be clear and very cold, with temperatures dropping into the low twenties overnight. The management team directed engineers to assess the possible effects of temperature on the launch. No critical issues were identified to management officials, and while evaluation continued, it was decided to proceed with the countdown and the fueling of the external tank.

Ice had accumulated in the launch pad area during the night and it caused considerable concern for the launch team. In reaction, the ice inspection team was sent to the launch pad at 01:35 A.M., January 28, and returned to the Launch Control Center at 03:00 A.M. After a meeting to consider the team's report, the space shuttle program manager decided to continue the countdown. Another ice inspection was scheduled at launch minus three hours.

Also, during the night, prior to fueling, a problem developed with a fire detector in the ground liquid hydrogen storage tank. Though it was ultimately tracked to a hardware fault and repaired, fueling was delayed by two and one-half hours. By continuing past a planned hold at launch minus three hours, however, the launch delay was reduced to one hour. Crew wake-up was rescheduled for 06:18 A.M., January 28, but by that time the crew was already up.

With an extra hour, the crew had more than sufficient time to eat breakfast, get a weather briefing and put on flight gear. At the weather briefing, the temperature and ice on the pad were discussed, but neither then nor in earlier weather discussions was the crew told of any concern about the effects of low temperature on the shuttle system. The seven crew members left the crew quarters and rode the astronaut van to launch pad B, arriving at 08:03. They were in their seats in the Challenger at 08:36 A.M.

At 08:44 A.M. the ice team completed its second inspection. After hearing the team's report, the program manager decided to allow additional time for ice to melt on the pad. He also decided to send the ice team to perform one final ice assessment at launch minus twenty minutes. When the count was resumed, launch had been delayed a second hour beyond the original lift off time of 09:38 A.M., Eastern Standard Time.

At 11:15 the ice inspection was completed, and during the hold at launch minus nine minutes, the mission 51-L crew and all members of the launch team gave their "go" for launch. The final flight of the Challenger began at 11:38:00.010 A.M., Eastern Standard Time, January 28, 1986.

From lift off until the signal from the shuttle was lost, no flight controller observed any indication of a problem. The shuttle's main engines throttled down to limit the maximum dynamic pressure, then throttled up to full thrust as expected. Voice communications with the crew were normal. The crew called to indicate the shuttle had begun its roll to head due east and to establish communication after launch. Fifty-seven seconds later, Mission Control informed the crew that the engines had successfully throttled up and all other systems were satisfactory. The commander's acknowledgment of this call was the last voice communication from the Challenger.

There were no alarms sounded in the cockpit. The crew apparently had no indication of a problem before the rapid break-up of the space shuttle

The Flight of the Challenger

The events that followed lift off were brief:

Launch Time	Event
−6.6 sec.	Space shuttle engines ignition
0 sec.	Solid rocket booster ignition
+7 sec.	"Roll program." (Challenger)
	"Roger, roll, Challenger." (Houston)
+24 sec.	Main engines throttled down to 94 percent
+42 sec.	Main engines throttled down to 65 percent
+59 sec.	Main engines throttled up to 104 percent
+65 sec.	"Challenger, go at throttled up." (Houston)
	"Roger. Go at throttle up." (Challenger)
+73 sec.	Loss of signal from Challenger

system. The first evidence of an accident came from live video coverage. Radar then began to track multiple objects. The flight dynamics officer in Houston confirmed to the flight director that "RSO [range safety officer] reports vehicle exploded," and thirty seconds later he added that the range safety officer had sent the destruct signal to the solid rocket boosters.

During the period of the flight when the solid rocket boosters are thrusting, there are no survivable abort options. There was nothing that either the crew or the ground controllers could have done to avert the catastrophe.

ANALYSIS OF THE INCIDENT

The Cause of the Accident

The consensus of the commission and participating investigative agencies is that the loss of the space shuttle Challenger was caused by a failure in the joint between the two lower segments of the right solid rocket motor. The specific failure was the destruction of the seals that are intended to prevent hot gases from leaking through the joint during the propellant burn of the rocket motor. The evidence assembled by the commission indicates that no other element of the space shuttle system contributed to this failure.

In arriving at this conclusion, the commission reviewed in detail all available data, reports, and records; directed and supervised numerous tests, analyses, and experiments by NASA, civilian contractors, and various government agencies; and then developed specific failure scenarios and the range of most probable causative factors. The sections that follow discuss the results of the investigation.

Findings

1. A combustion gas leak through the right solid rocket motor aft field joint initiated at or shortly after ignition eventually weakened and/or penetrated

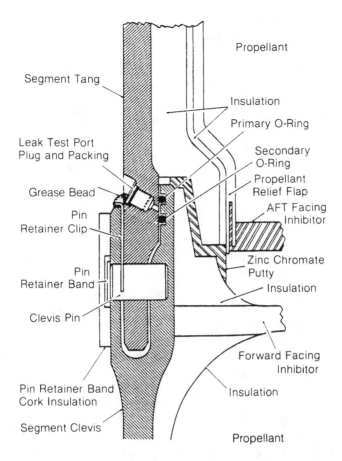

FIGURE 4   **SOLID ROCKET MOTOR CROSS SECTION SHOWS POSITIONS OF TANG, CLEVIS, AND O-RINGS. PUTTY LINES THE JOINT ON THE SIDE TOWARD THE PROPELLANT.**

the external tank initiating vehicle structural breakup and loss of the space shuttle Challenger during STS Mission 51-L.

2. The evidence shows that no other STS 51-L shuttle element or the payload contributed to the causes of the right solid rocket motor aft field joint combustion gas leak. Sabotage was not a factor.

3. Evidence examined in the review of space shuttle material, manufacturing, assembly, quality control, and processing of nonconformance reports found no flight hardware shipped to the launch site that fell outside the limits of shuttle design specifications.

4. Launch site activities, including assembly and preparation, from receipt of the flight hardware to launch, were generally in accord with established procedures and were not considered a factor in the accident.

5. Launch site records show that the right solid rocket motor segments were assembled using approved procedures. However, significant out-of-round conditions existed between the two segments joined at the right solid rocket motor aft field joint (the joint that failed).

6. The ambient temperature at time of launch was 36 degrees Fahrenheit, or 15 degrees lower than the next coldest previous launch.

- The temperature at the 300 degree position on the right aft field joint circumference was estimated to be 28 degrees ±5 degrees Fahrenheit. This was the coldest point on the joint.
- Temperature on the opposite side of the right solid rocket booster facing the sun was estimated to be about 50 degrees Fahrenheit.

[Findings 7 and 8 omitted]

9. O-ring resiliency is directly related to its temperature.

- A warm O-ring that has been compressed will return to its original shape much quicker than will a cold O-ring when compression is relieved. Thus, warm O-ring will follow the opening of the tang-to-clevis gap. A cold O-ring may not.
- A compressed O-ring at 75 degrees Fahrenheit is five times more responsive in returning to its uncompressed shape than a cold O-ring at 30 degrees Fahrenheit.
- As a result it is probable that the O-rings in the right solid booster aft field joint were not following the opening of the gap between the tang and clevis at time of ignition.

[Findings 10 and 11 omitted]

12. Of twenty-one launches with ambient temperatures of 61 degrees Fahrenheit or greater, only four showed signs of O-ring thermal distress; i.e., erosion or blow-by and soot. Each of the launches below 61 degrees Fahrenheit resulted in one or more O-rings showing signs of thermal distress.

[Finding 13 omitted]

14. A series of puffs of smoke were observed emanating from the 51-L aft field joint area of the right solid rocket booster between 0.678 and 2.500 seconds after ignition of the shuttle solid rocket motors.

- The puffs appeared at a frequency of about three puffs per second. This roughly matches the natural structural frequency of the solids at lift off and is reflected in slight cyclic changes of the tang-to-clevis gap opening.
- The puffs were seen to be moving upward along the surface of the booster above the aft field joint.
- The smoke was estimated to originate at a circumferential position of between 270 degrees and 315 degrees on the booster aft field joint, emerging from the top of the joint.

15. This smoke from the aft field joint at shuttle lift off was the first sign of the failure of the solid rocket booster O-ring seals on STS 51-L.

16. The leak was again clearly evident as a flame at approximately fifty eight seconds into the flight. It is possible that the leak was continuous but unobservable or non-existent in portions of the intervening period. It is possible in either case that thrust vectoring and normal vehicle response to wind shear as well as planned maneuvers reinitiated or magnified the leakage from a degraded seal in the period preceding the observed flames. The estimated position of the flame, centered at a point 307 degrees around the circumference of the aft field joint, was confirmed by the recovery of two fragments of the right solid rocket booster.

- A small leak could have been present that may have grown to breach the joint in flame at a time on the order of fifty-eight to sixty seconds after lift off.
- Alternatively, the O-ring gap could have been resealed by deposition of a fragile buildup of aluminum oxide and other combustion debris. This resealed section of the joint could have been disturbed by thrust vectoring space shuttle motion, and flight loads induced by changing winds aloft.

- The winds aloft caused control actions in the time interval of thirty-two seconds to sixty-two seconds into the flight that were typical of the largest values experienced on previous missions.

Conclusion

In view of the findings, the commission concluded that the cause of the Challenger accident was the failure of the pressure seal in the aft field joint of the right solid rocket motor. The failure was due to a faulty design unacceptably sensitive to a number of factors. These factors were the effects of temperature, physical dimensions, the character of materials, the effects of reusability, processing, and the reaction of the joint to dynamic loading.

THE CONTRIBUTING CAUSE OF THE ACCIDENT

The decision to launch the Challenger was flawed. Those who made that decision were unaware of the recent history of problems concerning the 0-rings and the joint and were unaware of the initial written recommendation of the contractor advising against the launch at temperatures below 53 degrees Fahrenheit and the continuing opposition of the engineers at Thiokol after the management reversed its position. They did not have a clear understanding of Rockwell's concern that it was not safe to launch because of ice on the pad. If the decision-makers had known all of the facts, it is highly unlikely that they would have decided to launch 51-L on January 28, 1986.

Flaws in the Decision-making Process

In addition to analyzing all available evidence concerning the material causes of the accident on January 28, the commission examined the chain of decisions that culminated in approval of the launch. It concluded that the decision-making process was flawed in several ways. The actual events that produced the information upon which the approval of launch was based are recounted and appraised in this section. The discussion that follows relies heavily on excerpts from the testimony of those involved in the management judgments that led to the launch of the Challenger under conditions described.

That testimony reveals failures in communication that resulted in a decision to launch 51-L based on incomplete and sometimes misleading information, a conflict between engineering data and management judgments, and a NASA management structure that permitted internal flight safety problems to bypass key shuttle managers.

The shuttle flight readiness review is a carefully planned, step-by-step activity, established by NASA program directive SPO-PD 710.5A, designed to certify the readiness of all components of the space shuttle assembly. The process is focused upon the Level I flight readiness review, held approximately two weeks before a launch. The Level I review is a conference chaired by the NASA associate administrator for space flight and supported by the NASA chief engineer, the program manager, the center directors, and project managers from Johnson, Marshall, and Kennedy, along with senior contractor representatives.

The formal portion of the process is initiated by directive from the associate administrator for space flight. The directive outlines the schedule for the Level I flight readiness review and for the steps that precede it. The process begins at

Level IV with the contractors formally certifying—in writing—the flight readiness of the elements for which they are responsible. Certification is made to the appropriate Level III NASA project managers at Johnson and Marshall. Additionally, at Marshall, the review is followed by a presentation directly to the center director. At Kennedy, the Level III review, chaired by the center director, verifies readiness of the launch support elements.

The next step in the process is the certification of high readiness to the Level II program manager at Johnson. In this review each space shuttle program element endorses that it has satisfactorily completed the manufacture, assembly, test and checkout of the pertinent element, including the contractors' certification that design and performance are up to standard. The flight readiness review process culminates in the Level I review.

In the initial notice of the review, the Level I directive establishes a mission management team for the particular mission. The team assumes responsibility for each shuttle's readiness for a period commencing forty-eight hours before launch and continuing through post-landing crew egress and the saving of the orbiter. On call throughout the entire period, the mission management team supports the associate administrator for space flight and the program manager.

A structured mission management team meeting—called L-I—is held twenty-four hours, or one day, prior to each scheduled launch. Its agenda includes closeout of any open work, a closeout of any flight readiness review action items, a discussion of new or continuing anomalies, and an updated briefing on anticipated weather conditions at the launch site and at the abort landing sites in different parts of the world. It is standard practice of Level I and II officials to encourage the reporting of new problems or concerns that might develop in the interval between the flight readiness review and the L-1 meeting, and between the L-1 and launch.

In a procedural sense, the process described was followed in the case of flight 51-L. However, in the launch preparation for 51-L relevant concerns of Level III NASA personnel and element contractors were not, in the following crucial areas, adequately communicated to the NASA Level I and II management responsible for the launch:

• The objections to launch voiced by Morton Thiokol engineers about the detrimental effect of cold temperatures on the performance of the solid rocket motor joint seal.

• The degree of concern of Thiokol and Marshall about the erosion of the joint seals in prior shuttle flights, notably 51-C (January 1985) and 51-B (April 1985). Since December 1982, the O-rings had been designated a "Criticality 1" feature of the solid rocket booster design, a term denoting a failure point—without back-up—that could cause a loss of life or vehicle if the component fails. In July, 1985, after a nozzle joint on STS 51-B showed erosion of a secondary O-ring, indicating that the primary seal failed, a launch constraint was placed on flight 51-F and subsequent launches. These constraints had been imposed and regularly waived by the solid rocket booster project manager at Marshall, Lawrence B. Mulloy.

Neither the launch constraint, the reason for it, or the six consecutive waivers prior to 51-L were known to Moore (Level 1) or Aldrich (Level II) or Thomas at the time of the flight readiness review process for 51-L.

In any event, no mention of the O-ring problems in the solid rocket booster joint appeared in the certification of flight readiness, signed for

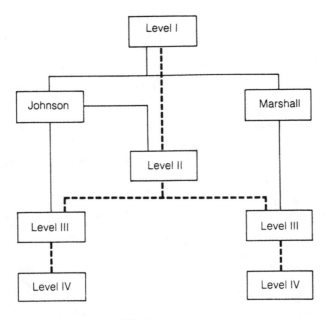

_____ Institutional Chain
---------- Program Chain

Level I: The associate administrator for Space Flight. Oversees budgets for Johnson, Marshall and Kennedy. Responsible for policy, budgetary and top-level technical matters for Shuttle program.

Level II: Manager, National Space Transportation Program. Responsible for Shuttle program baseline and requirements. Provides technical oversight on behalf of Level I.

Level III: Program managers for Orbiter, Solid Rocket Booster, External Tank and Space Shuttle Main Engine. Responsible for development, testing and delivery of hardware to launch site.

Level IV: Contractors for Shuttle elements. Responsible for design and production of hardware.

FIGURE 5   **SHUTTLE PROGRAM MANAGEMENT STRUCTURE**

Thiokol on January 9, 1986, by Joseph Kilminster, for the solid rocket booster set designated BI026.

Similarly, no mention appeared in the certification endorsement, signed on January 15, 1986, by Kilminster and by Mulloy. No mention appears in several inches of paper comprising the entire chain of readiness reviews for 51-L.

Findings

1. The commission concluded that there was a serious flaw in the decision-making process leading up to the launch of flight 51-L. A well-structured and managed system emphasizing safety would have flagged the rising doubts about the solid rocket booster joint seal. Had these matters been clearly stated and emphasized in the flight readiness process in terms reflecting the views of most of the Thiokol engineers and at least some of the Marshall engineers, it seems likely that the launch of 51-L might not have occurred when it did.

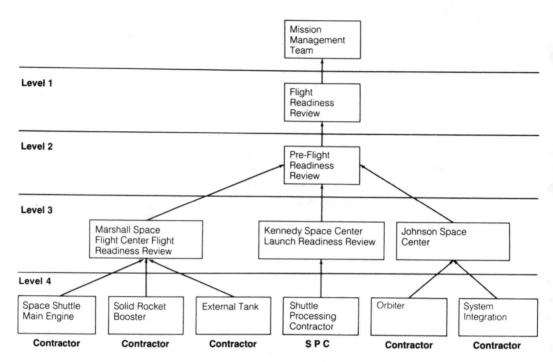

FIGURE 6   READINESS REVIEWS FOR BOTH THE LAUNCH AND THE FLIGHT OF A
SHUTTLE MISSION ARE CONDUCTED AT ASCENDING LEVELS THAT BEGIN
WITH CONTRACTORS

2. The waiving of launch constraints appears to have been at the expense of flight safety. There was no system which made it imperative that launch constraints and waivers of launch constraints be considered by all levels of management.

3. The commission is troubled by what appears to be a propensity of management at Marshall to contain potentially serious problems and to attempt to resolve them internally rather than communicate them forward. This tendency is altogether at odds with the need for Marshall to function as part of a system working toward successful flight missions, interfacing and communicating with the other parts of the system that work to the same end.

4. The commission concluded that the Thiokol management reversed its position and recommended the launch of 51-L at the urging of Marshall and contrary to the views of its engineers in order to accommodate a major customer.

THE SILENT SAFETY PROGRAM

The commission was surprised to realize after many hours of testimony that NASA's safety staff was never mentioned. No witness related the approval or disapproval of the reliability engineers, and none expressed the satisfaction or dissatisfaction of the quality assurance staff. No one thought to invite a safety representative or a reliability and quality assurance engineer to the January 27, 1986, teleconference between Marshall and Thiokol. Similarly, there was no representative of safety on the mission management team that made key decisions during the countdown on January 28, 1986. The commission is concerned about the symptoms that it sees.

The unrelenting pressure to meet the demands of an accelerating flight schedule might have been adequately handled by NASA if it had insisted upon the exactingly thorough procedures that were its hallmark during the Apollo program. An extensive and redundant safety program comprising interdependent safety, reliability, and quality assurance functions existed during and after the lunar program to discover any potential safety problems. Between that period and 1986, however, the program became ineffective. This loss of effectiveness seriously degraded the checks and balances essential for maintaining flight safety.

On April 3, 1986, Arnold Aldrich, the space shuttle program manager, appeared before the commission at a public hearing in Washington, D.C. He described five different communication or organization failures that affected the launch decision on January 28, 1986. Four of those failures relate directly to faults within the safety program. These faults include a lack of problem reporting requirements, inadequate trend analysis, misrepresentation of criticality, and lack of involvement in critical discussions. A properly staffed, supported, and robust safety organization might well have avoided these faults and thus eliminated the communication failures.

NASA has a safety program to ensure that the communication failures to which Mr. Aldrich referred do not occur. In the case of mission 51-L, that program fell short.

NASA's Safety Program

The NASA Safety, Reliability, and Quality Assurance Program should play an important role in agency activities, for the three concerns indicated in the program title are its functions. In general terms, the program monitors the status of equipment, validation of design, problem analysis, and system acceptability. Each of these has flight safety implications.

More specifically, safety includes the preparation and execution of plans for accident prevention, flight system safety, and industrial safety requirements. Within the shuttle program, safety analyses focus on potential hazards and the assessment of acceptable risks.

Reliability refers to processes for determining that particular components and systems can be relied on to work as planned. One product of such processes is a critical items list that identifies how serious the failure of a particular item or system would be.

Quality assurance is closely related to both safety and reliability. All NASA elements prepare plans and institute procedures to ensure that high standards of quality are maintained. To accomplish that goal, elements charged with responsibility for quality assurance establish procedural controls, assess inspection programs, and participate in a problem identification and reporting system.

The chief engineer at NASA headquarters has overall responsibility for safety, reliability, and quality assurance. The ability of the chief engineer to manage NASA's safety program is limited by the structure of safety, reliability, and quality assurance organizations within the agency. His limited staff of twenty persons includes only one who spends 25 percent of his time on shuttle maintainability, reliability, and quality assurance and another who spends 10 percent of his time on these vital aspects of flight safety.

At Johnson, a large number of government and contractor engineers support the safety, reliability, and quality assurance program, but needed expertise concerning Marshall hardware is absent. Thus the effectiveness of the oversight responsibilities at Level II was limited.

Kennedy has a myriad of safety, reliability, and quality assurance organizations. In most cases, these organizations report to supervisors who are responsible for processing. The clear implication of such a management structure is that it fails to provide the kind of independent role necessary for flight safety.

At Marshall, the director of reliability and quality assurance reports to the director of science and engineering who oversees the development of shuttle hardware. Again, this results in a lack of independence from the producer of hardware and is compounded by reductions in manpower, the net bringing about a decrease in effectiveness which has direct implications for flight safety.

Monitoring Safety Critical Items

As part of the safety, reliability, and quality assurance effort, components of the shuttle system are assigned to criticality categories as follows:

Criticality 1	Loss of life or vehicle if the component fails
Criticality 2	Loss of mission if the component fails
Criticality 3	All others
Criticality 1R	Redundant components; the failure of both could cause loss of life or vehicle
Criticality 2R	Redundant components; the failure of both could cause loss of mission.

The assignment of criticality follows a highly detailed analysis of each space shuttle component to determine the effect of various ways the component could fail. This analysis always assumes the most adverse conditions with the most conservative assumptions. Any component that does not meet the fail-safe design requirement is designated a Criticality 1 item and must receive a waiver for use. A critical items list is produced that contains information about all Criticality 1 components.

The inherent risk of the space shuttle program is defined by the combination of a highly dynamic environment, enormous energies, mechanical complexities, time-consuming preparations, and extremely time-critical decision-making. Complacency and failures in supervision and reporting seriously aggravate these risks.

Rather than weaken safety, reliability, and quality assurance programs through attrition and reorganization, NASA must elevate and strengthen these vital functions. In addition, NASA's traditional safety, reliability, and quality assurance efforts need to be augmented by an alert and vigorous organization that oversees the flight safety program.

Aerospace Safety Advisory Panel

The Aerospace Safety Advisory Panel (the "panel" in what follows) was established in the aftermath of the Apollo spacecraft fire January 27, 1967. Shortly thereafter the United States Congress enacted legislation (Section 6 of the NASA Authorization Act, 1968; 42 U.S.C. 2477) to establish the panel as a senior advisory committee to NASA.

The role of the panel has been defined and redefined. The efforts of this panel were not sufficiently specific and immediate to prevent the 51-L accident.

Space Shuttle Program Crew Safety Panel

The Space Shuttle Crew Safety Panel, established by space shuttle Program Directive 4A dated April 17, 1974, served an important function in NASA flight safety activities, until it went out of existence in 1981. If it were still in existence, it might have identified the kinds of problems now associated with the 51-L mission. The purpose of the panel was twofold: 1) to identify possible hazards to shuttle crews and 2) to provide guidance and advice to shuttle program management concerning the resolution of such conditions.

The panel effectively ceased to exist in 1980. After that point, the NASA shuttle program had no focal point for flight safety.

The Need for a New Safety Organization

The Aerospace Safety Advisory Panel unquestionably has provided NASA a valuable service, which has contributed to the safety of NASA's operations. Because of its breadth of activities, however, it cannot be expected to uncover all of the potential problems nor can it be charged with failure when accidents occur that in hindsight were clearly probable. The ability of any panel to function effectively depends on a focused scope of responsibilities. An acceptable level of operational safety coverage requires the total combination of NASA and contractor organizations, working more effectively on a coordinated basis at all levels. The commission believes, therefore, that a top-to-bottom emphasis on safety can best be achieved by a combination of a strong central authority and a working level panel devoted to the operational aspects of shuttle flight safety.

Findings

1. Reductions in the safety, reliability, and quality assurance work force at Marshall and NASA headquarters have seriously limited capability in those vital functions.

2. Organizational structures at Kennedy and Marshall have placed safety, reliability, and quality assurance offices under the supervision of the very organizations and activities whose efforts they are to check.

3. Problem reporting requirements are not concise and fail to get critical information to the proper levels of management.

4. Little or no trend analysis was performed on O-ring erosion and blow-by problems.

5. As the flight rate increased, the Marshall safety, reliability, and quality assurance work force was decreasing, which adversely affected mission safety.

6. Five weeks after the 51-L accident, the criticality of the solid rocket motor field joint was still not properly documented in the problem reporting system at Marshall.

AMBIGUITIES IN THE DECISION-MAKING PROCESS

During the night and early morning of January 28, another problem was developing due to the extreme cold weather, predicted to be in the low twenties for approximately eleven hours. Reaction control system heaters on the orbiter were activated and the solid rocket booster recovery batteries were checked and found to be functioning within specifications. There were no serious concerns regarding the external tank. The freeze protection plan for the launch pad was implemented, but the results were not what had been anticipated. The freeze protection plan usually involves completely draining the water system. However, this was not possible because of the imminent launch of 51-L. In order to prevent pipes from freezing, a decision was made to allow water to run slowly from the system. This had never been done before, and the combination of freezing temperatures and stiff winds caused large amounts of ice to form below the 240-foot level of the fixed service structure including the access to the crew emergency egress slide wire baskets. Ice also was forming in the water trays beneath the vehicle.

These conditions were first identified by the ice team at approximately 2:00 A.M. on January 28 and were assessed by management and engineering throughout the night, culminating with a mission management team meeting at 9:00 A.M. At this meeting, representatives for the orbiter prime contractor, Rockwell International, expressed their concern about what effects the ice might have on the orbiter during launch. Rockwell had been alerted about the icing conditions during the early morning and was working on the problem at its Downey, California, facility.

During commission hearings, the president of Rockwell's Space Transportation Systems Division, Dr. Rocco Petrone, and two of his vice presidents, Robert Glaysher and Martin Cioffoletti, all described the work done regarding the ice conditions and the Rockwell position at the 9:00 A.M. meeting with regard to launch. Dr. Petrone had arrived at Kennedy on Friday, January 24. On Monday the 27th he left to return to Rockwell's facility in California, but Glaysher and Cioffoletti remained at Kennedy. Dr. Petrone testified that he first heard about the ice at 4:00 A.M. Pacific Standard Time. (Detailed testimony is presented which supports the following findings. One conclusion that can be drawn from the testimony is that, while there was considerable concern about the ice on the equipment and whether it posed any risk to the shuttle or tanks, there was seemingly little concern about the temperature of these units. Thus, the potential O-ring problem did not appear to surface as a decision item.)

FINDINGS

The commission is concerned about three aspects of the ice-on-the-pad issue.

1. An analysis of all of the testimony and interviews establishes that Rockwell's recommendation on launch was ambiguous. The commission finds it difficult, as did Aldrich, to conclude that there was a no-launch recommendation. Moreover, all parties were asked specifically to contact Aldrich or Moore about launch objections due to weather. Rockwell made no phone calls or further objections to Aldrich or other NASA officials after the 9:00 A.M. mission management team meeting and subsequent to the resumption of the countdown.

2. The commission is also concerned about the NASA response to the Rockwell position at the 9:00 A.M. meeting. While it is understood that decisions have to be made in launching a shuttle, the commission is not convinced Levels I and II appropriately considered Rockwell's concern about the ice. However ambiguous Rockwell's position was, it is clear that it did tell NASA that the ice was an unknown condition. Given the extent of the ice on the pad, the admitted unknown effect of the solid rocket motor and space shuttle main engines ignition on the ice, as well as the fact that debris striking the orbiter was a potential flight safety hazard, the commission finds the decision to launch questionable under those circumstances. In this situation, NASA appeared to be requiring a contractor to prove that it was not safe to launch, rather than proving it was safe. Nevertheless, the commission has determined that the ice was not a cause of the 51-L accident and does not conclude that NASA's decision to launch specifically overrode a no-launch recommendation by an element contractor.

3. The commission concluded that the freeze protection plan for launch pad 39B was inadequate. The commission believes that the severe cold and presence of so much ice on the fixed service structure made it inadvisable to launch on the morning of January 28, and that margins of safety were whittled down too far.

Additionally, access to the crew emergency slide wire baskets was hazardous due to ice conditions. Had the crew been required to evacuate the orbiter on the launch pad, they would have been running on an icy surface. The commission believes the crew should have been made aware of the situation, and based on the seriousness of the condition, greater consideration should have been given to delaying the launch.

PRESSURES ON THE SYSTEM

With the 1982 completion of the orbital flight test series, NASA began a planned acceleration of the space shuttle launch schedule. One early plan contemplated an eventual rate of a mission a week, but realism forced several downward revisions. In 1985, NASA published a projection calling for an annual rate of twenty-four flights by 1990. Long before the Challenger accident, however, it was becoming obvious that even the modified goal of two flights a month was overambitious.

In establishing the schedule, NASA had not provided adequate resources for its attainment. As a result, the capabilities of the system were strained by the modest nine mission rate of 1985, and the evidence suggests that NASA would not have been able to accomplish the fifteen flights scheduled for 1986. These are the major conclusions of a commission examination of the pressures and problems attendant upon the accelerated launch schedule.

From the inception of the shuttle, NASA had been advertising a vehicle that would make space operations "routine and economical." The greater the annual number of flights, the greater the degree of routinization and economy, so heavy emphasis was placed on the schedule. However, the attempt to build up to twenty-four missions a year brought a number of difficulties, among them the compression of training schedules, the lack of spare parts, and the focusing of resources on near-term problems.

One effect of NASA's accelerated flight rate and the agency's determination to meet it was the dilution of the human and material resources that could be applied to any particular flight.

"Operational" Capabilities

For a long time during shuttle development, the program focused on a single flight, the first space shuttle mission. When the program became "operational," flights came more frequently, and the same resources that had been applied to one flight had to be applied to several flights concurrently. Accomplishing the more pressing immediate requirements diverted attention from what was happening to the system as a whole. That appears to be one of the many telling differences between a "research and development" program and an "operational program." Some of the differences are philosophical, some are attitudinal, and some are practical.

Elements within the shuttle program tried to adapt philosophy, attitude, and requirements to the "operational era." But that era came suddenly, and in some cases, there had not been enough preparation for what "operational" might entail. For example, routine and regular post-flight maintenance and inspections are critical in an operational program; spare parts are critical to flight readiness in an operational fleet; and the software tools and training facilities developed during a test program may not be suitable for the high volume of work required in an operational environment. In many respects, the system was not prepared to meet an "operational" schedule.

As the space shuttle system matured, with numerous changes and compromises, a comprehensive set of requirements was developed to ensure the success of a mission. What evolved was a system in which the preflight processing, flight planning, flight control, and flight training were accomplished with extreme care applied to every detail. This process checked and rechecked everything, and though it was both labor- and time-intensive, it was appropriate and necessary for a system still in the developmental phase. This process, however, was not capable of meeting the flight rate goals.

After the first series of flights, the system developed plans to accomplish what was required to support the flight rate. The challenge was to streamline the processes through automation, standardization, and centralized management, and to convert from the developmental phase to the mature system without a compromise in quality. It required that experts carefully analyze their areas to determine what could be standardized and automated, then take the time to do it.

But the increasing flight rate had priority—quality products had to be ready on time. Further, schedules and budgets for developing the needed facility improvements were not adequate. Only the time and resources left after supporting the flight schedule could be directed toward efforts to streamline and standardize. In 1985, NASA was attempting to develop the capabilities of a production system. But it was forced to do that while responding—with the same personnel—to a higher flight rate.

At the same time the flight rate was increasing, a variety of factors reduced the number of skilled personnel available to deal with it. These included retirements, hiring freezes, transfers to other programs like the space station, and transitioning to a single contractor for operations support.

The flight rate did not appear to be based on assessment of available resources and capabilities and was not reduced to accommodate the capacity of the work force. For example, on January 1, 1986, a new contract took effect at Johnson that consolidated the entire contractor work force under a single company. This transition was another disturbance at a time when the work force needed to be performing at full capacity to meet the 1986 flight rate. In some important areas, a significant fraction of workers elected not to change contractors. This reduced the work force and its capabilities, and necessitated intensive training programs to qualify the new personnel. According to projections, the work force would not have been back to full capacity until the summer of 1986. This drain on a critical part of the system came just as NASA was beginning the most challenging phase of its flight schedule.

Similarly, at Kennedy, the capabilities of the shuttle processing and facilities support work force became increasingly strained as the orbiter turnaround time decreased to accommodate the accelerated launch schedule. This factor has resulted in overtime percentages of almost 28 percent in some directorates. Numerous contract employees have worked seventy-two hours per week or longer and frequent twelve-hour shifts. The potential implications of such overtime for safety were made apparent during the attempted launch of mission 61-C on January 6, 1986, when fatigue and shift-work were cited as major contributing factors to a serious incident involving a liquid oxygen depletion that occurred less than five minutes before scheduled lift off.

Responding to Challenges and Changes

Another obstacle in the path toward accommodation of a higher flight rate is NASA's legendary "can-do" attitude. The attitude that enabled the agency to put men on the moon and to build the space shuttle will not allow it to pass up an exciting challenge—even though accepting the challenge may drain resources from the more mundane (but necessary) aspects of the program.

A recent example is NASA's decision to perform a spectacular retrieval of two communications satellites whose upper stage motors had failed to raise them to the proper geosynchronous orbit. NASA itself then proposed to the insurance companies who owned the failed satellites that the agency design a mission to rendezvous with them in turn and that an astronaut in a jet backpack fly over to escort the satellites into the shuttle's payload bay for a return to Earth.

The mission generated considerable excitement within NASA and required a substantial effort to develop the necessary techniques, hardware, and procedures. The mission was conceived, created, designed, and accomplished within ten months and was a resounding success.

Ten months after the first retrieval mission, NASA launched a mission to repair another communications satellite that had failed in low-Earth orbit. Again, the mission was developed and executed on relatively short notice and was resoundingly successful for both NASA and the satellite insurance industry.

The satellite retrieval missions were not isolated occurrences. Extraordinary efforts on NASA's part in developing and accomplishing missions will, and should, continue, but such efforts will be a substantial additional drain on resources. NASA cannot both accept the relatively spur-of-the-moment missions that its "can-do" attitude tends to generate and also maintain the planning and scheduling discipline required to operate as a "space truck" on a routine and cost-effective basis. As the flight rate increases, the cost in resources and the accompanying impact on future operations must be considered when infrequent but extraordinary efforts are undertaken. The system is still not sufficiently developed as a "production line" process in terms of planning or implementation procedures. It cannot routinely or even periodically accept major disruptions without considerable cost. NASA's attitude historically has reflected the position that "we can do anything," and while that may essentially be true, NASA's optimism must be tempered by the realization that it cannot do everything.

Attitude is important, and the word "operational" can mislead. Operational should not imply any less commitment to quality or safety, nor a dilution of resources. The attitude should be, "We are going to fly high risk flights this year; every one is going to be a challenge, and every one is going to involve some risk, so we had better be careful in our approach to each."

Effect of Flight Rate on Spare Parts

As the flight rate increases, the demand for spare parts increases. Since 1981, NASA has had logistics plans for shuttle flight rates of twelve and twenty-four flights a year. It was originally forecast (in mid-1983) that the supply of spares required to support twelve flights annually could be accomplished in the spring of 1986.

The spare parts plan to support twenty-four flights per year had called for completing inventory stockage by June 1987. By mid-1985, that schedule was in jeopardy.

The logistics plan could not be fully implemented because of budget reductions. In October 1985, the logistics funding requirement for the orbiter program, as determined by Level III management at Johnson, was $285.3 million. That funding was reduced by $83.3 million—a cut that necessitated major deferrals of spare parts purchases. Purchasing deferrals come at great cost. For example, a reduction due to deferral of $11.2 million in fiscal year 1986 would cost $11.2 million in fiscal year 1987, plus an additional $21.6 million in fiscal year 1988. This three-to-one ratio of future cost to current savings is not uncommon. Indeed, the ratio in many instances is as high as seven to one. This practice cannot make sense by any standard of good financial management.

Those actions resulted in a critical shortage of serviceable spare components. To provide parts required to support the flight rate, NASA had to resort to cannibalization.

Outside Pressure to Launch

After the accident, rumors appeared in the press to the effect that persons who made the decision to launch mission 51-L might have been subjected to outside pressure to launch. Such rumors concerning unnamed persons, emanating from anonymous sources about events that may never have happened, are difficult to disprove and dispel. Nonetheless, during the commission's hearings all persons who played key roles in that decision were questioned. Each one attested, under oath, that there had been no outside intervention or pressure of any kind leading up to the launch.

The commission concluded that the decision to launch the Challenger was made solely by the appropriate NASA officials without any outside intervention or pressure.

Findings

1. The capabilities of the system were stretched to the limit to support the flight rate in winter 1985/1986. Projections into the spring and summer of 1986 showed a clear trend; the system, as it existed, would have been unable to deliver crew training software for scheduled flights by the designated dates. The result would have been an unacceptable compression of the time available for the crews to accomplish their required training.

2. Spare parts are in critically short supply. The shuttle program made a conscious decision to postpone spare parts procurements in favor of budget items of perceived higher priority. Lack of spare parts would likely have limited flight operations in 1986.

3. Stated manifesting policies are not enforced. Numerous late manifest changes (after the care integration review) have been made to both major payloads and minor payloads throughout the shuttle program.
• Late changes to major payloads or program requirements can require extensive resources (money, manpower, facilities) to implement.
• If many late changes to "minor" payloads occur, resources are quickly absorbed.
• Payload specialists frequently were added to a flight well after announced deadlines.
• Late changes to a mission adversely affect the training and development of procedures for subsequent missions.

4. The scheduled flight rate did not accurately reflect the capabilities and resources.
• The flight rate was not reduced to accommodate periods of adjustment in the capacity of the work force. There was no margin in the system to accommodate unforeseen hardware problems.
• Resources were primarily directed toward supporting the flights and thus not enough were available to improve and expand facilities needed to support a higher flight rate.

5. Training simulators may be the limiting factor on the flight rate: the two current simulators cannot train crews for more than twelve to fifteen flights per year.

6. When flights come in rapid succession, current requirements do not ensure that critical anomalies occurring during one flight are identified and addressed appropriately before the next flight.

RECOMMENDATIONS OF THE COMMISSION

The commission has conducted an extensive investigation of the Challenger accident to determine the probable cause and necessary corrective actions. Based on the findings and determinations of its investigation, the commission has unanimously adopted recommendations to help assure the return to safe flight.

The commission urges that the administrator of NASA submit, one year from now, a report to the president of the progress that NASA has made in effecting the commission's recommendations set forth below.

I. Design

The faulty solid rocket motor joint and seal must be changed. This could be a new design eliminating the joint or a redesign of the current joint and seal.

No design options should be prematurely precluded because of schedule, cost, or reliance on existing hardware. All solid rocket motor joints should satisfy the following requirements:

- The joints should be fully understood, tested, and verified.
- The integrity of the structure and of the seals of all joints should be no less than that of the case walls throughout the design envelope.
- The integrity of the joints should be insensitive to:
  - dimensional tolerances
  - transportation and handling
  - assembly procedures
  - inspection and test procedures
  - environmental effects
  - internal case operating pressure
  - recovery and reuse effects
  - flight and water impact loads.
- The certification of the new design should include:
  - tests which duplicate the actual launch configuration as closely as possible
  - tests over the full range of operating conditions, including temperature
- Full consideration should be given to conducting static firings of the exact flight configuration in a vertical attitude.

Independent oversight. The administrator of NASA should request the National Research Council to form an independent solid rocket motor design oversight committee to implement the commission's design recommendations and oversee the design effort. This committee should:

- review and evaluate certification requirements
- provide technical oversight of the design, test program, and certification
- report to the administrator of NASA on the adequacy of the design and make appropriate recommendations.

II. Shuttle Management Structure

The shuttle program structure should be reviewed. The project managers for the various elements of the shuttle program felt more accountable to their center management than to the shuttle program organization. Shuttle element funding, work package definition, and vital program information frequently bypass the national STS (shuttle) program manager.

A redefinition of the program manager's responsibility is essential. This redefinition should give the program manager the requisite authority for all ongoing STS operations. Program funding and all shuttle program work at the centers should be placed clearly under the program manager's authority.

Astronauts in management. The commission observes that there appears to be a departure from the philosophy of the 1960s and 1970s relating to the use of astronauts in management positions. These individuals brought to their positions flight experience and a keen appreciation of operations and flight safety.

- NASA should encourage the transition of qualified astronauts into agency management positions.
- The function of the flight crew operations director should be elevated in the NASA organization structure.

Shuttle safety panel. NASA should establish an STS safety advisory panel reporting to the STS program manager. The charter of this panel should include shuttle operational issues, launch commit criteria, flight rules, flight readiness, and risk management. The panel should include representation from the safety organization, mission operations, and the astronaut office.

III. Criticality Review and Hazard Analysis

NASA and the primary shuttle contractors should review all Criticality 1, 1R, 2, and 2R items and hazard analyses. This review should identify those items that must be improved prior to flight to ensure mission success and flight safety. An audit panel, appointed by the National Research Council, should verify the adequacy of the effort and report directly to the administrator of NASA.

IV. Safety Organization

NASA should establish an Office of Safety, Reliability, and Quality Assurance to be headed by an associate administrator reporting directly to the NASA administrator. It would have direct authority for safety, reliability, and quality assurance throughout the agency. The office should be assigned the work force to ensure adequate oversight of its functions and should be independent of other NASA functional and program responsibilities.

The responsibilities of this office should include:
• the safety, reliability, and quality assurance functions as each relates to NASA's activities and programs
• direction of reporting and documentation of problems, problem resolution, and trends associated with flight safety.

V. Improved Communications

The commission found that Marshall Space Flight Center project managers, because of a tendency at Marshall to management isolation, failed to provide full and timely information bearing on the safety of flight 51-L to other vital elements of shuttle program management.
• NASA should take energetic steps to eliminate this tendency at Marshall Space Flight Center, whether by changes of personnel, organization, indoctrination, or all three.
• A policy should be developed which governs the imposition and removal of shuttle launch constraints.
• Flight readiness reviews and mission management team meetings should be recorded.
• The flight crew commander, or a designated representative, should attend the flight readiness review, participate in acceptance of the vehicle for flight, and certify that the crew is properly prepared for flight.

VI. Landing Safety

NASA must take actions to improve landing safety.
• The tire, brake, and nosewheel steering systems must be improved. These systems do not have sufficient safety margin, particularly at abort landing sites.
• The specific conditions under which planned landings at Kennedy would be acceptable should be determined. Criteria must be established for tires, brakes, and nosewheel steering. Until the systems meet those criteria in high fidelity testing that is verified at Edwards, landing at Kennedy should not be planned.

• Committing to a specific landing site requires that landing area weather be forecast more than an hour in advance. During unpredictable weather periods at Kennedy, program officials should plan on Edwards landings. Increased landings at Edwards may necessitate a dual ferry capability.

VII. Launch Abort and Crew Escape

The shuttle program management considered first-stage abort options and crew escape options several times during the history of the program, but because of limited utility, technical infeasibility, or program cost and schedule, no systems were implemented. The commission recommends that NASA:
• make all efforts to provide a crew escape system for use during controlled gliding flight
• make every effort to increase the range of flight conditions under which an emergency runway landing can be successfully conducted in the event that two or three main engines fail early in ascent.

VIII. Flight Rate

The nation's reliance on the shuttle as its principal space launch capability created a relentless pressure on NASA to increase the flight rate. Such reliance on a single launch capability should be avoided in the future.

NASA must establish a flight rate that is consistent with its resources. A firm payload assignment policy should be established. The policy should include rigorous controls on cargo manifest changes to limit the pressures such changes exert on schedules and crew training.

IX. Maintenance Safeguards

Installation, test, and maintenance procedures must be especially rigorous for space shuttle items designated Criticality 1. NASA should establish a system of analyzing and reporting performance trends of such items.

Maintenance procedures for such items should be specified in the critical items list, especially for those such as the liquid-fueled main engines, which require unstinting maintenance and overhaul.

With regard to the orbiters, NASA should:
• develop and execute a comprehensive maintenance inspection plan
• perform periodic structural inspections when scheduled and not permit them to be waived
• restore and support the maintenance and spare parts programs, and stop the practice of removing parts from one orbiter to supply another.

Concluding Thought

The commission urges that NASA continue to receive the support of the administration and the nation. The agency constitutes a national resource that plays a critical role in space exploration and development. It also provides a symbol of national pride and technological leadership.

The commission applauds NASA's spectacular achievements of the past and anticipates impressive achievements to come. The findings and recommendations presented in this report are intended to contribute to the future NASA successes that the nation both expects and requires as the Twenty-first Century approaches.

A Summary of Actions Taken

Little time was lost in taking corrective action following the January 28 disaster. The following is a chronology of events including, as appropriate, a summary of details relevant to the purposes of this article.

January 28, 1986. 11:39:13 A.M. End of Flight 51-L.

February 3, 1986. Appointment of Rogers Commission.

February 20, 1986. Appointment of Rear Admiral Richard H. Truly, a former astronaut, as associate administrator for space flight.

March 24, 1986. Implementation of "Strategy for Safely Returning the Space Shuttle to Flight Status," signed by Richard H. Truly. Topics covered were:

- Actions required prior to the next flight:
  - reassess entire program management structure and operation
  - solid rocket motor (SRM) joint redesign
  - design requirements reverification
  - complete critical items list/operational maintenance instruction review
  - complete operational maintenance requirements specification document review
  - launch/abort reassessment.
- First flight/first year operations
  - First flight. "The subject of first flight mission design will require extensive review to assure that we are proceeding in an orderly, conservative, safe manner. To permit the process to begin, the following specific planning guidance applies to the first planned mission:
    - daylight KSC launch
    - conservative flight design to minimize TAL exposure
    - repeat payload (not a new payload class)
    - no waiver on landing weight
    - conservative launch/launch abort/landing weather
    - NASA-only flight crew
    - engine thrust within the experience base
    - no active ascent/entry DTO's
    - conservative mission rules
    - early, *stable* flight plan with supporting flight software and training load
    - daylight EDW landing (lakebed or runway 22)."
- First year. "The planning of the flight schedule for the first year of operation will reflect a launch rate consistent with this conservative approach."
- Development of sustainable safe flight rate. Responsibility for reassessing the entire NSTS program management structure and organization was retained by the associate administrator for space flight. He appointed astronaut Robert L. Crippen to form a fact-finding group to accomplish this with its report due by August 15, 1986. The other items were assigned to the NSTS program manager at Johnson Space Center.

May 12, 1986. Appointment of Dr. James C. Fletcher as administrator, NASA. He had held this position previously from April 1971 to May 1977.

May 13, 1986. General Samuel C. Phillips, former Apollo program director, appointed to study every aspect of how NASA manages its programs.

June 9, 1986. "Report of the Presidential Commission on the Space Shuttle Challenger Accident."

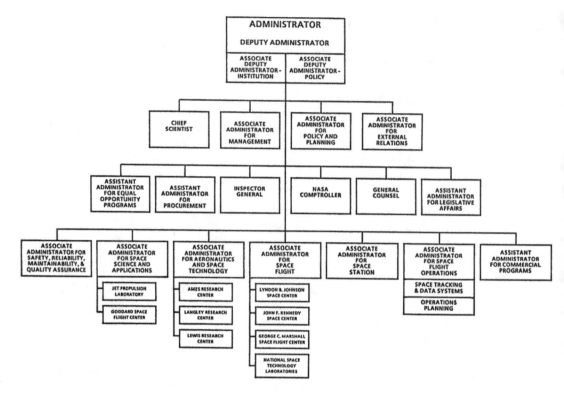

FIGURE 7   ORGANIZATION STRUCTURE RECOMMENDED FOR IMMEDIATE
IMPLEMENTATION

June 13, 1986. Directive for the "Implementation of Presidential Commission Recommendations."

July 8, 1986. Creation of the Safety, Reliability, Maintainability, and Quality Assurance Office, headed by Associate Administrator George A. Rodney, reporting directly to the administrator.

July 14, 1986. Report to the president, "Actions to Implement the Recommendations of the Presidential Commission on the Space Shuttle Challenger Accident." (These are summarized at the end of this chronology.)

November 5, 1986. Directive issued by associate administrator for space flight, entitled "Organization and Operation of the National Space Transportation System (NSTS) Program," in response to commission recommendations II (shuttle management structure) and V (communications). These resulted from recommendations of the Crippen study and were reviewed by the Phillips Study Group.

December 30, 1986. "Summary Report of the NASA Management Study Group Recommendations to the Administrator, NASA" from the General Samuel C. Phillips study group. This report includes recommendations in nine major areas. Among these are strengthening the program director of large multi-center space flight programs, establishing a formal planning process, and strengthening top management. Many of these are manifest in the recommended organization chart to be implemented immediately (see Figure 7).

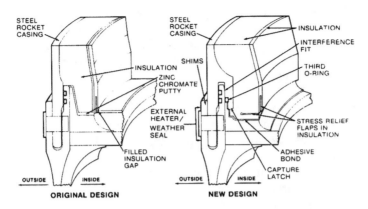

FIGURE 8   **SOLID ROCKET BOOSTER FIELD JOINT**

It was further recommended that, when appropriate, Kennedy Space Center be transferred to the associate administrator for space operations and the responsibility for the space station be absorbed by the associate administrator for space flight.

February 1, 1987. Report to the United States Senate Committee on Commerce, Science, and Transportation regarding the Rogers Commission Report. This was primarily an analysis of costs forecast to be necessary for fiscal years 1986 through 1991, to recover from the Challenger accident, a total of $460 to $560 million.

February 15, 1987. "Response to the Recommendations of the House of Representatives Committee on Science and Technology Report of the Investigation of the Challenger Accident."

(Pending) June 1987. A status report to the president on the implementation program.

Actions Taken to Date

The actions taken to date can be summarized in three categories: technical, planning, and organizational.

Technical. Under technical are included Recommendations I, III, and VII of the Rogers Commission. The first of these (I) was to redesign the joints between segments of the solid rocket booster. The results of this are shown in Figure 8—Solid Rocket Booster Field Joint. A third O-ring was incorporated along with a number of other details.

Recommendation III was to conduct a criticality review and hazard analysis. The immediate action was to cancel all Criticality 1 and 1R CIL waivers. This was followed by a detailed study and a number of design changes.

Under Recommendation VI, Landing Safety, and VII, Launch Abort and Crew Escape, a number of design and operating practice changes were made. Not the least of these was initiation of actions to improve weather forecasting.

Planning. Recommendation VIII was to set realistic flight rate objectives. As a result, projections are for four, nine, eleven and fourteen to sixteen flights in fiscal years 1988 to 1991, assuming the availability of a new orbiter in fiscal year 1991. This schedule provided for improvement of certain facilities as well as responding to Recommendation IX to improve maintenance safeguards, including minimizing the cannibalization of parts to sustain operations.

Organizational. NASA's responses to the organizational recommendations have been reviewed in the chronology above. In addition there were significant changes in the persons responsible for managing the NSTS program as well as NASA in general. Included in the changes in personnel and new positions are:

- administrator of NASA
- deputy administrator
- associate administrator for space flight
- associate administrator for safety, reliability, maintainability, and quality assurance
- center directors at Johnson, Kennedy, and Marshall centers
- deputy director at Johnson Space Center
- NSTS program manager
- NSTS deputy program managers (2) and at Marshall Space Flight Center
- director of shuttle projects
- solid rocket booster project manager
- director of science and engineering
- several other positions.

In addition, the reporting relationships of a number of positions were changed to substantially strengthen the NSTS program manager position.

For more detail, readers are invited to read any of the above mentioned reports which should be available at any library designated as a repository for federal government documents.

Ten Lessons From the Challenger Incident: Observations by the Author/Editor

Preface

The following thoughts are not offered as fact or tested hypotheses but as judgments by a practitioner/theorist based on a review of public documents obtained from NASA as well as general experience and study of project management. The documents are those identified in the above chronology.

We hope to emphasize the nature of some of the occurrences, events, and decisions which were associated with this incident and suggest that these occur with varying frequency and severity in most organizations and thus must be watched for constantly. The issues seem, to this writer, to be central to the profession of project management and the ethics thereof. While in no way discounting the magnitude of this disaster, it would be further regrettable if we failed to examine it rationally, to learn from this incident, and use the lessons learned to not only continue the exploration of space but also improve the management of projects of all types and sizes.

The Incident

What happened on January 28, 1986, was unique in history. Seven astronauts' lives were ended in full view of possibly more people than had ever witnessed such a traumatic event. Furthermore, these astronauts were probably considered by most viewers to be outstanding modern heroes and heroines.

Unlike many reports of disasters, these astronauts, in the prime of their lives, were doing good works for mankind. They were embarking on a mission which had been done successfully a sufficient number of times in the past to be perceived as routine and essentially risk free. We, the TV viewers, had perhaps even become blasé. It is possible that some members of the NSTS team also approached being blasé. Thus, we were deeply shocked when disaster struck.

The scene was repeated, almost incessantly, through the facilities of television. Indeed, it could be considered an ideal media event, one which attracted massive audiences and evoked strong feelings. And the television networks responded most effectively in covering this crisis. The event also invited the quick reactions of politicians to "point with pride and view with alarm." Project managers of every type must have winced at the thought of all the "help" that would be forthcoming.

Predictable Consequences

There are predictable consequences resulting from such an incident, regardless of the magnitude of the project. The Phillips report recognized this when it stated, "As a result of the Challenger accident, NASA faces increased critical scrutiny by Congress and the media, a long hiatus in space flights, and some unrealistic public expectations of risk free flight."

The exploration of space is not, and cannot be made, risk free. A public expectation of that is not only unrealistic but can be very expensive. Forecasted costs to recover from the Challenger incident are estimated at about one-half billion dollars. These are the directly identifiable costs. The indirect costs will never be known as they will likely be generated by "design safety factors" or "fudge factors" that exceed real requirements, by redundant components, by extra tests, by super cautious decisions, and the like. This is similar to the phenomenon which has been manifest in the practice of medicine in the United States as a result of malpractice law suits. Few people want to risk their jobs or reputations on such matters, let alone live with their consciences for having contributed to a disaster.

The direct costs of failure may be large, but are generally visible. The indirect costs may be larger but are generally not readily visible.

Further contributing to this phenomenon is the "help" that will be provided by Congress in the administration of NASA. The contrast between the level of detail of recommendations in the Rogers report (nine) and the similar report by the House of Representatives (seventy-three recommendations) is suggestive of what can be expected. Indeed, congratulations may well be in order for the members of the Rogers Commission for focusing on the key issues which demanded action and not meddling in the details which rightfully are the responsibility of the administrator in charge.

This may be the most important lesson to members of boards of directors and chief executive officers—identify objectives and policies and insist that the managers follow them. Failing this, consider replacing the manager.

The Safety Record

Two facts must be recognized about the safety record of the NSTS program. First, as clearly demonstrated in the Rogers Commission Report, a number of design features and operating practices needed review and correcting. The margins for error were narrower than may have been expected by the public.

The other fact is that in comparison to many, seemingly risk-free projects and operations, the NSTS program has had an extraordinary safety

Immediately after solid rocket motor ignition, dark smoke (arrow) swirled out between the right hand booster and the external tank. The smoke's origin, behavior, and duration was approximated by visual analysis and computer enhancement of film from five camera locations. Consensus: smoke was first discernible at .678 seconds mission elapsed time in the vicinity of the right booster's aft field joint.

record. A measure of this could be the number of lives lost per billion dollar spent. To date, the NSTS program has resulted in $27,000,000,000 in ex penditures. [In a conversation with Dick Young, public information office Kennedy Space Center, it was determined that, in addition to the seven as tronauts, there have been six fatalities directly associated with the NST program. Two of these were due to asphyxiation in a gaseous nitrogen envi ronment, two were as a result of electrical accidents, and two resulted from falling from the launch pad super structure. While no attempt was made t

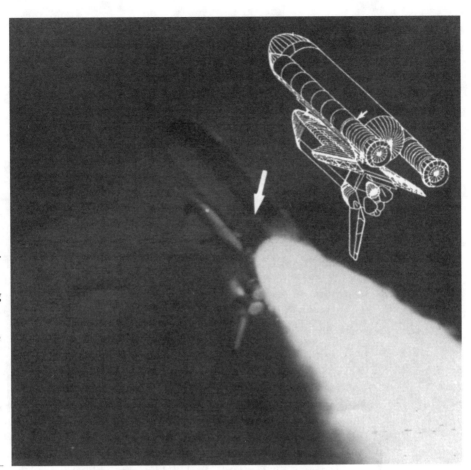

t 58.788
conds, the first
cker of flame
ppeared. Barely
sible above, it
ew into a large
ume and began
o impinge on the
xternal tank at
out 60 seconds.
ame is
npointed in the
omputer drawing
etweeen the
ght booster and
e tank, as in the
ise of earlier
noke puffs. At
r right (arrow),
apor is seen
scaping from the
oparently
reached external
ank.

contact other centers or suppliers to the NSTS program, it was considered likely that Young would have heard of any other fatalities due to his tenure as public information officer at Kennedy Space Center.] The number of fatalities has been thirteen. Thus, the ratio is approximately 0.48 per billion dollars. Many other human endeavors have resulted in much higher ratios than this, not the least of which is the rate at which lives are lost in automobile crashes, some of which might be attributable to faulty road or bridge design, or using them longer than appropriate.

The safety record on the NSTS program, rather than deserving condemnation, probably deserves commendation. We must accept that space is an extremely hostile environment and exploration of space is inherently risky.

We must be careful to make judgments about safety and other matters, until the facts are known. And then the judgments must be made in light of the level of risk and the significance of the project.

Incident versus Accident

We have chosen to entitle this project an "incident" as opposed to an "accident." This is done deliberately to emphasize that, at least in large part, it was a predictable event. From data in the Rogers Commission Report, it is reasonable to conclude that a probability distribution of successful performance of the O-ring seal could have been developed. Indeed, it is quite likely that it existed somewhere in the organization. What happened then?

Part of what happened can be explained by well understood organizational phenomena discussed in later sections. Two theoretical phenomena must be considered first.

The null hypothesis. The Rogers Commission report observed that concomitant with the transition from "development" mode to "operational" mode, an essential management attitude was reversed. Originally, the attitude was "prove to me that it is safe." The null hypothesis was that the mission is unsafe. Finding sufficient evidence to the contrary, for a specific flight, the alternative hypothesis was accepted. Over time, the attitude was "prove to me that it is not safe." The null hypothesis then becomes that the mission is safe and it is necessary to find evidence to refute it.

This is a natural phenomena for any product as it moves from the development phase to the operational phase, whether it be a new aircraft, a new pharmaceutical, a new automobile, or a new private dwelling after its final inspection. Thus, this is a common phenomena.

Beta (type II) error. A concomitant phenomena is the behavior of the beta or type II error in statistical decision theory. The focus of experimental control is generally on the alpha, or type I, error, i.e., rejecting the null hypothesis when it is in fact true. When the null hypothesis was that the system was unsafe, the focus of control was on the alpha error, i.e., concluding that the system was safe when it was in fact unsafe. Depending on the degree of "safety factor" in the design, the beta error, i.e., concluding that the *system was unsafe when it was in fact safe*, could be made quite small.

With the change in hypothesis, the focus of attention, while still on the alpha error, is now on the risk of concluding that the system was unsafe when in fact it was safe. With the same design and the same operating conditions, the beta error, i.e., now, the risk of concluding the system was safe when in fact it was unsafe, would still be quite low.

However, on January 28, 1986, operating conditions had changed substantially. It is reasonable to conclude that the "safety factor", i.e., the distance between the nominal design criterion and the distribution of the system performance, had narrowed, thus increasing the probability of the beta error. Indeed, it can be concluded that this narrowing of the safety margin was much more severe than it was perceived by management, resulting in a substantial increase in the probability of system failure.

Had the null hypothesis not been switched, it is possible that more attention would have been paid to temperature, more data collected, and thus the probability may have been increased for recognizing the very low temperature, and its potential impact, in the shaded area of the solid rocket booster.

From this, the lesson is, be cautious in moving from the development to the operational mode, for the beta error may catch you off guard.

Myopic Obsession

To complicate the matter further, there is at least a suggestion that the decision makers became obsessed with one problem to the near exclusion of another. Specifically, there was a heavy coating of ice on the shuttle system and the gantry. Several inspections were made to assess the possibility that ice loosened by vibrations during launch could damage the insulating tiles on the shuttle or penetrate the shell of the external tank. While temperature was considered, the testimony described in the Rogers Commission report suggests that the principle concern was with the ice.

It is generally recognized that, especially in project management, it is change that is most likely to cause problems. It is ironical that project management is the management of change and yet change is potentially the greatest pitfall in project management.

The project manager must be constantly alert to the effect of changes whether it is changes in plan, changes in environment, changes in design, changes in assumptions, or changes in personnel. It appears that in the case of 51-L, the decision-makers may have become so obsessed with the ice problem that they discounted the significance of the temperature problem. In actuality it was temperature which was the more significant problem.

This does not seem to be a phenomenon unique to 51-L. Indeed, becoming obsessed with a single problem to the exclusion of others only to have one of the others become critical, seems to be a common phenomenon. In the case of 51-L, it was changes in environmental conditions. In other instances it has been a single technical problem. In others, it has been a focus on the "critical path activities" to the exclusion of less critical activities which, all of a sudden, become critical to the point of delaying the project.

Project managers must be ever alert to change and keep a balanced perspective when analyzing the effects of change, whether it be in plans, environment, design, assumptions, or personnel, or any other aspect of the project.

Can-Do Attitude

The Rogers Commission report emphasized the effects of the "can-do attitude." This phenomenon is also not unique to the 51-L organization. Indeed, this is a characteristic which is sought and nurtured in project managers.

One of the vital decision areas of any manager is to assess the capabilities of her organization. In the case of 51-L, there were at least six factors which stretched the organization to near the breaking point. First, the flight schedule rate stretched the organization's capacity to the limit in terms of both people and equipment capabilities. Second, budget limitations resulted in shortage of spare parts which led to "cannibalizing" other shuttles in order to maintain schedule. Third, the changes to the manifest of 51-L stretched the organization's ability to cope. Fourth, changes to the 61-C schedule created scheduling conflicts which stretched the capacity of training equipment. Fifth, the changes in contractor at KSC created stress in the communications systems as well as reductions in the work force. And sixth, as a result of the reductions in the work force, personnel were working very long hours.

These conditions, despite the highest levels of morale and motivation, inevitably take their toll. They lead to performing the work a little faster, with a little less care, leading to seemingly insignificant imperfections in process or product. They lead to a slowing of mental capabilities resulting in failure to recognize "changes," less than optimal decision-making, and generally less efficiency and effectiveness. They lead to taking shortcuts. Often, these shortcuts are achieved by eliminating the checking and double checking necessary to ensure conformance with specifications.

It takes considerable mental discipline and self confidence to tell your boss—whether it be another manager, the board of directors, Congress, or the president of the United States—that you cannot perform a task adequately, on schedule, or in a safe manner. This is particularly true in project work where time is usually of the essence.

Project managers not only have the responsibility for completing the project but also to ensure it is completed effectively, efficiently, and safely. This is uniquely the PM's responsibility.

Project managers must continually asses the capabilities of their organizations and be willing to say "no" if the integrity of the project is at risk.

Bureaucratic Machinations

There were several manifestations of classical bureaucratic machinations. The most obvious of these is variously referred to as "turf protection" or "empire building." These inevitably lead to conflicts and "local optimization" and therefore "global sub-optimization." This phenomenon can be found in any bureaucratic organization and bureaucratic organizations are inevitable in projects of the magnitude of the NSTS program.

Top management must be ever alert to these phenomena and take action to counteract them. In this case, NASA has now increased the authority of the NSTS program manager to what might be termed a strong matrix organization as compared to what seemed to have been a weak matrix, if not almost a functional organization concept prior to 51-L.

Secondly, in an effort to maintain operational capabilities, i.e., achieve the accelerated flight rate, in the face of increasing budgetary restrictions, the quality and safety functions were sacrificed. This again is a familiar phenomenon. The essential question is, "Where can we most quickly save money with the least harm to operational capabilities?" Often, the answer has been in quality and safety. In prior days, when quality and safety were less serious than today, this strategy has been effective, at some time, in almost every organization.

Clearly, with hindsight—the more the state-of-the-art is being pushed, the more hazardous and risky the environment, the more the budget is under pressure—the more important it is to have that critical review and, sometimes it seems redundant, communication channel which can signal an alarm when the organization is moving too close to the precipice of disaster.

Management in general, and project managers in particular, must resist the temptation to find "easy money" at the risk of potential disaster.

Third, it may be tempting to criticize the relationship between NASA and its suppliers, in this case Morton Thiokol. The obvious conclusion might be that the relationship was too close and interdependent leading to reluctance to "displease" the client. It must be recognized that this close relationship is inevitable in projects of this type. The market for solid rocket boosters is hardly broad enough to rely on competition to ensure high quality at a low price. Rather, the relationship is more accurately described as the contracting for research and development, design, production, and management capacity of the vendor. Thus, in many respects, the vendor is just another element of the client's bureaucracy, subject to the same machinations. Corrections to the problems apparent in 51-L must come through more clearly, recognizing the bureaucratic manifestations and how they are exacerbated by the contractual relationship.

It is vital to recognize the economic and survival motivations of the contractor under the terms of the existing contract.

SUMMARY

The Challenger incident was indeed unfortunate. The opportunities to learn from it are abundant. Some of the lessons recognized by this writer are summarized below. It is hoped that these lessons will be of benefit to the aspiring student as well as the seasoned practitioner.

For Project Managers

Lesson 1. One of the risks of failure is "help" from the otherwise uninvolved who are quite willing to tell you what you should have done.

Lesson 2. The direct costs of failure may be large, but are visible. The indirect costs may be larger but are generally not readily visible.

Lesson 3. The change from developmental to operational mode must be done very carefully with full recognition of the implications of the associated null hypothesis and the concomitant beta error.

Lesson 4. While managing change itself, project managers must be alert to changes in the process of performing the project, maintain a balanced perspective on the project overall, and not become obsessed with a single facet of the project.

Lesson 5. Project managers must recognize their unique responsibility for the integrity of their projects and be willing to say "no" if appropriate.

Lesson 6. Be alert to the economic and survival motivations of contractors under the terms of the existing contract.

Lessons for Executives and Boards

Lesson 7. Board members and chief executive officers should limit themselves to establishing objectives and policies, insist that managers follow them, and evaluate performance. If performance is unsatisfactory, consider replacing the manager. Don't meddle!

Lesson 8. Be cautious in making judgments without adequate facts, and then only in light of the environment and circumstances.

Lesson 9. Be alert to the needs for direction of projects and ensure that the project manager has the authority to deal with the inevitable organizational conflicts such as "turf protection."

Lesson 10. Be cautious in seeking "easy money" by reducing or eliminating those functions and activities essential for preventing disaster.

Study Questions

THE SPACE SHUTTLE CHALLENGER INCIDENT

1. According to the *PMBOK Guide,* what is the concept of the work breakdown structure? Compare the planning process in this case to that of developing a work breakdown structure and describe some of the difficulties encountered when planning for the launch schedule.

2. Describe the problems existing in the shuttle program management structure and the communication process that contributed to the flawed launch decision.

3. Explain the organizational and environmental factors that lead to the overall decreased concern for safety, reliability, and quality assurance. How is this related to project risk management?

4. Describe the commission's recommendations aimed at improving the overall management of the shuttle program. Do you agree with these recommendations?

5. The National Space Transportation System (NSTS) project did not deliver what was intended. A successful project is one that not only fulfills the constraints of time, cost, and technical performance but fulfills other requirements such as minimal scope change and customer acceptance. Describe the requirements of a successful project.